HEALTH SECURITY
AND GOVERNANCE

HEALTH SECURITY AND GOVERNANCE

Critical Concepts in Military, Strategic, and Security Studies

Edited by
Nicholas Thomas

Volume II
Infectious Diseases and Security

Routledge
Taylor & Francis Group

LONDON AND NEW YORK

First published 2013
by Routledge
2 Park Square, Milton Park, Abingdon, Oxon OX14 4RN

Simultaneously published in the USA and Canada
by Routledge
711 Third Avenue, New York, NY 10017

Routledge is an imprint of the Taylor & Francis Group, an informa business

British Library Cataloguing in Publication Data
A catalogue record for this book is available from the British Library

Library of Congress Cataloging in Publication Data
Health security and governance : critical concepts in military, strategic, and security studies / edited by Nicholas Thomas.
    p. ; cm. – (Critical concepts in military, strategic, and security studies)
    Includes bibliographical references and index.
    ISBN 978-0-415-67104-0 (set : alk. paper) – ISBN 978-0-415-67105-7 (v. 1 : alk. paper) –
ISBN 978-0-415-67107-1 (v. 2 : alk. paper) – ISBN 978-0-415-67108-8 (v. 3 : alk. paper) –
ISBN 978-0-415-67109-5 (v. 4 : alk. paper)
    I. Thomas, Nicholas, 1970–   II. Series: Critical concepts in military, strategic, and security studies.
    [DNLM: 1. Health Policy.   2. Communicable Diseases, Emerging.   3. Human Rights.
4. Security Measures.   5. World Health. WA 530.1]
    LC classification not assigned
    362.1–dc23
                                                                    2011051203

ISBN: 978-0-415-67104-0 (Set)
ISBN: 978-0-415-67107-1 (Volume II)

Typeset in 10/12pt Times NR MT
by Graphicraft Limited, Hong Kong

Publisher's Note
References within each chapter are as they appear in the original complete work

Printed and bound in Great Britain by the MPG Books Group

CONTENTS

CONTENTS

CONTENTS

CONTENTS

ACKNOWLEDGEMENTS

The publishers would like to thank the following for permission to reprint their material:

Taylor & Francis for permission to reprint Peter Singer, 'AIDS and International Security', *Survival*, (Vol. 44, No. 1, Spring 2002), pp. 145–58.

Sage for permission to reprint Roxanna Sjöstedt, 'Exploring the Construction of Threats: The Securitization of HIV/AIDS in Russia,' *Security Dialogue*, (Vol. 39, No. 1, 2008), pp. 7–29.

Elsevier for permission to reprint Peter Piot, Michel Kazatchkine, Mark Dybul, Julian Lob-Levyt. 'AIDS: Lessons Learnt and Myths Dispelled', *The Lancet*, (Vol. 374, 20 March, 2009), pp. 260–3.

Wiley for permission to reprint Colin McInnes and Simon Rushton, 'HIV, AIDS and Security: Where Are We Now?', *International Affairs*, (Vol. 86, No. 1, 2010), pp. 225–45.

Wiley for permission to reprint Stefan Elbe, 'Should HIV/AIDS Be Securitized? The Ethical Dilemmas of Linking HIV/AIDS and Security', *International Studies Quarterly*, (Vol. 50, No. 1, 2006), pp. 119–44.

Taylor & Francis for permission to reprint Pieter Fourie, 'The Relationship between the AIDS Pandemic and State Fragility', *Global Change, Peace & Security*, (Vol. 19, No. 3, 2007), pp. 281–300.

Sage for permission to reprint Dennis Altman, 'AIDS and Security', *International Relations*, (Vol. 17, No. 4, 2003), pp. 417–27.

Wiley for permission to reprint Ann Swidler, 'Syncretism and Subversion in AIDS Governance: How Locals Cope with Global Demands', *International Affairs*, (Vol. 82, No. 2, 2006), pp. 269–84.

Taylor & Francis for permission to reprint Melissa Curley and Nicholas Thomas, 'Human Security and Public Health in Southeast Asia: the SARS Outbreak', *Australian Journal of International Affairs*, (Vol. 58, No. 1, 2004), pp. 17–32.

University of California Press for permission to reprint Mely Caballero-Anthony, 'SARS in Asia: Crisis, Vulnerabilities, and Regional Responses', *Asian Survey*, (Vol. 45, Issue 3, 2005), pp. 475–95.

Lynne Rienner Publishers for permission to reprint Simon Shen, 'The "SARS Diplomacy" of Beijing and Taipei: Competition Between the Chinese and Non-Chinese Orbits', *Asian Perspectives*, (Vol. 28, No. 1, 2004), pp. 45–65.

Social Alternatives for permission to reprint Frank L. Smith, 'WHO Governs? Limited Global Governance by the World Health Organization During the SARS Outbreak', *Social Alternatives*, (Vol. 28, No. 2, 2009), pp. 9–12.

Council of Foreign Relations for permission to reprint Laurie Garrett, 'The Next Pandemic?', *Foreign Affairs*, (Vol. 84, No. 4, July–August 2005), pp. 3–23.

Taylor & Francis for permission to reprint Julian Palmore, 'A Clear and Present Danger to International Security: Highly Pathogenic Avian Influenza', *Defense & Security Analysis*, (Vol. 22, No. 2, 2006), pp. 111–21.

University of California Press for permission to reprint Nicholas Thomas, 'The Regionalization of Avian Influenza in East Asia: Responding to the Next Pandemic(?)', *Asian Survey*, (Vol. 46, No. 6, November–December 2006), pp. 917–36.

Cambridge University Press for permission to reprint Melissa G. Curley and Jonathan Herington, 'The Securitisation of Avian Influenza: International Discourses and Domestic Politics in Asia', *Review of International Studies*, (Vol. 37, 2011), pp. 141–66.

Elsevier for permission to reprint Derek Gatherer, 'The 2009 H1N1 Influenza Outbreak in its Historical Context', *Journal of Clinical Virology*, (Vol. 45, 2009), pp. 174–8.

Elsevier for permission to reprint Matthew Thompson and Carl Heneghan, 'Antivirals for Pandemic Influenza: a Triumph of Policy over Evidence?', *Trends in Pharmacological Sciences*, (Vol. 31, No. 9, 2010), pp. 391–3.

BioMed Central for permission to reprint Antoine Flahault, Elisabeta Vergu and Pierre-Yves Boëlle, 'Potential for a Global Dynamic of Influenza A (H1N1)', *BMC Infectious Diseases*, (Vol. 9, No. 129, August 2009), 11 pp.

Oxford University Press for permission to reprint Kumanan Wilson, John S. Brownstein and David P. Fidler. 'Strengthening the International Health Regulations: Lessons from the H1N1 Pandemic', *Health Policy and Planning*, (Vol. 25, No. 6, November 2010), pp. 505–10.

Elsevier for permission to reprint G. J. Moran, D. A. Talan, F. M. Abrahamian, 'Biological Terrorism', *Infectious Disease Clinics of North America*, (Vol. 22, No. 1, 2008), pp. 148–87.

Lynne Rienner Publishers for permission to reprint Alexander Kelle, 'Securitization of International Public Health: Implications for Global Health Governance and the Biological Weapons Prohibition Regime', *Global Governance*, (Vol. 13, No. 2, 2007), pp. 217–35.

Oxford University Press for permission to reprint Christian Enemark, 'The Role of the Biological Weapons Convention in Disease Surveillance and Response', *Health Policy and Planning*, (Vol. 25, No. 6, November 2010), pp. 486–94.

Disclaimer

The publishers have made every effort to contact authors/copyright holders of works reprinted in *Health Security and Governance (Critical Concepts in Military, Strategic and Security Studies)*. This has not been possible in every case, however, and we would welcome correspondence from those individuals/companies whom we have been unable to trace.

INTRODUCTION

The disease–security nexus

Nicholas Thomas

No nation is immune to the growing global threat that can be posed by an isolated outbreak of infectious disease in a seemingly remote part of the world. Today, whether carried by an unknowing traveler or an opportunistic vector, human pathogens can rapidly arrive anywhere in the world.[1]

The link between diseases and security is nothing new. As noted in the previous volume, throughout history there has been an awareness of the devastation the unchecked spread of diseases can have on states, societies or their militaries. But these outbreaks were usually localized to a particular area or campaign. In 1347 the world experienced its first global epidemic. The Black Death, the plague, reached Europe from Asia through the port city of Genua (Genoa) after expanding through Asia. Over the next thirteen years the pandemic spread throughout Europe, where it was estimated to have killed up to two-thirds of the population. The Spanish influenza pandemic of 1918 echoed the devastation of the 1347 pandemic but reached a new continent – the Americas.

In the last three decades the world has seen four major infectious disease outbreaks on a global level – HIV/AIDS, SARS, HPAI H5N1 and H1N1. While none of these have matched the speed or severity of the two earlier pandemics, they have demonstrated a similar propensity to spread throughout the world on the back of trade and transportation networks. Indeed, as the world has globalized, the speed with which diseases can jump across continents has only grown faster – requiring ever-more effective surveillance and response networks. In the contemporary world, there are very few places that are more than a day away from anywhere else.

At the same time, global networks of information and technology now allow individuals and organizations to access biomedical data and use it for their own ends. Along with the threats posed by chemical and nuclear attacks, biological weapons also present a grave danger to human existence. Despite the presence of international conventions designed to safeguard humanity

1

against such threats, the reality is that such weapons – even built to a crude level – possess the capacity to kill and terrify populations.

The purpose of this volume is to explore the ways these four main diseases as well as biological weapons have (or have not) been securitized. It draws on the theoretical literature presented in the preceding volume, but each section is reviewed individually.

HIV/AIDS

HIV/AIDS – different strains of which have origins in Central and West African primates respectively – crossed the species barrier sometime towards the end of the nineteenth or early twentieth century. However, it was not until the late 1950s that it began to come to the attention of western physicians and it was not until the end of the following decade that it arrived in the United States and elsewhere in the developed world. Today it is a truly global disease. Of the four modern epidemics covered in this volume HIV/AIDS has been – by far – the most deadly. As of the end of 2010, global agencies estimated that there were 34 million people living with HIV/AIDS. Within the context of the pandemic, USAID calculated that over 60 million people have been infected since the 1980s with over 25 million people dying from their infection. Even as modern medical advances have reduced *in utero* infections and provided a better (and longer) quality of life for those who are infected, statistically this means that nearly one in every two people infected die.

The threat posed by HIV/AIDS led the United Nations in 2000 to adopt Security Council Resolution 1308, which specifically identified the disease as a security threat and marked the first time a health issue had been debated by the Security Council. This was echoed by numerous governments declaring the disease a serious threat to socio-economic and/or political stability, or even a threat to national security. As Dennis Altman argues in Chapter 31 of this volume, the impact of HIV/AIDS may rank it above both conventional and non-traditional security threats in terms of its impact, requiring an equally comprehensive response.

Unlike the three other diseases reviewed in this volume, there has been no reduction in the existential threat posed by HIV/AIDS. While recent medical advances hold the best hope that a cocktail of treatments may be able to effectively combat the disease, no country can yet declare itself 'free' of the virus. In terms of ongoing securitization responses HIV/AIDS, therefore, provides a useful benchmark against which to evaluate national and global responses to other infectious disease outbreaks.

Severe Acute Respiratory Syndrome (SARS)

The first known SARS case was detected in mid-November 2002 in Foshan city, Guangdong province, China. The main SARS inflection left mainland

China via 65-year-old Dr Liu Jianlun from Guangdong province, who came to Hong Kong after treating SARS patients. He checked in to a room on the 9th floor of the Metropole Hotel and subsequently infected other people staying on the floor. In returning to their home countries this group became the new index cases, spreading the disease to Singapore, Canada and Vietnam, as well as other parts of Hong Kong. Further outbreaks of the SARS virus occurred in South East Asia, in the Philippines, Malaysia and Thailand.

On 12 March 2003, after WHO had assessed the situation in Asia, a global health alert was issued regarding 'cases of severe atypical pneumonia with unknown etiology'. This was raised on 15 March 2003 to a rare emergency advisory. As the situation worsened, WHO recommended that all non-essential travel to Hong Kong and Guangdong province be postponed. Meanwhile, the virus was spread outside the region, to Europe and the United States, by infected air travellers. Following WHO's global alert, countries started to take a range of precautions against the further spread of SARS. These measures included temporarily banning flights from 'hot zones', temporarily stopping the issuance of visas to persons from these zones, health and temperature checks, and quarantining persons from infected countries for 10 days.

On 20 April China finally admitted to the spread of SARS from Guangdong to Beijing, with hundreds of cases as then unreported. China's silence as to its knowledge of SARS can be seen as the major cause of its rapid spread and deadly effect. However, soon afterwards, on 28 April 2003, Vietnam became the first country to be declared SARS-free – a clear demonstration that effective securitization strategies can yield rapid results. By mid-2003 all countries had either been declared free of the SARS virus or were finalizing their quarantine period. An isolated infection occurred in Singapore in September 2003, arising from a breach of laboratory safety protocols. Although limited to a single individual, who later recovered, of most concern was that this infection did not exhibit all the SARS symptoms. Should the virus re-occur, this mutable nature could make detection more problematic.

HPAI H5N1 (bird flu)

Highly Pathogenic Avian Influenza of the H5N1 strain is the longest running of the twenty-first-century epidemics. The original H5N1 strain of the current outbreak that has affected countries around the world first came to prominence in 1997 in Hong Kong. During that outbreak eighteen people were infected and six died as a result of contracting the virus. The virus re-emerged in Hong Kong in 2001 but without any human casualties. In 2003 it returned, killing two Hong Kong residents who had recently been in Fujian, with a different strain then appearing in ducks in South Korea.

At the same time as the South Korean and Japanese episodes were occurring, countries across South East Asia were also experiencing outbreaks of HPAI H5N1 and over the next twelve months it spread to a further four Asian countries. In a significant departure from protocols developed during the SARS outbreak, few countries in South East Asia immediately alerted either their regional neighbours or the relevant international organizations. It was only when the situation worsened (or was revealed by whistle-blowing officials), exceeding the capacities of the state, that the initial contact countries called for international assistance. In the eight years since the initial outbreak, this strain of H5N1 has spread around the world – moving between wild fowl to domesticated fowl populations and into humans and other species. As of November 2011, a total of 571 persons had been confirmed as being infected with H5N1 with 335 dying as a result of contracting the virus, making it more deadly than HIV/AIDS.

Throughout this period, no government has been able to entirely eliminate the virus. Concern is now being expressed by international organizations that these countries could be becoming reservoirs for a more lethal strain of the virus, one that can be passed by human-to-human contact, or that one of the H5N1 strains could mix with a strain of H1N1 to become even more lethal or transmissible.

H1N1 (swine flu)

Swine influenza – of various strains (H1N1, H3N2 and H1N2) – has been in circulation for over seventy-five years. Van Reeth notes that in Europe H1N1 (first identified in 1931) mixed genetically with avian influenza in the late 1970s, while in the Americas it has remained a 'more classical' strain.[2] In early 2009, a new form of the H1N1 strain was identified, one that demonstrated an ability to jump from human-to-human. What made this strain different was that it had started in the Americas, whereas the last two major epidemics were Asian in origin. It also possessed high transmissibility, a key factor in WHO's decision to upgrade the threat posed by this outbreak to Phase 6 (pandemic) in June 2009.

The first cohort of infections for the 2009 variant stemmed from the Mexican town of La Gloria in March. Initially it was believed that the virus was H3N2; subsequent tests showed that H1N1 was responsible. By April the virus had spread in North America and across to Europe, leading to countries around the world instituting travel bans against people going to or coming from the infected zones, and testing of persons travelling was widespread. Yet these numerous efforts had little effect. By early May the virus had reached Asia, with South Korea, Hong Kong, Japan and China all confirming cases. South and South East Asian infections began to be identified soon thereafter in mid-to-late May.

In contrast to the last two infectious diseases outbreaks, H1N1 had a markedly lower impact. Although the initial fear of a new viral outbreak was that its rapid spread would be accompanied by a mortality rate similar to SARS or H5N1, this proved not to be the case. With estimates varying by country H1N1 had a mortality rate of 0.9 per cent, although this figure is unclear given the misrepresentation of H1N1 and H3N2 symptoms. It also appeared to be more deadly in the developing world (especially Brazil and India) where the mortality rates ran in excess of 2 per cent of cases.[3] By the end of 2009 the H1N1 virus appeared to be in decline around the world. However, the capacity of the virus to mutate and – possibly – to recombine with other viruses means that this threat also bears continuous vigilance.

Bioterrorism

Beyond naturally occurring threats, are the challenges posed by artificially created disease outbreaks. As the name implies, biological terrorism is the use of biological agents to threaten or attack other states or populations by individuals or groups. Even indirectly, as the 2001 case of the anthrax letters in the United States clearly demonstrates, the perception of a threat can far outweigh the actual use of the weapon. This effectiveness, however, is mitigated by the unpredictability of the biological agent's behaviour once it is released. Nonetheless, as a reflection of their potential deadliness, biological attacks retain a high status in the threat hierarchy, equivalent to nuclear and chemical threats in their severity.

Although most states hold the technology to create such weapons, since the 1970s there has been a consistent effort by states to restrict such knowledge and to eliminate stockpiles of biological weapons. The Biological Weapons Convention was first established in 1972 and has now been signed and ratified by most states. However, outside the state, there remains the possibility that terrorist groups could weaponize biological agents as part of their non-traditional arsenal. To date, such attacks remain rare, although Aum Shinryko's attempted use of anthrax and the botulinum toxin (as well as Ebola) was an example of how such groups could develop and deploy such weapons. As successful international terrorist groups develop resources and weaponization capacity, the threat that a bio-weapon may be intentionally used against populations remains possible.

Conclusions

As the papers in this volume show, the challenge posed by infectious diseases is not a static threat but an ongoing existential threat to human existence. Every year new zoonotic diseases cross the species barrier. Although not every such disease develops into a pandemic, the globalized world continues to compress the space for human activity and for disease transmission. New forms of social and economic behaviour lead populations into contact with an ever-increasing array of viruses. Understanding how existing diseases have been securitized – and how successful such strategies have been – lays a foundation for responding to new threats in the future.

Notes

1 Stacey Knobler (ed.) *Impact of Globalization on Infectious Disease Emergence and Control: Exploring the Consequences and Opportunities, Workshop Summary – Forum on Microbial Threats*, Washington DC: National Academies Press, 2006, p. 1.
2 K. van Reeth, 'Avian and swine influenza viruses: our current understanding of the zoonotic risk', *Veterinary Research* 38 (2007): 243–60.
3 Toufiq Rashid, 'India tops H1N1 mortality rate', *Indian Express*, 1 September 2009.

Part 5

HIV/AIDS

25

AIDS AND INTERNATIONAL SECURITY

P. W. Singer

Source: *Survival*, 44:1 (2002), 145–58.

At the start of the new century, the AIDS epidemic is finally receiving high-level attention on the international stage. In 2001, the UN Security Council and General Assembly held special sessions on its dangers. Committees of the US Congress and the British Parliament held similar hearings. A meeting of African heads of state declared it 'a continental emergency'.[1] Emboldened by this attention, Kofi Annan, the UN Secretary-General, led a push to create a $10 billion fund to battle the spread of the disease, personally meeting nearly every major world leader. At the Davos meeting of the World Economic Forum, the annual gathering of the world's economic and political élite, Microsoft billionaire Bill Gates, the world's richest man, donated $100 million to the fund and urged the rest of the world's wealthy states and individuals to follow suit.

A recurring theme at all these meetings was the growing danger presented by the epidemic, not just in terms of direct victims of the disease itself, but to international security. Speaking at the UN Security Council session, James Wolfensohn, head of the World Bank, stated, 'Many of us used to think of AIDS as a health issue. We were wrong . . . nothing we have seen is a greater challenge to the peace and stability of African societies than the epidemic of AIDS . . . we face a major development crisis, and more than that, a security crisis'.[2] Indeed, a significant continuity between Clinton and Bush administration worldviews is the perception of a link between AIDS and increased instability and war. Following a CIA report on how the disease increased the prospects of 'revolutionary wars, ethnic wars, genocide, and disruptive regime transitions', the Clinton administration declared HIV/AIDS a 'national security threat' in 2000. The administration was initially accused of pandering to certain activist groups, but by the time of his confirmation hearings in 2001, the new Secretary of State Colin Powell was also declaring the disease a 'national security problem'.[3] Similarly, US Under-Secretary of State Paul Dobriansky stated that 'HIV/AIDS is a threat to security and global stability, plain and simple'.[4]

The looming security implications of AIDS, particularly within Africa, are now a baseline assumption. However, the mechanisms by which 'AIDS has changed the landscape of war' are barely understood.[5] This essay seeks to explain those mechanisms. AIDS not only threatens to heighten the risks of war, but also multiplies its impact. The disease will hollow out military capabilities, as well as state capacities in general, weakening both to the point of failure and collapse. Moreover, at these times of increased vulnerability, the disease also creates new pools of militant recruits, who portend even greater violence, as well as jeopardising certain pillars of international stability. In isolation, this increased risk of war around the globe is bad enough, but there are also certain types of cross-fertilisation between the disease and conflict, intensifying the threat. The ultimate dynamic of warfare and AIDS is that their combination makes both more likely and more devastating.

The direct danger of AIDS

More people will die from AIDS than from any other disease outbreak in human history, including the global influenza epidemic of 1918–19 and the bubonic plague in the 1300s.[6] Over 22 million people worldwide have already been killed and it is projected that, at current rates, another 100m more will be infected with HIV by 2005.[7]

Africa is at the epicentre of the AIDS epidemic. Of the world's 25 most AIDS-afflicted countries, 24 are in Africa, where seven countries already have infection rates above 20% of the population.[8] Over the next decade, many of the other countries, which now have far lower infection rates, can be expected to follow this pattern: South Africa went from 1% in 1990 to 20% in 2000, while Botswana rose to 38.5%. The impact of the disease is illustrated in what Secretary Powell described as the 'mind-boggling' drop that has taken place in African life expectancies, eliminating the gains of the last three decades of development.[9] Eventually, AIDS is expected to kill as many as 1 in 4 African adults.

The direct impact of AIDS will certainly not be limited to Africa. Rather, the continent provides the prelude to the disease's likely progression in Asia, the Caribbean, Central and South America, and the countries of the former Soviet Union.[10] In all of these areas, infection rates are rising steeply, showing patterns disturbingly similar to those in Africa 5–10 years ago. A number of nations hover just below the 5% infection rate. Once this point is passed, experience has shown that the disease's spread accelerates rapidly and becomes difficult to control.[11]

Within Asia and the Pacific, AIDS is growing at a rate that by 2010 could surpass Africa in the total number of infections. Already, many Indian cities

Projected demographic indicators for 2010 in selected African countries with and without AIDS.

Country	Projected Child Mortality Per 1,000 Live Births, 2010a		Projected Life Expectancy, 2010	
	With AIDS	Without	With AIDS	Without
Botswana	120	38	38	66
Burkina Faso	145	109	46	61
Burundi	129	91	45	61
Cameroon	108	78	50	63
Côte d'Ivoire	121	84	47	62
Dem. Rep. of Congo	116	97	52	60
Ethiopia	183	137	39	55
Kenya	105	45	44	69
Lesotho	122	71	45	66
Malawi	203	136	35	57
Namibia	119	38	39	70
Nigeria	113	68	46	65
Rwanda	166	106	38	59
South Africa	100	49	48	68
Swaziland	152	78	37	63
Tanzania	131	96	46	61
Uganda	121	92	48	60
Zambia	161	97	38	60
Zimbabwe	116	32	39	70

[a] Probable deaths before age 5.
Source: National Intelligence Council, 2001.

are at the 5% infection figure, while China should have over 10m cases by 2010.[12] AIDS also is spreading rapidly in Latin America, placing it third behind sub-Saharan Africa and Asia, with infection rates particularly high in Brazil and the Caribbean. The former Soviet Union is also a high-risk zone, with infection rising faster than in any other region in the world. Ukraine already has a 1% infection rate, while the HIV-positive population in Russia has doubled in the years 2000–01. Data is not as reliable for the Central Asian states, but infection rates there are assumed to be similarly high, due to poverty, poor health-care systems and significant populations of intravenous drug users.[13] The only region other than North America and Western Europe that is expected to keep a cap on the disease is the Middle East, primarily due to conservative social mores, but this area is also experiencing infection growth in high risk populations such as intravenous-drug users.

The death toll from AIDS has already been devastating and over the next decades it portends to kill at almost inconceivable rates. These figures, though, do not tell the full story of the disease's impact: these are fatalities without violence. The complete accounting of AIDS' toll will not just include the obvious direct victims of the disease, but also those who suffer from its wider consequences through warfare.

AIDS and the military

The primary connection between AIDS and conflict appears to come from the unique linkage between the disease and the institution of the military. Studies consistently find that the average infection rates of soldiers are significantly higher than equivalent age groups in the regular civilian population. This is true across the globe, whether in the US, UK, France, or in armies of the developing world where the problem is magnified. Recent studies in Africa have found that military infection rates are around four times that of the civilian population. During periods of war, this figure often soars to as much as 50 times higher.[14]

The reasons for this unhappy link are varied. In addition to being recruited from the most sexually active age groups, soldiers are typically posted away from their communities and families for long periods of time. Besides disconnecting them from traditional societal controls on behaviour, this also means that they are removed from contact with spouses or regular sexual partners. Personnel are often lonely or stressed and typically have more money than the local population, but little to spend it on. Their cloistering in bases thus tends to attract other high-risk populations, including prostitutes and drug dealers. Finally, soldiers live and work inside an institution and culture that tends to encourage risk-taking, so precautions against certain behaviour are often eschewed. In blunt terms, even in peacetime, military bases tend to attract prostitutes and soldiers usually don't use condoms. On deployment, this problem is heightened.[15]

The result is that many armies are the focal point of AIDS infection in their nation and are essentially under direct attack from the disease. The average infection rate of African militaries is about 30%, but is much higher for the states that have experienced AIDS for longer periods of time. Estimates of HIV infection rates among African armies are as high as 50% in the Congo and Angola, 66% in Uganda, 75% in Malawi and 80% in Zimbabwe.[16] It is the primary cause of death in many armies – even those, such as the Congo's, which have frequently been at war over the last decade.[17] It permeates the South African military to the extent that soldiers (as well as police) are prohibited from giving blood.

Militaries beyond the sub-Saharan African AIDS core – that is, from states with lower infection rates – are following this trend. For example, the army of Sierra Leone is, with British military assistance, attempting to remake itself into an effective fighting force. The discovery that as many as one in three in the army are now HIV-positive is making this more difficult.[18] Similarly, one in three Russian draftees is now rejected for various health reasons, compared to one in twenty 15 years ago.[19]

The results are devastating for the military as an institution and can lead to a dangerous weakening of its capabilities. As Colonel Kevin Beaton of the UK's Royal Army Medical Corps noted, 'History is littered with examples of armies falling apart for health reasons'.[20] Besides the effect on the regular troops and the general recruiting pool, the disease is particularly costly to military forces in terms of its draining effect on the skilled positions. AIDS is not only killing regular conscripts but also officers and NCOs – key personnel that military forces are least able to lose. Thus, leadership capacities and professional standards are directly suffering from the disease's scourge. Several armies, including those of Botswana, Uganda and Zimbabwe, are already facing serious gaps in their leadership cadres. In Malawi, at least half the general staff is thought to be HIV-positive, while the army's commander stated that he believed a quarter of his overall force would be dead from the disease within the next three years.[21] This hollowing-out of militaries, particularly at the leadership level, has a number of added implications for security. As human capacity is lost, military organisations' efforts to modernise are undermined. Preparedness and combat readiness deteriorate. Even if a new recruiting pool is found to replace sick troops, cohesion is compromised. As they lose their leadership to an unyielding, demoralising foe, the organisations themselves can unravel.

The higher risk within the military compounds the disease's impact by transferring it to the political level. Commanders in countries with high rates of infection already worry that they are now unable to field full contingents for deployment or to assist their nation's allies. AIDS-weakened militaries also pose the risk of domestic instability and may even invite foreign attack. Namibia's defence ministry, deeming AIDS to be a new form of strategic vulnerability, has treated military infection rates as classified information.[22]

AIDS and state failure

AIDS threatens not just the military but the whole state. As the disease spreads and becomes ever more pervasive, 'it destroys the very fibre of what constitutes a nation: individuals, families and communities, economic and political institutions, military and police forces'.[23] The manner in which AIDS can hollow out already weak states parallels its effect on militaries. In contrast to other epidemics, which tended to kill off the weak and infirm first, AIDS in the developing world tends to claim the lives of the more productive members of society, who are not easily replaced. Educated and well-off citizens are more mobile, and thus have often contracted the disease first. Many states have clusters of the disease in the middle and upper levels of management in both business and government, and AIDS is already being blamed for shortages of skilled workers in a number of countries.[24] For example, 10% of all African teachers are expected to die from AIDS by 2005, while between 25–50% of health-care workers in stricken states such as Malawi will similarly die from the disease.[25] In the words of Peter Piot, the head of UNAIDS, the UN organisation concerned with AIDS' global impact, the disease 'is devastating the ranks of the most productive members of society with an efficacy history has reserved for great armed conflicts'.[26]

The impact is felt not just in governance, but also in economic and social development. Besides acting as a new sort of tax on society, by increasing the health-care costs of business across the board, the disease also discourages foreign investment. Workforce productivity decreases, while revenues go down as the local consumer base is impoverished.[27] The disease increases budgetary needs at the same time as it shrinks the tax base. The consequences could well be shattering for already impoverished states. The World Bank considers AIDS to be the single biggest threat to economic development in Africa: it is expected to reduce GDP in many states by as much as 20%, in just the next decade. The rapid spread in poverty-stricken post-Soviet states, including those in Central Asia newly important to the war on terrorism, could be equally catastrophic.[28]

The precise security threat here is that AIDS causes dangerous weaknesses in the pillars of an otherwise stable state: its military; its governing institutions and economy. The disease is accordingly no longer just a symptom but a fundamental catalyst of state crisis.[29] As public institutions crumble and senior officials succumb to the disease, public confidence in governing bodies is further threatened.[30]

The weakening of state bodies at points of crisis has repeatedly been the spark for coups, revolts and other political and ethnic struggles to secure control over resources. As the recent collapse of the Democratic Republic of Congo (DRC) illustrates, warlords, plunderers and other violent actors will move in to fill the void left by a failing state. That the disease is concentrating in areas already undergoing tenuous political transitions – such as Africa and the former Soviet Union – only heightens the risk of instability and state failure.

The security danger presented by failed states extends beyond the simple human tragedy played out in the ensuing chaos and collapse. While stable states outside the region might imagine themselves secure and able to stand aside from failed states, the realities of the global system no longer permit this. Major powers have clear national interests in many of the regions most vulnerable to state failure generated or exacerbated by disease. The US, for example, has economic investments in at-risk areas in Africa that are, by some measures, comparable to investments in the Middle East or Eastern Europe.[31] Equally, a number of individual states at risk, such as Angola, Nigeria, and South Africa, are core regional allies, as well as critical suppliers of oil (roughly one-fifth of all US imports) and strategic minerals.[32]

The threats of economic and political collapse from the disease can also lead to new refugee flows. Besides facilitating the spread of the disease, the sudden and massive population movements such collapses provoke have led to heightened region-wide tension and destabilisation.[33] With AIDS likely to reach pandemic levels in the Caribbean and former Soviet Union, American and European governments will have to prepare for refugee crises reminiscent of the Haitian collapse and Balkan wars of the 1990s.

The more direct security threat is that failed states can become havens for the new enemies of global order. As the UN Special Envoy Lakhdar Brahimi noted, the events of 11 September were 'A wakeup call, [leading many] . . . to realize that even small countries, far away, like Afghanistan cannot be left to sink to the depths to which Afghanistan has sunk'.[34] Decaying states give extremist groups freedom of operation, with dangerous consequences a world away. This hazard applies even to seemingly disconnected state failures. Sierra Leone's collapse in the 1990s, for example, certainly was of little concern to policy-makers in Washington and had little connection to radical Islamic terrorist groups. Evidence has since emerged, however, that the tiny West African country is connected to al-Qaeda fundraising efforts involving the diamond trade.[35]

The new children of war

The AIDS epidemic also undermines security by creating new pools of combatants who are more likely to go to war. AIDS does not strike with equal weight across age groups. In a 'unique phenomenon in biology', the disease actually reverses death rates to strike hardest at mature, but not yet elderly, adults.[36] The consequence is that population curves shift, eliminating the typical middle-aged hump, almost directly opposite to the manner of previous epidemics.

Such demographic shifts have disturbing security implications. Recent research has found a strong correlation between violent outbreaks, ranging from wars to terrorism, and the ratio of a society's young male population in relation to its more mature segments.[37] Above a ratio of roughly 40 post-adolescent men to every 100 older males, violent conflict in a society becomes far more likely. In several states that are already close to this dangerous threshold, AIDS will likely tip the balance. Young men, psychologically more aggressive under normal circumstances, compete for both social and material resources, and are more easily harnessed to conflict when they outnumber other generational groups. Demagogues, warlords and criminals find it easier to recruit when the population is so distributed. Riots and other social crises are also more likely. Whatever the reason for the correlation, this worrying pattern has held true across history, from ancient times to recent outbreaks of violence in Rwanda, Yugoslavia and the Congo.

The new demographics of AIDS will also heighten security risks by creating a new pool of orphans, magnifying the child-soldier problem. By 2010, over 40m children will lose one or both of their parents to AIDS, including one-third of all children in the hardest-hit countries. These include 2.7m in Nigeria, 2.5m in Ethiopia and 1.8m in South Africa.[38] India, a country in which AIDS is not yet considered to have reached crisis levels, already has 120,000 AIDS orphans.

The stigma of the disease, as well as the sheer numbers of victims, will overwhelm the communities and extended families that would normally look after them. This cohort represents a new 'lost orphan generation'.[39] Its prospects are heartrending, as well as dangerous. Besides being malnourished, stigmatised and vulnerable to physical and sexual abuse, this mass of disconnected and disaffected children is particularly at risk of being exploited as child soldiers. Children in such straits are often targeted for recruitment, either through abduction or voluntary enlistment driven by desperation.

With recent changes in weapons technology that allow them to be effective fighters in low-intensity warfare, children represent an inexpensive way for warlords, guerrilla groups and other violent non-state actors to build up substantial forces.[40] This new ease of force generation means a likely increase in the number of internal rebellions and conflicts. Moreover, the doctrine behind the use of child-soldiers makes these conflicts inherently nastier. Such wars predominantly feature attacks on civilians, and atrocities are an inherent part of recruiting and indoctrination. At the same time, the lives of the child-soldiers themselves are considered cheap by those who utilise them; they tend to be deployed in a less disciplined manner, making their own losses much higher. Finally, the existence of child-soldiers is damaging to social fabric as well as their individual psyches, creating future problems down the road.

Child soldiers have appeared on contemporary battlefields without AIDS being present. The prevalence of a new, globalised mass of orphans, as well as a hollowing of local states and militaries, will make them more widespread. As a result, violent conflicts will be easier to start, greater in loss of life, harder to end and will lay the groundwork for their recurrence in succeeding generations.

Weakening global stability

Just as the disease endangers pillars of the nation-state, so too does it strike at pillars of international stability and governance. In particular, AIDS presents the institution of peacekeeping, a calming influence in many of the world's hot-spots, with a unique challenge.

As noted, a number of armies around the world have high infection rates among their rank and file as well as senior leadership. One of the heightening factors is frequency of deployment. During peacekeeping operations, forces from all over the world mix in a poor, post-conflict zone, where the sex industry is one of the few still in business. Not only are peacekeeping forces at risk of infection themselves, but they in turn present a new risk to the areas in which they are deployed and to their home states. Peacekeeping forces are in fact among the primary mechanisms of spreading the disease at a mass level to new areas. For example, in 1990s, West Africa had relatively low levels of AIDS infection. After the wars in Liberia and Sierra Leone brought in thousands of peacekeeping troops, the result was that the region became one of the new 'hot zones'.[41] Rates in the local populace skyrocketed, while troops from other contributing states, which had previously had low levels, became agents of spread back to their own homes.

A consequence of high AIDS prevalence in the military is that states will be less able and less willing to contribute their forces to peacekeeping operations. Around 40% of current UN peacekeepers come from countries with soaring infection rates.[42] For most of the last decade, the US has promoted a policy of training African peacekeepers to take on African conflicts, carried out under the auspices of the African Crisis Response Initiative. The greatest challenge to this programme's success is not a political one, but that many of the militaries participating in it, as well as other regional powers such as South Africa and Nigeria, are being decimated by AIDS.

The understandable reluctance of countries to accept peacekeepers from regions with high infection rates will thus make the already tough task of finding and deploying a robust peacekeeping operation even more difficult. The disease also provides a new stratagem for local parties to craft the makeup of peacekeeping forces to their own advantage. In the deployment of UNMEE (the UN Mission to Ethiopia and Eritrea), one of the parties used AIDS as a pretence to exclude troops from states that it felt would not be amenable to its own political agenda. The general result is that the already weak institution of peacekeeping is weakened further.

The new costs of war

The AIDS virus represents not only a new weapon of war, but one that makes the impact of war all the more catastrophic and enduring. AIDS has created a new tie between rape and genocide. Rape itself is certainly nothing new to warfare. In the last decade, however, it has become organised for political and strategic purposes.[43] In Bosnia there were camps designated for the purpose, while in Rwanda between 200,000 and 500,000 women were raped in a few short weeks. The introduction of AIDS makes such programs a genocidal practice.[44] The chance of disease transmission is especially high during rape, due to the violent nature of the act. It appears that rape is now being intentionally used to transfer AIDS to target populations. In the conflicts that have taken place over the last years in the Congo, for example, soldiers deliberately raped women of the enemy side with the stated intention of infecting them.[45] Their goal was to heighten the impact of their attacks and create long-lasting harm. Similarly, in Rwanda, soldiers taunted women after raping them: 'We are not killing you. We are giving you something worse. You will die a slow death'.[46] Likewise, the disease's spread to rural areas in Sierra Leone came from the thousands of women raped and infected by the Revolutionary United Front.

Disease has always been part of the true cost of war.[47] Epidemics decimated armies throughout ancient and biblical times and continued to do so well into the nineteenth century. Most of the combatant deaths during the Napoleonic Wars were from typhus. In the Crimean War, the Russians killed only a tenth as many British troops as did dysentery. Similar ratios held in the American Civil War.

The links between AIDS, militaries and warfare may make twenty-first century conflict no different. Of the countries with the highest infection rates in Africa, half are involved in conflict.[48] And during war, as noted above, infection rates within militaries often escalate. The rates within the seven armies that intervened into the Congo are estimated to have reached as high as 50–80%.[49] All these soldiers will die from the disease, making AIDS far more costly in lives than the limited combat that took place.

Such infected forces typically leave a swathe of disease in their wake. The original spread of infection in East Africa can be traced back to the movements made by individual units of the Tanzanian Army.[50] Moreover, the conditions of war hinder efforts to counter the disease's spread. In Sierra Leone and the Congo, for example, all efforts at AIDS prevention were put on hold by the breakdown of order during conflict.[51] Valuable windows of opportunity to arrest epidemics before they reach critical stages are lost.

Wars also lead to the uprooting and amalgamation of populations, bringing groups into contact that otherwise would be unlikely to mix. In the Congo war, for example, soldiers from all over Africa converged, while civilians from rural provinces were brought into urban centres. Such mixing promotes mutations in the virus itself. Researchers have found that the conflict in the Congo has created a veritable witch's brew of AIDS, bringing together various strains from around the continent. The resulting new strains are called 'strange recombinants'. One scientist noted, 'We are seeing variants [of HIV] never seen before'.[52]

The consequences reach far beyond the scope of the fighting. For those countries who can afford them, the recent development of new multi-drug therapies ('cocktails') have cut the risk of death from AIDS, leading many in the US to think that the disease is, in a sense, cured. Yet, there always remains the possibility of far more dangerous HIV strains: resistant to these latest treatments or even airborne. HIV has always displayed a high rate of genetic mutation, so this may happen regardless of wars or state collapse. That said, if such deadly new strains show up one day in the US or Europe, the multiple linkages of AIDS and warfare mean that its origin will likely be traced back to some ignored and faraway conflict.

Conclusion

The relationship between AIDS and increased threats of instability and war is complex, dynamic and very real. If the present trend of infection continues, the disease will kill at a rate that is almost unimaginable. The disease, however, also threatens those who are not at direct risk of infection. Its clustering in certain core social institutions threatens to set in motion events with wider political implications. Militaries could crumble, states could fall, wars could be more deadly, more frequent and harder to contain – all because of a tiny virus that targets the human immune system.

The prospects are dark, but not yet hopeless. The key phrase in the above assessment is 'if the present trend of infection continues'. AIDS is indeed a security threat and should be treated as such, with the high-level attention and resources necessary to defend against it. A number of states, including Senegal, Thailand, and Uganda, have acted to reverse their rates of infection, illustrating that, with a programmatic approach, success is possible. That said, nearly every country has denied or minimised the threat of AIDS over the last decade.[53]

Containing the disease and its security implications, on the contrary, will require clear talk, a consistent message and a coherent strategy. So the first task is to break the taboo of silence that still exists about the disease; as US Secretary of State Colin Powell has put it, 'Silence kills'.[54] Leaders in all walks of life – government, business, culture and religion – should repeat this message at every opportunity. An annual reassessment by the UN Security Council is one political mechanism that can help to keep the problem of AIDS and its security implications on the global agenda.

AIDS cannot be beaten on the cheap. Estimates are that an annual war-chest between $7–10bn is needed to fight its global spread, primarily to fund prevention programmes. The international community is nowhere near that goal, so far pledging around $1bn a year to the battle. A number of governments have donated small amounts: in May 2001, the US government gave $200m. However, if the world community is serious not only about saving lives, but preventing future chaos and calamity, it must do more than invest 'seed money'. Approximately $200bn was spent on fighting Y2K computer 'bugs' that did not strike with their anticipated impact. Given the stakes involved, the real threat, and proven impact, of the AIDS virus certainly deserves at least a fraction of that attention.

Funds and political capital are limited, so they must be used as effectively as possible. This means that certain programmes and target groups must receive greater support than others. This is a tragedy, but a reality. While the battle with pharmaceutical companies over drug treatment price-caps has received the bulk of publicity and effort, it has been a chimera of sorts. AIDS is an enemy that will be beaten only by prevention. In this, the military must be a priority, not only because of the institution's centrality to the spread of the disease, but also the associated security implications.

That military forces are generally problem areas for AIDS is a tragic irony, for the period of military service could be a window of opportunity for prevention. Armed forces offer a disciplined and highly organised environment geared to training. Adequately funded militaries can deliver prevention programmes to a captive audience, with significant potential for changing behaviour. The new AIDS-related code of conduct being drawn up by the Nigerian military and the joint training courses carried out under the auspices of UN peacekeepers by the Ethiopian and Eritrean armies are examples of positive and creative ways to address the disease.[55] The vetting of peacekeeping contingents for high infection rates, and the dedication of limited anti-viral drugs to critical military positions also merit exploration.

Finally, a new understanding of the disease–security nexus is required in order to rework old modes of military thinking. Intelligence agencies should update their threat-projection models to incorporate the disease, building in such possibilities as disease-weakened states and the threats of new strains.

Military aid programmes should also be similarly reassessed. If states genuinely cared about the capabilities and readiness of allied forces, they would integrate AIDS-prevention into military-assistance packages. A potential model is the $10m, two-year pilot Department of Defense HIV/AIDS Prevention Program (Africa), run by the US Navy Health Research Centre, which assists a small number of African militaries to establish AIDS-prevention programmes. Amazingly, this programme, which held benefits not only for the militaries but also for the local populations in general, was recently under consideration for cancellation rather than expansion.[56] Other possibilities are to incorporate AIDS-prevention training into traditional training and education exchanges (such as the US-run International Military Education and Training programme (IMET) and to run multilateral military anti-AIDS efforts through forces that already have an extensive military health presence in high-infection areas, such as the French have in Africa.

AIDS is a daunting threat, but not an unbeatable foe. It is a disease that is still preventable. The present challenge is to support those programmes and leaders who are facing the hard issues of AIDS, while encouraging those now shirking their duties to respond. Thinking about AIDS as a security threat helps clarify how this scourge reaches beyond individual lives and deaths into the realm of violence and war – and thus strengthens the case for serious action. Fighting AIDS is not just a matter of altruism, but enlightened self interest.

Notes

1 Raymond Copson, *AIDS in Africa*, Congressional Research Service Issue Brief IB10050, 14 May 2001.
2 James Wolfensohn, 'Impact of AIDS on Peace and Security in Africa', Speech delivered to the UN Security Council Special Session, 10 January 2000, www. un.org. Peter Piot, chairman of the Joint UN Program on HIV/AIDS (UNAIDS), similarly noted that 'conflicts and AIDS are linked like evil twins'. Peter Piot cited in 'AIDS in Africa: Exactly Which War Is That ?', *Le Monde*, 29 January 2000.

3 Senate Majority Leader Trent Lott has said that 'I don't view that as a national security threat, not to our national security interests, no'. He also claimed that Clinton was trying to make an appeal to 'certain groups', i.e., pandering to gay voters by making that AIDS a security threat. 'Clinton defends making AIDS a Security Threat', www.datalounge.com, 3 May 2000. Secretary of State Colin Powell, 'Text: Powell Address at UN Special Session on HIV/AIDS', 25 June 2001, http://usinfo.state.gov/topical/global/hiv/01062501.htm; 'Statement of the Secretary of State Designate Colin L. Powell, Prepared for the Confirmation Hearing of the US Senate Committee on Foreign Relations, 17 January 2001; 'AIDS a Security Threat Powell Says', Reuters, 4 February 2001.

4 US Department of State, 'Text: Under Secretary Dobriansky on US Role in Global AIDS Struggle', 22 June 2001, http://usinfo.state.gov.

5 Graca Machel, 'The Impact of Armed Conflict on Children', paper presented at the International Conference on War Affected Children, Winnipeg, Canada, 10 September 2000.

6 Harvard University Professor Jeffrey Sachs, quoted in Simon Baynham, 'African Military Capabilities in a Changing Security Environment', paper prepared for conference, 'The African Military in the New Millennium: Capabilities and Challenges', held in Washington DC, 28 June 2001.

7 International Crisis Group (ICG), *HIV/AIDS as a Security Threat*, 19 June 2001, www.intl-crisis-group.org.

8 J. Stephen Morrison, 'HIV/Aids in Africa: Opportunities and Critical Choices for US Foreign Policy', Center for Strategic and International Studies Working Paper, February 2001, www.csis.org.

9 'AIDS in the Classroom', US News and World Report, 14 February 2000; 'Statement of the Secretary of State Designate', 2001.

10 Morrison, 'HIV/Aids in Africa: Opportunities and Critical Choices for US Foreign Policy'.

11 *HIV/AIDS as a Security Threat*, ICG Report.

12 Figures from National Intelligence Council, *The Global Infectious Disease Threat and Its Implications for the United States*, NIE 99–17D, January 2000, http://www.cia.gov/cia/publications/nie/report/nie99–17d.html; 'India's AIDS Crisis', *New York Times*, 27 March 2001; 'India Underestimates AIDS Cases, Says Activist', *Washington Post, 7* March 2001.

13 World Bank, 'Former Soviet States Are Now AIDS Danger Zone', World Bank press release, 6 December 1999.

14 UNAIDS, *AIDS and the Military*, May 1998, www.unaids.org; 'Incidence of AIDS Higher Among Soldiers', *Voice of America*, 12 January 2001.

15 UNAIDS, *AIDS and the Military*, 1998. For example, research found that 45% of the Dutch sailors and marines serving in the peacekeeping mission in Cambodia had sexual contact with sex workers or the local population during just a five-month tour.

16 Claire Bisseker, 'Africa's Military Time Bomb', *Johannesburg Financial Mail*, 11 December 1998; Paul Kirk, 'Sixty Percent of Army May Be HIV Positive Reports', *The Daily Mail and Guardian*, 31 March 2000.

17 Lyne Mikangou, 'AIDS the Number One Cause of Death in the Army', *Interpress Service*, 10 January 2000.

18 James Astill, 'War Injects Aids into the Tragedy of Sierra Leone', *The Guardian*, 12 May 2001.

19 National Intelligence Council, *The Global Infectious Disease Threat and Its Implications for the United States*. The rejections are not just for AIDS but also other infectious disease, like TB, which are often linked with the disease.

20 Quoted in Astill, 'War Injects Aids into the Tragedy of Sierra Leone'.
21 Baynham, 'African Military Capabilities in a Changing Security Environment'.
22 'Aids An Intelligence Issue', *The Namibian*, 13 February 2001.
23 *HIV/AIDS as a Security Threat*, ICG Report, p. 1.
24 Copson, *AIDS in Africa*.
25 'Aids in the Classroom', US News and World Report.
26 *HIV/AIDS as a Security Threat*, ICG Report, p. 1.
27 *The Economic Impact of HIV/AIDS in Southern Africa*, Brookings Conference Report, No. 9, September 2001; 'HIV/Aids: The Impact on Social and Economic Development', *Report of Select committee on International Development*, British House of Commons, 29 March 2001; Copson, *AIDS in Africa*.
28 National Intelligence Council, *The Global Infectious Disease Threat and Its Implications for the United States*.
29 Helen Epstein, 'AIDS: The Lesson of Uganda', *The New York Review of Books*, 5 July 2001, www.nybooks.com/articles/14309.
30 For example in Ethiopia, there were recently large anti-government protests headed by children orphaned by AIDS. Three million Ethiopians are thought to be infected with HIV and about 900,000 Ethiopian children have been orphaned by the virus. 'Ethiopia: AIDS Orphans Demonstrate', UN Integrated Regional Information Networks (IRIN), 6 August 2001.
31 The US has a range of economic interests, from oil and gas, pharmaceuticals and telecoms, to soft drinks, amounting to just over $15 billion. Direct investment also showed a higher average return, roughly 30% for Africa compared to 17% for the Middle East.
32 'Africa: Clinton Legacy Alive Under Bush', IRIN, 8 February 2001.
33 National Intelligence Council, *The Global Infectious Disease Threat and Its Implications for the United States*; Alan Dowty and Gil Loescher, 'Refugee Flows as Grounds for International Action', *International Security*, vol. 21, issue 1, Summer 1996, pp. 43–71.
34 'UN Envoy Considering Taliban Meeting,' www.CNN.com, 30 October 2001.
35 The rebel RUF and agents of al-Qaeda traded in millions of dollars of 'blood diamonds', with a reported rise in purchasing before the 11 September attacks in New York and Washington DC as the group tried to gain hard assets. Douglas Farah, 'Al Qaeda Cash Tied to Diamond Trade', *Washington Post*, 2 November 2001.
36 Additionally, this is heightened for adult women, killing at even higher rates, such that the death rate for women in Africa in their 20s is twice that of women in their 60s. Rachel Swarns, 'Study Says AIDS is Now Chief Cause of Death in South Africa', www.CNN.com, 16 October, 2001.
37 Christian Mesquida, and Neil I. Warner, 'Male Age Composition and Severity of Conflicts', *Politics and Life Sciences*, vol. 18, no. 2, September 1999, pp. 181–89; Richard Morin, 'Boy Trouble', *Washington Post*, 24 June 2001; 'Natural Born Killers', *Profiles*, May 1999, www.yorku.ca. India, Pakistan and some African states are presently at risk if this demographic projection of conflict theory holds true.
38 Copson, *AIDS in Africa*; National Intelligence Council, *The Global Infectious Disease Threat and Its Implications for the United States*.
39 'South Africa AIDS Orphans Struggle to Survive', www.CNN.com, 21 June 2001; 'HIV/Aids: The Impact on Social and Economic Development', National Intelligence Council, *The Global Infectious Disease Threat and Its Implications for the United States*.
40 P. W. Singer, 'Caution: Children At War', *Parameters*, vol. 31, Winter 2001, pp. 40–56. http://carlisle-www.army.mil/usawc/Parameters/01winter/singer.htm.

41 Quoted in Astill, 'War Injects Aids into the Tragedy of Sierra Leone'; 'Armies Spread Aids in Africa', *Atlanta Journal Constitution*, 11 April 2001; 'Infected Troops Spread Scourge Worse than War', *San Jose Mercury*, 8 April 2001.

42 'Infected Troops Spread Scourge Worse than War'; *HIV/AIDS as a Security Threat*, ICG Report, p. 23.

43 Lisa Sharlach, 'Rape as Genocide: Bangladesh, the Former Yugoslavia, and Rwanda', *New Political Science*, vol. 22, no. 1, Spring, 2000, p. 98.

44 Vivianne Nathanson, 'Preventing and Limiting Suffering Should Conflict Break Out', *International Review of the Red Cross*, no. 839, 30 September 2000, pp. 601–15.

45 UNAIDS, 'Aids Becoming Africa's Top Human Security Issue, UN Warns', UNAIDS press release, 10 January 2000.

46 Margerate Owen, 'Widows Expose HIV War Threat', *Worldwomen News*, 12 June 2001.

47 See William McNeill, Plagues and Peoples (London: Penguin, 1976), p. 251; Arno Karlen, *Man and Microbes: Disease and Plagues in History and Modern Times* (New York: Touchstone Books, 1996); 'War and Disease', *Mindful*, vol. 1 no.7, March 1997, http://www.spusa.org/publications/mindfull/mindfull_wardis.pdf

48 Wolfensohn, 'Impact of AIDS on Peace and Security in Africa'.

49 Copson, *AIDS in Africa*.

50 Edward Hooper, *The River: A Journey Back to the Source of HIV and AIDS* (London: Penguin, 2000), pp. 42–4.

51 Lansana Fofana, 'Sierra Leone: Conflict Spurs the Spread of HIV/AIDS', *Interpress Service*, 5 July 1999.

52 Laurie Garrett, 'Allies of Aids: Among Warring Factions in Congo, Disease is Mutating', *Newsday*, 9 July 2000.

53 National Intelligence Council, *The Global Infectious Disease Threat and Its Implications for the United States*.

54 'Text: Powell Address at UN Special Session on HIV/AIDS'.

55 'Eritrea: UNMEE/EDF Start HIV AIDS Training Programme', *IRIN*, 25 July 2001.

56 Gerry Gilmore, 'Navy Targets AIDS in African Militaries', *American Forces Information Services*, 26 April 2001; Douglas Farah, 'Pentagon Role in Africa May End; Training Program Put Under Review', *Washington Post*, 3 July 2001. The recipient states, chosen on the basis of prior US military ties, are Benin, Ethiopia, Ghana, Kenya, Lesotho, Nigeria and Zambia. Angola was also included, as a means to open bilateral military relations.

26

EXPLORING THE CONSTRUCTION OF THREATS

The securitization of HIV/AIDS in Russia

Roxanna Sjöstedt*

Source: *Security Dialogue*, 39:1 (2008), 7–29.

In April 2006, Russian President Vladimir Putin publicly declared HIV/AIDS to be a threat to Russia's national security and proposed a guiding strategy to handle it. This move stood in sharp contrast to previous policies of the Russian goverment. Despite the fact that Russia has experienced one of the fastest growing rates of HIV/AIDS in the world since the turn of the millennium, the government's involvement had previously been minimal, not recognizing AIDS as a national security threat. The question then arises: when is a threat really threatening? This article contributes to the development of theories on threat-framing and security decisionmaking by suggesting an analytical framework that incorporates explanatory variables from different levels of analysis. The adoption of a broad theoretical position facilitates a comprehensive understanding of time and space variations in the securitization of issues. The article demonstrates that norms and identity constructions at the international and domestic levels, combined with their internalization by individual decisionmakers, can together explain Putin's move, and that these factors are of different importance at difference stages of the threat-construction process.

Introduction

At the State Council Presidium Meeting on 21 April 2006, Russian President Vladimir Putin declared that the HIV/AIDS epidemic in Russia had to be stopped. To achieve this, he suggested a number of major policy changes and allocated a twenty-fold increase in federal budget spending on the issue. Putin's announcement was a seminal event in Russian politics. A health issue such as AIDS had never previously been labelled a national threat by someone at this level of federal decisionmaking, even though the HIV/AIDS situation in Russia has been extremely serious since the late 1990s, with the country experiencing one of the world's most rapid rates of infection (Transatlantic Partners Against AIDS, 2003). Experts speak of the issue as an epidemiological crisis that will have grave consequences for various aspects of the Russian state. Furthermore, at the international level, HIV/AIDS has been labelled a security threat since the turn of the millennium. This raises the question, then, of why the Russian leadership has been so slow in internalizing the international norm on HIV/AIDS as a security threat.[1]

Yet, the situation is not unique. There are a multitude of other examples where decisionmakers have failed to recognize threats to national security.[2] Although the world presents decisionmakers with a range of complex situations that could be interpreted as threatening, only some of these issues generate socially constructed problem formulations. This raises the question of when is a threat really threatening – or, more precisely, what factors and mechanisms cause decisionmakers to construct an issue as a threat to national security?

This article argues that traditional monocausal approaches to international relations and security studies separately cannot capture the complexities of threat construction. It therefore attempts to make a theoretical contribution to the study of threats by suggesting an analytical framework that consists of both norms and identity constructions at the international and domestic levels, and decisionmakers' own internalization processes. The case of HIV/AIDS in Russia is used to illustrate the mechanisms of this framework and to demonstrate that, depending on the specificity of the case examined, these explanatory factors can be of varied importance at different stages of the threat-construction process. By addressing factors such as norms and identities, the article also attempts to complement existing discussions on HIV/AIDS in Russia, which often tend to focus solely on geopolitical and demographic elements.

The following section reviews previous research on security studies, particularly the broadened security agenda. Three factors drawn from this research form the theoretical basis of the present study: norms, identities and interalization are integrated into an analytical framework. The issue of HIV/AIDS in the Russian societal context is thereafter described. Finally, the framework is applied to the Russian discursive setting, and the implications of this discussed.

Threats and security decisionmaking

Despite frequent calls for a theoretical approach that examines variables 'from more than one level of analysis (*multilevel*)' (Hudson, 2005: 2; see also Carlsnaes, 2002), few studies within the fields of public, foreign or security policy analysis actually do so. This failure in explicitly addressing how structural factors interact with individual actors results in a general lacuna among studies that attempt to explain decisionmaking.

Within security studies, there is also a lacuna that concerns the relationship between threats and security. Although several studies deal with 'security policy' in the broader sense, there are remarkably few that attempt to problematize *why* certain issues are constructed as threats to national security. Traditional security studies are often coloured by the ideas of neorealism (for a discussion, see Knudsen, 2001), which leads to a failure to capture non-military and non-state threats. Neorealism also regards threats as objective and existing externally to individual perceptions, making the whole problematization of when an issue becomes a threat moot. The claims of realism have been challenged (e.g. Buzan, Wæver & de Wilde, 1998), and some recent empirical studies have employed other explanantia like norms and identities to analyse – albeit in a monocausal fashion – the construction of threats in the context of a national security setting (Farnham, 2003; Noreen & Sjöstedt, 2004).

The literature on so-called new threats like environmental issues and epidemics often incorporates a 'global' or a 'human' security dimension rather than a strictly 'national' one (Peterson, 2002).[3] Human security calls for a broadening and a deepening of the security concept through paying attention to the everyday security concerns of individuals, rather than focusing on the traditional security threats of high politics (UNDP, 1994). However, the concept has been criticized for being too vast and thereby having little analytical value (Paris, 2001). I make no distinction between 'human security' issues and 'traditional' national security threats. Instead, I argue that the broadened security agenda is most useful when applied to the national level of analysis, as this enables a comparison of the *securitization* of an issue like HIV/AIDS with the securitization of a more traditional threat to national security.

The three lacunae in previous research – the absence of multilevel approaches, the lack of studies looking into the construction of threats, and the analytical problems in addressing 'new' security issues – form a theoretical and analytical gap. This article attempts to make a contribution towards filling that gap.

The analytical framework

From issue to national security threat: the securitizing move

It has been increasingly recognized that issues like epidemics should be linked to a security discourse. HIV/AIDS, in particular, has serious consequences for national and international security (Singer, 2002). At the national level, AIDS can, for instance, contribute to the outbreak of military conflict by causing political and economic insecurity that brings about domestic instability or shifts in the balancing of power among states (Price-Smith, 2002).

Still, in order for an issue to be handled as a security threat, it needs to be recognized as such. Therefore, the focus here is on the *securitization* of HIV/AIDS (see Elbe, 2006; Vieira, 2006). Securitization is a rhetorical act that legitimizes the use of extraordinary measures, as well as justifying a high agenda position for an issue (Buzan, Wæver & de Wilde, 1998). This act can, but does not need to, concur with actual conditions.

The securitizing act is 'not simply a realm of instrumental rationality and rhetorical manipulation' (Williams, 2003: 522), but obligates and enables a certain subsequent behaviour to handle the securitized threat. In order to make the concept of securitization empirically applicable, I have modified some of the theoretical claims made about it.

The first change concerns the extent to which one traces the securitization process. According to securitization theory, a securitization cannot be seen as complete until an audience has accepted this threat construction. Until that has occurred, we can only talk about *securitizing moves*. Such a move is this article's analytical endpoint, and a measurement for determining whether or not an issue is constructed as a threat to national security. Since focus is on the process that causes decisionmakers to make such a move, it is beyond the scope of this investigation whether the move is successfully accepted by an audience (see Eriksson, 2000).

If we follow securitization theory literally, a securitizer should not only urge 'extraordinary measures' to be taken, but more or less disregard all institutionalized rules of conduct. I argue that this rather extreme conditional conceptualization severely delimits the theory's empirical applicability. With the exception of military matters, including terrorism, decisionmakers would rarely bypass normal democratic procedures of checks and balances to construct an issue as a threat. The securitizing move is therefore here operationalized as the public framing of an issue as a national threat, accompanied by a strategy to act.

What causes the move? Examining norms, identities and internalization

The setup of the analytical framework addresses a lacuna introduced above: the lack of multilevel explanations. Three explanantia from three levels of analysis are incorporated, and their interaction examined. Norms and identities are analysed at both international and domestic levels. To address the individual level, the internalization processes of individual decisionmakers are examined.

Theoretically, norms and identities are closely intertwined. Empirically, however, previous research has often focused on one of these concepts at a time, more or less viewing the impact of the other as given (e.g. Katzenstein, 1996). However, I argue that a comprehensive understanding of complex empirical phenomena requires that each concept be explicitly operationalized and analysed on its own premises before any reciprocated effects are explored (see Sjostedt, 2007).

My definition of *norms* follows the assumption that norms are *constitutive*, in the sense that they provide actors with an understanding of interests and thereby can change state behaviour (Checkel, 1999). An international norm can also constitute interest by reconceptualizing an issue – for instance, transforming HIV/AIDS from a health issue into an international security issue. Previous research has dealt with different phases of a norm's 'life-cycle', analysing either the formation or the diffusion of a norm (Finnemore & Sikkink, 1998: 896). This article focuses on the latter, that is, how an established norm diffuses to different actors, also called 'norm cascade' (Finnemore & Sikkink, 1998: 902).

Using norms as explanantia is not unproblematic, requiring clarity about 'which norms matter, the ways they matter, and how much they matter relative to other factors' (Legro, 1997: 31). As suggested by Legro, I assess the impact of norms by focusing on three features: First, the norm's *specificity* is determined. How well is the norm defined by norm entrepreneurs and inter-subjectively conceptualized by different actors? Second is the norm's *durability*, or how long it has been in effect. Finally, I assess the norm's *concordance*, that is, whether it is diffused to different audiences. Specificity, durability and concordance will be observed at the international level of analysis, as well as in the Russian domestic discourse.

Although the above design for measuring the diffusion of norms clearly structures the analysis, it does not fully capture this process. To understand why a norm is accepted by some actors while resisted by others also necessitates a determination of what major *identity constructions* were present in the international and domestic arenas. Norms are inseparable from identity in the sense that the identity relations between collectives not only affect the behaviour of these collectives but also their willingness and ability to internalize an international norm.

Identity in this article refers to collective identities and the constructed bonds that constitute them. Two kinds of particularly important identity distinctions are type identities, which concern social categorization, and role identities, which are the products of dyadic relationships between actors (Wendt, 1999). Although Wendt analyses the identity constructions at the international level, I argue that these concepts can also be applied to identity formations that exist on a domestic level. These identities are constructed in everyday domestic discourse and demonstrate various 'selves' and 'others' in society. Since policymakers also are members of the social community, they are as much affected by various domestic identities as any other individual, and their conceptions of threat are related to their understanding of these identity formations within their state (Hopf, 2002).

As I will illustrate later in this article using the case of Russia, identity can be empirically evaluated using the analytical tools of *predication* and *subject positioning* (Doty, 1993). The predications of Self and Other demonstrate the attributes assigned to different collective identities. Subject positioning indicates how identities are placed vis-à-vis each other. To explain why some actors are seen as competitors and others as allies, we need to take into account how they are positioned in relation to the in-group.

Although norms and identities are central in understanding how and why a securitizing move is initiated, a more complete explanation of this phenomenon requires an inclusion of the individual level of analysis. Including the latter helps to more explicitly account for how decisionmakers respond to and interact with constructed structural entities such as norms. By 'tracing processes of communication', we can see whether decisionmakers 'accept the validity and significance of norms in their discursive practices' (Risse & Sikkink, 1999: 13; see also Adler & Barnett, 1998: 40). If statements regarding a particular phenomenon have altered over time, it can be argued that this is a change of understanding, that is, *internalization*. This change is the result of a social learning process, that is, socialization. Normally such a process is discussed in collective terms, but it can also be traced at the individual level. Previous research has distinguished between instrumental internalization (i.e. an actor behaves in line with expectations) and deepened internalization (i.e. an actor accepts a particular norm and identity discourse) (Checkel, 2005). It is often assumed that an internalization process follows a particular order, with the instrumental phase preceding a deepened internalization. This distinction, however, is difficult to observe empirically. With perhaps the exception of in-depth psychological studies, most methodological approaches cannot capture whether an actor *truly* has internalized a norm. In this article, therefore, an observed discursive change is sufficient to conclude that some form of norm internalization has taken place.

The design of the analysis

Norms, identities and internalization are analysed through discourse analysis of texts from 2000 to mid-2006.[4] Statements from the UN and the World Bank are analysed to capture the international level. To reconstruct the domestic discourse, I analyse texts from the Russian media – for instance, the independent newspaper *Moscow News* – as well as other news sources, such as Ria Novosti and the BBC Monitoring Service. Statements by political actors outside Putin's immediate circle are also included in this category of text. Finally, to capture the individual level, statements and practices of key decisionmakers are analysed to assess whether there are any indications of an internalization process by President Putin and his advisers.

The following subsection gives a brief overview of the development of HIV/AIDS in Russia to provide context for the subsequent analysis.

AIDS in Russia

The case of Russia clearly demonstrates the military, economic and demographic implications of AIDS for the national security of a state. With regard to the military, 9,000 draftees have been rejected in the last five years owing to their being HIV positive. If this trend continues, Russia will face problems with recruiting new soldiers, and it has been claimed that 'Russia's HIV epidemic is already exacerbating an existing shortage of healthy individuals available for service' (Feldbaum, Lee & Patel, 2006: 5). Macroeconomic modelling predicts that AIDS will have negative effects on Russia's GDP, 'by increasing . . . mortality among the economy's most productive age groups, while at the same time driving up health and social protection costs' (Sharp, 2006: 90). Finally, there is the demography issue, which has pre-occupied Russian politicians and academics alike for almost two decades. Russia's population is decreasing rapidly, and 'HIV/AIDS will act as a prime accelerator' (Ambrosio, 2006: 11). The depopulation in Siberia and the far east can become a geopolitical security issue, expressed by 'fears of a sino-cization' (Ambrosio, 2006:13). In short, if Russia does not use extraordinary measures against the HIV/AIDS threat, there will be serious consequences for Russian and international security.

Even though AIDS in the Russian Federation has been 'spreading more quickly . . . than in any other country in the world' since the turn of the millennium (Peterson, 2002: 66), and even though it may have serious implications for national security, central political decisionmakers have been slow to respond. Russia experienced its first official case of HIV in 1987, and during the following ten years the virus spread slowly. It was limited to the homosexual community, the prison population and sex workers. Since in-travenous drug users began contracting the virus in the late 1990s, the epidemic has grown rapidly. According to official statistics, the 31,000 registered HIV cases in 1999 had skyrocketed to 315,000 in 2005 (Wallander, 2006). Experts argue that the actual number is more likely somewhere between 800,000 and 1.5 million (Transatlantic Partners Against AIDS, 2006). Russia, along with India and China, could form a 'second wave' of the AIDS epidemic, which could destabilize international security (Feldbaum, Lee & Patel, 2006).

Both international and domestic NGOs have tried to fight HIV/AIDS in Russia. Although they have made great contributions at the grass-roots level, their overall impact has been limited. Various sex-education projects in schools have been stopped, as have a number of anti-AIDS propaganda campaigns by foreign NGOs (Gomez, 2006). The federal government's engagement has been minimal, both in terms of educating the population as well as with regard to policies on HIV prevention and therapy for AIDS patients. Although some national AIDS programmes have been implemented, they have been allocated too little funding to make much of an impact. For example, the AIDS programme that started in 2002 spent only $6 million that year, compared with the $150 million spent on raising the *Kursk* submarine (Grisin & Wallander, 2002). A federal interagency body was founded in 2003, and a national Coordinating Committee/Council on HIV/AIDS was created in 2004. However, since no official from the presidential administration participates in either of these associations, they have had limited power and authority (Wallander, 2006). Russia is in several ways a political system with a 'vertical nature of government institutions and bureaucracies. . . . The system relies on policy direction from the top' (Wallander, 2006: 36). This means that, as long as the HIV/AIDS issue was not discussed by the key decisionmaking unit – that is, Putin and his closest advisory circle – there would be no significant changes in the way the issue was handled.

The implications of the AIDS epidemic on Russian national security, the government's neglect of the issue, and the constitution of the Russian political system demonstrate why Putin's securitizing move, expressed in a speech to the State Council Presidium on 21 April 2006, is given such importance by observers. Through its emphasis on several important dimensions with regard to HIV/AIDS, this securitizing move clearly contrasts with how the AIDS issue had previously been handled. First, it highlighted the scope of the epidemic, stressing its 'negative impact on the country's demographic situation'. The urgency of the matter was also stressed in unprecedented terms:

> This is a serious situation that requires us to take the appropriate action. We need more than words; we need action, and the whole of Russian society must get involved.
>
> (Putin, 2006b)

Moreover, Putin announced that he would initiate concrete measures to fight HIV/AIDS, which included an integrated and coordinated effort between the state, private business and different NGOs. He also allocated 3.1 billion roubles to the issue during 2006,[5] a substantial increase compared to previous years. Finally, Putin stated that, on Russia's initiative, the HIV/AIDS issue would be put on the agenda of the upcoming G-8 meeting in St Petersburg.

International expert agencies and the media responded in an overall enthusiastic manner, stressing that the declaration made on the 21 April

> marks a watershed in the fight against AIDS in Russia. This is the first time the issue of AIDS has been discussed by this senior group and the leadership of this important body is most welcome.
>
> (Tedstrom, 2006)

UNAIDS (2006), the joint United Nations programme on HIV/AIDS, was equally pleased, viewing Putin's action as a 'groundbreaking move', while the Russian Federation's chief sanitary physician/public health official, Gennadiy Onischenko, described it as 'historic' (RTR Russia TV/BBC Monitoring Service, 2006). Following the April event, there are indications that the issue of HIV/AIDS has taken a more central position on the Russian national agenda. In addition to its inclusion on the G-8 agenda, Russia also promised to contribute to the Global HIV Vaccine Enterprise and 'to involve Eastern

European and Central Asian Countries in its activities through the establishment of the corresponding regional coordination mechanism' (Putin, 2006a). Russia also doubled the 3.1 billion roubles budget allocation of 2006 to 7.7 billion in 2007 (Nowak, 2006). Putin's securitizing move clearly led to a flurry of activity in combating the problem.

Explaining the move

International and domestic norms

At the international level, HIV/AIDS has been discussed since the mid-1980s, initially as a health concern. The important milestone that shaped the HIV/AIDS norm took place at the turn of the millennium, when the UN Security Council dedicated a meeting entirely to AIDS. This was a seminal event, as it was 'the first time in the Council's history that it had designated a health issue as a threat to international security' (Elbe, 2006:121).

In terms of *specificity*, the norm on HIV/AIDS as a threat has since been clearly defined and intersubjectively understood at the international level. A number of different international actors have concurrently stated that the epidemic is not only a health problem but also a threat to international security and needs to be handled as such. Since the turn of the millennium, the international norm discourse on HIV/AIDS as a security matter has been more or less constant.

The World Bank, and its former president James D. Wolfensohn in particular, is one of the leading international norm entrepreneurs that has clearly shaped the specificity of the HIV/AIDS norm. In the first-ever appearance by a World Bank president at the UN Security Council, Wolfensohn declared a 'War on AIDS' and helped to establish the AIDS issue as a security matter:

> Many of us used to think of AIDS as a health issue. We were wrong. AIDS can no longer be confined to the health or the social sector portfolio. . . . In AIDS we face a war more debilitating than war itself.
>
> (Wolfensohn, 2005: 195)

The Joint United Nations Programme on HIV/AIDS (UNAIDS) was founded in 1995 as an organization coordinating the efforts of several UN bodies. Since the beginning of the 21st century, the organization has emphasized the security aspect of the epidemic. Executive Director Peter Piot has stressed that 'routine . . . approaches and financing are not sufficient as a response to the pandemic. AIDS is exceptional in so many ways that only an exceptional response will succeed' (cited in Vieira, 2006). The United States is a major transnational and international norm entrepreneur. Various governmental agencies – for instance, the CIA – have recognized the implications of the epidemic on national and international security (see, for example, Tenet, 2003), and the USA has initiated a number of programmes for raising awareness about AIDS.

As these examples indicate, the international norm on HIV/AIDS as a security issue is clearly specified among a number of actors. It has been settled since the turn of the millennium, and no major variations over time in the subsequent years can be traced. It can therefore be regarded as *durable*, at least within this limited time frame. While the establishment of this norm is an important factor for the Russian domestic recognition of AIDS as a security issue, it is not, as such, a sufficient factor. This norm had been in existence for at least six years prior to Putin's securitizing move without resulting in any form of Russian initiative. Hence, it is important to broaden the analysis and look to the norm's *concordance* to see how the internationally settled norm of HIV/AIDS as a security threat was viewed in the Russian domestic context.

During the initial years of the new millennium, Russian health officials discussed HIV/AIDS as a threat to states in sub-Saharan Africa and participated in international meetings on the issue. However, Gennadiy Onischenko, at that time the Russian Federation's first deputy minister of health, also hosted a seminar in Moscow in 2001 that reviewed the social and economic consequences of the HIV/AIDS epidemic in the Commonwealth of Independent States (CI S). Being a pioneer domestic norm entrepreneur, Onischenko tried to raise public and political awareness that AIDS had 'transcended the boundaries of a purely medical problem' (International Labour Organization, 2001: 10).

Still, Onischenko's efforts had limited effect on the overall Russian discourse. This has to a large extent to do with the 'low status' of the Ministry of Health in Russia (Honneland & Rowe, 2004: 25), which made initiatives from that ministry less likely to affect the inner circles of the Kremlin. One illuminating example of this is provided by the Task Force on Communicable Disease in the Baltic Sea Region. The Task Force was founded at the Baltic Sea Summit in April 2000, and one of its key elements was that health issues – ranging from primary healthcare to tuberculosis and HIV/AIDS – should not be restricted to the public health sector but be regarded in a larger political context. Despite this effort, the issues promoted by the Task Force were handled by the rank and file in the health ministries of the participating states and not by their respective ministries of foreign affairs. Thus, decisionmakers from the more central ministries were not engaged in the issue, limiting the Task Force's influence on Russia.

Turning to the general societal discourse, there are few indications that the international norm on AIDS diffused to Russia during the first years of investigation. A case in point is the Russian Orthodox Church, which clearly voiced its view on the matter by declaring that it was 'unacceptable to pander sin' at a 2003 conference on civil society's role on AIDS prevention (Gomez, 2006: 21). Searches in different media databases and analysis of issues of the weekly paper *Moscow News* show that the HIV/AIDS issue was fairly absent from news reporting. AIDS was mentioned in a piece on street children (Duron, 2002), and in an article on prostitution in Ukraine (Korolkov, 2002), but was otherwise rarely discussed, and certainly not in terms of being a national threat to Russia.

Over time, a change of norm concordance can be discerned, in the sense that the Russian domestic discourse began to pay greater attention to the epidemic. In 2004, AIDS was said to be a priority of the Russian government, although this claim was made by a first deputy minister from the previously mentioned low-ranked Ministry of Health (Gontmakher, 2004). More initiatives were, however, also taken by different societal groups. One example of this was the Russian Media Partnership that included representatives from a number of media groups, governmental officials and NGOs (Transatlantic Partners Against AIDS, 2005). Another example was the Stay Human Project, a nationwide attempt to fight 'prejudice against HIV-positive people' (Stolyarova, 2006). The Russian Orthodox Church also initiated a campaign that put 'emphasis on patronage and care of infected people', and issued a 'Concept To Stop the Spread of AIDS' (Soboleveskaya, 2005).

Through analysis of all issues of *Moscow News* in the final part of the investigated time period, it becomes apparent that articles on HIV/AIDS have not only slightly increased in quantitative terms compared to earlier years, but differ also in focus. AIDS is no longer mentioned in passing in relation to other problems to Russian society; instead, AIDS takes centre stage in the articles. They cover, for example, stories about the AIDS virus and its possible treatment (Kokurina, 2005), as well as people's experiences with the epidemic (Klimova, 2005). In an RIA Novosti story on HIV-positive Russians, interviewees say that they are experiencing less discrimination and greater understanding from society (Sobolevskaya, 2004). In short, recent years demonstrate an increased awareness about HIV/AIDS and how it threatens Russian society – in both the political and societal discourses.

International and domestic identity formations

Both in the Russian political discourse and in the Russian media, certain discursive patterns with regard to identity formations are evident. Throughout the period of investigation, there is one overall identity formation at the international level, where Russia is *subject positioned* vis-à-vis the USA in particular (e.g. Kondrashov, 2002). The *predications* of these two identities vary. The United States is seen as a strong superpower that sets the conditions for the international community in everything from trade issues to military matters (e.g. Stepanov, 2002). The predication of the USA is also somewhat contradictory: On the one hand, the USA is a partner and ally; on the other, it is a competitor and a bully. Similar mixed predications and subject positioning of other 'Western' identities are also evident throughout the entire period of investigation.

Russia is predicated as an actor of importance in the international arena – not a superpower but at least playing in the league of great powers. Economic and military alliances are important to Russia, but are also 'necessary for all other countries, for more effective ways of meeting new threats and preventing the United States from again slipping into the mindset of a world hegemony' (Karganov, 2002). One article claims that 'Russia has few external enemies today' (Urban, 2005), indicating that Russia's international role is one of friend and ally rather than competitor. Russia is often predicated as a bridge between East and West that warns against dividing the world 'on the religious/civilizational basis' (Primakov, 2006). This discourse is naturally not unanimous, and Russia is occasionally portrayed as an autocratic, backward state with a 'wretched economy' that has no business participating in the highest political circles of international affairs (Inozementsev, 2005).

This predication of Russia as a major player is particularly evident in the arena of international cooperation. For instance, at a meeting of the previously mentioned Task Force on Communicable Disease, delegates reportedly discussed a CIA report about HIV/AIDS-related developments in, among others, Russia, Ethiopia and India. The Russian comment appears to have been heavily coloured by a certain form of subject positioning:

> 'They compare us with those countries!' was the Russian reaction, combined with the exasperation that the HIV/AIDS threat from the USA 'never' seems to be an issue.
>
> (Honneland & Rowe, 2004: 58)

In many of these kinds of East–West encounters, there are similar responses by the representatives of Russian state agencies.

Along with these international identity formations, there are various domestic identity constructions in Russia. In the societal discourse of the first years of investigation, there is a fairly consistent pattern of constructing certain identities to which the HIV epidemic is believed to be confined. HIV-positive individuals are either foreigners (i.e. not ethnic Russians), homosexuals or drug users – groups that in various ways are predicated with negative attributes and alienated from the Russian domestic in-group. In an article on the alarming deficiency of donated blood in Russia, this view that AIDS is restricted to certain groups becomes evident, as Andrei Vorobyev, director of the Russian Academy of Medical Sciences Hematology Research Center, states that 'I have no guarantee except for a donor's word of honor that he is not a profligate, drug addict or homosexual' (cited in Skorobogatko, 2003). Another example of this clear distinction between *us* and *them* is found in the discussion regarding the development of an AIDS vaccine. According to one of the participating researchers, tests of the vaccine on humans would be limited to Russian prostitutes, homosexuals and drug addicts who have not yet contracted AIDS, since 'no *ordinary person* will agree to be vaccinated against AIDS' (*Kommersant*, 2004; emphasis mine).

There is a slight difference in this identity discourse over time. Although the aforementioned identities and the boundaries between them exist throughout the entire period of investigation, there appears to be an overall decrease in polarization between the Russian in-group and the identities assigned to people with HIV. In the latter part of the investigation period, there are several texts telling the stories of infected individuals that are ethnic Russians, heterosexual and do not use drugs. There is one story of how HIV-positive orphans are isolated from society, with 'officials trying to "seal them off" in closed homes, "forest park zones", not to be remembered . . . they become pariahs' (Korenchuk, 2004). RIA Novosti (2005) reported on a donor scandal in Voronezh, central Russia, where an 11-year-old boy and a 21-year-old woman contracted HIV from donated blood. One lengthy article in the *Moscow News* ran the story of how it is to be HIV-positive and have a child (Klimova, 2005). Mosnews.com (2005) ran a story on a young woman who won a beauty contest for women with HIV, 'Miss Positive of Russia'. Although these stories in many ways indicate that a certain stigma is still attached to AIDS, one could argue that the fact that they are brought to public attention is an indication of a discursive change. The boundaries between 'we' and 'they' become less clear-cut in the domestic discourse, since these articles suggest that it is possible for anyone to become infected.

Individual internalization

The previous subsection demonstrates that, just as there has been a change over time in the concordance of the norm of securitizing HIV/AIDS – with the ideas prominent in the international discourse slowly establishing themselves in the Russian domestic discourse – there has also been a gradual change in domestic identity constructions. To assess whether these two processes concur with an internalization by President Putin and his closest advisers, the present subsection attempts to trace that internalization by analysing statements and practices of individual decisionmakers.

Analysis over time shows that there initially was little or no shared understanding of the implications of AIDS for Russian national security. Quite surprisingly, however, then minister of foreign affairs Igor Ivanov (2003) admitted the following in a statement to the UN in September 2003:

HIV is a pressing problem for Russia, which goes through a serious demographic crisis. According to official statistics, the number of HIV-positives last June was 245 thousand. Unofficial data imply that the real numbers are 4–6 times higher. We clearly realize what damage AIDS is causing to our country today and what woes it may bring in the future.

This recognition, however, was not followed by any concrete measures, nor did it initiate any immediate acceptance of the international norm on HIV/AIDS. Over time, though, other actors contributed through their statements and practices to shaping the discourse – for example, Mikhail Grishankov (2004) of the Duma:

> Lately, as a member of the State Duma Deputies Interfactional Group on HIV/AIDS, I have been actively involved in the efforts to radically change the Government's attitude to this problem and to take urgent measures in order to prevent the spread of this disease in Russia. . . . Therefore, in the beginning of November, I sent a letter to the Administration of the President of the Russian Federation with the request to include this issue on the agenda of one of the State Council Sessions in 2005. As a matter of fact, a few days ago I got a reply that this issue was put on the list of problems for possible consideration at the State Council meeting.

During 2005, other senior ministers began mentioning HIV/AIDS. Foreign Minister Sergei Lavrov discussed new security threats with UN officials and hosted a conference on epidemics in the CIS (Ministry of Foreign Affairs, Information and Press Department, 2005). Deputy Prime Minister Alexander Zhukov declared that

> the spread of HIV/AIDS is beyond a medical problem, and in today's demographic situation, it has become an issue of strategic, social, and economic security of the country.
>
> (World Bank, 2005)

Turning to statements by President Putin, we find a gradual recognition of HIV/AIDS as a threat to Russian national security. Prior to his securitizing move in 2006, Putin had only publicly mentioned HIV /AIDS a few times. In 2001, in a speech on drug trafficking and drug addiction, he declared that the latter caused 'an avalanche-like spread of AIDS', but also that 90% of HIV-positive individuals were infected through intravenous drug use, thereby restricting the scope of the epidemic (Putin, 2001). Two years later, Putin (2003: 4) described the decline in the Russian population as one 'of the most serious threats we have identified', adding that 'the spread of new epidemics including . . . AIDS is only making the situation worse'. By 2005, Putin had mentioned AIDS on at least three different occasions. For example, in his annual address to the Federal Assembly, he emphasized that Russia would be a partner in fighting various global challenges, including 'the threat of the spread of

37

AIDS' (Putin, 2005a: 6). In his live television and radio dialogue with the nation, he declared that 'significant means will be allocated to the treatment of infectious diseases including AIDS' (Putin, 2005c: 23; see also Putin, 2005b).

Taken together, these statements indicate that from 2003 onwards there has been a discursive process among key decisionmakers in which HIV/AIDS has been recognized as a security threat to Russia. Putin's securitizing move can be viewed as the logical continuation of this internalization. The statements prior to the declaration of 2006 can thus be interpreted as a process moving in the direction of a shared understanding of the threat AIDS poses to national security. This understanding runs parallel to a similar process in the general domestic discourse.

Concluding discussion

The interplay between the international, the domestic and the individual

Having analysed norms and identities at the international and domestic levels, as well as the understanding of HIV/AIDS as a security issue among Putin and his advisers, we are able to identify some implications with regard to the case of AIDS in Russia, as well as to the theoretical framework presented here.

Despite the international recognition of HIV/ AIDS as a security issue since the turn of the millennium, there has been domestic resistance in Russia with regard to accepting this norm. International identity constructions can help us to understand this resistance, since Russia, according to one predominant discursive line, predicates itself as an important international power. Russia is predicated as active – not passive; a provider – not a receiver, and this is reflected in its reluctance to accept the suggestions of 'the West', including advice from international organizations perceived as products of 'the West'. Norms and identities make an important contribution to explaining the securitization puzzle: international norms demonstrate how the idea of assessing HIV/AIDS as a security issue is made possible in the first place, and are in this empirical case important for the domestic securitization of AIDS. As stated above, with regard to sub-Saharan Africa, Russian decisionmakers certainly agreed – both in statements and in practices – with the international norm on AIDS as a security issue. The reluctance to accept that the same norm would apply to Russia can be explained by the international identity constructions, along with the importance of self-image to actors. However, as both the international norm on AIDS and the predominant international identity constructions remain more or less constant throughout the investigated time period, they cannot on their own explain why the securitizing move occurred.

At the domestic level, we find greater dynamics in both norms and identities. Even though the predication of the Russian Self might have been an initial

obstacle in the acceptance of the international norm of securitizing HIV/
AIDS, this norm eventually reached some concordance in the Russian domestic
context. Although the texts do not clearly indicate that AIDS is seen as a
security threat, the issue has shifted from not being mentioned at all to
becoming increasingly politicized. When examining the relationship between
norms and identities at this level, it becomes evident that it is the collective
internalization of a norm that brings about a change in identity structures.
As AIDS is increasingly framed as a national problem for Russia, there is
less polarization between 'us' and 'them' on this issue. It is now recognized
that anyone can get AIDS, which is therefore a threat to a common Russian
identity – not just to a particular societal group. Hence, when comparing
the domestic level with the international level, we see that the effect of norms
on identities, and vice versa, differs between the two levels.

All four of the above discussed factors – domestic and international norms,
and domestic and international identities – affect to some extent the understanding of Putin and his key advisers and contribute to an internalization
process. This internalization is the key mechanism for demonstrating how
leaders construct issues as threats. An objection that might be made against
this proposition, though, is that we cannot know whether an individual actor
really has internalized a norm. As stated earlier, methodological limitations
do not allow us to assess from official statements whether an actor's discourse
and practices are a form of instrumental adaptation or whether they are a
deeper form of internalization. Some tentative conclusions might nevertheless
be drawn. If the present case were one of instrumental adaptation, we might
suggest that Putin's statements on the AIDS issue and his securitizing move
are not due to the internalization of a norm, but to rationally estimated gains
of some form (see Risse & Sikkink, 1999: 35). Although this might be a plausible
explanation in some cases, it is less likely here. Putin had no reason to act
in accordance with the wishes of the international community for the possibility of economical gains, as there are no known international economic
incentives preceding Putin's move. On the contrary, in 2001 the World Bank
offered $150 million for a project on HIV prevention. This was turned down
by the Russian government, and the HIV/AIDS issue was neglected for
another five years (Mendelson, Sawyer & Wallander, 2002).

It could still be argued that Putin's changed discursive practice is due to
another form of gain, namely power. Linked to power, and a common factor when explaining any form of Russian political behaviour, is the issue of
demography. In geopolitical terms, a decrease in the Russian population,
especially in the far east, would change the ratio between Russians and other
ethnic groups. This could in turn be a threat to the Russian Federation and
ultimately lead to a decrease in the Kremlin's power. However, as discussed
previously, the decline of the Russian population has been regarded a major
threat for years by the Russian political elite. It cannot therefore alone explain
why Putin brought AIDS onto the security agenda in 2006. On the contrary,

since there is no question that demography and AIDS are inextricably intertwined in the Russian discourse, AIDS – being an 'accelerator' to population decline – should have been securitized a long time ago (see Ambrosio, 2006). If anything, the demographic explanation, with its geopolitical implications, should be seen not as a contrasting but rather as a complementary view to the norm of understanding HIV/AIDS as a national security issue.

Instead, I suggest that the threat construction discussed in this article is more likely to be an example of a deeper type of internalization of an international norm. That the norm also has become established in the general domestic discourse, and that the domestic identity constructions have altered over time, are two important factors that make the internalization possible. Naturally, one might ask why this internalization took several years. Should not the political elite, with all facts at hand, have recognized the security implications of AIDS long before the societal discourse changed? One factor that might have contributed to the slow internalization process is Russia's political structure. The political administration is more or less divided into two branches. One is led by the prime minister and deals with 'low policy' – for instance, social issues. The 'power ministries', on the other hand, are headed by the president and handle national security issues and other 'high policies' (Lo & Trenin, 2005). This division is likely to impede internalization of issues that normally are associated with the 'lower' political sphere. That the Ministry of Health recognized the scope of the epidemic at the turn of the millennium did not necessarily aid the president's understanding of the issue as a threat to national security.

In conclusion, this article set out to explain the general puzzle of the social construction of threats. An analytical framework was presented and the Russian case used as an illustration of how this framework can be applied in an empirical setting. Dominant international and domestic discourses from the turn of the millennium to mid-2006 were reconstructed. A multilevel analysis of three different factors in the discourses – norms, identities and internalization – was performed, and this analysis helped to demonstrate why Putin and his closest ministers were slow to internalize the international norm of HIV/AIDS as a threat to national security. This study showed that a broad analytical approach provides a more comprehensive understanding of the complex phenomenon of issue securitization, as it explores different aspects of both structural features and individual action. Moreover, the study demonstrated that, depending on the contextual particularities of the case, the factors of the framework had different effects on one another in the process of threat construction. For instance, the diffusion of international norms can be deferred because of international identity constructions; the domestic establishment of an international norm can help to change domestic identities; individual internalization of norms was important in a case with a centralized and top-down form of decisionmaking process, and might thus be contingent on the structure of the political system. Whether these factors would play the same roles if applied to another empirical context remains to be seen.

The approach of this study has also contributed to addressing the three lacunae pointed out at the beginning of this article. It has shown that so-called new security threats can be analysed and problematized within the context of national security. Examining HIV/AIDS as a national security threat opens the possibility for comparison with the threat construction of other, more traditional, national security issues. The article has also explored the process of issue securitization, suggesting how a threat becomes threatening to decisionmakers. Finally, by employing a broad analytical framework, the study has attempted to demonstrate that a multifactorial approach provides us with the basis for a more refined analysis.

Notes

* An earlier version of the present article was presented at the Annual Convention of the International Studies Association in Chicago, IL, March 2007. The author would like to thank Erik Noreen, Kristine Eck, Thomas Ohlson, Johan Eriksson, Anders Nilsson, J. Peter Burgess and the three anonymous reviewers for excellent comments on this article. The author would also like to thank Stefano Guzzini and Claes Levinsson for their helpful suggestions on earlier versions.

1 This is particularly puzzling given that US President Bill Clinton did so already in 2000; see, for example, CNN (2000).
2 For instance, top US decisionmakers failed to act upon the terrorism warnings prior to 9/11, and underestimated the effects of environmental issues like Hurricane Katrina.
3 Previous work on AIDS as a global security issue has often been descriptive, discussing the global implications of the epidemic (Prins, 2004).
4 A list of all analysed texts is available in an online appendix at the author's web-page at http://www.pcr.uu.se/.
5 Approximately $113 million.

References

Adler, Emanuel & Michael N. Barnett, 1998. 'A Framework for the Study of Security Communities', in Emanuel Adler & Michael N. Barnett, eds, *Security Communities*. Cambridge: Cambridge University Press (29–65).

Ambrosio, Thomas, 2006. 'The Geopolitics of Demographic Decay: HIV/AIDS and Russia's Great-Power Status', *Post-Soviet Affairs* 22(1): 1–23.

Buzan, Barry; Ole Wæver & Jaap de Wilde, 1998. *Security: A New Framework for Analysis*. Boulder, CO: Lynne Rienner.

Carlsnaes, Walter, 2002. 'Foreign Policy', in Thomas Risse, Beth A. Simmons & Walter Carlsnaes, eds, *Handbook of International Relations*. London: Sage (331–349).

Checkel, Jeffrey T., 1999. 'Norms, Institutions, and National Identity in Contemporary Europe', *International Studies Quarterly* 43(1): 83–114.

Checkel, Jeffrey T., 2005. 'International Institutions and Socialization in Europe: Introduction and Framework', *International Organization* 59(4): 801–826.

CNN, 2000. 'Report: AIDS Pandemic Declared Threat to U.S. National Security', 30 April; available at http://archives.cnn.com/2000/US/04/30/aids.threat.02/ (accessed 20 January 2007).

Doty, Roxanne L., 1993. 'Foreign-Policy As Social Construction: A Post-Positivist Analysis of United-States Counterinsurgency Policy in the Philippines', *International Studies Quarterly* 37(3): 297–320.

Duron, Vincent, 2002. 'From Street to Street', *Moscow News* 20; available at http://english.mn.ru/english/printver.php?2002–20–26 (accessed 30 May 2006).

Elbe, Stefan, 2006. 'Should HIV/AIDS Be Securitized? The Ethical Dilemmas of Linking HIV/AIDS and Security', *International Studies Quarterly* 50(1): 119–144.

Eriksson, Johan, 2000. 'Agendas, Threats and Politics: Securitization in Sweden', Aberdeen Studies in Politics no. 7. Aberdeen: University of Aberdeen.

Farnham, Barbara, 2003. 'The Theory of Democratic Peace and Threat Perception', *International Studies Quarterly* 47(3): 395–415.

Feldbaum, Harley; Kelley Lee & Preeti Patel, 2006. 'The National Security Implications of HIV/AIDS' *Plos Medicine* 3(6): 774–778.

Finnemore, Martha & Kathryn Sikkink, 1998. 'International Norm Dynamics and Political Change', *International Organization* 52(4): 887–917.

Gomez, Eduardo J., 2006. 'The Politics of Government Response to HIV/AIDS in Russia and Brazil: Historical Institutions, Culture, and State Capacity', Harvard Initiative for Global Health, Working Paper no. 4. Boston, MA: Harvard School of Public Health.

Gontmakher, Yevgeni, 2004. 'Anti-AIDS Fight Among Russian Government's Priorities', RIA Novosti, 30 March; available at http://en.rian.ru/onlinenews/20040330/39912482.html (accessed 11 February 2007).

Grishankov, Mikhail, 2004. 'Chair of Committee on Security, Russian State Duma Takes Questions from Readers of UralPolit.ru', Transatlantic Partners Against AIDS, 23 November; available at www.tpaa.net/news/regionalnews/?id=687 (accessed 23 October 2007).

Grisin, Sarah A. & Celeste A. Wallander, 2002. 'Russia's HIV/AIDS Crisis: Confronting the Present and Facing the Future'. Washington, DC: CSIS HIV/AIDS Task Force, Center for Strategic and International Studies.

Honneland, Geir & Lars Rowe, 2004. *Health as International Politics: Combating Communicable Diseases in the Baltic Sea Region.* Aldershot: Ashgate.

Hopf, Ted, 2002. *Social Construction of International Politics: Identities & Foreign Policies, Moscow, 1955 & 1999.* Ithaca, NY: Cornell University Press.

Hudson, Valerie M., 2005. 'Foreign Policy Analysis: Actor-Specific Theory and the Ground of International Relations', *Foreign Policy Analysis* 1(1): 1–30.

Inozementsev, Vladislav, 2005. 'G8 as a Method Pacifying Moscow', *Moscow Times* 26; available at http://english.mn.ru/english/printver.php?2005–26–13 (accessed 31 May 2006).

International Labour Organization, 2001. 'HIV/AIDS Social and Economic Consequences in Countries of the Commonwealth of Independent States: Indicators for the World of Work', Report of a Tripartite Seminar. Moscow: International Labour Organization; available at www.ilo.ru/aids/docs/dec02/reports_eng.pdf.

Ivanov, Igor, 2003. 'Statement By His Excellency Igor S.Ivanov, Minister of Foreign Affairs of the Russian Federation at the High Level Plenary Meeting of the 58th Session of the UN General Assembly on HIV/AIDS', Ministry of

Foreign Affairs, 22 September; available at http://www.mid.ru/Brp_4.nsf/arh/ A62FC09ACD3B074143256DAB0050E25A? OpenDocument (accessed 15 December 2006).

Karganov, Sergei, 2002. 'Needed: An International Security Alliance', *Moscow News* 23; available at http://english.mn.ru/english/printver.php?2002–23–1 (accessed 31 May 2006).

Katzenstein, Peter J., ed., 1996. *The Culture of National Security: Norms and Identity in World Politics.* New York: Columbia University Press.

Klimova, Maria, 2005. 'Life With AIDS', *Moscow News* 8; available at http://english. mn.ru/english/printver.php?2005–8–23 (accessed 31 May 2006).

Knudsen, Olav F., 2001. 'Post-Copenhagen Security Studies: Desecuritizing Securitization', *Security Dialogue* 32(3): 355–368.

Kokurina, Yelena, 2005. 'Scientists Break Fresh Ground in Search for AIDS Cure', *Moscow News* 21; available at http://english.mn.ru/english/printver.php?2005–21– 28 (accessed 23 October 2007).

Kommersant, 2004. 'AIDS Vaccine in Russia', 3 June; reprinted by RIA Novosti; available at http://en.rian.ru/analysis/20040603/39762033.html (accessed 20 February 2007).

Kondrashov, Stanislav, 2002. 'Bush Whips Up Arms Race', *Moscow News* 6; available at http://english.mn.ru/english/printver.php?2002–26–2 (accessed 1 June 2006).

Korenchuk, Ksenia, 2004. 'In Russia AIDS Is a Social Problem', RIA Novosti, 25 November; available at http://en.rian.ru/onlinenews/20041125/39774231.html (accessed 16 January 2007).

Korolkov, Igor, 2002. 'Brothels-in-Law?', *Moscow News* 31; available at http://english. mn. ru/english.printver.php?2002–31–3 (accessed 11 May 2006).

Legro, Jeffrey W., 1997. 'Which Norms Matter? Revisiting the "Failure" of Internationalism', *International Organization* 51(1): 31–63.

Lo, Bobo & Dmitri Trenin, 2005. *The Landscape of Russian Foreign Policy Decision-Making.* Moscow: Carnegie Moscow Center; available at http://www.carnegie.ru/ en/pubs/books/9200doklad_fin.pdf (accessed 23 October 2007).

Mendelson, Sarah E.; Julie Sawyer & Celeste A. Wallander, 2002. 'The Security Implications of HIV/AIDS in Russia', Ponars Policy Memo No. 245. Washington, DC: Center for Strategic and International Studies.

Ministry of Foreign Affairs, Information and Press Department, 2005. 'Russian Minister of Foreign Affairs Sergey Lavrov Meets with Antonio Maria Costa, UN Under-Secretary-General and Executive Director of the United Nations Office on Drugs and Crime', Ministry of Foreign Affairs of the Russian Federation, 30 March; available at http://www.mid.ru/Brp_4.nsf/arh/6C76CA4531DE8A00C3256 FD50040117B?OpenDocument (accessed 15 January 2007).

Mosnews.com, 2005. 'Russian HIV Infected Woman Awarded "Miss Positive" Title on World AIDS Day', 1 December; available at www.mosnews.com/news/2005/12/01/ misspositive.shtml (accessed 30 May 2006).

Noreen, Erik & Roxanna Sjöstedt, 2004. 'Estonian Identity Formations and Threat Framing in the Post-Cold War Era', *Journal Of Peace Research* 41(6): 733–750.

Nowak, David, 2006. 'AIDS Spending Will Jump to $289M', *Moscow Times*, 15 November; available at http://www.moscowtimes.ru/stories/2006/11/15/001.html (accessed 18 February 2007).

Paris, Roland, 2001. 'Human Security: Paradigm Shift or Hot Air?', *International Security* 26(2): 87–102.

Peterson, Susan, 2002. 'Epidemic Disease and National Security', *Security Studies* 12(2): 43–81.

Price-Smith, Andrew T., 2002. *The Health of Nations: Infectious Disease, Environmental Change, and Their Effects on National Security and Development*. Cambridge, MA: MIT Press.

Primakov, Yevgeny, 2006. 'A New Threat', *Moscow News* 12; available at http://english.mn.ru/english/printver.php?2006–12–2 (accessed 31 May 2006).

Prins, Gwyn, 2004. 'AIDS and Global Security', *International Affairs* 80(5): 931–952.

Putin, Vladimir, 2001. 'Speech by President Vladimir Putin at a Meeting of the Security Council of the Russian Federation', Ministry of Foreign Affairs, 28 September; available at http://www.mid.ru/brp_4.nsf/78a48070f128a7b43256999005bcbb3/ 4cd8339743f900ee43256ad90039004d?OpenDocument (accessed 1 October 2006).

Putin, Vladimir, 2003. 'Annual Address to the Federal Assembly', President of Russia Official Web Portal, 16 May; available at http://www.kremlin.ru/eng/speeches/2003/05/16/0000_type70029type82912_44692.shtml (accessed 10 January 2007).

Putin, Vladimir, 2005a. 'Annual Address to the Federal Assembly', President of Russia Official Web Portal, 25 April; available at http://www.kremlin.ru/eng/speeches/2005/04/25/2031_type70029type82912_87086.shtml (accessed 11 January 2007).

Putin, Vladimir, 2005b. 'Opening Address at the Session of the State Council Presidium on Increasing the Availability and Quality of Medical Aid', President of Russia Official Web Portal, 11 October; available at http://www.kremlin.ru/eng/speeches/2005/10/11/2330_type82912type82913_95307.shtml (accessed 19 January 2007).

Putin, Vladimir, 2005c. 'President's Live Television and Radio Dialogue with the Nation', President of Russia Official Web Portal, 27 September; available at http://www.kremlin.ru/eng/speeches/2005/09/27/1955_type82912type82916type82917type84779_94321.shtml (accessed 10 January 2007).

Putin, Vladimir, 2006a. 'Chair's Summary of G8 Meeting', President of Russia Official Web Portal, 17 July; available at http://www.kremlin.ru/eng/text/docs/2006/07/108930.shtml (accessed 25 January 2007).

Putin, Vladimir, 2006b. 'Opening Words at the State Council Presidium Meeting on Urgent Measures To Combat the Spread of HIV-AIDS in the Russian Federation', President of Russia Official Web Portal, 21 April; available at http://www.kremlin.ru/eng/text/speeches/2006/04/21/2148_type82912type82913_104797.shtml (accessed 5 January 2007).

RIA Novosti, 2005. 'Voronezh Central Blood Bank Closed in HIV Scandal', RIA Novosti, 22 December; available at http://en.rian.ru/russia/20051222/42645699-print.html (accessed 10 February 2007).

Risse, Thomas & Kathryn Sikkink, 1999. 'The Socialization of International Human Rights Norms into Domestic Practices: Introduction', in Thomas Risse, Steve C. Ropp & Kathryn Sikkink, eds, *The Power of Human Rights: International Norms and Domestic Change*. Cambridge: Cambridge University Press (1–38).

RTR Russia TV/BBC Monitoring Service, 2006. 'Putin Stresses Moral Values in HIV Prevention', 21 April. Factiva database; available at http://global.factiva.com (accessed 23 October 2007).

Sharp, Shombi, 2006. 'Economic Impact of HIV/AIDS in Russia', in Judyth L. Twigg, ed., *HIV/AIDS in Russia and Eurasia*. New York: Palgrave Macmillan (77–102).

Singer, Peter W., 2002. 'AIDS and International Security', *Survival* 44(1): 145–158.

Sjöstedt, Roxanna, 2007. 'The Discursive Origins of a Doctrine: Norms, Identity and Securitization Under Harry S. Truman and George W. Bush', *Foreign Policy Analysis* 3(3): 233–254.

Skorobogatko, Tatyana, 2003. 'Donor Blood Pool Shrinks', *Moscow News* 8; available at http://english.mn.ru/english/printver.php?2003–8–10 (accessed 31 May 2006).

Sobolevskaya, Olga, 2004. 'Russian Society Is More Tolerant to People with HIV', Ria Novosti, 15 July; available at http://en.rian.ru/analysis/20040715/39765172-print.html (accessed 23 October 2007).

Sobolevskaya, Olga, 2005. 'Russian Orthodox Church Fighting HIV Epidemic', RIA Novosti, 7 September; available at http://en.rian.ru/analysis/20050907/41328725.html (accessed 10 January 2007).

Stepanov, Andrei, 2002. 'War-Time Policy', *Moscow News* 10; available at http://english. mn.ru/english/printver.php?2002–10–7 (accessed 23 October 2007).

Stolyarova, Galina, 2006. 'New Campaign Tackles HIV/AIDS Prejudice', *St. Petersburg Times,* 7 February; reprinted at Factiva Database; available at http://global.factiva.com/ (accessed 23 October 2007).

Tedstrom, John, 2006. 'President Putin Calls On Representatives of Business, Political Parties and Civil Society To Become More Actively Involved in AIDS Awareness Activities', press release, Transatlantic Partners Against AIDS; available at http://www.tpaa.net/news/pressreleases/?id=1970 (accessed 23 October 2007).

Tenet, George J., 2003. 'The Worldwide Threat in 2003: Evolving Dangers in a Complex World', Testimony of Director of Central Intelligence Before the Senate Select Committee on Intelligence, 11 February; available at https://www.cia.gov/news-information/speeches-testimony/2003/dci_speech_02112003.html (accessed 23 October, 2007).

Transatlantic Partners Against AIDS, 2003. 'On the Frontline of an Epidemic: The Need for Urgency in Russia's Fight Against AIDS'. New York: US–Russia Working Group Against AIDS, Transatlantic Partners Against AIDS; available at http://www.tpaa.net/files/upload/publications/829.pdf (accessed 23 October 2007).

Transatlantic Partners Against AIDS, 2005. 'Russian Media Partnership Annual Leadership Committee Meeting', Transatlantic Partners Against AIDS Events Briefing, 27 October; available at http://www.tpaa.net/events/?id=378 (accessed 23 October 2007).

Transatlantic Partners Against AIDS, 2006. 'Key Facts About HIV/AIDS in the Russian Federation', Transatlantic Partners Against AIDS Fact Sheet February 2006; available at http://www.tpaa.net/files/upload/publications/1873.pdf (accessed 23 October 2007).

UNAIDS, 2006. 'President Putin Calls for Urgent Measures To Stem the HIV Epidemic in Russia', 26 April; available at http://www.unaids.org/en/MediaCentre/PressMaterials/FeatureStory/20060426–russia.asp (accessed 23 October 2007).

United Nations Development Programme (UNDP), 1994. *Human Development Report 1994*. Oxford: Oxford University Press.

Urban, Vladimir, 2005. 'Kremlin Set To Reinforce Interior Troops', *Moscow Times* 20; available at http://english.mn.ru/english/printver.php?2005–20–19 (accessed 31 May 2006).

Vieira, Marco A., 2006. 'The Securitization of the HIV/AIDS Epidemic as a Norm: A Contribution to the Constructivist Scholarship on the Emergence and Diffusion of International Norms', paper presented at the 47th Annual Convention of the International Studies Association, San Diego, CA, 20–25 March.

Wallander, Celeste A., 2006. 'Russian Politics and HIV/AIDS: The Institutional and Leadership Sources of an Inadequate Policy', in Judyth L. Twigg, ed., *HIV/AIDS in Russia and Eurasia*. New York: Palgrave Macmillan (33–55).

Wendt, Alexander, 1999. *Social Theory of International Politics*. Cambridge: Cambridge University Press.

Williams, Michael C., 2003. 'Words, Images, Enemies: Securitization and International Polities', *International Studies Quarterly* 47(4): 511–531.

Wolfensohn, James D., 2005. *Voice for the World's Poor: Selected Speeches and Writings of World Bank President James D. Wolfensohn, 1995–2005*. Washington, DC: World Bank.

World Bank, 2005. 'Momentum To Fight AIDS Gains Pace in Moscow'. Washington, DC: World Bank; available at www.worldbank.org (accessed 12 May 2006).

27

AIDS

Lessons learnt and myths dispelled

Peter Piot, Michel Kazatchkine, Mark Dybul
and Julian Lob-Levyt

Source: *Lancet*, 374 (2009), 260–3.

Nearly 30 years into the AIDS epidemic, we are able to assess our progress in tackling the disease with both increased knowledge and the benefit of hindsight. This Viewpoint examines what we—the international community— got right, what we got wrong, and why we need to urgently dispel several emerging myths about the epidemic and the global response to it.

When HIV was emerging in the early 1980s, we clearly underestimated the global effect that the disease would have, and that in only a few decades, tens of millions of people worldwide would become infected. The epidemic nowadays is the result of what 30 years ago was an unpredictable—but tremendously potent—combination of intimate personal behaviours (notably, unprotected sex and needle sharing) and socioeconomic factors (including poverty, gender inequity, social exclusion, and migration) that have affected nearly every country worldwide.

We also underestimated the extent to which stigma and discrimination— against people living with HIV and those most vulnerable to it—would remain formidable obstacles to tackling AIDS. Although the introduction of antiretroviral treatment in developed countries 12 years ago and its dissemination to developing countries in recent years has largely changed the perception that AIDS is a so-called death sentence, people living with HIV/AIDS in many countries continue to experience ostracism, violence, eviction, loss of employment, and restrictions on their ability to travel. Stigma and fear of discrimination still prevent many people from accessing crucial prevention and treatment services, including HIV testing. Roughly 60 countries worldwide continue to deny or restrict entry to people living with HIV/AIDS, showing how differently HIV infection is perceived and treated compared with other diseases.

Notwithstanding these challenges, we can also say that, after years of inadequate action, we underestimated the sense of urgency and solidarity that would eventually develop in the global AIDS movement, leading to an unusual convergence of political will, money, and science. Since the UN General Assembly Special Session on AIDS in 2001, the international community has substantially increased resources available for AIDS by creating the Global Fund to Fight AIDS, Tuberculosis and Malaria. The USA has launched the US President's Emergency Plan for AIDS Relief (PEPFAR). As a result, more than 3 million people have now gained access to antiretroviral treatment, which was unimaginable only 5 years ago. People living with and affected by HIV, non-governmental organisations, civil society groups, and the private sector are more engaged in the response than ever before. However, in an unstable global political and economic environment, we will all have to work even harder than previously to ensure that this momentum is expanded and sustained.[1]

Some aspects of HIV/AIDS were also overestimated in the early years of the epidemic—notably, the pace with which HIV would spread in regions other than sub-Saharan Africa. For example, in the early 1990s, many were concerned that, left unchecked, HIV in Asia would spread quickly outside concentrated epidemics of sex workers, men who have sex with men, and injecting drug users, and that the disease would take on the proportions of the devastating generalised epidemics occurring in southern Africa.

Fortunately, this scenario has not yet happened, other than in Papua New Guinea, which now has a serious AIDS epidemic. Nevertheless, the Asian epidemic is showing its own worrying trends. A growing proportion of people with HIV in the region are women—notably married women. In Vietnam, women now account for a third of people infected.[2] At the same time, HIV prevalence in men who have sex with men is growing across Asia—eg, the proportion of men who have sex with men in Bangkok who are living with HIV increased from 17% to 28% between 2003 and 2005.[3] Because the continent of Asia has a very large population—more than 2.5 million people are living with HIV/AIDS in India alone—it will continue to demand substantial resources and intensive efforts to improve HIV prevention strategies and provide treatment to people who need it.

Meanwhile, our ability to estimate the number of people living with HIV/AIDS has become increasingly advanced. Estimates from UNAIDS/WHO are based on all relevant data available, including surveys of pregnant women attending antenatal clinics, population-based surveys, sentinel surveillance in populations at increased risk of HIV infection, case reporting, and registration systems. Different combinations of these approaches, and the consensus reached by leading experts nationally and internationally, are producing both improved data from country surveillance and steady advances in modelling methods. The overall result is increasingly accurate estimates.

Despite the remarkable innovations and successes of antiretroviral treatment, we have also overestimated our capacity to devise technological solutions to prevent HIV. Notwithstanding the optimistic projections of the US Health and Human Services Secretary Margaret Heckler in 1984, that an AIDS vaccine would be ready for testing in about 2 years, we still seem many years away from either a vaccine or a microbicide to protect against HIV transmission, especially after a recent series of disappointing trial results.[4,5] Nevertheless, much has been learned about how HIV enters and acts within the body, and continued investments in new prevention technology remain a crucial part of the AIDS research agenda. Encouragingly, in the past 2 years, studies have shown that male circumcision reduces HIV infection in men by up to 60%,[6] although it does not reduce transmission from men to women or between men.

One of the most common myths is that HIV prevention is not working. However, much evidence suggests that, in several countries, prevention programmes are effective. Between 2005 and 2007, coverage of services to prevent mother-to-child transmission of HIV increased from 14% to 33%.[7] As a result, in 2007, we noted for the first time a substantial decrease in the number of children born with HIV.

Prevention is, of course, about not only technology, but also behaviour. In many countries on several continents, changes in sexual behaviour (such as waiting longer to become sexually active, having fewer partners, and increased condom use) have been followed by reductions in the number of new HIV infections, providing evidence that efforts to change behaviour can and do work.[8]

However, sustaining behaviour change in the long term remains a major challenge. For example, the number of new HIV diagnoses in men who have sex with men doubled in Germany between 2002 and 2006, and increased by more than three-quarters in Switzerland.[2] These data could be attributable to complacency about AIDS and the sense that a treatable disease is somehow less threatening than are other diseases, and to a decrease in HIV prevention efforts in western Europe. Some developing countries that have previously had much success with HIV prevention, such as Uganda, have also had increases in rates of HIV transmission.[2]

Another major challenge is that, nearly 30 years into the epidemic, only about half of countries have national HIV prevention targets, whereas nearly 90% have targets for AIDS treatment. Furthermore, when prevention programmes do exist, they are often under-resourced and do not have the quality and scale that are needed to have a real effect in communities. They need to be better targeted to where the epidemic is, both in terms of populations at risk and geographic areas. Much has been published about the need for precise targeting of HIV prevention, especially in concentrated epidemics. But even saturation coverage of vulnerable groups will have little lasting effect without concerted and concrete efforts to change social standards and tackle social factors of the epidemic, such as homophobia and the low status of women in many societies. Programmes also need to be designed and managed more efficiently, including increased use of skills and practices from the business sector.[9,10]

An increasingly recurrent myth is that one solution, or a so-called silver bullet, will comprehensively prevent HIV transmission. Elimination of concurrent partnerships, circumcision of all men, focusing of prevention efforts on sex workers, universal HIV testing, and provision of antiretroviral therapy as soon as possible after infection, have all received attention as potential solutions for prevention of HIV transmission. Scaling up strategies for harm reduction, such as methadone substitution and the provision of clean needles for injecting drug users, remains neglected in many countries in which injection drug use is a major means of HIV transmission. Although these strategies are all important, no approach will be enough on its own, and the promotion of one solution is, in our view, irresponsible. If we have learned one lesson in the past 27 years, it is that effective HIV prevention depends on customising the right mix of interventions for every context and ensuring the necessary coverage of them.[8] If we are to successfully increase access to HIV prevention, we have to be prepared to come to terms with complexity, effectively use all the methods that are available, include affected communities, engage relevant business expertise, and foster leadership to help change harmful social norms.

Another prevailing misconception is that heterosexual transmission of HIV is uncommon outside Africa. Generalised epidemics are occurring in Haiti and Papua New Guinea, whereas heterosexual transmission drives the epidemic between sex workers, their partners, clients, and clients' partners in Asia and elsewhere. HIV infections in women are rising worldwide. The main method of transmission in Thailand is no longer between sex workers and their clients or between injecting drug users: it is between married couples.[3] Furthermore, AIDS remains the leading cause of death in African-American women in the USA.[11] To characterise all African epidemics as exclusively heterosexual is also incorrect. Methods of transmission and affected groups are many and varied. In Kenya, for example, HIV infections in men who have sex with men and injecting drug users are an increasing cause for concern.[12]

Although such observations neither indicate nor predict extensive or generalised HIV epidemic spread, they do draw attention to the fact that heterosexual transmission of HIV occurs in a wide range of settings. They also show that the HIV epidemic is constantly evolving, and continually surprising.

As we approach the fourth decade of the AIDS epidemic, new global challenges are competing for the attention of political leaders and donors at the same time as they face the present financial crisis. Alarmingly, a myth has begun to emerge that too much money is spent on AIDS. But AIDS remains the leading cause of death in Africa and the sixth highest cause of mortality worldwide.[13] It is fitting that investment in fighting AIDS has finally begun to increase substantially, rising from a paltry US$250 million in 1996 to around $14 billion in 2008.[14] Even so, UNAIDS estimates that available resources at present fall well short of what will be needed to reach coverage targets for 2010.[14] Moreover, mobilisation around AIDS has increased available resources for tuberculosis and malaria (largely through the Global Fund) to unprecedented amounts and generally contributed to an increase in global funding for health.

Increased resources are beginning to have an effect, as are antiretroviral treatment programmes, which have been established in developing countries for less than 5 years. Among the first was in Malawi, which recorded a 44% reduction in mortality in workers at the national electricity company—one of the country's largest employers—after the roll-out of antiretroviral treatment.[15] In Botswana, where HIV prevalence has reached 30%, mortality has begun to fall in the age groups most affected by AIDS since the introduction of antiretroviral treatment.[16]

Another major myth that needs to be dispelled is that investments in AIDS are being made at the expense of health systems that are chronically underfunded. Although AIDS has exposed weaknesses in health systems, funds for this disease are making a major contribution to the strengthening of health systems.

The Global Fund and PEPFAR are now among the biggest investors in health systems, joining other funders such as the GAVI Alliance. Although drugs and other commodities account for nearly half of Global Fund spending (figure 1), 35% of the Fund's financing for AIDS, tuberculosis, and malaria contributes directly to supporting human resources, infrastructure and equipment, and monitoring and evaluation: all key components of health systems. Overall, the Fund has committed more than $4 billion in these three areas. From 2004 to 2009, on the basis of conservative estimates, PEPFAR will commit more than $4 billion to health systems, including more than $1 billion in 2009 alone (figure 2).

The results of these investments are dearly noticeable on the ground, where AIDS resources are contributing to the refurbishment of health centres, the

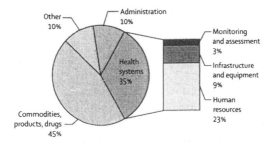

Figure 1 Direct funding of health systems through Global Fund grants.

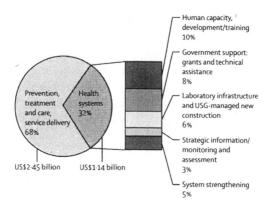

Figure 2 PEPFAR planned investments in health-systems-related programmes and bilateral programme support in 15 countries in 2009.

hiring of new health workers, and the establishment of local schemes for national health insurance. In Ethiopia, resources from the Global Fund and PEPFAR are strengthening the health system and enabling the rapid scale-up of diagnostic and treatment services for AIDS and tuberculosis.

AIDS programmes have other benefits for health systems. In many African countries, AIDS services and treatment keep health workers alive, healthy, and able to work. A study in Rwanda,[17] for example, showed that within 2 months of starting to provide antiretroviral treatment in PEPFAR-supported sites, the average number of new admissions at seven sites dropped by 21%, freeing up health workers and enabling valuable resources to be dedicated to other health-care needs. AIDS resources have greatly strengthened overall laboratory capacity and systems for distribution of drugs. In Nicaragua, new equipment financed by the Global Fund for the National Reference Laboratory enables not only processing of HIV tests, but also processing and storage of blood samples taken for other purposes.

A further myth that has emerged suggests that strengthening health services alone will solve the world's health problems, including AIDS. Improvements to health infrastructure and measures to tackle the human resources crisis for health are long overdue in many countries and deserve much support, especially since they will be essential for the further roll-out of antiretroviral treatment. At the same time, what might have happened to the 4 million people on antiretroviral therapy in developing countries if we had waited until health services had been strengthened before launching HIV treatment programmes is a sobering thought.

Improved health systems alone are not enough to end the AIDS epidemic. We have known since the early 1990s that, although the health sector has a major role in provision of HIV treatment, it cannot and does not meet the full range of needs. Whereas well functioning health and community services will be key to provision of antiretroviral therapy for decades to come—as well as services for the prevention of mother-to-child HIV transmission, blood safety, and male circumcision—most other HIV prevention activities are happening largely outside the health sector. This tenet is especially true in the case of programmes that reach populations at high risk and at the margins of society, youth, and injecting drug users, and programmes promoting social change.

AIDS funding is often used to lend support to the establishment of quality sex-education programmes in schools, efforts to eliminate violence against women, and care for orphans. The benefits of such activities extend far beyond an effective AIDS response.

A last myth is that AIDS has somehow been solved. However, we have only just begun to see a return on the investments of the past decade in the form of falling rates and fewer deaths, indicating a new phase in the AIDS response; it by no means suggests that the problem is anywhere near solved. This new phase is characterised by a new set of challenges that could well prove more difficult than any that we have encountered so far.

We need to recognise that AIDS is a long-term event. Tackling it is complex, but our successes so far indicate what is possible. In the future, we should pay far greater attention to epidemiological trends and to the social factors driving them. We have to identify now how to finance a sustained response to AIDS for another several decades, and develop longlasting links with broader efforts to strengthen health systems and health workforces as well as other development efforts, such as in education and food security. At the same time we have to continue to invest in research and development to produce improved diagnostic tests and less toxic and more effective drugs, in addition to microbicides and vaccines. A serious and concerted effort is also needed to tackle stigma and discrimination, ensuring that people most at risk actually receive the services that they need. Only when we have met all these aims will we be anywhere close to the point at which we can truthfully say that the fight against AIDS is being won.

Contributors

PP and MK jointly drafted the article, MD provided significant editorial input to the draft, and JL-L provided editorial input to the draft.

Conflict of interest statement

We declare that we have no conflict of interest.

Acknowledgments

We thank Sarah Russell, Ian Grubb, and Rebecca Affolder for their assistance in the preparation of this article.

References

1 Piot P., Russell S. Larson H. Good politics, bad politics: the experience of AIDS. *Am J Publ Health* 2007; 97:1934–36.

2 UNAIDS/WHO. AIDS epidemic update, 2007 Geneva: UNAIDS/WHO, 2007.

3 Commission on AIDS in Asia. Redefining AIDS in Asia: crafting an effective response. New Delhi: Oxford University Press, 2008.

4 Buchbinder S. P., Mehrotra D. V., Duerr A., et al, for the Step Study Protocol Team. Efficacy assessment of a cell-mediated immunity HIV-1 vaccine (the Step Study): a double-blind, randomised, placebo-controlled, test-of-concept trial. *Lancet* 2008; **372**: 1881–93.

5 McElrath M. J., De Rosa S. C., Moodie Z., et al, for the Step Study Protocol Team. HIV-1 vaccine-induced immunity in the test-of-concept Step Study: a case-cohort analysis. *Lancet* 2008; **372**: 1894–905.

6 Auvert B., Taljaard D., Lagarde E., Sobngwi-Tambekou J., Sitta R., Puren A. Randomized, controlled intervention trial of male circumcision for reduction of HIV infection risk: the ANRS 1265 Trial. *PLoS Med* 2005; **2**: e298.

7 WHO/UNAIDS. Towards universal access scaling up priority HIV/AIDS interventions in the health sector: progress report. June, 2008. http://www.who.int/hiv/pub/2008progressreport/en/index.html (accessed Feb 5, 2009).

8 Merson M. H., O'Malley J., Serwadda D., Apisuk C. The history and challenge of HIV prevention. *Lancet* 2008; **372**: 475–88.

9 Piot P., Bartos M., Larson H., Zewdie D., Mane P. Coming to terms with complexity: a call to action for HIV prevention. *Lancet* 2008; **372**: 845–59.

10 Bertozzi S. M., Laga M., Bautista-Arredondo S., Countinho A. Making HIV prevention programs work. *Lancet* 2008; **372**: 831–44.

11 US Centers for Disease Control and Prevention. Revised recommendations for HIV testing of adults, adolescents, and pregnant women in health-care settings. *MMWR Morb Mortal Wkly Rep* 2006; **55**: 1–17.

12 Gouws E., White P. J., Stover J., Brown T. Short term transmission estimates of adult HIV incidence by mode of transmission: Kenya and Thailand as examples. *Sex Transm Inf* 2006; **82**: 51–55.

13 WHO. The global burden of disease: 2004 update. Geneva: World Health Organization, 2008.

14 UNAIDS. What countries need: investments needed for 2010 targets. Geneva: UNAIDS, 2009.

15 The Global Fund to Fight AIDS, TB and Malaria. Partners in impact: results report. Geneva: The Global Fund to Fight AIDS, TB and Malaria, 2007.

16 Stoneburner R., Montagu D., Pervilhac C., et al. Declines in adult HIV mortality in Botswana, 2003–2005: evidence for an impact of antiretroviral therapy programs. Sixteenth International AIDS Conference, Toronto; 2006 (abstr THLB0507).

17 Price J. E., Micomyiza E., Nyeimana V., Tchupo J. Integrating HIV clinical services in primary health care centers in Rwanda: effect on the quantity on non-HIV services delivered. HIV Implemented Meeting; Kigali, Rwanda; June 17, 2007.

28

HIV, AIDS AND SECURITY

Where are we now?

Colin McInnes and Simon Rushton*

Source: *International Affairs*, 86:1 (2010), 225–45.

Over the course of the past three decades, HIV/AIDS has emerged as one of the greatest single causes of death and suffering on the planet.[1] The impact of the disease has been felt not only in the lives, lifestyles and livelihoods of millions of individuals and their families, but across whole societies as well. Over the last decade in particular the societal impact of HIV/AIDS has been widely discussed in terms of national and international security. The key moment in this development was the UN Security Council (UNSC) meeting in January 2000, and its subsequent passing of Resolution 1308. The Security Council's intervention appeared to act as a catalyst, changing the way in which the disease was thought about. It seemed to establish a new consensus over the disease, raising its international profile and enhancing the possibilities for action to combat its impact and further spread.

This article is partly a retrospective assessment of this securitizing move: ten years after UNSCR 1308, what has changed? Between 2000 and 2005 there was a widespread assumption, reflected both in the International Relations literature and in statements by key policy-makers, that HIV/AIDS had become well established as an international security issue. We suggest that in fact the strength of the international consensus over HIV/AIDS as a security issue tended to be overstated; that within a few years that consensus seemed to have dissipated (not least in the Security Council), and significant doubts had emerged over the evidence for the supposed links between HIV and security. In other words, we suggest that the securitizing move made by the UNSC in 2000 was at best only partially successful. Although there are some examples of HIV/AIDS appearing to have been framed as a security issue with possible policy implications, in other contexts the move appears to have had limited effect. After examining the manner in which this consensus was made and then broken we develop two arguments. First, we suggest that while links between HIV/AIDS and security do exist, they are more complex than was believed ten years ago. The fears articulated around the time of the Security Council's intervention—of militaries and conceivably whole states collapsing under the burden of the disease, and of the inexorable spread of HIV in areas of high conflict—were overstated; but there are risks, and they are still present. Second, we examine the consequences of the attempt to securitize HIV/AIDS and suggest that although there have been a number of positive developments over the last decade, many of these cannot be wholly explained by securitization. At the same time, the tendency of some actors to treat HIV/AIDS as a security issue has created a number of new tensions.

Making a consensus: from Washington to New York

The idea that AIDS poses a potential threat to security has been around for a surprisingly long time. As early as 1987—at which time only eleven sub-Saharan African states had reported over 100 cases, and many of the states which now have the highest prevalence levels had still reported under 100—a US Special National Intelligence Estimate examined the implications of the AIDS pandemic for the region in detail.[2] While the report noted that much of the information about the disease's spread in Africa was at that stage 'anecdotal or based on small medical research programs lacking a strong epidemiological basis',[3] there were clear concerns about the strategic and security implications of AIDS. Those concerns focused on two issues. The first was the now common set of claims about the ways in which AIDS threatens the security and stability of states: its disproportionate effect on elites; the economic consequences of lost productivity, reduced tourism and long-term demographic change; the implications for military capabilities; and the possibility of regional tensions being heightened by the reaction of neighbours to a state with high prevalence levels. The second issue, now absent from the discourse around AIDS and security but reflective of the very different times in which the report was produced, was the effort apparently under way by the Soviet Union to use the pandemic to stir up anti-US sentiment in the region by disseminating the idea that 'the United States developed and caused the spread of AIDS' and 'exploiting black African sensitivities to racism and so-called Western imperialism'.[4] For both these reasons, the report argued, US interests were at stake.

During the 1990s the AIDS–security linkage began to become more prominent in Washington policy circles, although some of those involved in pushing forward the case have complained that the Clinton administration was somewhat slow in the uptake.[5] The argument was gaining ground nonetheless. A 1992 report published by the Institute of Medicine did much to dramatize the threats posed to the US by infectious diseases, including HIV/AIDS.[6] The same year a Department of State memorandum entitled 'The global

AIDS disaster: implications for the 1990s' described AIDS as a 'time bomb' with severe economic, political and military ramifications.[7] Two years later Laurie Garrett's influential *The coming plague* put forward similar arguments.[8] In June 1996 a Presidential Decision Directive called for a greater degree of coordination in the US government's response to the security threats posed by infectious diseases. As part of this effort the National Intelligence Council produced a National Intelligence Estimate on 'The global infectious disease threat and its implications for the United States' (declassified in 2000). Although the report's scope was wider than HIV/AIDS, that was one of its key foci. Many of the claims that had appeared in the 1987 CIA report were repeated, particularly the concerns about the impact on militaries (now seen to include international peacekeeping forces), social cohesion and the potential for conflict, and the possibility that 'disease-related embargoes and restrictions on travel and immigration will cause frictions among and between developed and developing countries'.[9]

Reflecting these earlier discussions within the US, the Clinton administration was behind the first major push to assert the claim that AIDS was a security threat on the global stage. The key moment in this process came in January 2000 when, under the US presidency of the UNSC and during a month-long focus on Africa, the Council met to discuss the impact of AIDS on peace and security in Africa. Richard Holbrooke, Clinton's ambassador to the UN, played the central role in getting the issue onto the Council's agenda. Although Holbrooke has dated his awareness of the security implications of AIDS back to a 1992 trip to Cambodia,[10] the immediate precursor to the UNSC's involvement was his visit to southern Africa in December 1999. He then set about persuading key figures in the US administration and in the UN that AIDS should be discussed by the Council. In Washington he found a willing supporter in Al Gore, then Vice-President, who personally presided over the first Council session on the issue. Within the UN there was, initially at least, more scepticism. Gwyn Prins quotes Senator Russ Feingold's recollection of a telephone conversation between Holbrooke and Kofi Annan in December 1999. Holbrooke demanded a Security Council session on HIV/AIDS. 'We can't do that,' the Secretary-General reportedly replied; 'AIDS isn't a security issue.'[11] Steve Sternberg, the original source of the story, said that 'the Security Council meeting, held in January 2000, would change that notion forever'.[12] Certainly Annan's own view seems to have changed rapidly. On 10 January 2000, less than a month after his sceptical telephone conversation with Holbrooke, the Secretary-General told the Security Council that 'it is entirely appropriate that the Council should be devoting its first session [of the new millennium] to the problem of AIDS'.[13] Gore was even clearer in signalling the significance of the Council's initiative. In his opening address he thanked the members of the Council for

> their willingness to greet the dawn of this new millennium by exploring a brand-new definition of world security. Today marks the first time,

after more than 4,000 meetings stretching back more than half a
century, that the Security Council will discuss a health issue as a security threat. We tend to think of a threat to security in terms of war
and peace. Yet no one can doubt that the havoc wreaked and the
toll exacted by HIV/AIDS do threaten our security.[14]

Later in the same discussion Gore argued that

AIDS is not just a humanitarian crisis. It is a security crisis—because
it threatens not just individual citizens, but the very institutions that
define and defend the character of a society. This disease weakens
workforces and saps economic strength. AIDS strikes at teachers,
and denies education to their students. It strikes at the military, and
subverts the forces of order and peacekeeping.[15]

Many of those issues were discussed again later that year when the Security
Council passed Resolution 1308, focusing on the threat HIV/AIDS posed
to international peace and security. The Resolution argued that that the HIV/
AIDS pandemic, if unchecked, 'may pose a risk to stability and security' and
that its spread was 'exacerbated by conditions of violence and insecurity',
and expressed particular concerns over the risks to peacekeepers.[16] The
unanimous adoption of Resolution 1308 seemed to indicate a recognition
(at least among the 15 members of the Council) that AIDS constituted a
security threat. Given the Security Council's status within the UN, and in
world politics more broadly, its findings set the agenda for many of the
subsequent debates around HIV/AIDS as a national security issue. Its actions
in 2000 appeared to represent a powerful securitizing move, framing HIV/
AIDS as a threat to national and international security rather than as a
'mere' development or public health problem. In doing so the UNSC could
be seen to be acting as a policy entrepreneur both within the UN system (for
example, influencing actions of the Department of Peacekeeping Operations
and UNAIDS) and outside it (for example, in the G8). The Council returned
to the issue in 2001, 2003 and 2005. Interest in HIV/AIDS as a national
security problem continued in the wider UN context too, in much of the
work conducted by UNAIDS and the Department of Peacekeeping Operations,
while in December 2004 infectious disease (including HIV/AIDS) was highlighted as a new 'biosecurity' threat by the High Level Panel on Threats,
Challenges and Change established by the Secretary General.[17]

It is possible, then, to interpret the UNSC's intervention as the critical move
in constructing an international consensus around HIV/AIDS as a national
security problem demanding international attention and action. This move
rested on a series of arguments which, expressed in various ways, became
the orthodox set of linkages to which scholars and policy-makers alike pointed
in arguing for attention to be paid to the AIDS–security nexus, specifically:

- that uniformed militaries (including peacekeepers) were especially vulnerable to HIV and might act as agents in the spread of the disease (this argument was based on some empirical evidence, but more importantly on the identification of a range of risk factors specific to uniformed militaries);
- that state stability was at risk in high prevalence areas: economies might be devastated by the disease, while the social fabric of a nation could be ripped apart;
- that conflict (including the post-conflict phase) created significant risks for the spread of HIV (there was some empirical evidence for this, and also a range of readily identifiable risk factors).

HIV/AIDS was certainly moving rapidly up the agenda in the early 2000s, and a plethora of new policy initiatives emerged. Within a few months of Resolution 1308 came the adoption of the Millennium Development Goals (which explicitly included HIV/AIDS); the General Assembly conducted a Special Session on HIV/AIDS in June 2001; in 2002 the G8 established the Global Fund to Fight HIV/AIDS, Tuberculosis and Malaria; and in 2003 the Bush administration launched the President's Plan for Emergency AIDS Relief (PEPFAR), by far the largest national initiative to combat the global effects of HIV/AIDS. The disease's profile was almost unprecedented for a health issue. There was a clear and widespread sense of emergency and an almost universally recognized requirement for large-scale and sustained global action.

In this context it was natural that in the first half of the decade the Security Council's actions, with Resolution 1308 serving as the formal expression of its concern, were interpreted by many as a scene-changing intervention. Peter Piot, the executive director of UNAIDS, saw it as a 'milestone in the response to the epidemic'.[18] The AIDS–security linkage was seen in policy statements from major western governments and UN agencies; in academic articles, including those published by establishment outlets such as *International Security* and the International Institute for Strategic Studies; and in statements and reports from a range of NGOs and civil society organizations. Many took the view that this new perspective created the potential to gain a much higher international profile (and as a consequence greater resources) for the pandemic.[19] Others, however, highlighted the possible dangers of treating AIDS as a security issue.[20] Either way, all agreed that something really significant had happened.

Unmaking a consensus: doubts creep in

A decade on, the consensus that HIV/AIDS is a security issue (and that it ought to be treated as such) seems somewhat less robust. First, it is now clear that the degree of consensus was overstated from the beginning. There were doubts within the Council from the outset over the adoption of Resolution 1308, and subsequent actions both within and outside the Council have suggested that there is less than universal agreement on the status of HIV/AIDS as a security issue. Second, there has been a re-examination of the evidence underpinning the linkages identified above. In many cases the evidence has been found wanting, or the connections have turned out to be more complex than was originally supposed (an issue to which we return in more detail in the following section). This uncertainty has in turn further undermined what agreement there was initially.

On the face of it, the unanimous adoption of Resolution 1308 would appear to be definitive evidence of a consensus (in the Council at least) on the major securitizing claims. Yet there is ample evidence to suggest that the Resolution was a controversial one which the US had to steer skilfully through to adoption. Of the permanent members, Russia, China and France were all initially opposed to discussing HIV/AIDS in the Security Council, although they were ultimately persuaded to support the Resolution.[21] Even the UK—the one permanent Council member that publicly backed the Resolution—had private qualms. In the final days of negotiation over the wording of the Resolution the UK Foreign and Commonwealth Office (FCO) was concerned about the danger of exceeding the Security Council's remit. A telegram from the FCO to the mission in New York on 13 July noted: 'We remain concerned that the text as it stands does not obviously fall within the Security Council's competence. [text removed] . . . Nevertheless you should continue to support the US by shortening and amending the text.'[22] A similar message was included in the following day's telegram.[23] We also know that many of the countries that contribute most troops to UN peacekeeping operations were opposed to the Resolution. The UK mission's report on the meeting of 17 July at which Resolution 1308 was adopted notes: 'Only four non-Council members spoke, perhaps reflecting the opposition of many troop contributors to the resolution.'[24]

Despite these doubts, Holbrooke was successful in overcoming the opposition. As always, the US was able to exercise a large degree of influence over the Council. In this case, however, it was aided by the performance of Dr Peter Piot, the director of UNAIDS, who played an important and active role in the Council meetings and in the attempts to securitize HIV/AIDS more generally.[25] The US effort was also helped, no doubt, by the special status of HIV/AIDS as a global issue. Few states would wish to be seen to oppose action to combat it. Certainly no state would want to bear the political costs of unilaterally blocking international attempts to address the pandemic. The adoption of Resolution 1308 was not, then, simply the result of universal agreement on the securitizing claims. Even in the US case it has become clear that the desire to get AIDS onto the Security Council agenda was not solely a foreign policy consideration motivated by concerns over international security, but reflected a domestic agenda as well. US Vice-President Al

Gore saw the need to bolster support among those concerned with HIV/ AIDS in the US prior to the November presidential election in which he was the Democratic candidate and saw the Security Council's discussions as a platform for this. Moreover, Richard Holbrooke, who had aspirations to be Gore's Secretary of State, saw this as an opportunity to enhance his own reputation on the international stage.[26]

In subsequent years, and certainly since 2005, the Security Council seems to have backed away from the AIDS issue. Although it was stated following Resolution 1308 that AIDS had become a 'core issue' for the Security Council,[27] it now seems to have dropped off the agenda entirely. The pattern established by the Council's 2001, 2003 and 2005 meetings on HIV/AIDS has not continued and there has been no formal Council discussion of HIV/AIDS since 2005. It may be that the Council felt that it had already achieved its goal of highlighting the scale of the problem and addressing the specific issue relating to UN peacekeeping personnel. Yet the jettisoning of HIV from the Council agenda, coupled with a context in which the pandemic in Africa was getting no better,[28] sends out some very awkward signals for proponents of the security discourse. Wallensteen and Johansson have noted that at the turn of the millennium the Security Council had begun to see 'security' in a wider context, resulting in 'thematic Resolutions' not only on HIV/AIDS but also on other issues such as women and children. But, they go on to argue, this trend virtually disappeared as a result of the increased focus on terrorism (and the resulting return to more 'traditional' security concerns) which followed the events of 11 September 2001.[29] If this is so—and the record of Council Resolutions since 2001 seems to support the claim—it may be that HIV/AIDS became the subject of a Security Council Resolution not only due to the agency of Holbrooke and others but also because it happened to arise during a window of opportunity. The year 2000 offered perhaps uniquely fertile soil for attempts to frame AIDS as a security issue.

Away from the Council, the signs of universal agreement on the securitizing claims were scarcely more convincing. It is certainly the case that the security dimensions of HIV/AIDS have been a feature of policy statements from a variety of different sources, including states and multilateral bodies such as UNAIDS, the Global Fund and the G8. Yet it is questionable how many governments and agencies actually see and respond to the pandemic primarily in security terms. As we argue in the final section of this article, security seems to have been only one of the motivations for the proliferation of global initiatives to tackle the AIDS problem. In many ways it appears to be less significant than others, perhaps most notably international development. Comparisons of the approaches taken by the US (the prime instigator of securitization) and other states certainly suggest that security is not in all cases the dominant frame.[30]

The fragile agreement over HIV/AIDS as a security issue was further undermined by a second set of developments: namely, concerns over the empirical evidence supporting the claims. As seen above, HIV/AIDS was first identified as a security threat by the policy community, in particular by intelligence agencies such as the CIA. In some cases, most notably the CIA report of 1987, the evidence on which the purported links were based was recognized by the authors themselves as being incomplete. By the middle of the decade that had begun with the high points of a Security Council discussion and Resolution 1308, doubts were beginning to be expressed in the academic community, not least by Tony Barnett of the LSE and Alex de Waal of Harvard, over the evidence supporting these claims. In an influential 2005 report to UNAIDS, circulated to members of the Security Council, Barnett and Gwyn Prins argued that: 'Since the passage of Resolution 1308, year-on-year there has been an increasing flow of publication [sic] on the subject of AIDS and security . . . this is largely a literature of "inverted triangles" . . . balanced on narrow footings in terms of high quality hard evidence.'[31] For Barnett and Prins, however, it was not simply the thin basis of evidence available, but the nature of that evidence and the way it had been used which were problematic. In particular they criticized the widespread use of 'factoids' in the literature on HIV and security:

> 'Factoids' are the intellectual viruses of quick and dirty synthetic studies. They are soft opinions that have hardened into 'fact'. The term describes pieces of data that look credible at first glance but which are insecurely grounded in evidence. They achieve this status as a result of a form of pyramid selling by recycling through publications, grey literature and reports of meetings.[32]

It may well be that the Barnett and Prins report bolstered the resolve of those who were opposed to the issue being on the Council agenda in the first place, but at the very least it posed awkward questions over the strength of the case made.

Barnett's work then moved on to focus on the issue of HIV and state fragility. In a series of papers in the second half of the decade he developed a powerful critique of the link, suggesting that there was no direct relationship between high levels of HIV and state fragility.[33] Meanwhile, in 2005 Alex de Waal presented a paper on 'HIV/AIDS and the military' to a seminar organized by the Netherlands Ministry of Foreign Affairs at the Clingendael Institute in The Hague. In this he argued that the 'received wisdom' concerning high HIV levels in the military required greater scrutiny.[34] De Waal's scepticism was developed more fully the next year in an article he wrote with Alan Whiteside and Tsadkan Gebre-Tensae. Their conclusion was that 'the oft-cited claim that soldiers have prevalence rates two to five times higher than the civilian population is unsustainable and should no longer be cited . . . [and] there is remarkably little good evidence for conflict accelerating the spread of HIV/AIDS'.[35] In the AIDS and security field, however, de

Waal is perhaps best known for his leading role in the AIDS, Security and Conflict Initiative (ASCI).[36] As lead author of its concluding 2009 report, de Waal brings together a wide range of fieldwork, new data and reports commissioned by ASCI to criticize the generalized assumptions of the early years of the decade: 'The agenda has moved from the general to the specific . . . earlier more alarmist relationships that were assumed to exist between national-level state security and HIV and AIDS are not borne out by the evidence.'[37]

De Waal is careful not to dismiss the link entirely, however, instead arguing for an 'intermediary [level of analysis] between macro-level assumptions and micro-level behavioural and biomedical approaches'.[38] Local government structures, which are often primarily responsible for directly delivering services to the population, may be more immediately affected than national governments by HIV/AIDS. Work on the case of South Africa, for example, has suggested that the 'hollowing out' of government capacity is starting to be felt in local municipalities.[39] Yet this insight has not to date been widely reflected in the debates over the securitization of AIDS in either the policy or academic communities, both of which have tended to focus on national governments as crucial to the stability of states.

It is clear that the second half of the decade was marked by much more uncertainty over HIV/AIDS as a security issue. The apparent consensus over many of the claims which underpinned securitization has come under strain both in academia and in the policy world. What was originally seen as the securitization of HIV/AIDS now appears more as a securitizing move which has been at best only partially successful.

Building a new consensus: recognizing complexity

We suggest that the picture emerging is not one of there being no link between HIV/AIDS and security, but rather one indicating that we require a more nuanced understanding of this link. Moreover, we argue that the initial fears expressed over the security consequences of high HIV prevalence rates were overstated and not applicable in all circumstances. Again, what is needed is a better understanding, this time of the circumstances under which HIV can impact on national security. One of the most important reasons why the relationship between HIV and security is difficult to understand is that it is complex. This should have come as no surprise, since HIV generates not one but many epidemics, its impacts manifesting in diverse ways across different cultures and societies.[40] Whereas much of the literature on HIV and security in the early part of the decade portrayed the epidemic as one event encompassed by a single, grand narrative, the reality appears considerably more diverse with regard both to the nature of the epidemic and, more especially, to its social consequences. It is only more recently that the complexity in the relationship between HIV and security has been addressed. To illustrate this we re-examine the three key linkages raised earlier in this article as central to linking HIV and security: prevalence rates in the uniformed services (including peacekeepers); the impact of high prevalence rates on state stability; and the link between conflict and the spread of HIV.

Prevalence rates in armed services

At the time of UNSCR 1308 in 2000, it was accepted wisdom that the HIV prevalence rate within militaries in sub-Saharan Africa was between two and five times the rate of civilian populations, and that this disproportionate vulnerability impacted (or had the potential to impact) upon their operational capacity, thereby making HIV/AIDS a national security issue.[41] In 2005, however, UNAIDS admitted that 'little reliable information is available on levels of HIV infection among uniformed services. Few countries conduct systematic screening and public health surveillance systems are often weak.'[42] Nevertheless, in 2006 UNAIDS again repeated its belief that militaries 'are at risk of contracting HIV, and that AIDS impacts on their effectiveness'.[43] The claim that 'among male population groups, military and police report the highest risk behaviour and number of partners' and that this 'can seriously affect military readiness' remains present on its website to this day.[44]

Serious questions have been asked over the origins and generality of this assertion. The widely cited figure of prevalence two to five times as high as that of civilian populations appears to have originated in a single study from the early 1990s. As Whiteside and colleagues argue, 'While there was some evidence for this (with respect to HIV) in the early 1990s . . . it was uncritically accepted and repeated and is in fact demonstrably incorrect today [2006].'[45] Although there are reasons why prevalence rates in armed forces might be higher than in the civilian population, equally there were interventions available to the military which could reduce risk by raising awareness.[46] Depending on the success of these interventions, prevalence rates might vary considerably. Nor is a straightforward comparison between the adult civilian population and the armed forces satisfactory: age profile, location and socioeconomic status are all potentially significant variables in terms of risk of infection, and militaries are generally not representative of the general population by any of these measures.[47] Crucially, however, prevalence in the armed forces appears now to depend on a variety of factors including demography, structure, recruitment patterns, military ethos and training, delivery of awareness programmes and access to condoms, alcohol and drug abuse, and the stage and nature of the epidemic.[48]

Moreover, even if HIV were more prevalent in a country's armed forces, the impact upon their operational effectiveness would vary depending on factors such as the availability of replacements, discipline, and the significance of other security forces (including police and private security companies) in a given emergency. Nor is it apparent that the weakness of a state's armed forces is a causal agent in either internal or external aggression. It appears far more likely to be a contributory factor, and even then secrecy over combat readiness and HIV prevalence may limit the impression of weakness.[49] What these reflections suggest is that uniformed services (including peacekeepers) may be at greater risk of infection under certain circumstances, and that a high prevalence of HIV in the security forces may contribute to national security problems, but that both these possibilities are dependent on a wide range of variables, and the simple causal relationship suggested at the beginning of the decade does not accurately reflect the reality.

HIV and state stability

In his address to the UNSC's January 2000 session on HIV/AIDS, UN Secretary-General Kofi Annan argued that 'AIDS is causing socio-economic crises which in turn threaten political stability'.[50] The effects of the disease on economies and on governance were frequently highlighted by the UN and other commentators as potentially destabilizing. For these commentators, economic decline due to high HIV prevalence may increase income inequalities and poverty, exacerbating or creating social and political unrest. Equally worrying was the unusually high prevalence of HIV among skilled professionals, including civil servants, teachers, police and health workers, which threatened to undermine the institutions that make a state run effectively.[51]

Although it was perhaps understandable that a link was drawn between high prevalence and state instability in the early years of the decade—after all, state failure had been an international motif of the 1990s zeitgeist, and a set of risk factors were clearly identifiable—this link was clearly speculative since there had at that time been no example of a state failing as a result of high HIV prevalence. Ten years on, there is still none. Indeed, there is a noticeable *lack* of a correlation between those states with the highest levels of HIV in Africa and those that are most fragile.[52] Although Laurie Garrett has pointed out that the extended event horizon of the disease means that the full social and economic impact may be seen in decades, not months or years,[53] with the epidemic well into its third decade in Africa there seems to be little sign yet of states failing because of HIV. One of the major findings of the ASCI project was that there was no direct causal linkage between HIV and state fragility. Indeed, it was argued that the use of the concept 'state fragility' may actually undermine the effectiveness of international responses: 'fragile states' are not all fragile in the same way, or for the same reasons. Attempts to address HIV/AIDS must therefore recognize this diversity.[54]

Yet clearly high HIV prevalence creates the potential for negative economic and social impacts in some of the weakest states on earth. How, then, can we explain the apparent absence of a link between HIV and state failure? UNAIDS has suggested that the link is indirect, combining with or exacerbating other factors more obviously associated with state instability,[55] while in their Jaipur paradigm Barnett and Whiteside offer a more subtle understanding of the link, suggesting that it is only if such states also have *both* low social cohesion *and* high levels of poverty/unequal distribution of wealth that they may be at high risk of instability.[56] Other factors may also explain the poor correlation. These include the ability of states or the international community to respond, not least through aid or the provision of anti-retroviral therapies (ARTs); the possibility that the effects of HIV may be felt at the local or community level, where failure is not usually considered in measures of state stability; the tendency not to include unpaid costs of labour (especially that of women and children) in macroeconomic analyses of state performance; and the focus of state failure indices on short- to medium-term changes, not long-term ones.[57] In 2006 Whiteside and colleagues concluded that: 'The HIV/AIDS epidemic erodes institutional capacity, creates poverty and despair and intensifies dependence on international aid. These are all serious pressures which jeopardize the development of sound democratic governance and can intensify crisis.'[58] What has become apparent is that we do not fully understand whether and how this can lead to state failure.

Conflict and the spread of HIV[59]

As Stefan Elbe wrote in 2002, 'armed conflicts and their participants constitute an important vector of HIV/AIDS, a virus responsible for killing more than ten times as many people in Africa as the conflicts themselves'.[60] Similarly, a US Institute for Peace report baldly stated that 'no one denies the role of conflict in the spread of the virus'.[61] Perhaps the most significant contribution on this point, however, was the endorsement of the UN and especially the Security Council. In the preamble to Resolution 1308, the Security Council argued that the spread of HIV was 'exacerbated by conditions of violence and insecurity'.[62] Evidence for this link originated from several years earlier. In particular, the first major epidemic of HIV and AIDS, in Uganda, coincided with the invasion of that country.[63] More general conclusions were drawn from sub-Saharan Africa being an area of high instability and conflict during the 1970s and 1980s when HIV began to spread.[64] Reasons offered for this link included high HIV prevalence among uniformed services, which come into greater contact with civilian populations during conflict; human migration to avoid conflict and returning after conflict; changes in sexual behaviour, especially increased sexual violence towards women; the impact of conflict upon health provision; and risks which emerge after conflict, especially with regard to peacekeepers and human mobility.[65]

By the middle years of the current decade, however, further research suggested that the links were more complex than first imagined.[66] In some long conflicts little change in HIV prevalence was evident, while in others prevalence actually declined, suggesting that conflict might in some circumstances act as a brake on the spread of the disease. Not least, if conflict isolated a region and reduced the ability of people to move freely, then this directly affects one of the most significant vectors for the spread of the disease—human mobility. The case of Angola appeared particularly interesting in this respect. UNAIDS commented that 'largely due to the internal armed conflict, the Angolan HIV prevalence appears considerably lower than in neighbouring countries. This suggests that the restricted mobility as a result of the conflict may have slowed the spread of HIV in the country.'[67] Similarly, in Burundi prevalence rates in the capital actually fell during the period of conflict.[68] Initially such cases could be presented as exceptions, but as more evidence emerged of lower HIV rates in conflicts, so the picture became stronger.[69] In a major article in 2007, Paul Spiegel (the senior HIV officer at UNHCR) and colleagues argued that

> there is insufficient evidence that HIV transmission increases in populations affected by conflict. Furthermore, there are insufficient data to conclude that refugees fleeing conflict have a higher prevalence of HIV infection than do their surrounding host communities ... past assumptions that conflict and displacement increase prevalence of HIV infection were made from a few surveys, some of questionable quality and others with biased interpretation of results.[70]

Nevertheless, even Spiegel and his colleagues were unwilling to deny a possible link between conflict and HIV: 'Displaced populations and those affected by conflict are clearly at risk of HIV transmission. Furthermore, to expect that incidence of HIV infection will be high in survivors of conflict and rape is understandable.'[71] The work of Spiegel and others suggested that the link between conflict and the spread of HIV was not straightforward.[72] In particular, the reasons commonly offered for this link had begun to appear rather more nuanced and subject to variables than was originally believed,[73] while the empirical evidence was highly varied: in some conflicts prevalence increased, but in others it remained the same or even dropped. Conflict did not automatically lead to increased prevalence but was more accurately seen as a risk factor for the spread of HIV. The relationship was not straightforward but complex, and what was lacking was an explanation of when and how this risk factor translated into increased HIV prevalence. Just as HIV epidemics vary between different countries, so do conflicts. The extent to which conflict is a vector for HIV depends on the specificities of both the conflict and the epidemic in that state. This level of nuance was missing from the claims that were being made ten years ago, and was missing from Resolution 1308.

The mixed effects of securitizing HIV/AIDS

The above discussion suggests that the relationship between HIV/AIDS and national security is more complex than was originally suspected. This section examines the effect of the (partial) securitization on policy responses and discusses how securitizing HIV/AIDS may create new tensions. The desire to affect policy responses was central to the securitizing move. Presenting HIV as a security issue was not simply a recognition of the dangers the epidemic posed for societies; it was also a deliberate attempt to change the way in which the disease was thought about, leading to different possibilities for action. Gwyn Prins, for example, has argued that the prime mover behind the Security Council's discussion of HIV in January 2000, the US permanent representative Richard Holbrooke, was motivated by a realization that traditional approaches to disease rooted in medical and development paradigms were not working. By reframing HIV as a security issue, Holbrooke hoped to gain greater political attention and resources to combat the disease. Holbrooke was not alone at the time in seeing advantages in linking health to foreign and security policy.[74]

Yet the benefits of securitizing health in general and HIV in particular now appear more complex and nuanced, and a number of potential downsides have been highlighted.[75] Securitizing HIV creates three particular areas of tension. The first concerns ethics and the extent to which the rights of the individual should be given priority over the rights and interests of society. Securitizing HIV does something special here. In making HIV a security issue, a claim is being made that it is outside the realm of normal politics; and that, as an extreme event, it warrants extreme response measures, such as the suspension of certain civil liberties.[76] So the tension created is between the costs in terms of suspending rights and the benefits in terms of the public good; and it is tightest over issues such as the mandatory testing of security forces for HIV. Second, securitizing HIV may help to secure greater attention and resources, but the question is whether in so doing it changes the priorities for resource allocation, away from those in need and towards political benefits. Third, while considerable progress has been made in terms of how HIV and AIDS are perceived, in particular with regard to the stigmatization of people living with HIV or AIDS, securitizing HIV might run the risk of creating a new form of stigma: namely, that those living with the disease are not only health risks but security risks as well. In considering the extent to which security-based logics have come to underpin national and international responses to HIV/AIDS, it is important to be vigilant for signs that these potential problems are becoming apparent.[77]

However, any assessment of claims about the extent to which links between HIV and security have influenced such developments is hampered by the problem of tracing causation: what is being asked is not what has changed, but what has changed because of securitization as opposed to other possible causes. Given the difficulties in evidencing the independent effects of securitization, assessments of the security frame's contribution to global responses to HIV and AIDS are necessarily somewhat impressionistic. Nevertheless, here we briefly examine the impact of the AIDS–security linkage on national and global responses, and highlight some of the areas in which tensions have arisen.

As has been shown above, it was within US intelligence and security communities that the impetus to securitize AIDS first developed. It is no surprise, therefore, to find that it is within the US that security-based thinking has had the greatest policy purchase. A number of scholars have examined exactly how securitization has affected US policy approaches to HIV/AIDS and have argued that security concerns have been represented in PEPFAR, the centrepiece of US efforts to address AIDS.[78] Alan Ingram has described how the National Intelligence Council's concerns about the impact of AIDS in 'next wave' states combined with a number of other factors (including criticisms of the lack of US action on international development and lobbying by evangelical Christian groups and black congressional groups) to motivate President Bush's launching of PEPFAR.[79] A Council on Foreign Relations report argued that the linking of AIDS and security was crucial in building bipartisan support in Congress for PEPFAR, a foreign aid package of unprecedented size.[80] Indeed, the perceived benefits to US strategic interests are behind at least some of the backing PEPFAR continues to receive in Congress. During the Senate's debate on the reauthorization of PEPFAR in 2008 Senator Richard Lugar stated:

> We should understand that our investments in disease prevention programs have yielded enormous foreign policy benefits during the last five years. PEPFAR has helped to prevent instability and societal collapse in a number of at-risk countries; it has stimulated contributions from other wealthy nations to fight AIDS; it has facilitated deep partnerships with a new generation of African leaders; and it has improved attitudes toward the United States in Africa and other regions. In my judgment, the dollars spent on this program can be justified purely on the basis of the humanitarian results that we have achieved. But the value of this investment clearly extends to our national security and to our national reputation.[81]

There is evidence, however, that securitization has not only bolstered overall support for PEPFAR, but also affected the way in which money is spent. Ingram notes in his examination of PEPFAR in Nigeria that the Department of Defense plays a major implementation role through its work in support of the Nigerian military. For Ingram, this is an example of a broader trend in US policy in which militaries have come to be seen as 'strategic points at which to intervene against the pandemic while promoting security interests across the spectrum of national, international, global and human concerns'.[82] This is clearly reflected in the justification of the Department of Defense's HIV/AIDS Prevention Program (DHAPP) which involves collaborating with other countries to combat HIV/AIDS among their militaries on the basis that doing so 'has clear ties to security interests, regional stability, humanitarian concerns, and peacekeeping efforts'.[83]

The involvement of the US military in efforts to combat HIV/AIDS has not been limited to its work with other national militaries. It has also brought potentially significant advances in other (perhaps less obvious) ways, and in some cases these may have wider benefits. One example is vaccine research under the Department of Defense's US Military HIV Research Program.[84] This work captured global media attention when, in September 2009, results of a clinical trial backed by the US Army (but based in Thailand) of a prime-boost HIV vaccine regimen were released which suggested that the tested regimen was 'modestly effective at reducing the rate of HIV infection'.[85] The US Army Surgeon-General's statement on the trial was striking, and high-lighted some of the tensions that can arise when AIDS policy is linked to security policy. He said: 'The Army will continue to be an aggressive spon-sor and is committed to developing a globally effective HIV vaccine to protect US and allied troops from infection and to support the US National Security Strategy by reducing the global impact of the disease.'[86] Others have found that the targeting of US policy has been affected by geopolitical con-cerns in other ways. Denis Altman has explained Vietnam's inclusion as a PEPFAR 'focus country' as 'part of a larger American détente with a former enemy'.[87] While in some ways distinct from a direct concern with national security, this example does suggest that wider foreign policy interests at least play a part in determining where PEPFAR money is spent.

In the US, then, where over the last two decades HIV/AIDS has become deeply embedded as a security issue, there is evidence of securitization hav-ing a genuine impact on policy. The key security institutions (such as the Department of Defense, the CIA and the National Intelligence Council) recognize AIDS as being within their remit, and are taking steps to address it. Yet there has been little work demonstrating a comparable impact on the policies adopted by other countries, whose security policy institutions do not appear to have seized on the issue to the same extent. In the UK, for exam-ple, addressing the global problem of HIV/AIDS falls clearly within the mandate of the Department for International Development (DFID) rather than the Foreign and Commonwealth Office or the Ministry of Defence. Indeed, the UK has created 'institutional and legal firewalls' to prevent security policy concerns from affecting DFID's work.[88]

What about those countries that find their own security potentially at risk as a result of high HIV prevalence levels? Some states, as we have seen, have implemented programmes (often with support from the US Department of Defense) to limit the impact of HIV/AIDS on their militaries. But not all have taken the decisive action that might be expected of them: even some states that have a prima facie reason to be concerned about the security implications of HIV/AIDS have not made concerted efforts to address it. This includes some of the so-called 'next wave' states, such as Russia and China, which have been of considerable concern to the US security com-munity.[89] Feshbach has argued in the case of Russia that HIV/AIDS *is* having some impact on the state, in particular its military forces, albeit only as a contributory factor alongside larger problems of demographic trends and generally poor population health. The Russian military, he claims, rejects around 30 per cent of potential conscripts on medical grounds each year. While HIV infection ranks relatively low as a cause of rejection, far out-stripped by 'mental disorders' and drug addiction, the figures suggest that it is a growing problem, and also that it is linked to high levels of tuber-culosis in the military.[90] However, while Feshbach's report suggests that the Russian state is (belatedly) beginning to recognize these problems as poten-tial challenges to its future security,[91] action to address the problem (for example through the provision of ARTs) is still at an early stage of development. In short, the picture Feshbach presents is of a state that has begun to think about the problems poor health (including HIV infection) is posing to its security, but has not yet developed a sufficient sense of urgency to devote serious resources to combating it.

Global-level responses to HIV/AIDS have developed hugely in the last decade. The profile of the disease has been markedly accentuated, as the proponents of securitization hoped. In key bodies such as the UN and the G8, HIV (and Africa more generally) has become an important focus for political attention. HIV is sometimes referred to in these settings in security language, indicating that it is no longer seen as solely a humanitarian or development issue and suggesting that securitization has done at least some of the work in raising the political profile of the disease. In line with this sharper profile, global spending to address HIV/AIDS has risen exponentially since 2000. According to UNAIDS, global financing for AIDS has increased more than tenfold from 2000 to approximately US$13.8 billion in 2008.[92] Access to treatment has improved in the developing world, and the WHO's goal of 3 million people accessing anti-retroviral therapy has finally been met (albeit not by the target date of 2005). In 2008 UNAIDS reported the first decline in AIDS deaths since the virus was first identified in the 1980s.[93]

Despite these signs of progress, it seems fair to conclude that the security framing has played a genuinely significant role only in certain areas. Many of the most important global developments (including the Millennium Development Goals, the 2001 Declaration of Commitment on HIV/AIDS and the creation of the Global Fund) have not rested primarily on security considerations. Indeed, one of the ironies of the attempts by Holbrooke and others to show that HIV is not 'merely' a development problem is that it coincided with a resurgence in efforts to promote international development, expressed most concretely through the MDGs. While it seems probable that the MDG targets will not be met by 2015, development itself has become a major focus of political attention, and a major motivator of international action. Closely related to this have been a number of international attempts to address the problems facing Africa as a continent, seen most clearly in set-piece events including the UNSC's month on Africa, during which HIV/

AIDS was first discussed, and the Gleneagles G8 summit. HIV/AIDS has fed into both these (linked) foci of attention. The lesson of the last decade may be that securitization is not the only way of getting attention: 'developmentization' may work too.

Conclusion

The deliberations of the UNSC in January 2000, followed by Resolution 1308 later that year, seemed to mark a change in the way in which HIV/AIDS was framed. Although the security risks of the HIV/AIDS pandemic had been previously identified, not least in the US, the actions of the Security Council appeared to mark the successful securitization of the disease, confirming that it was now recognized as a security risk of such national and international concern that it should be viewed differently from other emergencies and was worthy of exceptional actions. In this article, however, we have argued that the political consensus behind the UNSC's actions was overestimated, and that it suffered at the hands of critics in the middle and later years of the decade who outlined the lack of evidence for the assertions made. Thus by the middle years of the decade the securitization of HIV/AIDS looked fragile, lacking both political support and a strong evidentiary base. This does not, however, mean either that there is no link between HIV/AIDS and security or that the securitizing move failed.

On the first of these points, it has become apparent that the links between HIV/AIDS and security are far from straightforward and a greater appreciation of nuances is required. Case sensitivities and intervening variables litter current understandings of the link. This insight demonstrates a much greater sophistication than was apparent a decade ago, and is also cause for some optimism over the societal effects of the disease: states are less likely than was previously thought to collapse because of the burden of HIV/AIDS, uniformed militaries and other security forces have less to fear from it in terms of their operational capabilities, and conflict does not automatically lead to the further spread of the disease. Some of the more dire predictions that were commonplace at the beginning of the last decade now appear overly alarmist. Nevertheless, the disease continues to spread, with millions of new infections each year, and large areas of uncertainty persist over the long-term consequences of this.

On the latter point, the case of HIV/AIDS highlights the fact that securitization is not a binary condition: there is a spectrum from failed, to partial, to successful securitization processes.[94] Nor are the results of a securitizing move homogeneous. Rather, some actors have accepted the designation of HIV/AIDS as a security issue more readily than others. This variation may in part be a reflection of the disease itself, for its effects are not homogeneous either, depending on context; but it also suggests that different actors (often at the level of ministries or even individuals) were more easily persuaded than others.

What, then, has been the effect of this partial securitization? Some actions aimed at groups at risk have reflected security concerns. Considerable work has been done, for example, to educate militaries, including UN peacekeepers and disaster relief workers, on preventing HIV infection, much of which can be traced back directly to the (partial) securitization of HIV. Nevertheless, the overall impression of the impact of securitization is one of disappointment. Despite the hopes expressed by many a decade ago, securitization has not changed the course of the pandemic. Where it has had an effect, this has mainly been either at the margins (e.g. educating military forces) or as a contributory factor in wider developments (e.g. PEPFAR). Indeed, HIV seems to some extent to have lost ground on the security agenda to other health issues. Pandemic influenza has become a more pressing concern for governments in developed western states, who find their own populations at risk from its uncontrollable cross-border spread. The threat of bioterrorism continues to worry the security community, and is a focus for major investment. The US has apparently spent between US$50 billion and US$60 billion on its biodefence programme since 9/11—more than the US$48 billion authorized for PEPFAR for the five years from FY 2009 to FY 2013 (and considerably more than the US$15 billion spent between FY 2004 and FY 2008). In a world where myriad health and non-health issues are competing for political priority, the high profile AIDS currently has cannot be taken for granted. Securitization may or may not be the most effective way of capturing the attention of policy-makers, but the human and social costs of the disease are such that there is a clear need to keep AIDS firmly on the radar.

Notes

* This article was first presented as a plenary address to the annual conference of the (Australian) National Centre for Biosecurity in February 2009. We are grateful to staff at the centre, and especially to Christian Enemark, for their support in this. The research leading to these results has received funding from the European Research Council under the European Community's Seventh Framework Programme—Ideas Grant 230489 GHG. All views expressed remain those of the authors.

1 For details, see UNAIDS, *2008 AIDS epidemic update* (Geneva: UNAIDS/WHO, 2008).
2 Central Intelligence Agency, 'Sub-Saharan Africa: implications of the AIDS pandemic', SNIE 70/1–87 (1987, approved for release May 2001).
3 CIA, 'Sub-Saharan Africa', p. 1.
4 CIA, 'Sub-Saharan Africa', p. 17.
5 Kenneth Brown, quoted in Barton Gellman, 'The belated global response to AIDS in Africa', *Washington Post*, 5 July 2000, p. A01.
6 Joshua Lederberg, Robert E. Shope and Stanley C. Oaks, Jr, eds. *Emerging infections: microbial threats to health in the United States* (Washington DC: Institute of Medicine/National Academy Press, 1992).
7 Department of State, 'The global AIDS disaster: implications for the 1990s', Washington DC, 1992.

8 Laurie Garrett, *The coming plague: newly emergent diseases in a world out of balance* (New York: Farrar, Straus & Giroux, 1994).

9 National Intelligence Council, 'The global infectious disease threat and its implications for the United States', NIE 99–17D (1999, released Jan. 2000).

10 Richard Holbrooke, 'Battling the AIDS pandemic', *Global Issues: An Electronic Journal of the US Department of State* 5: 2 (July 2000), pp. 9–11.

11 Gwyn Prins, 'AIDS and global security', *International Affairs* 80: 5, Sept. 2004, p. 941. See also Harley Feldbaum, 'The history of the HIV/AIDS–security nexus and its impact on global health', PhD diss., London School of Hygiene and Tropical Medicine, 2008, esp. ch. 5.

12 Steve Sternberg, 'Former diplomat Holbrooke takes on global AIDS', *USA Today*, 10 June 2002.

13 S/PV.4087, 10 Jan. 2000, p. 4.

14 S/PV.4087, 10 Jan. 2000, p. 2.

15 Vice-President Al Gore, Statement in the Security Council on AIDS in Africa, 10 Jan. 2000, http://www.un.int/usa/00_002.htm, accessed 27 Jan. 2006; cited in Laurie Garrett, *HIV and national security: where are the links?*(New York: Council on Foreign Relations, 2005), p. 14.

16 UNSC Resolution 1308, July 2000, p. 2, http://www.un.org/Docs/sc/unsc_resolutions. html, accessed 12 Oct. 2009.

17 Report of the High Level Panel on Threats, Challenges and Change, *A more secure world: our shared responsibility* (New York: United Nations, 2004), pp. 26–8, http://www.un.org/secureworld, accessed 12 Oct. 2005. See also introductory comments by UN Secretary-General Kofi Annan, esp. para. 8.

18 S/PV.5228, 18 July 2005, p. 5.

19 e.g. Denis Altman, 'AIDS and security', *International Relations* 17: 4, 2003, pp. 417–27; P. W. Singer, 'AIDS and international security', *Survival* 44: 1, 2002, pp. 145–58.

20 e.g. Marcella David, 'Rubber helmets: the certain pitfalls of marshaling Security Council resources to combat AIDS in Africa', *Human Rights Quarterly* 23: 0, 2001, pp. 560–82; Colleen O'Manique, 'The "securitization" of HIV/AIDS in sub-Saharan Africa: a critical feminist lens', in Sandra J. MacLean, David R. Black and Timothy M. Shaw, eds, *A decade of human security: global governance and new multilateralisms* (Aldershot: Ashgate, 2006); Stefan Elbe, 'Should HIV/ AIDS be securitized? The ethical dilemmas of linking HIV/AIDS and security', *International Studies Quarterly* 50: 1, March 2006, pp. 119–44.

21 Sternberg, 'Former diplomat Holbrooke takes on global AIDS'; Prins, 'AIDS and global security', p. 941.

22 Telegram from the FCO to the UK mission to the UN in New York, 13 July 2000 (released to the authors under the Freedom of Information Act 2000).

23 'We remain concerned that the resolution does not obviously fall within the Security Council's competence. We agree, therefore, that the statement [in the Security Council session] should be as short as possible.' Telegram from the FCO to the UK mission to the UN in New York, 14 July 2000 (released to the authors under the Freedom of Information Act 2000).

24 Telegram from the UK mission to the UN in New York to the FCO, 17 July 2000 (released to the authors under the Freedom of Information Act 2000).

25 Alan Ingram, 'HIV/AIDS, security and US strategic interests in Nigeria', *Review of International Political Economy* 14: 2, 2007, p. 515.

26 See Feldbaum, 'The history of the HIV/AIDS–security nexus', ch. 5. We are grateful to Harley Feldbaum for discussing this point further with us.

27 UNAIDS, 'AIDS now core issue at UN Security Council', press release, 19 Jan. 2001.

28 It was only in the 2008 UNAIDS report on the global pandemic that for the first time indications of stabilization were apparent in some African countries, though this was far from universally the case: UNAIDS, *2008 AIDS epidemic update*.

29 Peter Wallensteen and Patrik Johansson, 'Security Council decisions in perspective', in David M. Malone, ed., *The UN Security Council: from the Cold War to the 21st century* (Boulder, CO: Lynne Rienner, 2004).

30 e.g. Alan Ingram, 'Global leadership and global health: contending meta-narratives, divergent responses, fatal consequences', *International Relations* 19: 4, 2005, pp. 381–402.

31 Tony Barnett and Gwyn Prins, *HIV/AIDS and security: fact, fiction and evidence*, report to UNAIDS, 2005, p. 7, http://www.lse.ac.uk/lseaids, accessed 8 Oct. 2009. A version of the report was also published (London: LSEAIDS, 2005).

32 Barnett and Prins, *HIV/AIDS and security*, p. 7. It should be noted, however, that at least one of the major case studies used by Barnett and Prins to exemplify this phenomenon has subsequently been shown to have a rather more robust footing in the evidence than they find.

33 Tony Barnett and Indranil Dutta, *HIV and state failure: is HIV a security risk?* (2007), http://asci.researchhub.ssrc.org/hiv-and-state-failure-is-hiv-a-security-risk/resource_view, accessed 11 Nov. 2009.

34 Alex de Waal, 'HIV/AIDS and the military', background paper to expert seminar and policy conference, 'AIDS, security and democracy', Clingendael Institute, The Hague, 2–4 May 2005.

35 Alan Whiteside, Alex de Waal and Tsadkan Gebre-Tensae, 'AIDS, security and the military in Africa: a sober appraisal', *African Affairs* 105: 409, 2006, p. 216.

36 For details on ASCI, see http://asci.researchhub.ssrc.org/rdb/asci-hub, accessed 11 Nov. 2009.

37 ASCI, *HIV/AIDS, security and conflict: new realities, new responses*, p. 12, http://asci.researchhub.ssrc.org/rdb/asci-hub, accessed 11 Nov. 2009.

38 ASCI, *HIV/AIDS, security and conflict*, p. 12.

39 Kondwani Chirambo and Justin Steyn, 'AIDS and local government in South Africa: examining the impact of an epidemic on ward councillors', ASCI Research Report 25, Feb. 2009.

40 In 2006, for example, Whiteside et al. identified five different types of HIV epidemic, each of which had different implications for prevalence rates in the military: Whiteside et al., 'AIDS, security and the military in Africa', p. 208.

41 For example, UNAIDS, *Technical update: AIDS and the military, May 1998* (Geneva and New York, 1998); UNAIDS, *HIV/AIDS prevention and care among armed forces and UN peacekeepers: the case of Eritrea* (Geneva and New York, 2003), p. 8; National Intelligence Council, 'The global infectious disease threat'; Lindy Heinecken, 'Facing a merciless enemy: HIV/AIDS and the South African armed forces', *Armed Forces and Society* 29: 2, 2003, p. 784; Robert L. Ostergard Jr, 'Politics in the hot zone: AIDS and national security in Africa', *Third World Quarterly* 23: 2, 2002, p. 343; International Crisis Group, *HIV/AIDS as a security issue* (Brussels, 2001), pp. 9–13, ii.

42 UNAIDS, *On the front line*, 3rd edn (Geneva, 2005), p. 11.

43 UNAIDS Programme Coordinating Board, *AIDS, security and humanitarian response*, UNAIDS/PCB(19)/06.7 (2006), p. 9.

44 UNAIDS, 'Security and humanitarian response to AIDS', http://www.unaids.org/en/PolicyAndPractice/SecurityHumanitarianResponse/default.asp, accessed 13 Nov. 2009.

45 Whiteside et al., 'AIDS, security and the military in Africa', p. 202.

46 See Colin McInnes, 'HIV/AIDS and national security', in Nana K. Poku, Alan Whiteside and Bjorg Sandkjaer, eds, *AIDS and governance* (Aldershot: Ashgate,

2007), pp. 93–114, and 'HIV/AIDS and security', *International Affairs* 82: 2, March 2006, pp. 315–26.

47 For example, HIV is far more prevalent in young adults, which is the age range for the majority of the armed forces, than in the adult population as a whole: ASCI, *HIV/AIDS, security and conflict*, p. 34.

48 ASCI, *HIV/AIDS, security and conflict*, p. 33.

49 De Waal, 'HIV/AIDS and the military', p. 4. See also McInnes, 'HIV/AIDS and national security', pp. 98–101.

50 UNSC press release SC/6781, p. 1. See also Lee-Nah Hsu, 'HIV subverts national security', report from United Nations Development Programme, South-East Asia HIV and Development Project, Aug. 2001, p. 5.

51 See e.g. UN Secretariat, *The impact of AIDS*, report by the Population Division, Department of Economic and Social Affairs, 2 Sept. 2003 (New York: United Nations, 2003), pp. xiii, xiv, chs 4, 8; ICG, *HIV/AIDS as a security issue*, pp. 9–13; Ostergard, 'Politics in the hot zone', p. 344; S. Verstegen, 'HIV/AIDS: waking up to the challenge', working document prepared by Conflict Research Unit, Clingendael Institute, for the Netherlands Ministry of Foreign Affairs Special Ambassador for HIV/AIDS, March 2005, pp. 14–15; Mark Schneider and Michael Moodie, *The destabilising impact of HIV/AIDS* (Washington DC: Center for Strategic and International Studies, 2002), pp. 5–6. For an extensive review of the literature on the economic impact of HIV/AIDS, see Vinh-Kim Nguyen and Katherine Stovel, 'The social science of HIV/AIDS: a critical review and priorities for action', report prepared by the Social Science Research Council Working Group on HIV/AIDS, Oct. 2004, pp. 22–38.

52 ASCI, *HIV/AIDS, security and conflict*, p. 27, table 2.1.

53 Garrett, *HIV and national security*, p. 21.

54 Tony Barnett, 'HIV/AIDS and state fragility', ASCI synthesis paper, 2009, http://asci.researchhub.ssrc.org/working-papers/ASCI%20Synthesis%20Paper%20State%20Fragility.pdf, accessed 11 Nov. 2009.

55 e.g. UNAIDS, *AIDS, security and humanitarian response*, p. 8.

56 Tony Barnett and Alan Whiteside, 'The Jaipur paradigm: a conceptual framework for understanding social susceptibility and vulnerability to HIV', *South African Medical Journal* 90: 0, 2000, pp. 1098–101.

57 See e.g. ASCI, *HIV/AIDS, security and conflict*, pp. 24–7.

58 Whiteside et al., 'AIDS, security and the military in Africa', p. 216.

59 Our understanding of conflict here includes the post-conflict phase, where violence or the potential for violence still exists and reconstruction efforts have yet to return a state to 'normality'.

60 Stefan Elbe, 'HIV/AIDS and the changing landscape of war in Africa', *International Security* 27: 2, 2002, p. 174. See also e.g. Duane Bratt, 'Blue condoms: the use of international peacekeepers in the fight against AIDS', *International Peacekeeping* 9: 3, 2002, p. 72; Jeff Gow, 'The HIV/AIDS epidemic in Africa: implications for US policy', *Health Affairs* 21: 3, 2002, p. 65; Nancy B. Mock, Samba Duale, Lisanne F. Brown, Ellen Mathys, Heather C. O'Maonaigh, Nina K. L. Abul-Husn and Sterling Elliott, 'Conflict and HIV: a framework for risk assessment to prevent HIV in conflict-affected settings in Africa', *Emerging themes in epidemiology* 1: 6, 2004, available open access from BioMed Central. Subsequent page references to Mock et al. are from the open access version.

61 Timothy Docking, 'AIDS and violent conflict in Africa', USIP Special Report 75, http://ww.usip.org, accessed 11 Nov. 2009, p. 7.

62 UNSC Resolution 1308.

63 Paul B. Spiegel, Anne Rygaard Bennedsen, Johanna Claas, Lauire Bruns, Njogu Patterson, Dieudonne Yiweza and Marian Schilperoord, 'Prevalence of HIV infection in conflict-affected and displaced people in seven sub-Saharan African countries', *The Lancet*, no. 369, June 2007, p. 2191.

64 e.g. Spiegel et al., 'Prevalence of HIV infection', p. 2187; Gow, 'The HIV/AIDS epidemic in Africa', p. 65.

65 For a fuller discussion, see Colin McInnes, 'Conflict, HIV and AIDS: a new dynamic in warfare?', *Global Change, Peace and Security* 21: 1, Feb. 2009, pp. 99–114.

66 See e.g. Paul B. Spiegel, 'HIV/AIDS among conflict-affected and displaced populations: dispelling myths and taking action', *Disasters* 28, Sept. 2004, p. 323.

67 UNAIDS, *On the front line*, p. 26. See also UNAIDS, *Special report on HIV prevalence—AIDS epidemic update: December 2005* (Geneva: UNAIDS/WHO, 2005), p. 24.

68 Spiegel et al., 'Prevalence of HIV infection', p. 2192.

69 In 2005, for example, Alex de Waal argued that the evidence from other African conflicts (Sierra Leone, Sudan, Somalia, Uganda, northern Ethiopia and 'even' the DRC) was suggesting that, far from conflict spreading HIV, with a number of exceptions the reverse might actually prove to be the norm: de Waal, 'HIV/AIDS and the military', p. 8.

70 Spiegel et al., 'Prevalence of HIV infection' pp. 2192–3.

71 Spiegel et al., 'Prevalence of HIV infection', p. 2193.

72 See e.g. Nguyen and Stovel, 'The social science of HIV/AIDS', p. 12; Mock et al., 'Conflict and HIV', pp. 2–3.

73 For a discussion of this see McInnes, 'Conflict, HIV and AIDS'.

74 Prominent examples from the health community include Gro Harlem Brundtland (director of the WHO), John Wyn Owen (secretary of the UK health charity the Nuffield Trust) and Ken Shine (president of the US Institute of Medicine).

75 See e.g. Elbe, 'Should HIV/AIDS be securitized?'.

76 See e.g. Elbe, 'Should HIV be securitized?'.

77 Global Health Watch, 'Security and health', in *Global Health Watch 2: An alternative health report* (London: Zed, 2008).

78 e.g. Ricardo Pereira, 'PEPFAR as counterinsurgency technology: project, implementation, subversion', paper presented at the World Congress of Political Science, Santiago, Chile, 12–16 July 2009.

79 Ingram, 'HIV/AIDS, security and US strategic interests in Nigeria', pp. 523–4.

80 Council on Foreign Relations, *More than humanitarianism: a strategic US approach toward Africa*, Independent Task Force Report 56 (New York: Council on Foreign Relations, 2006), p. 65.

81 Sen. Richard Lugar, 'Senate floor speech highlights humanitarian duty to reauthorize PEPFAR', 14 July 2008, http://lugar.senate.gov/press/record.cfm?id=300627&&, accessed 20 Nov. 2009.

82 Ingram, 'HIV/AIDS, security and US strategic interests in Nigeria', p. 525.

83 US Africa Command, 'HIV/AIDS prevention program fact sheet', May 2009, www.africom.mil/getArticle.asp?art=3589, accessed 20 Nov. 2009.

84 http://www.hivresearch.org/, accessed 20 Nov. 2009.

85 Supachai Rerks-Ngarm et al., 'Vaccination with ALVAC and AIDSVAX to prevent HIV-1 infection in Thailand', *New England Journal of Medicine* 10: 1056, 20 Oct. 2009, pp. 1–12. The statistical significance of the results was later called into question. Jon Cohen, 'Unrevealed analysis weakens claim of AIDS vaccine "success" ', *Science*, 5 Oct. 2009.

86 Lt-Gen. Eric Schoomaker, quoted in Tiffany Holloway, 'US Army sponsors first HIV vaccine trial to show some effectiveness in preventing HIV', 24 Sept. 2009,

http://www.army.mil/-news/2009/09/24/27839-us-army-sponsors-first-hiv-vaccine-trial-to-show-some-effectiveness-in-preventing-hiv/, accessed 25 Sept. 2009.

87 Denis Altman, 'The political dimensions of responses to HIV/AIDS in Southeast Asia', ASCI Research Report 5, April 2008, p. 11.

88 Ingram, 'Global leadership and global health', p. 395.

89 National Intelligence Council, 'The next wave of HIV/AIDS: Nigeria, Ethiopia, Russia, India, and China', ICA 2002–04 D, Sept. 2002.

90 Murray Feshbach, 'Russian demography, health and the military: current and future issues', ASCI Research Report, April 2008, p. 14, http://asci.researchhub.ssrc.org/russian-demography-health-and-the-military-current-and-future-issues, accessed 20 Nov. 2009.

91 Feshbach, 'Russian demography, health and the military', p. 6.

92 UNAIDS, *2008 UNAIDS Annual Report: towards universal access* (Geneva, 2008), p. 42.

93 UNAIDS, *2008 UNAIDS Annual Report*, p. 9.

94 Ole Waever, 'Securitization: taking stock of a research programme in security studies', unpublished manuscript, Feb. 2003, http://media.fpn.bg.ac.yu/nacionalnaiglobalnabezbednost/03%20Socio%20konstruktivisticke%20teorije/03%20Literatura/Waever_2003_Securitisation_Taking_stock_of_a_research_programme_in_Securiry_Studies.doc, accessed 20 Nov. 2009.

29

SHOULD HIV/AIDS BE SECURITIZED?

The ethical dilemmas of linking HIV/AIDS and security

Stefan Elbe

Source: *International Studies Quarterly*, 50:1 (2006), 119–44.

Should the global AIDS pandemic be framed as an international security issue? Drawing on securitization theory, this article argues that there is a complex normative dilemma at the heart of recent attempts to formulate the global response to HIV/AIDS in the language of international security. Although "securitizing" the AIDS pandemic could bolster international AIDS initiatives by raising awareness and resources, the language of security simultaneously pushes responses to the disease away from civil society toward military and intelligence organizations with the power to override the civil liberties of persons living with HIV/AIDS. The security framework, moreover, brings into play a "threat-defense" logic that could undermine international efforts to address the pandemic because it makes such efforts a function of narrow national interest rather than of altruism, because it allows states to prioritize AIDS funding for their elites and armed forces who play a crucial role in maintaining security, and because portraying the illness as an overwhelming "threat" works against ongoing efforts to normalize social perceptions regarding HIV/AIDS. These overlooked dangers give rise to a profound ethical dilemma as to whether or not the global AIDS pandemic should be portrayed as a security issue. The article concludes that securitization theory cannot resolve this complex dilemma, but that raising awareness of its presence does allow policy makers, activists, and scholars to begin drawing the links between HIV/AIDS and security in ways that at least minimize some of these dangers.

Now in its third decade, HIV/AIDS is well poised to become one of the most devastating pandemics in modern history. Over the next years, many of the 42 million people living with HIV around the world will unfortunately join the 25 million who have already succumbed to AIDS-related illnesses. Every day the pandemic continues to kill three times as many people than died during the terrorist attacks of September 11, 2001, not least because in some southern African countries national HIV prevalence rates presently exceed a third of the adult population. Nor is the growth potential of the AIDS pandemic exhausted, as HIV rapidly spreads in parts of Asia, Latin America, the Caribbean, Russia, and Eastern Europe (Eberstadt 2002; Grisin and Wallander 2002; National Intelligence Council 2002). Scholars across a plethora of disciplines, ranging from economics and sociology to development studies and social policy, have rightly recognized that the effects of this pandemic will not be confined to individual human tragedies; HIV/AIDS will have a host of wider political, economic, and social ramifications around the globe that will need to be carefully considered and addressed (Garrett 1994; Bloom and Godwin 1997; Linge and Porter 1997; Godwin 1998; Hope 1999; Whiteside and Sunter 2000; Barnett and Whiteside 2002; Holden 2003; Seckinelgin 2003; Kalipeni 2004; Kauffman and Lindauer 2004). Despite the international scope of the AIDS pandemic, and the growing involvement of a number of prominent international organizations in its management, the discipline of international relations still lags notably behind many of these related fields in studying these effects.[1] Only very recently has the AIDS pandemic begun to make inroads into the core of the field through the efforts of a small group of scholars exploring the implications of the pandemic for international security (Ostergard 2005).

This article wishes to expand the discipline's engagement with the global AIDS pandemic by opening up a novel, normative debate on HIV/AIDS and security. It does so through identifying and outlining a complex ethical dilemma at the heart of recent attempts to frame the global AIDS pandemic as a security issue. On the one hand, a successful "securitization"[2] of HIV/AIDS could accrue vital economic, social, and political benefits for millions of affected people by raising awareness of the pandemic's debilitating global consequences and by bolstering resources for international AIDS initiatives. These benefits cannot be easily dismissed and make a strong case in favor of presenting HIV/AIDS as a security issue. Through the novel application of securitization theory, however, this article also shows how such use of security language is simultaneously accompanied by two very serious and hitherto overlooked normative dangers. First, the securitization of HIV/AIDS could push national and international responses to the disease away from civil society toward state institutions such as the military and the intelligence community with the power to override human rights and civil liberties— including those of persons living with HIV/AIDS. Second, the language of security also brings a "threat-defense" logic to bear on HIV/AIDS, which may ultimately prove counterproductive to international efforts to stem the pandemic because (i) this logic makes such efforts not a function of altruism but of more restrictive and narrow national interests, (ii) because it allows states to prioritize AIDS funding for their armed forces and elites who play a crucial role in maintaining security, and (iii) because the portrayal of the illness as an overwhelming security "threat" works against the efforts of many grassroots AIDS activists seeking to normalize social perceptions regarding persons living with HIV/AIDS. These dangers in turn strongly caution against framing HIV/AIDS as a security issue, giving rise to a profound ethical dilemma at the heart of recent efforts to securitize the global AIDS pandemic. The article concludes that securitization theory cannot, in the end, resolve this complex dilemma, but raising awareness of its presence does allow policy makers, activists, and scholars to begin drawing the links between security and HIV/AIDS in ways that at least minimize some of these dangers.

HIV/AIDS and security: the need for a normative debate

HIV/AIDS is increasingly being portrayed by a range of international organizations, national governments, non-governmental organizations, and scholars of international relations as having important security implications. This was not always so. In the first two decades since the discovery of HIV/AIDS in the mid-1980s, the disease was conceptualized primarily as a public health and development issue. Although the links between HIV/AIDS and security were sporadically explored in the 1990s by a small number of analysts in the U.S. Central Intelligence Agency and in some security think tanks, the major international turning point in terms of conceptualizing HIV/AIDS as a security issue did not occur until 2000. On January 10 of that year, at the behest of U.S. Ambassador Richard Holbrook and Vice-President Al Gore, the United Nations Security Council officially designated HIV/AIDS as a threat to international peace and security in Africa.[3] It was an immensely symbolic occasion because this was the first meeting of the Council in the new millennium and because it was the first time in the Council's history that it had designated a health issue as a threat to international security. In his position as president of the World Bank, James Wolfensohn (2000) argued on this occasion that "[m]any of us used to think of AIDS as a health issue. We were wrong. . . . Nothing we have seen is a greater challenge to the peace and stability of African societies than the epidemic of AIDS. . . . We face a major development crisis, and more than that, a security crisis." The meeting was accompanied by the declassification of a National Intelligence Estimate entitled *The Global Infectious Disease Threat and Its Implications for the United States*. This estimate spelled out the debilitating impact of HIV/AIDS and other infectious diseases on U.S. national security in sufficient detail to merit the Clinton administration's designation of HIV/AIDS as a threat to the national security of the United States in the spring of that same year.[4] The securitization of HIV/AIDS had begun in earnest.

Since that watershed meeting, there have been a plethora of reports and scholarly studies mapping out the implications of HIV/AIDS for security in greater detail. These studies have sought to assess empirically the multiple ways in which HIV/AIDS has ramifications for human security[5] (Kristoffersson 2000; Fourie and Schönteich 2001; Piot 2001; Chen 2003; Leen 2004), national security (Price-Smith 1998, 2001, 2002; Harker 2001; Heinecken 2001a; Yeager and Kingma 2001; CSIS 2002; Ostergard 2002; Sarin 2003), and international security (National Intelligence Council 2000; Singer 2002; Elbe 2003; Prins 2004).[6] They argue that the social, economic, and political stability of communities (and even entire states) can be undermined in the long run by HIV prevalence rates ranging between 10% and 40% of the adult population (ICG 2001; Pharaoh and Schönteich 2003; ICG 2004), that in some African armed forces HIV prevalence rates are estimated to be between 40% and 60%, raising concerns about their combat effectiveness (Heinecken 2001b; Mills 2000; Elbe 2002), and that HIV/AIDS even has important ramifications for international peacekeeping operations, which because they are staffed by members of these same armed forces, can serve as a vector of the illness where and when they are deployed (Bazergan 2001, 2003; U.S. Government Accountability Office 2001; Bratt 2002; Tripodi and Patel 2002). Although a few scholars (David 2001; Mock 2002; Peterson 2002/2003; Elbe 2003; Bazergan 2003) have since begun to raise questions about the unproblematic way in which some of these empirical relationships are increasingly posited, arguments about the security implications of HIV/AIDS have clearly not fallen on deaf ears. "The national security dimension of the virus is plain," the Director of the Central Intelligence Agency (Tenet 2003) could be heard arguing before a Senate intelligence panel in 2003, "[i]t can undermine economic growth, exacerbate social tensions, diminish military preparedness, create huge social welfare costs, and further weaken already beleaguered states." The United Nations Security Council, moreover, has held three further meetings on HIV/AIDS subsequent to its first one in January 2000 and is planning to have further meetings on this issue in the future—rendering the AIDS pandemic the latest in a long line of wider social issues to become framed as an international security concern.

Despite the evident importance of continuing to empirically assess the security implications of HIV/AIDS, the debate about HIV/AIDS and security cannot be conducted on such narrow empirical grounds alone. This debate urgently needs to be widened because recent attempts to bring the language and analytic apparatus of international security to bear on the global AIDS pandemic raise equally important normative questions about the long-term benefits and drawbacks of using such a security framework to respond to the disease. Amidst the pressing efforts to assess the complex impact of HIV/AIDS on international security, scholars and policy makers in this area have yet to engage in a more comprehensive, systematic, and open debate about the ethical tradeoffs inherent in pursuing such a strategy.[7] This is a striking silence, given that normative concerns clearly form an integral part of the debate about HIV/AIDS and security, never lurking far from its surface. Many of those drawing the links between HIV/AIDS and security do so instrumentally in the hope that this will accrue important humanitarian benefits by bolstering international efforts to combat the spread of the disease. Peter W. Singer (2002:158) argues that presenting HIV/AIDS as a security threat "strengthens the call for serious action against the menace of AIDS. It is not just a matter of altruism, but simple cold self-interest." Many policy makers agree, including the director of the Joint United Nations Program on HIV/AIDS (UNAIDS), who has similarly argued (Piot 2000) that framing HIV/AIDS as a security issue is not merely an academic exercise but "defines how we respond to the epidemic, how much is allocated to combating it, and what sectors of government are involved in the response." In the debate on HIV/AIDS and security, scholarly interest in understanding the wider social dynamics of the AIDS pandemic frequently goes hand-in-hand with an underlying normative commitment to scaling up international efforts to respond to the disease.

This progressive belief in the humanitarian benefits of framing HIV/AIDS as a security issue has not gone entirely unchallenged, however. Taking her cue from earlier debates seeking to link environmental concerns with national security, Susan Peterson (2002/2003:81) has warned that "[i]f well-intentioned people seek to rally support among western governments for anti-AIDS efforts in Africa, portraying disease as a security issue may be exactly the wrong strategy to employ." In her view, such a strategy is unlikely to achieve its objectives because the empirical security implications of HIV/AIDS for the United States are insufficiently strong to motivate a sustained commitment to the issue, and because such a strategy may even begin to trigger novel security dilemmas, fueling further suspicion and rivalry between states, rather than encouraging the more open and multilateral policy approaches needed to address the illness on a global scale. Moreover, even in heavily affected countries, she finds that these security implications pale in comparison with the much more pressing impact of HIV/AIDS on health, human rights, and development, as well as social and economic justice—making these alternative, non-security framings much more fruitful to pursue in the long run.[8] Crucially, however, Peterson does not only challenge the political efficacy of using security language; in the conclusion to her article she also begins to raise important *normative* reservations about the long-term effects of pursuing such language in relation to HIV/AIDS. Rather than bolstering international efforts to reduce the spread of the disease, she is concerned that such moves may paradoxically end up absolving states from any moral responsibility to react to diseases in the developing world that do not engage their essential national interests. Instead of going through the complicated and ambiguous route of securitizing AIDS, the world should instead "face AIDS for what it is and will be for the foreseeable future—a health tragedy of unprecedented and staggering proportions that cries out for international and transnational humanitarian assistance, not for the garrisoning of states behind national boundaries and national security rhetoric (Peterson 2002/2003:81)." Peterson thus raises for the first time the possibility that the normative aspects involved in framing HIV/AIDS as a security issue may be much more complex and complicated than has hitherto been assumed by participants in the debate, and hence require further analysis.

A more detailed exploration on the ethical implications of securitizing HIV/AIDS becomes unavoidable, then, for at least two reasons. First, as is the case with so many discussions revolving around this highly politicized illness, the debate on the security implications of HIV/AIDS is already deeply invested and infused with a host of subtle normative commitments that need to be brought to the fore and debated more openly.[9] Second, as Peterson's intervention shows, strongly divergent views about the ethical consequences of framing HIV/AIDS as a security issue are beginning to emerge, necessitating more systematic attention to the possible benefits and drawbacks of framing the disease in this manner. Over the past decade, such normative debates have proved similarly unavoidable in relation to a wide variety of other non-military issues framed by the international community as security concerns—ranging from the environment (Deudney 1990; Kakonen 1994; Litfin 1999; Ney 1999; Ostrauskaite 2001) and migration (Weiner 1992/1993; Wæver et al. 1993; Huysmans 1995, 2000; Bigo 1998; Doty 1998; Ceyhan and Tsoukala 2002), to the "war on drugs" (Husak 1992; Aradau 2001), transnational crime (Emmers 2003), and even development more generally (Duffield 2001). Given the growing policy resonance of arguments about the security implications of HIV/AIDS, the time has come to reflect more thoroughly on how such a framing of the pandemic could facilitate international efforts to reduce its spread and how this framing might also be counterproductive to these efforts. This is undoubtedly an enormous task encompassing a multiplicity of actors, issues, and arguments, and one that easily exceeds the limits of a single article; yet it is a task that must be begun if the discipline of international relations is not to restrict itself to merely tracing the impact of HIV/AIDS on international security, but to also actively contribute to finding the most appropriate ways for international political actors to respond to the pandemic.

Securitization theory and HIV/AIDS

How, then, does one begin such a normative debate? Even though there has been an immense resurgence in normative theorizing in international relations over the past decade (Brown 1992, 2002; Nardin and Mapel 1993; Bonanate, Puchala, and Kegley 1995; Frost 1996; Keim 2000; Seckinelgin and Shinoda 2001; Odysseos 2002, 2003), there has been markedly less engagement with the particular ethical tradeoffs involved in bringing the language of international security to bear on wider social issues. For those interested in such questions, the *locus classicus* has quickly become the influential study by Barry Buzan, Ole Wæver, and Jaap de Wilde (1998) entitled *Security: A New Framework for Analysis*.[10] Not only is the "securitization" theory presented in this framework widely considered to be among the most important, original, and controversial contributions to the field of security studies in recent years (Huysmans 1998:480), it also remains the only systematic scholarly study of the ethical implications of widening the security agenda to include an array of non-military issues—making it a natural starting point for a more sustained normative debate about the securitization of HIV/AIDS. Although securitization theory is not exclusively concerned with normative questions, and also has important analytical interests in tracing the detailed social processes through which security threats become constructed by political actors, it is predominantly this normative dimension of the framework that remains indispensable for opening up a wider ethical debate about framing HIV/AIDS as an international security issue.[11]

Indeed, securitization theory can address these normative questions more readily than many longer standing neorealist or neoliberal approaches to international security, because its constructivist account of security remains highly sensitive to the intersubjective and performative nature of portraying social issues as security concerns, that is, of "speaking" security.[12] Securitization theory forms part of a growing body of literature bringing the insights of speech act theory—as pioneered by J. L. Austin (1962) at Harvard University in the 1950s and subsequently developed by several other prominent philosophers and linguists (Searle 1969)—to bear on social and political analysis. Austin (1962:1) famously argued that the point of speech act theory was to challenge the assumption that "the business of a 'statement' can only be to 'describe' some state of affairs, or to 'state some fact,' which it must do either truly or falsely." Even though language certainly encodes information, speech act theory illustrates that language can also do much more than just convey information, and that even when it is used primarily to convey information, language often conveys more than just the literal meaning of the words. Austin became particularly interested in phrases that in themselves constitute a form of action or social activity, that is phrases such as saying "thank you," "you are fired," "I promise," "I bet," "I nominate," etc. These are instances in which a speaker is using language not just for the purposes of description, but also for actually *doing* something with considerable social significance—hence the term speech *acts*. In saying "thank you," for example, one is not making a statement that is either true or false, but is undertaking the act of thanking somebody.

By way of extension, for Buzan, Wæver, and de Wilde, labeling an issue a security issue also constitutes such a performative speech act. For them (1998:26) security "is not interesting as a sign referring to something more real; it is the utterance itself that is the act. By saying the words, something is done (like betting, giving a promise, naming a ship)." Security is thus not viewed by these three scholars as something that exists independently of its discursive articulation,[13] but rather as a particular form of performative speech act; security is a social quality political actors, such as intelligence agencies, government officials, and international organizations, inject into issues by publicly portraying them as existential threats (Buzan, Wæver, and de Wilde 1998:204). Whereas more traditional approaches to security operate within a specific definition of security, revolving for example around the deployment of armed force in world politics, and then seek to ascertain empirically whether an issue *genuinely* represents a security threat, for secur-itization theory the designation of an issue as a security threat is primarily an intersubjective practice undertaken by security policy makers. "It is a choice to phrase things in security . . . terms, not an objective feature of the issue. . . ." (Buzan, Wæver, and de Wilde 1998:211); or, as Wæver (1995:65) put it elsewhere, the "[u]se of the security label does not merely reflect whether a problem *is* a security problem, it is also a political choice, that is, a decision for conceptualization in a special way." The leader of a political party, for example, can choose whether to portray immigration as a security issue or as a human rights issue. Similarly, leaders of international organizations can choose whether they portray HIV/AIDS as a health issue, as a development issue, or, as they have done more recently, as an international security issue.

According to the framework of Buzan, Wæver, and de Wilde, the deter-mination of which issues end up on the international security agenda cannot consequently be made solely on the basis of empirical criteria. Much security analysis entails making speculative predictions about future developments, necessitates prioritizing between competing claims with imperfect information, and, especially when it comes to wider social issues, requires deciding about whether an issue is best addressed under the heading of security rather than another competing framework. Inevitably, there is a considerable element of politics involved in determining how a social issue is presented in public debate. An issue can either remain non-politicized if it is not made an issue of public debate or decision, or it can become politicized if it is successfully made part of public policy and subject to a public decision. Finally, in the extreme case, an issue can become "securitized," by which Buzan, Wæver, and de Wilde (1998:23–24) mean very specifically that it is "presented as an existential threat requiring emergency measures and justifying actions outside the normal bounds of political procedure." The security quality of an issue thus does not reside for them in the nature of the issue itself or in the anticipated empirical effects of a particular phenomenon, but it derives from the specific way in which an issue or phenomenon is presented in public debate.

Buzan, Wæver, and de Wilde provide their framework with a high degree of analytical focus by further specifying the precise conditions that collectively make up this "security" speech act. Rather than addressing all instances in which the word "security" is used, or all wider calls for the adoption of emergency measures, securitization theory applies only to those issues that are presented according to the particular logic or grammar of the security speech act (Buzan, Wæver, and de Wilde 1998:25). The four constituent components of this security speech act (Buzan, Wæver, and de Wilde 1998:24, 36) are presence of the following: (i) *securitizing actors* (such as political leaders, intelligence experts, etc.), declaring (ii) a *referent object* (such as a state)[14] to be (iii) *existentially threatened* (e.g., by an immanent invasion), and who make a persuasive call for the adoption of (iv) *emergency measures* to counter this threat (e.g., declare war or impose a curfew). The framework advanced by Buzan, Wæver, and de Wilde confines itself to analyzing only those issues—be they of a military or non-military nature—that are presented in a manner conforming to all four of these criteria. The term *securitization*, in turn, formally refers to the process whereby an issue is taken out of its non-politicized or politicized status and is elevated to the security sphere by portraying it in a way that meets these four criteria. This is precisely what has happened to the issue of HIV/AIDS in recent years, where arguments have shifted from humanitarian and public health ones to officials in international organizations, governments, and non-governmental organizations (*securitizing actors*) increasingly arguing that beyond these humanitarian considerations, the survival of communities, states, and militaries (*referent objects*) is now being undermined (*existentially threatened*), unless drastic measures (*emergency measures*) are undertaken by national and international actors to better address the global pandemic.[15] HIV/AIDS has become securitized.

This radically constructivist view of security also generates important new tasks for security analysts, who must now begin to reflect in greater depth on the normative consequences of securitizing a particular issue. "Our approach," Buzan, Wæver, and de Wilde (1998:212) insist, "has the basic merit of conceptualizing security as a labeling for which actors can be held responsible rather than an objective feature of threats"; securitization theory "serves to underline the responsibility of talking security, the responsibility of actors as well as of analysts who choose to frame an issue as a security issue. They cannot hide behind the claim that anything in itself constitutes a security issue (Buzan, Wæver, and de Wilde 1998:34)." Because security analysts have a choice about whether or not to present a given issue in the language of security, they need to reflect on the wider consequences of doing so. This also means that the debate about HIV/AIDS and security cannot be waged solely on empirical grounds; for if there is an inevitable choice to "speaking" security in relation to HIV/AIDS, then the debate about the security implications of the disease will remain incomplete, unless the wider normative implications of using such language are assessed as well. Securitization theory was designed with a view to this very task; with its help "it is possible to ask with some force whether it is a good idea to make this issue a security issue—to transfer it to the agenda of panic politics—or whether it is better handled within normal politics" (Buzan, Wæver, and de Wilde 1998:34). Yet because the global AIDS pandemic was securitized only after the publication of their study, this line of inquiry has not yet been pursued specifically in relation to HIV/AIDS.

Raising this normative dimension is all the more important because Buzan, Wæver, and de Wilde think scholars would be mistaken in simply assuming that bringing the language of security to bear on the growing number of social issues is always a favorable political development. After the end of the Cold War, some security scholars quickly faulted such an expansion of the international security agenda on the grounds of the inability of security studies to accommodate such a wide variety of issues without losing analytical focus as a result. Stephen Walt (1991:213) famously argued that expanding the field of security studies to include issues such as pollution, diseases, and economic recessions "would destroy its intellectual coherence and make it more difficult to devise solutions to any of these important problems." From a different theoretical perspective, Daniel Deudney (1990:464) echoed that "[i]f everything that causes a decline in human well-being is labeled a 'security' threat, the term loses any analytical usefulness and becomes a loose synonym of 'bad'". Buzan, Wæver, and de Wilde, by contrast, have criticized such an expansion on different, normative grounds. Already on the first page of their study, they warn readers of serious intellectual and political dangers involved in securitizing social issues, and hence in widening the security agenda. "Basically, security should be seen as negative, as a failure to deal with issues as normal politics. Ideally, politics should be able to unfold according to routine procedures without this extraordinary elevation of specific 'threats' to prepolitical immediacy" (Buzan, Wæver, and de Wilde 1998:29; Williams 2003:523). In the conclusion to their study (1998:208), they again point to the dangers of securitization, insisting that "[a]voiding excessive and irrational securitization is thus a legitimate social, political, and economic objective of considerable importance." By highlighting the normative choices that are always involved in framing issues as security issues and by warning of potential dangers inherent in doing so, their framework marks an ideal starting point for a deeper debate on the ethical implications of using the language of international security to respond to the global AIDS pandemic.

The dangers of securitizing AIDS

What, then, are the specific normative dangers Buzan, Wæver, and de Wilde identify, and how do they pertain to the ongoing securitization of HIV/AIDS? Based on their selection of case studies, such as the securitization of migration in Europe in the 1990s, two general dangers emerge. Both of these dangers result from the unique connotations of the word "security," about which Wæver (1995:47) has observed elsewhere that it "carries with it a history and a set of connotations that it cannot escape. At the heart of the concept we still find something to do with defense and the state. As a result, addressing an issue in security terms still evokes an image of threat-defense, allocating to the state an important role in addressing it. This is not always an improvement." This passage expresses in summary form both the major normative concerns that securitization theorists have about securitization processes, namely that (i) these processes usually lead to a greater level of state mobilization, enabling the state to encroach on an increasing proportion of social life where it might not be desirable (Buzan, Wæver, and de Wilde 1998:4), and (ii) that the language of security attaches to issues a particular "threat-defense" logic that may not always be appropriate or beneficial for addressing these issues. It is worth exploring these two concerns in greater detail.

In many ways, this first concern about excessive state mobilization is deeply liberal, in that it assumes an a priori preference for a minimalist state that maximizes individual liberty, rather than for a state that is heavily involved in the management of social life. Although this is not explicitly mentioned in their framework, Buzan and Wæver have pointed to the liberal nature of such an objection elsewhere when they observe that classical liberalism can itself be understood as a project that seeks to narrow the range of things seen as security threats, so as to enlarge the realm of "normal politics" and to reduce as far as possible the areas of social life within which force could be used (Buzan and Wæver 1998:4; Buzan, Wæver, and de Wilde 1998:210). More specifically, Buzan, Wæver, and de Wilde wish to highlight two concrete threats to democratic politics inherent in using security language in order to incite state mobilization. First, states can use the language of security in order to remove an issue from routine democratic considerations and push it into the higher echelons of the state's inner circles of power, where there is less political transparency and hence also less democratic scrutiny of issues. Second, state representatives often also invoke the term "security" to justify the use of any necessary means to confront the threatening condition or to silence opposition to the state (Buzan, Wæver, and de Wilde 1998:21). Any emergency measures taken by the state can thus be used to override the rule of law and infringe upon valued civil liberties. Hence, Buzan, Wæver, and de Wilde (1998:29) are generally concerned about how the language of security has historically served to silence opposition to the state, how it has given state representatives special powers that could be exploited for domestic purposes, and how it can lead to the suspension of important democratic control mechanisms.

Even though this danger of excessive state involvement has not been hitherto acknowledged in the debate on AIDS and security, advocates of the securitization of HIV/AIDS will need to devote greater attention to this outcome of past securitization processes. In the case of HIV/AIDS, too, framing the issue as a security issue pushes responses to the disease away from civil society toward the much less transparent workings of military and intelligence organizations, which also possess the power to override human rights and civil liberties—including those of persons living with HIV/AIDS. One analyst (Chowka 2000) has pointed out that the designation of HIV/ AIDS as a security issue is "a bit frightening and a bit scary . . . [b]ecause that means you're going to begin to call in the FBI, you can call in the CIA. If people are talking about things which are decided to be a national security issue, they in fact can be spied upon and civil rights protections can be suspended." Not everyone would go this far, but it is certainly true that in the United States the armed forces and the CIA are becoming increasingly involved in assessing the security implications of HIV/AIDS. It is also true that historically state responses to the disease have frequently been undemocratic and have been characterized by periods of great insensitivity toward persons living with the virus. Calls for quarantining such people, subjecting them to various forms of violence, attempting to bar them from serving in state institutions, and refusing to issue visas to HIV-positive foreigners are only a few of the examples in which persons living with HIV/AIDS have been ostracized and even persecuted by some states for their illness. In the early stages of HIV/AIDS in the United States, Haitians were variously denied housing, required to undergo tests before entering the country, dismissed from jobs, and so forth. In Europe and Russia, moreover, many Africans were similarly targeted because of the perception that they were disease carriers (Schoepf 2004). Portraying HIV/AIDS as a national and international security threat risks fueling such exclusionary and dehumanizing responses and could serve as an implicit legitimization of any harsh or unjust "emergency" policies that states may adopt in relation to persons living with the virus. After all, examples of such measures are not confined to the dustbin of history. In the United States, the Institute of Medicine not long ago proposed a policy of introducing mandatory screening for tuberculosis—a common condition for people living with HIV—for immigrants from countries with high prevalence rates, and it even made the case in favor of linking the permanent residence card (green card) to taking preventative treatment (Coker 2003:2). As recently as February 2003, the British government similarly considered implementing compulsory HIV screening for prospective immigrants amid alleged worries that HIV-positive foreigners are traveling to the United Kingdom to seek treatment (Hinsliff 2003:2). Such moves undoubtedly justify the first normative concern of Buzan, Wæver, and de Wilde that the involvement of the state in the management of wider social issues can also have detrimental effects in terms of placing the management of such an issue behind closed doors, and by paving the way for civil liberties to be overridden if this is deemed necessary by the state.[16]

Participants in this debate will also need to reflect more deeply on the second danger inherent in their efforts to portray the pandemic as an international security issue, namely that such efforts bring the unique "threat-defense" logic of security to bear on an ever-growing range of social issues. Buzan, Wæver, and de Wilde observe on a deeper level how the immense increase in the number of securitization processes occurring over the past decade collectively construes the notion of "security" as a universally good thing—as a desirable condition toward which to push all social relations. The cumulative social effect of this proliferation of securitization processes, of which HIV/AIDS is only the latest manifestation, is thus to convey the impression that working toward a condition of security is always socially beneficial—that "more security" is always better. Buzan, Wæver, and de Wilde (1998:29) find this to be a dangerously narrow view, because the connotations of security also attach a specific "threat-defense" logic to issues that may not always be appropriate or beneficial for their resolution.

This too is a valid normative concern in the case of HIV/AIDS, where the "threat-defense" logic entailed in the language of security can have three detrimental consequences. First, the securitization of the disease removes the issue from the more cosmopolitan and altruistic frameworks of health and development, locating it instead within a state-centric framework, where states are primarily concerned with maximizing power and security, rather than with addressing wider humanitarian concerns. In such a context, national and international action taken on HIV/AIDS is likely to be confined to those instances where it touches upon the selfish security interests of states. States may take action to defend their core security interests, but they are unlikely to undertake measures extending much beyond these narrow concerns. As Susan Peterson points out, responding to HIV/AIDS as a security issue transforms the logic of international action on HIV/AIDS into one based on narrow self-interest, which historically has not proved very effective in terms of addressing global health issues. Indeed it creates the impression that global health issues are not worth addressing in their own right, but only to the extent that they touch upon the core security interests of states, which may mean that in the long run, states will cease to be concerned about global health in areas where it does not concern their core national security interests (Peterson 2002/2003:46, 80). This is an important side effect of the language of security that needs to be borne in mind by those drawing the links between HIV/AIDS and security.

A second and closely related effect of the "threat-defense" logic in the case of HIV/AIDS is that it may adversely shift the identification of national and international funding priorities. Within a security framework, concern about HIV/AIDS will not revolve primarily around how HIV/AIDS affects civilian populations, but around how it affects the core institutions of the state, including the armed forces. In low-income countries in particular, this may mean that scarce resources for medicines are provided on a priority basis to the armed forces and state elites rather than to civilian populations as a whole, or, in the worst case, are diverted from civilian programs to military programs as a result of the portrayal of HIV/AIDS as a security issue. Examples of the latter have not yet been officially documented by NGOs or civil-society organizations, but there is certainly evidence that in many countries members of the armed forces routinely enjoy preferential access to medicines vis-à-vis the civilian population, or have at least moved to the front of the line in terms of receiving access to expensive antiretroviral medicines (ARVs). In Zambia, for example, members of the military have begun to argue that the armed forces should have priority access to more government funding for ARVs, because the military and their families are more at risk because of the nature of their job and because this would contribute to world peace (Allocate More ARVs to Military Personnel, 2003). Similarly, in Rwanda, high-ranking officers increasingly have access to ARVs, but the general population does not (Amnesty International 2004). This is part of a wider development in Africa, whereby the soldiers of many countries now have greater or better access to health care and AIDS medicines than the civilian population.[17] As Radhika Sarin (in Conklin 2003) argues, "quite a few African militaries are committed to providing treatment for their soldiers, such as the Ugandan People's Defense Forces and Nigeria's Armed Forces. These militaries do try and work with military spouses and civilian communities to provide HIV prevention education. However, access to antiretrovirals is very low in many African nations." The portrayal of HIV/AIDS as a security issue thus plays into the hands of those who already have the greatest chances of access to medicines, rather than into the hands of those who are currently least likely to receive such access. Indeed, it may inadvertently help to ensure that soldiers and elites who play a crucial role in the maintenance of national and international security receive access to treatment, without being able to ensure that such treatment is also provided democratically and universally to all who need it. This too is an important normative drawback that needs to be reflected upon in a more sustained manner.

Finally, the "threat-defense" logic inherent in the securitization of HIV/AIDS also works against the grassroots efforts undertaken by many non-governmental organizations and AIDS charities over the past decade in terms of normalizing societal attitudes regarding people living with HIV/AIDS. The goal of many of these groups has been to move away from the perception that people living with HIV/AIDS are dangerous "outsiders" and a threat to society. Rather than avoiding contact with such persons in the quest to be completely safe and secure from the virus, what is needed instead is more tolerance and a better understanding of the illness. Already in the 1980s the writer Susan Sontag described how the view of disease as "invader" is a perennial feature of many public pronouncements about the "war on AIDS," and she famously made the case for abandoning the military metaphor—both in terms of portraying the illness as something that invades the person and that invades entire societies. She (1998:94) felt that the military metaphor "overmobilizes" and "powerfully contributes to the excommunicating and stigmatizing of the ill." In such a context, a strategy of normalization can, from an ethical standpoint grounded in the lived experiences of those living with HIV/AIDS, easily be seen as highly advantageous in terms of cultivating a more inclusive and supportive public posture toward those persons. Ongoing efforts to securitize HIV/AIDS, by contrast, once again work against this goal by portraying the illness as a destructive and debilitating threat, and risk reversing important advances made to date regarding societal attitudes about the illness. In this way, the language of security deployed in international organizations also has important implications at the grassroots level.

The contribution, then, that securitization theory can make toward an ethical debate about whether the global AIDS pandemic should be framed as a security issue is not just methodological but also substantive. While its unique methodological standpoint highlights particularly clearly the choice that analysts have in terms of whether they frame issues such as HIV/AIDS in security terms, its wider normative concerns about excessive state mobilization and its questioning of the usefulness of using the "threat-defense" logic of security to respond to a growing range of social issues help to highlight important and previously overlooked normative dangers inherent in the ongoing securitization of HIV/AIDS—and this despite the fact that securitization theory was formulated well in advance of these more recent efforts. It is also precisely because of such dangers that Buzan, Wæver, and de Wilde (1998:4) generally do not believe that scholars should eagerly rush to publicly present an ever-growing range of issues as security issues; they should aim instead for "desecuritization," that is for shifting issues out of the emergency mode and returning them to routine political processes. Securitization theory thus compels those linking HIV/AIDS and security to think more deeply about whether, upon reflection, such efforts should best be abandoned, resisted, and reversed because of these adverse effects. At this stage, the answer to the question of whether HIV/AIDS should be securitized might well be "no." As the next section illustrates, however, such a conclusion would be premature, because in the case of HIV/AIDS, uncovering these ethical dangers does not mark the end of the normative debate about its securitization, but only the beginning of a much more complex and complicated ethical terrain that begins to unfold.

The benefits of securitizing AIDS

Taking securitization theory's ethical imperative seriously also necessitates reflecting on the possible benefits a successful securitization of HIV/AIDS could have for persons living with the illness. Buzan, Wæver, and de Wilde (1998:29) insist that although desecuritization remains the abstract ideal of their framework, "one has to weigh the always problematic side effects of applying a mind-set of security against the possible advantages of focus, attention, and mobilization." Pursuing this line of thought shows that the ethical concerns identified above in fact only apply in a qualified manner in the case of HIV/AIDS and that they also have to be balanced with a plethora of competing political, economic, and legal advantages that a successful securitization of the AIDS pandemic could accrue for persons living with HIV/AIDS. For example, although the concern raised by Buzan, Wæver, and de Wilde about excessive state mobilization certainly resonates within the context of a liberal democracy where the state should, *ceteris paribus*, not seek to forcefully interfere with democratic deliberation processes, outside the context of Western democracies, the relationship between state, society, and security is often more complex, so their findings in this regard may consequently be less readily applicable.

In some of the countries most seriously affected by the AIDS pandemic, it is not excessive state mobilization that poses the main problem, but, on the contrary, the utter absence of a meaningful state response to the disease. In several southern African countries there is a widespread desire among persons living with HIV/AIDS for more action to be taken to ensure the provision of medicines—a prominent example of which is the Treatment Action Campaign in South Africa.[18] In many other African countries there are millions of people who do not even have the privilege of being informed about this illness, let alone knowing whether they have contracted the virus or not; yet, their governments remain unable or unwilling to demonstrate leadership on the issue, or to make such medical provisions, or even to prioritize their illness politically. Over the past years, Thabo Mbeki's refusal to instruct the South African government to prioritize efforts to address the AIDS pandemic has been a case in point and continues to receive widespread media attention. It is, unfortunately, only one case among many. Because of the stigmatized nature of the illness, and the long illness cycle, the strategy of denial has been particularly convenient for many governments to pursue in the past, albeit with catastrophic social consequences. What is more, many scholars and AIDS activists view the minimalist (neoliberal) state promoted in Africa through the structural adjustment programs favored by several international political and financial institutions over the past decade as part of the underlying structural conditions facilitating the emergence of the AIDS pandemic, and as contributing to the limited health care infrastructure currently available in many of the countries seriously affected by HIV/AIDS (Lurie 2004). In such a context, where a devastating illness remains largely ignored by states and where a minimalist conception of the state promoted by the international community is not helping the situation, the concern of many political AIDS activists understandably does not revolve around fears of excessive state mobilization, but, on the contrary, around the utter absence of adequate state involvement. What is needed is an urgent attempt by the international community and by governments to respond to the disease, which is what those framing HIV/AIDS as a security issue are actively trying to provoke.

The securitization of HIV/AIDS through the United Nations Security Council, because of its high public profile and unique status in international law, is one way of working toward this goal; it tries to increase the political pressure on governments to begin addressing the issue in a way that would help to ensure the survival of millions of persons living with HIV/AIDS, and it tries to encourage them to do so through early and prompt responses to the pandemic. Thus, where Buzan, Wæver, and de Wilde see dangers to democracy emanating from securitization processes because of the potentially oppressive role they accord to the security institutions of states, for some AIDS activists, compelling states hitherto unresponsive to the needs of their people into greater action is an equally important political goal with a strong democratic dimension. However imperfect, it is a way of representing the ignored political voice of those with HIV/AIDS at the highest levels of government.[19] Speaking at the UN Security Council in January 2001, Dr. Peter Piot, Executive Director of UNAIDS (2001), argued that "[t]he simple fact that the Security Council regards AIDS as a significant problem sends a powerful message: AIDS is a serious matter for the global community." In the case of HIV/AIDS, then, the key normative question does not revolve around the quantity or intensity of state involvement, because some state involvement is undoubtedly needed, but around the mode and nature of such state responses.[20] Securitization, in this instance, is not intended to remove the issue of HIV/AIDS from the political sphere and to shift it into the security sphere, but instead to shift it out of its non-politicized status in many countries and to begin a proper politicization of the issue.

By way of extension, where Buzan, Wæver, and de Wilde generally see dangers with pushing issues higher up the echelons of state bureaucracies—and thus away from civilian control—many AIDS activists see this as precisely what is needed for getting many African governments to undertake more sustained efforts and to commit more resources to addressing a pandemic that is already affecting more than 40 million people. To date, the securitization of AIDS at the international level has encouraged political actors to break the silence surrounding HIV/AIDS. For example, the Abuja Declaration on HIV/AIDS, Tuberculosis and other Related Infectious Diseases adopted by several African heads of state and by the Organisation of African Unity in 2001 reasoned that it was necessary to break the silence around HIV/AIDS because HIV/AIDS is not just a health issue, but also a threat to Africa's political stability, and that fighting illnesses such as HIV/AIDS must consequently form a part of Africa's strategy for ensuring durable peace and political security on the continent (OAU 2001). In some instances, moreover, the securitization of HIV/AIDS has also allowed states to shift responsibility for addressing the issue from ministries with only very little political clout to political bodies with greater influence on the political process. Denis Altman (2000) has observed that in countries such as Nigeria, Cote d'Ivoire, and South Africa, where health ministries only enjoy a modest degree of political influence and are perennially short of financial resources, the securitization of the pandemic has helped to move the issue higher up the political agenda, and HIV/AIDS has subsequently become the responsibility of ministries or committees with a greater degree of political clout and with more resources at their disposal. By illustrating that HIV/AIDS is not only a humanitarian concern but also a security concern affecting the core institutions of states, the securitization of HIV/AIDS can increase the political priority accorded to the issue by governments, which in turn could benefit those living with HIV/AIDS if this is translated into the scaling up of treatment programs.

Finally, where Buzan, Wæver, and de Wilde point to the danger of security arguments being used to override the rule of law, and hence also to threaten civil liberties, from an economic perspective this ability of security concerns to override certain legal provisions is deemed to be a potential advantage. The patents on many AIDS medicines are presently protected by the World Trade Organization's Agreement on Trade-Related Aspects of Intellectual Property (TRIPS)—barring poorer countries from producing generic antiretroviral therapies and other medicines at lower prices, or even importing them from other countries who can procure them at lower costs. Those countries who try to circumvent these restrictions can subsequently be threatened with a variety of political, economic, and legal sanctions. In 1997, some 39 different pharmaceutical companies attempted to legally challenge the South African Medicines and Related Substances Control Amendment Act, which would have enabled South Africa to "parallel" import much cheaper generic HIV/AIDS medicines. The securitization of HIV/AIDS assists groups wishing to weaken the grip of patents on life-saving medicines because these patents could potentially be overridden in light of national security considerations. The TRIPS agreement contains an important set of "security exceptions," including Article 73(b), which notes that nothing contained in the agreement should be construed to "prevent a Member from taking any action which it considers necessary for the protection of its essential security interests" (World Trade Organization 1994). Although no dispute has yet occurred under Article 73 since the establishment of the World Trade Organization, the devastating social and economic impact of HIV/AIDS is raising the possibility of invoking these security provisions. A recent report by the United Nations (Roffe and Melendez-Ortiz 2005:10) has noted that it might be possible to invoke the security exceptions of TRIPS because "it could be argued that pandemics such as HIV affect a nation far beyond purely economic interests and might therefore justify action otherwise inconsistent with the TRIPS Agreement." If states do wish to override these patents on expensive life-saving medicines in the future, or at least maintain pressure on the pharmaceutical companies when negotiating prices, it will be essential for them to demonstrate that the AIDS pandemic constitutes an emergency affecting the security of states, especially as attempts to protect such access to medicines through widening the public health provisions of TRIPS agreed at Doha in 2001 are proving increasingly ineffective and are being actively side-stepped through bilateral free trade agreements

(Oxfam 2004; Medecins Sans Frontiers 2005). Some participants in the United Nations Security Council debates on AIDS and international security have already been able to use that forum in order to make precisely this point. The Indian representative (Sharma 2001) has urged the Security Council, in line with its responsibility of maintaining international peace and security, "to rule that Article 73 of the TRIPS Agreement must be invoked to urgently provide affordable medicines that help in the treatment of the epidemic."

This legal dimension to the securitization of HIV/AIDS is becoming even more important because of the strong role that Indian pharmaceuticals have recently been playing in providing generic and affordable AIDS medicines to many developing countries. Because India's Patent Act of 1970 did not apply to medicines, Indian pharmaceuticals have been able to produce generic versions of AIDS drugs for some time. The pressure of their generic products has meant that prices for ARVs have dropped from over U.S.$10,000 annually to, in some instances, U.S.$140 annually, but this has only been possible because some of the provisions of the TRIPS agreement have hitherto not applied to India. What is more, Indian pharmaceuticals have also been at the forefront of developing the three-in-one cocktail pill, which means that patients only need to take two pills instead of six pills a day, making their administration considerably easier. However, as members of the Affordable Medicines and Treatment Campaign point out, India is in the process of changing its Patent Act in a way that would comply with TRIPS, which requires all governments to grant developed countries a 20-year monopoly patent on all essential medicines, including HIV/AIDS drugs. There are several proposed amendments to the Act that would potentially impede generic competition. If the supply of cheap Indian medicines dries up in the near future, this will make the ability to invoke the security exceptions of TRIPS all the more pressing (Grover 2004). In this way, the securitization of AIDS continues to play into the hands of those countries that might wish to invoke legal provisions necessary for procuring life-saving medicines at lower costs, maintaining background pressure on pharmaceutical companies. This illustrates how securitization processes can have normative benefits beyond merely raising attention and resources. Furthermore, it means that where Buzan, Wæver, and de Wilde—coming from a political perspective concerned with civil liberties—point to the dangers of security arguments being used to override the rule of law, from an economic perspective grounded in the attempts of poorer states to access cheap generic medicines, this same ability of security concerns to override legal provisions is deemed to be a crucial potential advantage, and something that the language of security can uniquely bring to the debate in a way that health or development language cannot. In either case, the point here is not that the concern of Buzan, Wæver, and de Wilde is not justified, but rather that in the context of HIV/AIDS, the advantages and disadvantages for those persons living with HIV/AIDS are much more evenly balanced than their normative criticism about excessive state involvement would initially seem to suggest.

The same is true regarding their other warning about the appropriateness of applying security's unique "threat-defense" logic to an ever-growing range of issues, such as HIV/AIDS. Although concern is clearly justified here as well, upon reflection, all three of the adverse side affects that this logic can have in the case of HIV/AIDS emerge in a much more complex form. The state-centric and self-interested nature of security, for example, is not seen by many of those advocating the links between HIV/AIDS and security as a drawback, but on the contrary, as an important asset that can mobilize global responses to HIV/AIDS. "It is a simple truth," Alex de Waal (2003) notes in reflecting on his experience with many African governments over the past decades, "that governments act when they perceive real threats to their power. This is a lesson from government famine prevention strategies: the political impulse is primary . . . To date, few African governments have recognized the political threat posed by the HIV/AIDS pandemic." Where humanitarian development or other more altruistically inclined international initiatives have failed to generate sufficient political will and resources, for those advocating the HIV/AIDS-security nexus, the appeal to the naked self-interest of states is the only strategy left in light of the pressing daily humanitarian implications of the pandemic.

Indeed, appealing to the self-interest of states through the language of security can be economically useful in terms of increasing the amount of international attention the AIDS pandemic receives. Securitizing the illness could assist in freeing up more scarce resources for preventing the transmission of HIV in the future, as well as for purchasing medicines to treat those persons already suffering from AIDS. In the United States, arguments about the long-term security implications of AIDS reportedly already informed President Bush's decision to launch his five-year U.S.$ 15 billion Emergency Plan for AIDS Relief (Stolberg 2003).[21] There has been much controversy about the strings attached to this money, about its emphasis on bilateral rather than multilateral programs, as well as the considerable delay in its appropriation, indicating that this was a shrewdly calculated political move, but such resources will undoubtedly be necessary for international efforts to respond to the global pandemic. This shows the ability of leaders to use security arguments in order to justify appropriating such considerable sums and the general expansion in AIDS funding that has taken place in recent years.[22] The logic of security can thus help to maintain such funding in the years ahead as will be necessary for treatment and prevention programs.

The securitization of HIV/AIDS is not only useful in terms of increasing international aid for HIV/AIDS, but it is also an important tool in terms of provoking African governments themselves into taking the issue more seriously within their domestic politics, that is to prioritize HIV/AIDS efforts on their own political agendas and budgets. Highlighting the security implications of

HIV on the armed forces, for example, can even serve as an important initial trigger for placing HIV/AIDS on the political agenda (UNAIDS 1998; Elbe 2002). There is evidence from countries such as Uganda, Ethiopia, and Malawi that highlighting this military relationship was crucial in securing wider political leadership on the issue of HIV/AIDS. In Uganda, President Museveni began to take the issue seriously when, in 1986, Fidel Castro took him aside at a meeting of the Non-Aligned Movement in Harare and informed him that 18 out of the 60 military staff that Museveni had sent to Cuba for military training were HIV positive. This spurned Museveni into commencing a wider social program on HIV/AIDS in Uganda (Museveni 1995). Commenting on the response to HIV/AIDS by the Ethiopian army in 1996, de Waal (2003:22) similarly observes how "within the military such as the quasi-democratic 'council of commanders,' a legacy of the army's roots as a revolutionary guerrilla army, allowed the institution to develop and implement its own distinctive AIDS program." There is also some evidence from Malawi indicating that the impact of HIV/AIDS on the army and members of parliament was crucial in prompting political leadership on this issue (Lwanda 2004:40). In this way, highlighting the impact of HIV/AIDS on the armed forces undermines the ability of political leaders to deny the importance of the problem and can present a very obvious way of putting HIV/AIDS on the political agenda, as well as marking an entry point for wider HIV/AIDS programs and efforts. Thus, although in an ideal world HIV/AIDS would be addressed as a humanitarian and altruistic issue, outlining how HIV/AIDS programs would also benefit the national interests of states can help to increase international funding and can spur heavily affected states into action in a way that more altruistic health and development frameworks have not been able to do over the past decade.

This still leaves unresolved, however, the second problem: that the "threat-defense" logic could lead to the redirection of funding priorities toward the core institutions of the state. Will such a security framing not simply shift funding to the elites and the armed forces at the expense of more universal programs? Here, too, there are factors complicating the picture; for even when money is allocated to the military, this money can have a wider beneficial impact. The securitization of HIV/AIDS spurred Congress to allocate $10 million to begin setting up a program to address the spread of HIV/AIDS in selected African militaries. In 2001, this culminated in the Department of Defense HIV/AIDS Prevention Program, which has secured funding in excess of U.S.$35 million through fiscal year 2004 (U.S. Department of Defense 2005). Through this program, the Department of Defense has assisted 35 countries in developing HIV/AIDS prevention programs in the armed forces. Although these programs primarily focus on military personnel, and their levels of funding are small compared with other expenditures undertaken by the Department of Defense, they can have a broader impact. In Kenya, for example, the U.S. military HIV/AIDS program also extends to soldiers' dependents, with the result that 1,500 Kenyans, half of whom are not soldiers, are now receiving treatment through the program—a program which has also helped train many HIV counselors (Fisher-Thompson 2005). A similar program is currently underway in Tanzania, and a further one is planned for Nigeria. As long as such funding does not come at the expense of funding for civilian programs, the securitization of HIV/AIDS could generate new resources that are crucial for building the health care infra-structure in poor countries and thus for international efforts to mitigate the spread of HIV/AIDS. What is more, as an organization, the armed forces also have a duty to protect the health of their soldiers when deployed abroad. This means that unlike many commercial pharmaceutical companies that lack economic incentives to develop medicines for illnesses affecting the developing world, the U.S. military continues to be engaged in vaccine research for strands of HIV that predominate in Asia and Africa in order to protect troops that might contract HIV while deployed abroad. Historically, many of the medical advances that people still benefit from today originally emerged from military research.

What is more, drawing attention to the role of HIV/AIDS in the armed forces will invariably have to form an important part of international efforts to respond to HIV/AIDS. Although many would clearly oppose privileged access to treatment for the armed forces of developing countries, when the issue of HIV/AIDS is approached from the angle of prevention, a slightly different picture emerges. In a recent overview of new security issues, James Wirtz (2002:311) notes that "it is not clear how military action can help stop the [AIDS] epidemic that is sweeping Africa and other parts of the world." Yet around the world members of the security sector are not only profoundly affected by, but are also important actors in, the AIDS pandemic. Although Wirtz is thus correct in the sense that the security sector cannot (and indeed should not) co-ordinate national or international responses to HIV/AIDS, it is similarly true that such efforts to mitigate the spread of the virus are unlikely to succeed unless they incorporate strategies for targeting members of the security sector. In many countries members of the armed forces mark a high-risk group, and prevalence rates in several militaries around the world are thought to range between two and five times that of comparable civilian populations. A study carried out regarding gonorrhea and chlamydia infections at the Fort Bragg U.S. Army installation in North Carolina, for example, found that even after standardization of rates by age, race, and sex, the adjusted rates for Fort Bragg were higher than state or national averages (Sena et al. 2000). Around the world it is suspected that this is true in many militaries regarding levels of HIV as well, given that one of the transmission routes is through unprotected sexual intercourse. In some African militaries, average HIV prevalence rates are even thought to have reached between forty and sixty percent of the armed forces (National Intelligence Council 2000). Soldiers that are of a sexually active age, and that are very mobile and stationed away from home for long periods of time often valorize violent and risky behavior, can have frequent opportunities for casual sexual relations, and often seek to relieve themselves from the stress of combat. Members of the armed forces can thus be an important vector for transmitting the virus, and will have to play a vital role—not in leading or orchestrating national and international AIDS policy—but rather in terms of taking seriously their role in the pandemic and undertaking responsible steps to reduce the transmission of HIV both within and outside of the ranks. Again, this is not to insist that the armed forces should enjoy privileged access to medicines, but rather to suggest that, given the prominent role of the military sector in the pandemic, international efforts to prevent the spread of the pandemic are unlikely to succeed in the absence of a strategy for also addressing HIV/AIDS in the military. It makes a big difference, therefore, whether the issue of HIV/AIDS in the military is approached from the perspective of treatment or prevention. Although highlighting HIV/AIDS in the military could thus be seen as detrimental if it leads to privileged access to treatment, from the perspective of global prevention efforts, drawing attention to the role of HIV/AIDS in the armed forces seems inevitable—mitigating against this second problem inherent in bringing the "threat-defense" logic of security to bear on HIV/AIDS.

What, then, of the third concern about the impact of the "threat-defense" logic on grassroots attempts to normalize social responses to the illness? Does the portrayal of HIV/AIDS as a debilitating security threat not just further stigmatize those living with the illness? Here, too, the normative picture becomes much more complicated when the threat is not seen to emanate from a group of persons, but rather from the *virus*. Although many would find the portrayal of persons living with HIV as a security threat to be ethically abhorrent and as something to be avoided at all costs, the question of whether such an assessment is also appropriate regarding the virus itself is much less certain. There is a crucial difference between arguing that "people with HIV/AIDS are a security threat" and arguing that "AIDS is a security threat": while the former aims to be politically exclusionary, and would bring into play a host of normative concerns already outlined by other scholars (Huysmans 1995, 2000) in relation to the securitization of migrants in many countries, the latter can be understood as a more inclusive gesture arguing that those living with HIV/AIDS should receive assistance if they so desire. It is also the latter claim that predominates among those linking HIV/AIDS and security.

What is more, one may well be skeptical about whether, in order to avoid the "threat-defense" logic of security, the optimal long-term relationship between people and the HIV virus really is one of complete normalization and "desecuritization." A certain normalization regarding the perception of people living with the illness would, of course, serve to reduce stigma and discrimination, but it might also culminate in an increased "threat" to life if, as a result, people begin to underestimate the lethal nature of the virus and cease to the take precautions against its transmission. In Western countries, where public reactions to people living with HIV/AIDS have become slightly more normalized compared with much of the 1980s, transmission rates are again increasing—even though there is no cure for HIV/AIDS and the virus may well become drug resistant in the long run (UNAIDS 2002:25). In this way, aiming for normalization regarding the HIV virus might have more adverse side effects. Again, the point here is not that the normative concern of securitization theory is not justified—especially as many political actors may not be able to differentiate at this level of detail and might perceive people living with HIV/AIDS as a threat rather than the key to reversing the global pandemic; the point is that in the case of HIV/AIDS, there are, depending on where precisely the threat is seen to emanate from, also strong arguments complicating any hasty rejection of the securitization of HIV/AIDS. In the case of HIV/AIDS, the ethical picture rapidly becomes much more complex.

In all of these aforementioned instances, then, linking HIV/AIDS and security can also have important benefits for those living with HIV/AIDS, especially in terms of reinforcing national and international efforts to stem the spread of HIV and treating those already suffering from AIDS-related illnesses. Many of these advantages are also unique to the language and apparatus of security, that is benefits that a securitization of HIV/AIDS could bring to the international debate on HIV/AIDS in a way that, as the first two decades of the pandemic's history have shown, portraying HIV/AIDS primarily as a health issue or as a development issue has not been able to achieve. In terms of securing high-level political leadership and increased funding, the framing of HIV/AIDS as a security issue is clearly useful; it is essential in terms of potentially overriding the TRIPS provisions and politicizing the role of the security sector in the pandemic. Given these competing normative benefits and drawbacks of framing the international response to the global AIDS pandemic in the language of security, participants in the debate are left confronting a profound and complex ethical dilemma about whether they should continue to frame HIV/AIDS as a security issue.[23] Indeed, just as there are clear normative dangers inherent in presenting HIV/AIDS as a security issue, there appear to be equally important normative costs involved in not doing so. All of this generates a much more complex and unyielding normative terrain surrounding the securitization of AIDS. At this stage, the answer to the question of whether HIV/AIDS should be securitized could justifiably be both "yes" and "no."

Conclusion

Can this ethical dilemma be resolved? It is not actually the intention of securitization theory to solve this dilemma on behalf of individual policy makers, activists, and scholars. Rather, its purpose is to cultivate among all of these audiences a deeper ethical sensibility about "speaking" security and to encourage them to reflect more thoroughly on whether the language of security is the most appropriate avenue for addressing any particular social issue. Securitization theory, Wæver (1999:334) notes, "puts an ethical question at the feet of analysts, decision makers and political activists alike: why do you call this a security issue? What are the implications of doing this—or of not doing it?" This article has sought to take this challenge seriously and to outline both the possible benefits and dangers of framing HIV/AIDS as a security issue. Yet securitization theory is also very cautious not to prejudge the complexity of issues such as HIV/AIDS. While Buzan, Wæver, and de Wilde (1998:29) have a general preference for resisting securitization processes, they also grant that "although in the abstract desecuritization is the ideal, in specific situations one can choose securitization, only one should not believe this is an innocent reflection of the issue *being* a security threat; it is always a political choice to securitize or to accept a securitization." In the end this choice about whether to endorse or reject securitization processes cannot be made *for* analysts and scholars; it must be made *by* them— independently and with respect to each particular securitization they encounter, as well as with the particular audiences they engage.

What an awareness of this dilemma can do in the case of HIV/AIDS, however, is spur those advocating the links between HIV/AIDS and security to at least do so in ways that seek to minimize some of these aforementioned dangers. There are three ways in which this could be achieved. First, those presenting HIV/AIDS as a security issue could be sure to insist that it is not *exclusively* a security issue, but rather a security issue *in addition* to also being a health issue, a development issue, an economic issue, a social issue, a political issue, a gender issue, etc. In this way, insisting on the security implications of HIV/AIDS does not unreflectively reify the traditional hierarchy between achieving security and the attainment of other social values, such as health. Nor does it simply replace an altruistic logic with a self-interested one. The security dimension of HIV/AIDS could then complement, rather than supersede, existing frameworks, and it would not undermine alternative rationales for global health initiatives, or unduly prioritize the needs of the security community over those of civil society. Second, the ethical dangers of securitizing AIDS could be further minimized by framing the illness as a security *issue*, or as an issue with an important security *dimension*, rather than as a dangerous and overwhelming security *threat*. This would still add considerable political *gravitas* to international efforts to respond to HIV/AIDS. It would probably also suffice in terms of invoking the security exceptions within TRIPS should this become necessary in the years ahead, and would similarly allow for the role of the security sector in the pandemic to be politicized, without doing so at the cost of playing on excessive fears and further stigmatizing persons living with HIV/AIDS. Finally, those framing HIV/AIDS as a security issue could also take great care to indicate that their primary concern lies with those people living with HIV/AIDS—that the problem lies not with the people living with the virus, but with the virus itself.

Here, then, the uniqueness of the case of HIV/AIDS in relation to previous securitization processes also begins to emerge particularly clearly. For it is a "danger" residing within the human body. If, as a result of the securitization of HIV/AIDS, *persons* living with the virus come to be seen as the threat, then many of the dangers already highlighted by scholars in relation to the securitization of migration and its detrimental effects on migrants come into play. If, however, it is the *virus* that is seen to be the threat, then these concerns are much less applicable, and the parallels reside much closer to environmental security, where nature is part of that which is being securitized. In this case, people living with HIV/AIDS would not be the enemy of global efforts to reduce the pandemic's debilitating consequences, but in fact would be the only hope for achieving viable improvements in the future. Consequently, they would have to be included in these efforts in a way that does not infringe upon their human rights or civil liberties. Precisely because the virus resides inside the human body, however, the case of HIV/AIDS in the end neatly parallels neither the securitization of the environment nor that of migration; it reaffirms instead the need for security analysts to continually assess the effects of linking security and wider social issues with due consideration of the specificities of each particular issue. All of this requires participants in the debate on HIV/AIDS and security to at least follow securitization theory's ethical imperative of thinking much more carefully about the intended audience, about the way in which the term security is used, and about the general language deployed in relation to HIV/AIDS. In the end, however, the securitization of HIV/AIDS undoubtedly remains a gamble on the ability of those presenting HIV/AIDS as a security issue to maintain control over the uses to which this language will be put—albeit a gamble that has perhaps become necessary because of the particular vicissitudes of contemporary world politics.

Author's note

This article was first presented at the 44th Annual Convention of the International Studies Association, Portland, Oregon, February 2003. The author would like to thank members of the Africa Research Group at the London School of Economics, members of the Security Research Group at the University of Wales, Aberystwyth, members of the Africa Research Group at King's College, London, participants in the Twenty-First Century Trust Conference on Disease and Security, as well as Andrew Price-Smith, Robert Ostergard Jr., Alex de Waal, Christopher Coker, Louiza Odysseos, and three anonymous reviewers for their valuable feedback on previous versions of this article.

Notes

1 For two rare attempts to probe the implications of health for international relations, see Fidler (1998) and Youde (2005).

2 The term securitization refers to the process whereby HIV/AIDS is presented by officials of national and international institutions not just as a health or development issue, but also as a pressing matter of national and international security requiring the adoption of emergency measures. See also the more detailed discussion of securitization in "Securitization Theory and HIV/AIDS" of this article.

3 For an account of the genesis of this meeting, see Sternberg (2002).

4 That same year, the Clinton administration also invoked national security justifications for other non-military purposes, such as granting China "normal" trading status with the United States. Several decades earlier, in 1955, Dwight Eisenhower had similarly tried to promote his administration's National System of Interstate and Defense Highways on the basis of a national security justification, arguing that such a highway network would be essential for evacuation plans and mobilizing defenses. See Sanger (2000).

5 For competing definitions of "human security," see United Nations Development Program (United Nations Development Program 1994); Commission on Human Security (2003); and the special issue of *Security Dialogue* (Vol. 35, No. 3; September 2004) on human security.

6 I have explored competing definitions and meanings of human, national, and international security, as well as the ways in which HIV/AIDS bears on them, in greater detail in Elbe (2005). For other accounts of human and national security, see Fidler (2003) and Peterson (2002/2003).

7 For two notable exceptions, see the brief discussion in Altman (2000) and Peterson (2002/2003).

8 These arguments closely parallel those in Deudney (1990).

9 For more general reflections on the normative questions the AIDS pandemic gives rise to, see Harris and Siplon (2001), and the special section on "Health and Global Justice" in *Ethics and International Affairs* 16 (2), Fall 2002. For pieces on the ethics of conducting research into HIV/AIDS see Kesby (2004) and Craddock (2004).

10 See also Wæver (1995) and Williams (2003).

11 A more comprehensive analysis of the securitizing actors, agendas, and strategies has already been undertaken by Sheehan (2002).

12 In this way, their study forms part of a larger research effort to view security issues as being socially constructed. See, for example, Wendt (1992, 1999), Finnemore (1996), Katzenstein (1996), Adler (1997), Hopf (1998), Barnett and Finnemore (1999).

13 On this point see also Hansen (2000:288).

14 Referent objects of security do not necessarily have to be states or militaries, but more generally "things that are seen to be existentially threatened and that have a legitimate claim to survival" (Buzan, Wæver, and de Wilde 1998:36). Examples of this security grammar can thus be found operating both in regard to military issues and throughout the wider security agenda. For example, it is just as possible for non-governmental organizations (securitizing actors) to declare humanity or the biosphere (referent objects) existentially threatened by greenhouse gases, requiring drastic social changes. Of course, Buzan, Wæver, and de Wilde are aware that, in practice, there are important constraints on which actors can successfully securitize issues. Although it remains a theoretical possibility, they find that individuals and small groups of people are rarely able to establish a wider security legitimacy in their own right. Nevertheless, this flexibility in their framework in principle allows it to be applied to the wider security agenda, including HIV/AIDS, without losing analytic focus as a result.

15 These specific and narrow criteria also set the securitization of HIV/AIDS distinctly apart from other emergency responses to HIV/AIDS that have occurred within

the contexts of public health, development, or even disaster relief, such as the Ryan White Comprehensive AIDS Resource Emergency Act in the United States. The latter clearly calls for emergency measures that provide health care and support for those persons living with HIV/AIDS, whose health needs would otherwise remain unmet. This act, however, is not intended to protect the United States from an existential threat, but instead to "reduce the use of more costly inpatient care, increase access to care for underserved populations, and improve the quality of life for those affected by the epidemic" (U.S. Department of Health and Human Services 2005). In this case, there are no securitizing actors arguing that a referent object is existentially threatened.

16 Indeed, this danger is not only inherent in relations between the state and the civilian population, but also *within* state institutions, such as the armed forces. In many of the world's armed forces, security arguments have already been cited for no longer accepting HIV-positive applicants for service.

17 For a more comprehensive list of medical provision for HIV/AIDS in the civilian and military populations of African countries, see www.uniformservices.unaids.org/

18 For a good overview, see Sell and Prakash (2004).

19 This is part of deeper tension inherent in securitization theory. By grounding their normative framework in speech act theory, the framework encounters difficulties when dealing with social groups that are not able to voice their views due, for example, to political marginalization. On this point see Hansen (2000:287).

20 Even among theorists of democracy, there is considerable disagreement regarding the role the state should perform in social life, with some models arguing in favor of a role restricted to the provision of security and with others suggesting that the state must make important social provisions and perform redistributive functions.

21 Another important factor was the push for action by evangelical Christian religious groups in the United States. See Burkhalter (2004).

22 It also seems to parallel an insight expounded by William H. Foege, the former director of the Center for Disease Control in Atlanta, Georgia: one must "[t]ie the needs of the poor with the fears of the rich. When the rich lose their fear, they are not willing to invest in the problems of the poor." Quoted in Gellman (2002).

23 Nor are there clear historical precedents that one could turn to. There are certainly historical precedents for diseases shaping the unfolding of human history, and indeed influencing battle outcomes. See, for example. Cartwright (1972), Diamond (1997), McNeill (1998), Oldstone (2000), Watts (1997), and Zinsser (1953). There are, however, no diseases in recent history that match the experience of HIV/AIDS in terms of transmission methods, geographic extent, demographic impact, and disease pattern.

References

ADLER, EMMANUEL. (1997) Seizing the Middle Ground: Constructivism in World Politics. *European Journal of International Relations* 3(3):319–365.

ALLOCATE MORE, ARVS TO MILITARY PERSONNEL. (2003) Times of Zambia, November 17. <http://www.times.co.zm> (June 28, 2005).

ALTMAN, DENNIS. (2000) Understanding HIV/AIDS as a Global Security Issue. In *Health Impacts of Globalization: Towards Global Governance*, edited by Lee Kelley. London: Palgrave.

AMNESTY INTERNATIONAL. (2004) Marked for Death: Rape Survivors Living with HIV/AIDS in Rwanda. Report AFR 47/007/2004. Available at <http://web.amnesty.org/library/index/engafr470072004> (Accessed June 28, 2005).

ARADAU, CLAUDIA. (2001) Beyond Good and Evil: Ethics and Securitization/Dese-curitization Techniques. *Rubikon*. Available at <http://venus.ci.uw.edu.pl/~rubikon/forum/claudia2.htm> (Accessed June 28, 2005).

AUSTIN, JOHN. (1962) *How to Do Things with Words*. Cambridge: Harvard University Press.

BARNETT, MICHAEL, AND MARTHA FINNEMORE. (1999) The Politics, Power and Pathologies of International Organizations. *International Organization* 53(4): 699–732.

BARNETT, TONY, AND ALAN WHITESIDE. (2002) *AIDS in the Twenty-First Century: Disease and Globalization*. Basingstoke: Palgrave.

BAZERGAN, ROXANNE. (2001) UN Peacekeepers and HIV/AIDS. *World Today* 57(5): 6–8.

BAZERGAN, ROXANNE. (2003) Intervention and Intercourse: HIV/AIDS and Peace-keepers. *Conflict, Security and Development* 3(1):27–51.

BIGO, DIDIER. (1998) Sécurité et immigration: vers une gouvernementalité par l'inquiétude. *Cultures el Conflits* 31–32:13–38.

BLOOM, DAVID E., AND PETER GODWIN, EDS. (1997) *The Economics of HIV and AIDS: The Case of South and South East Asia*. New York: Oxford University Press.

BONANATE, LUIGI, DONALD PUCHALA, AND CHARLES W. KEGLEY JR., EDS. (1995) *Ethics and International Politics*. Columbia: University of South Carolina Press.

BRATT, DUANE. (2002) Blue Condoms: The Use of International Peacekeepers in the Fight Against AIDS. *International Peacekeeping* 9(3):67–86.

BROWN, CHRIS. (1992) *International Relations Theory: New Normative Approaches*. New York: Columbia University Press.

BROWN, CHRIS. (2002) *Sovereignty, Rights and Justice: International Political Theory Today*. Cambridge: Polity.

BURKHALTER, HOLLY. (2004) The Politics of AIDS: Engaging Conservative Activists. *Foreign Affairs* 83:8–14.

BUZAN, BARRY, AND OLE WÆVER. (1998) Liberalism and Security: The Contradictions of the Liberal Leviathan. Working papers no. 23, Copenhagen Peace Research Insti-tute, Copenhagen. Available at <http://www.ciaonet.org/wps/bub02/> (Accessed June 28, 2005).

BUZAN, BARRY, OLE WÆVER, AND JAAP DE WILDE. (1998) *Security: A New Framework for Analysis*. Boulder: Lynne Rienner.

CARTWRIGHT, FREDERICK. (1972) *Disease and History*. New York: Barnes & Noble.

CEYHAN, AYSE, AND ANASTASSIA TSOUKALA. (2002) The Securitization of Migration in Western Societies: Ambivalent Discourses and Policies. *Alternatives* 27(1):21–39.

CHEN, LINCOLN, *et al.*, EDS. (2003) *Global Health Challenges for Human Security*. Cambridge: Harvard University Press.

CHOWKA, PETER. (2000) AIDS Deemed a "National Security" Threat by U.S. as South African President Challenges Medical Orthodoxy. Natural Healthline, May 1. Available at <http://www.naturalhealthvillage.com/newsletter/01may00/aids.htm> (Accessed June 28, 2005).

COKER, RICHARD. (2003) Migration, Public Health and Compulsory Screening for TB and HIV. Asylum and migration working paper 1, Institute for Public Policy Research, London.

COMMISSION ON HUMAN SECURITY. (2003) Human Security Now. Available at <http://www.humansecurity-chs.org/finalreport/FinalReport.pdf> (Accessed June 28, 2005).

CONKLIN, STEVE. (2003) Interview with Radhika Sarin, Author of the Enemy Within: AIDS in the Military. World Watch Institute, Washington, March 28. Available at <http://www.worldwatch.org/live/discussion/70/> (Accessed June 28, 2005).

CRADDOCK, SUSAN. (2004) AIDS and Ethics: Clinical Trials, Pharmaceuticals, and Global Scientific Practice. In *HIV and AIDS in Africa: Beyond Epidemiology*, edited by Ezekiel Kalipeni, *et al.* Oxford: Blackwell.

CSIS. (2002) *The Destabilizing Impacts of HIV/AIDS*. Washington: Center for Strategic and International Studies. Available at <http://www.csis.org/africa/destabilizing_aids.pdf>.

DAVID, MARCELLA. (2001) Rubber Helmets: The Certain Pitfalls of Marshalling Security Council Resources to Combat AIDS in Africa. *Human Rights Quarterly* 23(3):560–582.

DEUDNEY, DANIEL. (1990) The Case Against Linking Environmental Degradation and National Security. *Millennium* 19(3):461–476.

DE WAAL, ALEX. (2003) How Will HIV/AIDS Transform African Governance? *African Affairs* 102:1–23.

DIAMOND, JARED. (1997) *Guns, Germs and Steel: The Fates of Human Societies*. New York: Norton.

DOTY, ROXANNE. (1998) Immigration and the Politics of Security. *Security Studies* 8(2–3):71–93.

DUFFIELD, MARK. (2001) *Global Governance and the New Wars: The Merging of Development and Security*. London: Zed Books.

EBERSTADT, NICHOLAS. (2002) The Future of AIDS. *Foreign Affairs* 81(6):22–45.

ELBE, STEFAN. (2002) HIV/AIDS and the Changing Landscape of War in Africa. *International Security* 27(2):159–177.

ELBE, STEFAN. (2003) *The Strategic Dimensions of HIV/AIDS. International Institute for Strategic Studies*. Oxford: Oxford University Press.

ELBE, STEFAN. (2005) HIV/AIDS: The International Security Dimensions. In *New Threats and New Actors in International Security*, edited by Elke Krahmann. New York: Palgrave.

EMMERS, RALF. (2003) ASEAN and the Securitization of Transnational Crime in Southeast Asia. *Pacific Review* 16(3):419–438.

FIDLER, DAVID. (1998) Microbialpolitik: Infectious Diseases and International Relations. *American University International Law Review* 14(1):1–11.

FIDLER, DAVID. (2003) Public Health and National Security in the Global Age: Infectious Diseases, Bioterrorism, and Realpolitik. *George Washington International Law Review* 35:787–856.

FINNEMORE, MARTHA. (1996) *National Interests in International Society*. Ithaca: Cornell University Press.

FISHER-THOMPSON, JIM. (2005) Kenya Provides Firm Ground for U.S. Military AIDS Partnership. U.S. Department of State Information Service (USINFO), Washington, February 18. Available at <http://usinfo.state.gov/gi/Archive/2005/Feb/22-541177.html> (Accessed June 28, 2005).

FOURIE, PIETER, AND MARTIN SCHÖNTEICH. (2001) Africa's New Security Threat: HIV/AIDS and Human Security in Southern Africa. *African Security Review* 10(4). Available at <http://www.iss.co.za> (Accessed June 28, 2005).

FROST, MERVYN. (1996) *Ethics in International Relations: A Constitutive Theory*. Cambridge: Cambridge University Press.

GARRETT, LAURIE. (1994) *The Coming Plague: Newly Emerging Diseases in a World out of Balance.* New York: Penguin Books.

GELLMAN, BARTON. (2000) World Shunned Signs of the Coming Plague. *Washington Post*, July 5.

GRISIN, SARAH, AND CELESTE WALLANDER. (2002) *Russia's HIV/AIDS Crisis: Confronting the Present and Facing the Future.* Washington: Center for Strategic and International Studies.

GODWIN, PETER, ED. (1998) *The Looming Epidemic: The Impact of HIV and AIDS in India.* London: Hurst & Company.

GROVER, ANAND. (2004) Letter from the Affordable Medicines Treatment Campaign to India's National Human Rights Commission. Human Rights News, Human Rights Watch, October 11. Available at <http://www.hrw.org/english/docs/2004/10/22/india9556.htm> (Accessed June 28, 2005).

HANSEN, LENE. (2000) The Little Mermaid's Silent Security Dilemma and the Absence of Gender in the Copenhagen School. *Millennium* 29(2):285–306.

HARKER, JOHN. (2001) HIV/AIDS and the Security Sector in Africa: A Threat to Canada. Canadian Security Intelligence Service, Ottawa. Available at <http://www.csis-scrs.gc.ca/eng/comment/com80_e.html> (Accessed June 28, 2005).

HARRIS, PAUL, AND PATRICIA SIPLON. (2001) International Obligation and Human Health: Evolving Policy Responses to HIV/AIDS. *Ethics and International Affairs* 15(2):29–52.

HEINECKEN, LINDY. (2001a) Strategic implications of HIV/AIDS in South Africa. *Conflict, Security and Development* 1(1):109–113.

HEINECKEN, LINDY. (2001b) Living in Terror: The Looming Security Threat to Southern Africa. *African Security Review* 10(4):7–17.

HOLDEN, SUE. (2003) *AIDS on the Agenda: Adapting Development and Humanitarian Programmes to Meet the Challenge of HIV/AIDS.* Oxford: Oxfam.

HINSLIFF, GABY. (2003) Britain Slams the Door on Foreign NHS Cheats. *The Observer*, February 9.

HOPE, KEMPE RONALD, ED. (1999) *AIDS and Development in Africa: A Social Science Perspective.* New York: The Haworth Press.

HOPF, TED. (1998) The Promise of Constructivism in International Relations Theory. *International Security* 23(1):171–200.

HUSAK, DOUGLAS. (1992) *Drugs and Rights.* Cambridge: Cambridge University Press.

HUYSMANS, JEFF. (1995) Migrants as a Security Problem: Dangers of "Securitizing" Societal Issues. In *Migration and European Integration*, edited by Robert Miles and Dietrich Thranhardt. London: Pinter.

HUYSMANS, JEFF. (1998) Revisiting Copenhagen: Or, on the Creative Development of a Security Studies Agenda in Europe. *European Journal of International Relations* 4(4):479–505.

HUYSMANS, JEFF. (2000) The European Union and the Securitization of Migration. *Journal of Common Market Studies* 38(5):751–777.

ICG. (2001) *HIV/AIDS as a Security Issue.* Washington: International Crisis Group.

ICG. (2004) *HIV/AIDS as a Security Issue in Africa: Lessons From Uganda.* Kampala, Uganda: International Crisis Group.

KAKONEN, JYRKI, ED. (1994) *Green Security or Militarized Environment.* Aldershot: Dartmouth Publishing Company.

KALIPENI, EZEKIEL, *et al.*, EDS. (2004) *HIV and AIDS in Africa: Beyond Epidemiology.* Oxford: Blackwell.

KATZENSTEIN, PETER, ED. (1996) *The Culture of National Security: Norms and Identity in World Politics.* New York: Columbia University Press.

KAUFFMAN, KYLE, AND DAVID LINDAUER, EDS. (2004) *AIDS and South Africa: The Social Expression of a Pandemic.* Basingstoke: Palgrave.

KEIM, WILLARD. (2000) *Ethics, Morality and International Affairs.* Lanham: University Press of America.

KESBY, MIKE. (2004) Participatory Diagramming and the Ethical and Practical Challenges of Helping Themselves to Move HIV Work "Beyond Epidemiology." In *HIV and AIDS in Africa: Beyond Epidemiology*, edited by Ezekiel Kalipeni, *et al.* Oxford: Blackwell.

KRISTOFFERSSON, ULF. (2000) HIV/AIDS as a Human Security Issue: A Gender Perspective. Paper presented at the expert group meeting on "The HIV/AIDS Pandemic and Its Gender Implications," 13–17 November, Windhoek, Namibia.

LEEN, MAURA. (2004) *The European Union, HIV/AIDS and Human Security.* Dublin: Dochas.

LINGE, GODFREY, AND DOUG PORTER, EDS. (1997) *No Place for Borders: The HIV/AIDS Epidemic and Development in Asia and the Pacific.* New York: St. Martin's Press.

LITFIN, KAREN. (1999) Constructing Environmental Security and Ecological Interdependence. *Global Governance* 5(3):359–378.

LURIE, PETER, PERCY C. HINTZEN, AND ROBERT A. LOWE. (2004) Socioeconomic Obstacles to HIV Prevention in Developing Countries: The Roles of the International Monetary Fund and the World Bank. In *HIV and AIDS in Africa: Beyond Epidemiology*, edited by Ezekiel Kalipeni, Susan Craddock, Joseph R. Oppong, and Jayati Ghosh. Oxford: Blackwell.

LWANDA, JOHN LLOYD. (2004) Politics, Culture, and Medicine: An Unholy Trinity. In *HIV and AIDS in Africa: Beyond Epidemiology*, edited by Ezekiel Kalipeni, *et al.* Oxford: Blackwell.

MCNEILL, WILLIAM. (1998) *Plagues and People.* New York: Anchor Books.

MEDECINS SANS FRONTIERS. (2005) A Guide to the Post-2005 World: TRIPS, R&D and Access to Medicines. Available at <http://www.msf.org/msfinternational/content/advocacy/accesstoessentialmedicinescampaign/index.cfm> (Accessed June 28, 2005).

MILLS, GREG. (2000) AIDS and the South African Military: Timeworn Cliché or Timebomb? In *HIV/AIDS: A Threat to the African Renaissance?*, edited by Michael Lange. Johannesburg: Konrad Adenauer Foundation.

MOCK, NANCY. (2002) HIV/AIDS in our Ranks. Presentation to the Woodrow Wilson Center, Washington, June 4. Available at <http://www.certi.org/strategy/military/role_of_the_military.htm> (Accessed June 28, 2005).

MUSEVENI, YOWERI. (1995) Opening Speech at the Ninth International Conference on AIDS and STDs in Africa. Kampala, Uganda, December 10. Available at <http://www.museveni.co.ug> (Accessed March 15, 2005).

NARDIN, TERRY, AND DAVID MAPEL, EDS. (1993) *Traditions of International Ethics.* Cambridge: Cambridge University Press.

NATIONAL INTELLIGENCE COUNCIL. (2000) The Global Infectious Disease Threat and Its Implications for the U.S. Washington DC. Available at <http://www.cia.gov/cia/reports/nie/report/nie99-17d.html>.

NATIONAL INTELLIGENCE COUNCIL. (2002) The Next Wave of HIV/AIDS: Nigeria, Ethiopia, Russia, India, and China. Washington, DC. Available at <http://www. cia.gov/nic/special_nextwaveHIV.html>.

NEY, STEVEN. (1999) Environmental Security: A Critical Overview. *Innovation: The European Journal of Social Sciences* 12(1):7–30.

OAU. (2001) *Abuja Declaration on HIV/AIDS, Tuberculosis and other Related Infectious Diseases*. Abuja, Nigeria: Organisation of African Unity. Available at <www. un.org/ga/aids/pdf/abuja_declaration.pdf> (Accessed June 28, 2005).

ODYSSEOS, LOUIZA. (2002) Dangerous Ontologies: The Ethos of Survival and Ethical Theorising in International Relations. *Review of International Studies* 28(2):403–418.

ODYSSEOS, LOUIZA. (2003) On the Way to Global Ethics? Cosmopolitanism, Ethical Selfhood and Otherness. *European Journal of Political Theory* 2(2):187–207.

OLDSTONE, MICHAEL. (2000) *Viruses, Plagues, and History*. Oxford: Oxford University Press.

OSTERGARD, ROBERT L. JR. (2002) Politics in the Hot Zone: AIDS and National Security in Africa. *Third World Quarterly* 23(2):333–350.

OSTERGARD, ROBERT L. JR., ED. (2005) *HIV, AIDS and the Threat to National and International Security*. London: Palgrave.

OSTRAUSKAITE, RASA. (2001) Environmental Security as an Ambiguous Symbol: Can We Securitize the Environment? *Rubikon*. Available at <http://venus.ci.uw.edu.pl/ ~rubikon/forum/rasa2.htm> (Accessed June 28, 2005).

OXFAM. (2004) Undermining Access to Medicines: Comparison of Five US FTAs. A Technical Note. Available at <http://www.oxfam.org.uk/what_we_do/issues/health/ downloads/undermining_access_ftas.pdf> (Accessed June 28, 2005).

PETERSON, SUSAN. (2002/2003) Epidemic Disease and National Security. *Security Studies* 12(2):43–81.

PHARAOH, ROBYN, AND MARTIN SCHÖNTEICH. (2003) *AIDS, Security and Governance in Southern Africa: Exploring the Impact*. Pretoria: Institute for Security Studies.

PIOT, PETER. (2000) Global AIDS Pandemic: Time to Turn the Tide. *Science* 288:2176–2178.

PIOT, PETER. (2001) AIDS and Human Security. Speech delivered at the United Nations University. Tokyo, October 2. Available at <http://www.unaids.org/html/pub/media/ speeches01/piot_tokyo_02oct01_en_doc.htm> (Accessed June 28, 2005).

PRICE-SMITH, ANDREW. (1998) Ghosts of Kigali: Infectious Disease and Global Stability at the Turn of the Century. *International Journal* 54:426–442.

PRICE-SMITH, ANDREW. (2001) *The Health of Nations: Infectious Disease, Environmental Change, and Their Effects on National Security and Development*. Cambridge: MIT Press.

PRICE-SMITH, ANDREW. (2002) *Pretoria's Shadow: The HIV/AIDS Pandemic and National Security in South Africa*. Washington: Chemical and Biological Arms Control Institute.

PRINS, GWYN. (2004) AIDS and Global Security. *International Affairs* 80(5):931–952.

ROFFE, PEDRO, AND RICARDO MELENDEZ-ORTIZ. (2005) *Resource Book on TRIPS and Development: An Authoritative and Practical Guide to the TRIPS Agreement*. Geneva: The United Nations Conference on Trade and Development and The International Centre for Trade and Sustainable Development. Available at <http://www.iprsonline. org/unctadictsd/ResourceBookIndex.htm> (Accessed June 28, 2005).

SANGER, DAVID. (2000) Sometimes, National Security Says It All. *New York Times*, May 7.

SARIN, RADHIKA. (2003) A New Security Threat: HIV/AIDS in the Military. *World Watch* (March/April), 17–22.

SCHOEPF, BROOKE GRUNDFEST. (2004) AIDS, History, and Struggles over Meaning. In *HIV and AIDS in Africa: Beyond Epidemiology*, edited by Ezekiel Kalipeni, *et al.* Oxford: Blackwell.

SEARLE, JOHN. (1969) *Speech Acts: An Essay in the Philosophy of Language.* Cambridge: Cambridge University Press.

SECKINELGIN, HAKAN. (2003) HIV/AIDS, Global Civil Society and People's Politics: An Update. In *Global Civil Society Yearbook*, edited by Mary Kaldor, *et al.* Oxford: Oxford University Press.

SECKINELGIN, HAKAN, AND HIDEAKI SHINODA, EDS. (2001) *Ethics and International Relations.* London: Palgrave.

SELL, S., AND A. PRAKASH. (2004) Using Ideas Strategically: The Contest Between Business and NGO Networks in Intellectual Property Rights. *International Studies Quarterly* 48(1):143–175.

SENA, A., W. MILLER, I. HOFFMAN, M. COHEN, P. JENKINS, AND J. MCKEE. (2000) Trends of Gonorrhoea and Chlamydial Infections During 1985–1996 Among Active Duty Soldiers at a US Army Installation. *Clinical Infectious Diseases* 30: 742–748.

SHARMA, KAMALESH. (2001) Statement by Mr. Kamalesh Sharma, Permanent Representative at the Open Meeting of the Security Council on the Responsibility of the Security Council in the Maintenance of International Peace and Security: HIV/AIDS and International Peacekeeping Operations, January 19. Available at <http://www.un.int/india/ind499.htm> (Accessed June 28, 2005).

SHEEHAN, CARRIE. (2002) Securitizing Global Health Issues: HIV/AIDS in Africa as a U.S. National Security Threat. Paper presented at the International Studies Association, New Orleans, LA, 26 March.

SINGER, PETER. (2002) AIDS and International Security. *Survival* 44(1):145–158.

SONTAG, SUSAN. (1988) *AIDS and Its Metaphors.* New York: Farrar, Straus and Giroux.

STERNBERG, STEVE. (2002) Former Diplomat Holbrooke Takes on Global AIDS. *USA Today*, June 10.

STOLBERG, SHERYL. (2003) Bush Proposal on AIDS Funds Shows Concern about Security. *New York Times*, January 29.

TENET, GEORGE J. (2003) Testimony of Director of Central Intelligence George J. Tenet before the Senate Select Committee on Intelligence. Washington, February 11.

TRIPODI, PAOLO, AND PREETI PATEL. (2002) The Global Impact of HIV/AIDS on Peace Support Operations. *International Peacekeeping* 9(3):51–66.

UNAIDS. (1998) *AIDS and the Military.* Geneva: UNAIDS.

UNAIDS. (2001) AIDS Now Core Issue at UN Security Council. Press Release, New York, January 19.

UNAIDS. (2002) AIDS Epidemic Update: December 2002, Geneva.

UNITED NATIONS DEVELOPMENT PROGRAM. (1994) *Human Development Report, 1994: New Dimensions of Human Security.* New York: Oxford University Press.

U.S. DEPARTMENT OF DEFENSE. (2005) Background Information on HIV/AIDS Prevention Program. Available at <http://www.nhrc.navy.mil/programs/dhapp/background/background.html> (Accessed June 28, 2005).

U.S. DEPARTMENT OF HEALTH AND HUMAN SERVICES. (2005) Ryan White Comprehensive AIDS Resources Emergency (CARE) Act. Available at <http://hab.hrsa.gov/history.htm> (Accessed June 28, 2005).

U.S. GOVERNMENT ACCOUNTABILITY OFFICE. (2001) *U. N. Peacekeeping: United Nations Faces Challenges in Responding to the Impact of HIV/AIDS on Peacekeeping Operations*. Washington: U.S. Government Accountability Office.

WÆVER, OLE. (1995) Securitization and Desecuritization. In *On Security*, edited by Ronnie Lipschutz. New York: Columbia University Press.

WÆVER, OLE. (1999) Securitizing Sectors? Reply to Eriksson. *Cooperation and Conflict* 34(3):334–340.

WÆVER, OLE, BARRY, BUZAN, MORTEN, KELSTRUP AND PIERRE, LEMAITRE. (1993) *Identity, Migration and the New Security Agenda in Europe*. New York: St. Martin's Press.

WALT, STEPHEN. (1991) The Renaissance of Security Studies. *International Studies Quarterly* 35(2):211–239.

WATTS, SHELDON. (1997) *Epidemics and. History: Disease, Power, and Imperialism*. New Haven: Yale University Press.

WEINER, MYRON. (1992/1993) Security, Stability and International Migration. *International Security* 17(3):91–126.

WENDT, ALEXANDER. (1992) Anarchy Is What States Make of It: The Social Construction of Power Politics. *International Organization* 46(2):335–370.

WENDT, ALEXANDER. (1999) *A Social Theory of International Politics*. Cambridge: Cambridge University Press.

WHITESIDE, ALAN, AND CLEM SUNTER. (2000) *AIDS: The Challenge for South Africa*. Cape Town: Human & Rousseau.

WILLIAMS, MICHAEL. (2003) Words, Images, Enemies: Securitization and International Politics. *International Studies Quarterly* 47(4):511–531.

WIRTZ, JAMES J. (2002) A New Agenda for Security and Strategy? In *Strategy in the Contemporary World*, edited by John Baylis, *et al.* Oxford: Oxford University Press.

WOLFENSOHN, JAMES. (2000) Speech delivered to the UN Security Council. New York, January 10.

WORLD TRADE ORGANISATION. (1994) The Agreement on Trade-Related Aspects of Intellectual Property Rights. Available at <http://www.wto.org/english/docs_e/legal_e/27-trips_01_e.htm>.

YEAGER, RODGER, AND STUART KINGMA. (2001) HIVAIDS: Destabilizing National Security and the Multi-National Response. *International Review of the Armed Forces Medical Services* 74(1–3):3–12.

YOUDE, JEREMY. (2005) Enter the Fourth Horseman: Health Security and International Relations Theory. *Whitehead Journal of Diplomacy and International Relations* 6(1):193–208.

ZINSSER, HANS. (1953) *Rats, Lice, and History*. Boston: Little, Brown and Company.

30

THE RELATIONSHIP BETWEEN THE AIDS PANDEMIC AND STATE FRAGILITY[1]

Pieter Fourie

Source: *Global Change, Peace & Security*, 19:3 (2007), 281–300.

Despite high levels of AIDS in Africa, there are few indications that the pandemic is directly leading to imminent state failure amongst those countries on the continent that manifest exceptionally high AIDS prevalence. Of the factors that threaten the ability of governments to govern, AIDS (or any other health threat, for that matter) is seen to be a derivative threat—at most. However, there has been significant conjecture about the purported link between the pandemic and state fragility. This polemic has been fuelled by the securitization of disease that has become so prevalent in the multilateral arena since 9/11 in particular. However, social science has for the most part left the key concepts in this arena uncomfortably unexplored, and there have been few attempts to speak intelligently about empirical or other indices of the epidemic's impact at the macro (state) level. This article is an attempt to come to grips with some of these issues, specifically in the context of the mature epidemics ravaging Africa.

Introduction

On 5 June 1981 the Centre for Disease Control (CDC) in the United States published its *Weekly Morbidity and Mortality Report*, chronicling for the first time the symptoms amongst a few urban gay men of what was set to become the most deadly plague known to humanity. That was over 25 years ago, and the AIDS[2] pandemic has since then killed around 30 million individuals worldwide. More than 40 million people are currently infected globally; of these, 25 million live in Africa south of the Sahara, making this continent the most infected and worst-affected region in the world.[3]

Table 1 HIV/AIDS prevalence levels in Southern Africa.

Country	Adults and children living with HIV	HIV prevalence rate (%) in adults aged 15–49	AIDS deaths (adults and children) in 2005	Number of orphans (0–17 years) due to AIDS
Angola	320,000	3.7	30,000	160,000
Botswana	270,000	24.1	18,000	120,000
Congo Kinshasa	1,000,000	3.2	90,000	680,000
Lesotho	270,000	23.2	23,000	97,000
Madagascar	49,000	0.5	2,900	13,000
Malawi	940,000	14.1	78,000	550,000
Mozambique	1,800,000	16.1	140,000	510,000
Namibia	230,000	19.6	17,000	85,000
South Africa	5,500,000	18.8	320,000	1,200,000
Swaziland	220,000	33.4	16,000	63,000
Tanzania	1,400,000	6.5	140,000	1,100,000
Zambia	1,100,000	17.0	98,000	710,000
Zimbabwe	1,700,000	20.1	180,000	1,100,000
Total/average	14,799,000	15.4	1,152,900	6,388,000

According to the global report published by the Joint United Nations Programme on AIDS (UNAIDS) in mid-2006 some data for the proximate Southern African region can be summarized as shown in Table 1.[4]

In terms of mortality this translates into more than 3000 deaths amongst Southern African Development Community (SADC) states' citizens *every single day*—and this number is steadily increasing. To put this in comparative perspective, these numbers mean that SADC experiences the equivalent of a 9/11 attack every day of the year, all year round.

To make matters worse, epidemiologists tell us that the AIDS epidemic (since it results from HIV, a lentivirus, meaning that it acts slowly) is a 'long-wave event'. Amongst other implications, this means that we are faced with an insidious phenomenon that might take up to 130 years to play itself out.[5] The conventional parameters of such an event and the programmatic responses to such a 'crisis in slow motion' are simply unknown. Long-wave events share a number of distinguishing features:[6]

- One is usually unaware of their starting point.
- Once awareness is there, it is difficult to stop and turn the progress and impact of the long-wave crisis/event around.
- People with power (such as politicians) find it difficult to face such crises, since their own terms in office are normally for a much shorter time, and it is difficult to mobilize the appropriate amount of resources to counter the crisis.

- There are few precedents for such events, which means that there is little experience or 'best practice' to fall back on—leading to a sense of fatalism and impotence.
- Such events tend to threaten any realistic impact that any governmental administration might have to oppose it.
- Short-term responses taken in haste may act as band-aid solutions that work counter to more effective, longer-term changes in the long run.
- A holistic response to such long-wave events requires long-term thinking that challenges the contemporary short-term way of doing things among current epistemic and political elites.

Simply put, humanity has never experienced anything comparable with this, and we simply do not know what the long-term impact of the pandemic will be. How does one respond to such a threat in an effective and appropriately scaled way? One key response has been to polemicize the epidemic; a master narrative has been created to 'securitize' AIDS. By making appeals to *states'* security, and by crafting AIDS as an 'enemy' that needs to be 'battled' and 'defeated' (note the securocratic register or the language of war applied here), a number of effects can be achieved. These include the inculcation of a sense of imminent threat, the creation of an identifiable and common villain, the rapid mobilization of the required state/governmental resources required to respond to that threat, as well as mythmaking around who the saviours or victors might be.

Since AIDS first made headlines in the early 1980s this narrative or culture of securitization has come to be associated with the epidemic, and one purpose of this article to analyse the implications of such securitization. In the context of the 'war against terror' after 11 September 2001 we are becoming increasingly familiar with the super-patriotic proclivities and nationalistic pathologies that securitization can enable, so a closer look at the powerful constructivist role of specific conceptualizations of the pandemic is in order, and timely. One analyst[7] observes that

> [i]n the aftermath of September 11, 2001, the United States tends to define all national security concerns through the prism of terrorism. That framework is overly limited even for the United States, and an absurdly narrow template to apply to the security of most other countries. The HIV/AIDS pandemic is aggravating a laundry list of underlying tensions in developing, declining, and failed states. As the burden of death due to HIV/AIDS skyrockets around the world over the next five to ten years, the disease may well play a more profound role on the security stage of many nations, and present the wealthy world with a challenge the likes of which it has never experienced. How countries, rich and poor, frame HIV/AIDS within their national security debates today may well determine how well

they respond to the massive grief, demographic destruction, and security threats that the pandemic will present tomorrow.

There has, of course, been significant academic interest in the construction of metaphors and myths (including the securitization) of disease and also the AIDS epidemic in recent years.[8] This is happening within the context of a mostly discreet yet exceedingly influential battle between individual state sovereignty and its concomitant epidemic response imperatives on the one hand, and the multilateralization (via the World Bank's Millennium AIDS Program [MAP], the US President's Emergency Program for AIDS Relief [PEPFAR] as well as Global Fund initiatives [not to mention UNAIDS]) of the pandemic on the other.

The scene is set for great tension between autonomous, state-centred interventions on the one hand, and multilateral initiatives on the other. Discursively, one of the ways in which this tension has been manifesting has been through appeals to either a (hard) securitization agenda that emphasizes the dangers that AIDS implies for state survival, or an agenda that appeals more directly to a softer, human security approach that underlines the nefarious implications of the epidemic for individual human rights to health. The latter approach has been most closely associated with a developmental agenda.

The polemic

As AIDS only appeared on the public agenda in the 1980s, this context of contestation regarding the securitization of AIDS is a fairly recent phenomenon. The result has been that various AIDS watchers have been making claims and counter-claims regarding the link between the pandemic and its impacts. This discourse is constantly revised—a process that takes place in an increasingly political global and particularly multilateral environment; this is understandable given the high stakes: billions of dollars have been made available to counter AIDS and other chronic diseases. This has given rise to a nascent AIDS industry (in both financial and ideological terms) as the battle for the control over who can and should shape global efforts to combat AIDS has taken hold.[9] In the high political discursive environment regarding the purported link between AIDS and state security there have been significant developments:

- In 1990 the US Central Intelligence Agency (CIA) added HIV to its 'state failure watchlist' as a variable that contributes to state collapse.[10]
- In 2002 the US National Security Strategy identified failing states as the US's main threat, arguing that failed or failing states provide a fertile breeding ground for terrorism, and also leading to regional spillover effects,[11] dragging more than only the failing states into a condition of

anarchy—this conclusion was reiterated by the 2006 US National Security Strategy document;[12] but at the same time

- in 2005 the US National Intelligence Council (NIC) stated that 'it is not clear if AIDS can be directly tied to state collapse in the way that was feared and anticipated a few years ago'.[13]

Even in the US homeland security environment there thus appears to be no consensus regarding the link between AIDS and state fragility. This in itself is not problematic, given that Kuhnian scientific revolutions are based on the testing and revision of theses; however, what is problematic is that the discourse is shaped by a surprising lack of attention to conceptual clarity and, importantly, empirical enquiry. As discussed below, the result has been that the debates about the purported link between AIDS and state fragility has been informed by (mostly unsubstantiated) normative and ideological agendas.

The central polemic can thus be summarized as follows:

1   Firstly, loose and unsubstantiated statements are made about the covariance of mature AIDS epidemics on the one hand, and state fragility on the other. In other words, there is an assumption that state fragility in itself creates an enabling environment for the vectoring of HIV. Rising prevalence levels in turn are seen to be contributing to state fragility and ultimate state collapse. This first polemic is for the most part untested.
2   Integrated with this first polemic is an implied polemic that provides the ideological environment for a broader *problematique*: state fragility in itself is seen as contributing to global insecurity (particularly as it is seen to act as a vector for terrorism).[14] In turn it is argued that this global insecurity provides an enabling environment for further instances of state fragility and eventual collapse.

Given the obfuscation and contestation associated with these arguments and the general AIDS/state failure discourse thus far, it is worth exploring what states are, in fact, supposed to do, as well as what is meant by 'state fragility'. Once this has been more firmly established, one should be able to speak more confidently to the possible impact of AIDS on state stability.

States and fragility

It is challenging to find a balance between not getting mired in the minutiae or tangentialism of opposing ideological debates about state functions on the one hand, and the imperative to do justice to the essential characteristics of functioning, effective statehood on the other. Political economy can assist by succinctly introducing the core high political intellectual input of three éminences grises: according to Adam Smith it is the role of a benign, effective state to facilitate economic growth and the allocation of scarce resources in society by championing the 'invisible hand' of the market; Karl Marx would add that this should be done with a focus on human development, fairly and equitably, with minimal exploitation and social class stratification; Max Weber would say that the creation of effective governance or implementing institutions is essential in all of this, and that the state should ensure order by using its monopoly on the use of violence.

Essentially, then, the core functions of the state are to provide physical security to everyone living in its area of jurisdiction; to build and maintain legitimate political institutions to implement government programmes and sustain the whole; to provide sound and consistent economic management; and to provide mechanisms of social welfare to those who need them.[15] In this logic those who argue that AIDS is weakening the state should be able demonstrate that the pandemic is directly eroding and reversing the state functions as prescribed by Smith, Marx and Weber, as well as the application of those roles as described here.

In the literature on state fragility an important distinction is made between *capacity* and *will* as determinants of state weakness.[16] The key message is that states should manifest both of these aspects when judged as to their robustness. Some states may have the capacity to fulfil all of the functions of statehood, but may lack the will to provide all of them to certain sections of society; conversely, some states may be perfectly willing and even eager to provide these services and functions to their constituents, but may simply be unable to. What is the effect of AIDS on such governance modalities? As pointed out below, the pandemic may lead to stratification in societies and the strengthening of neo-patrimonial linkages between the state and certain sections of society, resulting in effective statehood for some and not for others—the result of will rather than of capacity. The distinction between capacity and will as determinants of state weakness has led to the development of a tacit typology of state resilience. This includes 'good performers', 'weak but willing', 'strong but unresponsive' and 'weak–weak' states.[17] Again, when addressing the link between the AIDS pandemic and state fragility, one should take into account this differentiation of determinants of state weakness; in a worst-case scenario AIDS would negatively affect both the capacity and the will of states to execute their core functions.

Analysts of state fragility stress a number of qualifications to be borne in mind. For instance, one should not assume that the weakest states are necessarily the poorest; weak states tend to have bouts of political instability in common; state weakness spillovers are not linear, but vary by threat.[18] In other words, any analysis of state fragility as an independent variable is contingent; except for the manifestation of political instability state fragility manifests in exceedingly granular ways. It is thus easier to initially describe fragile states in terms of what they are not: stable or resilient states have effective institutions, the political will and capacity to fulfil the core statal functions referred to above, achieve and maintain a greater degree of social cohesion, social equality, as well as an ability to withstand exogenous and endogenous shocks. Fragile states on the other hand are broadly associated with social dissent, lack of border control, predation by the state on their own constituents, flawed institutions, deteriorating infrastructure, endemic corruption, a declining gross domestic product (GDP), food shortages, loss of legitimacy, an increase in infant mortality, a closed economic system and a general informalization of the economy towards localized subsistence rather than commercial surplus production.[19]

In his recent analysis of state-building, Francis Fukuyama[20] re-emphasizes the Weberian imperative: the crafting and maintenance of state institutions are seen as central to the state project, and any threat to it is seen as exacerbating and hastening state failure. Here are a few quotations from Fukuyama's book to illustrate:

- 'State-building is the creation of new government institutions and the strengthening of existing ones.'
- 'Weak or failed states are the sources of many of the world's most serious problems, from poverty to AIDS to drugs to terrorism.'
- 'The essence of stateness is enforcement.'
- 'Since the end of the Cold War, weak or failing states have arguably become the single most important problem for international order.'
- 'Since September 11 . . . they shelter international terrorists who can do significant damage to the United States and other developed countries.'
- 'The failed state problem that was seen previously as largely a humanitarian or human rights issue suddenly took on a major security dimension.'

These quotations are significant in that they restate the state fragility/insecurity/terrorism nexus, and of course the link to AIDS is made explicit as well. However, amongst those states about which there is general consensus regarding their fragility or their danger of failing,[21] it is important to note that AIDS does not appear as a common feature. In fact, for the most part AIDS is not a major public issue.[22] Given this reality, it is prudent to ask whether the link between AIDS and state fragility in general is not in fact more a matter of ideology than description:

> At bottom, the entire literature on fragile or failed states assumes a particular normative model of the state—a liberal democratic state that is market-friendly, transparent, and accountable, with very specific institutional requirements—without analysing that model at all. It is a given in identifying failure.[23]

Significantly, the meta-theoretical or ideological prescriptions resulting from this normative model also form the basis of an evolving multilateral or 'Geneva Consensus' for not only good governance but also good AIDS governance (see below). This has exceedingly political implications for the purported links between HIV and democracy, democratic remedies/vaccines against HIV, the inferred links between HIV and fragile states, and (as mentioned above) the evolution of the discourse of securitization regarding both state failure and HIV post-9/11.

Given this context, let us move to interrogate the individual aspects of how HIV has been proffered as a variable that directly causes or exacerbates state fragility. These include discourses on HIV and increased manifestations of violence, HIV and curtailed governance capacity, HIV and economic atrophy, as well as the covariance of the pandemic and liberal democracy.

AIDS and violence

The central argument regarding the relationship between mature AIDS pandemics and an increase in violence in high-prevalence states pertains to the implications of derivative demographic changes. These analyses emphasize the Weberian tenet that the state should have a monopoly on violence in society, the implied premise being that AIDS would dilute that monopoly, emasculate the state, and vest the ability for violence in different sectors and actors in society.

Figures 1–3 and Table 2 illustrate the demographic impact that mature AIDS pandemics are having on populations. These figures demonstrate fundamental features of mature AIDS epidemics, including:

- a spike in the mortality rates amongst younger, economically active population cohorts; this means that more people in their twenties to their forties die than older people, women being affected more severely and also earlier than men (see the Figures 1–2);[24]
- radically reduced life expectancy at birth (LEB) and life expectancy upon reaching adulthood (LEA) (see Figure 2, which demonstrates such impact in Swaziland);[25]
- the creation of a drastically altered population pyramid for entire populations—this leads to a demographic 'chimney affect', leaving a vast youth bulge and the elderly (this is dramatically demonstrated by the last figure, which reflects the projected impact in Botswana by 2020).[26]

Those who argue that AIDS will lead to more violent societies point to these three key demographic shifts and justifiably question whether social order is sustainable under such an extended catastrophe. It is clear that the pandemic is already changing societies in profound ways. However, the societies noted in these figures do not appear to be collapsing; so far state-level collapse simply has not occurred.

Crime is used as one possible proxy indicator of such collapse, or, rather, as an indication of the state's loss of the Weberian monopoly on violence.[27] This proxy linked the so-called 'security demographic' of a youth bulge and a

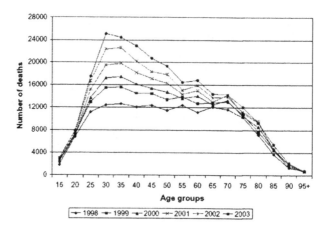

Figure 1 Male mortality in South Africa.

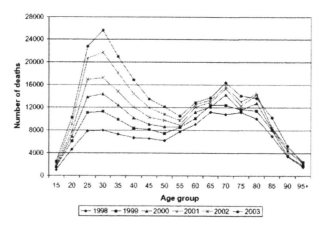

Figure 2 Female mortality in South Africa.

generation of AIDS orphans and vulnerable children (OVCs) in particular as a potential threat to social order—a 'Lord of the Flies' scenario has been presupposed in which it is feared that youths will discount their much abridged futures and thus will have less qualms about engaging in violent criminal behaviour. Again, the actual data that are available do not support this thesis, although one analyst in 2006 reported some evidence that property crime in particular may be linked to an increase in AIDS prevalence in South Africa.[28]

However, there is no evidence to support a direct link between OVCs and violent crime. This finding should, of course, be qualified by pointing out the reality that (as noted above) in epidemiological terms these are early days yet; we do not know what the indirect effect can be of increases in criminality due

122

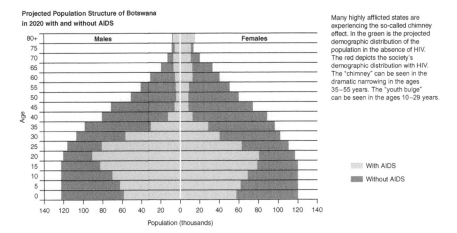

Projected Population Structure of Botswana in 2020 with and without AIDS

Many highly afflicted states are experiencing the so-called chimney effect. In the green is the projected demographic distribution of the population in the absence of HIV. The red depicts the society's demographic distribution with HIV. The "chimney" can be seen in the dramatic narrowing in the ages 35–55 years. The "youth bulge" can be seen in the ages 10–29 years.

Figure 3 The 'security demographic': projected population structure of Botswana in 2020 with and without AIDS. Many highly affected states are experiencing the so-called 'chimney effect'. The 'chimney' can be seen in the dramatic narrowing in the ages 35–55 years. The 'youth bulge' in the ages 10–29 years.

Table 2 Projected life expectancy (in years) in Swaziland.

Year	Without AIDS	With AIDS	Difference (%)
2004	64.2	37.5	41.6
2005	64.5	37.4	42.0
2006	64.9	35.3	45.5
2007	65.2	33.7	48.3
2008	65.6	32.5	50.4
2009	65.9	31.7	51.9
2010	66.2	31.3	52.7
2011	66.5	31.2	53.0
2012	66.8	31.4	53.0
2013	67.1	31.6	52.9
2014	67.3	32.0	52.5
2015	67.6	32.5	51.9

to AIDS-related breakdowns in national criminal justice systems and corruption. In terms of the current manifestation of the supposed impact of AIDS on social criminality and its link to OVCs and the security demographic, however, it seems as though analysts have thus far underestimated OVCs' ability to adapt to or absorb the impact of the pandemic.[29] Clearly AIDS watchers should revisit notions regarding 'the family' and positive socialization; one should not assume that such socialization only takes place in nuclear families.

The impact of AIDS on uniformed forces in general and armies in particular is also mentioned as a factor that could not only contribute to the vectoring of HIV (particularly during armed conflicts), but also erode the state's monopoly on violence. Thus far these claims were based on anecdotal 'evidence' regarding HIV prevalence in armies of three or four times that found in the general population. The argument was that the epidemic adversely affects the combat readiness and overall discipline of armed forces, and that soldiers, due to their age, income levels, and culture of aggression, act as vectors of the epidemic—particularly during operational duty. In so doing, a discourse was created equating the virus with the uniformed individual, and thus with 'the enemy'.

Most seriously, the inevitable breakdown in the ranks was therefore seen as an eventual threat to the state itself. However, as is the case with OVCs these grim anecdotes and predictions simply have not materialized; in the Democratic Republic of the Congo (DRC) and Angola (two states in Southern Africa recently emerging from long histories of violent armed conflict) AIDS prevalence rates are amongst the lowest in Sub-Saharan Africa.[30] It may be that the disciplined ethos found in most militaries mitigates against the impact of the epidemic; also, armies have built-in redundancy, with lower ranks ready to fill vacancies where AIDS leads to structural attrition; it may be that the public health interventions that are less concerned with individual human rights and focus on excluding infected recruits have had positive consequences.[31] Whatever the case may be, the scaremongering about infected militaries contributing to state collapse simply has not happened.

A recent study for UNAIDS[32] has also clarified and debunked some of the myths associating AIDS with uniformed forces. The main finding is that military groups appear to have HIV prevalence levels no higher than their age cohorts amongst the general population. Again there is a disconcerting lack of data about prevalence levels amongst uniformed personnel everywhere, and therefore '[i]t is premature to generalize about the direction or the dynamic of the relationship between uniformed forces and the spread of HIV'.[33]

> Suggestions either that AIDS is a threat to 'national security' or that it necessarily leads to political and governance problems are facile and self-fulfilling. We can speculate but we just do not have the evidence on this, either way, for countries in sub-Saharan Africa or, for that matter, anywhere else.[34]

AIDS and governance

The available evidence regarding a direct link between AIDS and governance attrition for the most part supports this last conclusion, casting doubt on those who equate the pandemic with 'Weber or Fukuyama in reverse'. That said, the literature on the impact of AIDS on effective governance has produced some conclusions regarding procedural governance practices such as elections.[35] The main conclusion of these studies is that AIDS is a long-term threat to the efficacy of electoral processes, eroding actual electioneering and also curtailing parliamentarians' ability to do their work. For instance, in Kenya

85 per cent of parliamentarians estimate that most of their fundraising engagement is devoted to the medical requirements of constituents.[36] Also, this is taking place in a context where there is an increase in absenteeism amongst members of parliament (MPs). Any conclusion regarding 'Africa' should, of course, be qualified: the continent consists of 53 countries with widely varied AIDS epidemics; generalizations are not useful.

The recent studies mentioned here provide a more nuanced analysis of the impact of AIDS in various mature epidemics, and some conclusions are possible. These include warnings that the impact of AIDS on LEA in particular does have an adverse effect on democratic consolidation: mortality levels amongst registered voters in the 30–49-years age range are increasing dramatically, and decreasing voting ratios may mean that political mandates are weakening.[37] The pandemic is thus changing the voting demographics in some countries. This necessitates AIDS-related reforms of electoral processes for the longer term. For instance, the Westminster system of first-past-the-post (FPTP) elections may no longer be appropriate in many countries, given that there is increasing mortality amongst elected representatives and by-elections are expensive; a proportional (list) system may thus be more appropriate in mature epidemics, as this will bypass the need for by-elections.[38] However, such an intervention needs to be balanced against the implications for the direct accountability of MPs.

Although no electoral crisis seems to be looming, the Institute for Democracy in South Africa (IDASA) and studies elsewhere on AIDS and electoral politics do indicate that the impact of the pandemic is most severe at the local government level: Africans tend to equate democracy with delivery, and thus any breakdown at this coalface of governance could be dangerous in the longer term; by-elections are more inevitable and have become more frequent at the local government level; any lack of formal representation is seen as denying constituents a sense of direct input into the system of governance; it becomes easy to politicize even trivial matters at the local government level; increasingly there are instances where AIDS has been used as a political football during local government elections, for instance to demonize political opponents.[39] IDASA's Afrobarometer project surveys the opinions of Africans in 18 countries in Sub-Saharan Africa, and their findings over the last few years with regards to public perceptions about AIDS and governance are telling:

> As delivery is deemed to be more important than abstract aspirations regarding democracy, elections *per se* are not viewed as that important for accountability. However, there does appear to be a gradual erosion of trust in democracy on the whole, and levels of satisfaction with democracy are declining sharply in Nigeria, Malawi, Zambia and Zimbabwe (however, in the latter case this is linked to hunger more than any other factor). Also, HIV lags behind employment,

the state of the national economy, crime and security, health services, poverty and hunger as a political priority. As individual levels of poverty increase, people become less likely to cite HIV as an important problem; two-thirds of those interviewed approve of their governments' management of HIV. Also, mainly elites are interested in and mobilising around HIV, and there appears to be little pressure on governments regarding HIV.[40]

Importantly, then, state legitimacy in Africa does not appear to face serious challenges due to citizen's perceptions regarding the impact of AIDS in mature epidemics and governments' inability or unwillingness to counter such impact. However, populations have increasing misgivings about the performance of local governments. This conclusion leads the authors of the Afrobarometer reports to speculate that '[p]erhaps . . . Africans see HIV/ AIDS as a problem for families and communities, and not for governments'.[41]

Reviewing the relationship between AIDS and governance, the main conclusion has to be that '[t]he lack of a coherent theory has led some analysts to rely on statistical correlations between measures of state capacity and indications of disease, but, however impressive the statistics, these tell us little about causal relationships'.[42] This early into the pandemic there are few certainties: we do know that there is a massive and sustained reduction in LEB and LEA; we also know that existing models for democratization and good governance are premised on different and inappropriate assumptions about LEA. However, by varying the longevity factor, one can speculate about some likely impacts:

- There is and will continue to be some measurable erosion of parliaments, some public sectors, members of civil society and electoral processes.
- However, there has been little empirical study of these impacts.
- Governments should be particularly concerned by reduced institutional efficacy, particularly at the local government level.
- The curtailed LEA of bureaucrats may lead to a strengthening of neo-patrimonialism.
- There are direct costs associated with the rollout of health and other social services.
- This necessitates some policy and programmatic triage.

AIDS and economic atrophy

Those who claim that AIDS is leading to state collapse seek to demonstrate that the pandemic is reversing national GDP growth and development to such an extent that the state becomes incapable of sustaining its population. In such analyses AIDS would nullify the ideological prescriptions of either Adam Smith or Karl Marx. Although it is not the purpose of this article to ridicule the 'dismal science' for its lack of accuracy, it is surprising that econometrics has not, apparently, been able to offer much that is either definite or supportable by quantifiable evidence—at least not at the macro (state) level. Most of the studies regarding the impact of AIDS on states' economies are sectoral and suggest qualitative inferences regarding 'AIDS' versus 'no-AIDS' scenarios. Little modelling is done at the macroeconomic level. I am not suggesting that economics is at fault: again one should note that AIDS has only been with us for 25 years; this is an unprecedented event; the worst is yet to come.

The conclusions that are appearing regarding macroeconomic impact are surprisingly counter-intuitive. Most economists are in agreement that AIDS may be causing a 0.3–1.5 per cent contraction in GDP in the worst-affected economies.[43] Given that even the worst epidemics are currently manifesting in developing economies that for the most part are expanding at rates in excess of five or even ten per cent per annum, this impact does not in itself constitute a crisis—at least not in terms of threatening states' capacity to self-perpetuate. In fact, a perverse statistic is developing where AIDS mortality occurring in contexts of high economic growth may actually have the effect of an increased GDP per capita.[44] Macroeconomic models focus on the size of economies and tend to neglect changes in the overall long-term structure of economies—not because of a weakness inherent to the discipline; the reality is that economists (like all AIDS analysts) simply do not have any clear understanding of how AIDS is impacting on the systemic variables that drive patterns and events in various societies. Of course, this problem is not unique to the economic modelling of AIDS: there are weaknesses in macro-modelling in general,[45] suggesting that economists do not really understand processes that drive growth. Growth models tend to perform poorly at prediction, and problems with assessing HIV and AIDS provide a specific (albeit important) example of this general problem.

One welcome exception is a recent study that conceptualizes an 'overlapping generations framework'.[46] The model attempts to measure the impact of AIDS in South Africa across several generations. This is done by quantifying the socio-economic impact of the pandemic which results from the resultant loss of human capital. The assumption is that every generation teaches the next generation valuable skills in terms of sustaining and developing its production structure. The model logically assumes that, due to contracting LEB and LEA, this generational (memetic)[47] transfer will be eroded to such an extent that there will be concomitant attrition in society as a whole, resulting in an inability to adapt to the realities of AIDS. This will make socio-economic learning increasingly difficult, shorten the socio-generational time horizon, and systemically increase inequalities. The result will be sociopolitical collapse in South Africa a few generations hence.

The key lessons from attempts at macroeconomic modelling on the impact of the pandemic are twofold:

1   For the moment AIDS does not appear to be significantly contributing to state collapse at the macro level.
2   However, models that measure this impact need to be adjusted—with a much longer time horizon in mind.

Although it falls beyond the ambit of this article, the impact of AIDS at the household economic level is significantly easier to demonstrate—and here the pandemic has devastating consequences that are readily quantifiable. The following quotation suffices for our purposes:

> A man is taken ill. While nursing him, the wife can't weed the maize and cotton fields, mulch and pare the banana trees, dry the coffee or harvest the rice. This means less food crops and less income from cash crops. Trips to town for medical treatment, hospital fees and medicines consume savings. Traditional healers are paid in livestock. The man dies. Farm tools, sometimes cattle, are sold to pay burial expenses. Mourning practices forbid farming for several days. Precious time for farm chores is lost. In the next season, unable to hire casual labour, the family plants a smaller area. Without pesticides, weeds and bugs multiply. Children leave school to weed and harvest. Again yields are lower. With little home-grown food and without cash to buy fish or meat, family nutrition and health suffer. If the mother becomes ill with AIDS, the cycle of asset and labour loss is repeated. Families withdraw into subsistence farming. Overall production of cash crops drops.[48]

Tragic as this illustration is, there is no indication that the household impact of AIDS provides a threat to the state in terms of 'reversing' Adam Smith, Karl Marx, or Max Weber. However, what this dynamic does contribute to is a 'new variant famine'[49]—and famines are exceedingly frightening to governments, since they can provide a direct threat to socio-political stability. Simply put, the 'new variant famine' thesis states that '[t]he nature of food crises in Africa is changing on account of the co-occurrence of a generalized epidemic of HIV/AIDS and other concurrent shocks such as drought'.[50] By weakening the productive and regenerative capacity of micro economies (households), AIDS may be creating a 'Swiss cheese' pattern of vulnerability: one household, unaffected by AIDS, lives in abundance (within a larger, national context of food sufficiency), whilst those households in which HIV is present suffer food shortages.

New variant famine thus describes a context in which HIV is not causing famine at the macro level, but it is exacerbating chronic food insecurity for some. The new variant famine thesis is only a few years old and justifies further study, but for the moment it does serve to emphasize the complexity of the impact of AIDS. The latter has severe consequences—but it is supremely significant where one looks, how one measures impact, and which level of analysis is under scrutiny. Generalizations regarding macroeconomics run the danger of ignoring the daily tragedies in individual households. However, on the whole hunger from AIDS is diffuse rather than concentrated, and thus does not pose a threat to governments.[51] Also, as noted elsewhere,[52] governments' response to famine also depends on the political and economic power of those starving.

AIDS and democracy

As noted above, the Washington and Geneva consensuses regarding state survival tacitly but also explicitly link governance capacity and resilience to a liberal democratic prescription. Any threat to this Western conception of liberal democratic practice is deemed as an insidious and direct threat to state survival, and a discourse has emerged that casts such threats (including AIDS) as a vector of global insecurity. However, the problem with this liberal construct is that its fixation on state institutions and rules (the formal applications of contemporary Westphalian power) discounts informal centres of authority in the contexts of mature epidemics. For instance, in Africa chiefs, healers, and other traditional centres of authority have significant influence on how people live their lives. These traditional centres of authority (which increasingly include Pentecostal religion) create contexts of moral conservatism in which a sweeping liberal statist prescription regarding the governance of HIV is anachronistic and inappropriate. This does create a fascinating but challenging social juxtaposition of modern and traditional centres of power that may actually be counter-productive in terms of the exigencies of AIDS. The Geneva Consensus (with the tacit endorsement of those in Washington) presents liberal democracy as a 'political vaccine' against AIDS:

> AIDS was pronounced an epidemiological Rorschach test whose handling revealed the essence of our culture. In selecting preventive strategies against the epidemic, society was also revealing its core values. Individual rights, liberty, and democracy, on the one hand, or compulsion, exclusion, and force, on the other: thus ran the Manichaean choice offered by many observers.[53]

The assumption is that this ideology and its governance applications provide the best sociopolitical environment in which the pandemic and its effects can be neutralized and reversed. As noted above, this is an equation of the 'good governance' agenda with a 'good AIDS governance' agenda, which is ideologically driven, and most closely linked to an emphasis on the so-called 'best practice' of human rights interventions in combating AIDS. It is erroneous to equate this human rights approach with 'democracy', as the typology of measures that states can apply against AIDS is more nuanced. For instance, it is perfectly acceptable for different democratic states to have a variety of political measures against AIDS—these include the idealistic human rights approach, which insists that AIDS is exceptional and should therefore not be managed in ways similar to other chronic pathologies, to the more directive or 'authoritative' approach, which 'limits one or more of the democratic ideals with the argument that such limitations will enable the government to respond more effectively in the interest of public health'.[54]

This latter approach was implemented by several democratic states in the West during the zenith of their AIDS crises.[55] AIDS-watchers should thus be cautious not to fall into the trap of equating a human rights approach with democracy or 'best practice' per se. Such normative-ideological generalizations and prescriptions do not reflect the reality that several democratic states have applied public health rather than human rights interventions against AIDS, and that these have been effective against their epidemics. Just as one should be cautious not to equate the loaded 'good governance' with 'good AIDS governance', one should also not equate 'authoritative' interventions with 'authoritarian' interventions, or, ultimately, aspirations with description. 'The fact that Western countries all managed to contain the epidemic despite that they . . . responded with different governance approaches suggests that the type of governance had little to do with that success.'[56] The political management of mature epidemics in Africa underline this point:

> social constraint has been a key aspect of what has [been effective in Botswana and Uganda] . . . Botswana has followed the accepted line in HIV intervention with its stress on voluntarism, confidentiality, gentle persuasion and encouragement. Only now, with the population facing meltdown, are more coercive measures being advocated and even then in the face of intense opposition from outside agencies. In parts of Uganda, on the other hand, sexual-behavioural change has been regulated by local groups . . . human behaviour rarely changes because of health education alone. Change is facilitated when information is linked to procedures of compliance.[57]

Adaptation and resilience

The normative-ideological hardwiring of analyses regarding the impact of AIDS in the broad field of political science has led to a situation where AIDS-watchers have come to equate 'impact' with highly contingent and inductive research and conclusions regarding social attrition. No one doubts that the pandemic can be associated with a barrage of governance erosion and development reversals, but one should not stop there. It is clear that HIV kills, but it changes individuals, households, societies, states, governments, and cultures in other ways as well. Some analysts have already pointed out that the pandemic can be thought of as a 'Darwinian event',[58] which has profoundly systemic, long-term, and as yet unknown consequences for humanity as a whole.

Social science as a whole should regard the disease and 'impact' in ways that go beyond searching for instances of political and other pathologies. For instance, waves of AIDS have occurred parallel to the consolidation of democracy in mature African epidemics; many OVCs and other vulnerable communities have learnt to adapt to it remarkably well; as the pandemic has evolved, so can societies. Rather than thinking in Malthusian terms regarding the 'survival of the fittest', one should turn to thinking in terms of the 'survival of the best adapted', and try to learn from this. Such insights may lead to improved policy triage for governments in contexts of severely limited resources.

It has become a cliché to compare AIDS today to the Black Death in Europe in the Middle Ages. However, instead of only focusing on demographic doom comparisons, one can also learn from the broader socio-political consequences of earlier plagues.[59] Yes, the Black Death exacerbated tensions between rich and poor, but it also led to changes that to some extent were managed. There are inevitable surprises that AIDS and the Black Death may have in common; changes that governments need not just await as emasculated observers:

- Depletion of the agricultural labour force, resulting in decades of crop and livestock deficiencies; this led to a revolution in the European agricultural production structure in the decades and centuries following the Black Death. Will the agricultural production structure in Africa also be transformed for the better?
- Loss of faith in the Catholic Church due to priests' failure to perform last rites; this led to authority shifts and, eventually, the Reformation and secularization. Funeral rituals and grieving periods in many African contexts have already changed; will AIDS galvanize similar questioning of the power and authority of traditional healers, or will we see an increase in supernaturalism and social conservatism as a response to the pandemic?
- Erosion of feudal control. Will rural Africans also insist on empowerment and property rights rather than vesting power in traditional leaders?
- Property disputes due to disrupted lineages of power. In Zambia, widows of AIDS causalities are often victim to instances of 'property-grabbing'— the law allowing or tolerating in-laws who claim the land of the diseased husband.[60]

The point is that it may be possible for societies to respond to HIV in ways that may enhance social and state resilience rather than lead to inevitable state collapse—the trajectory is not necessarily as linear and negative as the current discourse would have it. Other possibilities of AIDS as a transformative socio-political agent include a questioning of what Richard Dawkins calls 'skyhooks'[61]—those traditional centres of authority such as customary leaders, supernatural moralisms, and religiosity that at times act to fan the pandemic. Admittedly, at the moment the prognosis for this is not good, as there seems to be an increase in social conservatism and moralism surrounding AIDS in Africa.[62] However, one should remain mindful that this is a long-wave event, and lessons can still be learnt. These lessons may lead to revolutions in traditional understandings regarding the links between HIV and AIDS, including timely debates between proponents of contagionism versus those who invoke supernaturalism.

Ideally the reality of AIDS would galvanize positive changes in sexual and gender politics. Other positive changes have included insights regarding more suitable levels of analysis: 'social clusters'[63] are deemed more appropriate than outdated notions regarding nuclear family units, in particular as they relate to local or household political economies.[64] Constructive changes in political culture are possible as well: the Treatment Action Campaign (TAC) in South Africa is seen by some as an example of civil society evolving from a single-issue organization to one addressing broader matters regarding social inequalities[65] (this in itself may be strengthening democratic participation in that country); societies are learning to build new political palimpsests: new kinds of patrimonial relationships have to co-exist side by side with legal-rational bureaucracies. These can be examples of positive sociopolitical evolution related to AIDS, rather than any 'predestined' collapse.

One of the key elements of galvanizing such adaptation and resilience would be the development of social mechanisms to anticipate shocks and/or changes, since this enables improved planning and a deeper understanding of altered time horizons. Conversely, the inability to anticipate or a failure to respond to an altered reality may result from a number of variables.[66] For example, maintaining the status quo may be good for some people (usually those with power), and society and centres of authority and power may not have any experience in dealing with proactive change. Also, appropriate planning may fall prey to reasoning by false or inappropriate analogy (climate change, for instance), and hence society may fail to perceive a problem that has already arrived. This may be the result of looking for signs in the wrong place (for instance, an obsession with macro (state) level collapse which ignores fragility at the household or local government levels). There may also be an overbearing presence of distant managers who fail to understand the nuances of specific contexts (some would argue that PEPFAR[67] or the Catholic Church's prescriptions regarding condoms is one example of this). In addition, AIDS could manifest as a slow trend concealed by wide up-and-down fluctuations (cyclical elements of attrition during the 'long wave'), which blinds analysts who have a shorter time horizon. Ultimately, then, this could establish a sense of 'creeping normalcy' about AIDS, for instance in that death or morbidity becomes everyday and acceptable.[68] Furthermore, those in power may also suffer from 'landscape amnesia', forgetting how different things looked 10 or 20 years ago (for instance, in South Africa there has been a dramatic increase in the number of OVCs begging at traffic lights; this has become 'normal', but this normality was absent just a few years ago).

A number of other manifestations of denial can also inhibit positive learning from AIDS, as well as the transformation that it may enable. Firstly, there can be 'involution': short-term adaptation that becomes fixed.[69] There may also be 'interpretative denial': 'the existence of AIDS in acknowledged, but the implication that one might need to change one's personal beliefs and behaviour is not'.[70] Supernatural cosmologies may also prevail: sorcery, witchcraft, traditionalism, religiosity, and moralism, rather than rational, biomedical understandings of the pandemic. Lastly, the human rights script can also be applied as a mode of denial: where high levels of health awareness, a climate of liberal individualism, and universal access to good-quality health services are lacking, 'the principle of voluntariness is less meaningful and can become an excuse for failing to acknowledge and deal with the social structures that determine behaviour'.[71] For instance, some analysts have noted how human rights activism has hindered the implementation of urgent public health measures in mature AIDS epidemics.[72]

The point is that the difference between state fragility or collapse on the one hand and societal resilience and evolution on the other is not necessarily a given, or as absolute or Manichaean as has been constructed; even in the context of mature AIDS epidemics behaviour change can decrease the gradient of the HIV incidence curve, treatment measures can bend the AIDS mortality curve downwards, and little appears to be truly inevitable regarding the impact curve.

Key lessons

This article offers three sets of lessons; all are related to AIDS as a political construct.

Firstly, analysts have to be more respectful of the plurality of the AIDS pandemic. Just as 'Africa' or the 'developing world' is not a monolith with a single kind of epidemic, so too do we need to pluralize our thinking about AIDS and its impacts: we need greater differentiation *amongst* countries as well as *within* countries. The implication is that we should guard against the tyranny of 'best practice' rhetoric[73]—even the most well-meaning prescriptions are drenched in ideology, and the current master narrative is driven by the Geneva Consensus.

It follows that one should not regard liberal democracy as a natural political vaccine/panacea in all contexts; 'good governance' does not equate with 'good AIDS governance'. In fact, just as AIDS demands fundamental individual behaviour change, it also requires a new social contract;[74] liberalism is appropriate in many instances, but one should not be blinded by its proclivity to focus mainly at the state institution and legal levels. Part of this new social contract and spirit of analytical pluralization may be a focus on the imperative to secularize the pandemic, rather than the insipid and ostensibly noble (and liberal) tolerance for 'skyhooks'.[75]

Secondly, we must internalize the implications of AIDS as a 'long-wave' event. This means that pseudo-quantitative analyses on short-term impacts are insufficient; analysts need to adjust their time horizons. In the context of this article, this implies that if AIDS is a 130-year event, then maybe 'collapse' should also be thought of as something that may happen gradually rather than instantly or dramatically. However, given the absence of reliable empirical data about such impacts, it is imperative not to become complacent, to regress into denial, or to implement dangerous quick-fix solutions that end up doing more harm than good.

Thirdly, the link between AIDS and uniform notions regarding democracy which has become such a central feature of the discursive environment within which the pandemic is couched warrants much closer and respectful analysis. Democracy is an ideology, not a tactic; the human rights approach should not be equated with a democratic (and therefore 'good') approach—the typology is more varied. Rather than as a condition, democracy should be thought of as a process—and the same is true of AIDS in a human ecological context.

It is demonstrated above that democracy also allows for directive approaches to AIDS, and thus more profound debate is required regarding the context of rights-based interventions.[76] In terms of governance, more careful analysis is needed of impact levels that dip beneath that of the national state. This narrow focus has been the result of political science's embrace of liberalism and its derived weakness for institutions and rules at this level of analysis; local government in particular has been neglected.

Conclusion

The manifestations of state fragility—broad reversals of economic growth and development, a loss of the state's monopoly on violence, and a weakening of government institutions as well as the concomitant implications thereof for responses to the political management of the pandemic—can contribute to the vectoring of HIV as well as exacerbate the negative impacts of AIDS.

However, there is little reliable evidence to suggest that HIV by itself causes state fragility or collapse. 'Rather, like the effect of HIV on the human body, an "AIDS-related national crisis" will consist of a range of pre-existing social and political pathologies, rendered more common and more severe by the underlying vulnerability caused by human resource losses due to AIDS.'[77]

Separating AIDS as an independent variable for study from its wider socio-political ecology is like trying to separate a dancer from the dance; this has particularly challenging implications for generating reliable data regarding the impact of this long-wave event. AIDS as a political construct is not in itself an objectively separable, visible, morally salient, and tractable issue, which makes it particularly challenging for collective action.[78]

However, we do know for certain that AIDS is creating demographic pressures (a youth bulge, decreasing LEB and LEA, rapid urbanization into underdeveloped cities, as well as new variant famine), which are variables that should be taken very seriously as indices of possible future stresses on the state.

Given these realities, as well as the fact that AIDS is set to be a permanent presence in our lives, the moral imperative remains for states and individuals to maintain a sense of urgency and purpose—as Susan Sontag writes, 'That even an apocalypse can be made to seem part of the ordinary horizon of expectation constitutes an unparalleled violence that is being done to our sense of reality, to our humanity.'[79]

Notes

1 This article is the result of a research fellowship with the Institute for Advanced Study at La Trobe University, Melbourne. I am particularly grateful to Dennis Altman and Michael O'Keefe for sharing ideas on this topic; of course the responsibility for the contents and any errors remains my own.
2 In the AIDS literature there is debate and contestation regarding the use of 'AIDS', 'HIV', 'HIV/AIDS', and 'HIV and AIDS' when referring to different aspects of the pandemic. In this article these terms are used interchangeably.
3 UNAIDS, *Report on the Global AIDS Epidemic*, (New York and Geneva, 2006).
4 UNAIDS, *Report on the Global AIDS Epidemic*, pp. 505–540.
5 Tony Barnett, 'A Long-Wave Event. HIV/AIDS, Politics, Governance and "Security": Sundering the Intergenerational Bond?', *International Affairs*, 82, 2, (2006), p. 304.
6 Barnett, 'A Long-Wave Event', pp. 302–303.
7 Laurie Garrett, 'The Lessons of HIV/AIDS', *Foreign Affairs*, 84, 4, (2005), p. 64.
8 For instance, see the following: Stefan Elbe, 'Should HIV/AIDS Be Securitized? The Ethical Dilemmas of Linking HIV/AIDS and Security', *International Studies Quarterly*, 50, 1, (2006), pp. 119–44, Dennis Altman, 'HIV and Security', *International Relations*, 17, 4, (2003), pp. 417–27; Susan Sontag, *Illness as Metaphor & AIDS and Its Metaphors*, (London: Penguin Books, 2002), Dennis Altman, 'AIDS and Questions of Global Governance', *Pacifica Review*, 11, 2, (1999), pp. 195–212; Pieter Fourie and Martin Schönteich, 'Africa's New Security Threat', *African Security Review*, 10, 4, (2001), pp. 29–44; Lindy Heinecken, 'Living in Terror: The Looming Security Threat to Southern Africa', *African Security Review*, 10, 4, (2001), pp. 7–18.
9 Laurie Garrett, 'The Challenge of Global Health', *Foreign Affairs*, 86, 1, (2007).
10 CIA, Interagency Intelligence Memorandum 91-10005, (1990).
11 Stefan Wolff, 'State Failure in a Regional Context', research report, University of Bath, UK, (2006).
12 Stewart Patrick and Kaysie Brown, 'Fragile States and US Foreign Assistance: Show Me the Money', Center for Global Development, Working Paper No. 96, (August 2006), p. 2; David Carment, 'Assessing State Failure: Implications for Theory and Policy', *Third World Quarterly*, 24, 3, (2003), p. 407.
13 NIC, 'Mapping Sub-Saharan Africa's Future', paper summarizing a one-day conference of US experts on Africa convened in January 2005 and sponsored by the National Intelligence Council, CR 2005-02, (March 2005), p. 2.

14 Stephen D. Krasner & Carlos Pascual, 'Addressing State Failure', *Foreign Affairs*, 84, 4, (2005).

15 Stewart Patrick, 'Weak States and Global Threats: Fact or Fiction?', *Washington Quarterly*, 29, 2, (2006), p. 29; Stuart E. Eizenstat, John Edward Porter, and Jeremy M. Weinstein, 'Rebuilding Weak States', *Foreign Affairs*, 84, 1, (2005), p. 136.

16 Department for International Development (DFID), *Why We Need to Work More Effectively in Fragile States*, (London, 2005), p. 8; Patrick, 'Weak States and Global Threats', p. 30.

17 DFID, *Why We Need to Work More Effectively in Fragile States*, p. 8.

18 Patrick, 'Weak States and Global Threats: Fact or Fiction?', pp. 31–32.

19 Patrick, 'Weak States and Global Threats: Fact or Fiction?', pp. 45–49; Claire Vallings and Magui Moreno-Torres, 'Drivers of Fragility: What Makes States Fragile?', Department for International Development PRDE Working Paper no. 7, (London: April 2005), p. 4. Of course, these characteristics may not be agreed by all. For example, although a 'closed economic system' is associated with weak or failing states, 'openness' does not equate to economic robustness—see for example evidence on a number of poor performing African states that have very open trade systems, many of which states also appear in lists of failing states. For a general discussion on openness and growth, see J. A. Oscampo and L. Taylor, 'Why Trade Liberalisation in Developing Economies: Modest Benefits but Problems with Productivity Growth, Macro Prices, and Income Distribution', *Economic Journal*, 108, (September 1998), pp. 1523–1546.

20 Francis Fukuyama, *State Building: Governance and World Order in the Twenty-First Century*, (London: Profile Books, 2004).

21 Prominent recent studies to develop more quantifiable methodologies regarding fragile states include the following: World Bank Independent Evaluation Group, *Engaging with Fragile States: An IEG Review of World Bank Support to Low-Income Countries under Stress*, (Washington: World Bank, 2006); Fund for Peace, 'Failed State Index 2006', <http://www.fundforpeace.org/programs/fsi/fsindex2006.php> (accessed 16 December 2006). Although there is no universally agreed definition of weak and failing states, there seems to be consensus that the following states are fragile or in danger of failing: Afghanistan, Angola, Bangladesh, Burkina Faso, Burundi, Cambodia, Cameroon, Central African Republic, Chad, Comoros, Congo Kinshasa, Congo Brazzaville, Côte d'Ivoire, Djibouti, Eritrea, Ethiopia, Guinea, Guinea-Bissau, Haiti, Iraq, Kenya, Lao People's Democratic Republic Lesotho, Liberia, Madagascar, Malawi, Mali, Mauritania, Moldova, Mozambique, Myanmar, Nepal, Niger, Nigeria, North Korea, Pakistan, Papua New Guinea, Rwanda, Senegal, Sierra Leone, Solomon Islands, Somalia, Sudan, Tajikistan, Timor-Leste, Togo, Uganda, Uzbekistan, Yemen, Zambia, and Zimbabwe. See Patrick and Brown, 'Fragile States and US Foreign Assistance', p. 6.

22 For a discussion on the relationship between wealth and HIV prevalence, see Simon Gregson, Heather Waddell and Step Chandiwana, 'School education and HIV control', *Journal of International Development*, 13, 4, (2001). Evidence for Africa suggests a complex relationship between wealth and prevalence; many African countries with relatively high per capita incomes have the highest HIV prevalence levels on the continent (although some with lower incomes also have high HIV prevalence). Interestingly, this complexity is also true at the micro level—see for example Janet Bujra, 'Class Relations: AIDS & Socio-economic Privilege in Africa', *Review of African Political Economy*, 107, (2006), pp. 113–129.

23 Susan Woodward, 'Fragile States', paper presented to the 'States and Security' Learning Group at the Peace and Social Justice meeting of the Ford Foundation, Rio de Janeiro, (29 November 2004), p. 6.

24 Statistics South Africa, *Mortality and Causes of Death in South Africa, 1997–2003: Findings from Death Notification*, P0309.3, (18 February 2005).

25 Alan Whiteside, Catarina Andrade, Lisa Arrehag, Solomon Dlamini, Themba Ginindza and Anokhi Parikh, *The Socio-economic Impact of HIV/AIDS in Swaziland*, (Mbabane, Swaziland: National Emergency Response Council on HIV/AIDS; Durban: Health, Economics & HIV/AIDS Research Division, 2006), p. 10.

26 Tony Barnett and Gwyn Prins, *HIV/AIDS and Security: Fact, Fiction and Evidence*, (Geneva: UNAIDS, 2006), p. 62. Analysts know very little about the real demographics; there are data available (e.g. for the Rakai project in Uganda) that could be analysed to demonstrate actual effects, but for the most part the analysis is not done.

27 Martin Schönteich, 'Age and AIDS: South Africa's Crime Timebomb?', *African Security Review*, 8, 4, (1999).

28 Julian Naidoo, 'The Impact of HIV/AIDS on Crime in South Africa', <http://www.sarpn.org.za> (accessed 16 December 2006).

29 This conclusion finds support from studies that show that the impact of orphanhood on education depends greatly on government policy and household wealth. That means that some OVCs are able to continue with their education, depending on what education policy is and how wealthy their households are. This supports the contention that different households will be able to bear the burden of AIDS differently, as well as that a rise in the number of OVCs will not always lead to the social/economic breakdown predicted. See Martha Ainsworth and Deon Filmer, 'Poverty, AIDS and Children's Schooling: A Targeting Dilemma', World Bank Policy Working Paper no. WPS2885, (September 2002).

30 The mentioned lack of empirical evidence regarding the link between AIDS and state fragility also extends to the evidence on HIV prevalence. Witness debates over HIV prevalence in Kenya, South Africa, and Zambia, where population-based surveys have found quite difference prevalence levels to those of UNAIDS. For example, see Paul Bennell, 'HIV/AIDS in Sub-Saharan Africa: The Growing Epidemic?', ELDIS discussion paper, (2003), <http://www.eldis.org/fulltext/BennellHIVAfrica.pdf> (accessed 21 July 2007). For this reason, it is likely that the margins of error are high.

31 UNAIDS, 'AIDS, Security and Humanitarian Response', report from the 19th Meeting of the UNAIDS Programme Coordinating Board, Lusaka, (6–8 December 2006); Alan Whiteside, Alex de Waal, and Tsadkan Gebre-Tensae, 'AIDS, Security and the Military in Africa: A Sober Appraisal', *African Affairs*, 105, 419, (2006), p. 211.

32 Tony Barnett and Gwyn Prins, *HIV/AIDS and Security: Fact, Fiction and Evidence*; Taddesse Berhe, Hagos Gemechu, and Alex de Waal, 'War and HIV Prevalence', *African Security Review*, 14, 3, (2005).

33 Barnett and Prins, *HIV/AIDS and Security*, p. 64.

34 Barnett, 'A Long-Wave Event', p. 313.

35 Kondwani Chirambo, 'Democratization in the Age of HIV/AIDS: Understanding the Impact of a Pandemic on the Electoral Process in Africa', paper delivered at the South African Association of Political Studies' Biannual Conference, Cape Town, (August 2006); Per Strand, 'AIDS and Elections in Southern Africa: Is the Epidemic Undermining Its Democratic Remedy?', ISS Occasional Paper No. 110, (2005), <http://ww.iss.co.za/pubs/papers/110/Paper110.htm> (accessed 9 January 2007).

36 Ephraim Kimotho, 'HIV/AIDS and Governance in Kenya', report for Justice Africa, London, (December 2005), p. 3.

37 Per Strand, Khabele Matlesa, Ann Strode and Kondwani Chirambo, *HIV/AIDS and Democratic Governance in South Africa: Illustrating the Impact on Electoral Processes*, (Pretoria: IDASA, 2004).

38 Strand, 'AIDS and Elections in Southern Africa', p. 5.

39 Michael Bratton and Mxoliso Sibanyoni, 'Delivery or Responsiveness? A Popular Scorecard of Local Government Performance in South Africa", IDASA Afrobarometer Working Paper no. 62, (August 2006); Mary Caesar-Katsenga and Marietjie Myburg, *Parliament, Politics and AIDS: A Comparative Study of Five African Countries*, (Cape Town: IDASA, 2006).

40 Michael Bratton and Carolyn Logan, 'Voters but Not Yet Citizens: The Weak Demand for Political Accountability in Africa's Unclaimed Democracies', Afrobarometer Working Paper No. 63, (September 2006); Michael Bratton and Wonbin Cho, 'Where Is Africa Going? Views from Below', Afrobarometer Paper No. 60, (May 2006); Carolyn Logan, Tetsuya Fujiwara, and Virginia Parish, 'Citizens and the State in Africa: New Results from Afrobarometer Round 3', Afrobarometer Paper No. 61, (May 2006); IDASA, "The Public Agenda: Change and Stability in South Africans' Ratings of National Priorities', Afrobarometer Briefing Paper No. 45, (June 2006); IDASA, 'AIDS and Public Opinion in South Africa', Afrobarometer Briefing Paper No. 14, (August 2005); IDASA, 'Public Opinion and HIV/AIDS: Facing up to the Future?', Afrobarometer Briefing Paper No. 12, (April 2004).

41 Alan Whiteside, Robert Mattes, Samantha Willan, and Ryann Manning, 'Examining HIV/AIDS in Southern Africa through the Eyes of Ordinary Southern Africans', Afrobarometer Paper No. 21, (August 2002), p. 26.

42 Alex de Waal, 'How Will HIV/AIDS Transform African Governance?', *African Affairs*, 102, (2003), p. 2. The impressive statistics are based on historical relationships between prevalence and state capacity. However, full impacts of prevalence have only been felt in a few countries at most (e.g. Uganda). In all others, impacts have yet to be fully played out, and so it is inappropriate to extrapolate past correlations of prevalence and state capacity. No African country has yet experienced the full impact of the likely demographic changes and so the current reality provides no basis for modelling these effects. See Malcom McPherson, 'Macroeconomic Models of the Impact of HIV/AIDS', Background Paper, Center for Business and Government, Harvard University, (2003), <http://www.ksg.harvard.edu/m-rcbg/hiv-aids/ksg/McPherson_Macroeconomic.models.pdf> (accessed 21 July 2007).

43 Tony Barnett and Alan Whiteside, *AIDS in the Twenty-First Century: Disease and Globalization*, 2nd edn, (Basingstoke, UK/New York: Palgrave Macmillan, 2006), p. 305; Katrina Quattek, 'The Economic Impact of AIDS in South Africa: A Dark Cloud on the Horizon', in *HIV and AIDS: A Threat to the African Renaissance?*, (Johannesburg: Konrad Adenauer Foundation, 2000).

44 De Waal, 'How Will HIV/AIDS Transform African Governance?', p. 7. Another study recently predicted that GDP per capita will rise in South Africa (i.e. that higher mortality will bring economic benefits). See Alwyn Young, 'The Gift of the Dying: The Tragedy of AIDS and the Welfare of Future African Generations', *Quarterly Journal of Economics*, 120, 2, (2005), pp. 423–466.

45 For a good discussion of the lack of robustness of growth models in general, see Charles Kenny and David Williams, 'What Do We Know about Economic Growth? or, Why Don't We Know Very Much?', *World Development*, 29, 1, (2001), pp. 1–22.

46 Clive Bell, Shantayanan Devarajan, and Hans Gersbach, 'The Long-Run Economic Costs of AIDS: A Model with an Application to South Africa', *World Bank Economic Review*, 20, 1, (2006).

47 Although the Bell, Devarajan, and Gersbach study does not refer to 'memes' per se, these are instructive constructs that at their simplest conceptual level refer to 'units of cultural inheritance' or replication essential for social evolution—see Richard Dawkins, *The God Delusion*, (London: Bantam Press, 2006), pp. 191–201.

48 Quoted in Pieter Fourie, *The Political Management of HIV and AIDS in South Africa: One Burden Too Many?*, (Basingstoke, UK/New York: Palgrave Macmillan, 2006), p. 39.

49 Alex de Waal and Alan Whiteside, 'New Variant Famine: AIDS and Food Crisis in Southern Africa', *Lancet*, 362, (2003).

50 Alex de Waal, 'Evidence for the "New Variant Famine" Hypothesis in Africa', Justice Africa, <http://www.justiceafrica.org> (accessed 16 December 2006), p. 1.

51 Alex de Waal, *AIDS and Power: Why There Is No Political Crisis—Yet*, (London & New York: Zed Books, 2006), p. 92.

52 David Keen, The Benefits of Famine: A Political Economy of Famine and Relief in Southwestern Sudan, 1983–89, (Princeton, NJ: Princeton University Press, 1994).

53 Peter Baldwin, *Disease and Democracy: The Industrialized World Faces AIDS*, (Berkeley: University of California Press, 2005), p. 11.

54 Per Strand, 'Comparing AIDS Governance: A Research Agenda on Responses to the AIDS Epidemic', research paper due for publication in 2007, p. 8.

55 Baldwin, *Disease and Democracy*.

56 Strand, 'Comparing AIDS Governance', p. 14.

57 Tim Allen and Suzette Heald, 'HIV/AIDS Policy in Africa: What Has Worked in Uganda and What Has Failed in Botswana?', *Journal of International Development*, 16, (2004), p. 1152.

58 Alex de Waal and Alan Whiteside, 'AIDS: A Darwinian Event?', in Phillippe Denis and Charles Becker (eds), *The HIV/AIDS Epidemic in Sub-Saharan Africa in a Historical Perspective*, online edn, <www.refer.sn/rds/IMG/pdf/08 WAAL-WHITESIDE.pdf> (2006).

59 Laurie Garrett, *HIV and National Security: Where Are the Links?*, (New York: CFR, 2005), p. 18.

60 Fourie, *The Political Management of HIV and AIDS in South Africa*, p. 44.

61 Dawkins, *The God Delusion*, p. 73.

62 John Iliffe, *The African AIDS Epidemic: A History*, (Oxford: James Currey, 2006), pp. 113–114.

63 Fiona Samuels, Michael Drinkwater, and Margaret McEwan, 'Understanding HIV/AIDS and Livelihoods: The Contribution of Longitudinal Data and Cluster Analysis', Overseas Development Institute Briefing Paper No. 8, (August 2006).

64 Hein Marais, *Buckling: The Impact of AIDS in South Africa*, (Pretoria: Centre for the Study of AIDS, 2005), p. 52.

65 De Waal, *AIDS and Power*, p. 39; Steven Friedman and Shauna Mottiar, 'A Rewarding Engagement? The Treatment Action Campaign and the Politics of HIV/AIDS', *Politics & Society*, 33, 4, (2005), p. 511.

66 Jared Diamond, *Collapse: How Societies Choose to Fail or Survive*, (London: Penguin Books, 2005), pp. 421–440.

67 Garrett, 'The Challenge of Global Health', p. 30.

68 Alex de Waal describes this 'normalization as the most sophisticated form of denial'—see De Waal, *AIDS and Power*, p. 18.

69 De Waal, *AIDS and Power*, p. 19.

70 De Waal, *AIDS and Power*, p. 22.

71 De Waal, *AIDS and Power*, p. 102.
72 Allen and Heald, 'HIV/AIDS Policy in Africa', p. 1152.
73 Suzette Heald, 'Abstain or Die: The Development of HIV/AIDS Policy in Botswana', *Journal of Biosocial Science*, 38, (2006), p. 29; Douglas Webb, 'Legitimate Actors? The Future Roles for NGOs against HIV/AIDS in Sub-Saharan Africa', in Nana Poku and Alan Whiteside (eds), *The Political Economy of AIDS in Africa*, (Aldershot, UK: Ashgate, 2004).
74 Lee-Nah Hsu, 'Building Dynamic Democratic Governance and HIV-Resilient Societies', paper presented at the Oslo Governance Centre, (3 November 2003), p. 45.
75 Pieter Fourie, 'For a Secular Response to AIDS', *Mail & Guardian*, 27 October 2006.
76 Edwin Cameron, 'Normalising Testing—Normalising AIDS', Ronald Louw Memorial Lecture, University of KwaZulu-Natal, Durban, South Africa (4 May 2006), pp. 5–7.
77 De Waal, "How Will HIV/AIDS Transform African Governance?', p. 21.
78 Alex de Waal, 'Issue Paper 2: HIV/AIDS and Democratic Governance', Expert Seminar on AIDS, Security and Democracy, Clingendael Institute, The Hague, (2–5 May 2005), p. 3.
79 Quoted in De Waal, *AIDS and Power*, p. 123.

31

AIDS AND SECURITY

Dennis Altman

Source: *International Relations*, 17:4 (2003), 417–27.

Abstract

The war on terrorism has drawn attention to non-conventional threats to security, even as it led to conventional warfare in the case of the attack on Iraq. HIV/AIDS is arguably an even greater threat to security, with the effect of destabilizing the social and economic order to the extent that the very survival of entire nations is at stake. This article examines both the security implications of AIDS, and the various international responses aimed at slowing its spread and mitigating its impact.

The defense this nation seeks involves a great deal more than building airplanes, ships, guns and bombs. We cannot be a strong nation unless we are a healthy nation.

President Roosevelt, 1940[1]

In mid-1999, the South African government placed orders for three new submarines for approximately US$680 million dollars. At the time, something like 1500 people a day were becoming infected by HIV, and the government was increasingly criticized for its failures in both prevention and treatment. South Africa is a particularly appropriate example of the larger political aspects of the epidemic because its government has sought to engage with the larger dimensions of the epidemic, while enraging many activists through its specific responses. South Africa has experienced bitter domestic debates on the adequacy of its response, particularly around the reluctance of the government to provide anti-retroviral therapy (indeed, whether HIV is the primary cause of AIDS).[2] In 2001, the South African government used the courts to battle attempts by international pharmaceutical companies to place restrictions

141

on the availability of generic drugs, but this has not necessarily resulted in the sort of national plan for access to both treatments and prevention associated with Brazil.[3] One might legitimately ask whether the money spent on expanding its naval forces would not more appropriately be spent on fighting HIV/AIDS.

If the primary aim of the state is to protect the lives of its citizens, then risks to security can come in many forms other than those of conventional warfare. The discipline of International Relations has gradually been coming to terms with this argument, although with some reluctance, given its continued dependence on seeing states and the relations between them as central, which makes it difficult to see factors such as environmental degradation, refugee flows or infectious diseases as threats to security comparable to tanks or supersonic missiles. In contemporary attempts to redefine security, it is now common to list a number of items (for example, environmental degradation, international terrorism, drug trafficking, and growing refugee flows), to which epidemics of infectious diseases are often added. The fear of new infectious diseases from the 'third world' insidiously attacking the rich world is an increasingly popular theme, moving from fiction and movies to such widely read journalism as Laurie Garrett's *The Coming Plague*, and the American political commentator, Joe Klein, writes of new 'viral threats' which 'attack the global community insidiously'.[4] The outbreak of SARS at the beginning of 2003 created an international panic, but also gave the World Health Organization a chance to display leadership in promoting international responses to a potential global epidemic.

For 20th-century strategists, the impact of two world wars and the succeeding 50 years of the Cold War meant that security was defined almost entirely in military terms. With the end of the Cold War the short-lived hope for a 'peace dividend' was quickly replaced by a recognition that the world was no safer, just more unpredictable. Increasingly, wars became civil conflicts, with escalating civilian casualties and sometimes belated attempts by international coalitions (as in the former Yugoslavia or East Timor) to impose an end to the carnage. At the same time, there is a growing recognition that the lines between military and non-military threats to security are blurred, as in the case of terrorism (the most striking contemporary example) and organized crime. It is increasingly difficult to perceive conventional military threats to either western Europe or North America, and increasingly their military power is likely to be involved in interventions in unstable poor countries, as in the recent Afghan and Iraqi wars, aimed at replacing regimes seen as posing threats to global order.

Growing global interdependence creates new security threats. Collapse of civil order in one country leads to massive population movements: indeed, recent western European interventions in the Balkans and Africa have been fuelled by a fear of uncontrollable refugee flows as much as by humanitarian impulses. The alleged links between terrorists and 'rogue states' have been invoked to justify the overthrow of 'hostile' governments. The outbreak of a contagious disease in one part of the world will spread extremely rapidly, due to the volume and speed of travel. A nuclear accident (such as the Chernobyl power station) or environmental pollution (for example, acid rain and the poisoning of waterways) will quickly impact on neighbouring countries. Some environmentalists speak of 'natural security' (basic access to food, health care, and a safe environment)[5] as more useful than 'national security', in an era when national boundaries are increasingly unable to protect against many threats to human well-being and survival.

In one sense, the 'new' security threats are not new. The spread of the Black Death (bubonic plague) through Europe and Asia in the Middle Ages, or the movement of diseases such as syphilis and measles as part of the expansion of European empires into the rest of the world are precursors to today's problems. What is new is both the instant transmission of news and information, and the growing acceptance that national sovereignty cannot be relied upon to respond to problems of international significance. Thus one finds reports such as that compiled jointly by the Chemical and Biological Arms Control Institute and the Center for Strategic and International Studies in the USA which claimed 'directly [to] link health and global security for the first time'. The report stressed the rapidity with which infections can spread; the threat of biological weapons; and the consequences for health of regional conflicts and failing states.[6] Indeed, there is evidence that officers in the CIA had been pushing their superiors to consider the impact of HIV/AIDS on national and international stability since 1990.[7]

The United Nations Development Programme (UNDP) has developed the concept of human security, locating the concept of security within a framework of 'the legitimate concerns of ordinary people', and encompassing safety from chronic threats of hunger, disease, and repression and protection from sudden disruptions in the patterns of everyday life. In brief, human security places the emphasis on protecting individuals and communities rather than merely state boundaries. More recently, the UNDP in 1993 has linked these definitions of human security to the rapid changes and insecurities brought about through globalization: 'In the globalizing world of shrinking time, shrinking space and disappearing borders, people are confronting new threats to human security – sudden and hurtful disruptions in the pattern of daily life'.[8] In some ways, this conceptualization appears to echo the currently fashionable idea of 'risk society', a term which is often used to characterize the contemporary condition. One analysis of 'human security' counterposes an emphasis on the community and individual, socio-economic and environmental threats, and unstructured violence to the state-centred approach of more traditional concepts of security.[9]

There are strikingly different ways in which the concern with new security threats can be deployed. The concern of the US government is largely based on preserving stability and protecting its own citizens from contamination from abroad. A quite different perspective begins with the conditions in the poor world that are leading to the rapid spread of infectious diseases, and argues for a greater global response to eliminate these.

HIV/AIDS as exemplar of a new form of global security threat

The first attempts to create a framework for the international control of HIV/AIDS grew out of the 'new public health' and the Ottawa Charter, with its emphasis on community participation and a move away from an overly medicalized view of health. The Ottawa Charter was a statement adopted by 38 countries in 1986 which identified good health as resting upon 'the empowerment of communities, their ownership and control of their own endeavours and destinies'.[10]

The first director of the Global Programme on AIDS (GPA), Jonathan Mann, perceived a strong connection between human rights and vulnerability to HIV, and both human rights and support for non-governmental and community-based organizations were centrepieces of his policies. Simultaneously, there developed a stress on the linkages between HIV and development, which was significant in the decision of the Economic and Social Council of the United Nations to establish UNAIDS as a 'joint and co-sponsored program' of a number of key United Nations agencies.[11] Whereas Mann stressed the link between vulnerability to infection and the lack of human rights, others have stressed the linkages between vulnerability and poverty, noting that widespread HIV is often the result of the massive dislocations brought about by global economic forces.[12]

More recently, the enormity of the epidemic – and the need to focus political attention on its implications – has led to some pressure to reconceptualize it as a political/security issue. Thus a spokesman for South Africa's President Mbeki asserted: 'He has broken the tradition that seeks to make the disease just a health problem. HIV/AIDS is a socio-economic problem. It is a political problem that has reached the proportion of an international crisis. It threatens to destroy nations and continents'.[13] By 2001, when the United Nations General Assembly organized a Special Session on AIDS (UNGASS), this rhetoric had become a commonplace of political speak, if not yet of academic work. Only a small number of mainstream writers on security and international relations have incorporated HIV/AIDS into their analyses.[14]

The spread of and the response to AIDS is itself a product of globalization, with dislocations caused by rapid population movements, urbanization, the rapid spread of ideas and information, and the changes in government policies, often as a result of policies imposed by external organizations, all relevant factors.[15] There is an irony in the World Bank putting increasing sums of money into AIDS work in countries such as Brazil and India, where the Bank's own policies had helped weaken the health structures which might have already helped prevent the spread of HIV. One of the most telling examples of how structural adjustment affected the spread of AIDS is data from Kenya, which showed a steep drop in attendance at STI clinics after the World Bank enforced charges for such visits.[16]

Gradually the international political system has come to recognize the larger political implications of HIV/AIDS. In January 2000, the United Nations Security Council held a debate on the impact of HIV/AIDS on Africa, thus recognizing the implicit connection between security and the scale of the epidemic. At that meeting Mark Malloch Brown of the UNDP pointed out:

> HIV/AIDS has a qualitatively different impact than a traditional health killer such as malaria. It rips across social structures, target-ing a young continent's young people, particularly its girls; by cutting deep into all sectors of society it undermines vital economic growth – perhaps reducing future national GDP size in the region by a third over the next twenty years. And by putting huge additional demand on already weak, hard to access, public services it is setting up the terms of a desperate conflict over inadequate resources.[17]

Already across large parts of southern and eastern Africa, more than a quarter of the adult population is infected with HIV, with rapidly increasing figures for other parts of the developing world, including India, China, Thailand, Cambodia, Papua New Guinea, parts of the Caribbean, and some of the former Soviet Union. That AIDS predominantly affects young adults means it hits the most productive and volatile members of society, which has considerable social, economic, and political consequences.

The epidemic is inextricably connected with war and civil unrest. Wars fuel the epidemic, as Peter Piot pointed out: 'War is the instrument of AIDS and rape is an instrument of war'.[18] Summing up the impact of war on the spread of HIV, a Nigerian commentator identified six factors as relevant: widespread rape by soldiers; massive and uncontrollable population move-ments; the creation of large refugee camps and the conditions making for unprotected and forced sex within them; poverty leading to an increase in commercial sex; decline of literacy and access to basic prevention informa-tion; and the collapse of health services, leading to lesser ability to follow infection protection guidelines.[19] All of these factors can be clearly identified in recent civil strife and warfare in the Congo, Sierra Leone, Rwanda, East Timor, and so on. Sierra Leone now has a growing HIV epidemic, with estimates of widespread rape and a positive rate of almost 25 percent among army recruits.[20] The post-Afghan war refugee camps in Pakistan are likely to be fertile breeding grounds for HIV, given the high needle use in the region.

There is arguably a close relationship between high HIV rates and civil disorder. A report from the US National Intelligence Agency estimated that HIV prevalence among militia in Angola and the Democratic Republic of the Congo was between 40 and 60 percent, and earlier reports linked the brutal killings in Rwanda in the late 1990s to widespread HIV infection.[21] In Cambodia and Honduras, it is claimed that the presence of foreign troops has been a major factor in leading to the introduction of HIV[22] and there is concern about the ways in which peacekeeping forces might help spread HIV. At the same time, HIV helps create economic and social crises which in turn threaten stability and civic order. It seems possible that the political hysteria to which President Mugabe appealed in Zimbabwe during the election campaign of 2000, and the violence directed against white settlers, was connected in various ways to the high rate of HIV infection, not least as a way of denying the gravity of the epidemic. I write 'seems possible' quite deliberately, as there is great reluctance to discuss publicly this hypothesis. (Laurie Garrett reports that she has had death threats from ZANU thugs merely for asking about government failure to address HIV.[23]) Even Doris Lessing's widely publicized critique of Mugabe in early 2003 barely mentioned the extent of HIV, though it is clearly a contributory factor to the collapse of social and economic order in Zimbabwe.[24]

Given the high rate of casual sex engaged in by military personnel, HIV will have special implications for the military, who have to develop policies as to how they can best deal with the threat of large numbers of their members becoming infected, and the concomitant costs this poses. Thailand began early in developing programmes to deal with HIV within its military, but most countries have been very slow and often extremely reluctant to confront the problem. Given the reality that the military is the primary source of political power and social order in many of the world's poorest countries, the existence of the widespread prevalence of HIV among military personnel threatens political and social stability.

For the broader society, AIDS reduces life expectancy, distorts health budgets, and creates a new generation of orphans for whom adequate care is almost impossible. It is already having an impact on the economic future of many countries because it attacks those who are most productive, and increases the burden of care on others. In many parts of sub-Saharan Africa – and potentially in other parts of the world – the loss of skilled workers and professionals is leading to a measurable decline in living standards, compounded by the growing burden on already under-resourced health systems, and exacerbating the threat of famine.[25] (The development of elaborate and expensive treatments for HIV is merely increasing the gap between the epidemic of the rich minority and the poor majority, and fuelling a growing anger against the major pharmaceutical manufacturers.) In more and more villages, the care of children is falling upon grandparents, as the intermediate adult generation becomes sick and dies. In much of Africa, teachers, nurses, police, and public servants are dying of AIDS faster than they can be replaced, and there is a general belief that GDP is declining by about 1 percent per year in the worst-affected countries. This may, however, seriously underestimate the medium- and long-term loss of human capital caused by the epidemic.[26]

The implications of the perceptions of HIV/AIDS

Does it matter if HIV/AIDS is understood as a matter of security, rather than, say, health or development? Yes, because how we conceptualize the epidemic will immediately impact on the extent of political commitment governments bring to dealing with it. Defining AIDS as a health issue limits it to the province of one ministry, often without much political clout. Redefining it to encompass security issues almost inevitably pushes it far higher up governmental agendas, making it a first-order concern. This is now happening, as in the decision of recently democratized Nigeria to bring AIDS under the control of a committee headed by the president himself or in the creation of a special ministry for HIV/AIDS in Cote d'Ivoire. Without such political mobilization it is unlikely that the response to HIV/AIDS will encompass the full range of programmes for prevention, treatment care and support, and campaigns against the stigma associated with the condition that not only furthers the burdens of those who are positive, but makes testing and prevention programmes difficult to implement.

Since UNGASS there has been some increase in resources to fight AIDS through establishment of a Global Fund against AIDS, TB, and Malaria, intended to provide international resources for prevention and treatment in poor countries. The fund has had a difficult beginning, and while it has signed agreements with nearly 30 countries, it had only disbursed US$20 million by April 2003. Of course, resources are crucial, but resources by themselves are insufficient. Effective HIV prevention requires, above all, the political will to break down barriers imposed in the name of culture, religion, and tradition. (Under strong religious pressure UNGASS refused to vote to name men who have sex with men, drug users, and sex workers as among those who are most vulnerable to HIV.) And while there has been considerable success in lowering the price of anti-retroviral drugs in the developing world, successful HIV treatments require a complex infrastructure which few poor countries can provide (although impressive gains have been made in a few, such as Botswana).

The great irony is that we know how to prevent transmission of HIV, and it is neither technically difficult nor expensive. Most HIV transmission can be stopped by the widespread use of condoms and clean needles (only in terms of blood screening does prevention involve the use of costly technology). But for this to happen requires major changes in behaviour, both individual and collective, which in turn require support for programmes which often infringe cherished religious and cultural beliefs. Effective HIV prevention requires governments to acknowledge a whole set of behaviours which they would rather ignore, and a willingness to support, and indeed empower, groups practising such behaviours. This requires major shifts in the conception of what is criminalized, and a willingness to recognize that a great deal of behaviour which is proscribed nonetheless exists, and that the more it is stigmatized, the more difficult it is effectively to prevent HIV transmission. In other cases, most particularly widespread forced sexual intercourse, it may mean an increase in policing activities. As John Caldwell has argued: 'The central plank in the victory over AIDS is the recognition by African governments of social and sexual reality. Millions of people are being allowed to die on the grounds that the only way they can be saved is by adopting a more "moral" way of life, indeed a way of life that is not their morality'.[27]

Thus, effective measures against HIV may involve changes to existing structures of power, which threaten those who have most to lose. At some level politicians understand that to speak of empowering women, of abolishing stigmas based on unpopular behaviour and status, threatens the status quo from which they benefit. The development of peer education programmes or community health measures can, in turn, open up space for ideas of popular involvement in policymaking and question the allocation of governmental resources in ways which are potentially quite revolutionary. Where governments either depend upon or fear the power of organized religion, the major need for basic prevention information around frank discussion of sexuality is likely to be extremely difficult. HIV/AIDS is simultaneously an example of new paradigms in understanding security and an issue which requires state leadership to intervene in areas often regarded as both natural and private.

Barnett and Whiteside have argued that there is a link between HIV and the degree of social cohesion and the overall level of wealth in a society, arguing that the worst combination is low social cohesion and very unequal distribution of wealth. They also draw an important distinction between various forms of social cohesion, distinguishing that which may derive from civil society and that which stems from authoritarian political or cultural systems. In the short run, it is possible that the latter will be more effective in controlling the spread of the epidemic (a good example is Cuba, whose policies were criticized as unnecessarily restrictive of human rights, but which nonetheless managed to limit the spread of HIV through policies of compulsory quarantine). In the longer run, as is now evident in China and Vietnam, authoritarian governments can force risky behaviour underground, but are unlikely to be able to prevent it.

The global response to AIDS

Perhaps the one bright note in what too often seems a tale of unmitigated failures and stupidity is the international solidarity which has been created in response to the AIDS epidemic. The response of the United Nations system has been matched by the development of a whole set of regional and global community-based networks, with considerable ongoing links to multilateral and bilateral agencies. The biennial international conferences, of which the most recent in Barcelona (July 2002) generated very considerable global media coverage, have become significant symbolic expressions of global solidarity.

While 'solidarity' can easily become a meaningless shibboleth, the HIV/AIDS epidemic has created an extraordinary number of concrete examples, ranging from the development of community-based sex-worker and gay organizations, 'buyers' clubs' in rich countries that collect HIV treatments to send to people in poor ones, through to international business and multilateral organizations.

As is true of other areas of global concern, AIDS has opened up possibilities for non-governmental actors to influence and work with both governments and international agencies. From its inception UNAIDS sought to work in conjunction with community-based organizations, and to avoid the formal and bureaucratic processes of the United Nations system. It created a place for 'NGO delegates' (not representatives) on its governing body, the Policy Coordinating Board, and sought to establish ways of consulting with all significant NGO networks to choose such delegates. Probably more important has been a steady recruitment of people from the community sector to work for UNAIDS, and a greater day-to-day engagement with AIDS organizations than is usual for international organizations.

Yet UNAIDS is caught in a contradiction it cannot resolve: its success depends on establishing cooperation between the UN agencies which are its co-sponsors, where territorial claims are often more important than policy outcomes. For UNAIDS to coordinate, say, the World Bank and UNESCO is rather akin to asking a sparrow to direct a herd of elephants. Increasingly, it has come to act as a focal point for international activities, providing information and contacts, and in some countries directly influencing policy from both donors and governments. Such in-country success depends on establishing a good relationship between its own representative (there are UNAIDS country officers in close to 50 countries), the chair of the United Nations theme groups (comprising the various UN co-sponsors of UNAIDS), and the officers of the country's own AIDS bureaucracies.

Just as significant is the positioning of AIDS on the global agenda. Under Peter Piot UNAIDS has been able to capture some of the moral weight which Jonathan Mann gave the Global Program on AIDS, and to win significant support from both Secretary General Annan and US Secretary of State Powell. While AIDS clearly cannot be contained by national boundaries, an effective response depends heavily on the will of national governments. However much international support and solidarity may be generated, governments have to be willing to allow effective prevention, counselling, and treatment programmes, which in turn require the use of community organizations to mobilize often marginalized and disempowered populations.[28] The UNGASS meeting revealed that many governments were uneasy about anything other than the most token involvement of PLWHAs and civil society organizations in policy debates around the epidemic.

But UNGASS did illustrate that the security concerns around HIV/AIDS had begun to affect governments, particularly those from sub-Saharan Africa (there was some concern at the absence of senior political figures attending from countries in Asia and eastern Europe with potentially huge epidemics). By declaring AIDS 'a global emergency' and with the creation of the Global Fund the Special Session marked the final break from defining AIDS in purely health terms, putting it on the agenda of governments as a whole. While the wars in Afghanistan and Iraq have seemed to direct attention back to a more conventional focus on security, the Bush administration remains committed to major international initiatives on HIV/AIDS. It remains unclear how far domestic political pressures will make such US support conditional on ignoring what UNAIDS regards as 'best practice' on issues such as needle exchange and sex education.[29]

Only if governments see fighting the epidemic as a matter of national survival are they likely to provide the degree of resources, both political and financial, which are required and which cannot be met by international effort alone. Indeed, the paradox is that while governments may often seem too weak to provide effective social programmes, they are usually strong enough to create extraordinary barriers against anyone else who might provide them. (Thus Burma, whose government knows the potential threat of the epidemic, places considerable obstacles in the way of both domestic and international efforts against HIV.) Stronger governments, which means governments with the support of their citizens, will feel less threatened by international efforts and by regional and international NGOs, and will be able, in turn, to create supportive environments within which international and non-governmental efforts are most effective.

As I write, current estimates suggest that there are more than 40 million HIV-positive people in the world. In absolute numbers, infections in Asia will probably exceed the African figures within a decade. Estimates of infections in India and China are very imprecise, but no one disputes they are already in the millions. In Cambodia, 10,000 people will die each year for the next decade from HIV, while Papua New Guinea faces a huge crisis which former Prime Minister Sir Mekere Morauta identified as having the potential to undermine the survival of the country. Former Soviet republics such as Russia and Ukraine face rapidly increasing infection through the sharing of needles. We do not know enough about the Middle East and western Asia, but there are suggestions of rapid growth, due again to needle use in Afghanistan and Iran.

The impact of a spreading epidemic will be disastrous in terms of the social and economic stability of increasing numbers of countries, with an extraordinary potential to destabilize already fragile political systems across much of the poor world. Three years ago, in a discussion with Australian defence forces personnel, I agreed that the impact of HIV on Indonesia was likely to be slight. With the rapid increase of HIV in Indonesia in the past couple of years[30] the epidemic looms as much of a threat to its national survival as do movements for regional autonomy and religious fundamentalism.

Acknowledgement

An earlier version of this article appeared in Kelley Lee (ed.) (2003) *Health Impacts of Globalisation*, pp.33–46. Basingstoke: Palgrave Macmillan. Research for this article was supported by a grant from the Australian Research Council.

Notes

1 James Fallows (1999) 'The Political Scientist', *New Yorker*, 7 June.
2 See Hein Marais (2000) 'To the Edge', *AIDS Review 2000*. Pretoria: University of Pretoria; Helen Schneider and Joanne Stein (2001) 'Implementing AIDS Policy in Post-Apartheid South Africa', *Social Science and Medicine* 52: 723–31; Virginia van der Vliet (2001) 'AIDS: Losing "The New Struggle"?', *Daedalus*, winter: 151–84; D. Fassin and H. Schneider (2003) 'The Politics of AIDS in South Africa', *BMJ* 326: 495–7; Samantha Power (2003) 'The AIDS Rebel', *New Yorker*, 19 May: 54–67.
3 See Jane Galvao (2002) 'Access to Antiretroviral Drugs in Brazil', *The Lancet* 360: 1862–5; Tina Rosenberg (2001) 'The Brazilian Solution', *New York Times Magazine*, 28 January: 26–31, 52–5.
4 Laurie Garrett (1994) *The Coming Plague*. New York: Farrar Strauss; Joe Klein (2003) 'How to Build a Better Democrat', *Time Magazine*, 19 May: 26.
5 Risa Hontiveros-Braquel (1996) 'Gender and Security'. Paper presented at the 10th Asia-Pacific Roundtable, June, Kuala Lumpur.
6 Chemical and Biological Arms Control Institute and Center for Strategic and International Studies (2000) *Conflict and Contagion: Health as a Global Security Challenge*. Washington, DC.
7 Barton Gellman (2000) 'Death Watch: The Belated Global Response to AIDS in Africa', *Washington Post*, 5 July.
8 Caroline Thomas (2000) *Global Governance, Development and Human Security*, pp.5–6. London: Pluto; UNDP (1999) *Human Development Report: Overview*. New York.
9 W. Tow and R. Trood (2000) 'Linkages Between Traditional Security and Human Security', in W. Tow, R. Thakur and I. Hyuen (eds) *Asia's Emerging Regional Order*, p.20. Tokyo: Tokyo United Nations University.
10 WHO (1986) *Ottawa Charter for Health Promotion*. Health and Welfare Canada, Canadian Public Health Association.
11 Dennis Altman (1999) 'AIDS and Questions of Global Governance', *Pacifica Review*, 2 June, 11: 195–211.
12 See, for example, Dennis Altman (1999) 'Globalization, Political Economy and HIV/AIDS', *Theory and Society* 28: 559–84; Tony Barnett and Alan Whiteside (2002) *AIDS in the Twenty First Century*. Basingstoke: Palgrave Macmillan; Kelley Lee (ed.) (2003) *Health Impacts of Globalisation*. Basingstoke: Palgrave Macmillan.
13 Parks Mankahlana (2000) Press release, Parks Mankahlana, Head of Communications, President Mbeki's office, 24 March.
14 The most influential example is probably Nicholas Eberstadt (2002) 'The Future of AIDS', *Foreign Affairs*, November–December.

15 Alan Whiteside and Tony Barnett (1998) 'AIDS in Africa: Socio-Economic Determinants and Development Impact', *IAS Newsletter* (9), 8–11 March.
16 P. Lurie, P. Hintzen and R. Lowe (1995) 'Socioeconomic Obstacles to HIV Prevention and Treatment in Developing Countries', *AIDS* 9(6); Helen Epstein (2001) 'Time of Indifference', *New York Review of Books*, 12 April: 33–8.
17 Mark Malloch Brown (2000) Statement at Security Council Meeting, 10 January.
18 Peter Piot (2000) Statement at Security Council Meeting on HIV/AIDS in Africa, 10 January.
19 Ruku Oyaku (2001) 'Wars and HIV/AIDS Spread in Sub-Saharan Africa', posting to *Break the Silence*, URL: (19 April) break-the-silence@hdnet.org.
20 Simon Robinson (2001) 'Battle Ahead', *Time Magazine*, Australian edn., 16 July: 40.
21 S. M. Bertozzi (1996) 'The Impact of Human Immunodeficiency Virus/AIDS', *Journal of Infectious Diseases*, Supplement 2: 174.
22 Chris Beyrer (1998) 'Burma and Cambodia: Human Rights, Social Disruption and the Spread of HIV/AIDS', *Health and Human Rights* 2(4): 85–96; Stephanie Kane (1993) 'Prostitution and the Military: Planning AIDS Intervention in Belize', *Social Science and Medicine* 36(7): 965–79.
23 Laurie Garrett (2000) 'You Just Signed His Death Warrant', *Columbia Journalism Review*, URL (November–December): http://cjr.org/year/00/4/garrett.asp.
24 Doris Lessing (2003) 'The Jewel of Africa', *New York Review of Books*, 10 April: 6–10.
25 Martin Schonteich (2002) 'Impact of Aids on Security in Southern Africa'. Poster presentation at the Barcelona International AIDS Conference.
26 For an analysis of this argument, see *The Economist* (2003) 'Epidemics and Economies', 10 April.
27 John Caldwell (2000) 'Rethinking the African AIDS Epidemic', *Population and Development Review* 26(1): 130.
28 See Dennis Altman (1994) *Power and Community*. London: Falmer.
29 Jodi Jacobsen (2003) 'The Dis-Integration of U.S. Global AIDS Funding'. Washington, DC: Foreign Policy in Focus. URL: http://www.fpif.org.
30 UNAIDS (2002) *Report on the Global HIV/AIDS Epidemic*, p.30. Geneva.

32

SYNCRETISM AND SUBVERSION IN AIDS GOVERNANCE

How locals cope with global demands

Ann Swidler*

Source: *International Affairs*, 82:2 (2006), 269–84.

AIDS is changing the face of Africa, bringing life expectancies in parts of southern and eastern Africa, which had begun to approach First World standards, down to 38–40 years. But also, and perhaps more consequentially, the definition of the AIDS pandemic as an epochal crisis is generating an organizational response that may alter patterns of governance across Africa. We know something about the effects of the pandemic on life, health and education, and on matters like food security and defence, but hardly anyone has analysed the epidemic's effects on forms and cultures of governance.

This article attempts to lay out a set of broad theoretical questions, illustrated with material from two visits to sub-Saharan Africa (Botswana in July 2003 and Malawi in June and July 2004), including interviews with government officials and international organization representatives in Botswana and Malawi, about 70 interviews with staff from AIDS NGOs across sub-Saharan Africa, and an initial effort at mapping the universe of organizations responding to Africa's AIDS pandemic. The article focuses on four issues: (1) the nature of the organizations responding to AIDS in Africa; (2) the relation of AIDS governance to existing patterns of African governance, including the possibilities of syncretism and, conversely, a stand-off between the organizational models created by AIDS NGOs and existing patterns of authority and cooperation in African societies; (3) the problems and possibilities of 'cultural match' between existing repertoires of 'collective action schemas' and those proffered by NGOs and international organizations;[1] and (4) the slippery matter of the play of power, money and identity in a field of power with very unequal players.

African governance

While AIDS and the global response to the epidemic are worldwide phenomena, they have distinctive effects in Africa; and African governance in turn has fundamental lessons to teach about the nature of politics, governance and institutional change. Post-colonial African states have typically been both more porous (easily penetrated) and less deeply integrated into the societies they govern than western states.[2] Thus in Africa generally, and in dealing with AIDS in particular, one cannot think about the local without considering the global. While African states vary enormously in the integrity and effectiveness of their national governments, many are so weak or so poor that they depend on outside organizations to fund, and sometimes to administer, their AIDS and other public health programmes.[3] Some African states are relatively strong and effective; but, ironically, these more effective states then attract the largest number of donors and NGO partners who, in turn, seek to alter elements of governance and policy.

How is AIDS governance tracked and managed at local levels?

The AIDS pandemic is tracked and 'managed' by an enormous, world-spanning collection of organizations, some loosely coordinated through the UNAIDS umbrella and now the Global Fund to Fight AIDS, Tuberculosis and Malaria (GFATM); some funded by major international organizations such as the World Bank, the United Nations Population Fund (UNFPA) and the WHO; many funded directly or indirectly by USAID (and now the President's Emergency Plan for AIDS Relief, PEPFAR), the Danish International Development Agency (DANIDA), the Norwegian Agency for Development Cooperation (NORAD), the UK Department for International Development, and the other major bilateral donors; and others funded by a hodge-podge of smaller groups and foundations, basically freelancers, many with their own funds and their own ideas and interests.

Even a brief look at what the 'structure' of such an organizational universe might look like illustrates the complexity of this system. Just to map this universe is an enormous challenge. All sorts of organizations—upstart freelancers, pseudo-independent NGOs, and many 'consort' organizations from universities to traditional foundations to church and missionary organizations (e.g. Catholic AIDS Alliance or World Vision)—have jumped into the AIDS fight. This universe is organized partly as a hierarchy, with the big funders and the regulatory organizations like the Global Fund, WHO, the World Bank and UNAIDS at the top; but it is also organized as a network of 'partnerships' and projects, often with specialized focuses or target groups. And then in many respects it is unorganized, with entrepreneurial actors at all levels inventing (or reinventing) themselves as actors in the AIDS drama.

In the AIDS arena, as with development, human rights, peace, women's rights and environmental movements, complex networks of international and locally based NGOs define issues, carry out projects, mobilize local activists, and lobby in international forums.[4] However we define the relevant system, multiple levels are interacting simultaneously, and our usual ways of thinking about boundaries, or even about nested hierarchies of social processes (local, regional, national, international, global, for example), do not work very well.[5]

African governance is deeply interpenetrated with international actors, but the degree to which such actors actually influence governance is much more ambiguous. Three brief examples will illustrate how complex such processes are.

An internal report advising the government of Uganda on decentralization begins with a list of 32 'Abbreviations and Acronyms' for various political units, officials and programmes of the Ugandan government, but also includes CARE, CUAMM (Italian Cooperation), DANIDA, SNV-Netherlands, United Nations Capital Fund and USAID. Thus Uganda cannot even discuss its own governance structures without frequent reference to the international organizations with which it interpenetrates.

A second example is a 'Monitoring and Evaluation' report for Malawi's National AIDS Commission, produced with funding (and a consultant) from the World Bank, to develop a reporting system for all of Malawi's AIDS programmes.[6] This Monitoring and Evaluation system was a prerequisite for grants from the Global Fund (GFATM) and from an international donor pool supporting Malawi's anti-retroviral (ARV) drug programme.[7] Thus, to get resources from global donors, Malawi had to mobilize local actors to enact organizational forms and procedures required by global actors. (I take up below the question to what extent the organizational isomorphism such requirements would imply is actually achieved in practice.)

The third example is simpler, but perhaps even more typical. A volunteer for a small NGO bringing international students to do AIDS work in Kenya for a few months reported that she ended up writing and then helping to promote a new AIDS curriculum for the local school system because the region, having not supported Kenya's ruling party, had received no curricular materials to carry out government-mandated AIDS education.

These examples illustrate both that African governments are dependent on and interpenetrated with international actors, and also that those actors may often be used to advance very local agendas.

Paradoxes of permeability

African states differ, however, in how permeable they are, and thus indirectly in how NGOs function and how they relate to government. An intriguing contrast is that between Zambia and Botswana. The director of a Zambian AIDS hospice—the first in the country and highly regarded—explained that her organization had operated for more than ten years without licensing or regulation because Zambia had no licensing category for hospices. The local government administrators, village headmen, police and hospital personnel have a good relationship with the hospice, but its integration into both state and community is essentially informal. Botswana, in contrast, has a remarkably effective, organized, administratively coherent and non-corrupt government. But ACHAP (the African Comprehensive HIV/AIDS Partnership), a $100 million AIDS initiative funded by the Gates and Merck foundations, has felt hampered, and sometimes hamstrung, by the very government competence and integrity that have made Botswana such a magnet for outside foundations, international organizations and bilateral funding.

One issue illustrates the paradox of Botswana's competence and Zambia's relative incompetence. Botswana, like most African countries, has a shortage of trained medical personnel. Thus one obstacle to rapid 'scaling up' of ARV treatment has been the shortage of doctors, nurses, laboratories and so forth.[8] Botswana also has a comprehensive system of professional regulation, according to which only physicians (and, on the ground, nurses) can draw blood, an essential part of AIDS treatment. But ACHAP's suggestion that phlebotomists—specialists in drawing blood, but without other medical training—might reduce the pressures on medical personnel were met with fierce, and ultimately successful, resistance by Botswana's licensed medical professionals. At the same time, in Zambia, no one was regulating what medical professionals as opposed to volunteers and other workers in medical settings could do. Indeed, after hearing how the dearth of medical professionals and the extensive lab work required for ARV therapy were limiting Botswana's options, I learned from the Zambian hospice director that she (an American college graduate with no formal medical training) had, in collaboration with the hospice's part-time physician, 'just written' the (quite simple, thus manageable) protocol that would guide her hospice's ARV treatment programme.

Institutional isomorphism

One effect of the ramified global universe of AIDS organizations has been to create a proliferation of organizations and a homogenization of organizational forms across the AIDS terrain. UNAIDS has, for example, insisted on 'multisectoral' approaches to coordinating AIDS prevention and treatment, often marginalizing traditional ministries of health, while generating national, regional and local-level coordinating bodies, the NACs, DACCs and VACs (National AIDS Commissions, District AIDS Coordinating Committees and Village AIDS Committees) that populate the AIDS landscape. The 'Monitoring and Evaluation' specialists dispatched from the World Bank as countries line up for funding from the GFATM provide another example of nearly all the processes DiMaggio and Powell saw as producing 'institutional isomorphism'—the development of similar organizational forms, professional titles and programme labels.[9] But it is not clear how much this proliferation of organizational forms actually affects what happens on the ground.

John Meyer and his collaborators suggest far-reaching 'institutional' effects of current international and transnational activities. John Boli, Meyer and colleagues have written about an emergent world cultural order, a world agenda of human rights, gender equality and democratic participation advanced by the NGOs that have proliferated across the globe.[10] The global NGO order certainly presses its understanding of gender equality, human rights and community participation, but these interact on the ground with local understandings in ways that often differ from the paper trail international organizations leave in their mission statements. Indeed, the West has been trying to reshape Africa along lines it thought appropriate for centuries, and only some of those efforts at institutional transformation have taken root, often in ways far removed from what their authors imagined.

Syncretism and subversion

While there is an enormous literature on religious syncretism, we know remarkably little about syncretism at the level of organizational form and content. Some recent studies of economic institutions—and especially of the 'economic transition' in formerly communist economies—have asked how imported institutional forms fare when transplanted to new soil.[11] But we lack a culturally rich theory about when and why transplanted institutional forms sometimes take root and flourish but so often wither or become deformed.

Ultimately such a theory will have to incorporate both the 'cultural match' arguments discussed below and an understanding of how groups with particular interests invest in institutions and how institutions become embedded as they get 'filled up' with the aspirations and agendas of particular interest groups.[12] For now, however, I want to start with an inventory of some of the organizational forms NGOs attempt to use in their AIDS work. (In part this provides an answer to what people mean when they talk about 'AIDS prevention' on the ground.)

Social marketing

One of the most widespread—and, in its own terms, 'successful'—innovations in service delivery has been the development of 'social marketing', particularly the marketing of condoms by organizations like Population Services International. Such programmes both presume markets (and market actors) and induce them to distribute subsidized versions of goods the donors regard as desirable. This involves marketing campaigns (focus groups to choose the name—e.g. the 'Chisango' ['shield' in Swahili] condom; elsewhere the 'panther' as a logo; staging publicity campaigns; and working through existing community leaders to persuade people to seek and use condoms) and the notion that condoms will achieve wider distribution if every actor in the chain of distribution makes a profit from marketing the product. Social marketing has met with wide success in a number of areas. But we should remember that, rather than introducing a completely new concept into African societies, 'social marketing' of course piggybacks on the enormous importance of petty trading across most of Africa.[13]

Volunteering

It was clear from both my interviews and my observations that the most widespread form of AIDS intervention on the ground is the establishment of volunteer 'clubs' of various sorts. In rural Malawi, Save the Children (USA) established 'AIDS Toto' ('stop AIDS') clubs in many villages. Similarly, World Vision founded its own village youth clubs, targeted on youth of different ages. Some clubs were supposed to mount drama groups to spread the AIDS message to young people in other villages. Other youth were to be drawn in by netball competitions. The Malawi Broadcasting Company organized a set of innovative radio programmes, meant to encourage even illiterate villagers to discuss AIDS and to develop their own suggestions for doing something about it. The broadcasters establish village-level clubs that meet during the weekly radio broadcast to listen together and then to formulate their own programme through discussion.

Such volunteer groups—sometimes women's groups, sometimes youth clubs, and sometimes mobilizing through churches, in schools, or across age and gender lines—were an important feature of Uganda's successful mobilization against AIDS. Zambia developed the remarkable Society for Women and AIDS in Zambia (SWAAZ), a volunteer organization now claiming a membership of about 10,000 women organized in chapters all over Zambia, that has held meetings to educate market women, factory workers, villagers, school pupils and so forth across the country about AIDS. Indeed, I have argued elsewhere that the mobilization of volunteers may itself matter much more in successful AIDS prevention than whether the mobilization promotes condoms, abstinence, fidelity or simply 'information and education'.[14]

Clubs are only one aspect of the very widespread reliance on volunteer workers as the core staff of many NGO interventions—those like World Vision's Area Development Projects, family planning programmes, and many AIDS interventions, from youth drama clubs to village AIDS committees. A widespread way of delivering medical care, for example, is 'home-based care', dependent on the volunteer efforts of local women who visit the sick and their caregivers. On the one hand, such volunteer mobilization is a remarkable example of a kind of synergy between the organizational forms western donors understand and promote, on the one hand, and existing patterns of African social life on the other, most important among them expectations of 'generalized reciprocity' that make people obligated to other members of their own families, clans or villages when there are shortages or crises. On the other hand, such arrangements illustrate where slippage and subversion can occur as embedded understandings alter the meanings of organizational forms.

Turning informal obligations to family, clan or neighbours into more organizationally distinct clubs, projects or programmes—as many development projects from micro-lending organizations to women's cooperatives to community health projects do—has proved surprisingly successful. But it is not clear that the international sponsors of such programmes understand very well the kind of cultural/organizational syncretism that has occurred there. I offer a few speculative suggestions about how the understandings of western AIDS workers (many of whom are themselves 'volunteers') about 'volunteer' activities may intersect those of local actors. First, it is clear that, despite the appearance of pure volunteerism, some hope of access to resources— money for transportation, possible access to a bicycle, food or an outing for a youth group, an actual soccer ball—is a critical complement to volunteering for those from societies so poor that any extra resource is enormously valuable.[15] Second, volunteer participation in organizations that involve international personnel create the ever-present possibility of contact with and help from the outside. This is, on a local level, the same pattern that Bayart has called 'extraversion', when African political leaders plead their nations' neediness as a way of generating external resources for themselves.[16]

More important than specific resources may be the possibility (like winning the lottery) of contact with outsiders that might lead to almost unimaginable benefits. The local director of a small AIDS NGO operating in Kenya was careful to cultivate the local district commissioner, who let it be understood that he wanted to be consulted about the NGO's projects—in essence, incorporating them into his patronage network. No bribes were requested or offered, but he wanted to be kept informed and to be consulted about decisions such as which local families might house the organization's idealistic young volunteers who, in addition to their volunteer labour, could potentially offer contacts of enormous value. One young volunteer reported that she became so attached to the family she lived with that she became the godmother of the youngest child and committed herself to pay the child's school fees. Another volunteer in her programme arranged a full scholarship for the son of his Kenyan host family to attend an American university.

The enormous disparity in resources between the international organization's personnel (however modestly they live and however poorly funded the organization) and the local community is, in Africa, the inescapable background against which all interactions between international organizations and the local society have to be understood. A fascinating paper by Harri Englund on Malawian Pentecostals argues that conflict and schisms among Pentecostals often occur because religious leaders keep for themselves the material and spiritual goods that outside sponsors potentially offer, so that others break away to try to establish a purer, uncorrupted tie to those external sources of value.[17] Thus local people at all levels, at least initially, inevitably regard an international organization as a potential source of money, goods or contacts that are otherwise unavailable.

Patron–client ties

The hope—even the distant hope—of material benefit is not all that accounts for the wide diffusion and the frequent success of forms of 'volunteer' organization in successful NGO projects. When international initiatives recruit influential local women to distribute condoms or to act as staff on a community health programme, they are tapping into another important form of local social organization, what I will refer to broadly as patron–client ties. Even in our own society, as Peter Blau noted long ago, being a person who can offer help to others, who then feel gratitude or consider themselves indebted to the helper, is at minimum a source of psychological gratification and status.[18] But village communities—not only in many parts of Africa, but in many other communities as well—are often organized around fundamental patterns of unequal interdependence.[19] Amy Kaler and Susan Watkins, in a study of community-based distributors (CBD) of birth control in rural Kenya, noted just such a pattern of patron–client ties among women volunteers and their clients. They note:

> In this context, CBD work is a means for women to earn respect and obligation from other people, where earning money is difficult. The GTZ/MOH CBD program may enable these women to attain a measure of power and respect by giving them new ways to take advantage of one of the few avenues open to women. International and national agendas and resources are thus being drawn into a local, historically rooted dynamic.[20]

The possibility of relationships of exchange or of interdependence among unequal partners may account for the ease with which international NGOs of many sorts establish working relationships with local communities. Interviews with staff in very different sorts of local NGOs suggest that these NGO workers found ways to ally themselves with members of the local community by becoming both patrons and clients of those they could help and who could help them. The director of the Zambian hospice arranged to enrol the families of the local police in the hospice's clinic, and the van they sent out to pick up patients who had fallen ill in the local villages often stayed to provide vaccinations and other medical services to village children. The hospice depended on a network of volunteers in the ten local villages and compounds in its catchment area, who looked out for those living at home with AIDS and notified the hospice when one of their patients needed acute care. The hospice carefully cultivated good relations with the chiefs and headmen of local villages and with the physician who also worked at the local hospital. A young Peace Corps volunteer in Côte d'Ivoire similarly depended on the cooperation and help of the head of the local men's organization (the Président des Jeunes) to help her initiate projects, and she was unable to advance AIDS-related projects until she won his assent. The volunteer working on an AIDS curriculum in Kenya was in a sense a client of the district commissioner, who allowed her organization to work in his district, and effectively a patron to the local superintendent of schools, for whom she provided AIDS-related curricular materials for his schools.

If the friendships and alliances that NGO staff, both country nationals and outsiders, form with local leaders and clients account for how NGO organizational models sometimes form a reasonable symbiosis with local patterns, the absence or failure of such processes may also help to explain cases where there appears to be a misfit or mismatch with local patterns of authority, influence or community.[21]

Bureaucratic controls

The example I described above of Malawi's plans for 'Monitoring and Evaluation' of its AIDS programs suggests something of the feel of centralized 'administration' of AIDS programming. But where the actual services are provided by a motley assortment of organizations, most of which have their own sources of funding, and their own schedules, priorities and local contacts, it is unlikely that bureaucratic administration will apply to more than the attempt to collect information in some—at least ostensibly—centralized place. Malawi's National AIDS Commission seems to have taken its role in 'monitoring' AIDS organizations seriously. It has produced a comprehensive list of all AIDS NGOs, faith-based organizations, community organizations and government AIDS projects, organized by district; and each year every organization is sent a form asking for an update on their programmes, numbers of people served, and so forth.[22] But the local branches of key NGOs like Save the Children, World Vision and PLAN (an international development organization focused on children) get much of their money from child sponsorship by individual donors who are moved to sponsor a child or a family. At the local World Vision office we visited, we were shown a picture on the wall of an American couple who had sponsored a major share of its programming. And in classical patron–client style, when the visiting foreigners—Germans, Dutch, Swedish, American—come, the local World Vision workers take them out to meet the families whom they have helped, to see the AIDS club perform a drama, or to watch a netball match.

It takes only a brief period on the ground in Malawi to run into groups of American church members who are travelling around the country looking for villages that need boreholes (deep wells) dug, a group of international students doing a summer AIDS project in a village, or Japanese engineers designing an irrigation project. And when we paid the obligatory visit to a local chief (the 'traditional authority' over more than a hundred villages), after initial civilities he asked us, the visiting researchers, whether we might help his people acquire fertilizer and seeds and whether we might have ARV drugs for the family members of one of his headmen. So bureaucracy at the top often monitors a bevy of independent actors on the ground. Paperwork may flow both to the national and international offices of the NGO and to the government, describing the number of programmes under way each month or each quarter, the number of youth involved or homes visited and so forth,[23] but the actual practices on the ground are closer to a patron–client arrangement in which what the clients provide their NGO patrons is evidence that the programme actually has participants, households, or needy children that it serves.

Indeed, in Malawi responsibility for implementing the complex new reporting system at the district level falls to five 'umbrella organizations'—ActionAID, World Vision, CPAR (Canadian Physicians for Aid and Relief), PLAN and Save the Children (USA)—each of which is responsible for data collection (and for the 'training of trainers' required to teach local organizations the forms of reporting required) in several of Malawi's 28 districts. These organizations are already skilled at turning in monthly, quarterly and annual reports enumerating numbers of children served, numbers attending programmes, numbers attending school, and so forth, by compiling reports duly submitted by their field personnel. But these personnel are rewarded for turning in the reports without much scrutiny from the home office staff. So in the long run, what these organizations really need to provide in order to survive are enough children; so that when the infrequent visitor comes, local relationships can be used to mobilize an acceptable number of children or adults to demonstrate that something is happening on the ground.[24]

Such an example demonstrates the real limitations of the institutional theorists' stress on 'isomorphism' in institutional form. Although each country is supposed to have a 'national AIDS commission', and they all employ a 'multi-sectoral approach', even to enact these formulas local actors do not so much 'resist' as discover that they must mobilize other actors who in turn have their own agendas and priorities.

Cultural match

In an important series of papers, Stephen Cornell and Joseph Kalt have explored the causes and consequences of effective governance among American Indian groups.[25] They suggest that the degree of 'cultural match' between original forms of governance and current forms best explains why some groups are well governed while others are not. The fragmentary data I have collected so far do not equip me to test such arguments. Indeed, the variety of African cultural groups and the diversity of forms of traditional governance, as well as the upheavals of colonial experience, would make any direct effort to 'match' contemporary forms of NGO governance with traditional forms a chimera.

Nonetheless, I want to suggest that at least thinking about 'cultural match' may help us understand some of the paradoxes and frustration of current global AIDS campaigns. First I want to return to a problem I have discussed elsewhere: Uganda's success in AIDS prevention, despite a history of dictatorship and civil war and its relative poverty, in contrast to Botswana's stunning failure to lower the highest HIV prevalence in the world, despite its administrative competence and integrity, its stable democracy and its relative wealth.[26] At the most superficial level one might say that Uganda's situation was so desperate that when Yoweri Museveni came to power as president in 1986 and recognized the threat AIDS posed he had no choice but to mobilize his population and to welcome AIDS prevention efforts from every quarter, including international NGOs, local churches and community organizations of all sorts. Botswana, in contrast, followed international advice with its usual care, but has been highly resistant to organizations operating independently of government. Indeed, it has followed the 'good government' principles that brought it peace, prosperity and stability, such as limiting the growth of government spending,[27] even when these have frustrated outsiders who see AIDS as an overriding emergency.

We can also think about the contrast between Botswana and Uganda at a deeper level, however. In very interesting work unrelated to Uganda's AIDS fight, Mikael Karlström has argued that the National Revolutionary Movement, the political party that was formed during Uganda's civil war and has ruled the country since 1986, has deep cultural resonances with traditional Buganda political forms, so that Uganda's one-party 'democracy', with election of the best individual but no party competition, is understood in the rural areas as being 'the same' as the civility, clan loyalty and rule by responsive chiefs that are considered the Buganda political legacy.[28] In the Buganda areas Museveni has brought back the chiefs (who fled into exile under Idi Amin and Milton Obote) to provide local rule and enhanced political legitimacy.

In a similar way, Botswana's extraordinary democracy and political stability are attributable in part to the continuity in its political culture and its forms of political leadership.[29] It has a bicameral legislature with an elected Congress and a House of Chiefs made up of the hereditary chiefs of the eight main Tswana tribes. Its democratic traditions derive in part from the traditional role of the chief or *kgosi* and the village council or *kgotla*.[30] Before independence, Botswana managed to avoid colonization by British settlers, and its traditional political forms were little disrupted by the benign indifference of a nominal British protectorate. Its first president, Sir Seretse Khama, was simultaneously an Oxford-educated national hero, the paramount chief of a major Tswana tribe and the grandson of King Khama III, whose diplomacy had preserved his nation's 'autonomy from white-settler rule'.[31] But Botswana's democratic stability is also directly linked to its heavy reliance on a centralized bureaucracy for policy decisions.[32]

Botswana's political system thus also seems to have a 'cultural match' between traditional and contemporary political culture and institutions. But this is not a system that encourages NGOs. Indeed, the effectiveness of government and prestige of the civil service make outspoken demands from below seem like threats to stability. And this lack of a robust non-governmental sector of local NGOs and community organizations may explain why Botswana has failed so completely in its AIDS prevention efforts, despite ample outside funding and a strong commitment to AIDS education and treatment on the part of government.

Current developments in Botswana offer a fascinating suggestion of the importance of cultural match. To summarize a complex story, Botswana's advantages of small population, excellent public health infrastructure and political stability made it an ideal place to roll out a radically ambitious project to give free ARV drugs to everyone who could benefit. Backed by $100 million from the Gates and Merck foundations, and with additional contributions of money, lab facilities, drugs and technical expertise from Bristol-Meyers Squibb, Harvard and Baylor College of Medicine, among others, ACHAP began in 2000.[33] Reports from the first three years of this programme were disconcertingly disappointing. ACHAP enrolled only a fraction of the patients anticipated, and it appeared that the combination of bureaucratic inertia, 'stigma' that kept Batswana from coming forward for treatment, and the inability of ACHAP's international staff to relate to the local population was leading an ambitious and much-heralded experiment to a dismal conclusion.[34] But Botswana has had something of a breakthrough. In January 2004 Botswana began making HIV testing 'routine', rather than following the American-promoted VCT approach (voluntary counselling and testing): 'Instead of simply offering H.I.V. tests to those who sought them, [Botswana's president, Festus Mogae] ordered routine tests of everyone who came into a hospital or clinic, unless the patient objected.'[35] This routinization, unlike all the government's and private foundations' earlier efforts to reduce stigma, seems to have changed the entire dynamic of AIDS testing and treatment. The numbers in treatment have started to soar, and the sense of stigma and isolation seems to be dissipating.[36] So Botswana, which has not been able to respond adequately to AIDS through the models promoted by the international NGO ideology—informed individual choice, human rights, participation and VCT—has found a very 'Botswanan' way to meet the epidemic.

Power, money and identity

The NGO presence in Africa can reasonably be seen, for good or ill, as the latest successor of earlier colonial penetrations. The enormous disparity in wealth and power between the donor countries and African recipients, compounded by the frightening, often overwhelming, aspects of the AIDS pandemic, make NGOs certain that their procedures and policies are right, that the crisis is urgent, and that resistance to their programmes is madness or malice.

On the whole, I share the view of the urgency of the crisis, despite awareness that many of those dying of AIDS might otherwise die of malaria or tuberculosis—or indeed cancer or heart disease—and that if AIDS were suddenly to disappear many if not most Africans would once again find themselves of little interest and no 'value' to the wider world. Indeed, the cynic in me thinks that AIDS philanthropy, AIDS research and what might be called AIDS tourism have become Africa's most successful 'export' and certainly a major source of foreign exchange.

Earlier European interventions in Africa, both the well- and the ill-intentioned, would not suggest optimism about the current round. Much of the institutional legacy that Europe sought to impose or bequeath was from the beginning a kind of catch-22. Jeffrey Herbst has argued that the European state form never fit African circumstances.[37] But before Africans had the possibility of forming modern states, they had already been pillaged, their populations displaced, and their indigenous political institutions ravaged. For most of the twentieth century, when the West paid attention to Africa at all, it was to prop up leaders who were responsive to their external sponsors rather than to their own people, or to undermine or destroy African political formations that did not serve the interests of western powers.[38]

The current moment is unusual only because the AIDS crisis has focused the world's attention on Africa. I would argue that for AIDS, as for every other form of participation in the modern world, effective governance is probably the fundamental precursor to all other forms of progress.[39] But governance cannot be directly imported. All the external pressure—for 'transparency', 'democracy', 'human rights' and other goods valued in the global arena—has accomplished very little. And indeed, that pressure, which is aimed at fostering stronger, more capable states that could advance and protect their citizens, is constantly undermined by the aspiration of western capital for prostrate states that leave their markets unprotected.

This is a period of the reconfiguration of power and politics at the global level. While 'nation-building' may be a bitter joke, there is massive institutional and cultural reconfiguration afoot at the global level in which Africa and Africans may yet be able to play new roles. In part, the very variety of forms of contact and connection between global actors and local systems makes traditional nation-state politics more difficult but creates more degrees of freedom for actors at other levels of the system. In such a world it is possible for institutional forms that make local sense—like the patron–client ties that sometimes indigenize what start as foreign-inspired NGOs, or policy inventions like Botswana's routine AIDS testing—to emerge and thrive, not in spite of the inequalities of power and resources that separate Africans and the West, but at the intersection where institutional and cultural forms meet, sometimes taking syncretic forms that come to have a vibrant life of their own.

Notes

* I would like to thank Gabe Chodorow-Reich, Sarah Gilman, Keyvan Kashkooli, Kate Krontiris and Rachel Sullivan for valuable research assistance. I am also grateful to the Canadian Institute for Advanced Research, the Malawi Diffusion and Ideational Change Project (MDICP), and the University of California at Berkeley's Committee on Research, Center for African Studies, and Center for Health Research for supporting this research. An earlier version of this paper was presented at Annual Meetings of the American Sociological Association, San Francisco, 14–17 Aug. 2004.

1 Stephen Cornell and Joseph P. Kalt, 'Where's the glue? Institutional and cultural foundations of American Indian economic development', *Journal of Socio-Economics* 29, 2000, pp. 443–70; Ann Swidler, 'Out of our minds: where cognition and culture intersect', paper prepared for Sociology of Culture Mini-Conference session on 'Culture and cognition', George Mason University, 2000; Ann Swidler, *Talk of love: how culture matters* (Chicago: University of Chicago Press, 2001).

2 Thomas M. Callaghy, Ronald Kassimir, et al., eds. *Intervention and transnationalism in Africa: global–local networks of power* (Cambridge: Cambridge University Press, 2001).

3 Jeffrey Herbst, *States and power in Africa: comparative lessons in authority and control* (Princeton, NJ: Princeton University Press, 2000); Jean François Bayart, *The state in Africa: the politics of the belly* (New York: Longmans, 1993).

4 See e.g. Sanjeev Khagram, James V. Riker, et al. eds, *Restructuring world politics: transnational social movements, networks and norms* (Minneapolis: University of Minnesota Press, 2002); Erica Bornstein, *The spirit of development: Protestant NGOs, morality, and economics in Zimbabwe* (New York: Routledge, 2003).

5 Callaghy and Kassimir, *Intervention and transnationalism in Africa.*

6 Malawi National AIDS Commission, 'Technical support for operationalisation of Malawi's M&E system: end of mission report' (Lilongwe, 2004).

7 The report's author, a 'Member of M&E Country Support Team, The World Bank Global HIV/AIDS Program', describes the genesis of the report as follows:

> One of the priorities for the Malawi National AIDS Commission and its partners has been the set up of an HIV/AIDS monitoring and evaluation system. The need for this M&E system was not only driven by external demand from pool donors and the GFATM, but also by internal demand within NAC to drive the establishment of a system through which the NAC can track the progress made with Malawi's response to HIV/AIDS, within a multisectoral context.

8 Michael Grunwald, 'A small nation's big effort against AIDS: Botswana spreads message and tree drugs, but old attitudes persist', *Washington Post*, p. A1, 2 Dec. 2002.

9 Paul J. DiMaggio and Walter W. Powell, 'The iron cage revisited: institutional isomorphism and collective rationality in organization fields', *American Sociological Review* 48, 1983, pp. 147–60.

10 John Boli and George M. Thomas, 'The world polity under construction: a century of international non-governmental organizing', *American Sociological Review* 62, April 1997, pp. 171–90; John Boli and George M. Thomas, eds, *Constructing*

world culture: international nongovernmental organizations since 1875 (Stanford, CA: Stanford University Press, 1999).

11 Peter Evans, *Embedded autonomy: states and industrial transformation* (Princeton, NJ: Princeton University Press, 1995); Doug Guthrie, *Dragon in a three-piece suit: the emergence of capitalism in China* (Princeton, NJ: Princeton University Press, 1999); Neil Fligstein, *The architecture of markets: an economic sociology of twenty-first century capitalist societies* (Princeton, NJ: Princeton University Press, 2001).

12 Kathleen Thelen, in an important new book, *How institutions evolve: the political economy of skills in Germany, Britain, the United States and Japan* (Cambridge: Cambridge University Press, 2004), explores how an institutional complex—in this case, the institutions of skill formation in industrial democracies—can change over time as political conflict and the clash of interest groups either graft 'new elements onto an otherwise stable institutional framework' (p. 35) or 'convert' the institution when 'the adoption of new goals or the incorporation of new groups into the coalitions on which institutions are founded can drive a change in the functions these institutions serve or the roles they perform' (p. 36). This may mean that an institution's current 'functions' have little or nothing to do with its origins. Thelen's model also suggests that institutions become more established and robust as new groups invest them with their own interests and purposes. In this sense contestation might lead to more stability as institutions recruit new participants. Joel Migdal's work on weak states (Joel S. Migdal, *State in society: studying how states and societies transform and constitute one another* (Cambridge: Cambridge University Press, 2001)) describes the opposite dynamic, in which state institutions never become effective enough to persuade important groups to invest the state with their core interests, so state institutions never become robust.

13 The importance of petty trading should not be confused with 'market relations' more generally. The sale of labour as a commodity usually originated in coercive systems of labour control and the often brutal efforts of colonial powers to impose wage labour under the most unequal conditions, from slavery and direct coercion to the imposition of the head tax and migrant labour systems meant to force workers into the cash economy.

14 Ann Swidler, 'The politics of AIDS in sub-Saharan Africa', paper presented at the American Sociological Association Annual Meeting, Atlanta, GA, August, 2003. The idea that collective moral mobilization may be more important for successful AIDS prevention than particular prevention programmes is sobering. If the whole A, B or C debate is a distraction from the real issue, then public health experts don't know what formula or technique to promote, what to fund, or even how to generate useful research. The fascinating study by Catherine Campbell, *'Letting them die': why HIV/AIDS prevention programmes fail* (Bloomington, IN: Indiana University Press, 2003) of the failure of a 'gold standard' South African project that was supposed to generate stakeholder commitment and community buy-in is a chilling reminder of how little we understand why some forms of collective action—in Uganda, and to a lesser degree in Zambia and regions of Tanzania—succeeded when so many AIDS-prevention efforts have had no apparent effect on AIDS prevalence (see Edward C. Green, *Rethinking AIDS prevention learning from successes in developing countries*, Westport, CN: Praeger, 2003; Norman Hearst and Sanny Chen, 'Condoms for AIDS prevention in the developing world: is it working?'. *Studies in Family Planning* 35: 1, March 2004, pp. 39–47).

15 Daniel Jordan Smith, 'Patronage, per diems and "the workshop mentality": the practice of family planning programs in southeastern Nigeria', *World Development* 31: 4, 2003, pp. 703–15.

16 Bayart, *The state in Africa*; Jean François Bayart, 'Africa in the world: a history of extraversion', *African Affairs* 99: 200, pp. 217–67.
17 Harri Englund, 'Christian independency and global membership: Pentecostal extraversions in Malawi', *Journal of Religion in Africa* 33: 1, 2003, pp. 83–111.
18 Peter M. Blau, *Exchange and power in social life* (New York: John Wiley, 1964).
19 S. N. Eisenstadt and L. Roniger, *Patrons, clients, and friends: interpersonal relations and the structure of trust in society* (New York: Cambridge University Press, 1984); Sandra T. Barnes, *Patrons and power: creating a political community in metropolitan Lagos* (Manchester: Manchester University Press, 1986); Luis Roniger, *Hierarchy and trust in modern Mexico and Brazil* (New York: Praeger, 1990).
20 Amy Kaler and Susan Cotts Watkins, 'Disobedient distributors: street-level bureaucrats and would-be patrons in community-based family planning programs in rural Kenya', *Studies in Family Planning* 32: 3, September 2001, p. 261.
21 One additional issue makes it difficult for Americans and Europeans to think fruitfully about the importance of patron–client ties in Third World settings. We tend to think of love and money as opposites, and to cast 'genuine' relationships as those that are free of self-interest (see Jane Fishburne Collier, *From duty to desire: remaking families in a Spanish village*, Princeton, NJ: Princeton University Press, 1997), but we know that for most societies throughout most of human history, ties of personal dependence combined deep emotional connection with economic, social and personal dependence (Max Weber, *Economy and society: an outline of interpretive sociology*, Berkeley, CA: University of California Press, 1968; Marc Bloch, *Feudal society*, Chicago: University of Chicago Press, 1961).
22 National AIDS Commission, 'Organizations working with AIDS in Malawi: 2003 update', Lilongwe, Malawi, 2003.
23 In a recent article, Helen Epstein ('The lost children of AIDS', *New York Review of Books* 52, 2005, pp. 41–6) shows how internationally funded projects can try to beef up the reported numbers of 'Orphans and Vulnerable Children' helped, while failing to provide actual funding or services.
24 Malawi National AIDS Commission, 'Technical support for operationalisation of Malawi's M&E system: end of mission report'.
25 Cornell and Kalt, 'Where's the glue?'; Stephen Cornell, Joseph P. Kalt et al., *Seizing the future: why some native nations do and others don't* (Cambridge, MA: Harvard Project on American Indian Economic Development, 2003).
26 Swidler, 'The politics of AIDS in sub-Saharan Africa'.
27 J. Clark Leith, *Why Botswana prospered: behind the success of Africa's sole economically prosperous democracy* (Montreal and Kingston, ON: McGill-Queen's University Press, 2005); Daron Acemoglu, Simon Johnson and James A. Robinson, 'An African success story: Botswana', in Dan Rodrik, ed., *In search of prosperity: analytical narratives on economic growth* (Princeton, NJ: Princeton University Press, 2003).
28 Mikael Karlström, 'Imagining democracy: the political culture and democratisation in Buganda', *Africa* 66: 4, 1996, pp. 485–506: Mikael Karlström, 'Civil society and its presuppositions: lessons from Uganda', in J. L. Comaroff, ed., *Civil society and the political imagination in Africa: critical perspectives* (Chicago: University of Chicago Press, 1999), pp. 104–23.
29 John Holm and Patrick Molutsi, eds, *Democracy in Botswana* (Athens, Ohio: Botswana Society, University of Botswana, Ohio University Press, 1989).
30 Holm and Molutsi, *Democracy in Botswana*.
31 Neil Parsons, *King Khama, Emperor Joe, and the great white queen: Victorian Britain through African eyes* (Chicago: University of Chicago Press, 1998).

32 Mpho G. Molomo, 'The bureaucracy and democracy in Botswana', pp. 237–43 in Holm and Molutsi, *Democracy in Botswana*; P. P. Molutsi, 'The ruling class and democracy in Botswana', pp. 103–15 in Holm and Molutsi, *Democracy in Botswana*.

33 Banu Khan, 'Perspective from a public–private partnership: the Botswana comprehensive HIV/AIDS partnerships', presentation to Global Alliance for Women's Health in partnership with Merck and Co., Inc., New York, 25 June 2001; Julian Meldrum, 'Scaling up antiretroviral therapy: learning from Botswana', aidsmap. com news, NAM publications, 9 July 2002.

34 Michael Grunwald, 'A small nation's big effort against AIDS: Botswana spreads message and free drugs, but old attitudes persist', *Washington Post*, 2 Dec. 2002, p. A1; John Donnelly, 'A battle line in Botswana AIDS fight', *Boston Globe*, 24 Oct. 2003, p. A8; John Donnelly, 'Reluctance to face tests slows Botswana AIDS fight', *Boston Globe*, 8 Nov. 2003; Sello Motseta, 'Stigma hampers effort to get free AIDS drugs to infected in Botswana', 1 June 2003, *Associated Press*; National AIDS Coordinating Agency (NACA), 'Botswana 2003 second generation HIV/AIDS surveillance: a technical report', Dec. 2003, Gaborone, Botswana.

35 Sharon LaFraniere, 'Mandatory testing bolsters Botswana in combating AIDS', *New York Times*, 14 June 2004.

36 Alaistair Leithead, 'Hope out of pain: Botswana's AIDS story', BBC News World Edition, 13 July 2004.

37 Jeffrey Herbst, 'Responding to state failure in Africa', *International Security* 21: 3, 1996–7, pp. 120–44.

38 Mahmood Mamdani, *Citizen and subject: contemporary Africa and the legacy of late colonialism* (Princeton, NJ: Princeton University Press, 1996).

39 Peter Evans, *Embedded autonomy: states and industrial transformation* (Princeton, NJ: Princeton University Press, 1995); Peter Evans, ed., *State–society synergy: government action and social capital in development* (Berkeley, CA: University of California, International and Area Studies Publications, 1997); Peter Evans, 'The eclipse of the state? Reflections on stateness in an era of globalization', *World Politics* 50, Oct. 1997, pp. 62–87.

Part 6

SARS

33

HUMAN SECURITY AND PUBLIC HEALTH IN SOUTHEAST ASIA

The SARS outbreak

Melissa Curley and Nicholas Thomas

Source: *Australian Journal of International Affairs*, 58:1 (2004), 17–32.

Severe acute respiratory syndrome (SARS) is now a global public health threat with many medical, ethical, social, economic, political, and legal implications.

(Abdullah et al. 2003)

No man is an island.

(John Donne)

The security of the state is dependent on the security of its individual citizens. If they are not secure, the state is not secure. Traditional, state-dominant, conceptions of security are ill-equipped to provide understanding into the array of security concerns that now confront nation-states. In November 2002, one of these new security concerns, a corona pulmonary virus jumped the species barrier to begin infecting people in southern China. Three months later this virus was unwittingly transmitted from mainland China to Hong Kong. From there it spread rapidly throughout most of Southeast Asia as well as through parts of the Americas and Europe. Now known as the SARS—Severe Acute Respiratory Syndrome—virus, it became a major threat to the stability and prosperity of Southeast Asian countries. This article reviews the spread and impact of the SARS virus within Southeast Asia from a human security perspective. It is intended that the utilisation of human security in this instance will not only provide a better understanding of the impact of SARS on regional states but will also advance the conceptualisation of the human security model.

Introduction

The security of the state resides in the security of the individual. In recent years the security of East Asia has been threatened by a number of crises, which have had a region-wide impact. In November 2002, the latest crisis—Severe Acute Respiratory Syndrome (SARS)—broke out in southern China. Though it was thought contained, an index case travelled to Hong Kong where he unwittingly passed on the virus to nine others. From this small beginning a major threat to public health spread rapidly across Southeast Asia and throughout the world. Such crises represent a non-traditional threat to regional security. Drawing on the SARS virus as the case study, this article will seek to show how public health matters can cross national boundaries to threaten the security of neighbouring states.

This article begins by placing human security within the constellation of contemporary security studies, and then showing how major public health issues can, in some instances, evolve into security threats. A history of the outbreak of the SARS virus is briefly viewed, before exploring the impact the virus had in a number of Southeast Asian countries, as well as on the ASEAN group as a regional organisation. During this exploration, some of the key issues arising from the experiences in different Southeast Asian countries, as well as from the attempts of the ASEAN group, in addressing the threat of SARS will be examined. The final section of the article will be an analysis of the lessons learned from the outbreak and their utility in addressing other human security threats.

Human security and public health

After the Cold War, the contemporary debate in International Relations on security burgeoned to accommodate the diversification of what could be considered a 'threat' to state security. At the same time, it is true to say that the conceptual clarity of security within International Relations has atrophied in response to theoretical and methodology debates within the discipline that have questioned the utility of traditional concepts of security within realist and neo-realist constructions. This conceptual debate has been driven by the changing international environment, which presents a more fluid challenge to nation-states than was the case in the bipolar world order that characterised the Cold War period. Alternative sub-concepts of security—such as human security—have now emerged to accommodate and incorporate a variety of issues and processes considered outside of the 'traditional' framework.

Human security is a classically liberal concept, where a state's security rests on the premise that its citizens must be secure. Initially coming to prominence via the 1994 United Nations Development Report entitled *New Dimensions of Human Security*, (UNDP 1994) this concept was adopted by the IR community as a new mechanism for understanding security in the post-Cold War period; 'one that could cope with multidimensional threats that did not emanate from a state nor were necessarily directed against state interests but which nonetheless detracted from the security of a state' (Shannon & Thomas 2004). Human security concerns are therefore of interest to a wide range of actors, not only including states, but also international organisations, international non-governmental organisations (INGOs), domestic organisations, and the individual. Scholars and policy-makers have used the term to refer to the diverse array of issues that fall outside the purview of traditional military-centric security concerns.

However, the broad definitions used by the United Nations in the 1994 report created a problem for those seeking the theoretical clarity that had once been assumed during the Cold War era. It has been argued elsewhere that the transnational component of the human security concept offers a way of accruing 'greater analytical and policy value'. (Thomas & Tow 2002) To achieve this clarity requires acknowledgement of three factors, namely that (1) insecurity arises from 'inadequacies in internal state systems [that] make individuals and groups within [other] states more vulnerable'; (2) that affected states and individuals frequently cannot address these threats unilaterally; and (3) that because of this some form of international assistance or intervention is required (Thomas & Tow 2002: 178).

Thus, when evaluating an event as a human security threat it is necessary that the issue emerge from within a domestic setting before crossing national boundaries to negatively affect other states or associated groups or individuals. The nature of a human security threat is such that affected states do have the capacity to resolve them by themselves but need to rely, to varying extents, on other states, international organisations and/or individuals. This is especially the case when threats become non-linear—'where causes and effects beyond the immediate area of the threat must be considered' (Thomas & Tow: 179).

Within East Asia, national security interests are still dominated by traditional security concerns of sovereignty and territoriality, governed by the belief in a structured order of states in the international system. Within Southeast Asia this system is, if anything, even stronger. The 'ASEAN Way' assiduously promotes non-interference and consensual decision-making as core principles of state behaviour; making attempts to resolve transnational human security threats difficult and regional responses to such threats from ASEAN problematic. However, in the last five years, there has been a growing recognition among the Southeast Asian countries that non-traditional security issues did threaten the stability and prosperity of the region. Despite this, because of its liberalist origins, few regional countries have been willing to shift to human security modelling of current or future threats.[1] Nevertheless, public health concerns such as HIV/AIDS or, most recently, Severe Acute Respiratory Syndrome (SARS) have forced states to go beyond such conceptions to consider human security responses to incipient or potential threats.

The recognition that health issues are vitally important to the human security of individuals and the security interests of states is not new. Pirages and Runci commented that,

> Viruses, bacteria, and various kinds of plants and animals have never respected national borders. They have travelled across frontiers with the winds, waters, explorers, merchants, and mercenaries. Most of the time these crossings have been quite innocent, but occasionally whole societies or ecosystems have been reshaped by them. Now there is growing concern over the impact of increasing globalisation on the potential development and spread of new and resurgent diseases across increasingly porous borders.
>
> (Pirages & Runci 2000: 176)

This comment is supported by Cusimano, who concluded that 'while open society, open economy, and open technology forces can help contribute resources to combat the spread of infectious disease, these dynamics also create an infrastructure that allows and encourages diseases to spread' (Cusimano 2000: 174).

In other areas of the health-security nexus, scholars and international organisations such as the World Health Organisation (WHO) have identified health and well-being as an important causal variable in conflict situations. One example of this is the Program on Human Security at Harvard University's Centre for Basic Research in the Social Sciences that has explored causal relationships between public health and conflict, in particular how various types of conflict (intra-state, ethnic, civil war) and their duration impact on the public health of civilian populations (Program on Human Security n.d.).

The twinned questions that then arise are how and why health issues develop into human security threats? The answer to the first question is complex and relates to the specific disease or virus being investigated. In broad terms, SARS, although still not yet finally confirmed, appears to be a crossover virus; one that normally resides in the civet cat (Peiris *et al.* 2003; Drosten *et al.* 2003; Günther *et al.* 2003). The civet cat is also a Southern Chinese delicacy. At some point in recent times the virus jumped the species divide, probably during the harvesting or consumption of the cats. (This is not the first lethal cross-over virus that the area has experienced. A strain of avian influenza, H5N1, has appeared several times in the last decade). Once the civet cats were identified as the most likely source of the SARS virus they were pulled from local menus. However, as the incidence of SARS declined, the Chinese authorities have again allowed the cat back on provincial tables. That decision, when coupled with wintry and unhygienic conditions, may yet see a return of the virus.

The second question can be ultimately answered as a failure—at some level or levels—of the host nation-state, which if left unchecked, can spillover into other states. Colebatch and Larmour identify three sectors where such failures can occur: the bureaucracy, the market, or the community (Colebatch & Larmour 1993: 28–39). Bureaucratic failure occurs when time constraints and information requirements do not meet the needs of a particular case. This may be compounded by conflicting requirements between the central authorities and those implementing the policies at 'street level'. This failure may also come up when different organisational units have conflicting goals (Colebatch & Larmour 1993: 33–34). Market failure occurs when an information gap is present or when externalities are generated. It can also fail when the goods (in this case public health) are controlled by a narrower group of people than those immediately threatened (Colebatch & Larmour 1993: 29–33). Community failure can transpire when individuals' overlapping needs and identities cause them to all not 'pull in the same direction', destabilising the nation-state (Colebatch & Larmour 1993: 35).

Thus, when considering where threats emerge to challenge state security, and given that it is 'inadequacies in internal state systems' that create vulnerabilities, this approach provides a model from which the origins of human security threat could be ascertained. Further, in a transnational setting, the identification of a threat emanating from a failed sector could assist in the identification of sectors most at risk in other states. Colebatch and Larmour conclude that for a resolution not to be a failure it generally requires a mix of at least two other sectors, if not in addition to the remaining capacity from the failed sector. In other words, a market failure could require the combined resources of the bureaucratic and community sectors, and may even require market resources from other parts of the sector, to be successfully overcome.

To test this model with the human security concept we will examine the domestic impact of the virus in the most affected Southeast countries before exploring the effectiveness of the organisational response at the regional level. After analysing the events and issues surrounding the SARS outbreak in Southeast Asia, the key lessons learned from this event will be reviewed. First, however, it is important to understand the manner by which the virus spread.

An overview of the outbreak

The first known SARS case was detected in mid-November 2002 in Foshan city, Guangdong province, China. However the World Health Organisation (WHO) only received a report from the Chinese authorities on 11 February 2003 stating that there had been an outbreak of atypical pneumonia in the province that had affected 305 persons and resulted in five deaths (Communicable Disease Surveillance and Response (CDSR 2003)). The WHO was officially made aware of the existence of a severe form of atypical pneumonia with no known cause on 28 February 2003 when Dr Carlo Urbani alerted the WHO regional offices following the review of an American patient in the French Hospital who had contracted the virus (CDSR 2003).

The main SARS infection left mainland China via 65-year-old Dr Liu Jianlun from Guangdong province, who came to Hong Kong after treating SARS patients. He checked in to a room on the 9th floor of the Metropole Hotel, and subsequently infected other people staying on the floor. In returning to their home countries this group became the new index cases, spreading the disease to Singapore, Canada and Vietnam, as well as other parts of Hong Kong. Further outbreaks of the SARS virus occurred in Southeast Asia, in the Philippines, Malaysia and Thailand; though no local transmission of the disease was ever confirmed in Thailand.

On 12 March 2003, after the WHO had assessed the situation in Asia a global health alert was issued regarding 'cases of severe atypical pneumonia with unknown etiology that appeared to place health workers at high risk' (CDSR 2003). This was raised on 15 March 2003 to a rare emergency advisory. As the situation worsened, the WHO recommended that all non-essential travel to Hong Kong and Guangdong province be postponed.

Meanwhile, the virus spread outside the region, to Europe and the United States, by infected air travellers. Following the WHO's global alert, countries started to take a range of precautions against the further spread of SARS. These measures included the temporary banning of flights from 'hot zones' (those areas most infected); temporarily stopping the issuance of visas to persons from these zones; health and temperature checks; and quarantining persons from infected countries for 10 days.

On 20 April China finally admitted to the spread of SARS from Guangdong to Beijing, with hundreds of cases as yet unreported. Although the Chinese Health Minister, Zhang Wenkang, and the Mayor of Beijing, Meng Xuenong, were both sacked for their lapse, this move was seen proverbially as 'scaring the chickens to catch the monkey'; a Chinese idiom meaning 'to create a fuss to deflect blame from those more senior in power'. This action came two-and-half weeks after WHO officials were allowed access to the main infectious sites in southern China (3 April), and nearly a month after the WHO made the preliminary identification of the index case coming from Foshan city in Guangdong province (28 March).[2] China's silence as to its knowledge of SARS can be seen as the major causes of its rapid spread and deadly effect.

On 28 April, Vietnam became the first country to be declared SARS-free. By mid-2003 all countries had either been declared free of the SARS virus or were finalising their quarantine period. An isolated infection occurred in Singapore in September 2003, arising from a breach of laboratory safety protocols. Although limited to a single individual, who later recovered, of most concern was that this infection did not exhibit all the SARS symptoms. Should the virus reoccur, its mutable nature could possibly make detection more problematic.

Incidence of SARS: country and regional case studies

In reviewing the Southeast countries affected by the SARS outbreak, Singapore and Vietnam stand out as the most severely threatened states. Other regional states such as Malaysia, the Philippines, or Thailand were also affected, but to a much lesser extent. Of those others that were affected, Thailand provides a good example of the negative impact popular opinion can have in a crisis situation. As was the case with the Asian Financial Crisis in 1997–98, similar problems in a number of Southeast Asian countries created the impression that SARS was a regional issue, one where ASEAN should play a role.

Vietnam

Vietnam was the first Southeast Asian country to deal with the SARS epidemic in late February, and the first country in the world to contain the highly contagious disease. At the same time as Dr Urbani alerted the WHO to the existence of the atypical pneumonia he met with officials from the Vietnamese Ministry of Health and proposed strict quarantine measures (Savioli 2003). In addition to the quarantine measures, the Vietnamese government also established a cross-ministerial committee to monitor and respond to any developments. It was this rapid response that limited the spread of the virus, both in Vietnam as well as internationally. However, despite these efforts, by the time the outbreak was finished Vietnam had registered 63 SARS cases, including five fatalities (*Vietnam News Briefs* 2003–21 October).

As was the case with other countries affected by the outbreak, the impact of SARS quickly moved beyond a health issue, to become a political and economic threat as well as major foreign policy challenge. In addition to the health protocols enforced at the French Hospital in Hanoi, the Vietnamese government moved quickly with a public information campaign. While official sources claimed that this campaign had reduced public concerns, regional press reported that Hanoi residents were being discriminated against, while ethnic Chinese tourists were being shunned (*Vietnam News Briefs* 2003–22 April). In fact, once China was identified as the index country, additional troops were placed on the border to prevent the unchecked entry of any infected Chinese persons (*Channel News Asia* 2003).

Economically, no sector of Vietnam's economy was left unscathed by the virus, with hospitality and tourism-related operations the most affected. Since the first case of SARS was discovered in Hanoi in late February, the country's tourism and air travel sectors have been badly affected. Vietnam's economic loss was estimated to be in excess of US$220 million, which was compounded by an estimated 120,750 redundancies. In GDP terms this meant that SARS cut 1.1 percent from Vietnam's economic growth in 2003 (*Vietnam News Briefs* 2003–21 October).

The main lesson that can be drawn from the Vietnamese experience with SARS is that hospital staff need to be trained to make informed decisions, and have the authority to act on them in a preventative manner. Further, it is essential that hospitals have good lines of communication with relevant health ministries, and are not afraid to issue alerts when required. Finally, the decision by the Vietnamese government to create an inter-ministerial committee capable of coordinating policy responses across different sectors was a key tool in the government's fight against SARS.

Singapore

The SARS outbreak in Singapore presented the government with a major social, economic and political challenge, at a time when the country was distracted by other economic and security issues. In reviewing the SARS outbreak in Singapore a number of important issues stand out. First, Singapore's location as a major regional transport hub makes it particularly exposed for rapidly transmitted, human-borne diseases. At a practical level, there is little the local authorities can do to prevent further viral outbreaks. Despite this exposure, Singapore dealt with a major medical crisis and managed to avoid the travel sanctions imposed on other affected areas, thereby partly protecting the economy; though many travellers simply stayed away. It should be acknowledged that Singapore was in a better position than either Vietnam or Hong Kong in that there was a transmission lag between the severity of the virus being realised and SARS arriving in Singapore. That caveat aside, the Singaporean government was quick to implement political, medical, economic and public relations strategies to counter the virus.

Even with the time lag, the first three SARS cases were confirmed on 13 March, all of whom had stayed in the Metropole Hotel. Less than two weeks later the first death had been recorded and the government was forced to close all schools and issue quarantine orders for 740 people, amid rising public concern. In late March, the Singaporean Health Ministry invoked the Infectious Diseases Act (IDA) to isolate everyone known to have been in contact with anyone who had fallen sick with SARS. This was quickly followed by the Home Affairs Minister, Wong Kan Seng, heading a ministerial-rank task force to deal with all aspects of the SARS outbreak. As with Vietnam, the power delegated to the cross-ministerial committee to decide policies that cut across individual departments was an important factor in helping Singapore stem the SARS outbreak. In addition to the public policy and quarantine programs, in late April the government also began restricting the movements of health workers, during office hours as well as at home.

In terms of medical responses, the government moved swiftly to designate hospitals for quarantine, and to disseminate guidelines to private doctors and clinics on how to handle suspected SARS cases. At the height of the outbreak it went further, creating barriers against cross-hospital transmission by requiring hospital staff to reside only with other staff from the same hospital. However, it is unclear how effective this policy was, as it was slow to be implemented and the virus was largely contained by the time it was being properly enacted.

In an effort to address the economic impact of the SARS virus, in April the Singapore government unveiled a S$230 million rescue package for those sectors most affected; namely tourism and the transport-related industries. Of the S$230 million, S$155 million was used to help tourism-related businesses like hotels, travel agents, retailers and restaurants—with almost S$74 million set aside for airlines, cruise operators and taxi drivers, who saw fewer passengers. The Singapore Tourism Board (STB) also announced a short-term financing programme for local SMEs in SARS-affected tourism-related sectors. Domestic reaction to the SARS outbreak was calm, relative to public sentiment witnessed in mainland China or Hong Kong. To a large extent this was due to two factors: (1) the public control of the outbreak agenda by the government, and (2) the close relationship between the local media and the government, which allowed the government to direct the information flow. There were a number of instances where members of the local population did not heed the numerous warnings and advice regarding appropriate SARS behaviour. Such breaches were dealt with increasing severity as the crisis unfolded. Outside these two factors, the government also engaged social organisations, in the dissemination of information and home detection kits (Hooi 2003b), and the private sector, in the daily testing of employees (Hooi 2003a).

In sum, Singapore's responses were aided, from the bottom up, by highly effective channels of communication between frontline medical staff, hospital management, and health officials. In turn, the rapid creation of a ministerial-level committee to provide oversight for all SARS-related government activities, on a daily basis, ensured that top-down management of the crisis across all political, economic and social sectors was efficiently implemented. This whole-society approach was more necessary in Singapore than in Vietnam because the geographical area was much smaller, allowing the virus easier access to all areas of the country. The higher threat to Singapore from SARS is reflected in the final toll, 33 people dead from the virus out of 238 infections. (Ling Chang Hong 2003).

Thailand

Thailand is a good example of how the perception of a threat can—in some instances—be as damaging as the threat itself. During the regional outbreak of SARS, Thailand reported only eight cases, with two reported deaths and no domestic transmission of the disease. Thai Prime Minister Thaksin was, from the outset, acutely aware of the potential damage the outbreak of SARS could do to the Thai economy. As the crisis unfolded, Thaksin made much effort to promote Thailand as a 'SARS zero-transmission country' in an attempt to limit the damage to the tourism industry and the wider economy.

The most obvious impact of SARS virus on the Thai economy was a downturn in tourist arrivals, flowing into the retail sales and hotel/entertainment sectors of the economy. Despite the fact that Thailand was not as severely affected by the virus, its tourism industry nevertheless suffered considerably by regional association. March tourist arrivals declined by 12.5 percent year-on-year, April by 46 percent, while the number of arrivals to late May was down by nearly 55 percent. As a result, the government launched a range of measures to reinvigorate the tourism sector, focusing on promoting Thailand as a 'SARS Free' destination. While these measures included the standard hotel and airfare discounts, and subsidised holiday packages, it also included the more controversial program to offer US$100,000 in compensation to any foreign tourist who was infected with SARS in Thailand and subsequently died (*Financial Times Information* 2003).

Thailand's understanding of the regional nature of the crisis pushed it to call for regional responses to the crisis. Thailand was very active in pushing other ASEAN members to approach the threat from a regional perspective, with the accompanying recognition that the region was now increasingly interconnected in sectors beyond economics, trade or politics.

Regional responses

Regional responses to the SARS outbreak were not as rapid as those taken by individual Southeast Asian countries. While both ASEAN and, to a lesser extent, APEC attempted to develop coordinated multilateral strategies to address the threat posed by the SARS virus, two issues emerge. First, at least with this particular crisis, states were the main agents of prevention and response. Second, stemming from this, both regional organisations were very passive actors, unable to enforce a collective will on states that did not agree with the policies under discussion.

The ASEAN + 3 (ASEAN plus China, Japan and South Korea) Ministers of Health Special Meeting on SARS was held in Kuala Lumpur on 26 April. The ministerial meeting agreed that a comprehensive cross-border approach was required to contain and prevent the spread of the disease but that such measures should take the form of 'isolate and contain' strategies rather than blanket bans. The ministers also agreed to: (a) request the ASEAN Expert Group on Communicable Diseases (under the ASEAN Senior Officials Meeting on Health Development), in collaboration with their counterparts from China, Japan and South Korea, to develop a work plan for regional cooperation as well as evaluating the setting up of an ASEAN centre of excellence for disease control; (b) request Indonesia, as coordinator of the ASEAN Disease Surveillance Net, to look into using the Web to support the exchange of information among the ASEAN + 3 Countries; (c) request Thailand, as the coordinator of the ASEAN Epidemiologic Network to strengthen regional capacity for epidemiological surveillance; and (d) request Malaysia to implement the ASEAN project on Strengthening Laboratory Capacity and Quality Assurance for Disease Surveillance (*New Straits Times* 2003a). While critics of ASEAN often deride its meetings as little more than talk shops, the difference with this meeting was that it was focused on practical outcomes rather than a reiteration of regional ambitions.

The Special ASEAN Leaders' Meeting on SARS on 29 April 2003, initiated by Singapore, was the first such meeting since the group's creation. The Heads of ASEAN states and the leaders of the + 3 countries, as well as Hong Kong, met to exchange information and approve initiatives drawn up earlier by regional health ministers and senior officials to address the SARS outbreak. The leaders approved the establishment of an ad-hoc ministerial-level Joint Task Force to follow-up the decisions made and the creation of an ASEAN SARS Containment Information Network to share information. The meeting also endorsed pre-departure health control procedures for travellers, 'despite some initial objections from Cambodia, Laos and Myanmar who feared that tourism would be affected' (*New Straits Times* 2003b).

Although the summit reaffirmed ASEAN as the most relevant group to combat SARS, it was unable to enforce a uniform approach among its members. Malaysia insisted on placing a 10-day quarantine on foreign students entering Malaysia from SARS-affected areas and Filipino migrant workers to prevent them from spreading the SARS virus. Other regional countries also imposed a range of other unilateral measures (*New Straits Times* 2003b).

The annual ASEAN Labour Ministers meeting held on 8–9 May in Mataram discussed the challenges of SARS on labour-related issues. The ministers agreed to ask the senior officials to convene a special meeting to discuss among other things the impact of SARS on labour, employment, human resources and occupational safety and health. The ASEAN Labour Ministers also had a separate meeting with their + 3 counterparts on this issue the day after their main meeting (*Borneo Bulletin* 2003).

ASEAN + 3 Airport Officials met in Pampanga in the Philippines on 15–16 May. Responding to a Philippines proposal, ASEAN + 3 airport officials agreed to adopt standardised prevention and immunisation measures and procedures in order to prevent the spread of SARS through civil aviation. These measures included the use of health declaration cards for all departing and arriving passengers and for temperature screening at both ends of any route that touched a SARS affected area, starting from 15 June. Starting from 15 August, all officials, except Japan, agreed that all departing passengers and passengers arriving from countries and regions affected with SARS would have their temperatures taken. The airport authorities had also agreed that all passengers suspected of having SARS would not be denied entry into the country of arrival, but rather would be provided with appropriate medical treatment in that country (Xinhua 2003).

However, soon after these agreements were made, Singapore was criticised by Malaysia, for turning back a Malaysian man entering Singapore at their common land border on 18 May. Singapore replied that the agreement among ASEAN members not to refuse entry to SARS cases and treat them in the country where they arrive in applies to travellers who land at the airport and said the Malaysian official 'might have mistakenly referred to the common protocol agreed upon for air travel' (*Agence France Presse* 2003).

The APEC Trade Ministers met between 2 and 3 June in Khon Kaen in Thailand, where they approved an emergency plan to protect their economies from SARS and terrorism. Regarding the SARS-related outcomes, a public relations campaign was suggested to boost regional tourism. Members also agreed to establish common health screening measures at borders and airports, while exchanging information about SARS cases (*Deutsche Presse-Agentur* 2003). Though this was simply a reflection of what was already being done within the ASEAN and ASEAN + 3 group and, given the timing of the meeting, it was of little use to the region.

ASEAN + 3 countries then met again for a high-level symposium on SARS in Beijing on 2–6 June, designed to exchange information between ASEAN + 3 experts as well as international organisations and researchers (Wang Qian 2003). Ahead of the Beijing meeting, China and ASEAN signed a joint action plan to strengthen quarantine measures at border checkpoints to control the spread of SARS. Under the agreement, travellers from China and ASEAN member countries are required to undergo temperature checks, answer medical inquiries and complete a health declaration form when passing through customs. When a SARS suspect is detected at the border checkpoint of a country other than his own, the passenger's country of origin will be notified immediately. China and the ASEAN countries also agreed to set up effective communications channels; facilitate customs clearing for medicines, remedial equipment and other goods used for the prevention and treatment of SARS; and allow ships carrying a SARS suspect to stop at the nearest port for emergency medical help. Finally, any country intending to temporarily close its border checkpoints due to SARS has to notify all the other countries concerned in advance (*Asia Pulse* 2003).

In sum, these meetings covered the period of greatest impact from the SARS virus, from April to June 2003. Although the decisions reached in the ASEAN and ASEAN + 3 meetings were largely reactive, they have created an information-sharing network that can be utilised in the event of another regional public health threat. Beyond the network is an increased capacity of regional states to protect themselves against other health or biosafety threats. Further, the speed with which these meetings were called and the decisions reached is unprecedented in the history of ASEAN; an indication that the organisation has learnt from the mistakes of the Asian Financial Crisis to respond in a timely fashion. However, inasmuch as ASEAN was able to respond relatively quickly to the crisis, the delay in an institutional response from APEC only serves to highlight its irrelevancy to region-building processes that, by their very nature, must be both responsive to regional needs and go beyond a narrowly-focused agenda. Additionally, the outcomes from these meetings show that self-interest from regional states can still prevent collective action being taken.

Lessons learned

When reviewing the programs implemented in the affected countries a number of factors stand out in their successful eradication of the virus. Indeed, seldom 'have intersections between politics, economic development, and public health been more graphically demonstrated' (Breiman *et al.* 2003). First, there were good channels of communication. Especially in the cases of Vietnam and Singapore, there were clear and effective channels of communication between medical staff and authorities. Good lines of communication were also established between the government and the people. These lines of communication and support were also extended to the domestic private sector. Second, within the governments there was a rapid response in creating a high-level body able to coordinate information and policies horizontally across all government departments. In some cases these bodies met daily, sometimes twice daily, sometimes weekly or as needed. Together, these two factors helped foster a third factor: the maintenance of public trust and state legitimacy. In other words, even as states were under attack from an unforeseen threat, with an unknown pathology, they undertook measures to strengthen their capacities. With the state as the lead actor, markets and societies were engaged in an effort to ensure that any sectoral failures stemming from the SARS virus were isolated and did not become systemic.

Going beyond the state, it is clear that as states engage in regional (or even global) processes of engagement they must simultaneously protect themselves against threats that are more intense as geographical areas become smaller. Southeast Asia had already experienced this intensity at the regional level during the 1997–98 Asian Financial Crisis, as well as with the environmental 'haze' threat, which emerged at the same time. With the SARS virus, a major public health threat crossed national boundaries to challenge the security of regional states, economies and societies. Therefore, given this intensity, it could be concluded that, in a regional setting, states have a self-interested obligation to their counterparts to act in such a manner as to not threaten regional stability and prosperity.

It follows that, as part of this obligation, states have to act to ensure that their processes of governance do not fail or, if they do, that the processes are sufficiently transparent for neighbouring states to take preventative actions to address any potential threats that may subsequently arise. In the example of the 2003 SARS outbreak, China's failure to ensure that its public were protected by the timely provision of information relating to the virus only served to start a failure that cascaded through its bureaucratic, market and community sectors. With the transborder movement of people, it was only a matter of time before an infected person took the SARS virus outside mainland China. At this point, China's internal inadequacies unwittingly created a human security threat of regional and global proportions. Thus, one of the key lessons to be drawn from this crisis is that, while it is still may be a matter of debate to what extent states benefit domestically from good governance, it is clear that there are tangible benefits—in the form of enhanced security and prosperity—to be gained at the regional level for enacting such processes.

Conclusion

SARS was the latest crisis to engulf Southeast Asian states—domestically as well as at the regional level. Unlike the Asian Financial Crisis or the 'haze', SARS originated outside Southeast Asia and was not the result of any pre-existing systemic weakness in the regional states' structures. However, as with the two earlier crises, what began as a problem in one area of one state quickly spread across boundaries to challenge the ability of other regional states to engage in their normal daily operations. It was at this point that a failure due to one state's internal inadequacy became a human security threat. Further, as also occurred in the last two crises, the threat perception was so great that even states not seriously affected by the virus, suffered by association. This perception not only served to increase the magnitude of the threat—and, hence, the difficulty in addressing it—but also served to underline the regional nature of contemporary Southeast Asia.

In understanding such crises, traditional, state-dominant conceptions of security are insufficient to meet the international community's needs. What is required is a reformulation of what it means to be secure, and then an understanding of how such security can be achieved. This article has argued that security can be achieved by acknowledging the role market groups, civil society organisations, and even individuals can play in both detracting from and enhancing a nation-state. Beyond a single state, this article has also argued that such actors can also both cause insecurity or create greater security in secondary states. Such an effect is stronger where the geographical area is smaller. Thus, the effect is most intense at the domestic level, and weakest at the global level. In the case of regions, the intensity can be said to depend on the level of integration, both real and perceived.

If the diverse threats that are now seen to threaten the security of states (for example, economic, food, environmental, or health insecurities) are to be properly met, then a security model that, at least, attempts to consider how and why such threats emerge should be advanced. The human security concept offers one possible model that can equitably meet the analytic needs of the international community without devaluing or distorting its myriad elements.

In conclusion, there is an old saying that 'no man is an island'. I believe that none of us can afford to exist in isolation. We must build bridges between us, we must communicate and support each other. If we do this now, we will be better able to respond to the next challenge.

—*Mr Stephen Ip, Secretary for Economic Development and Labour, Hong Kong SAR. 15 July 2003*

Notes

1 During Thai Foreign Minister Surin Pitsuwan's time in office, Thailand strongly promoted human security. Since then, the regional dialogue has preferenced non-traditional security approaches over human security models; largely because of the latter's individual-centricism.
2 For more information refer to: *Financial Times Information*, 2003 (15 June). The Chinese idiom and its interpretation were provided by a Chinese scholar in the wake of the sackings.

References

Abdullah, A. S. M. *et al.*, 2003. 'Lessons from the severe acute respiratory syndrome outbreak in Hong Kong', *Emerging Infectious Diseases Journal [online]*. September. Available from: URL: http://www.cdc.gov/ncidod/EID/vol9no9/03-0366.htm

Agence France Presse, 2003. 'Singapore rejects Malaysian allegation it breached SARS accord', 21 May.

Asia Pulse, 2003. 'China, ASEAN Build Entry-Exit Quarantine Cooperation Mechanism', 2 June.

Borneo Bulletin, 2003. 'Brunei: ASEAN Labour Ministers Meet', 11 May.

Breiman, R. F. *et al.*, 2003. 'Role of China in the quest to define and control severe acute respiratory syndrome', *Emerging Infectious Disease Journal [online]* September. Available from: URL: http://www.cdc.gov/ncidod/EID/vol9no9/03-0390.htm

Channel News Asia 2003, Asia Pacific. 'Expert warns SARS may revisit Vietnam if border with southern China is not well guarded', 2 May.

Colebatch, Hal, 1993 and Larmour. Peter *Market, Bureaucracy and Community* (London: Pluto Press).

Communicable Disease Surveillance and Response (CDSR), 2003. *Severe Acute Respiratory Syndrome* (SARS): *Status of the outbreak and lessons for the immediate future.* (Geneva: World Health Organisation). 20 May.

Cusimano, Maryann, 2000 'Editor's Preface to Chapter Seven', Maryann Cusimano (ed). *Beyond Sovereignty: Issues for a Global Agenda.* (New York: St Martins Press), p. 174.

Deutsche Presse-Agentur, 2003. 'APEC ministers agree to cooperate to free trade and fight SARS', 3 June.

Drosten, C. *et al.*, 2003. 'Identification of a novel coronavirus in patients with severe acute respiratory syndrome'. (10 April). Available from: URL: www.nejm.org.

Financial Times Information 2003 (3 June). Global News Wire. 'Thailand to Conduct Global Campaign to Confirm SARS-Free Status'.

Günther, S. *et al.*, 2003. 'Identification of a novel coronavirus in patients with severe acute respiratory syndrome', 10 April. Available from www.nejm.org.

——. 2003 (15 June). 'Chronology of Worldwide SARS outbreak 11 Feb–2 Jun'.

Hooi, Alexis, 2003a. 'WHAT'S HOT: 2-second fever scan WHAT'S COOL: Hotels, retailers', *The Straits Times*, 30 April.

——. 2003b '385,000 SARS kits yet to be collected', *The Straits Times*, 12 July.

Ling Chang Hong, 2003. 'Harsh lessons from SARS' *The Straits Times*, 4 August.

New Straits Times, 2003a. 'Pre-travel checks for ASEAN'. 27 April.

——. 2003b. 'ASEAN must not fail SARS test', 2 May.

Peiris, J. S. M. *et al.* 2003. 'Coronavirus as a possible cause of severe acute respiratory syndrome' (8 April). Available from: URL: www.thelancet.com

Pirages, Dennis and Runci, Paul 2000. 'Ecological Interdependence and the Spread of Infectious Disease', in Maryann Cusimano (ed.) *Beyond Sovereignty: Issues for a Global Agenda* (New York: St Martins Press) 2000. p 176.

Program on Human Security n.d outline, online at http://www.cbrss.harvard.edu/programs/hsecurity.htm

Savioli, Lorenzo, 2003. 'Obituary: Carlo Urbani', *The Guardian*, 21 April, p. 19.

Shannon, Julie and Thomas, Nicholas 2004 (forthcoming). 'Human Security and Cybersecurity: operationalising a transnational policy framework', in Broadhurst, R. (ed.) *Cyber Crime: The Challenge in Asia*. (Hong Kong: University of Hong Kong Press).

Thomas, Nicholas and Tow, William 2002. 'The Utility of Human Security', *Security Dialogue*. 33(2) June, pp. 177–192.

UNDR (United Nations Development Program) (HDR), 1994, *New Dimensions of Human Security*. (New York: Oxford University Press).

Vietnam News Briefs, 2003 (22 April), Tourism. 'Vietnam's Northern Border Province Stops Receiving Chinese Tourists Amid SARS Spread'.

——. 2003 (21 October), Health & Environment. 'Health Ministry seeks $5.2 MLN More for SARS Prevention'.

Wang Qian, 2003. 'High-level Symposium on SARS Held in Beijing', www.china.org.cn. 6 June.

Xinhua, 2003. 'ASEAN, China, Japan, South Korea Approve SARS Border controls', 16 May.

34

SARS IN ASIA

Crisis, vulnerabilities, and regional responses

Mely Caballero-Anthony

Source: *Asian Survey*, 45:3 (2005), 475–95.

Abstract

This article examines lessons learned from the recent Severe Acute Respiratory Syndrome crisis in East and Southeast Asia, arguing that the wide-ranging impact of infectious diseases makes it imperative for states to treat these diseases as security concerns. "Securitizing" infectious diseases provides urgency for mobilizing resources and strengthening regional cooperation. Adding infectious diseases to the security agenda allows for better handling of sudden outbreaks that endanger lives and threaten the survival of nation-states; this is also in line with the region's concept of comprehensive security.

Introduction

No sooner had East and Southeast Asia begun to recover from the impact of the Iraq War when Severe Acute Respiratory Syndrome (SARS) suddenly hit the region in early 2003. Fatally infectious, the disease brought not only a serious threat to weakened economies but its appearance and spread also awakened countries to a clear and present danger, making affected nations aware of how vulnerable their security could be—something beyond even what their military defenses could guarantee.

If the world changed after the September 11, 2001, terrorist attacks in the United States, so has the impact of infectious diseases on security in most countries, particularly in Asia—the region most affected by SARS.[1] From the first known outbreak in late February 2003 until the end of June that year, the disease spawned crises in a number of states. By the time it was contained, SARS had infected about 8,300 people, causing 783 reported deaths in 28 countries. With no known cure in sight, SARS saw medical teams around the globe working feverishly to contain the problem as the

189

death toll rose. The rapid spread of SARS across borders, not to mention the attendant disruptions in business and travel, caught many governments by surprise, to the extent that containing the spread became the immediate task. Member states of the Association of Southeast Asian Nations (ASEAN), together with China, Japan, and Korea, convened special emergency meetings to put in place regional mechanisms to handle the health crisis. Although the World Health Organization (WHO) declared on July 5 that the global outbreak of SARS had finally been contained, it cautioned that the threat remains. WHO has therefore warned that "continued global vigilance for SARS is crucial for the foreseeable future [because] the world is not yet SARS-free."[2]

The main objective of this article is to analyze the lessons that states in Asia can learn from the region's recent experience with SARS. This study suggests that given the multidimensional threats to national security posed by infectious diseases such as SARS, it is imperative that states treat these diseases within a security framework. Although the concept of security, particularly in Southeast Asia, has been expanded to include both conventional and non-conventional threats—hence the prevailing notion of comprehensive security—the idea of health security has not been included in the region's security lexicon. The recent episode should be seen as a wake-up call for how security should be re-conceptualized to account for new and serious threats. By framing infectious diseases as a matter of national security, governments and their people would be better prepared to handle sudden outbreaks that endanger human lives and threaten the existence and survival of nation-states.

In arguing for the inclusion of infectious diseases in the security agenda of the region, this article assesses critically current security thinking in Asia and suggests that comprehensive security should not be seen as a static concept. Instead, building on the idea of non-traditional security that is not alien to the region, the elements of comprehensive security thinking should reflect the realities and challenges faced by states and communities. While the study challenges current security thinking, it does not attempt to replace the current notions of comprehensive and cooperative security that are rooted in regional practice.

The article begins with a brief review of how security has been conceptualized in Asia within the region's various security discourses and in light of significant developments that have affected national and regional security. This is followed by a brief narrative outlining how SARS turned out to be one of the most devastating and feared diseases in modern history, both tracing the medical crisis as it unfolded in affected countries and examining the economic, political, and socio-psychological impact of SARS and the ways governments handled their responses to it. The remainder of the article culls the lessons learned from SARS to support the argument that infectious diseases/health should be factored into regional security thinking. Finally, the article explores prospects for strengthening regional cooperation in Asia in containing and fighting infectious diseases.

Revisiting regional notions of comprehensive security

The current literature on security studies reflects recent changes in the conceptualization of security that move beyond conventional notions of military and state security. This qualitative change can be seen in the way security is defined and the expansion of the types of threats, the core values to the secured, and the referent objects.[3] Scholars such as Richard Ullman in 1983 called for a redefinition of security to include economic, environmental, and other non-military dimensions.[4] The end of the Cold War added impetus to calls for inclusion of other non-military concerns for several reasons, including structural changes, higher incidence of intrastate than interstate conflict, and rising concern over failed states. Many scholars such as Ken Booth, Simon Dalby, and Barry Buzan have argued not only for expansion of security issues but also for reconsideration of the security referent to include people or human collectivities instead of the state. According to these writers, security encompasses issues at both domestic and international levels that affect the emancipation or interests of the people.[5]

While security discourses since the early 1990s have led to alternative and much broader views of the topic, this type of thinking was neither novel nor uncommon in Asian countries, particularly in Southeast Asia. Although Japan was the first to coin the phrase "comprehensive security," the term was also articulated among ASEAN states. At least three—Indonesia, Malaysia, and Singapore—developed their own versions of comprehensive security. Indonesia's was expressed in the idea of Ketahanan Nasional (national resilience), which became its security doctrine starting from the Suharto era in the mid-1960s. In its promulgation, Ketahanan Nasional presented a comprehensive view of security to include political, economic, socio-cultural, and military aspects covering both the domestic and international environment. Resilience was to be attained through a multi-dimensional approach to security, with particular attention given to economic development.[6] Malaysia's articulation of comprehensive security was similar. In 1986, then-Prime Minister Mahathir Mohamad declared that "national security is inseparable from political stability, economic success and social harmony."[7] Singapore, on the other hand, has pursued a comprehensive approach to its security through the concept of "Total Defense," covering five constituent elements: psychological, social, economic, civil, and military defense. Similar themes can also be found in the security policies of Brunei, the Philippines, and Thailand. As noted by Alagappa, comprehensive security, regardless of the labels and varied interpretations accompanying the term, implies that security "goes beyond (but does not exclude) the military to embrace the political, economic and socio-cultural dimensions."[8] This kind of broad security thinking is also shared by China, which has strongly emphasized economic development in the belief that the country's national security depends on its overall strength, not only its military might. According to Wu Xinbo, one of the significant features of China's security practice is the pursuit of national security through international cooperation, which its political elites have promoted.[9]

By 1995, the concept of comprehensive security had found added articulation among influential non-governmental organizations such as the Council for Security Cooperation in the Asia Pacific (CSCAP), a track-two institution comprising several research institutes in the Asia/Pacific region.[10] This effort was an attempt by CSCAP to come up with an organizing concept on comprehensive security by bringing together the common themes of the region's varying conceptualizations of security, including those of East Asian nations and especially, those of ASEAN states. CSCAP's definition stated that "comprehensive security is the pursuit of sustainable security in all fields (personal, political, economic, social, cultural, military, environmental) in both the domestic and external spheres, essentially through cooperative means."[11]

The definition outlined several principles, including mutual interdependence, cooperative and shared security, and good citizenship.[12] These underscored the importance placed on cooperative security approaches by both ASEAN members and also states outside Southeast Asia. However, in spite of these notions of comprehensive and cooperative security, there remains a missing element in the types of security concerns articulated by states and governments in the region. While economic security and development have indeed been emphasized as integral to national security, we should note that *health security* has not been featured in the discourse over contemporary challenges. Yet, considering the rapidly changing global and strategic environment, the SARS crisis and its impact in the region provide important lessons to ponder and present a mechanism for expanding the scope of security concerns to reflect current threats. Moreover, considering the limited capacities of states to handle this kind of transnational menace, the SARS crisis also offers opportunities to improve regional responses and cooperation in areas of "new" non-conventional security threats. This is discussed in detail below.

SARS: the unfolding of a health crisis

Numerous accounts have been published on the devastating impact of SARS, particularly the havoc it has wreaked in affected Asian countries. Most narratives on the SARS episode trace the outbreak of this highly virulent disease to the Chinese province of Guangdong as early as November 2002.[13] But although the outbreak may have started then, it was not until March 12, 2003, that the WHO issued a global health alert, followed three days later by an emergency travel advisory. So by the time the alert came out, the disease had already spread to many parts of China, Hong Kong, Singapore, Taiwan, and Vietnam.

This time lag was attributed to the failure of the Chinese authorities to promptly inform the WHO. China has been severely criticized for initially playing down the seriousness of the problem. As a consequence of the inaction and delay, by the time the WHO had set up its teams in affected areas, China and Hong Kong had registered the highest number of reported SARS cases—making up approximately 80% of global SARS cases and deaths.

China and the fear of economic fallout

Two factors have emerged to explain China's belated response. One was concern by Chinese authorities about the economic fallout if information about SARS were to be leaked.[14] There were reports that when word about the disease began to spread across China, officials from Beijing ignored the problem, hoping that it would go away.[15] Apparently, Chinese officials, including Premier Wen Jiabao, initially went out of their way to say that China was safe, while state-run television was ordered to broadcast images of happy tourists traveling around the country.[16] When China admitted the appearance of SARS, authorities initially reported only 10 cases in the capital. Even as late as April 15, the official number still stayed at a paltry 37.[17] Not until the party leadership faced "blistering rebukes" from the WHO and its own medical community did it finally admit on April 20 that its authorities had concealed the true extent of the crisis, upping the number of confirmed cases to 339. By May 9, the number of cases reported in Beijing rose to over 2,177, with 114 deaths.[18]

Prevailing attitudes

The other significant reason for the delay derived from prevailing Chinese attitudes toward infectious diseases. China, perhaps like most countries, treats infectious diseases as medical problems, meriting a medical response. This could explain why it was four and a half months after the first known cases of SARS emerged before Chinese authorities alerted the WHO. The delay was reportedly incurred because of bureaucratic procedures that first required classification of SARS as a "Category B" disease, that is, highly infectious and requiring compulsory reporting, before local authorities could report it to the central government. Moreover, there was the problem of how to handle this class of disease, that is, whether it fell under the framework of the International Health Regulations (IHR) that make reporting of infectious diseases to WHO mandatory. Considering that the present IHR covers only three infectious diseases—cholera, yellow fever, and plague—it was not surprising that SARS did not initially make it to the list. These bureaucratic procedures had been exacerbated by the lack of coordination occurring at both local and national levels in alerting the international community to the nature of the emerging health crisis.[19]

Thus, it was not altogether surprising that the actual health alert came not from China but from a WHO staffer working at a hospital in Hanoi, Vietnam. Dr. Carlo Urbani, an Italian doctor working on infectious diseases, suspected something was amiss when several medical staffers at the Hanoi French Hospital fell ill. Investigations showed that these health workers began to fall sick after the hospital treated an American businessman who had come from Hong Kong. By the time WHO's Urbani alerted the world to the emerging epidemic, 36 hospital workers had fallen ill—more than half the staff.[20] Urbani later died of SARS in a Bangkok hospital.

Further investigation revealed that the American patient in Hanoi had stayed at the Metropole Hotel in Hong Kong, where the first index case was traced. Reports also showed that a Chinese lung specialist from Guangzhou's Zhongshan No. 2 Hospital had attended his nephew's wedding in Hong Kong. Prior to his trip, the doctor treated a SARS patient at the Zhongshan Hospital who was highly infectious and had already infected dozens of health workers. At the Metropole Hotel where he stayed, the doctor passed on SARS to other guests, including two Canadians, the American businessman, a Hong Kong man, and three young women from Singapore.[21] Until that time, it had appeared that SARS was confined to the Chinese mainland; then it was "unleashed" on the world.[22] Between mid-March and the end of April 2003, the SARS cases multiplied—this time spreading to more countries. China accounted for more than 3,460 probable cases of the global total of 5,663; by early May, cumulative cases surpassed 6,000.[23]

Impact of SARS: more than a health crisis

With the uncharacteristic nature of the spread and reach of SARS, it became clear that the pandemic was more than a health crisis. The impact of SARS was not limited to loss of life but extended to other areas—socio-economic, political, and security. The extent of the impact and the efforts by the state to contain SARS in affected countries are discussed below.

Economic impact

Unlike other infectious diseases, SARS seemed to have spread more easily than first believed, aided by the fluid borders of a highly mobile and interconnected world. Countries found themselves bracing for the worst to come: fear and panic set in. Travel alerts to SARS-affected countries were issued first by WHO, followed by several countries that advised their citizens against nonessential travel to SARS-stricken places. These included China and Hong Kong, Vietnam, Singapore, and Canada. As the disease spread, the list was expanded to include Taiwan and the Philippines.

The extent of the economic impact of SARS was reflected in the sudden disruption of economic activity in several Asian economies, notably in Hong Kong, Singapore, and in China, particularly Guangdong Province, Beijing, and Shanghai. Travel advisories prompted a drastic fall in tourism and travel, generally making these two sectors the worst hit. Exacerbating this was the fear of a possible domino effect. Starting with a fall in consumer confidence, a drop in domestic demand, and pessimism over business prospects, many firms were threatened with collapse as the cost of SARS started to rise. Economic growth prospects began to be reassessed as forecasts of gross domestic product (GDP) growth in some places were reduced to between 0.5% and 1%. In Hong Kong, for example, which recorded the second-highest number of SARS cases, government estimates placed the cost of SARS at about US$1.7 billion, while in Singapore, the government forecast indicated that SARS could shave as much as one-half to one percentage point off expected GDP growth.[24] The WHO put the cost of SARS to the Asian region at $30 billion; another analysis estimated the figure at around $60 billion.[25]

Within three months of the outbreak, in the period between mid-March and mid-May, the tourism and travel sectors hit an unprecedented low as people began to shy away from traveling to China, Hong Kong, Singapore, and Vietnam. Tourist data from Hong Kong indicated that inbound tourist figures fell by 70%–80%, while outbound tourists were down 20%. Since early April, airline passenger traffic on Hong Kong's flag carrier, Cathay Pacific, decreased by around 75%.[26] In Singapore, tourist arrivals fell to 70% of previous levels.[27] In the first few week of April, Singapore Airlines' passenger traffic also declined by 25%.[28] Added to this was the impact of reduced travel on the hotel industry, with many countries reporting occupancy rates of below 10%–30%. Topping this was the huge slump in retail industry, which saw a 20%–50% drop in business for many countries.[29]

Social and psychological impact

The severity of the economic effects cited above was caused largely by the social and psychological impact of SARS. In fact, one of the major questions that emerged throughout the health crisis was why SARS triggered so much fear. Compared with other infectious diseases, the death toll from SARS was far less than that from malaria or AIDS.[30] From most analyses, two common factors emerged that seemed to explain why the kind of fear that SARS generated appeared to be grossly disproportional in relation to its low mortality rate. First was a lack of medical information about the disease.[31] SARS was not only contagious but also could be fatal, yet the means of transmission remained far from clear. There is no known cure for it. Second, coverage of SARS infections and deaths dominated the media. Thus, juxtaposing the massive publicity about SARS against the medical unknowns boosted feelings of uncertainty and contributed to what could have been an overreaction, in some cases.[32]

For SARS-stricken countries, an uneasy atmosphere of fear and apprehension prevailed. Within a short but significant period, SARS had drastically altered many lives. People's mobility within their environment, normally taken for granted, suddenly changed as the psychological fear of possible exposure and infection in public places loomed. Even traveling from one's home to other places became problematic because of concerns over not having adequate protection. Wearing face masks became de rigueur in places like Hong Kong and China. Television and print images of people wearing masks—not just in hospitals but also while traveling on buses, trains, and planes or walking in streets, shopping malls, and other public places—triggered a chain reaction of mass panic. This concern prompted governments to take drastic steps to stem the tide of panic that theatened to disrupt public life.

On the medical front, SARS patients were quarantined and specific hospitals were officially designated to attend only to SARS cases in an effort to stop the chain of infection. Home quarantine orders were also issued to families and friends of SARS patients who had come into close contact with them. Hospitals set up triage areas as procedures were drawn up for screening, transport, admission, and protection of health care staff. For health care workers serving in the front line in the battle against SARS, strict protocols were adopted, including wearing layers of protective gowns, masks, gloves, visors, caps, and shoe covers.[33]

Preventive measures outside hospitals were also set in place. These included closure of schools as anxious parents worried about possible exposure of their children to the SARS virus. In Beijing, for example, elementary and high schools were closed for a month beginning in mid-April and college classes were canceled.[34] Similar measures were adopted in Singapore and Hong Kong. Entertainment venues such as bars and restaurants were closed or avoided. Trade fairs, conferences, and business meetings were canceled or postponed indefinitely.

Political impact

SARS also caused political ripples, particularly in China, which was blamed for mismanaging the outbreak. With its credibility seriously undermined by poor handling of SARS in the epidemic's early stages, China was forced to demonstrate its resolve in the fight to contain the disease. After having downplayed the seriousness of the health crisis, Premier Wen Jiabao openly admitted on April 20, that the situation in China remained "grave." Three days earlier, Health Minister Zhang Wenkang and Beijing Mayor Meng Xuenong were fired for negligence; another 120 Chinese officials were also reported to have been fired, demoted, or reprimanded during that month.[35] The government also acted quickly to appoint a top Chinese technocrat, Ms. Wu Yi, a deputy prime minister and former trade negotiator, to run the Health Ministry and Beijing's anti-SARS campaign. President Hu Jintao and Premier Wen toured the country exhorting people to fight SARS.[36]

Prior to China's official admission of the crisis, the WHO had lamented the lack of cooperation received from Chinese authorities. In late March, when the WHO requested China to allow its medical team to go to Guangdong Province where the infectious pathogen was said to have originated, the government vacillated so much that former WHO Director-General Gro Harlem Brundtland remarked that had the Chinese authorities acted earlier and with more openness, the outbreak of the disease would have taken a different course.[37] To win back confidence from the international community, Chinese health officials held press conferences daily to report on the number of SARS cases in China.

The Chinese government also took drastic steps to control the movement of people in and out of Beijing. While the country was gearing up for its May Day holiday period, officials announced new steps to discourage ill people from boarding planes, buses, and trains.[38] Reports circulated that people were leaving the cities in droves to go to villages considered safe from SARS. Meanwhile, some villages near Beijing were reported to have also closed their entry points to keep the infection out.[39]

Beyond China, several countries adopted stringent measures to screen and control visitors coming from SARS-affected countries. Thermal imagers were installed in airports and other entry/exit points to scan and bar passengers with fevers. More stringent measures were introduced, but later reconsidered. Thailand and Malaysia at one point banned the entry of tourists from China but withdrew the rule after quiet protests from Beijing, which in turn retaliated, by preventing its citizens from traveling to Malaysia, Singapore, and Thailand. Nonetheless, a policy by Bangkok and Kuala Lumpur requiring their own citizens arriving from China and other SARS-affected areas to go into voluntary quarantine for seven to 10 days remained in place until the WHO gradually removed the countries from its list of SARS-affected areas where the travel advisory applied.

The other significant impact was how crisis management measures, particularly mandatory quarantine, were viewed as a curtailment of civil liberties. Anecdotal incidents of people resisting and violating quarantine laws were reported in several countries, and the question of how far authorities could go in imposing quarantines became a nagging issue because governments tended to revive quarantine laws that in many countries predate World War Two.[40] Other measures such as home surveillance and monitoring of quarantined people, adopted in Singapore, China, and to some extent Hong Kong, were widely viewed as draconian and having serious repercussions for civil liberties.

It is beyond the scope of this study to give a comprehensive account of the full impact of the SARS crisis. The foregoing discussion on economic, socio-psychological, and political impacts is certainly not exhaustive. It is nonetheless indicative of how a health crisis brought on by an infectious disease can wreak great havoc and suffering on people and societies. To sum up, SARS has—at the very least—generated tremendous fear and anxiety among people across the globe. As the SARS experience has revealed, it did not take much to convince anyone that SARS presented a clear and present danger to human lives. Whether fears of SARS were rational or not, the crisis that hit the region was certainly comparable to, if not worse than, the 1997 Asian financial crisis, leading some observers to ask whether the SARS episode was the region's own version of September 11.

Regional responses to contain SARS

As affected states grappled with how to contain SARS, the crisis generated unprecedented coordination among ASEAN countries, together with China, Japan, and Korea (together known as ASEAN + 3), as seen in hastily convened meetings among heads of governments and officials. Singapore Prime Minister Goh Chok Tong and Thai Prime Minister Thaksin Shinawatra gathered their regional counterparts to address the crisis. Following the ASEAN + 3 health ministers' meeting held in Kuala Lumpur on April 26, 2003, a Special ASEAN Summit on SARS and a Special ASEAN-China Leaders' Meeting were held, back to back, in Bangkok on April 29. Several measures were outlined to put in place regional mechanisms to address the multiplicity of issues brought on by the SARS crisis. Immediate measures agreed upon involved the exchange of information and best practices in containing infectious diseases; strengthening of cooperation among front-line enforcement agencies, such as health, immigration, customs, transport, and law enforcement; and harmonization of travel procedures to ensure proper health screening at points of origin. Another significant concern was identifying foreign nationals who are suspected of carrying SARS.[41]

Short-to-mid-term measures involved deepening cooperation between ASEAN and the WHO, as well as exploring the possibility of developing a regional framework of rapid response to outbreaks of infectious diseases. Malaysia, for example, has proposed setting up a regional center for disease control (CDC); efforts are underway to further develop <ASEAN-Disease-Surveillance.net>, which coincidentally was set up in April 2003 at the height of the SARS crisis (see Figure 1). Moreover, a special ASEAN SARS fund was set up, with China offering to contribute $1.2 million. The special ASEAN-China meeting was significant in that it provided an avenue for China to reassure the region of its cooperation in the fight against SARS. This enabled Beijing to make amends for its failure to respond promptly to international calls for action to contain the disease. Premier Wen expressed

<ASEAN-Disease Surveillance.net> is a website set up in April 2003 to facilitate regional cooperation in Southeast Asia and provide timely dissemination of information on disease outbreaks. This website was established with financial and technical support from the U.S. Naval Medical Research Unit 2 (NAMRU-2) and is maintained by the Indonesian Ministry of Health.

The <ASEAN-Disease Surveillance.net> website is an Internet-based system onto which participating countries post syndromic data gathered via the Early Warning Outbreak Recognition System (EWORS). It operates like a hub-and-spokes monitoring system wherein local data are uploaded to a central hospital computer and then processed to determine whether disease is present; local public health personnel are automatically alerted. Plans are in progress to link <ASEAN-Disease Surveillance.net> with the Pacific Disease Surveillance Network (PANCET).

Figure 1 About <ASEAN-Disease Surveillance.net>.
Source: ASEAN Surveillance Network at <http://www.asean.diseases-surveillance-net/ASNHistory.asp.

his gratitude for ASEAN's support and understanding, noting that the ASEAN-China summit did not turn into a "finger pointing" session.[42] Similarly, the ASEAN meetings strengthened bilateral cooperation among states such as Singapore (the ASEAN country most affected by SARS) and Malaysia. Given the huge number of people crossing the border daily—making the two states into a virtually contiguous area—it became imperative to agree to strengthen consultation and communication between their health ministries and other relevant agencies to monitor and contain the disease.

Since the convening of the regional leaders' meetings on SARS, efforts at bilateral and regional levels to monitor the disease are continuing; it would be premature at this stage to provide a more definitive assessment of regional efforts. However, what is interesting to note in these evolving regional efforts is the trend toward adopting a region-wide surveillance mechanism for monitoring infectious diseases. This could complement efforts to monitor diseases worldwide by the WHO, which in 1997 had initiated the Global Outbreak Alert and Response Network, the only equivalent of an international mechanism providing global disease surveillance and control. Maintained by Health Canada, this surveillance body boasts a network of 100 laboratories and disease reporting systems worldwide. However, obtaining international cooperation at both local and national levels is crucial. In this regard, ASEAN's plan to build a regional disease surveillance mechanism is a significant development in global disease control. For new infectious diseases such as SARS, for which there is much to be learned about epidemiology and treatment, an imperative exists for multilateral coordination at many levels. This point is elaborated below.

Lessons from SARS: strengthening regional cooperation in fighting infectious diseases

The SARS episode forced many states to adjust to new realities of fighting new types of potentially transnational infectious diseases. With no known cure, the battle is far from over. Hence, the recent SARS crisis may be seen as an eye-opener for the international community and the ASEAN region. It presents an opportunity to reflect on salient issues that the region's governments and political elites may have overlooked and/or taken for granted in dealing with health issues and their impact on national security. In other words, the crisis forces one to rethink security.

Within the frameworks of comprehensive and non-traditional security, one can argue that good health is an important component of the security of individuals and the state. But much contention has arisen over whether infectious diseases such as SARS should be considered a matter of national or international security, as opposed to simply a public health concern. At one end of the spectrum are analysts who regard infectious diseases as health matters; at the other end are those who see such diseases as national security issues *only if* the microbes undermine military, economic, and political capabilities of states—and consequently, the foundations of power. A state's failure to recognize and act on the security component of infectious disease would also indirectly affect other states' strategic interests when military, political, or economic instability exists.[43]

This article suggests that the threats of infectious diseases require urgent responses. The regional community and states need not wait for the worst-case scenario of state failure before infectious diseases can be considered as a matter of national security. Hence, there is a need to "securitize." If one applies the Copenhagen School's approach, an issue is "securitized" if it is presented as an "existential threat" to a "referent object."[44] Based on this criterion, infectious diseases can be securitized because they pose existential threats to people and states (the referent objects). The main objectives of the act and process of securitizing infectious diseases are to alert concerned actors within and outside a state to the threats and dangers that could arise, particularly if there are no known treatments. More important, the action allows the state to marshal attention and resources to address the complex issues that are intertwined with the threats of infectious diseases at different levels.[45]

There is sufficient reason to build a case for securitizing infectious diseases. Firstly, with globalization, the scale, speed, and extent of movement of people and goods are without parallel. According to the WHO, new diseases are emerging at an unprecedented rate of one per year. Examples include ebola hemorrhagic fever in Africa, the West Nile-hantavirus pulmonary syndrome in the U.S., and Nipah encephalitis in Southeast Asia. Older diseases such as cholera and tuberculosis have re-emerged. Cholera, in fact, is in its seventh pandemic year, having returned to Peru in 1991 and recently manifested itself in the "Black Plague" hitting India in 1994. Recurring diseases such as tuberculosis have returned in more virulent strains resistant to currently available first-line antibiotic drugs.[46] New strains have appeared of food-borne diseases such as Creutzfeldt-Jacob (mad cow) disease, first detected in 1996, and highly unstable forms of flu virus—SARS being one of these.

Secondly, aside from globalization, there are "artificial" disease force-multipliers that greatly exacerbate not only the incidence but also the spread of infectious disease. These include modern medical practices, accelerating urbanization, climate change resulting from global warming, and new social and behavioral patterns.[47]

Thirdly, the threat from infectious pathogens is greater today than ever. As the case of SARS clearly demonstrates, infectious diseases not only threaten the health of individuals, their spread can also have catastrophic economic impact, weaken social order, and undermine public confidence in government. The outbreak or even resurgence of infectious diseases can in fact undermine a state's control of what happens within its territory and may also threaten regional stability. Diseases such as SARS have made countries aware of their vulnerability to the threats of infectious pathogens, which can easily cross borders in ways that defy traditional military defense. And, as the SARS experience has borne out, while countries can tighten immigration controls to turn away travelers who might be carriers, this measure fails to stem the spread of the virus. As aptly described by a virologist at Hong Kong's Queen Mary Hospital, "[V]irus[es] do not carry passports."[48]

But what is the added value of securitizing infectious diseases and how does this relate to current security thinking and approaches in the region? One way to answer this is to reframe the question and ask: How does adding a security label to infectious diseases better address the threats they carry? While the ASEAN governments, in collaboration with China, Japan, and Korea, have instituted a number of collaborative measures to contain SARS, more can still be done to address the broader problem of infectious diseases and health security. *To begin with, it is important to bring the health component into comprehensive security.*

Bringing the health component into comprehensive security

One of the main lessons to be learned from the SARS experience is the need to appreciate the close nexus between health and security. While East Asia's and/or ASEAN's notion of comprehensive security extended beyond the military to include political, economic, environmental, and sociocultural aspects of security—i.e., non-traditional security—health security has not become a part of the region's security lexicon. At least in ASEAN, it was not until the concept of human security (economic, food, environmental, personal, community, and political security) was introduced and included in the development discourse that health was added as an element.[49] Even then, this type of discourse has found a limited voice in the region, mostly articulated by non-state actors.[50]

Yet, SARS has been a good barometer of the depth and extent that infectious diseases impact on most, if not all, elements subsumed in the concept of comprehensive security. As discussed earlier, given the lack of medical knowledge about SARS and the way the disease threatened to stretch the medical infrastructure even in countries with developed medical facilities such as Canada and Singapore, states and communities can become extremely vulnerable if a disease spins out of control.

Hence, any failure to appreciate the depth, extent, and externalities brought on by infectious diseases can have catastrophic consequence. The case of AIDS is a good example. Within a few years of its discovery, AIDS had spread to every country across the globe, killing productive adults. In heavily infected countries such as in Sub-Saharan Africa, HIV/AIDS is already depleting the ranks of skilled workers, teachers, nurses, police officers, and civil servants—not to mention the loss of health staff, as high as 40%.[51] A recent study on HIV/AIDS in Southern Africa showed that infection rates in the armed forces range from 16% and 20% in Namibia and South Africa, respectively, to 50% and 60%, respectively, in the Democratic Republic of Congo and Zambia.[52]

Although the United Nations Security Council finally declared AIDS to be a national security threat in 2000, the battle to securitize AIDS was not easy because many countries regarded it as a health problem and domestic issue, not a security threat. When the United States first pushed for HIV/AIDS to be discussed in the Security Council, many nations protested for procedural reasons—they felt that the Council was not the appropriate forum for what were perceived as "social and economic issues."[53] It was therefore more than a political victory to put AIDS on the security agenda of the international community.

The threat of AIDS remains very real. The U.S. National Intelligence Council recently released projections of the "next wave" of the HIV/AIDS epidemic in four populous countries, China, Ethiopia, Nigeria, and Russia. The Council estimated that the number of people infected with HIV in these countries is likely to soar from 14 million–23 million today to 50 million–75 million in 2010.[54] Similar reports highlight the potential for an explosion of AIDS cases in Asia. In China, for example, the Department of Disease Control of the Ministry of Health has warned that if the AIDS epidemic is not dealt with efficiently, by 2010 there could be more than 10 million HIV/AIDS patients in China.[55] In Cambodia, HIV/AIDS is reported to be the country's new "killing field." A senior Cambodian health official has predicted that by 2010, more than half a million of the country's 11.5 million population will suffer or die from AIDS.[56]

However, in spite of this alarming information, the case for including infectious diseases or health security among the list of security priorities in the East/Southeast Asian region has not been made. And while the idea of comprehensive security is promoted in security thinking there, many states in and outside ASEAN have yet to include health security in their list of non-conventional threats—*until SARS*. But even in states such as China where health has now become a security issue, the nature of the discourse has still been muted. But the risks of infectious diseases are no longer only a domestic concern. SARS has demonstrated the urgency of addressing this problem in a multilateral and integrated way, as domestic efforts have proved inadequate in addressing it. Securitizing infectious diseases offers innovative ways to address such threats, including the following:

Adopting an integrated, multilateral approach in fighting infectious diseases   Integrating health as a component in the region's notion of comprehensive security allows for adopting an integrated, multilateral approach in fighting infectious diseases. This involves bringing together different actors to work with the medical community to cope with the immense problem of infectious diseases. This means that health is no longer just a "medical" concern but also a national security concern. This requires a change of mind-set in coordinating agencies in, for example, agriculture, environment, and defense to work with public health experts to create multidimensional approaches to containing infectious diseases. This effort would also include the participation of civil society organizations that can fill in the gaps between states and societies. A change of mind-set would also remove an artificial distinction existing between health and security that has been the norm in many parts of the world.

Developing and promoting international regimes to avert health disasters   An integrated, multilateral approach also requires addressing the challenge of building a good mechanism for global disease surveillance and control. This would require strict observance of relevant health protocols and compliance with international conventions. This is one area where ASEAN, China, and the rest of Asia could play a crucial role, such as supporting the existing global surveillance mechanism—Global Outbreak Alert and Response Network— in timely reporting of outbreaks and in providing crucial information to the WHO. China has paid a high price for its initial secrecy and, despite its leaders' pledges of greater transparency, has faced a credibility problem both abroad and domestically.

Similarly, progress in ASEAN toward disease surveillance would be significant. In order for this regional mechanism to work, cooperation at both the local and national levels is important. This brings us back to tricky issues of transparency and compliance by states. As noted by a senior official at the ASEAN Secretariat, health matters have always been regarded as falling under the authority of national domain.[57] Hence, unless countries in the region

203

can navigate these rough waters in getting members states to cooperate, this could yet be another uphill challenge.

Providing good public health systems   In strengthening cooperation at various levels—local, national, regional, and global—the centrality of providing good public health systems must be emphasized. In this regard, the record of primary health care in many parts of Asia bears closer scrutiny; the picture that emerges is often dismal. Many parts of developing Asia too often lack basic health care facilities. This problem stems from inadequate resources allocated to public health, particularly for primary health care facilities.[58] Part of the reason is that in the hierarchy of national priorities, primary health care is not considered as critical as jobs or military security. More often, as far as public expenditure is concerned, defense budgets far exceed those for health (see Tables 1 and 2). But this need not be a constant feature. For regional disease surveillance mechanisms to be effective, building

Table 1 Health expenditures in 1995 in selected ASEAN countries.

	Total (% of GDP)	*Public Sector (% of GDP)*	*Public Sector (% of Total)*
Brunei	—	2.2	—
Cambodia	7.2	0.7	10.0
Indonesia	1.8	0.6	37.0
Malaysia	2.5	1.5	60.0
Philippines	2.4	1.3	56.0
Singapore	3.5	1.3	37.0
Thailand	5.3	1.4	26.0
Vietnam	5.2	1.1	22.0

Table 2 Government health and defense expenditure in 1995 in selected ASEAN countries.

	Health (% of GDP)	*Defense (% of GDP)*
Brunei	2.2	5.5
Cambodia	0.7	5.9
Indonesia	0.6	1.3
Malaysia	1.5	2.7
Philippines	1.3	1.4
Singapore	1.3	4.7
Thailand	1.4	2.2
Vietnam	1.1	7.2

Sources: WHO, World Health Report, 1999–2001; and IISS, The Military Balance, 1995–2000.
Note: 1995 data are used to facilitate a comparative analysis for government expenditures on health and defense in selected countries.

local surveillance and laboratory capacities among member states is critical. Inevitably, this would underscore the importance of providing more resources for building good public health systems. For countries with inadequate resources, multilateral institutions could be enjoined to help.

Attention to poverty and development issues   Last but certainly not least is the need for the region to revisit the issue of poverty and its linkages with infectious diseases. The most vulnerable in many societies are the poor, who clearly are at a disadvantage in protecting themselves. It is widely known that the burden of infectious diseases such as HIV/AIDs, malaria, and tuberculosis falls overwhelmingly on the world's poorest regions, where the tendency is not to seek professional help but to self-treat or avoid treatment altogether.

One need not go into the complex relationship between poverty and infectious diseases. Needless to say, poverty and infectious diseases are fellow-travelers, each feeding on the other. The risks of poverty-related diseases are compounded by malnutrition and environmental threats, especially the lack of clean water and sanitation. Given crowded conditions and poor hygiene, these places become perfect breeding grounds for infectious diseases.[59] In summary, adding infectious diseases to the security agenda, as well as considering innovative approaches—both integrated and multilateral—to contain diseases, plus building and promoting international regimes for global health, providing public health infrastructure, and attending to the issues of poverty and development are all part and parcel of the rethinking of security in the region.

Conclusion

This article has highlighted the serious risks of infectious diseases such as SARS to national and regional stability in East and Southeast Asia. The discussion has shown that infectious diseases not only impinge on traditional conceptions of state security but also directly undermine the survival and well-being of communities. The article suggested that the concept of comprehensive security, as propagated by ASEAN and some other Asian states, must be reassessed in the light of new challenges and threats, especially because domestic responses are no longer adequate to address these issues. Infectious diseases—broadly, health security—must therefore be included in the new security agenda. The suggestion that comprehensive security needs to be revisited underscores that fact that the definition of security is anything but static. Attempts at rethinking security are not simply exercises in inventing neologisms but are borne out of the need to reflect the realities of states and societies.

The article has also suggested a way of framing this non-conventional threat, arguing that attempts at "securitization" might influence the efficacy of responses and help develop informed ways to mitigate the impact of infectious diseases. Hence, when health authorities warn of the impending return of SARS—or any other infectious disease—it may be that the global community can be spared from added anxiety about the insidious risks of these new threats.

Notes

1 Note, in this article, "Asia" refers generally to the East and Southeast Asian region.
2 "SARS Outbreak Contained Worldwide," WHO press release, July 5, 2003, <http://www.who.int/mediacetre/releases/2003/pr56/en/print.html>. Isolated reports of SARS cases in China have re-emerged, however, again raising concerns that the disease is making a comeback. See WHO Update 4, "China Confirms SARS Infection in Two Previously Reported Cases," April 29, 2004, <http://www.who.int/csr/don/2004_04_29/en/print.html>, accessed July 23, 2004.
3 Qualitative change in core values refers to the expansion of this list of values beyond issues such as sovereignty and autonomy to the protection of human rights, environment, etc. Similarly, referent objects—units or things seen to be existentially threatened—are no longer confined to states but may also include individuals and communities. See, for example, Barry Buzan, Ole Wæver, and Jaap de Wilde, *Security: A New Framework of Analysis* (Boulder, Colo.: Lynne Rienner, 1998).
4 Richard Ullman, "Redefining Security," *International Security* 8:1 (Summer 1983), pp. 128–53.
5 For an excellent review of contestation in security discourses, see Muthiah Alagappa, ed., *Asian Security Practice: Material and Ideational Influences* (Stanford: Stanford University Press, 1998), pp. 27–64.
6 Muthiah Alagappa, "Comprehensive Security: Interpretations in ASEAN Countries," in Robert Scalapino et al., eds., *Asian Security Issues: Regional and Global* (Berkeley: Institute of East Asian Studies, University of California, 1989), pp. 50–78.
7 Keynote address of Dr. Mahathir Mohamad at the First ISIS National Conference on Security, *ISIS Focus, no. 17* (Kuala Lumpur: Institute of Strategic and International Studies, August 1986), p. 16.
8 Alagappa, *Asian Security Practice*, p. 624.
9 See Wu Xinbo, "China: Security Practice of a Modernizing and Ascending Power," in ibid., pp. 115–56.
10 For a detailed discussion on CSCAP, see Desmond Ball, *The Council for Security Cooperation in the Asia Pacific: Its Record and Prospects* (Canberra: Strategic and Defence Studies Centre, Australian National University, 2000).
11 See *CSCAP Memorandum No. 3: The Concepts of Comprehensive and Cooperative Security* (Kuala Lumpur: Institute of Strategic and International Studies, 1995).
12 Ibid.
13 WHO Update 95: "SARS: Chronology of a Serial Killer," <http://www.who.int/csr/doc/2003_07_04/en/html>, accessed April 10, 2003.
14 See, for example, "Epidemic Is a 'Test' for China's Leadership," *Washington Post*, April 22, 2003, <http://www.washingtonpost.com/ac2/wp.dyn/A7272-2003April21/html>, and "For China, a Crisis of Epidemic, Image," *Boston Globe Online*, April 23, 2003, <http://www.boston.com/dailyglobe2/113/nation/>.
15 "Virus Badly Underreported in Beijing, WHO Team Finds," *New York Times*, April 17, 2003, <http://www.nytimes.com/2003/04/17/science/17BEIJ.html/>.

16 See "For China, a Crisis of Epidemic, Image."
17 "Dictatorships and Disease," *New York Times*, April 17, 2003. See also "Deception, by the Numbers," *Asia Times Online*, June 5, 2003, <http://www.atimes/China/EFOFAd05.html>.
18 See Neil J. Beck, "What Does SARS Mean for China?" *National Bureau of Asian Research*, no. 13, May 9, 2003, <http://www.nbr.org/publications/briefing/no.13-SARS/beck.html>.
19 David Lague et al., "The China Virus," *Far Eastern Economic Review (FEER)*, April 10, 2003.
20 Ellen Nakashima, "Vietnamese Celebrate Progress against Virus," *Washington Post*, May 1, 2003, accessed from <JoyoIndonews@aol.com>, May 1, 2003. See also Seth Mydans, "Hanoi SARS Survivor," *International Herald Tribune*, May 7, 2003, <http://www.iht.com/cgi-bin/generic.cgi/articleID-95487/>.
21 SARS spreads from close contact through respiratory droplets expelled during coughing or sneezing and by direct exchange of bodily fluids. See "SARS—Epidemiological Findings, and Case Management," <http://www.wpro.who.int/sars/doc/interimguidelines/part2.asp>, accessed July 23, 2003. See also Elisabeth Rosenthal, "China Provides Clues on Origins of SARS," *International Herald Tribune*, April 28, 2003, <http://www.iht.com/cgi-bin/generic.cgi/articleID-94642>, accessed April 28, 2003; and WHO, "SARS: Breaking the Chain of Transmission," <http://www.who.int/features/2003/07/en/print.html>.
22 Ibid.
23 WHO Update 95, "SARS: Chronology of a Serial Killer."
24 See "The Cost of SARS: US$11 Billion and Rising," *FEER*, April 24, 2003.
25 See "Assessing the Impact and Cost of SARS in Developing Asia," *Asian Development Outlook 2003 Update* (Manila: Asian Development Bank [ADB], 2003).
26 See *GIC* (Government Investment Corporation) *Daily Bulletin*, Singapore, May 26, 2003, p. 4.
27 Nizam Idris, "The Impact of SARS on Singapore's Economy," IDEAglobal Ltd., Singapore, May 2003 (unpublished paper).
28 *GIC Daily Bulletin*, May 26, 2003, p. 4.
29 *FEER*, "The Cost of SARS."
30 According to the WHO, the death rate for SARS is less than 1% for people aged 24 and below but could be 50% for those over 65, making the overall case fatality ratio 14%–15%. See WHO Update 49: "SARS Case Fatality Ratio," May 7, 2003, <http://www.int/csr/sars/2003_05_07a/en/>, accessed May 23, 2003.
31 "Severe Acute Respiratory Syndrome: Status of the Outbreak and Lessons for the Immediate Future," *WHO Communicable Disease Surveillance and Response* (Geneva: WHO, May 20, 2003).
32 See, for example, "Epidemic of Fear," *Boston Globe*, June 1, 2003, <http://www.boston.com/globe/magazine/2003/0601/coverstory_entire.html>, accessed June 6, 2003; Xiang Bao and Theresa Wong, "SARS: Public Health and Social Science Perspectives," *Economic and Political Weekly* (Mumbai), June 21, 2003. See also Emma Xiaoqin Fan, "SARS: Economic Impacts and Implications," Economic and Research Department (ERD) Policy Brief Series, no. 15, *ADB*, May 20, 2003, <http://www.adb.org/economics>.
33 "Staying Cool on the SARS Battlefield," *New Sunday Times* (Kuala Lumpur), May 18, 2003.
34 "SARS Inciting 'Mass Panic' in Beijing," *Washington Post*, May 1, 2003, <http://www.washingtonpost.com/>, accessed May 3, 2003.

35 "Outbreak Gave China's Hu an Opening," ibid., May 13, 2003, <http://www.washingtonpost.com/wp-dyn/articles/A47408.2003May12/html>. See also Beck, "What Does SARS Mean for China?"

36 "SARS Shakes Complacent Mood in China," *New York Times*, May 13, 2003, <http://www.nytimes.com/2003/05/13/international/asia/13CHN.html>.

37 "China: It's Cooperating Now: By WHO," *Straits Times*, April 8, 2003.

38 "Virus Badly Underreported in Beijing, WHO Teams Finds."

39 "SARS Inciting 'Mass Panic' in Beijing."

40 In Hong Kong, for example, there were reported incidents where police met stiff resistance in tracing the whereabouts of people exposed to SARS patients and those who had been issued home confinement orders. See "Hong Kong Police Take on Expanded Role in Fighting SARS," *New York Times*, April 24, 2003, <http://www.nytimes.com/2003/04/05/sciencespecial/20Hong.html>, accessed April 25, 2003; "Macapagal Bares Tough Measures to Fight SARS," Inquirer News Service (Philippines), April 25, 2003, <http://www.inq7.net/2003/apr/text/nat-2-1p.html>; "Laws Not up to SARS Epidemic," *Washington Post*, April 26, 2003, <http://www.washingtonpost.com/wp-dn/articles/A39436-2003 April 25.html>.

41 See *Joint Statements of ASEAN + 3 Ministers of Health Special Meeting on SARS*, Kuala Lumpur, April 26, 2003; *Joint Statement of the Special ASEAN Leaders' Meeting on SARS*, Bangkok, April 29, 2003; and the *Joint Statement on the Special ASEAN-China Leaders' Meeting on SARS*, Bangkok, April 26, 2003, at <http://www.aseansec.org/14824.htm>.

42 "SARS Crisis: China Bids to Reassure Region," *The Nation Online*, <http://www.nationmultimedia.com/page.news.php3>.

43 See, for example, Shannon Selin, "The Security Implications of SARS," Canadian Consortium on Asia Pacific Security, *CANCAPS Bulletin*, no. 37, May 2003, pp. 9–13.

44 See Buzan, Wæver, and de Wilde, *Security: A New Framework for Analysis*, p. 5.

45 For more on the process of securitization, see Ole Wæver, "Securitization and Desecuritization," in *On Security*, ed. Ronnie Lipschutz (New York: Columbia University Press, 1995), pp. 46–86.

46 See "Global Defense against the Infectious Disease Threat," in *Communicable Diseases 2002*, ed. Mary Kay Kindhauser (Geneva: WHO, 2003).

47 For an excellent discussion of the interrelatedness of these factors, see Jennifer Brower and Peter Chalk, *The Global Threat of New and Re-emerging Infectious Diseases: Reconciling U.S. National Security and Public Health Policy* (Santa Monica, Calif.: RAND, 2003), pp. 13–30.

48 Dr. Malik Peiris, CNN International interview, May 7, 2003.

49 This is based on the United Nations Development Program's (UNDP) definition of human security, discussed comprehensively in UNDP, *UNDP Human Development Report 1994* (New York: Oxford University Press, 1994).

50 In ASEAN, track-two organizations such as CSCAP and the ASEAN-International Institute of Strategic Studies (ASEAN-IISS) have started to use the concept of human security. Former Thai Foreign Minister Surin Pitsuwan used the concept frequently during the height of the Asian financial crisis. Although Japan started to use human security as a platform of its foreign policy during the leadership of the late Prime Minister Keizo Obuchi (1998–2000) and had started a Human Security Fund, human security has not really found its way into the country's official national security discourse.

51 See Olive Shinana, Nompumelelo Zungu-Dirwayi, and William Shinana, "AIDS: A Threat to Human Security," in Lincoln Chen, Jennifer Leaning, and Vasant

Nahasimha, eds., *Global Health Challenges for Human Security* (Boston, Mass.: Harvard University Press, 2003), pp. 141–60.

52 Ibid., pp. 150–51.

53 See *United Nations Chronicle*, 38:1 (2001), <http://www.un.org/Pubs/chronicla/2001/issuel/0101p10.htm>.

54 Cited in *Human Security Now* (New York: Commission on Human Security, 2003), p. 99.

55 See "China on the Verge of AIDS Epidemic," *Straits Times Interactive*, September 6, 2002, <http://wwww.straitstimes.asial.com.sg>.

56 "More than 500,000 AIDS Victims in Cambodia by 2010," ibid., September 30, 2002.

57 Author's interview with ASEAN officials, April 26, 2003, Jakarta.

58 For a more extensive discussion, see Mely Caballero-Anthony, "Health and Human Security in Asia: Realities and Challenges," in Chen et al., *Global Health Challenges for Human Security*, pp. 233–56.

59 Mely Caballero-Anthony, "Health and Human Security in Asia."

35

THE "SARS DIPLOMACY" OF BEIJING AND TAIPEI

Competition between the Chinese and non-Chinese orbits

Simon Shen

Source: *Asian Perspectives*, 28:1 (2004), 45–65.

The article tries to prove how SARS has exceeded mere health and humanitarian levels from the viewpoint of different political entities among the Chinese population. Examining the "SARS Diplomacy" between the People's Republic of China and the Republic of China/Taiwan—that is, how each side of the Strait spoke to one another during the epidemic crisis—may enable us to gauge the potential for the formation of the Chinese orbit in the era of globalization. The greatest threat posed to the Chinese people from SARS Diplomacy is the stirred up populist sentiments on both sides of the Strait, with the agenda to hold a "preventive referendum" against the mainland threat on one side, and the escalated nationalism with an increasing level of distrust toward Taiwan on the other.

Introduction

After several months of worldwide hysteria, SARS is still viewed as an epidemic spread by the Chinese in the Western world.[1] However, the Chinese population did not form a holistic bloc in the crisis. Beijing, Taipei, Hong Kong, Macau, Singapore, and (to a lesser extent) the overseas Chinese all had different agendas to pursue in their respective anti-SARS campaigns. Although their official policies were conveyed to the world in an explicit manner, their implicit meanings have yet to be fully reviewed. Along with the different casualties suffered by China and Taiwan,[2] their policies on the diplomatic stage diverged sharply.

By examining the "SARS Diplomacy" between the People's Republic of China (PRC) and the Republic of China (ROC/Taiwan), this article will analyze the potential, and the potential frictions impeding, the formation of the Chinese orbit in the era of globalization. The cross-Strait interactions during the SARS crisis will be divided into two sections, with the responses from Beijing to be reviewed first, followed by the Taipei reactions. A conclusion will be made to assess the prospects of the Chinese orbit mentioned.[3]

Beijing's foreign policy during the SARS crisis

The first indications, from the time when the first case was reported in Guangdong province in November 2002, was that Beijing's efforts were fundamentally flawed. The early bureaucratic coverup—and Guangdong's habit of blaming neighboring Hong Kong for epidemics—provided limited confidence in the Chinese leadership. A closed-door SARS policy was at once implemented, when Zhang Wenkang, the Minister of Health, guaranteed the World Health Organization (WHO) in March 2003 that SARS was "well under control" and the number of infections was declining.[4] Beijing was telling WHO and the international community that this was a Chinese problem, not an international problem, and that China would solve it. Everything was under control, in short.

However, after Zhang and Beijing Mayor Meng Xuenong were removed on April 20 for the implementation of this policy, a new round of SARS Diplomacy began to emerge in Beijing. The article will show how Beijing emphasized three themes after the u-turn: depicting China as an internationally responsible state; making friendly gestures toward Taiwan under the "one-country framework"; and emphasizing the sovereignty issue in the SARS crisis. They together conveyed a single message: Beijing would no longer protest against its label as the origin of SARS. Instead, China would try demonstrating to the world its responsibility in containing "its" epidemic, in the hope of strengthening the inevitability of Greater China's integration.

China as a "responsible state"

Dating back to the Mao and the early Deng Xiaoping eras, "Red China" was regarded as a steady source of global instability by contemporary scholars such as Philip Snow[5] and politicians such as Ronald Reagan.[6] Even after the end of the cold war, the remark made by President George W. Bush that the U.S. pilots involved in the Sino-American spy plane incident over Hainan in April 2001 were "patriotic" once again reminded the world that a strong China was an unwelcome challenger to Western domination.[7] Granted, Sino-American relations greatly improved after the 9/11 attacks, yet the "China Threat Theory" is still popular in the Western world.[8]

On the Chinese side, Beijing has tried hard to assign itself a new role since the 1990s: to be a "responsible state" in the world. The foreign policy motto given by Deng Xiaoping after the Tiananmen Incident, instructing his successors to "conceal China's capabilities and not to take the lead to challenge the Western world," has already paved the way for China to cooperate, and assimilate, with the globalized—or even Westernized—world order.[9] Some scholars now credit the PRC with being an emergent power that is acting as a responsible state. Rosemary Foot, for instance, considers that contemporary Chinese foreign policy reflects an emphasis among the new generation of Chinese Communist Party (CCP) leaders on sharing human responsibility. In acknowledging the new world order, these leaders see China's role not as a challenger but as a preserver of order.[10] During the SARS crisis, Beijing indeed acted more in accordance with the latter than the former role.

On April 14, 2003, Premier Wen Jiabao for the first time linked the credibility of the anti-SARS campaign to the international reputation of China.[11] Less than a week later, the removal of the minister of health was confirmed. From then on, Wen and the Vice-Premier and new Minister of Health Wu Yi repeatedly promised the Chinese people as well as to the outside world that SARS would be contained. All "Chinese brothers" would be united to "win the battle of vitality and fatality."[12]

Once Wu took over the ministry, body temperature checking was implemented for all Chinese citizens leaving the country. Apparently, transparent figures of SARS cases were disclosed to the worldwide press at daily press conferences—a very unusual circumstance in Chinese politics. WHO representatives were welcomed as de facto supervisors of the Chinese anti-SARS campaign. Hence, the standards of WHO, such as its definition of "infected areas," became China's standards for assessing its own effectiveness. In sharp contrast with official Chinese responses to charges of pirated markets, ethnic repression, and human-rights violations, in the case of SARS, Beijing leaders did not complain about "external forces interfering in Chinese internal policy." In short, Beijing tried its best to act as a responsible member of the world family during the SARS crisis, if we ignore the initial responses.

Initiation of cross-strait anti-SARS cooperation

Since Beijing claims to be the only legitimate Chinese regime in the world, its responsibility to combat SARS for the well-being of all Chinese people naturally includes the population in Taiwan. In order to visualize cross-Strait cooperation against the "Chinese epidemic," three policies were formulated. These not only embraced friendly gestures toward the Taiwanese population, but also, interestingly, yielded a kind of green light to Taipei's autonomy.

First, the Taiwan Affairs Office of the State Council (TAO) initiated a direct exchange of SARS information with Taipei. Cross-Strait anti-SARS conferences, which hosted medical experts and technocrats from Taiwan, were repeatedly organized by Beijing from April 23, 2003 onward. Earlier, on April 11, Premier Wen had already urged a better utilization of unofficial channels to generate cross-Strait anti-SARS cooperation.[13] Since it was difficult to sharply differentiate epidemic and administrative information, the message behind the information sharing went beyond the sharing itself. In the same way that Tony Blair told the Yugoslavian President Slobodan Milosevic during the Kosovo civil war in 1999 that "human rights should be higher than sovereignty," Beijing hoped to convince Taipei that humanitarianism should be placed higher than politics in the SARS crisis.

Beijing also attempted to provide tangible humanitarian aid to Taiwan. In early May, 5,000 Chinese-made masks were sent to Taiwan-ruled Jinmen (Quemoy) island through Taiwan's Jinmen-Matsu Cross-Strait Communication Association.[14] On May 12, Wang Lizhong, vice-chairman of the Chinese branch of the Red Cross, offered a limited amount of medical equipment to Chen Chang-wen, his counterpart in Taiwan.[15] The largest-scale offer was made on May 23, during the peak of Taiwan's SARS crisis, when the semi-official Association for Relations Across the Taiwan Strait (ARATS) offered to donate 200,000 sets of anti-SARS jackets, 100,000 N95-standard masks, five ambulances, and a team of mainland experts to Taiwan's Strait Exchange Foundation (SEF).[16] In addition, Taiwan businessmen on the mainland, like foreigners, were given preferential treatment after TAO chairman Chen Yunlin and ARATS vice-chairman Li Bingcai paid a high-profile visit to Taiwan-owned enterprises on April 28, and used it as a platform to instruct Chinese officials to "take special care of the Taiwanese businessmen."[17] The above gestures were in line with Beijing's revised principle of pushing unification via economic integration—ahead of intensive political debates—an idea that was first introduced at the 16th CCP Party Congress in December 2002.

As a more pragmatic gift to Taipei, Beijing on May 4 surprisingly gave the green light to WHO experts who wished to visit Taiwan to investigate the condition of the SARS outbreak there.[18] Borrowing from Beijing's logic, since it is the only valid government representing the Chinese population, the situation of Taiwan should theoretically have been reported to WHO via Beijing. From Taiwan's point of view, the green light was in fact a major step forward since its departure from the United Nations (UN) in 1971, as direct communication between Taipei and international associations was thus reactivated by the SARS crisis. However, from Beijing's point of view, the green light was probably given amidst contradictory considerations: While it risked enhancing Taiwan's "sovereignty" by allowing Taipei to have direct contact with WHO, Beijing also dismissed the idea of Taiwan's joining WHO as a full member.

The above gestures all pointed in the same direction. As long as Taiwan was walking within the Chinese orbit, its autonomy—but not its sovereignty—would still have room for expansion, as Beijing's bottom line on Taiwan's autonomy was clearly more flexible than what it openly declared. Scholars like Kenichi Ohmae went a step further to suggest that the admission of Taiwan into the United Nations would not be impossible so long as its clear submission to Beijing was guaranteed. At that time, he wrote, Beijing might apply the "Ukrainian Model" of the USSR to nominate Taiwan to join the UN.[19] Although Ohmae's suggestion is too remote a possibility, if valid at all, the WHO green light was indeed given under a similar rationale. Beijing hoped to convey the message that Taiwan would gain functional advantages by participating in the international arena so long as it did not claim full sovereignty. More Taiwanese people would then side with the pro-unification "Pan-Blue" lobby on the island in the next election.

SARS as an issue of sovereign states

The chief focus of Beijing's SARS Diplomacy was the issue of sovereignty—the sovereignty of Beijing as the effective regime representing all Chinese territories. All gestures—or even concessions—to Taipei were made under the assumption that SARS was an internal Chinese affair. Any need for Taiwan, as a result of SARS, to join the social club of sovereign states, such as the United Nations or WHO, was strongly dismissed by Beijing.

After Taiwan's President Chen Shui-bian made the first official request for Taiwan to join WHO to safeguard his citizens from SARS, which will be discussed in the next section, the mainland's response remained consistently stern but calm. On the one hand, not only did Beijing allow the visit of WHO experts to Taiwan, it showed flexibility about helping Taiwan join WHO in other formats—a "willingness to provide other WHO-related information and help" as was also hinted at by Vice-Premier Wu when she attended the WHO annual conference in May.[20] The hint was based on the following logic: Technically, a nongovernmental organization (NGO) can join WHO as an Associate Member,[21] thus Beijing might well nominate Taiwan's participation as an NGO instead of as an "observer" as Taiwan proposed. If cross-Strait understanding on this issue could be achieved, it would presumably solve the sovereignty issue.

On the other hand, however, Beijing's rhetoric from Vice-Premier Wu and her ousted predecessor always tied Chen's WHO proposal to his Taiwanese independence plot. To preempt such a "plot," Beijing not only prevented Taiwan from joining WHO, but also pressured the World Trade Organization (WTO) on May 27 to downgrade the status of Taiwan officials from "delegates" to "representatives."[22] Even Andrew Hsia, Taiwan's representative in New York, was barred from reporting Taiwan's SARS condition to the United Nations on May 24 after UN General Secretary Kofi Annan was pressured by Beijing.[23] It is a combination of carrot and stick, Beijing-style: Sovereignty is nonnegotiable, yet being submissive to the Chinese orbit may potentially generate more autonomy for Taipei.[24] The strategy might well have logical flaws, as Beijing's humanitarianism is not mere humanitarianism but *political* humanitarianism. Nonetheless, it is the bottom line of SARS Diplomacy of Beijing.

Foreign policy of Taipei during the SARS crisis

Since the electoral victory of the pro-independence Democratic People's Party (DPP) in 2000, Taipei has been accused by Beijing of walking gradually down the road to independence. While Beijing tried its best to present its SARS Diplomacy as a humanitarian and internal affair, Taipei took an opposing viewpoint. DPP President Chen regarded SARS as a political and external affair, and took the opportunity to withdraw Taiwan from the Chinese orbit. Long before the outbreak of SARS in Taiwan, Chen Shui-bian's China policy included badmouthing China as an "irresponsible state" to the world; minimizing cross-Strait cooperation in the anti-SARS campaign and cutting back the existing cross-Strait linkages; and emphasizing the non-sovereign globalized nature of SARS.

China as an "irresponsible state"

While Beijing was portraying itself as a responsible state, the DPP government of Taiwan offered plenty of evidence to prove Beijing's irresponsibility. Given the time gap of five months between the first reported SARS case in the PRC and in Taiwan, the Taiwanese people had little doubt that SARS was spread by Taiwanese businessmen returning from the mainland or Hong Kong, especially after the case of an infected SARS patient from Hong Kong's Amoy Garden who had gone to Taiwan to worship his Taiwanese ancestors in March.[25] The import of the "Chinese disease"—"their epidemic"—was then elevated to a moral high ground by Taiwanese leaders. For instance, when SARS began to lose control in Taiwan on April 12, Vice-President Annette Lu emotionally criticized Beijing for "sending foot-and-mouth disease and SARS to Taiwan" and "ignoring the loss of lives."[26] The list of ailments to blame as a result of frequent cross-Strait contact was extended on June 2 by the president's adviser, Huang Tien-lin, to include dengue fever, anthrax, avian flu, hantavirus, and other "epidemics that have not been seen for decades."[27] Following this logic, Beijing's responsibility for setting a bad hygiene standard for the mainland to nurture epidemics was inescapable.

Further proof of Beijing's irresponsibility was its opaque political system. In order to quantify such opaqueness, President Chen told the world on April 20, without any valid source, that the real number of SARS infected cases on the mainland should be "five times higher than the official figure." This comment suggested that everything in Beijing was still covert, and that such a lack of transparency would only create further crises for the whole world.[28] To visualize the conspiracy for the public, Taiwan's Department of Health even designed a notorious advertisement in April that equated

SARS with those communist spies hiding in Taiwan. A slogan was shown everywhere: "the number of SARS is far less than the number of communist spies in Taiwan."[29]

These pieces of so-called "evidence" were targeted at supporting the "One Country on Each Side" Theory (*yibian yiguo lun*), which was proposed by President Chen in 2002 to claim that each side of the Strait is "a country." According to the theory, in the SARS crisis, one side is the sender, the other is the receiver; one side is the conspirer, the other is the victim. We can now observe how Taipei designed its SARS Diplomacy to situate itself in a win-win scenario: In the early days of "zero infection" and "zero casualties," the achievement was quoted to support the effective cross-Strait alienation from March on.[30] However, when Taipei lost control of SARS on April 21, when medical staff in Hoping Hospital were cross-infected en masse, the crisis was quoted to support the horror of cross-Strait contact, despite its logical refutation of the earlier argument.[31]

As a result, no matter how hard Beijing tried to frame its reunification context in terms of humanitarianism during the SARS crisis, Taipei remained sensitive toward this tactic and still regarded Beijing as an irresponsible player—for the export of its epidemic to Taiwan, for its problematic figures, and for its "political language and unfriendly gestures derived from a non-factual basis," as concluded by Mainland Affairs Council (MAC) Chairlady Tsai Ing-wen's *Post-SARS Era Cross-Strait Economic Development New Strategy Report* on July 17, 2003.[32] On July 3, in an even higher profile report by the Japanese newspaper *Asahi Shimbun*, a personal interview with President Chen revealed his disappointment with Chinese President Hu Jintao at a personal level. This disappointment resulted from Hu's lack of apology for spreading SARS to Taiwan, his rejection of Taiwan's entry into WHO, and his rejection of Taiwan's legitimate international aspirations.[33] As a matter of fact, given the day-to-day sense of helplessness of Taiwan during the SARS crisis, the Taiwanese people were easily convinced of the irresponsibility of Beijing. With the "big brother" of the Greater China Region demeaned as a bully, the DPP leaders could then look for patrons elsewhere to actualize their gradual move toward independence.

Restrictions on cross-strait anti-SARS cooperation

Taipei not only highlighted the irresponsibility of Beijing, but also artificially amplified the nature of such "irresponsibility" by freezing remaining cross-Strait contact during the SARS crisis. Just as Beijing had a hidden agenda of reunification and expansion of the Chinese order, Taipei's policies were formulated not as a result of humanitarian concerns, but instead with political considerations in mind. They were, arguably, designed to dissociate Taiwan from the Greater Chinese Region, and to present the lone island as victim—an abandoned orphan of the world community.

First, cross-Strait anti-SARS conferences, official- or academic-based, were openly discouraged by Taipei. As disclosed by Taiwanese medical scholar Chen Yimin, Taiwan's Department of Health had advised indigenous scholars not to attend Beijing's anti-SARS conference on April 23. At the same time, the anti-SARS conference organized by Taipei on April 20, which was organized in haste to precede the mainland one, technically barred mainland scholars from attending.[34]

In addition, as a unilateral practice with few equivalents from the mainland or Hong Kong, a ten-day quarantine period was imposed on April 27 on all travelers coming from infected areas, particularly referring to the "Chinese."[35] Although the quarantine was undisputedly humanitarian, the unfriendly reception given to people from China and Hong Kong further alienated Taiwan's Chinese neighbors. For instance, an outcry developed when a thirty-two-member Hong Kong tour was forced into quarantine on April 25, simply owing to a six-year-old girl being found to have suffered from mild fever in the morning.[36]

In a dramatic manner, almost all humanitarian aid offered by the mainland was rejected by Taipei. On May 13, the Taiwan representative of the Red Cross turned down the help offered by the mainland's Red Cross.[37] Moreover, provoking Beijing in a more serious manner, on May 26 SEF used "popular reaction" as a reason to reject all mainland materials provided by ARATS.[38] The response was dubbed a Taipei conspiracy, since according to an ARATS official it was SEF that first hinted at wanting the mainland's help: "we express our gratitude toward the equipment donated by the mainland owing to SARS."[39] Beijing's anger was received by President Chen with delight: Commenting on the ARATS offer, Chen called it the mainland's "shameful help of Taiwan."[40]

Chen's implicit message was clear: When Beijing failed to offer a single hand in Taiwan, and Taipei did not offer any substantial help to Beijing as well, the relations between Taiwan and the PRC had no special nature at all. The fact of "no special nature" is one more step away from the so-called "special country-to-country relations" doctrine (Two-State Theory, *liangguolun*) expressed by ex-president Lee Teng-hui in 1999, which Beijing already regarded as a quasi-declaration of independence.

Furthermore, the restriction of cross-Strait cooperation was extended to other originally irrelevant agendas. The entry permit for Hong Kong citizens to enter Taiwan ceased to function on April 25, 2003.[41] Prior to this, on March 31, the cross-Strait "Little Three Direct Links"—mainly concerning direct transportation between Jinmen and Xiamen—had already been halted by MAC.[42] The pro-independence lobby—the so-called "Pan-Green" Camp—even urged a slowdown of the building of the "Three Direct Links."[43] The backlash was echoed by MAC's delay in evaluating the prospect of the links on August 15, 2003, which was supposed to be revealed in November 2002. As the ultimate solution to dissociate from the mainland, President Chen set up a "Presidential Economic Advisory Committee" on May 23 as part of the SARS recovery program. The aim of the committee was to transform Taiwan into an "Asian-Pacific Operations Hub."[44] As stated by Vice-President Lu: "if Taiwan became the Asian-Pacific Operations Hub, Taiwanese businessmen would no longer have to invest in China."[45]

SARS as an issue of globalization: the WHO entry proposal

Since the spread of SARS was interpreted as an unwanted import of the globalized era following frequent cross-Strait contact, a sensible solution for Taiwan would be to play a more formal role in this globalized world order. The most controversial attempt to achieve such a solution was Taiwan's intention to use SARS as a way to enter WHO—an international organization of sovereign states—as an Associate Member. Taiwan had made the same request for seven consecutive years, as a parallel and futile attempt to join the United Nations. Unlike previous tries that featured only political incentives, the current bid was camouflaged under a "humanitarian clause" because Taiwan regarded the mainland as an ineffective protector against SARS.

The attempt achieved preliminary success with the formal endorsement of the U.S. House of Representatives on May 14.[46] A bill to support Taiwan's entry was signed by President George W. Bush on May 29.[47] Japanese Foreign Minister Kawaguchi Yoriko also provided verbal support.[48] As Taiwan Minister of Foreign Affairs Eugene Chien made clear at the time: SARS is both a crisis and an opportunity for Taiwan.[49]

As expected, after Beijing's strong sense of disapproval of the Taiwanese entry became clear, the preliminary success proved insufficient to sway international opinion. As in 2002, the American and Japanese representatives did not give any actual support to Taiwan when the entry proposal was put forward at Geneva's World Health Association (WHA) by Taiwan's ally, the Marshall Islands, on May 19. The proposal was defeated again; only seven WHO members supported it.

Such an expected defeat, however, generated a disproportionately vigorous response in Taiwan. On May 20, Foreign Minister Chien described the failure as a "matter of life or death," and criticized the role of Beijing for violating the basic human rights of the Taiwanese people.[50] On May 25, President Chen escalated the official rhetoric; he called Beijing's role a "deliberate, barbaric maneuver to isolate Taiwan."[51] DPP Deputy Secretary-General Lee Chin-yung spoke of Beijing's "hegemonic nature" on May 26.[52] Populist sentiment was stirred up against Beijing's aggression towards Taiwan's *Lebensraum*. Even the "Pan-Blue" Camp found it unacceptable: Helping Taiwan to join WHO became a new item on Pan-Blue's platform for the 2004 presidential election.[53] Eloquently capturing the moment,

President Chen proposed to hold a referendum to decide whether Taiwan should join WHO.[54] Beijing viewed this idea with grave concern, as the first step toward a referendum to decide upon the future of Taiwanese sovereignty.[55]

The WHO proposal was not the only attempt by Taipei to exploit SARS as a means to distance itself from the Chinese sphere of influence. On April 24, DPP Legislative Councilor Trong Chai suggested that Taipei should make use of the "worldwide anti-Chinese momentum" brought about by SARS to issue a new Taiwanese passport, which should display the term "Taiwan" on its "Republic of China" cover.[56] The suggestion was endorsed by the Department of Foreign Affairs,[57] and the new passport was issued on September 1, 2003. In a parallel effort, China was formally regarded as a "foreign country" when Taiwan's Ministry of Foreign Affairs labeled it as a "Post-SARS Travel Warning Zone" on August 25. This was the first time the Ministry of Foreign Affairs bypassed the MAC, which is responsible for handling cross-Strait issues, to deal with the PRC.[58]

In fact, the response generated from the WHO defeat is already, ironically, more beneficial to the DPP than a success might have been. From the unfolding of SARS to the WHO entry proposal, the referendum, and the new passport, the DPP regime clearly had a strategy for guiding Taiwan into a non-Chinese orbit. Just as the friendliness of Beijing to Taipei was intended to convey China's "internal affairs" agenda, Taipei's unfriendliness was intended to convey its "external affairs" agenda. Its motive was to extend Taiwan's non-Chinese identity and self-sovereignty to the international arena, with the ultimate goal of achieving independence in a non-Chinese sphere of influence.

Chinese or non-Chinese orbit?
Macro framework of the SARS diplomacy

When the SARS crisis began to wane in July 2003, some of the measures implemented in the previous months were reviewed. The quarantine policy of Taiwan against people coming from infected areas was repudiated on June 25;[59] the Entry Permit for Hong Kong citizens to enter Taiwan was reissued on July 14;[60] and the "Little Three Direct Links" were finally reinstated on July 16.[61]

Thus, apparently, Beijing did not regard SARS as a modifier of cross-Strait relations, as revealed by the official rhetoric of Tang Shubei, former ARATS chairman, at the 4th Cross-Strait Relations Forum on July 18.[62] However, Taiwan's MAC viewed it contradictorily, and believed SARS "has provided certain challenges to cross-Strait relations and has led to the waning of the recent 'Mainland Craze' as a fashion in Taiwan."[63] The two evaluations prove the reality of the different preferred orbits that Beijing and Taipei are trying to build.

Two different orbits in the SARS diplomacy

According to Beijing, the Chinese populations across the whole world, and particularly across the Strait, should unite under its leadership to cope with their own epidemic. Since the origin of SARS was in China, and the spread of the epidemic proved unstoppable in the era of globalization, the choice of Beijing was to cope with—instead of challenge—the spread of globalization, and to use the crisis as a cause to visualize and consolidate the existence of the Greater Chinese integration in its sphere of influence. Were other political entities willing to acknowledge the central position of Beijing in this orbit, Beijing in turn would be willing to acknowledge a certain degree of autonomy—or "face"—to junior members. Despite their different levels, Beijing's strategy is comparable to Brussels' handling of the BSE (Mad Cow Disease) crisis: The European Union was willing to sacrifice some "face" to the national sovereignty of Britain if the latter were more submissive to its central policy regarding the British-originated BSE.

In contrast, despite Beijing's effort to consolidate its orbit by smiling, though never dismissing the possibility of solving the Taiwan question militarily as a last resort, Taipei pushed for a completely different agenda and chose to employ hostility to dissociate itself from Greater China. According to the *Mainland Work Report* released by MAC on May 31, Taiwan regarded SARS as a messenger to disclose four deficits of the mainland system: the discredited medical system, the opaque political system, bureaucratism, and institutional factionalism.[64] When the anti-SARS campaign of Taipei failed to give any credit to Beijing, and the locus from which Taipei sought help was the Western-dominated international community (e.g., the American and Japanese help in the WHO entry), Taiwan's eagerness to look beyond the region—i.e., to the non-Chinese orbit—in the era of globalization was clearly revealed. The "Western orbit" might not be particularly welcoming to Taiwan, but as long as it can provide a viable alternative for the DPP regime to the Chinese orbit, it is still the preferable one.

Prospects and limitations of Beijing's Chinese orbit

Beijing's agenda achieved a certain level of success during the SARS crisis, for the symbolic importance of Beijing in the Greater China region was repeatedly proven. For instance, regardless of Taiwan's response, the direct WHO-Taipei contact was made possible only with Beijing's approval. Humanitarian aid to Taiwan and Hong Kong, despite rejection from the former, demonstrated Beijing's parental position in its orbit. The removal of Hong Kong from WHO's travel warning and infected area list was forcefully pushed by Chinese Vice-Premier Wu in WHO.[65] Beijing was also the major backstage broker behind the multilateral anti-SARS agreements reached by twelve Southeastern Asian countries in Kuala Lumpur.[66] In short,

Beijing's position as the center of the Chinese orbit was strengthened through anti-SARS humanitarianism, a strategy comparable to the Chinese decision not to devalue the renminbi during the Asian Financial Crisis in 1997. When Chinese unification was tied to the cross-Strait anti-SARS campaign in the post-SARS recovery conferences in July, the parallel was even acknowledged by the "Pan-Blue" attendants from Taiwan.[67]

However, the prospect of such a Chinese orbit is subject to one major constraint: the inability of the Chinese umbrella to cover all humanitarian intentions of the people living within its sphere of influence. This was suggested by Taiwan's response to the WHO controversy. It was not due to any Beijing measure to bar humanitarian aid to Taiwan; instead, ironically, Taiwan's response derived from the inevitable political statements embedded in Beijing's not-so-genuine humanitarianism. As long as the Chinese communities remain divided among different political entities, not to mention other potential members within the Chinese orbit who are still cautious of the rising power of Beijing, full humanitarian cooperation among them will remain difficult to achieve.

Prospects and limitations of Taipei's non-Chinese orbit

The DPP regime of Taiwan also achieved some success in internationalizing its local SARS crisis via SARS Diplomacy. The symbolic American and Japanese support of Taiwan's entry into WHO gave the Taiwanese people a glimmer of hope that they might be able to turn away from mainland Chinese influence and to the Western world. Moreover, SARS—and the SARS Diplomacy of Taipei—successfully transcended all political parties: even the "Pan-Blue" Camp could not openly resist the non-Chinese direction for fear of being labeled with "betraying Taiwan."[68] Thus, despite the ineffectiveness of the anti-SARS campaign on the humanitarian battlefront, the DPP effectively turned the crisis into a platform to generate universal hostility toward Beijing, and further transformed such hostility into a mandate for Taipei to search for alternative patrons in the world.

However, although Taiwan tried to label itself as a member of the non-Chinese, Western world orbit by characterizing itself as another scapegoat of the "Chinese disease," along with Toronto and Bangkok, the argument of differentiating the Taiwanese from mainland Chinese was not well accepted by Western audiences. For instance, Taipei's heavily politicized verbal attack on Beijing was viewed with contempt by WHO officials. As expressed by WHO spokesman Allen Thompson, Taipei's protest against WHO after its self-declared "anti-SARS D-Day" was not rectified by the latter[69] generated mutual mistrust between Taipei and WHO.[70] As a coincidence, since its enlistment on March 18, Taiwan was the last place to be removed from the WHO infected area list (on July 5), despite having suffered lighter casualties than Beijing or Hong Kong (which were removed from the list on June 24 and June 23 respectively).

Moreover, no matter how hard the DPP regime tried to tie Taiwan to Japan and the United States, the existence of Beijing pressure, representing the ever-present linkage of the two sides of the Strait, was always a reminder of the limits of Taiwan's diplomacy. Just as President Chen was badmouthing Beijing in his SARS Diplomacy, George W. Bush was openly praising China's anti-SARS effort under Hu Jintao's leadership.[71] Realistically, from the Western point of view, Taiwan might be a fair tool to balance against Beijing, but it is more likely to be a tool belonging to "their world," instead of a family-member of "our world."

To conclude, SARS has far exceeded mere health and humanitarian issues from the viewpoint of different political entities among the Chinese population. The greatest threat posed to the Chinese people from SARS Diplomacy is the stirred up populist sentiments on both sides of the Strait, with the agenda to hold a "preventive referendum" against the mainland threat on one side, and the escalated nationalism with an increasing level of distrust toward Taiwan on the other. If there is another SARS crisis or its equivalent in the future, it will probably generate similar policies from Beijing and Taipei, with one targeting Greater Chinese integration and the other moving toward the non-Chinese and very possibly the Western orbit. Although the contents of the two agendas might seem impulsive at times, since they might include exceptionally friendly or unfriendly representations, their ultimate motivations are crystal clear. The worrisome reality is that, despite the impossibility of achieving both agendas, Beijing and Taipei considers them irresistible missions in the new century.

Notes

1 "China Lags in Sharing SARS Background," *Washington Times*, August 5, 2003.
2 The total number of reported SARS cases in China was 5,327, including 349 fatalities. The number of reported SARS cases in Taiwan was 665, with a total number of 180 deaths.
3 In the following, the "SARS crisis" is dated from November 16, 2002, when the first case was reported on the mainland, to August 16, 2003, when the last SARS patient in Inner Mongolia was discharged from the hospital. The duration overlaps with both the beginning (March 14, 2003) and the end (July 5, 2003) of SARS in Taiwan. April to June 2003 saw the peak of the epidemic, as well as the peak of the SARS Diplomacy.
4 "Zang Wenkang Met with WHO Representatives in China," *Guangming Daily*, March 20, 2003.
5 Philip Snow, "China and Africa: Consensus and Camouflage," in David Shambaugh, ed., *Chinese Foreign Policy: Theory and Practice* (Oxford: Clarendon Press, 1994).
6 Lou Cannon, *President Reagan: the Role of a Lifetime* (New York: Public Affairs, 2000), pp. 479–80.
7 "In N.C., Bush Cheered Over Crew Release," *Washington Post*, April 12, 2001.

8 Steven Mosher, *Hegemon—China's Plan to Dominate Asia and the World*, trans. Li Weiyi (Taiwan: New Century Publishing Co., 2001).

9 Qiufa Li, Jianyi Xu, and Jinzhu Zhuang, *The Compass of International Challenge: the Diplomatic Strategic Thoughts of Deng Xiaoping* (Beijing: Lantian, 1998).

10 Rosemary Foot, "Chinese Power and the Idea of a Responsible State," *China Journal*, vol. 45 (January, 2001), pp. 1–19.

11 "Wen Jiabao Convened State Council General Conference," *Renmin ribao* (People's Daily, Beijing), April 15, 2003.

12 "Wu Yi Reported Anti-SARS Process to National People's Congress Standing Committee," *Renmin ribao*, April 25, 2003.

13 "Cross-Strait Experts Combating SARS Together," *Macau Daily News*, April 12, 2003.

14 "Xiamen Gave 5,000 Masks to Jinmen," *Zhongyang ribao*, May 10, 2003.

15 "China Red Cross Expressed Concern of Taiwan's Epidemic," *Renmin ribao*, May 13, 2003.

16 "ARATS Sent Letter to SEF to Express Concern Over Taiwan's Epidemic," *Renmin ribao*, May 24, 2003.

17 "TAO and ARATS Leaders Urged Cross-Strait Anti-SARS Cooperation," *Renmin ribao*, April 29, 2003.

18 "Beijing to Allow WHO to Send Team to Taiwan," *Washington Post*, May 4, 2003.

19 Kenichi Ohmae, *Emergence of the United States of Chunghwa* (Japan: PHP Publishing Co., 2002).

20 "Wu Yi: China Strongly Opposes," *Xinhua Macau Daily News*, May 20, 2003.

21 According to the constitution of the World Health Organization, Article 4, "Members of the United Nations may become Members of the Organization by signing or otherwise accepting this Constitution in accordance with the provisions of Chapter XIX [of the United Nations Charter] and in accordance with their constitutional processes." And Article 8 states: "Territories or groups of territories which are not responsible for the conduct of their international relations may be admitted as Associate Members by the Health Assembly upon application made on behalf of such territory or group of territories by the Member or other authority having responsibility for their international relations." Current Associate Members include the Vatican and Palestine. See online at www.yale.edu/lawweb/avalon/decade/decad051.htm.

22 "Taiwan Cannot Kowtow to the Barbaric 'De-legitimizing' Attempt of China in WTO," *Taiwan Daily News*, May 28, 2003.

23 "Barbaric China," *Taiwan Daily News*, May 25, 2003.

24 For instance, if Taiwan acknowledges the so-called "92-Consensus" reached by SEF and ARATS in 1992, featuring the "One China Principle with different interpretations by both sides allowed," it would be considered as being "submissive" to Beijing.

25 "Amoy Resident from Hong Kong Suspected of SARS Symptoms in Taiwan," *Ming Pao*, April 21, 2003.

26 "Annette Lu Elaborated on SARS," *Takungpao*, April 21, 2003.

27 "Taiwan Should Cut Ties with China," *Taipei Times*, June 2, 2003.

28 "Chen Shui-bian Criticized CCP for Caring Only for Face Instead of Lives," *Taiwan Shin Sheng Daily News*, April 21, 2003.

29 "Is SARS a Communist Spy?" *United Daily News*, April 1, 2003.

30 "The Setback of 'Chinese Assimilation,'" *Taiwan Daily News*, March 17, 2003.

31 "Combating SARS, Combating People from China and Hong Kong," *Commons Daily*, April 26, 2003.

32 Ing-wen Tsai, *Post-SARS Era Cross-Strait Economic Development New Strategy Report* (Taiwan: Taiwan Chinese Economic Research Institute, 2003).

33 "Interview with President Chen Shui-bian of Taiwan," *Asahi Shimbun* (Tokyo), July 3, 2003.

34 "Taiwan Scholars Urge Cross-Strait Cooperative Anti-SARS Program," *Takungpao*, April 24, 2003.

35 "Hong Kong Government Regarded Quarantine in Taiwan as Unnecessary," *Xinhua Macau Daily News*, April 28, 2003.

36 "Hong Kong Government Rented Chartered Flight to Take Back Quarantined Tourists from Taiwan," *Ming Pao*, May 1, 2003.

37 "Is Mainland Really Taking Care of Taiwan?" *United Daily News*, May 24, 2003.

38 "ARCTS Criticized Taiwan's Limbo," *United Daily News*, May 26, 2003.

39 The SEF letter was revealed by an anonymous ARATS official in the Hong Kong leftist newspaper Wen Weipao, May 27, 2003.

40 "Chen Shui-bian Blamed China for being Barbaric and Shameful," *Taiwan Daily News*, May 26, 2003.

41 "Taiwan Paused Hong Kong's Entry Permit for One Month," *Ming Pao*, April 26, 2003.

42 "Little Three Direct Links at Jinmen and Matsu Paused," *United Daily News*, April 1, 2003.

43 On April 21, Hu Shan-jen, an Administrative Officer of the Executive Yuan, used SARS as an excuse to propose taking a more prudent attitude toward the Three Direct Links. "Slowed Down Disclosure of Direct Flight Evaluation," *Taiwan Economic Daily News*, April 22, 2003.

44 "Vincent Siew Invited to Chair Presidential Economic Advisory Panel," *United Daily News*, May 24, 2003.

45 "Annette Lu Advises Not to Invest in China in the Post-SARS Era," *Xinhua Macau Daily News*, May 31, 2003.

46 "USA Helps Us to Join WHO," *China Times*, May 14, 2003.

47 "Bush Signs Bill to Support Taiwanese Entry into WHO," *Oriental Daily News*, May 31, 2003.

48 "Japanese Foreign Minister Supports Our Participation in WHO," *Central Daily News*, 13 May 2003.

49 "Minister Chien: WHO Entry Campaign Better than Last Year," *Taiwan Shin Sheng Daily News*, May 8, 2003.

50 "Minister Chien Press Conference," *Commons Daily*, May 21, 2003.

51 "Chen Shui-bian Criticizes China's Barbaric Pressure," *Central Daily News*, May 26, 2003.

52 "DPP: Beijing Harms Cross-Strait Friendship," *Xinhua Macau Daily News*, May 27, 2003.

53 James Soong, chairman of the People's First Party (PFP), and the candidate for vice-president in 2004 on the "Pan-Blue" ticket, promised on May 30 to help Taiwan enter WHO in 2004 were the list elected. "James Soong Guarantees that Taiwan Will Join WHO in Two Years," *Xinhua Macau Daily News*, May 31, 2003.

54 "Chen Shui-bian Proposes Joining WHO by Referendum," *Central Daily News*, May 21, 2003.

55 "Taiwan Referendum Against Rationality and Emotion," *Wenweipao*, May 22, 2003.

56 "Trong Chai Proposes Taiwan Passport," *Takungpao*, April 25, 2003.

57 "New Passport Cover Printed 'Taiwan,'" *Taiwan Daily News*, June 12, 2003.

58 "Taiwan Regards China as a 'Foreign Country,'" *Oriental Daily News*, August 25, 2003.

59 "Quarantine for Hong Kong and Macau Citizens Lifted," *Wenweipao*, June 26, 2003.
60 "Taiwan Resumes Hong Kong Citizen's Entry Permit," *Shing Pao*, July 13, 2003.
61 "Little Three Direct Links Fully Recovered," *Commons Daily*, July 17, 2003.
62 "Beijing Stresses Uncompromising One China Principle," *Xinhua Macau Daily News*, July 19, 2003.
63 Post-SARS Era Cross-Strait Economic Development New Strategy Report.
64 "MAC Evaluated the Impacts of SARS on Mainland in This Way," *Xinhua Macau Daily News*, May 31, 2003.
65 "Wu Yi Supports Hong Kong and Urges WHO to Withdraw Travel Warning," *Oriental Daily*, May 20, 2003.
66 "Twelve Asian Countries Discuss United Anti-SARS Measures," *Takungpao*, April 26, 2003.
67 For instance, refer to the 4th Cross-Strait Relations Forum, held in Yunnan on July 18, 2003.
68 "PFP Promotes Anti-Betraying Taiwan Bill," *Taiwan Economic Daily News*, July 9, 2003.
69 "Taiwan Lost Again to be Removed from Travel Warning," *Commons Daily*, June 11, 2003.
70 Taiwan suspected the non-rectification of its "anti-SARS D-Day" was owing to an unfriendly intervention from Beijing. WHO spokesman Allen Thompson clarified on June 12 that the only criterion to assess whether to list Taiwan's warning was "knowledge on public health." "WHO Strongly Dismissed Unfair Treatment to Taiwan," *Takungpao*, June 12, 2003.
71 "Bush Calls Hu Jintao to Praise China's Anti-SARS Measures," *Ming Pao*, April 28, 2003.

36

WHO GOVERNS?

Limited global governance by the World Health Organization during the SARS outbreak

Frank L. Smith

Source: *Social Alternatives*, 28:2 (2009), 9–12.

Did the World Health Organization's response to Severe Acute Respiratory Syndrome represent a radical change in global health governance? The short answer is no. Granted, some scholars have argued that global health governance was radically transformed because WHO appeared to exercise unprecedented power and change state behaviour regarding SARS. Yet global governance by WHO was actually of limited content and consequence during this outbreak. State and local governments, in contrast, governed the most important public health actions, namely medical treatment and infection control. While these findings may curtail optimism about global governance, they have important implications for understanding the international response to transnational outbreaks of infectious diseases.

In 2003, a mysterious and lethal disease started to spread around the world. Caused by a previously unknown virus, Severe Acute Respiratory Syndrome (SARS) infected thousands of people and left hundreds dead. In response, the World Health Organization (WHO) issued global alerts and travel advisories, mobilized the world's medical and research community, and pressured states to cooperate with disease surveillance and reporting in order to fight this deadly outbreak. Fortunately, the spread of infection was stopped less than a year after SARS first emerged – a remarkable accomplishment that is often attributed to intervention by WHO.

Scholars of global health governance were quick to draw lessons from SARS. Shortly after the disease was contained, key literature argued that SARS demonstrated that globalisation has changed global health governance to such an extent that now transnational outbreaks are effectively governed by non-state actors like WHO. For example, according to David Fidler,

> No country, not even the United States, could have produced on its own or in conjunction with a few other countries the global response led and coordinated by WHO on SARS.
>
> (Fidler 2004, 189)

If true, then the WHO response to SARS would represent a radical turning point in the rule or regulation of infectious disease and demonstrate the transformative effect that globalisation has on global governance.

However, this article revisits the history of SARS and argues that global governance by the WHO was of limited content and consequence during this outbreak. State and local governments governed the most important public health actions, not the WHO or other non-state actors. Consequently, the response to SARS offers little evidence of any radical change in global health governance, although it does provide valuable lessons about the respective roles of states and WHO during transnational outbreaks of infectious diseases.

Background: WHO and SARS

Founded in 1948, WHO is an agency of the United Nations dedicated to improving global health. It is funded primarily through voluntary contributions by its member states with an annual budget of about $3 billion USD in recent years. WHO is involved with a variety of public health initiatives, providing technical support and sometimes material aid to help fight chronic and infectious diseases. One such initiative occurred during 2003, in response to a previously unknown and occasionally fatal atypical pneumonia that was dubbed SARS as it spread around the world.

SARS first emerged late the previous year in the Chinese province of Guangdong. Although provincial health officials and the Chinese government were probably aware of this outbreak by January 2003, they did not report it to the WHO (Saich 2006, 74). Nevertheless, rumours about a 'fatal flu' quickly spread through unofficial channels such as text messages and email, prompting the WHO to request information from China about the disease in early February. While Chinese officials reported that the outbreak was limited and under control, a sick physician from Guangdong accidentally infected several other travellers while visiting Hong Kong in late February. SARS subsequently spread around the world, with large numbers of cases reported in China, Taiwan, Canada, Singapore, and Vietnam.

According to conventional wisdom, WHO was the hero in the story about SARS because it supposedly governed this outbreak by issuing global alerts and travel advisories, mobilising the world's medical and research community, and pressuring China to stop lying about the epidemic. In contrast, China was seen as the villain because it covered up the initial outbreak and lied about SARS for months while other states shared information with WHO.

China suffered many more cases of SARS than any other country. By the end of June 2003, however, the Chinese government had successfully extinguished SARS and the WHO lifted all of its travel advisories against China – even before Taiwan and Toronto were removed from the WHO list of areas with local transmission. The last case was isolated in mid-June, which effectively ended this outbreak (Whaley and Mansoor 2006). All told, more than 8,000 people were infected with SARS worldwide and almost 800 people died from the disease (WHO 2003a).

A radical change in global health governance?

Before SARS, it was widely recognised that states governed outbreaks of infectious disease inside their borders. This state-centric approach to governing public health is often associated with Westphalian principles of sovereignty, whereby state governments are assumed to have ultimate authority over their own domestic affairs. Conversely, non-state actors were traditionally weak or irrelevant and international organisations like the WHO had little independent power or authority.

However, some scholars argue that global governance of SARS by the WHO was radically different from the state-centric approach that preceded this outbreak. First, the WHO issued an unprecedented series of global alerts and travel advisories to help control SARS – in some cases, without prior approval from the states that were adversely affected by these warnings. Here the WHO might be seen as bypassing state governments and speaking directly to the people, perhaps in accordance with norms such as human rights to health that transcend state sovereignty (Fidler 2004, 38; Zacher 2007, 19). These alerts and advisories also indicate the independent authority of WHO and its willingness to consider unofficial or non-state sources of information.

Second, the WHO helped mobilize the world's medical and research community to identify and contain SARS. It also collected and reported data from disease surveillance that is often assumed to be necessary for governing transnational outbreaks (Fidler 2004, 62). Finally, the WHO pressured China to stop lying about SARS, and remarkably, the Chinese government is portrayed as having buckled in response. After all, the Chinese Minster of Health and the Mayor of Beijing were fired and China started reporting realistic figures about the epidemic only a few days after WHO officials publically accused China of underreporting SARS on April 16 (Pomfret 2003b). This sequence of events seems to suggest that the power and authority of WHO was sufficient to override Chinese sovereignty.

Given the humbling of Chinese sovereignty, mobilization of the world's medical and research community, and unprecedented alerts and advisories, some literature argues that the WHO response to SARS represents a radical change in global health governance. If true, then what caused this change? According to this line of argument, globalisation has drastically increased global health governance, particularly through disease surveillance and reporting by the WHO. In short, globalisation is associated with a proliferation of non-state actors and free flows of information, both of which empower international organisations like the WHO to act with far greater independence and authority than ever before. As a result, globalisation has allegedly caused a fundamental change in world order, whereby state sovereignty over public health is now constrained by the WHO – producing what some scholars describe as a 'post Westphalian' system of global health governance (Fidler 2004; Aginam 2007, 162).

SARS revisited: the more things change, the more they stay the same

Since a radical change in global health governance would be important for theory and practice alike, the WHO response to SARS warrants further investigation. However, a closer examination of history reveals that little evidence supports optimistic conclusions about radical change. If global governance is defined as transnational rule or regulation, then global governance by WHO was of limited content and consequence during the SARS outbreak. Despite globalisation, state and local governments still governed the most important actions associated with medical treatment and infection control.

First, a handful of global alerts and travel advisories is hardly sufficient proof of a fundamental change in world order. While unprecedented for the WHO, these alerts and advisories were also rather innocuous. For example, a WHO 'emergency travel advisory' for SARS issued in March 2003 was the first of its kind but made 'no recommendation for people to restrict travel to any location' (WHO 2003d). Irrespective of norms about human rights to health, WHO did not actually start advising against non-essential travel to places where SARS was spreading until after government authorities in the United States and elsewhere had issued their own warnings (Stein 2003; Stein and Brown 2003). Therefore, it is difficult to distinguish the effect of WHO alerts and advisories from similar warnings issued by states, and neither represents a radical or effective form of global governance since SARS still continued to spread.

Second, medical research and disease surveillance were tangential to the actual provision of healthcare, which the WHO had virtually no capacity to deliver. As in the past, only state and local governments had the resources necessary to treat the sick and control the spread of infection. Unlike medical treatment and infection control, the research and surveillance data collected and shared by WHO was not the most important aspect of outbreak response. As a WHO team leader in Beijing during 2003 observed,

> The SARS outbreak . . . demonstrated the overwhelming and predominant significance of national responses to global outbreaks of disease. In the end, it was what China did that mattered most.
>
> (Schnur 2006, 50)

Finally, it is doubtful that 'naming and shaming' by WHO officials was the decisive factor in changing Chinese policy. Domestic pressure inside China to acknowledge SARS was at least as significant as international pressure to cooperate with WHO (see Cheung 2003; Jakes 2003). In addition, leaders within the Chinese government started preparing to change policy in early April, when the head of China's Center for Disease Control apologized for failing to inform the public about SARS (Pomfret 2003a; Saich 2006, 80–81). This occurred well before naming and shaming by WHO.

Pressure from the WHO was therefore insufficient to change state behaviour. Furthermore, states like Canada were able to change WHO behaviour regarding SARS – not the other way around. For example, pressure from the Canadian government caused the WHO to prematurely lift its advisory against travel to Toronto, even while SARS was still spreading there (WHO 2003b, c). By bowing to this political pressure, the WHO demonstrated its limited independence and marginal role in ruling or regulating transnational outbreaks.

Implications for governing transnational outbreaks of infectious diseases

A good argument can be made that there should be a radical change in global health governance, given the failure of states to more fully relieve the burden of infectious disease around the world. However, this is a normative claim rather than a descriptive statement of fact. While no such change occurred during the SARS outbreak, this history still provides important lessons about the governance of transnational outbreaks by states and WHO.

For their part, state and local governments typically govern medical treatment and infection control in the aftermath of an outbreak. These are the most important public health actions for the sick and susceptible. As a result, health security resembles national security during transnational outbreaks because states cannot rely on international organisations like the WHO or other states to treat their sick or control the spread of infection for them. In other words, medical treatment and infection control are 'self help' problems for states.

One consequence of the self help nature of outbreak response is that differences in state capacity matter. Contrary to the popular cliché about globalisation and disease that says 'germs do not recognise borders,' the prevalence and severity of diseases do correspond to borders that reflect real differences in state capacity. Transnational outbreaks cross these borders, by definition, but the most important actions and outcomes for public health still depend on the resources that individual states have to provide healthcare within their own borders.

In contrast, global governance by WHO has been of limited content and consequence, at least during transnational outbreaks in the recent past. While its prominence in news and scholarship indicates that WHO is seen as a legitimate source of information about disease, visibility is not the same as ability to govern important actions like treatment and control. Similarly, WHO surveillance and reporting are not the same as governing transnational outbreaks in any respect other than a voyeuristic 'look but don't touch' approach to global health governance.

This is not to say that WHO is irrelevant – it provides important information and serves as a useful focal point for international cooperation. Yet these are traditional rather than revolutionary roles for international organizations. Furthermore, WHO cannot force states to comply with it except through inherently weak threats of naming and shaming. Even in a world of perfect compliance with WHO rules and regulations for surveillance and reporting, however, states would still have to rely on self help for treatment and control.

Likewise, 'globalization is not irrelevant to global governance, but it is not transformative either' (Drezner 2007, xiv). There is little evidence to suggest that globalisation caused a radical change in global governance by WHO or other non-state actors during the SARS outbreak in 2003. As a result, concepts like a 'post Westphalian' system of global health governance are provocative but misguided. Transnational outbreaks of infectious diseases are still governed by state and local governments.

References

Aginam, Obijiofor. 2007. 'Global Governance'. In *Macrosocial Determinants of Population Health*, ed. Sandro Galea. New York: Springer.

Cheung, Gary. 2003. 'NPC deputies call on the mainland to release details'. *South China Morning Post* (Hong Kong), 2 April 2003.

Drezner, Daniel W. 2007. *All Politics Is Global: Explaining International Regulatory Regimes*. Princeton: Princeton University Press.

Fidler, David P. 2004. SARS, *Governance and the Globalization of Disease*. New York: Palgrave Macmillan.

Jakes, Susan. 2003. 'Beijing's SARS Attack'. *Time Magazine*, 8 April 2003.

Pomfret, John. 2003a. 'Official Says China Erred on Outbreak: Rare Apology Cites "Poor Coordination".'. *The Washington Post*, 5 April 2003.

Pomfret, John. 2003b. 'Underreporting, Secrecy Fuel SARS in Beijing, WHO Says.' *The Washington Post*, 16 April 2003.

Saich, Tony. 2006. 'Is SARS China's Chernobyl or Much Ado About Nothing?' In *SARS in China: Prelude to Pandemic*, eds. Arthur Kleinman and James L. Watson. Stanford CA: Stanford University Press.

Schnur, Alan. 2006. 'The Role of the World Health Organization in Combating SARS, Focusing on the Effort in China.' In *SARS in China: Prelude to Pandemic?*, eds. Arthur Kleinman and James L. Watson. Stanford CA: Stanford University Press.

Stein, Rob. 2003. 'At CDC, Big Steps To Stem Epidemic; Warnings Cover Travel, Treatment.' *The Washington Post*, 30 March 2003.

Stein, Rob and DeNeen Brown. 2003. 'Illness May Have Spread on Plane; Respiratory Infection of Chinese Tourists Would be 1st Transmission on Flight.' *The Washington Post*, 26 March 2003.

Whaley, Floyd and Osman David Mansoor. 2006. 'SARS Chronology.' In *SARS: How a global epidemic was stopped.* Geneva: WHO Press.

WHO. 2003a. 'Summary of probable SARS cases with onset of illness from 1 November 2002 to 31 July 2003.' http://www.who.int/csr/sars/country/table2004_04_21/en/print.html. Viewed July 2009.

WHO. 2003b. 'Update 37 – WHO extends its SARS-related travel advice to Beijing and Shanxi Province in China and to Toronto Canada.' http://www.who.int/csr/sars/archive/2003_04_23/en/. Viewed July 2009.

WHO. 2003c. 'Update 42 – Travel advice for Toronto, situation in China.' http://www.who.int/csr/sars/archive/2003_04_29/en/. Viewed July 2009.

WHO. 2003d. 'World Health Organization issues emergency travel advisory.' http://www.who.int/csr/sars/archive/2003_03_15/en/. Viewed July 2009.

Zacher, Mark W. 2007. 'The Transformation in Global Health Collaboration since the 1990s.' In *Governing Global Health*, eds. Andrew F. Cooper, John J. Kirton and Ted Schrecker. Burlington, VT: Ashgate.

Part 7

HPAI H5N1

37

THE NEXT PANDEMIC?

Laurie Garrett

Source: *Foreign Affairs*, 84:4 (2005), 3–23.

Probable cause

Scientists have long forecast the appearance of an influenza virus capable of infecting 40 percent of the world's human population and killing unimaginable numbers. Recently, a new strain, H5N1 avian influenza, has shown all the earmarks of becoming that disease. Until now, it has largely been confined to certain bird species, but that may be changing.

The havoc such a disease could wreak is commonly compared to the devastation of the 1918–19 Spanish flu, which killed 50 million people in 18 months. But avian flu is far more dangerous. It kills 100 percent of the domesticated chickens it infects, and among humans the disease is also lethal: as of May 1, about 109 people were known to have contracted it, and it killed 54 percent (although this statistic does not include any milder cases that may have gone unreported). Since it first appeared in southern China in 1997, the virus has mutated, becoming heartier and deadlier and killing a wider range of species. According to the March 2005 National Academy of Science's Institute of Medicine flu report, the "current ongoing epidemic of H5N1 avian influenza in Asia is unprecedented in its scale, in its spread, and in the economic losses it has caused."

In short, doom may loom. But note the "may." If the relentlessly evolving virus becomes capable of human-to-human transmission, develops a power of contagion typical of human influenzas, and maintains its extraordinary virulence, humanity could well face a pandemic unlike any ever witnessed. Or nothing at all could happen. Scientists cannot predict with certainty what this H5N1 influenza will do. Evolution does not function on a knowable timetable, and influenza is one of the sloppiest, most mutation-prone pathogens in nature's storehouse.

Such absolute uncertainty, coupled with the profound potential danger, is disturbing for those whose job it is to ensure the health of their community, their nation, and broader humanity. According to the Centers for Disease Control and Prevention (CDC), in a normal flu season about 200,000 Americans are hospitalized, 38,000 of whom die from the disease, with an overall mortality rate of .008 percent for those infected. Most of those deaths occur among people older than 65; on average, 98 of every 100,000 seniors with the flu die. Influenza costs the U.S. economy about $12 billion annually in direct medical costs and loss of productivity.

Yet this level of damage hardly approaches the catastrophe that the United States would face in a severe flu pandemic. The CDC predicts that a "medium-level epidemic" could kill up to 207,000 Americans, hospitalize 734,000, and sicken about a third of the U.S. population. Direct medical costs would top $166 billion, not including the costs of vaccination. An H5N1 avian influenza that is transmittable from human to human could be even more devastating: assuming a mortality rate of 20 percent and 80 million illnesses, the United States could be looking at 16 million deaths and unimaginable economic costs. This extreme outcome is a worst-case scenario; it assumes failure to produce an effective vaccine rapidly enough to make a difference and a virus that remains impervious to some antiflu drugs. But the 207,000 reckoning is clearly a conservative guess.

The entire world would experience similar levels of viral carnage, and those areas ravaged by HIV and home to millions of immunocompromised individuals might witness even greater death tolls. In response, some countries might impose useless but highly disruptive quarantines or close borders and airports, perhaps for months. Such closures would disrupt trade, travel, and productivity. No doubt the world's stock markets would teeter and perhaps fall precipitously. Aside from economics, the disease would likely directly affect global security, reducing troop strength and capacity for all armed forces, UN peacekeeping operations, and police worldwide.

In a world where most of the wealth is concentrated in less than a dozen nations representing a distinct minority of the total population, the capacity to respond to global threats is, to put it politely, severely imbalanced. The majority of the world's governments not only lack sufficient funds to respond to a superflu; they also have no health infrastructure to handle the burdens of disease, social disruption, and panic. The international community would look to the United States, Canada, Japan, and Europe for answers, vaccines, cures, cash, and hope. How these wealthy governments responded, and how radically the death rates differed along worldwide fault lines of poverty, would resonate for years thereafter.

What once was lost

Nearly half of all deaths in the United States in 1918 were flu related. Some 675,000 Americans—about six percent of the population of 105 million and the equivalent of 2 million American deaths today—perished from the Spanish flu. The average life expectancy for Americans born in 1918 was just 37 years, down from 55 in 1917. Although doctors then lacked the technology to test people's blood for flu infections, scientists reckon that the Spanish flu had a mortality rate of just less than one percent of those who took ill in the United States. It would have been much worse had there not been milder flu epidemics in the 1850s and in 1889, caused by similar but less virulent viruses, which made most elderly Americans immune to the 1918–19 strain. The highest death tolls were among young adults, ages 20–35.

The Spanish flu got its name because Spain suffered from an early and acute outbreak, but it did not originate there. Its actual origin remains uncertain. The first strain was mild enough to prompt most World War I military forces to dismiss it as a pesky ailment. When the second strain hit North America in the summer of 1918, however, the virus caused a surge of deaths. First hit was Camp Funston, an army base in Kansas, where young soldiers were preparing for deployment to Europe. The virus then spread swiftly to other camps and on troop ships crossing the Atlantic, killing 43,000 U.S. military personnel in about three months. Despite the entreaties of the military's surgeons general, President Woodrow Wilson ordered continued shipments of troops aboard crowded naval transports, which soldiers came to call "death ships." By late September 1918, so overwhelmed was the War Department by influenza that the military could not assist in controlling civic disorder at home, including riots caused by epidemic hysteria. Worse, so many doctors, scientists, and lab technicians had been drafted into military service that civilian operations were hamstrung.

Under these conditions, influenza swept from the most populous U.S. cities to extraordinarily remote rural areas. Explorers discovered empty Inuit villages in what are now Alaska and the Yukon Territory, their entire populations having succumbed to the flu. Many deaths were never included in the pandemic's official death toll—such as the majority of victims in Africa, Latin America, Indonesia, the Pacific Islands, and Russia (then still in the throes of revolution). What is known about the toll in these regions is staggering. For example, influenza killed 5 percent of the population of Ghana in only two months, and nearly 20 percent of the people of Western Samoa died. The official estimate of 40–50 million total deaths is believed to be a conservative extrapolation of European and American records. In fact, many historians and biologists believe that nearly a third of all humans suffered from influenza in 1918–19—and that of these, 100 million died.

In the last years of the nineteenth century and the early years of the twentieth, a series of important scientific discoveries spawned a revolution in biology and medicine and led pioneers such as Hermann Biggs, a New York City doctor, to create entire legal and health systems based on the identification and control of germs. By 1917, the United States and much of Europe had become enthralled by the hygiene movement. Impressive new public health infrastructures had been built in many cities, tens of thousands of tuberculosis victims were isolated in sanatoriums, the incidences of child-killing diseases such as diphtheria and typhoid fever had plummeted, and cholera epidemics had become rare events in the industrialized world. There was great optimism that modern science held the key to perfect health.

Influenza's arrival shattered the hope; scientists still had virtually no understanding of viruses generally, and of influenza in particular. The hygienic

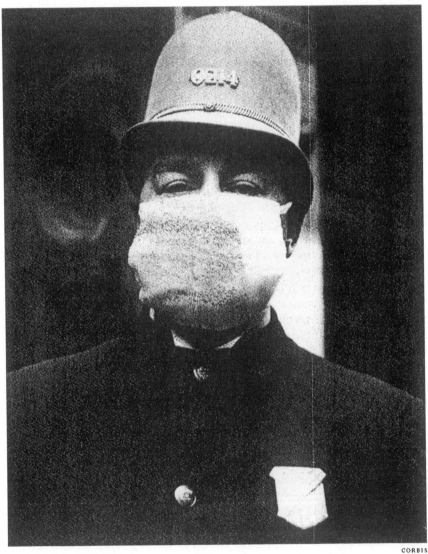

On guard: antiflu precautions, 1918

precautions and quarantines that had proved so effective in holding back the tide of bacterial diseases in the United States proved useless, even harmful, in the face of the Spanish flu. As the epidemic spread, top physicians and scientists claimed its cause was everything from tiny plants to old dusty books to something called "cosmic influence." It was not until 1933 that a British research team finally isolated and identified the influenza virus.

Most strains of the flu do not kill people directly; rather, death is caused by bacteria, which surge into the embattled lungs of the victim. But the Spanish flu that circulated in 1918–19 was a direct killer. Victims suffered from acute cyanosis, a blue discoloration of the skin and mucous membranes. They vomited and coughed up blood, which also poured uncontrollably from their noses and, in the case of women, from their genitals. The highest death toll occurred among pregnant women: as many as 71 percent of those infected died. If the woman survived, the fetus invariably did not. Many young people suffered from encephalitis, as the virus chewed away at their brains and spinal cords. And millions experienced acute respiratory distress syndrome, an immunological condition in which disease-fighting cells so overwhelm the lungs in their battle against the invaders that the lung cells themselves become collateral damage, and the victims suffocate. Had antibiotics existed, they may not have been much help.

Oops

In January 1976, 18-year-old Private David Lewis staggered his way through a forced march during basic training in a brutal New Jersey winter. By the time his unit returned to base at Fort Dix, Lewis was dying. He collapsed and did not respond to his sergeant's attempts at mouth-to-mouth resuscitation.

In subsequent weeks, U.S. Army and CDC scientists discovered that the virus that had killed Lewis was swine flu. Although no other soldiers at Fort Dix died, health officials panicked. F. David Matthews, then secretary of health, education, and welfare, promptly declared, "There is evidence there will be a major flu epidemic this coming fall. The indication is that we will see a return of the 1918 flu virus that is the most virulent form of flu. In 1918, a half million people died [in the United States]. The projections are that this virus will kill one million Americans in 1976."

At the time, it was widely believed that influenza appeared in cycles, with especially lethal forms surfacing at relatively predictable intervals. Since 1918–19, the United States had suffered through influenza pandemics in 1957–58 and 1968–69; the first caused 70,000 deaths and the second 34,000. In 1976, scientists believed the world was overdue for a more lethal cycle, and the apparent emergence of swine flu at Fort Dix seemed to signal that another wave had come. The leaders of the CDC and the Department of Health, Education, and Welfare (HEW) warned the White House that there was a reasonably high probability that a catastrophic flu pandemic was about to hit. But opinion was hardly unanimous, and many European and Australian health authorities scoffed at the Americans' concern. Unsure of how to gauge the threat, President Gerald Ford summoned the polio-fighting heroes Jonas Salk and Albert Sabin to Washington and found the long-time adversaries in remarkable accord: a flu pandemic might truly be on the way.

On March 24, 1976, Ford went on national television. "I have just concluded a meeting on a subject of vast importance to all Americans," he announced. "I have been advised that there is a very real possibility that unless we take effective counteractions, there could be an epidemic of this dangerous disease next fall and winter here in the United States. . . . I am asking Congress to appropriate $135 million, prior to the April recess, for the production of sufficient vaccine to inoculate every man, woman, and child in the United States."

Vaccine producers immediately complained that they could not manufacture sufficient doses of vaccine in such haste without special liability protection. Congress responded, passing a law in April that made the government responsible for the companies' liability. When the campaign to vaccinate the U.S. population started four months later, there were almost immediate claims of side effects, including the neurologically debilitating Guillain Barré Syndrome. Most of the lawsuits—with claims totaling $3.2 billion—were settled or dismissed, but the U.S. government still ended up paying claimants around $90 million.

Swine flu, however, never appeared. The head of the CDC was asked to resign, and Congress never again considered assuming the liability of pharmaceutical companies during a potential epidemic. The experience weakened U.S. credibility in public health and helped undermine the stature of President Ford. Subsequently, an official assessment of what went wrong was performed for HEW by Dr. Harvey Fineberg, a Harvard professor who is currently president of the Institute of Medicine. Fineberg concluded:

> In this case the consequences of being wrong about an epidemic were so devastating in people's minds that it wasn't possible to focus properly on the issue of likelihood. Nobody could really estimate likelihood then, or now. The challenge in such circumstances is to be able to distinguish things so you can rationally talk about it. In 1976, some policymakers were simply overwhelmed by the consequences of being wrong. And at a higher level [in the White House] the two—likelihood and consequence—got meshed.

Fineberg's warnings are well worth remembering today, as scientists nervously consider H5N1 avian influenza in Asia. The consequences of a form of this virus that is transmittable from human to human, particularly if it retains its unprecedented virulence, would be disastrous. But what is the likelihood that such a virus will appear?

Devolution

Understanding the risks requires understanding the nature of H5N1 avian flu specifically and influenza in general. Influenza originates with aquatic birds and is normally carried by migratory ducks, geese, and herons, usually without harm to them. As the birds migrate, they can pass the viruses on to domesticated birds—chickens, for example—via feces or during competitions over food, territory, and water. Throughout history, this connection between birds and the flu has spawned epidemics in Asia, especially southern China. Aquatic flu viruses are more likely to pass into domestic animals—and then into humans—in China than anywhere else in the world. Dense concentrations of humans and livestock have left little of China's original migratory route for birds intact. Birds that annually travel from Indonesia to Siberia and back are forced to land and search for sustenance in farms, city parks, and industrial sites. For centuries, Chinese farmers have raised chickens, ducks, and pigs together, in miniscule pens surrounding their homes, greatly increasing the chance of contamination: influenza can spread from migrating to domestic birds and then to swine, mutating and eventually infecting human beings.

Ominously, as China's GDP grows, so do the expensive appetites of the country's 1.3 billion people, more of whom can afford to eat chicken regularly. Today, China annually raises about 13 billion chickens, 60 percent of them on small farms. Chicken farming is quickly morphing into a major industry, with some commercial poultry plants rivaling those in Arkansas and Georgia in scale—but lagging behind in hygienic standards. These factors favor rapid influenza evolution. By the close of the twentieth century, at least two new types of human-to-human flu spread around the world every year.

Influenza viruses contain eight genes, composed of RNA and packaged loosely in protective proteins. Like most RNA viruses, influenza reproduces sloppily: its genes readily fall apart, and it can absorb different genetic material and get mixed up in a process called reassortment. When influenza successfully infects a new species—say, pigs—it can reassort, and may switch from being an avian virus to a mammalian one. When that occurs, a human epidemic can result. The transmission cycles and the constant evolution are key to influenza's continued survival, for were it to remain identical year after year, most animals would develop immunity, and the flu would die out. This changing form explains why influenza is a seasonal disease. Vaccines made one year are generally useless the following.

Among the eight influenza genes there are two, dubbed H and N, that provide the code for proteins recognized by the human immune system. Scientists have numbered the many types of H and N proteins and use this system to classify a virus. A different viral combination of H and N proteins will trigger a different human immune response. For example, if a strain of H2N3 influenza circulates one year, followed by a different variety of H2N3 the next year, most people will be at least partially immune to the second strain. But if an H2N3 season is followed by an outbreak of H3N5 influenza, few people will have any immunity to the second virus, and the epidemic could be enormous. But a widespread epidemic need not be a severe or particularly deadly one: a virus' virulence depends on genes other than the two that control the H and N proteins.

Scientists first started saving flu virus samples in the early twentieth century. Since that time, an H5N1 influenza has never spread among human beings. According to the World Health Organization (WHO), "No virus of the H5 subtype has probably ever circulated among humans, and certainly not within the lifetime of today's world population. Population vulnerability to an H5N1-like pandemic virus would be universal." As for virulence, within about 48 hours of infection, H5N1 avian influenza kills 100 percent of infected chickens—although the virulence of a potential human-to-human transmissible H5N1 is impossible to predict.

A team of Chinese scientists has been tracking the H5N1 virus since it first emerged in Hong Kong in 1997, killing 6 people and sickening 18 others. The strain came out of southern China's Guangdong Province, where it apparently was carried by ducks, and hit Hong Kong's chicken population hard. After authorities there killed 1.5 million chickens—almost every single one in Hong Kong—the outbreak seemed to stop. But the virus had not disappeared; rather, it had retreated to China's Guangdong, Hunan, and Yunnan provinces, spreading once again to aquatic birds.

From 1998 to 2001 the virus went through multiple reassortments and moved back to domestic birds, spreading almost unnoticed in Chinese chicken flocks. It continued to evolve at high speed: 17 more reassortments occurred, and in January 2003 the "z" virus emerged, a mutant powerhouse that had become tougher, capable of withstanding a wider range of environmental challenges. The z virus spread to Vietnam and Thailand, where it evolved further, becoming resistant to one of the two classes of antiflu drugs, known as amantadines, or M2-inhibitors.

In early 2004, it became supervirulent and capable of killing a broad range of species, including rodents and humans. That permutation of the virus was dubbed "z+." In the first three weeks of January 2004, z+ killed 11 million chickens in Vietnam and Thailand. By April 2004, 120 million chickens in Asia had died of flu or been exterminated to slow the influenza brushfire. The avian epidemic stopped for a while, but in July another 1 million chickens died from the disease. The z+ virus was causing massive internal bleeding in the birds. By the beginning of 2005, with chickens dying and customers shying away from what remained, the Asian poultry industry had lost nearly $15 billion.

By April 2005, the H5N1 virus had also moved to pigs. Scientists isolated the disease from swine in a part of Indonesia where pigs are raised underneath elevated wood-slatted platforms that house chickens. Less rigorous investigations had previously indicated that pigs in China and Vietnam may also have been infected by H5N1 influenza. The discovery in Indonesia provided disturbing evidence that the virus was infecting mammals, although it was not yet known how widely the swine disease had spread or how lethal it was for the animals.

Hard to kill

Over the course of this brief but rapid evolution, the H5N1 virus developed in ways unprecedented in influenza research. It is not only incredibly deadly but also incredibly difficult to contain. The virus apparently now has the ability to survive in chicken feces and the meat of dead animals, despite the lack of blood flow and living cells; raw chicken meat fed to tigers in Thailand zoos resulted in the deaths of 147 out of a total of 418. The virus has also found ways to vastly increase the range of species it can infect and kill. Most strains of influenza are not lethal in lab mice, but z+ is lethal in 100 percent of them. It even kills the very types of wild migratory birds that normally host influenza strains harmlessly. Yet domestic ducks, for unknown reasons, carry the virus without a problem, which may explain where z+ hides between outbreaks among chickens.

Traditional Asian methods of buying, slaughtering, and cooking meat make it hard to track the spread of an influenza virus—and tracking it is critical to preventing the disease from spreading. In Asia, consumers prefer to buy live chickens and other live animals at the market, slaughtering them in home kitchens. Asians thus have a high level of exposure to potentially disease-carrying animals, both in their homes and as they pass through the markets that line the streets of densely packed urban centers. For someone trying to trace a disease, Asia is a nightmare: with people daily exposed to live chickens in so many different environments, how can a sleuth tell whether an ailing flu victim was infected by a chicken, a duck, a migratory heron— or another human being?

Although most of the 109 known human H5N1 infections have been ascribed to some type of contact with chickens, mysteries abound, and many cases remain unsolved. "The virus is no longer causing large and highly conspicuous outbreaks on commercial farms," a 2005 WHO summary of the human z+ cases states. "Nor have poultry workers or cullers turned out to be an important risk group that could be targeted for protection. Instead, the virus has become stealthier: human cases are now occurring with no discernible exposure to H5N1 through contact with diseased or dead birds."

If proximity to infected animals is the key, why have there been no deaths among chicken handlers, poultry workers, or live-chicken dealers? The majority of the infected have been young adults and children. And there has been one documented case of human-to-human transmission of the z+ strain of the H5N1 virus—in late 2004, in Thailand. Several more such cases are suspected but cannot be confirmed. According to the WHO, there is "no scientific explanation for the unusual disease pattern."

Assessing and understanding H5N1's virulence in humans has also proved elusive. When it first appeared in Hong Kong in 1997, the virus killed 35 percent of those it was known to have infected. (Less severe cases may not have been reported.) The z strain of the disease, which emerged in early 2003, killed 68 percent of those known to have been infected. In H5N1 cases since December 2004, however, the mortality has been 36 percent. How can the fluctuation over time be explained? One disturbing possibility is that H5N1 has begun adapting to its human hosts, becoming less deadly but easier to spread. In the spring of 2005, in fact, H5N1 infected 17 people throughout Vietnam, resulting in only three deaths. Leading flu experts argue that this sort of phenomenon has in the past been a prelude to human influenza epidemics.

The medical histories of those who have died from H5N1 influenza are disturbingly similar to accounts of sufferers of the Spanish flu in 1918–19. Otherwise healthy people are completely overcome by the virus, developing all of the classic flu symptoms: coughing, headache, muscle pain, nausea, dizziness, diarrhea, high fever, depression, and loss of appetite. But these are just some of the effects. Victims also suffer from pneumonia, encephalitis, meningitis, acute respiratory distress, and internal bleeding and hemorrhaging. An autopsy of a child who died of the disease in Thailand last year revealed that the youth's lungs had been torn apart in the all-out war between disease-fighting cells and the virus.

Bad medicine

According to test-tube studies, z+ ought to be vulnerable to the antiflu drug oseltamivir, which the Roche pharmaceuticals company markets in the United States under the brand name Tamiflu. Yet Tamiflu was given to many of those who ultimately succumbed to the virus; it is believed that medical complications induced by the virus, including acute respiratory distress syndrome, may have prevented the drug from helping. It is also difficult to tell whether the drug contributed to the survival of those who took it and lived, although higher doses and more prolonged treatment may have a greater impact in fighting the disease. A team of Thai clinicians recently concluded that "the optimal treatment for case-patients with suspected H5 infection is not known." Lacking any better options, the WHO has recommended that countries stockpile Tamiflu to the best of their ability. The U.S. Department of Health and Human Services is doing so, but supplies of the drug are limited and it is hard to manufacture.

What about developing a z+ vaccine? Unfortunately, there is only more gloom in the forecast. The total number of companies willing to produce influenza vaccines has plummeted in recent years, from more than two dozen in 1980 to just a handful in 2004. There are many reasons for the decline in vaccine producers. A spate of corporate mergers in the 1990s, for example, reduced the number of major international pharmaceutical companies. The financial risk of investing in vaccines is also a key factor. In 2003, the entire market for all vaccines—from polio to measles to hepatitis to influenza—amounted to just $5.4 billion. Although that sum may seem considerable, it is less than two percent of the global pharmaceutical market of $337.3 billion. Unlike chemical compounds, vaccines and most other biological products are difficult to make and can easily become contaminated. There is also a large and litigious antivaccine constituency—some people believe that vaccines cause harmful side effects such as Alzheimer's disease and autism—adding considerable liability costs to manufacturers' bottom lines.

The production of influenza vaccines holds particular drawbacks for companies. Flu vaccines must be made rapidly, increasing the risk of contamination or other errors. Because of the seasonal nature of the flu, a new batch of influenza vaccines must be produced each year. Should sales in a given year prove disappointing, flu vaccines cannot be stockpiled for sale in a subsequent season because by then the viruses will have evolved. In addition, the manufacturing process of flu vaccines is uniquely complex: pharmaceutical companies must grow viral samples on live chicken eggs, which must be reared under rigorous hygienic conditions. Research is under way on reverse genetics and cellular-level production techniques that might prove cheaper, faster, and less contamination-prone than using eggs, but for the foreseeable future manufacturers are stuck with the current laborious method. After cultivation, samples of the viruses must be harvested, the H and N characteristics must be shown to produce antibodies in test animals and human volunteers, and tests must prove that the vaccine is not contaminated. Only then can mass production commence.

The H5N1 strain of avian flu poses an additional problem: the virus is 100 percent lethal to chickens—and that includes chicken eggs. It took researchers five years of hard work to devise a way to grow the 1997 version of the H5N1 virus on eggs without killing them; although there have been technological improvements since then, there is no guarantee that an emerging pandemic strain could be cultivated fast enough.

In the current system, all influenza vaccines must be quickly made following a WHO meeting of flu experts held every February. At that gathering, scientists scrutinize all available information on the flu strains known to be circulating in the world. They then try to predict which strains are most likely to spread across every continent in the next six to nine months. (This year the WHO committee chose three human flu strains, of types H3N2 and H1N1, to be the basis of the next vaccine.) Samples of the chosen strains are delivered to pharmaceutical companies around the world for vaccine production, and the vaccines are hopefully available to the public by September or October—a few months after influenza typically strikes Asia, in the early summer. Europe and the Americas are usually hit shortly after, in September. Because viruses constantly change themselves, the process cannot be executed earlier in the year.

Although new technology may allow an increase in production capacity, manufacturers have never made more than 300 million doses of flu vaccine

in a single year. The slow pace of production means that in the event of an
H5N1 flu pandemic millions of people would likely be infected well before
vaccines could be distributed.

Global reach

The scarcity of flu vaccine, although a serious problem, is actually of little
relevance to most of the world. Even if pharmaceutical companies managed
to produce enough effective vaccine in time to save some privileged lives in
Europe, North America, Japan, and a few other wealthy nations, more than
six billion people in developing countries would go unvaccinated. Stockpiles
of Tamiflu and other anti-influenza drugs would also do nothing for those
six billion, at least 30 percent of whom—and possibly half—would likely get
infected in such a pandemic.

Resources are so scarce that both wealthy and poor countries would be
foolish to count on the generosity of their neighbors during a global outbreak.
Were the United States to miraculously overcome its vaccine production
problems and produce ample supplies for U.S. citizens, Washington would
probably deny the vaccine to neighbors such as Mexico, since governments
tend to reserve vaccine supplies for their own citizens during emergencies.
Were the United States to falter, it would probably not be able to rely on
Canadian or European generosity, as it did just last year. When the United
Kingdom suspended the license for the Chiron Corporations U.K. production
facility for flu vaccine due to contamination problems, Canada and Germany
bailed the United States out, supplying additional doses until the French
company Sanofi Pasteur could manufacture more. Even with this assistance,
however, the United States' vaccine needs were not fully met until February
2005—the tail end of the flu season.

In the event of a deadly influenza pandemic, it is doubtful that any of
the world's wealthy nations would be able to meet the needs of their own
citizenry—much less those of other countries. Domestic vaccine purchasing
and distribution schemes currently assume that only the very young, the
elderly, and the immunocompromised are at serious risk of dying from the flu.
That assumption would have led health leaders in 1918 to vaccinate all of
the wrong people. Then, the young and the old fared relatively well, while
those aged 20 to 35—today typically the lowest priority for vaccination—suffered
the most deaths from the Spanish flu. And so far, H5N1 influenza looks like
it could have a similar effect: its human victims have all fallen into age groups
that would not be on national vaccine priority lists, and because H5N1 has
never circulated among humans before, it is highly conceivable that all ages
could be susceptible. Every year, trusting that the flu will kill only the usual risk
groups, the United States plans for 185 million vaccine doses. If that guess
were wrong—if all Americans were at risk—the nation would need at least
300 million doses. That is what the entire world typically produces each year.

There would thus be a global scramble for vaccine. Some governments might well block foreign access to supplies produced on their soil and bar vaccine export. Since little vaccine is actually made in the United States, this could prove a problem for Americans in particular. Facing such limited supplies, the U.S., European, and Japanese governments might give priority to vaccinating heads of state around the world in hopes of limiting social chaos. But who among the elite would be eligible? Would their families be included? How could such a global triage be executed justly?

A similar calculus might be necessary for countries engaged in significant military operations. Troop movements would certainly help spread the disease, just as World War I aided the growth of the 1918–19 Spanish flu. Back then, the flu wreaked havoc on combatant nations. In the summer of 1918, influenza killed far more soldiers than did bombs, bullets, or mustard gas. By October, some 46 percent of the French army was off the field of battle—ailing, dying, or caring for flu victims. Influenza death tolls among the various military forces generally ranged from 5 to 10 percent, but some segments fared even worse: historian John Barry has reported that 22 percent of the Indian members of the British military died.

In the event of a modern pandemic, the U.S. Department of Defense, with the lessons of World War I in mind, would undoubtedly insist that U.S. troops in Iraq and Afghanistan be given top access to vaccines and antiflu drugs. About 170,000 U.S. forces are currently stationed in Iraq and Afghanistan, while 200,000 more are permanently based elsewhere overseas. All of them would potentially be in danger: in late March, for example, North Korea conceded it was suffering a large-scale H7N1 outbreak—taking place within miles of some 41,000 U.S. military forces. It is impossible to predict how such a pandemic influenza would affect U.S. operations in Iraq, Afghanistan, Colombia, or any other place.

Armed forces throughout the world would face similar issues. Most would no doubt pressure their governments for preferential access to vaccine and medications. In addition, more than a quarter of some African armies and police forces are HIV positive, perhaps making them especially vulnerable to influenza's lethal impact. Social instability resulting from troop and police losses there would likely be particularly acute.

Such a devastating disease would clearly have profound implications for international relations and the global economy. With death tolls rising, vaccines and drugs in short supply, and the potential for the virus to spread further, governments would feel obliged to take drastic measures that could inhibit travel, limit worldwide trade, and alienate their neighbors. In fact, the z+ virus has already demonstrated its disruptive potential on a limited scale. In July 2004, for example, when the z+ strain reemerged in Vietnam after a three-month hiatus, officials in the northern province of Bac Giang charged that Chinese smugglers were selling old and sickly birds in Vietnamese markets— where more than ten tons of chickens are smuggled daily. Chinese authorities in charge of policing their side of the porous border, more than 1,000 kilometers long, countered that it was impossible to inspect all the shipments. Such conflicts are now limited to the movement of livestock, but if a pandemic develops they could well escalate to a ban on trade and human movement.

Although there is little evidence that isolation measures have ever slowed the spread of influenza—it is just too contagious—most governments would likely resort to quarantines in a pandemic crisis. Indeed, on April 1, 2005, President George W. Bush issued an executive order authorizing the use of quarantines inside the United States and permitting the isolation of international visitors suspected of carrying influenza. If one country implements such orders, others will follow suit, bringing legal international travel to a standstill. The SARS (severe acute respiratory syndrome) virus, which was less dangerous than a pandemic flu by several orders of magnitude, virtually shut down Asian travel for three months.

As great as they would be, the economic consequences of travel restrictions, quarantines, and medical care would be well outstripped by productivity losses. In a typical flu season, productivity costs are ten times greater than all other flu-related costs combined. The decline in productivity is usually due directly to worker illness and absenteeism. During a pandemic, productivity losses would be even more disproportionate because entire workplaces— schools, theaters, and public facilities—would be shut down to limit human-to-human spread of the virus. Workers' illnesses also would likely be even more severe and last even longer than normal. Frankly, no models of social response to such a pandemic have managed to factor in fully the potential effect on human productivity. It is therefore impossible to reckon accurately the potential global economic impact.

Ailing

The potential for a pandemic comes at a time when the world's public health systems are severely taxed and have long been in decline. This is true in both rich and poor countries.

The Bush administration recognized this weakness following the anthrax scare of 2001, which underscored the poor ability of federal and local health agencies to respond to bioterrorism or epidemic threats. Since that year, Congress has approved $3.7 billion to strengthen the nation's public health infrastructure. In 2003, the White House also took several steps to improve the nation's capacity to respond to a flu pandemic: it increased funding for the CDC's flu program by 242 percent, to $41.6 million in 2004; gave the National Institutes of Health an additional 320 percent in funds for flu-related research and development, for a total of $65.9 million; increased spending on the Food and Drug Administration's licensing capacity for flu vaccines and drugs by 173 percent, to $2.6 million; and spent an additional $80 million to create new stockpiles of Tamiflu and other anti-influenza drugs. On August 4, 2004, the

Department of Health and Human Services also issued its pandemic flu plan, detailing further steps that would be taken by federal and state agencies in the event of a pandemic. Several other countries have released similar plans of action.

But despite all this, a recent event underscored the United States' tremendous vulnerability. In October 2004, the American College of Pathologists mailed a collection of mystery microbes prepared by a private lab to almost 5,000 labs in 18 countries for them to test as part of their recertification. The mailing should have been routine procedure; instead, in March 2005 a Canadian lab discovered that the test kits included a sample of H2N2 flu—a strain that had killed four million people worldwide in 1957. H2N2 has not been in circulation since 1968, meaning that hundreds of millions of people lack immunity to it. Had any of the samples leaked or been exposed to the environment, the results could have been devastating. On learning of the error, the WHO called for the immediate destruction of all the test kits. Miraculously, none of the virus managed to escape any of the labs.

But the snafu raises serious questions: If billions have been spent to improve laboratory capabilities since 2001, why did nobody notice the H2N2 flu until about six months after the kits had been shipped? Why did a private company possess samples of the virulent flu? Why was the sample included in the kits? In the aftermath of the September 11, 2001, attacks and the anthrax scare, many countries reclassified 1957–58 and 1968–69 influenza strains as Level 3 pathogens, requiring extreme care in their handling, distribution, and storage— why did the United States still consider H2N2 to be a mere Level 2 pathogen, a type frequently mailed and studied? Finally, around the world, what other labs—public and private—currently possess samples of such lethal influenza viruses? The official CDC answer to these questions is, "We don't know."

Even with all of these gaps, probably the greatest weakness that each nation must individually address is the inability of their hospitals to cope with a sudden surge of new patients. Medical cost cutting has resulted in a tremendous reduction in the numbers of staffed hospital beds in the wealthy world, especially in the United States. Even during a normal flu season, hospitals located in popular retirement areas have great difficulty meeting the demand. In a pandemic, it is doubtful that any nation would have adequate medical facilities and personnel to meet the extra need.

National policymakers would be wise to plan now for worst-case scenarios involving quarantines, weakened armed services, and dwindling hospital space and vaccine supplies. But at the end of the day, effectively combating influenza will require multilateral and global mechanisms. Chief among them, of course, is the WHO, which since 1947 has maintained a worldwide network that conducts influenza surveillance. The WHO system oversees laboratories all over the world, chases (and sometimes refutes) rumors of pandemics, pushes for government transparency regarding human and avian flu cases, and acts as an arbiter in negotiations over vaccine production, trade embargoes, and border disputes. Its companion UN agency, the Food and Agriculture

Organization (FAO), working closely with the World Organization for Animal Health, monitors flu outbreaks in animal populations and advises governments on culling flocks and herds, cross-border animal trade, animal husbandry and slaughter, and livestock quarantine and vaccination. All of these organizations have published lengthy guidelines on how to respond to a pandemic flu, lists of answers to commonly asked questions, and descriptions of their research priorities—most of which have been posted on their Web sites.

The efforts of these agencies should be bolstered, both with expertise and dollars. The WHO, for example, has an annual core budget of just $400 million, a tiny increment of which is spent on influenza- and epidemic-response programs. (In comparison, the annual budget of New York City's health department exceeds $1.2 billion.) An unpublished internal study estimates that the agency would require at least another $600 million for its flu program were a pandemic to erupt. It is in every government's interest to give the WHO and the FAO the authority to act as impartial voices during a pandemic, able (theoretically) to assess objectively the epidemic's progress and rapidly evaluate research claims. The WHO in particular must have adequate funding and personnel to serve as an accurate clearinghouse of information about the disease, thereby preventing the spread of false rumors and global panic. No nation can erect a fortress against influenza—not even the world's wealthiest country.

Few members of the U.S. Congress or its legislative counterparts around the world were alive when the great Spanish flu swept the planet. There may be some who lost parents, aunts, or uncles to the 1918–19 pandemic, and perhaps even more have heard the horror stories that were passed down. But politics breeds shortsightedness, and for decades the threat of an influenza pandemic has been easily forgotten, and therefore ignored at budget time. Politicians and health leaders made many serious errors in 1918–19; some historians say that President Wilson sent 43,000 soldiers to their deaths by forcing them aboard crowded ships to join a war he had already won. But in those days, human beings had no understanding of their influenza foe.

In 1971, the great American public health leader Alexander Langmuir likened flu forecasting to trying to predict the weather, arguing that "as with hurricanes, pandemics can be identified and their probable course projected so that warnings can be issued. Epidemics, however, are more variable [than hurricanes], and the best that can be done is to estimate probabilities."

Since Langmuir's time a quarter of a century ago, weather forecasting has gained a stunning level of precision. And although scientists cannot tell political leaders when an influenza pandemic will occur, researchers today are able to guide policymakers with information and analysis exponentially richer than that which informed the decisions of President Ford and the 1976 Congress. Whether or not this particular H5N1 influenza mutates into a human-to-human pandemic form, the scientific evidence points to the potential that such an event will take place, perhaps soon. Those responsible for foreign policy and national security, the world over, cannot afford to ignore the warning.

38

A CLEAR AND PRESENT DANGER TO INTERNATIONAL SECURITY

Highly Pathogenic Avian Influenza

Julian Palmore

Source: *Defense & Security Analysis*, 22:2 (2006), 111–21.

Introduction

It is the author's premise that natural disasters, especially pandemics, can and do affect international security in many ways. They can have disastrous effects on countries' economies, infrastructures, populations, public health and stability. As a consequence of natural disasters, governments may be hard pressed to respond adequately and populations may be decimated. Thus, planning for international security needs must take into account the effects of natural disasters. Since avian influenza is of utmost concern in Asia and in many other parts of the world, it is imperative that states' governments and non-governmental organizations (NGOs) pay attention to the evolution of the Highly Pathogenic Avian Influenza (HPAI) H5N1 virus. As 2005 came to a close, the world was faced with the prospect of a global pandemic caused, hosted and spread by birds on international flyways.

Planning for a pandemic arising from avian influenza is currently under way. Many conferences are being held, devoted to pandemic planning, surveillance and tracking of infectious diseases. In the case of bird flu, the "vectors" may be the flyways of the migratory birds. Much research has to be done before the epidemiology of the disease is clear. There is no better time to discuss these issues than before a pandemic appears.

Preparedness in the United States

At present, the preparedness plans for 2006 in the United States call for an expenditure of several billions of dollars on the following: $1 billion for research, $1 billion for vaccine acquisition, $3 billion for acquiring vaccine production facilities and strengthening production of a yet-to-be-determined specific vaccine to protect against the mutated avian influenza virus, $0.6 billion for state and local preparedness plans. These expenditures are yearly for the next several years.

One of the major problems with vaccines is that they have to be tailored to a specific virus and the avian flu virus to protect against has not appeared in the form in which human-to-human transmission occurs. Thus, great uncertainty exists with regard to providing the infrastructure to respond rapidly to the demands placed on the system when the virus finally appears. Another major problem is that the time to acquire protective measures may be too long compared to the mutation rate of the avian flu virus. We may not have a year to prepare for a pandemic.

The Center for Disease Control (CDC) in Atlanta suggests three actions for individuals to minimize transmission of influenza: wash your hands, cover your mouth (while sneezing, coughing), and stay out of groups. These simple procedures can greatly reduce the transmission of avian influenza by human-to-human contact.

International security concerns

With natural disasters looming large on our horizons – tsunamis, earthquakes, hurricanes, typhoons, volcanic eruptions, avian influenza, pandemics – we are reminded of the need for disaster preparations in the event of natural disasters, and, coincidentally, attacks by terrorists using weapons of mass destruction.

In various statements issued after the Katrina hurricane of August 2005, the US President George W. Bush said that America needs to be prepared for disasters and terrorist attacks. In the President's address to the nation on 1 November 2005 about the possibility of an avian flu pandemic, he mentioned once again the need for preparing for the consequences of terrorists using weapons of mass destruction. Clearly, there is a need for disaster preparations; and just as clearly, there is a need to remind ourselves that natural disasters can inflict potentially more damage economically and in human deaths on a wider scale than any attack by humans on humans, other than a nuclear war.

The US, as with all other states, needs to better equip its public health systems, communications and surveillance infrastructures and first responders to deal with any biological incident. Birds migrating from Asia to Europe and, on different bird migration flyways, to the United States through Alaska and Canada, pose a significant delivery system for avian influenza as they infect domestic birds, then animals by droppings laden with viruses. We cannot stop or divert this delivery system. What we can do is detect and prevent transmission from domesticated animals to humans as animal infections become apparent through intensive surveillance.[1]

Alaska and migration flyways

Alaska is at the crossroads of birds flying from Asia and the Americas. Thus, it is important to maintain an alert at this juncture of flyways. Sampling various species of birds, both wild birds and domestic animals, must be done frequently, with the results tested for all types of avian influenza. Plans are under way for intensive sampling in 2006. If the highly pathogenic avian influenza (HPAI) H5N1 virus mutates into a form that allows for significant human-to-human transmission and additionally is capable of infecting specific species of migratory birds that can intermingle with domestic waterfowl along certain flyways, then we have a severe problem on our hands that must be met with vaccines. In that case, with the technology and production capabilities at hand currently, many millions will die from lack of vaccines.[2]

The principal bird migration flyways for North America are the Mississippi flyway, the Atlantic flyway, the Pacific Coast flyway, and the Central flyway. In addition, for the Americas there are the Pacific Americas flyway, the Atlantic Americas flyway and the Mississippi Americas flyway. The East Asia Australian flyway enters a mixing bowl over Alaska where it intersects the Mississippi Americas and Pacific Americas flyways. Alaska is the location where cross-species infection is most likely to occur, since the East Asia Australian flyway passes near countries in which the avian influenza virus H5N1 has infected poultry and birds. These include Thailand, Vietnam and Indonesia.

Research problems associated with avian influenza

There are two problems that need to be studied and solved quickly. The first is to answer the question: what species of wild birds carry influenza viruses? If the virus is transmissible by wild waterfowl, then it is important to identify the carriers of the avian flu virus. If the route of transmission is by other means, then it is important to identify these routes and vectors as soon as possible.

Second: what flyways do the asymptomatic migratory wild birds use? This question is based on transmission by infected waterfowl. It is possible that there are many paths of transmission so that we need to know what vectors are possible. The reason these questions must be answered is that migratory wild birds are one means of delivery of avian influenza around the world. Principal flyways are well known and track water-resting locations, marshes, shorelines and coastlines.

The highly pathogenic avian influenza virus H5N1 has infected many species. These are chickens, turkeys, ducks, geese (Russia); swans (Croatia); ducks, swans, hen, heron (Romania); chicken, duck, goose, quail, turkey, stork (Thailand); chicken, crow (Japan); chicken, quail, duck, moscovy duck (Vietnam); chicken, duck, quail and pig (Indonesia); geese, ducks (Kazakhstan);

chicken, duck, goose, turkey, guinea fowl, wild bird (Cambodia); Peregrine falcon, Gray heron, Chinese pond heron (Hong Kong SAR); Layer, duck, magpie (Republic of Korea); wild duck (Egypt); chicken, duck and quail (Lao PDR).[3]

Low pathogenic avian influenza (including H7N3, H7N2, H2N2) have been found in Canada and the United States, primarily in chickens. LPAI virus is not a threat but must be watched so that any mutation into a HPAI virus is detected immediately.

What we need to know

As in all scientific research, it is of utmost importance to ask relevant questions – answers will come eventually. In an Op-Ed piece in the *New York Times* in February 2005, Hans Troedsson and Anton Rychener, representatives in Vietnam of WHO and FAO respectively, asked several questions regarding avian flu:

- Why, for instance, did none of the many thousands of farm workers culling sick birds without wearing protective equipment contract the disease?
- Why are children and young people predominantly infected and not older people?
- Why do some ducks infected with the virus not show any symptoms?
- What is the role of these animals in the transmission of the virus?"

These questions are important and will dominate discussions and research on bird flu as time progresses.

Statistics on human cases

As of 20 February 2006, according to the World Health Organization there has been a total of 170 cases and 92 deaths (included in the case count).[4] "Laboratory-confirmed human cases" means that there is laboratory confirmation from within the country and an independent confirmation by a laboratory outside the country, in the UK for example. Two deaths in Turkey are the first laboratory-confirmed human cases outside of East Asia. There have been many more people hospitalized in Turkey who are suspected of being infected by the H5N1 virus. An unofficial but reliable count places the number of human infections in Turkey at 18 as of 12 January 2006, and confirmed by the Turkish health laboratory in Ankara. This raises concerns that avian flu is on the march westward with consequences for humans.

A new concern has been voiced by the World Health Organization in mid-January 2006 that the H5N1 virus is mutating – several cases in Turkey have detected this change; it is unclear of the extent to which the mutated virus can pass between humans. The cases are being investigated currently.

Three waves of avian flu outbreaks

There have been three waves of outbreaks, starting in 1997 when the virus was first identified in an outbreak of poultry infections in Hong Kong. Significantly, the Hong Kong outbreak was contained within three days by the culling of many millions of poultry.[5] In the most recent third wave we have seen more deaths over a wider region than waves I and II. The virus has been carried by migratory birds to European countries – Turkey, Romania and Greece – as well as other parts of Asia. Alaska and Canada are on several bird migration flyways so the alert level of WHO is high in these areas.

As noted above, the route of an avian influenza virus from Asia to the western United States is through Alaska providing a mixing bowl of viruses among birds using different flyways that intersect in Alaska. The principal flyway from Asia is the East Asia Australian flyway. This intersects the Mississippi Americas flyway and the Pacific Americas flyway there.

Pandemic alert levels

Avian influenza has already posed a clear and present danger to the well-being of hundreds of millions of poultry and birds in Asia, and consequently, food stocks and Asian economies. As the virus travels westward toward Europe new concerns are raised. In Turkey, health officials are concerned about simultaneous outbreaks in many of the country's 81 provinces.

Experts at WHO and elsewhere believe that the world is now closer to another influenza pandemic than at any time since 1968, when the last of the previous century's three pandemics occurred. WHO uses a series of six phases of pandemic alert as a system for informing the world of the seriousness of the threat and of the need to launch progressively more intense preparedness activities (see Table 1).

The world is presently in phase 3: a new influenza virus subtype is causing disease in humans, but is not yet spreading efficiently and sustainably among humans. In the *New York Times* of 6 November there is an article entitled "Sentries in US seek early signs of avian flu". It is about wildlife groups who are on the lookout in the United States for diseased birds and in particular those which might be carrying avian influenza. The estimates of damage from an avian flu pandemic vary but it is clear that migratory birds are carrying the virus from Asia to other parts of the world. Migratory birds from Asia are known to mingle with US wildlife in Alaska. These in turn migrate south into Canada and the western United States. Also, the virus has spread west to Europe. There is an effort under way to set up a US

255

Table 1 Phases of alert for pandemics.

Alert	Phase	Description
1	Inter-pandemic phase	Low risk of human cases
2	New virus in animals; no human cases	Higher risk of human cases
3	**Pandemic alert**	**No or very limited human-to-human transmission**
4	New virus causes human cases	Evidence of increased human-to-human transmission
5	New virus causes human cases	Evidence of significant human-to-human transmission
6	Pandemic	Efficient and sustained human-to-human transmission

national surveillance system to monitor birds for avian flu. This system would use volunteers, medical and veterinary doctors and other health specialists who would be trained to take specimen samples from birds routinely captured and released for this purpose.

Even were the virus not to infect people by human-to-human transmission, it would spread to animal populations. In turn, infected animals, especially poultry, would pose a potential risk for humans. Clearly, the avian flu and its delivery system represent a clear and present danger to the world's animals and, most likely, humans. It will be necessary to be on the alert for this virus for many years to come. It will not be contained or damped out without the virus mutating to a less virulent form. It is to be hoped that the combination of virus and delivery system will naturally cease to be a threat to humans.

WHO issues advice on the current state of disease incidents and the latest on avian flu is dated 10 January, 2006. The total number of laboratory-confirmed human cases is 147 and the number of deaths is 78. The latest cases occurred in Turkey and China. The three waves may be dated as Wave I: 26 December 2003–10 March, 2004; Wave II: 19 July 2004–8 October 2004 and Wave III: 16 December 2004 to the present. The total number of laboratory-confirmed human cases occurring in WAVE III in 2005 is 93, with 41 deaths. A further several cases and deaths have been seen in Turkey and China in 2006. It is suspected by unconfirmed counts that the number of H5N1 human infections is significantly higher in under-reported rural areas of Turkey.

Although the number of laboratory-confirmed cases and deaths is still small, the potential for the virus to mutate into a form of human-to-human transmittal is great. The ratio of deaths to cases (74:142) is slightly greater than 50 percent. This shows the great virulence of avian influenza compared to that of Spanish influenza in 1918, in which deaths occurred in approximately 2.5 percent of cases worldwide.[6] In some parts of the world the mortality rose to around 5 percent of total cases.

The effect of the virus on animals is unquestionably significant – and one might say that the risk of an animal/bird pandemic is great. Recently, China has destroyed millions of poultry in a two-mile radius of an infected area. We may see more infestations and destruction of birds, wild and domestic, by the hundreds of millions. In the future, the virus has more chance to infect humans by animal-to-human transmissions.

The Bush pandemic plan

President Bush announced on 1 November 2005 that he is making the following requests from Congress as part of his influenza pandemic plan:

1. $251 million to help foreign partners train medical personnel, develop monitoring capabilities to detect outbreaks and draw up preparedness plans.
2. $1.2 billion to purchase enough vaccine developed by the National Institutes of Health against current bird flu strain to vaccinate 20 million people.
3. $1 billion to stockpile additional antiviral medications to provide enough to treat first responders and other key personnel.
4. $2.8 billion for a "crash program" to accelerate cell culture technology, which Bush said would produce enough vaccine for all Americans within six months.
5. Relief from the "burden of litigation" for vaccine manufacturers.
6. $583 million for pandemic preparedness, including $100 million to help states complete and exercise their pandemic plans.[7]

Table 2 shows the World Health Organization's count of laboratory-confirmed human cases of H5N1 for the years 2003, 2004, 2005 and 2006 that have been reported from Cambodia, China, Indonesia, Thailand, Turkey and Vietnam since late 2003. The bar chart (Figure 1), an adaptation from that of the OIE (World Organization for Animal Health), gives the 30 December 2005 count of *outbreaks* in various countries. This graph is brought up to date on a

Table 2 The situation at 2 February 2006.

Country	2003		2004		2005		2006		Total	
	Cases	Deaths	Cases	Deaths	Cases	Deaths	Cases	Deaths	Cases	Deaths
Cambodia	0	0	0	0	4	4	0	0	4	4
China	0	0	0	0	8	5	2	2	10	7
Indonesia	0	0	0	0	16	11	3	3	19	14
Iraq	0	0	0	0	0	0	1	1	1	1
Thailand	0	0	17	12	5	2	0	0	22	14
Turkey	0	0	0	0	0	0	12	4	12	4
Vietnam	3	3	29	20	61	19	0	0	93	42
Total	3	3	46	32	94	41	18	10	161	86

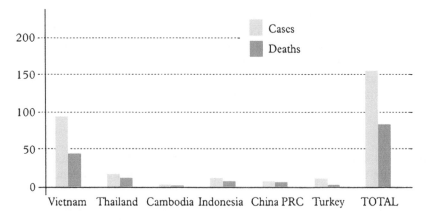

Figure 1 Incidents of deaths from avian flu cases.

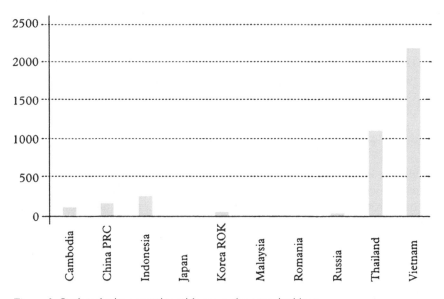

Figure 2 Outbreaks in countries with more than ten incidents.

weekly basis. Vietnam has experienced more HPAI outbreaks than any other country, with Thailand experiencing the second-most number of outbreaks.

Figure 2 shows the number of outbreaks (among animals/poultry) in selected countries that have had more than ten outbreaks since 2003. Although the virus is more widespread geographically among other countries, there have not been significant outbreaks. Other countries in which avian influenza outbreaks have been found in less significant numbers are: Croatia, Hong Kong (SAR), Kazakhstan, Laos, Mongolia, Romania and Turkey. LPAI viruses have been found in North America in the United States and Canada.

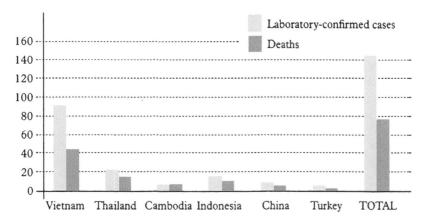

Figure 3 Laboratory-confirmed human cases of HPA1 H5N1, December 2003 to
January 2006.

Figure 3 shows a time-line sequence of *laboratory-confirmed human cases*
of HPAI H5N1 from December 2003 until January 2006, starting with
Vietnam and Thailand. The third country in the time sequence to have human
cases is Cambodia in February 2005, with Indonesia following in July 2005
and China in November 2005. Cases in Turkey came in January 2006. Since
January, cases of avian flu have been reported in Hungary, Germany, Austria,
Italy, Greece, Slovenia, Bulgaria, Denmark and France.[8] Of particular concern
has been the discovery of avian flu in Nigeria, demonstrating that the virus
can travel long distances, across continents and, effectively, world-wide.[9] A
death in Iraq in the middle of January 2006 has prompted intense scrutiny
and surveillance of parts of Northern Iraq near the Turkish border which
to date has been free of the virus.

Virus mutations

There are two main processes of concern in virus mutation. One is called
antigenic drift, and the other *antigenic shift*. Antigen drift is a normal process
of variation caused by slight mutations of the virus. Antigen shift is a sudden
abrupt mutation.

Antigenic drift refers to small, gradual changes that occur through point
mutations in the two genes that contain the genetic material to produce the
main surface proteins, hemagglutinin and neuraminidase. These point mutations
occur unpredictably and result in minor changes to these surface proteins.
Antigenic drift produces new virus strains that may not be recognized by
antibodies to earlier influenza strains. This process works as follows: a person
infected with a particular influenza virus strain develops antibody against
that strain. As newer virus strains appear, the antibodies against the older

259

strains might not recognize the "newer" virus, and infection with a new strain can occur. This is one of the main reasons why people can become infected with influenza viruses more than one time and why global surveillance is critical.

Antigenic shift refers to an abrupt, major change to produce a novel influenza A virus subtype in humans that was not currently circulating among people. Antigenic shift can occur either through direct animal (poultry)-to-human transmission or through a mixing of human influenza A and animal influenza A virus genes to create a new human influenza A subtype virus through a process called genetic reassortment. Antigenic shift results in a new human influenza A subtype.[10]

Global pandemics

A global influenza pandemic may occur if three conditions are met:

1. A new subtype of influenza A virus is introduced into the human population.
2. The virus causes serious illness in humans.
3. The virus can spread easily from person to person in a *sustained and efficient manner.*[11]

The third criterion is important. Without efficient transmission the virus will burn out in affected regions. It is also important that the means of delivery, wild waterfowl, be asymptomatic so that migratory birds can carry it over intercontinental flyways. From an epidemiological view the vector must be well defined and sustainable within the delivery system. And the delivery system must be global, as with migratory birds that can travel thousands of miles across vast regions.

Current state of pandemic alert

Conditions favorable for the emergence of antigenic shift have long been thought to involve humans living in close proximity to domestic poultry and pigs. Because pigs are susceptible to infection with both avian and mammalian viruses, including human strains, they can serve as a "mixing vessel" for the scrambling of genetic material from human and avian viruses, resulting in the emergence of a novel subtype. Recent events, however, have identified a second possible mechanism. Evidence is mounting that, for at least some of the 15 avian influenza virus subtypes circulating in bird populations, humans themselves can serve as the "mixing vessel".[12]

Conclusions

Since Alaska is at the forefront of detection for avian species that fly between Asia and North America it is important to monitor and sample species for all types of avian influenza. This should be an ongoing experiment and observation that currently is being planned.[13] East Asia and South Asia can be considered the *incubator* for avian influenza and Alaska can be considered a *mixing bowl* for influenza transmission among wild bird species flying between Asia and the Americas. These facts tell us where surveillance and detection are most important for defining an outbreak and spread of a global pandemic.

Several questions remain high on the list of priorities. How to prepare for a pandemic? What can national health planners do? What can individuals do to prepare?

By strengthening the surveillance and detection of avian influenza the public health organizations will provide an early warning to the onset of an avian influenza epidemic. In turn this warning may provide the opportunity to limit the spread of a virus that has mutated into a form that allows efficient human-to-human transmission, thereby thwarting a pandemic.[14]

Recently, there have been reports from Turkey and Vietnam of people infected with the H5N1 strain who have developed milder symptoms than the cases reported by WHO under the heading of laboratory-confirmed human cases. It may be that better sampling of cases needs to be accomplished so that a balanced picture emerges of the avian influenza, how it is transmitted and to what extent it is lethal. These are epidemiologic questions that remain to be answered.[15]

A pressing question about highly pathogenic avian influenza is whether H5N1 can infect people without causing severe symptoms and, if so, how often does it do this? Another is whether the virus mutations increase or decrease the lethality of H5N1. The international community is right to recognize the threat posed by international terrorism, but not at the expense of threats such as avian influenza. For this reason the threat to human life, world-wide, must be prioritized and resources allocated accordingly.

Note: A useful recent quotation attributed to Michael Leavitt, US Secretary of Health and Human Services, is: "At this point, if you're a bird, it's a pandemic. If you're a human being, it's not!"

Notes

1 There are two subtypes of avian influenza A. These are the H and N subtypes. The letters H (hemagglutinin) and N (neuraminidase) refer to proteins on the surface of the viruses. The H variant gives rise to subtypes H1, ..., H16 and the N variant gives rise to subtypes N1, ..., N9. There is a total of 144 subtypes of which H5N1 is a highly pathogenic avian influenza (HPAI). "Avian influenza A H5 and H7 viruses can be distinguished as 'low pathogenic' and 'high pathogenic' forms on the basis of genetic features of the virus and the severity of the illness they cause in poultry; influenza H9 virus has been identified only in a 'low pathogenicity' form. Each of these three avian influenza A viruses (H5, H7 and H9) theoretically can be partnered with any one of nine neuraminidase surface

proteins; thus, there are potentially nine different forms of each subtype (e.g., H5N1, H5N2, H5N3, . . . , H5N9)."

2 "Sentries in US seek early signs of avian flu", *New York Times*, 6 November 2005.

3 FAO AIDE news 5 November/2005. FAO is the Food and Agricultural Organization of the World Health Organization.

4 The number of countries in which H5N1 has been found in birds rose by three over the weekend 18–19 February. It is hard to keep track in print as the numbers change daily – follow the WHO website.

5 World Health Organization. For updates on laboratory-confirmed cases go to "Cumulative Number of Confirmed Human Cases of Avian Influenza A (H5N1) Reported to WHO" at http://www.who.int/csr/disease/avian_influenza/country/en/. Website for the Center for Infectious Disease Research and Policy (CIDRAP) is http://www.cidrap.umn.edu/cidrap/content/influenza/avianflu/case-count/avflucount.html

6 John M. Barry, *The Great Influenza*, New York: Viking, 2004.

7 CNN, 1 November 2005.

8 Valerie Elliott and Nigel Hawkes, "No-go areas Planned as Bird Flu Closes In", *The Times*, 16 February 2006, pp. 1 and 11.

9 http://www.mydna.com/health/diseases/avian/news/news_20050216_bird_flu_terrorism_comparison.html.

10 http://en.wikipedia.org/wiki/Antigenic_drift.

11 World Health Organization, Geneva, and Center for Disease Control, Atlanta, Georgia.

12 World Health Organization, Geneva, 2005.

13 Workshop held in University of Alaska, Fairbanks, October 2005.

14 Julian Palmore, "On Setting Priorities for International Security", *Defense & Security Analysis*, Vol. 22 No. 1, March 2006. This critical commentary was written to alert readers to the breadth of a global problem: avian influenza – a problem that might reach pandemic proportions if the highly pathogenic avian influenza virus (H5N1) mutates into a form that provides for "efficient and sustained human to human transmission" of the disease. When this happens the World Health Organization will declare a pandemic: a Stage 6 phase of alert, the highest form of alert. See also "Bird Flu Not Yet Migrating with Wild Fowl", *The Associated Press*, 28 December 2005.

15 See "Scientific Puzzle: Some Turks Have Bird Flu but Aren't Sick", *New York Times*, at http://www.nytimes.com/2006/01/11/international/europe/11flu.html?emc=eta1. Also, *Archives of Internal Medicine*, January 2006, at http://archinte.ama-assn.org/cgi/content/abstract/166/1/119.

39

THE REGIONALIZATION OF AVIAN INFLUENZA IN EAST ASIA

Responding to the next pandemic(?)

Nicholas Thomas

Source: *Asian Survey*, 46:6 (2006), 917–36.

Abstract

In 2003, a highly pathogenic version of an avian influenza virus—H5N1—began to emerge in a number of countries in Southeast Asia. The subsequent spread of this virus to nearly all parts of the world has raised concerns about a possible pandemic. This article explores how the virus spread and the policy implications for regional states.

The interaction between human and animal health is not a new phenomenon. However, the scope, scale, and world-wide impact of zoonoses we are facing today have no historical precedent. Central to the profound changes . . . are both the birth of a new era of emerging and re-emerging diseases and the significant potential impact of these diseases on public health.
　　　　　—Bernard Vallat, "Emerging and Re-emerging Zoonoses"

Introduction

The threat from infectious diseases is nothing new.[1] Throughout the ages, populations have struggled to overcome the debilitating effects of disease outbreaks, few of which have been subject to sovereign limitations. During the past century, infectious disease outbreaks continued to ravage societies across the world. Between 1918 and 1919, the outbreak of Spanish Flu is estimated to have infected one-fifth of the world's population, killing up to 40 million people. In the decades that followed, the Asian Flu outbreak

(1958–59) is estimated to have killed in excess of one million people worldwide, while the Hong Kong Flu outbreak (1968–69) brought approximately 750,000 deaths worldwide. These major outbreaks were followed by other—comparatively minor—influenza outbreaks such as Swine Flu (1976) and Russian Flu (1977). In all of these cases, the epidemics were largely left to run their course. Now, on the possible brink of another pandemic, little has changed.

As the East Asian region moves to deepen ties among neighboring states, there has been a concomitant rise in intra-regional population flows. At the same time, global processes are leading to more people traveling from the region to other parts of the world. On the one hand, these enhanced ties bring a range of benefits to the participating states, markets, and societies. Deeper regional integration in East Asia could lead to the formation of a stable and prosperous regional community better able to meet the needs of its attendant societies than the present situation allows for. Closer ties could also mean a greater sharing of state capacity. Where one state cannot address a particular issue (such as good economic governance) unilaterally, a regional grouping can collectively work toward a solution. On the other hand, as the region moves closer together threats within a particular state can more readily cross national borders to become a problem for other states. Although this has always been seen where contiguous national borders meant shared natural concerns (in terms of the use of resources or in addressing such issues as air pollution), more human-centric threats (such as drug trafficking, illegal immigration, or small-arms smuggling) have emerged as problems with a regional, or even global, scope.

Another challenge shared by all regional states is the threat posed by newly emergent infectious diseases. Even in pre-modern times, diseases spread through human contact along trading routes and from key cities. This is still the case today, except that as the region integrates further and global processes expand, the time frame for the spread of the disease (and thus for detection and preventive action) has shortened dramatically. The outbreak of Severe Acute Respiratory Syndrome (SARS), for example, showed how quickly regional and global connectivity could be subverted in the spread of infectious diseases beyond national borders.

Highly Pathogenic Avian Influenza (HPAI), of the subtype H5N1, first resulted in human fatalities in Asia in Hong Kong in 1997.[2] The rapid response of Hong Kong health officials limited the impact of that outbreak, preventing it from spreading to other locations. In its present form, HPAI H5N1 reemerged possibly as early as 2003 and has now been detected in all regional countries as well as a growing number of other nations. The objective of this paper is to explore the impact that the reemergence of this virus has had on East Asian countries and how those countries have coordinated their response through existing or new regional institutions or mechanisms. This study also seeks to ascertain from where the main policy pressure for action against the virus is emanating—from within the nation-state, from other regional states or institutions, or from international organizations. The paper will first review the integrative processes taking place among East Asian states and the impact this has had on the public health sector at the regional level. Public policy responses to the current outbreak of avian flu in Thailand and Vietnam, as well as from the Association of Southeast Asian Nations (ASEAN), will be explored. These states were chosen because they were also involved in the regional responses to the 2003 SARS outbreak. Drawing on this analysis, the key issues arising from these domestic and regional responses will be reviewed, before drawing conclusions.

East Asian regionalization and public health

In December 2005, the first East Asian Summit, hosted by ASEAN, was held in Kuala Lumpur. This summit, designed to bring all regional countries together as equals, was a step forward in creating an East Asian Community. This region-building process began over three decades ago when the then-five-member ASEAN group opened a bilateral dialogue with South Korea. Over the next two decades, ASEAN expanded to encompass all 10 Southeast Asian states; its bilateral dialogues grew to encompass Japan and China as well as Korea in what became known as the ASEAN+3 process. However, it was only when the 1997 financial crisis spread that the regional governments were truly catalyzed into undertaking collective public policy programs among all 13 states. Although these activities were initially centered on enhancing economic and financial capacity at both the domestic and regional levels, they have since expanded into a wide range of policy areas. It was an expansion that emerged from recognition that the future for Southeast Asian and Northeast Asian states was intrinsically linked by common challenges and issues.

Beyond the core political, economic, and financial areas, ASEAN+3 countries have also been cooperating in a variety of functional areas. To date these have included educational initiatives, environmental concerns, labor issues, and security threats, to name only a fraction. However, unlike these other sectors, public health was not developed at the regional level until 2003. Transnational cooperation in public health issues occurred via membership of different international organizations such as the World Health Organization (WHO) or through training programs initiated by the more developed regional states for their less developed brethren. This all changed after the SARS outbreak. As with the 1997 financial crisis, SARS demonstrated how quickly a domestic issue could transcend national boundaries and how, at the regional level, time and space were compressed, requiring faster response times and a better understanding of the situation in neighboring countries.

The recognition that public health issues could transcend boundaries and affect the stability and prosperity of other states is not new. Pirages and Runci have commented that

[v]iruses, bacteria, and various kinds of plants and animals have never respected national borders. They have travelled across frontiers with the winds, waters, explorers, merchants, and mercenaries. Most of the time these crossings have been quite innocent, but occasionally whole societies or ecosystems have been reshaped by them. Now there is growing concern over the impact of increasing globalisation on the potential development and spread of new and resurgent diseases across increasingly porous borders.[3]

This view is supported by Cusimano, who concluded that "while open society, open economy, and open technology forces can help contribute resources to combat the spread of infectious disease, these dynamics also create an infrastructure that allows and encourages diseases to spread."[4]

The two questions that then arise are how—and why—domestic health issues develop into regional health threats. The answer to the first question is complex and relates to the specific disease or virus being investigated. The reasons incorporate different aspects of "globalization, modern medical practices, unsustained urbanization, environmental factors, and the changes in social and behavioral patterns."[5] Of these aspects, the last two—changes to the environment and alterations to social and behavioral patterns—have played key roles in both the SARS and HPAI H5N1 outbreaks. At the same time, man-made alterations to species habitats have disrupted the patterns of interaction between domesticated and wild animal species and humans. Thus, another condition, the changing patterns of animal husbandry, should be included. This could be seen as a sub-factor in several of the above conditions. But as competition over land use grows, the greater interaction between animals and humans (often in unhygienic conditions) has been so pivotal to both the SARS and HPAI H5N1 outbreaks that it constitutes a separate condition. In the case of SARS, the proximity of humans to the civet population—especially in urban areas where civets were marketed as food—was a key condition allowing the virus to cross the species barrier. Once civets were identified as the most likely source of the SARS virus, they were withdrawn from local market stalls and menus, diminishing the opportunity for the disease to cross species. At the regional level, the public health challenges inherent in these six aspects is intensified as cross-border trade flows increase and with them the movement (regulated and otherwise) of wildlife and livestock.

The second question is why do domestic health problems sometimes become regional crises? Ultimately, this can be explained as a failure on some level of the disease host state that spills over the border into other nations. States effectively conterminous via borders or other conduits are more susceptible to transmission than more distant states.

Colebatch and Larmour identify three meso-level sectors where such failures can occur: the bureaucracy, the market, or the community.[6] Bureaucratic failure occurs when time constraints and information requirements fail to meet the needs of a particular case. This may be compounded by conflicting requirements between the central authorities and those implementing the policies at street level. Such failures may also arise when different organizational units have conflicting goals. Market failure can occur when an information gap is present or when decisions generate unforeseen consequences. Community failure can transpire when the overlapping needs and identities of individuals pull people in varying directions, placing the society at risk. In the East Asian responses to HPAI H5N1, it will be shown how failures in all three sectors—domestically and in terms of regional responses—have led to the current situation. First, however, it is necessary to understand the characteristics of the virus and the way it has spread.

Avian flu in East Asia: a brief overview

All influenza is avian in origin and in most of its variations it does not present a threat to humans. Some influenza viruses, however, have evolved a greater affinity for humans. Others have done so for horses, dogs, cats, or seals. This is an ever-developing pool of viruses. Normally, avian strains do not readily infect humans and vice versa. Despite this, over the past 100 years different strains of the avian influenza virus have crossed the species barrier causing millions of deaths around the world. The Spanish, Asian, and Hong Kong flus were all caused by mutated avian influenza strains—respectively, H1N1, H2N2, and H3N2. Moreover, an intermingling of human and avian genes is suspected to have played a role in the development of the latter two strains.[7]

The strain of the current outbreak, HPAI H5N1, that is affecting a large number of East Asian countries first came to prominence in 1997 in Hong Kong. During that outbreak, 18 people were infected by the virus and six died from it. To prevent the virus from spreading, authorities slaughtered every chicken—approximately 1.4 million—in Hong Kong.

In late 2000, the virus changed genetically, incorporating new genes from other influenza viruses. These genes were believed to be from influenza viruses derived from aquatic birds. As reported by the U.N.'s Food and Agriculture Organization (FAO), "(V)iruses isolated from a goose and a duck in December 2000 have acquired NS, PA, M, and PB2 genes from the aquatic avian influenza gene pool through reassortment. For pandemic preparedness, it is important to monitor whether these reassortant viruses have the capacity for interspecies transmission to terrestrial poultry or mammals."[8]

The virus reemerged in Hong Kong in 2001 but without any human casualties. As before, the entire local stock of chickens older than 75 days as well as related fowls (ducks, geese, pigeons, and quail) were culled. The importation of stock from mainland China was banned, although no evidence of the virus was ever revealed by Chinese authorities.[9] However, at the same time the strain was again found in duck meat that had been imported to

South Korea from China,[10] lending credence to the notion that there was an uncontained (and unreported) outbreak in China. The most recent Hong Kong-centered emergence of human infection occurred in February 2003, when a limited outbreak of HPAI H5N1 hit two family members, killing one of them.[11] While it is known that the two Hong Kong residents had travelled to China's Fujian Province immediately prior to becoming ill, no cases of the virus were reported by authorities in either Fujian or adjacent Guangdong Province.[12] Hence, the source of this outbreak was never confirmed.[13]

Regionally, HPAI H5N1 next emerged in South Korea in mid-December 2003.[14] Unlike during the earlier episodes in Hong Kong, the main carrier of the South Korean virus was ducks, not chickens, although both were heavily culled across a number of provinces as a precautionary measure. Interestingly, the South Korean virus was identified as being genetically different from the other, more lethal strains of HPAI H5N1. This is indicative of a second reservoir of the disease and may also account for why no people died.[15] One month after the South Korean outbreak, the disease was detected on a farm in Ato, Yamaguchi Prefecture, Japan. This was the first outbreak of poultry influenza in Japan since 1925.[16] The Japanese episode was limited compared with outbreaks in other countries and quickly contained.[17] Since these initial outbreaks, both countries have experienced repeat episodes, particularly in wild fowl species.

At the same time as the South Korean and Japanese episodes were occurring, Southeast Asian countries were also experiencing outbreaks of HPAI H5N1. Between November 2003 and January 2004, Cambodia, Laos, Thailand, and Vietnam all reported instances of the virus. Over the next 12 months, it spread to four more Asian countries. In a significant departure from protocols developed during the SARS outbreak, few countries in Southeast Asia immediately alerted either their regional neighbors or the relevant international organizations. It was only when the situation worsened, exceeding the state's capacity to handle it (or was revealed by whistle-blowing officials), that the initial contact countries called for international assistance. Between December 2003 and June 2006, the outbreak of HPAI H5N1 has resulted in 101 deaths in Southeast Asia, compared with 12 deaths in China and 17 deaths elsewhere (see Table 1). Throughout this period, few of these Southeast Asian governments have been able to entirely eliminate the prevalence of the virus in domesticated and wild fowl populations. The concern is now being expressed by international organizations that these countries could be becoming reservoirs for a more lethal strain of the virus, one that can be passed by human-to-human contact. The frequent reemergence of the virus across Asia suggests that it has been established there for at least a decade. In understanding how this situation has developed, it is appropriate to examine the public policy responses undertaken by different countries in their efforts to contain and eradicate the virus.

Table 1 Cumulative number of confirmed human cases of avian influenza A/(H5N1) reported to WHO.

	2003		2004		2005		2006		Total	
	Cases	Deaths	Cases	Deaths	Cases	Deaths	Cases	Deaths	Cases	Deaths
Azerbaijan	0	0	0	0	0	0	8	5	8	5
Cambodia	0	0	0	0	4	4	2	2	6	6
China	0	0	0	0	8	5	11	7	19	12
Djibouti	0	0	0	0	0	0	1	0	1	0
Egypt	0	0	0	0	0	0	14	6	14	6
Indonesia	0	0	0	0	17	11	34	28	51	39
Iraq	0	0	0	0	0	0	2	2	2	2
Thailand	0	0	17	12	5	2	0	0	22	14
Turkey	0	0	0	0	0	0	12	4	12	4
Vietnam	3	3	29	20	61	19	0	0	93	42
Total	3	3	46	32	95	41	84	54	228	130

Source: WHO, "Epidemic and Pandemic Alert and Response, Cumulative Number of Confirmed Human Cases of Avian Influenza A/(H5N1) Reported to WHO," <http://www.who.int/csr/disease/avian_influenza/country/cases_table_2006_06_20/en/index.html>, accessed June 29, 2006.
Note: Total numbers of cases, including the number of deaths, are from laboratory-confirmed cases only (June 29, 2006).

Responses to avian flu

National level

Thailand

Despite the lessons learned during the SARS crisis, Thailand initially sought to downplay the possibility of an outbreak of HPAI H5N1, with the deputy agriculture minister describing it as chicken cholera and denying that it could be transmitted to humans. However, even as this official position was being promulgated, local media in central Thailand were getting farmers' statements describing the outbreak as HPAI H5N1.[18] In an overly optimistic move to reassure both the local population as well as export partners, then-Prime Minister Thaksin Shinawatra declared in early January 2004 that "I can certify that the country is free of bird flu, the country is safe, the government has paid attention to this issue for a long time, we have checked the suspected places and killed all chickens infected by disease, even though it's not bird flu."[19] This statement was soon contradicted by Senator Nirun Phitakwatchara who announced later that month that the first case of HPAI H5N1 had already been verified. The government subsequently confirmed that Thailand indeed had the virus.[20] From this confused starting point, the country played catch-up. However, the delay meant that the outbreak was allowed to spread much further than should have been the case, with 29 of 76 provinces declared infected soon after Senator Nirun's statement.

Of all the regional countries affected by HPAI H5N1, Thailand has the largest poultry sector for both domestic consumption and international export. "The country's earnings from exports of chickens and chicken products in 2003 totaled more than 60 billion baht ($1.5 billion) while about 20,000 people are involved in the entire industry."[21] Although no concrete figures have been provided, a review of government estimates puts the cost of directly combating the virus in the billions of dollars. Indirect costs—providing compensation for affected industries—will also rise the longer the outbreak continues.[22] The value of the poultry industry has itself hampered the implementation of government policies, with notable resistance coming from the provinces and within the industry. During the current outbreak, corruption has also been reported, with some officials being offered inducements not to cull infected birds.[23]

As shown in Table 1, the Thai government's efforts to stem and eradicate the instances of avian-human infections have met with uneven success. Although the mortality rate declined over 2005 (and there are yet to be any new cases as of June 2006), the situation has still not yet fully stabilized, with a variety of non-domesticated birds, such as sparrows and pigeons, being found to carry the virus.[24] These wild birds often live in and around infected poultry and may share feed and water supplies, thereby possibly extending the time needed to eradicate the disease at infected sites. Nonetheless, the fact that incidences of confirmed avian flu have been trending down suggests that the new policies, designed to limit the virus's spread and curb its opportunities to cross the species barrier, are meeting with success. Examples of such policies include widespread culling of avian stocks, bans on the movement of avian stocks, as well as the introduction of closed farms to prevent further transmission of the virus between domesticated and wild avian species. This was particularly necessary with the duck population, where studies have shown that "of the nation's estimated 4,000 duck flocks, around 30% are infected with avian flu although most do not display any symptoms."[25] However, not all of the policies have succeeded. A community-based program to encourage villagers to cull chickens had great potential but offered only the equivalent of US$1 per kilogram of poultry handed in. This led many participants to simply keep the birds to eat or sell, boosting the risk of exposure.[26]

Beyond its domestic policies, Thailand has actively supported sub-regional and bilateral programs to monitor and eradicate avian flu. Through its membership in the Ayeyawady-Chao Phraya-Mekong Economic Cooperation Strategy group, Thailand has provided funds to help neighboring countries combat avian flu. At the same time, Bangkok has worked with communities and refugee groups along the Thai-Myanmar border to implement health protocols in more remote areas. Although these programs serve to recognize the transnational nature of the threat, particularly in peninsular Southeast Asia, many of them were started only in 2005, well after nations and societies there were exposed to the virus.

Vietnam

At the same time HPAI H5N1 was being confirmed in Thailand, Vietnam also began reporting infections. This was not, however, the first outbreak there. Soon after Vietnamese authorities called for international assistance, they confirmed that an earlier outbreak had been detected in July 2003. However, for political and economic reasons (Vietnam was preparing to stage the 22nd Southeast Asian Games) the authorities elected not to publicize the matter. That outbreak, in northern Vietnam, lasted from July to September.[27] In this case, Vietnam demonstrated a notably different procedure for dealing with infectious diseases than was the case with SARS.

For the current outbreak, the virus was first detected in the southern provinces of Tien Giang and Long An, but it "subsequently spread to other Mekong Delta provinces and Ho Chi Minh City as a result of panic selling [of chickens] by local farmers."[28] Within two weeks of HPAI H5N1 being officially announced, three people were confirmed dead and over one million chickens had either been killed by the virus or culled by authorities.[29] Further tests showed that the virus was present in 20 of Vietnam's 64 provinces.

In the wake of these initial outbreaks, the virus spread throughout Vietnam and caused the highest number of deaths per country (despite the authorities claiming several times to have contained the virus).[30] Of most concern was that the pattern of the disease spread suggested the virus could be clustering, with limited human-to-human transmission. This pattern is suggestive of a pre-pandemic stage of a virus and may thus be of greater concern than the outbreaks in other regional countries.

Methods to control the initial outbreaks met with limited success because of policy shortcomings as well as gaps in technical capacities. For example, the Vietnamese government instituted a compensation policy, offering 5,000 dong ($0.30) per culled bird. This was problematic in two ways.[31] First, the level of compensation was below market prices, so farmers were not provided with an incentive to cooperate with the government; rather, they tried to recoup likely losses by lowering prices. Second, the policy only covered culled birds. No funds were allocated for birds that died as a result of the disease. This further hampered reporting practices. The decision not to immediately alert the population to the disease also meant that those who were in a position to take proactive measures (farmers and local health officials) were not equipped with the necessary information to do so. In addition, when the public was eventually alerted, the virus had already spread through nearly one-third of Vietnam's provinces, exceeding the state's capacity to address the threat.

Since reaching a peak in 2005, the number of cases in Vietnam has fallen sharply, with no new cases as of the end of June 2006. However, this assessment was based only on reported cases of human and avian infections. Not only is it possible for the virus to persist in the local environment outside a living host but other species, such as ducks, may be carriers without showing symptoms. Moreover, given Vietnam's geographic location, reintroduction of the virus from neighboring countries where it is still prevalent cannot be ruled out. Indeed, in early 2006 a number of infected poultry shipments, which had been smuggled in from China, were found in Vietnam's northern provinces of Lang Song and Quang Ninh, jeopardizing the country's disease-free status.[32]

Responses to avian flu

Regional level

The avian influenza at the moment is a crisis of Asian dimensions. . . . Every country is really encouraged to do more than they do at the moment.
—Dr. Hans Wagner, FAO

As was the case at the national level, the mechanisms by which regional organizations responded to the current outbreak of avian flu derived in part from methods adopted in response to the SARS outbreak in early 2003.[33] Although ASEAN's responses in principle reflect the needs of its members, the organization was largely passive as member states attempted to address the issue without significant regional involvement. Nonetheless, since the current outbreak began a variety of meetings have been held between regional political leaderships, parliamentarians, health officials, and medical specialists from the ASEAN, ASEAN+1, and ASEAN+3 groups.

In the cases of ASEAN and ASEAN+3, regional-level responses to avian flu have been limited, in part reflecting member states' policies. This stemmed in part from resistance by different regional states to declaring a HPAI H5N1 outbreak, which officials feared would hurt domestic and export poultry markets. Nonetheless, the Seventh ASEAN Health Ministers' Meeting held in late April 2004 was immediately followed by the First ASEAN+3 Health Ministers' Meeting. This proximity reflected the growing seriousness of the threat posed by infectious diseases—and also the interconnected-ness of Southeast and Northeast Asian populations with respect to public health challenges. Attendees agreed to set up an emerging infectious disease (EID) program and to deepen regional public health cooperation. They also reached accord on the need to develop a standard operating procedure for all regional states in handling communicable diseases. This expanded meeting had been preceded by an ASEAN+1 meeting in Beijing in March to improve communication and cooperation between China and ASEAN on avian influenza issues.[34] Regional health ministers met again in Bangkok in late November to further coordinate responses to the outbreak and agreed to ensure the "transparent exchange of ideas, mutual assistance, and the development of researchers to investigate the spread of the disease," in conjunction with the WHO.[35]

In response to the growing threat posed by HPAI H5N1—and in light of individual countries' inability to eradicate the virus—in December 2004 ASEAN established a task force to address the threat posed by the outbreak. Responsibility for combating the disease was divided among the five founding members, with each country taking on a specific role. As reported in the *Straits Times*,

> Thailand will coordinate the surveillance and diagnosis of the disease, while Indonesia will deal with policy and vaccinations. Malaysia will be in charge of containment measures—such as quarantine and border control—as well as the establishment of disease-free zones to facilitate the resumption of exports. Malaysia will also deal with emergency response plans. Singapore will coordinate the sharing of information on bird flu around the region, while the Philippines will handle efforts to raise public awareness and communication to help control the threat.[36]

The task force is the best example of a regional approach to the HPAI H5N1 outbreak. However, as with earlier efforts, it is limited by being disaggregated among five of the 10 ASEAN countries. Although this reflects the sites of greatest capacity within the region, it is still limited and cannot be considered a truly regional approach to the problem.

Since the task force was formed, other meetings have been held on the outbreak. In April 2005, ASEAN held a training meeting of epidemiologists from its member states and the +3 states as well as from the WHO and the U.S. Centers for Disease Control (CDC). This meeting was part of the EID program that had been agreed upon at the 2004 ASEAN+ 3 Health Ministers Meeting. This was followed by a meeting of regional politicians from eight of the ASEAN+3 countries. The purpose of the meeting was not only information sharing but also developing political networks that would allow for greater transparency in policy and research development. Although such networks are of limited efficacy in authoritarian or partially democratic regimes, their existence may indicate a deepening of regional political ties on public health issues in general and HPAI H5N1 in particular.

At the East Asian Summit in December 2005, the pressing nature of the avian flu threat led regional states to agree on establishing an international network for monitoring the virus. Even though this is a step forward in exchanging information and best practices, it is still predicated on all member states supplying accurate and timely information. As the two country studies above suggest, this may not always be the case. The two-year lag in setting up such a regional network is an indictment of ASEAN+3 and its dialogue partners for failure to take the initiative, coming just as the outbreak may be ending in some countries.

During the first half of 2006, regional countries began exploring more ways to address the threat posed by the HPAI H5N1 outbreak. Indonesia, Thailand, and Vietnam have embarked on a two-year study on finding effective ways to treat the virus. Vietnam and Indonesia are also exploring possible bilateral programs in addressing new outbreaks and ensuring vaccine supplies for affected populations. The Asian Development Bank (ADB) also announced a new project to strengthen regional capacity and cooperation in detecting and controlling existing and future outbreaks. Even though ASEAN and its partners have been slow to respond institutionally to this problem, it is also likely that the issue will remain high on the agenda of most regional meetings for the foreseeable future.

Issues raised

A key concern is the probability of the current outbreak of HPAI H5N1 developing into a global pandemic. Among the more conservative estimates are between 7.4 million and 50 million dead if the virus mutates into a form spread from human to human.[37] Some analyses suggest that if the current outbreak were to evolve into a pandemic mirroring the Spanish Flu catastrophe, the death toll would be far greater. Globalization, coupled with the lower cost of international travel, means that carriers can disseminate the virus rapidly, exposing all countries to the threat. Even considering technological advances in the detection and treatment of infected persons, WHO and other U.N. officials have suggested that totals could reach 100 million to 150 million dead.[38] Southeast Asia and China are likely to be the places from which such a pandemic would emerge; given the region's generally low public health care capacity, it is reasonable to conclude that most deaths would occur there.

What is now believed is that the current outbreak of the virus began in one of three fowl populations (geese, duck, or quail), spreading among all three before infecting chickens. Ducks, for example, can generally carry HPAI H5N1 without showing any symptoms; yet, the virus is lethal to chickens. Cross-infections among these four species and clean populations allowed the virus to spread further, as did the infection of wild fowl groups. Moreover, H9N2 co-infection or inoculation can mask symptoms of HPAI H5N1 even though the HPAI H5N1 virus particles are still excreted, paving the way for re-emergence of the virus in an otherwise "clean" site.

As has been seen in the recent spread of the virus through Africa, West Asia, and South Asia, the potential for migratory avian species to carry the virus to new regions and to intermix with other species is a particular concern for public health officials, although the main transmission vector remains exports of infected livestock. In the African outbreaks, for example, it is now thought that transmission was through poultry exports from China of infected one-day old chicks because there have been almost no outbreaks in the Rift

Valley (Kenya) or the Okavango Delta (Botswana), the main migratory destinations. Further, wild migration routes tend to be north-south, but spread of HPAI H5N1 has been mostly east-west, suggesting that poultry movements are more responsible, infecting wild populations along the way. Both pathways then overlap, continuing transmission of the virus.

However, even as HPAI H5N1 was detected in an increasing number of avian species it had not, until recently, been detected in other animals. Of special concern was the possible acquisition by pigs.[39] This has always been a concern with the current outbreak, because pigs are genetically similar to humans and may act as a "mixing vessel," carrying and recombining human and other animal diseases into new, more lethal strains. The 1979 outbreak of avian influenza (H1N1) in Europe became established in pig populations, while the 1993 influenza outbreak in the Netherlands was shown to be caused by the H3N2 virus circulating in European swine.[40] In Asia a 1996 study identified the presence of H1N1 in pigs from southern and central China.[41] Going back further, pigs have probably been mixing vessels for avian influenza viruses for over 100 years.

No genetic mutations are required for pure avian viruses and pure human viruses to infect pigs. Once a pig is co-infected, opportunities exist for both viruses to swap genes, generating potentially new strains. Other species, such as humans or other mammals are aberrant hosts, not the preferred hosts. Aberrant hosts make the virus work harder to survive and thereby can drive in aberrant species the evolution of viruses, sometimes increasing their virulence, lethality, or transmissibility among human beings. Humans being aberrant hosts are not easily infected with current strains of H5N1 and transmissibility between humans takes place only on rare occasions. Indeed, ever since the outbreak of HPAI H5N1 was confirmed, the WHO has stated that its main mission is to minimize the evolution of human-to-human transmissible strains.

Once the virus was officially acknowledged in Vietnam, local and WHO authorities were quick to warn people to stay away from pig manure to prevent transmission of the virus "from chickens to pigs to humans."[42] Despite such warnings, in early 2005 Indonesian authorities confirmed the first cases of HPAI H5N1 in pigs. The virus was limited to traces rather than provoking a full-body infection.[43] On May 10, pigs on a farm in Java—adjacent to a poultry farm—were confirmed to be infected with HPAI H5N1.[44] Until this point, the fact that the virus had not yet spread from avian species to pigs was believed to be one limiting factor in the development of a pandemic.[45] Although no pig-to-human cases have been confirmed, the presence of the virus in these pigs clearly demonstrates the potential of the H5N1 virus to mutate across species. Data from tests carried out in Thailand and Vietnam in 2004 indicate that HPAI H5N1 is not readily transmitted between pigs, suggesting that—unlike the H1N1 virus—there may be more restrictions on viral capacity to cross this particular species barrier,[46] although the virus easily infects cats, ferrets, and martens and can easily spread between cats.

Even as they become more regionally integrated, most East Asian states are still building advanced political and economic systems. The underdeveloped nature of these countries has meant that they face a significant shortfall in their capacity to deal with infectious diseases. This capacity gap has been revealed in a variety of ways in different countries as the current outbreak has progressed. In a number of instances, information was not passed among central, provincial, and/or local authorities in a timely manner. Nor was it transmitted quickly to the relevant international or regional organizations, even though all regional states are members of the OIE (Office International des Epizooties, World Organization for Animal Health) and WHO and most are members of the FAO and have agreed to abide by agreed upon protocols.[47]

Problems have also arisen in terms of the technical capacity of frontline medical staff to identify and treat avian flu cases; many of the poorer countries also lack appropriate testing and training facilities. In Vietnam in April 2005, for example, Japanese researchers retested 30 blood samples of people declared to be free of the virus only to discover that seven had actually been infected.[48] Beyond issues of surveillance, equipment, and staff training is the simple fact that the underdeveloped nature of these countries means they have limited surplus financial capacity to redirect or stem the outbreak. While it is in these areas that regional and international cooperation can bolster a state's ability to respond to an infectious disease outbreak, ultimately it is state policies and practices that will have to eradicate the virus.

One area where governments have been quick to respond to the threat of contagion has been in the banning of imported poultry products from countries with confirmed outbreaks. Smuggling, though, remains largely unchecked. Although prohibition is a sensible measure it gives rise to the question of what should be the appropriate set of responses if a pandemic occurs. With the SARS outbreak as well as with earlier epidemics, the movement of people and goods was either restricted or forbidden. However, as the region becomes more deeply integrated, and as its countries become more intertwined with global processes, similarly severe measures could cripple national economies. As a 2004 ADB analysis concluded, "If the epidemic remains confined to animals, as has been the case up to now, it is likely that the aggregate impact on the economies of the region will be relatively limited and hardly perceptible given the underlying strong growth trends projected for the Asian and Pacific region in 2004." However if HPAI H5N1 were to mutate to allow human-to-human transmission, the economic impact would be far greater. The ADB analysis noted that

> the impact of the SARS epidemic lasting one quarter was of a magnitude of about $18 billion in terms of regional GDP (0.8%) or $59 billion in terms of business losses (measured as total final expenditures). It

is clear that if the avian influenza mutates to a human virus, these estimates would provide a floor for expected losses.[49]

Measures and their effect

Apart from future macro-level calculations on the impact of an avian flu pandemic, current control measures are already generating economic consequences in affected communities. In Thailand and Vietnam, in particular, where poultry is a key domestic and export industry, the culling of livestock and change in consumption patterns are materially affecting the poorer urban and rural populations. People on the economic margins are slipping into poverty, and this process could spill over to harm other sectors. As was shown in the country studies, the unwillingness of the Bangkok and Hanoi governments to pay a reasonable price for culled poultry diminished the effectiveness of policies designed to limit the spread of diseased fowl. The impact these policies are having on people's livelihoods is an especially pressing concern in Southeast Asian countries and China, where significant percentages of the populations are employed in low-paid, rural-based industries.

Public awareness and the engagement of civil society are important factors in combating the spread of HPAI H5N1. As the country level case studies show, the unwillingness of governments to appropriately inform the public and respond to contradictory concerns raised at the grassroots level directly contributed to the spread of the virus and can be considered a significant factor in the early deaths. Conflicting data distributed in the early stages of the outbreak by governments, on the one hand, and local groups, on the other, also encouraged an imperfect understanding of the crisis, which may have exacerbated individual responses to the virus's presence (for example, the panic selling of infected poultry by Vietnamese farmers). In addressing underlying social customs, it is critical for governments to engage their societies. In Thailand and Indonesia, social support for the sport of cockfighting helped to thwart efforts to restrict shipments of domesticated avian species between infected and non-infected areas. And in Vietnam, the continued consumption of duckblood pudding also potentially exposes people to new infections.

Conversely, at the regional level there has been a clear willingness to draw upon expert groups and to form region-wide communities of medical specialists, public health officials, policymakers, and researchers. Although the nature of the overarching regional body affects the effectiveness of communities formed, within ASEAN these groups have played (and continue to play) a significant role in advising on responses to the outbreak. This domestic/regional disjuncture is another issue that needs to be addressed, not only to resolve the current threat but also successfully to combat future infectious disease outbreaks. In Thailand and Vietnam both governments have sought to address these issues outside of a domestic framework through bilateral meetings of government officials and health specialists. Within regional civil society, Red Cross organizations in Cambodia, Laos, and Vietnam have begun to develop co-operative programs to address avian flu across their borders.[50]

According to the Asia-Pacific Economic Cooperation (APEC) group, "[R]egional strategies of prevention and control are critical as avian infections have spread across borders, and results of mathematical modeling suggest that if an avian strain developed the ability to spread between people, efforts to contain the outbreak would need to be implemented regionally in order to be successful."[51] Developing such a standard regional approach to the challenges a virus can pose to state systems is a key issue arising from the current avian flu outbreak. This can be seen in the regional debate over whether to vaccinate people against the spread of HPAI H5N1. Although a number of states favored vaccination, Thailand chose not to follow suit, on the basis that its trading partners would then ban imports of Thai poultry. Without a common approach on such issues, regional states risk creating reservoirs of the virus in non-vaccinated populations. And imperfect vaccination regimes could produce virus strains that are resistant to prophylactic measures, augmenting the threat to the region and beyond. To develop a common approach across East Asia is more problematic because concrete action would require a compromise—or even surrender—of sovereignty that many states oppose.

A related problem is underreporting of infectious disease outbreaks. As the examples of Thailand and Vietnam clearly demonstrate, domestic politics and economics can easily play a decisive role in whether or not a country declares an infectious outbreak. Such decisions not only endanger the lives of the local citizenry but—given the numerous channels through which a virus can transcend national boundaries—the citizens of other states as well. With higher transmission risks existing among contiguous states, such decisions directly jeopardize the stability and prosperity of an infected state's regional partners, although broader trade flows can allow diseases to jump to more distant locales. These phenomena suggest that a mechanism for monitoring infectious disease outbreaks—beyond the immediate purview of a state—is required. A network was proposed at the East Asian Summit, but as the post-SARS experience demonstrates, any such structure should focus on prevention and address all types of infectious disease outbreaks, not just avian flu.

Conclusion

Historically, influenza viruses have repeatedly mutated, crossing species barriers and causing tens of millions of human and poultry deaths. The current outbreak of HPAI H5N1 has not yet reached this degree of lethality but there are concerns that it retains the potential to do so. Since mid-2003, successive waves of the virus have spread the disease throughout most of East Asia, moving from domesticated water fowl to chickens as well as wild avian species. Most recently new mutations have allowed the virus to infect other mammals. The capacity of pigs to easily accommodate both avian and human influenza viruses boosts the risk of gene mixing and the emergence of a reassorted virus with pandemic potential.

Since the SARS crisis in early 2003, East Asia has understood how quickly infectious diseases can spread around the region and to the wider world. The SARS experience showed that only by dealing with disease outbreaks in an open and timely manner can such diseases be stopped. To do otherwise, jeopardizes not only the safety of the infected state's citizens but also populations outside its borders, posing a moral as well as a political responsibility. These lessons appear to have been forgotten with HPAI H5N1. Domestic political and economic considerations combined to stop governments from reporting the virus in its early stages, allowing it to spread across borders and species.

The delay in state-level responses meant regional organizations were slow to react to the crisis. This ensured that states—often with insufficient bureaucratic, economic, or human resource capacities—together with some support from international organizations dealt with the virus in a primarily unilateral mode. Yet, the lesson from both SARS and HPAI H5N1 is that it is more efficient to deal with an infectious disease collaboratively than individually. It is a lesson supported by other regional crises, financial, environmental, or security-related, that East Asia has faced in the past decade. The conclusion therefore is that despite the pressure to the contrary, East Asia has yet to effectively regionalize its approaches to public health challenges. As with the other crises, the failure of East Asian states in general and Southeast Asian states in particular to collectively address the avian influenza threat leaves a sorry legacy of greater damage over a longer period of time than should have been the case.

Notes

Nicholas Thomas wishes to thank Richard Fielding and an anonymous reviewer for their help in preparing this article.

1 Bernard Vallat, "Emerging and Re-emerging Zoonoses," *World Organization for Animal Health*, editorial, November 2004, <http://www.oie.int/eng/Edito/en_edito_nov04.htm>, accessed December 2004. Zoonoses are communicable diseases occurring between humans and animals.
2 Note: there are non-highly pathogenic strains of H5N1 in circulation, but the focus of this paper is on HPAI H5N1.
3 Dennis Pirages and Paul Runci, "Ecological Interdependence and the Spread of Infectious Disease," in *Beyond Sovereignty: Issues for a Global Agenda*, ed. Maryann Cusimano (New York: St. Martins Press, 2000), p. 176.
4 Cusimano, "Editors Preface to Chapter Seven," in ibid., p. 174.
5 Nanyang Technological University, Institute of Defense and Strategic Studies, "Workshop Report: Dynamics and Securitization in Asia," <http://www.idss-nts.org/PDF/NTS%20Workshop%20report.pdf>, accessed March 14, 2006.
6 Hal Colebatch and Peter Larmour, *Market, Bureaucracy, and Community* (London: Pluto Press, 1993), pp. 28–39.

7 Nature.com, "Avian Flu Timeline," <http://www.nature.com/nature/focus/avianflu/timeline.html>, accessed June 15, 2005.

8 FAO, "History of H5N1 Virus Circulation in South-East Asia before 2004," <http://www.fao.org>, accessed May 2005. Reassortment occurs when viruses exchange genes during replication; such mutations can allow old viruses to act in new ways.

9 "HK to Resume Imports of Live Chickens from Mainland China," Japan Economic Newswire, June 11, 2001.

10 T. M. Tumpey, D. L. Suarez, L. E. L. Perkins, D. A. Senne, J. G. Lee, Y. J. Lee, I. P. Mo, H. W. Sung, and D. E. Swayne, "Characterization of a Highly Pathogenic H5N1 Avian Influenza A Virus Isolated from Duck Meat," *Journal of Virology* 76:12 (June 2002), pp. 6344–55.

11 Frank Ching, "A Pox on Chicken," *South China Morning Post*, March 1, 2003. Although these figures are technically correct—insofar as only one person died in Hong Kong during this outbreak—they cover up the fact that the daughter died on the mainland of pneumonia (a possible misdiagnosis of HPAI H5N1). See Mary Ann Benitez, "Migratory Birds Linked to Avian Flu Virus: Dead Geese and Ducks Have Been Found in Four Locations across Hong Kong," ibid., February 25, 2003.

12 Leu Siew-ying, "We Have No Cases, Say Fujian and Guangzhou," ibid., February 20, 2003.

13 It is, however, worth noting that in late 2005 reports from Chinese health authorities acknowledged that two siblings who died in 2003 after traveling to Fujian Province contracted H5N1 of the same strain that first appeared in Hong Kong in 1997. The stability of this strain may lend further weight to the argument that the HPAI H5N1 strain has probably been responsible for human fatalities in mainland China for a far longer period of time than has been officially acknowledged. See Mary Ann Benitez, "Mainland Bird Flu Close to HK Type," ibid., December 21, 2005.

14 In-between the 2003 Hong Kong and South Korean outbreaks, another strain of avian influenza, H7N7, emerged in the Netherlands, infecting 83 people with flu symptoms and conjunctivitis. One person died.

15 "New Bird Flu Case Confirmed as South Korean Poultry Consumption Falls," *Financial Times Information*, February 6, 2004.

16 "1st Bird Flu Plague since '25," Asahi News Service, January 13, 2004.

17 "Tests Point to Avian Flu in 28,000 Chicken Deaths," ibid., February 24, 2004. Shortly after the first Japanese case was noted, Taiwan also declared an outbreak of avian influenza. However, tests revealed a less pathogenic strain of H5N2.

18 "Thailand Insists Its Chickens Free of Bird Flu," Deutsche Presse-Agentur, January 14, 2004.

19 "Thailand Free of Bird Flu: PM," Xinhua News Agency, January 15, 2004.

20 "Senator Says Thailand Has Its 1st Bird Flu Case," Japan Economic Newswire, January 22, 2004.

21 "Thailand to Train Officials on Bird Flu Controlling," Xinhua, August 28, 2004.

22 For a summary of the ways in which the Thai government is providing assistance to industry, see "Government Extends Help to Poultry Related Businesses Affected by Bird Flu Outbreak," Global News Wire—Asia Africa Intelligence Wire, October 11, 2004.

23 See, for example, "Government Insists Bird Flu Will Not Mutate," ibid., July 12, 2004.

24 "Thailand: Sparrows, Pigeons Found with Bird Flu Virus," ibid., October 20, 2005.

25 "BT50 Million for Bird Flu Vaccine Research," ibid., February 21, 2005.
26 "Thai Villagers Mobilized to Cull Poultry," Channel News Asia, November 7, 2005.
27 "Chicken Imports Banned, Vietnamese Officials Admit Earlier Knowledge of Bird Flu," Deutsche Presse-Agentur, January 13, 2004.
28 "Vietnam Says It Will Ask for Help to Identify Mystery Poultry Virus," Agence France-Presse, January 8, 2004. I use the term "current outbreak" here; however, given the lack of verifiable data, there remains the possibility that the incidence in mid-2003 continued on to become what is otherwise identified as the 2004 outbreak.
29 "Vietnam Appeals for UN Help over Bird Flu, Asia on Alert," Channel News Asia, January 13, 2004.
30 On the latter point, see, for example, Hoang Cuong, "Bird Flu under Control, Says Minister," *Saigon Times Daily*, February 26, 2004; Hoang Cuong, "Bird Flu Basically Contained," ibid., March 2, 2004; and "Agriculture; Vietnam Contains Returned Bird Flu," Vietnam News Briefs, October 6, 2004.
31 FAO Workshop on Social and Economic Impacts of Avian Influenza Control, December 2004, <http://www.fao.org/ag/againfo/subjects/documents/AIReport.pdf>, p. 42, accessed May 2005.
32 "Agriculture Vietnam to Collaborate with China in Poultry Smuggling Control," *Financial Times Information*, April 11, 2006.
33 Comment in epigraph by Dr. Hans Wagner, FAO, as reported in Alexis Hooi, "Warning Goes Out: Fight Bird Flu Together; Health Experts Say Coordinated Approach Needed to Avert Pandemic," *Straits Times*, December 21, 2004.
34 "China, ASEAN Agree to Step Up Cooperation on Curbing Bird Flu Virus," Agence France-Presse, March 2, 2004.
35 "ASEAN+3 Joins Hands to Combat Bird Flu," Thai Press Reports, November 29, 2004.
36 "ASEAN Action Plan to Fight Bird Flu," *Straits Times*, December 22, 2004.
37 "Thailand Drafts Emergency Plan Warning Bird Flu Pandemic 'Imminent'," BBC Monitoring Asia Pacific—Political, January 25, 2005.
38 Eugene Low, "Yes; UN Official Sticks to His Warning of 150m Deaths If Avian Flu Takes Hold," *Straits Times*, October 29, 2005.
39 For more on this point, see Ian Brown, "The Pig as an Intermediate Host for Influenza A Viruses between Birds and Humans," *International Congress Series* 1219 (2001), pp. 173–78.
40 Y. Guan, K. F. Shortridge, S. Krauss, P. H. Li, Y. Kawaoka, and R. G. Webster, "Emergence of Avian H1N1 Influenza Viruses in Pigs in China," *Journal of Virology* 70:11 (November 1996), pp. 8041–46; and E. C. J. Claas, Y. Kawaoka, J. C. de Jong, N. Masurel, and R. G. Webster, "Infection of Children with Avian-Human Reassortant Influenza Virus from Pigs in Europe," *Virology* 204:1 (October 1994), pp. 453–57.
41 Y. Guan et al., "Emergence of Avian H1N1 Influenza Viruses in Pigs in China." In terms of the transnational spread of infectious diseases, it is important to highlight that while these pigs were from mainland China, they were sampled in Hong Kong, demonstrating that it is not just birds that can carry diseases across borders.
42 Ben Rowse, "Vietnam Appeals for UN Help to Contain Worsening Bird Flu Epidemic," Agence France-Presse, January 13, 2004.
43 "Indonesia Detects Bird Flu in Pigs," Global News Wire—Asia Africa Intelligence Wire, April 13, 2005. In another case, in mid-2004 a Chinese official declared that H5N1 had been detected in pigs in China but no followup was made to this announcement. See Keith Bradsher, "Avian Flu Jumps to Pig Herds in China;

Official Disclosure Raises Worry on Risk of Human Infection," *International Herald Tribune*, August 21, 2004.

44 Chris Brummitt, "Indonesia Finds Bird Flu in Pigs, Raising Fears It Could Easily Spread to Humans," Associated Press, May 14, 2005.

45 Another way this could happen is if the virus jumped from an infected person into a pig.

46 Y. K. Choi, T. D. Nguyen, H. Ozaki, R. Webby, P. Puthavathana, C. Buranathal, A. Chaisingh, P. Auewarakul, N. Hanh, S. Ma, P. Hui, Y. Huan, M. Peiris, and R. G. Webster, "Studies of H5N1 Influenza Virus Infection of Pigs by Using Viruses Isolated in Vietnam and Thailand in 2004," *Journal of Virology* 79:16 (August 2005), pp. 10821–25.

47 See Jason Gale, "Asian Bird Flu Cases Not Being Reported Fast Enough, Donors say," Bloomberg, June 6, 2006.

48 Charles Piller, "Many Scientists Fear Bird Flu Cases Exceed Data; Minimal Reports from Laos and Cambodia and Unreliable Test Results Elsewhere Suggest that the Virus' Progress Has Been Underestimated," *Los Angeles Times*, March 16, 2005.

49 John-Pierre Verbeist and Charissa Castillo, *Avian Flu: An Economic Assessment for Selected Developing Countries in Asia*, ERD (Economics and Research Department) Policy Brief Series, no. 24 (Manila: ADB, March 2004), pp. 6–7.

50 "Vietnamese, Lao, and Cambodian Red Crosses Promote Cooperation," Thai Press Reports, January 18, 2006.

51 USA APEC, "Progress Report: Pandemic Influenza Planning and Preparedness Situation Assessment," Second Health Task Force Meeting (Seoul), February 28, 2005.

40

THE SECURITISATION OF AVIAN INFLUENZA

International discourses and domestic politics in Asia

*Melissa G. Curley and Jonathan Herington**

Source: *Review of International Studies*, 37 (2011), 141–66.

Abstract

Infectious disease outbreaks primarily affect communities of individuals with little reference to the political borders which contain them; yet, the state is still the primary provider of public health capacity. This duality has profound effects for the way disease is framed as a security issue, and how international organisations, such as the World Health Organization, assist affected countries. The article seeks to explore the role that domestic political relationships play in mediating the treatment of diseases as security issues. Drawing upon an analysis of the securitisation of avian influenza in Vietnam and Indonesia, the article discusses the effect that legitimacy, competing referents and audiences have on the external and internal policy reactions of states to infectious diseases, specifically in their interpretation of disease as a security threat. In doing so, we extend upon existing debates on the Copenhagen School's securitisation framework, particularly on the impact of domestic political structures on securitisation processes in non-Western, non-democratic and transitional states.

Major outbreaks of infectious disease affect communities of individuals with little reference to the political borders overlaid upon them. Although this has always been the case, the rapid pace of globalisation has meant that in recent times regional disease epidemics are no longer contained by even those natural borders, such as oceans and mountain ranges, which once were effective.

Some infectious diseases can now travel at a frightening pace around the world, spurred on by the frequency of trade and the speed of air travel. Public health practitioners have advocated that the problems raised by the globalisation of infectious disease should be addressed with global solutions.[1] However, the state remains the most significant actor within the political arena of global public health protection and the guardian of the resources and organisational capacity to respond effectively. Motivating states to respond to emergent infectious disease threats, such as avian influenza, is thus seen as critical to the maintenance of global public health.

Some, both academics and policy-makers, have argued that the securitisation of health is the most efficacious way to garner resources and attention to global strategies for disease control.[2] The great potential of constructing infectious disease as a security issue is that it promises the appropriation of considerable resources for the defence of people's well-being; regardless of a state's attitude to public health. The argument proceeds that all states value security, whether or not they value the health of their citizens. While there is a strong case to be made for such a claim, there are also significant caveats which we believe are borne out in the study of empirical cases.

This article begins with the premise that the securitisation of health issues within the international community cannot be treated as a monolithic process. The domestic political and social context within states drives their responses to infectious disease as much, or more so, than the international discourse of health security. A corresponding gulf has emerged between the hopes of the developed world, who initiated the global securitisation of health, and the actions taken by some countries in the developing world. States thus respond to infectious disease emergencies in diverse (and potentially unproductive) ways, even when they embrace the language of security.

Although the literature contains a number of theoretical deconstructions of the link between security and health, empirical analyses of key cases remain scarce. To this end, we examine the case of avian influenza in Vietnam and Indonesia against the backdrop of the international discourse. Drawing from the Copenhagen School's securitisation framework, we analyse the process of securitisation within two countries to present empirical data on how the ostensible shift towards the securitisation of infectious disease is being operationalised in countries facing infectious disease emergencies. The empirical case analysis interrogates how local securitisation processes, that aim to operationalise international public health discourses, rely on fragile state legitimacy, use competing referents and utilise language that is heavily contingent upon the audience to which they are appealing. We suggest that the analysis of such facilitating conditions when studying securitisation processes promotes insights which help us to understand the policy challenges of implementing the global discourse of infectious disease securitisation at the domestic level.

In forwarding the argument, the article is structured into five main sections. The first reviews recent debates linking infectious disease with security; by interrogating discussions on which conditions facilitate disease securitisation, and by identifying gaps within the literature on the types of audiences which are present in that process at the domestic and international level. The second section presents key themes present in recent literature on securitisation processes in non-Western and non-democratic or transitional contexts. Here we review two main aspects of pertinent critiques of securitisation, namely its Eurocentricism, and its focus on linguistic speech act methodology, to establish important conceptual parameters for our discussion of empirical cases in Southeast Asia. The third section presents the empirical cases of Vietnam and Indonesia, focusing on the social and political context in shaping the securitisation process within these polities. Section four discusses how analyses of political legitimacy, domestic referents and audience interaction facilitate greater understanding of the securitisation process, particularly in non-Western, non-democratic and transitional states. Finally, we explore the article's implications for the global public health securitisation agenda, and the role of domestic political structures within the securitisation framework.

Disease as a security issue

Most recent scholarship on disease and security has focused on the context in which disease becomes a security issue. However it has done so by focusing on which diseases have security potential, rather than the socio-political environment in which these securitisations occur. Traditionally, diseases have been the subject of security analysis when they have had an effect on the relative power of the state, particularly during conflict. Conversely, advocates of human security, particularly those of the 'freedom from want' agenda, have proposed that almost any disease is a potential security threat due to its ability to significantly affect the quality of life of an individual.[3] Such paradigms have sought to establish the objective 'security-ness' of disease, and play an important role in making sense of the arguments forwarded by actors, but they offer little analytical utility when seeking to explain the interplay between the global and local politics of infectious disease control.

Following the Copenhagen School's work on securitisation, we believe that the crucial component in seeking to understand the plurality of policies is whether the disease can credibly be termed a security issue and hence be accepted by an audience as an existential threat to a referent object.[4] According to Buzan, Wæver and de Wilde this requires that a set of 'facilitating conditions' be met in order for the disease to be credible as a security issue. Thus coherent analyses of the subject must be able to form a rationale for why some disease outbreaks are accepted as security issues, while others are not.

For the most part, these rationales have focused on the diseases themselves, and have tended to overlook differences between the disease-affected communities. McInnes suggests that, amongst other facilitating conditions, in order for a disease to be successfully securitised: 'it must be perceived as an *extreme threat* to social well being, going beyond the individual to the community'.[5] A key factor which accelerates this process is the degree to which Western, developed societies have become 'individuated', creating a heightened perception of uncertainty and risk surrounding disease.[6] Enemark provides a complementary explanation, positing that: 'the health threats most suitable for securitisation are *outbreaks* of infectious diseases – specifically, those that inspire a level of dread disproportionate to their ability to cause illness and death'.[7] Such pronouncements tend to produce a list of candidate maladies, which include: SARS, HIV/AIDS, Ebola, variant Creutzfeldt-Jakob disease (vCJD) and pandemic influenza.[8]

While McInnes and Enemark's exploration of fear's role in securitising disease might correctly identify *which* diseases are securitised, it raises an equally important question: in *whom* do these diseases inspire dread? How do audiences come to fear these diseases and view them as security threats? McInnes' emphasis on the 'risk society' is a well rounded dissection of how certain diseases become securitised within the developed world, but it is unclear what utility it possesses outside of risk societies, or even outside of the Western-context.[9] While McInnes has therefore dealt with the 'facilitating conditions' which inform the reaction of a developed world audience to securitising attempts, the lack of a systemic discussion on the role of audiences within his framework hampers the applicability of the analysis to non-risk society contexts.

Audiences, be they groups of individuals or communities, are widely divergent in the way that they understand threats and the way they become fearful. For Buzan, Wæver and de Wilde, the audience is the primary judge of whether an issue warrants security attention, and in order for that imprimatur to be given, the securitising actor must convince the audience that the issue represents an existential threat to a referent *they* value.[10] This process, as we discuss below and as is recounted in detail elsewhere, should not be understood as merely an act of persuasion; there are critical questions of social structuring and linguistic legitimacy which inform this process. It is important to note, however, that within securitisation studies generally, the role that the audience plays in the construction of threats is seldom acknowledged, and its relationship to the state, the threat being constructed, and the securitising actor is rarely analysed.[11] The focus has rather been on the securitising actor (what speech they use, how *they* securitise) and the objective facets of threats which make them conducive to securitising processes.

In line with this critique of securitisation theory, a growing body of literature, from both theoretical and empirical perspectives, has questioned the ability of Buzan, Wæver and de Wilde's framework to adequately incorporate the social and political context within which securitisation processes occur. Two aspects of the critique of the securitisation framework are useful in our discussion of disease and health. The first relates generally to the Eurocentrism and 'democratic bias' of the framework, which suggests that processes of

securitisation proceed in different, and possibly non-linear and more fragmented ways, than in democratic systems. The second relates to securitisation's
supposed over-emphasis on linguistic speech acts as the primary evidence to locate
cases of securitisation, neglecting other potentially viable and important non-
verbal ways in which the audience responds to the securitising goals of the state.

We believe, along with others,[12] that supplementary concepts – such as
non-verbal forms of political communication – do not pose a methodological
challenge to the fundamental concept of securitisation *per se*. However, we
suggest that the application of a purely linguistic analysis in non-democratic
and transitional East Asian contexts does not adequately take into account
the specific negotiated relationships between the 'audience' and political elites
(or senders and receivers of speech acts), such that corresponding analysis
of empirical cases are devoid of hermeneutic depth and recognition of the
situated audience. The article does not attempt to undertake an exhaustive
analysis of the degree of, and factors responsible for, H5N1 securitisation in
the case studies. Rather the comparative case analysis informs our argument
about the need to better understand the complexity of audience situatedness
in the process of securitising infectious disease, specifically in relation to the
interplay between global public health discourse and its impact on, and
implementation within, the state. In sum then, our critique is directed towards
the analytical prejudices of securitisation theory, using empirical insights
from cases in Southeast Asia to support our contention.

Securitisation studies in non-Western/non-democratic contexts

Critiques of the securitisation framework are not new and an extensive review
of these theoretical discussions can be found elsewhere.[13] More attention has
been paid in recent debates to the application of securitisation outside the
European context. Critiques relating to the framework's Eurocentrism –
and the fact that little work has been done on processes of securitisation
in non-Western, non-democratic, or indeed Asian contexts – are becoming
more apparent. Wilkinson for example has argued that despite claims to the contrary, the Copenhagen School is yet to escape what she calls the 'Westphalian
straitjacket' because of an institutionalised Eurocentrism.[14] This is most
obvious she argues when the Euro-American model of the state and its
political culture are assumed to be valid globally. The model assumes the
presence of democratic processes, where 'the "state" and "society" take on
a normative dimension, the assumption being that they can be used directly
and are understood in "Western" rather than local terms and contexts'.[15] An
important methodological implication is that when expectations of securitisation theory meet empirical evidence, this so-called straitjacket "acts as an
editor, highlighting similarities to the Euro-American model, rephrasing to
better suit Western understanding and excising specificities deemed irrelevant
to the Western model'.[16]

These recent debates have been explored empirically for example in the context of post-Soviet Russia and USSR successor states,[17] newly independent Central Asian states,[18] and in South Asia in relation to Bangladeshi migrants to India.[19] Common themes of these works illustrate that the state is by no means a unitary actor, and there remain various influences over state policy and its capacity to implement security policy. Furthermore, multiple sources of 'threats' compete for attention as referent objects of security within the state apparatus. In some cases defining the referent object of security in post-colonial and transitional states becomes a reflection of wider contestations over state-building and other internal power struggles between competing social groups and elites.[20] The implications of competing referent objects for the securitisation of infectious disease will be taken up later in the case study analysis and in the conclusion.

While Buzan and Wæver's work, *Regions and Powers* (2003), goes some way to recognise the need for securitisation theory to be more fluid – by emphasising the importance of diverse security sectors and levels of analysis – its overall focus has been criticised for paying scant attention to actually developing those ideas.[21] As Hoogensen suggests, while Buzan and Wæver argue that 'leaders and peoples have considerable freedom to determine what they do and do not define as security threats [. . .] these ideas receive little attention [. . .] because these dynamics largely transcend traditional, state-based security thinking (whether from above or from below).'[22] The implication is that other levels and forms of politics (such as clan ties, personal networks of influence, and informal regime behaviour) need to be incorporated methodologically when analysing the production of security discourses.

This resonates particularly within the context of Indonesia, where a geographically fragmented state faces the challenge of implementing health policies uniformly over provinces, and where local political relationships may hinder or render national level policy dictates ineffectual. As in many transitional and post-colonial state contexts, the degree of communication possible between state elites and citizens at the grassroots level varies. Divergences in socio-economic and political conditions clearly impact on state-civil society relations, and the capacity and ability of citizens to protest and voice opinions over state security speech acts. The degree to which one can say that an 'audience' accepts securitising speech acts in these polities is challenged by the nature and 'volume' of the communication of the existential threat. This in turn can be limited by state responses, geographical distance, and political willingness on the part of local officials.

The second major critique of relevance is securitisation's emphasis on linguistic speech acts as the main vehicle for identifying and validating cases of securitisation. Like others, we argue that an overly linguistic rule-generating approach to determining securitisation marginalises the ways in which the audience responds to, and resists or ignores, securitising attempts by the state, or an international organisation. As Balzacq notes, securitisation is perhaps better understood as a 'strategic (pragmatic) practice that occurs within, and as part of, a configuration of circumstances, including the context, psycho-cultural disposition of the audience, and the power that both speaker and listener bring to the interaction'.[23] Balzacq's aim is to relocate securitisation away from speech act theory, which he believes is theoretically unsuited to dealing comprehensively with the audience-centred nature of the construction process.[24]

The debate about domestic context and securitisation fundamentally relates to the question of audience acceptance – an important part of how securit-isation is identified and validated.[25] Vuori has been interested in examining how the securitisation framework's dichotomy of 'normal' and 'special' (or security) politics functions in non-democratic contexts.[26] He notes that the definition of 'audience acceptance' in the Copenhagen school's work on securitisation is left 'undefined'.[27] He argues that understanding the dynamics of securitisation in non-democratic political orders – via his empirical work on China – is crucial if securitisation theory is to be a theory about security discourse formation. Like Wilkinson, he argues securitisation has a bias towards democratic decision-making systems and that it is tempting to believe that 'special politics' is not applicable to non-democratic systems because 'there are no democratic process to begin with'.[28] On the contrary, he argues that non-democratic systems also need to justify and participate in securitising rhetoric, because the desire for political legitimacy is a common factor across both democratic and non-democratic systems.[29]

Furthermore, recent work on securitisation in Asia suggests that it is difficult to define the location of 'normal' political practice in post-colonial states.[30] Separating 'security' politics from 'normal' politics is problematic when they appear at times to be mutually constitutive.[31] Vuori, for example, criticises the category of 'special' politics, asserting that, what this 'special' kind of politics means has 'largely been left undefined' by the Copenhagen School.[32] He usefully suggests that special politics has conceptual utility in non-democratic systems, in that it does not *necessarily* have to represent securitisation in terms of 'breaking rules' (read democratic ones); but rather that in totalitarian socialist systems such as China and Vietnam, 'struggle and antagonistic contradiction among enemies can sometimes be con-sidered "normal" politics, or politics following the "rules"'.[33] Furthermore, his use of Kluver's work on the three different audiences for propaganda in China can tentatively identify different audiences in Vietnam for application in our case analysis. These are: '(1) officials for whom official language is a game and a tool for social impact, (2) intellectuals for whom official language is a tool of aggression and defence, and (3) the masses for whom official languages is transformatory, it legitimates and delegitimates different forms of action.'[34] Although we analyse security discourses around infectious disease and not party propaganda, these categorisations help to differentiate between audience types within Vietnam's authoritarian domestic political structure, which is markedly different from that analysed in the democratising, transitional state of Indonesia.

In sum, this brief review has illustrated that when considering the securitisation of international health discourses in domestic contexts, one must take into account local factors which impact on the process of securitisation. Here, critiques of securitisation methodology illustrate two points. Firstly, that caution must be paid to how securitisation proceeds in non-democratic systems; in terms of the ability and capacity of citizens to understand and then 'accept' securitising rhetoric, but also in analysing the motives that elites have in securitising disease. Secondly, emphasis on the speech act alone to identify and validate health securitisation omits other potentially useful sources of action/resistance. These are in addition to other contextual factors, such as geo-political considerations and state-periphery relations, which in turn are interconnected to methods of internal state communication and control. The discussion of 'normal' and 'security' politics suggests that attempts to locate and 'prove' that international health norms have been securitised face considerable complexity in the face of the above factors.

The WHO and the 'Health Security' agenda

The WHO and the World Organisation for Animal Health (OIE) are the two primary international organisations charged with providing technical advice and assistance to avian influenza affected countries. Additionally, the Global Influenza Surveillance Network (GISN), whose technical laboratories are located primarily in a small number of developed states and which is coordinated by the WHO, provides the scientific support and surveillance infrastructure for monitoring the spread of the disease.[35] Importantly, the surveillance aspect of this network primarily relies upon the cooperation of member states in notifying the WHO or OIE when outbreaks in either humans or animals occur.[36] This network, along with the WHO and OIE more generally, form the basis of the international community's assistance and coordination network for avian influenza.

Although a number of discourses operate within global health governance,[37] the WHO and GISN have recently seen a marked shift in the rhetoric which guides their response to infectious disease emergencies, such as pandemic influenza. With its roots in earlier debates surrounding human security, and spurred on by the securitisation of HIV/AIDS in the late 1990s and the emergence of SARS in 2002, the securitisation of infectious disease emergencies has become one of the dominant features of global health governance.[38] The 2007 World Health Report, entitled *A Safer Future: Global Public Health Security in the 21st Century*, entrenches the link between the language of security and the practice of public health within the global health governance agenda.[39] Focusing on emerging microbial threats and catastrophic disasters it embraces security language, a threat assessment methodology and even a 'security aesthetic' (see, for instance, the stamped stencil motif throughout the report, reminiscent of military intelligence reports). The creation of the Global Outbreak Alert and Response Network (GOARN) in 2002, coupled with an expansion of the powers of the WHO under the revised International Health Regulations of 2005, have also been suggested as key signs of increasing securitisation.[40] Accompanying this change in the global health governance discourse have been similar shifts in the national policies of many developed nations to incorporate a significant security dimension into their health initiatives.[41] These developments amongst the international community have been of critical importance in generating a strong link between infectious disease and security amongst a wider cross-section of policy practitioners than was previously the case.

Few accounts have analysed how this discourse has been operationalised in countries affected by an epidemic that threatens international public health.[42] To address this gap, we evaluate the response of Vietnam and Indonesia, to the outbreak of H5N1 influenza amongst their poultry. In analysing to what degree, and which, domestic factors account for variance in response to the securitisation of global public health, we examine bureaucratic and community resistance, core-periphery relations and socio-political discourses as variables that impact on the state's capacity and motivation to securitise infectious disease.

Vietnam, Indonesia and the control of avian influenza

Vietnam and Indonesia provide useful contexts in which to interrogate the universality of the construction of security issues as is usually modelled in the paradigmatic version of securitisation studies. Neither case is a liberal democratic state of the type frequently present in European securitisation studies. In this sense, they provide a good opportunity to test some of the theoretical critiques and innovations enumerated above. It should be noted that by focusing on Southeast Asian states we do not deny that the process of constructing security in Western democratic states could be similarly fraught and contested. Nor should this article be viewed as an exhaustive study of securitisation in non-democratic contexts. We therefore merely view the following cases as suggestive of theoretical silences which studies of securitisation in non-democratic, transitional and non-Western contexts must be careful to examine.

From a methodological point of view, Indonesia and Vietnam provide fertile ground for comparison of moves to securitise infectious disease. Both are developing countries with high growth economies and large populations, the demographics of which are changing from largely agrarian to urbanised societies.[43] Both have significant poultry sectors and a history of subsistence farming using poultry as a basis.[44] Most importantly, both nations have been, at differing times, the epicentre of human and avian cases of H5N1 influenza.[45]

Therefore, the threat which they faced from avian influenza, although it peaked at different times, can be said to be roughly similar for the purposes of a macro level political discussion. For a study which seeks to interrogate the 'facilitating conditions' of political legitimacy, audience acceptance and claims to 'security-ness', the comparability of the threat faced by the two polities is important.

Equally important is that the states under consideration have some important differences in their political structure and processes, the role of civil society and the media, and the domestic and international legitimacy of their leaders. We do not claim to make definitive causal statements about the relationship between such variables and the degree and nature of H5N1 securitisation during the period under analysis. Rather, by investigating these 'non-threat facilitating conditions' we provide empirical evidence on the fraught nature of securitising processes outside the Western-democratic state, and outline future avenues for research on the securitisation of infectious disease in those environments.

Throughout the case studies, speech acts, resource allocations, administrative changes, policy 'action', and audience 'reaction' are used as indicators of the process of securitisation. This approach does not seek to provide proof that avian influenza has, or has not been securitised 'successfully'; rather it places the securitising moves (or lack thereof) of the government against the role of political structures and audience reactions in influencing the overall outcome of health securitisation.

Vietnam

Since 2003, Vietnam has suffered two major outbreaks of the H5N1 virus in humans, corresponding to the northern hemisphere winter and spring.[46] The first, occurring in the first few months of 2004, resulted in 23 human cases of the disease. The second, occurring from late 2004 until the middle of 2005, resulted in a further 62 cases. From December 2005, Vietnam reported no cases of human infection for almost two years, before a small number of isolated cases since July 2007.

Importantly, while the human cases form the nexus of concern for the WHO and GISN, the epidemic has a far greater reach amongst Vietnam's poultry industry and domestic waterfowl. Vietnam's traditional agricultural system is uniquely suited to sustained, and sometimes undetectable, transmission of the H5N1 virus amongst birds.[47] Not surprisingly, outbreaks amongst poultry have been a regular feature of Vietnam's provinces since 2003, even when no new human cases were emerging. At one point, 20 per cent of the country's poultry were slaughtered in an effort to control the disease – a massive blow to the short-term economic stability of rural agricultural areas, where 80 per cent of Vietnam's population resides.[48]

The Vietnamese government's response to the outbreak of avian influenza started slowly. In 2003, as the first sporadic cases of H5N1 influenza appeared, provincial governments struggled to identify the disease and notify central and international authorities.[49] Likely to a combination of deliberate bureaucratic obfuscation and a lack of capacity, the response to these initial avian and human outbreaks in disparate provinces was sluggish and pursued through an under-resourced public health apparatus.[50]

However, once the gravity and scale of the outbreak became apparent – and impossible to quarantine from the oversight of international organisations – in January 2004, efforts to securitise the disease were swift. Chairing a Politburo-level National Steering Committee on Avian Influenza, the Prime Minister demanded that the epidemic be contained by the end of February through a widespread culling programme, which would involve 'all State apparatuses and administrative bodies of all levels'.[51] From this point forward, the Vietnamese central government's rhetoric and the tone of its response remained remarkably consistent. From 2004 until 2008 security language was frequently invoked, comparatively large budgetary allocations were made and the central government reinforced its control by limiting resistance to emergency measures. Its cooperation with the WHO and OIE, although occasionally plagued by capacity constraints, was also consistently good.[52]

In the context of an ongoing and severe avian epidemic, the government's domestic rhetoric surrounding bird flu since February 2004 has been highly securitised, and focused on placing the economic wellbeing of the Vietnamese state as the referent object. In May 2005, after multiple bouts of culling in infected areas, the Vietnamese government began an extraordinary effort to vaccinate all 212 million poultry in the country against H5N1 subtypes with a view to minimising the economic impact of the outbreaks.[53] However, despite the initiation of this effort, avian epidemics continued to occur in the northern and southern river deltas in late 2005. The response to these avian epidemics is indicative of the types of securitising moves which were made. Throughout this period, newspaper articles about the poultry farms affected by the virus and the government's control efforts appeared daily; variously referring to avian influenza as an 'imminent danger', a 'deadly threat' to Vietnam, or even a 'global threat'.[54] Such pronouncements underscored the government's desire to 'mobilise the entire political system' in the 'fight against the H5N1-virus'.[55] High pressure statements were followed by regulations and directives,[56] including one from the Prime Minister which sought to mobilise the state, its security forces, its citizens and every resource available against the threat:

> The formulation and implementation of such urgent action plans (against bird flu) must be considered an unexpected and urgent task of Party committees and administrations of all levels and a duty of each citizen and, therefore, the strength of the whole political system should be mobilized for this task [. . .] To take initiative in making all necessary preparations and mobilizing every resource to prevent

and combat the type-A (H5N1) influenza among humans [. . .] the Ministry of Health, concerned ministries and branches and localities shall guide all medical units and establishments (even the army and police forces) from the central to provincial, municipal, district and communal levels.[57]

Typical of the media statements and directives during subsequent avian outbreaks in 2006 and 2007, such language was indicative of the Vietnamese government's conviction that 'the fight against bird flu is an uninterrupted war'.[58] The urgency with which the government sought to act is, in our view, a product of the avian epidemic's potential to impact negatively upon the legitimacy of the government amongst both international and domestic audiences.

The 2002 and 2003 SARS epidemic taught the Vietnamese government valuable lessons about its ability to control information flows to the international community and consequently control its image as a good-faith actor in the global public health sphere. In particular, the praise it received for openly and competently controlling the epidemic stood in strong contrast to the opprobrium over China's evasiveness.[59] This resonates with the empirical evidence suggesting that, although Vietnamese officials tried to quietly deal with the initial, small-scale avian outbreaks in mid-2003, they began cooperating with the WHO and international community at the point at which the outbreaks became a national (and hence potentially international) problem. Reinforcing this logic was the need to appear competent to avoid severe consequences for the tourism industry and foreign direct investment.

The pressures from the international sphere appear to coincide with domestic sources with the potential to threaten domestic political legitimacy. Since the late 1980s, the legitimacy of one-party communist rule has been increasingly linked to its ability to bring economic prosperity and development to Vietnam, a phenomena known as 'performance legitimacy'.[60] Through the process of *doi moi*, Vietnam's version of economic liberalisation, the maintenance of economic growth has become central to the stability of the Communist Party.[61] As the demographics of Vietnam shift towards a population base which does not recall the nationalist struggle of the mid-twentieth century, the ability to provide stability and economic progress is becoming increasingly central to continued Vietnamese Communist Party legitimacy.[62] For Vietnam's elites, threats to this growth destabilise the current political order and consequently economic crises are met with large resource allocations and mobilisations of the apparatus of government.

Given the political and social context of Vietnam just outlined, it is unsurprising that the economy was made the referent object of a number of the securitising speech acts made by government officials. The Green Book highlighted 'large-scale loss of life and livelihoods' as the primary threat posed by a human influenza pandemic, but then re-iterated that 'the effects of sickness and mortality on potential output' would be the first-order concern of the government.[63] Control programmes to stem the avian epidemic were framed as a cost-benefit analysis against short and long-term economic hardship, not the potential loss of life. The reasoning for a widespread cull of all poultry in and around Hanoi in November of 2005, as enunciated by one of the Deputy Prime Ministers, was that:

> a potential pandemic would damage not only Vietnam's agriculture but also 'almost all other fields,' he said. The threat of a bird flu epidemic and a potential human pandemic was 'clear before our eyes,' Dzung stressed, adding that Vietnam would use all resources to fight them 'even if it hurt growth'.[64]

These declarations, designed both to shore up legitimacy and exercise control, were followed by consistent injections of money and energy by the central government. The Prime Minister himself frequently chaired the control programme committee, and his two Deputies were each given responsibility for control in the North and the South respectively.[65]

The centralised nature of Vietnam's bureaucracy is a key factor in the apparent success of the securitisation discourse and implementation of control measures. When limited pockets of dissent presented themselves in the Southern Mekong delta, primarily amongst provincial officials seeking to limit the impact of control measures on the livelihoods of rural producers, the intervention of a Deputy Prime Minister instituted even tougher measures than previously mandated.[66]

Financially, between 2006 and 2007, the Vietnamese government allocated US $266 million to control both the agricultural and human health implications of the H5N1 epidemic.[67] This represented an increase of almost a fifth on the total health budget for each year, and dwarfed the resource allocations to other diseases of concern such as tuberculosis and HIV, which received US $10 and US $5 million respectively.[68] The bulk of this allocation has been spent on a highly effective campaign of area-culling of poultry, including a well funded compensation programme for citizens who lost poultry (and thus a large slice of their livelihood) to the control efforts.[69] If we are to take resource allocation as an indicator of commitment to control programmes, and the urgency of the task, then the Vietnamese central government was strongly committed to implementing its securitising rhetoric.

In the language of traditional representations of securitisation theory, Vietnamese leaders made a claim that avian influenza existentially threatened the economic security of Vietnam, and this necessitated emergency measures to contain the disease.[70]

While it is difficult to accurately assess the degree of resistance to government policy within a state whose media is heavily controlled, sporadic episodes of resistance at the provincial and village level seem to have occurred.[71] The tension between enacting proper control measures and limiting their economic impact (which was concentrated in the poor, rural areas of Vietnam – a traditional support base for the Communist Party) is one of the primary reasons for these episodes of resistance. Recent work has identified significant tension amongst central policy dictates and the actions of local bureaucrats, particularly in the Southern provinces surrounding Ho Chi Minh City.[72] These instances of resistance to the central government's control programmes by provincial bureaucrats and their constituents, rather than derailing the securitising acts of the government, precipitated the swift intervention of the State and Party apparatus and a re-doubling of rhetorical and bureaucratic discipline.[73]

Overall, the balance of evidence indicates that the Vietnamese central government initiated a process of securitisation, and that strong control measures were pursued by the central government in order to meet the declared threat. Furthermore, the processes, and their outcomes, were heavily influenced by the fact that by controlling the disease, the Vietnamese Communist Party was able to reinforce its control of social order and protect political legitimacy.

Indonesia

In contrast to the unified and swift response of the Vietnamese government, the Indonesian government has seemingly taken little action domestically, while demanding international assistance to deal with the effects of a pandemic. Statements by government officials to domestic media sources alternatively denied the existence of the epidemic, downplayed its impact or recommended control programmes which were largely ineffective. In contrast, the approach taken when dealing with international organisations has been to emphasise the threat of a pandemic and to use whatever political or material leverage possible to urge the securitisation of the problem of vaccine availability.

Since 2003, Indonesia has experienced a widespread epidemic of H5N1 amongst its poultry and domestic birds.[74] From a human health perspective, the archipelago has also produced some of the most alarming statistics and cases of human infection with the strain since its emergence in Hong Kong in 1997. Since 2005, 141 human cases of the disease have been reported by Indonesia, 115 of which have been fatal.[75] These cases have included a major 'cluster' in the province of Northern Sumatra, which was likely caused by human-to-human transmission of the virus between family members who had no contact with infected poultry.[76]

Despite the ferocity of the initial outbreak, and in contrast to Vietnam's frank and honest approach to the reporting of the disease to the GISN, Indonesia instead reported outbreaks of avian flu as Newcastle disease – a devastating poultry disease but crucially without the ability to infect humans. This misreporting, allegedly performed at the behest of poultry industry pressure, was a key feature of Indonesia's early response to the epidemic and was only discontinued late in January 2004.[77]

From this beginning, the tone and substance of Indonesia's reaction to avian influenza was set, and has continued throughout the epidemic. The Agriculture Ministry, at various times, declared that the strain of H5N1 in Indonesia was incapable of being transmitted from poultry to humans.[78] Spokespersons additionally implied that the primary responsibility for control lay with the under-resourced provincial authorities and claimed that only visibly infected poultry needed to be culled.[79]

These statements were reinforced by Indonesian resource allocations to control programmes. For the years 2006 and 2007, some of the severest periods of the epidemic so far, average government expenditure on avian influenza control was only US $57.5 million, or 1.7 per cent of the US $3.5 billion of government health expenditure in 2006.[80] Institutional attention and support to control programmes has also been very weak. The belated creation of a 'National Commission on Avian Influenza Control' in 2006 was supposed to enable new levels of cooperation between ministries and provincial authorities.[81] Although composed of the majority of the Indonesian cabinet it possessed neither Presidential nor provincial involvement and hence lacked priority as an important domestic issue.[82]

Coupled with the relative passivity of the Indonesian government's domestic response was an active resistance campaign emanating from, and structured by, domestic political relationships. The most salient examples of overt bureaucratic resistance to securitising moves have come from the Agriculture Ministry of the Indonesian government.[83] This is perhaps best illustrated by the dismissal of the National Director for Animal Health (well respected in the international animal health community); after she made allegations that bird flu outbreaks had been 'secretly contained' at the behest of poultry industry insiders with personal ties to senior Agriculture Ministry officials.[84] Significant resistance to central directives and culling operations was also demonstrated by district officials, in many cases denying the severity or existence of the disease in their area.[85] As Paul Forster notes in his recent study of the politics of avian influenza in Indonesia, 'national guidelines are only implemented when local officials think it is necessary and have the funds and local support to do so'.[86] In this way, the locally powerful district officials acted as filters, selectively reinforcing or contradicting potential securitising acts by the central government.

In contrast to the domestic situation, the Indonesian government performed a number of securitising moves on the international stage. In particular, the government embarked upon a policy of withholding H5N1 virus samples extracted from Indonesian patients from the world scientific community. This violated the 55 year old influenza virus sharing agreement at the heart of the GISN pandemic alert and surveillance programme and caused significant consternation within the WHO and the scientific community more broadly.[87] By breaking such an agreement, Indonesia sought to accelerate the accommodation of its demands for more access to vaccines and antivirals.

It declared, through its actions, that emergency measures were required to force a solution to inequitable distribution of the benefits of the GISN.

This securitising act was reinforced and explained by subsequent speech acts directed towards the international community. Speaking at the World Health Assembly (WHA), the peak representative body of the WHO, Indonesian Health Minister Supari suggested that inequalities in vaccine production capacity between the developed and the developing world would result in unjustifiable inequalities in the distribution of vaccines and would undermine 'the battle we have to wage against the pandemic threat' and that 'the unfairness (sic) [. . .] could threaten global health security'.[88] She justified Indonesia's withdrawal from the virus-sharing system on the grounds that Indonesia would receive no benefit, in terms of access to vaccines, from participation in GISN and in a subsequent book claimed that the lack of transparency within GISN meant that the Indonesian virus samples could potentially be used for biological weapons research.[89] Indeed, the securitisation of avian influenza at a global level was challenged directly by Supari, when she declared that 'the current unfair access to vaccines worsens the global inequality between the rich and the poor, between the North and the South – and I think that is more dangerous than a pandemic'.[90] Indonesia subsequently demanded, and achieved, the establishment of an international pandemic vaccine stockpile to be allocated to developing nations in the event of a pandemic.[91]

The statements of the Indonesian government have thus been directed at, and distinguished for, two audiences: on the one hand the domestic constituency and on the other the international community. The two seemingly contradictory policy routes are, in our view, driven by the political situation within Indonesia as well as the international discourse of 'health security'.

The key domestic factor in Indonesia's governance of the avian influenza problem has been the inability to garner support for emergency measures from its provincial and district governments. This is not a new problem for Indonesia, and much has been written regarding it, but it is especially salient in the context of Vuori's criticisms of the securitisation framework.[92] Since the end of the Suharto regime in 1999, the archipelago has undertaken democratic reforms, decentralisation of power to the districts, and has struggled with the effects of a number of separatist movements.[93] Of these reforms, the decentralisation process has likely had the biggest impact upon Indonesia's capacity to control disease outbreaks, not least because authority over public health issues was among the first of the administrative responsibilities that were devolved to the control of the 456 autonomous districts.[94]

Hadiz argues that the process of decentralisation (undertaken to settle secessionist tendencies and promote accountability) has resulted in serious confusion over authority, revenue and responsibility within Indonesia's government.[95] The result of this process, within the context of avian influenza, has been tension between the Agricultural and Health bureaucracies – with Agriculture ultimately assuming a dominant role in, and antagonistic relationship towards, the administration of poultry culling programmes.[96] Additionally, devolution of power to the districts has allowed for local power structures and interest groups, many of whom rely economically on the poultry industry, to regain influence and shape not only the policy of provincial governments, but also that of the central bureaucracy.[97] Indeed, pressure to minimise culling operations seems to have been brought upon provincial governors by the poultry industry.[98] In this way, decentralisation of political legitimacy in the area of public health, and weak or antagonistic relationships between central and provincial authorities have had a profound impact upon the securitisation process in Indonesia.

Health Minister Supari herself alluded to the difficulty in creating policy consensus in a state plagued by internal governance tensions. Asked whether she accepted the criticism of many international observers that Indonesia had not done enough to stem the epidemic, she replied:

> Vietnam, as a centralised socialist country, can get high compliance on national policies and so has succeeded, for example, in implementing rapid culling of birds [. . .] In contrast, Indonesia is in transition towards a decentralized democracy after three decades of authoritarian national rule. We are still on a learning curve, and compliance of the relatively independent regional authorities with national policies is often poor.[99]

The result, explored here, has been paralysis when local political priorities did not coincide with central public health policy, or when central bureaucracies could not come to a consensus. In short, the possibility for action to contain the epidemic, through securitisation of the epidemic for a domestic audience and mobilisation of the internal power structures, was severely inhibited by domestic political concerns.

Coupled with an inability to act domestically was the Indonesian government's effort to divert the securitisation of avian influenza towards the securitisation of vaccine access. A deep post-colonial rhetoric has been a hallmark of Indonesian politics since independence; a civic-nationalism defined largely by external threats was frequently invoked throughout the Sukarno/Suharto years in order to bind the fractious state together. Such a tool remains attractive to Indonesia's modern leaders as they struggle to imprint their legitimacy on the disparate districts.[100] Such political predispositions underlie Indonesia's justification for withholding virus samples; whereby it claimed that the developed world was (once again) exploiting its resources.[101] In this sense, the interplay of domestic factors with global pressure to act produced a set of policy outcomes wholly divergent from those seen in Vietnam.

Case analysis: legitimacy, referents and audiences

The above empirical analysis supports the proposition that state and sub-state factors are fundamentally important to the implementation of the global discourse of public health security. In particular we identify, along with recent empirical work independent to our own, that decentralisation and national discourses of political legitimacy may have played a critical role in the disease control efforts of both states.[102] Of critical importance are the composition of the audience, and the situating of both actor and audience in political and social contexts. Our analysis has implications for the success of the global health security discourse, as well as the utility of the securitisation framework in assessing the construction of security issues in non-democratic, transitional and non-European contexts. Whether or not both countries constitute a 'positive' case of securitisation, it is clear that they have responded to the international discourse which links security with infectious disease in different ways. Their policy responses to avian influenza, some of which have invoked security, have been markedly different. Indeed, there appears to be a degree of contestation over, not only the response to the threat, but the nature and severity of the threat itself. It is therefore useful to disaggregate this process to better understand the interplay between actors, referent objects, and the audiences with which securitising actors interact.

Legitimacy

Key to our analysis is the issue of political and linguistic legitimacy – both as a facilitating condition of securitisation and, following from the critiques, a motivation for, and benefit of, securitisation. As Stritzel notes, 'actors may have some sort of official, delegated or enforced, ability to define meaning so that their power capacity may come close to a monopoly'.[103] In the case of Vietnam, the state did have this monopoly, articulated through the Party, which utilised and also bolstered the rhetoric force of its legitimacy as the economic provider for the nation. However, the contingent nature of this official linguistic power is illustrated by the case of Indonesia, where political sensitivities over policy imposition by the central government, devolution of political power to district leaders and the active resistance of sections of the bureaucracy stifled the coherency (perhaps the initiation) of securitising moves. Simply because governments traditionally possess (and sometimes monopolise) the political legitimacy to articulate security speech, does not mean that this legitimacy can be universally assumed.

The search for political legitimacy can also *motivate* securitising moves. Vietnam has utilised its greater bureaucratic unity and centralised power structure to securitise in order to safeguard the 'performance legitimacy' of the government. Borne of the Vietnamese Communist Party's tight associa-tion with the state, the securitisation process was, on the surface, relatively

300

similar to that described by a paradigmatic version of the Copenhagen School. However, the motivations behind the securitisation of avian influenza, and the clear use of it as a strategic manoeuvre to shore up the threatened legitimacy of the domestic political system, are not well accounted for by the traditional models. A better explanation draws from what Vuori calls 'securitisation for legitimating past acts of the securitising actor' – in this case reaffirming a publicly responsible decision-maker, where 'the audience is the *evaluator* of political legitimacy'.[104]

As the leaders of a transitional and fractious democratic state, the central government of Indonesia may also have been seeking to safeguard domestic political legitimacy. A securitised response to the epidemic, which coerced provincial and local governments, bypassing the 'normal' processes of political bargaining, would have undercut the foundations of the central government's political legitimacy in the post-Suharto environment. However, externalisation of the threat by moving the focus from provincial farming practices to international vaccine inequalities avoids the domestic political sensitivities (particularly regarding 'Javanese domination') and structural impediments (such as that of decentralisation previously discussed) while offering potential benefits. Post-colonial rhetoric has, in the past, been a key foundation of the unity of the Indonesian state.[105] Therefore, one avenue to demonstrate authority and legitimacy was to re-cast the security threat in the international arena.

In this respect, the motivation for a securitising act and the ability to perform it coincide. The contested politics of possessing the legitimacy to make a securitising move are less evident in international forums. In the international environment, states, by the very fact of being states, possess the legitimacy to articulate security threats.[106] International organisations, operating on the assumption of a unitary Westphalian state, are fertile ground for states to make claims about 'their' security interests regardless of whether the constituency they speak for is unitary or whether it has legitimated the state's interpretation of security. A state's legitimacy to speak for 'itself' (and the implied unitary 'it' which that represents) is assumed. Thus, while unable to operationalise the international discourse of health security domestically, the Indonesian government was able to pursue a policy which sought to securitise the problem of vaccine availability.

This problematises the utility of international discourses which attempt to generalise the link between avian influenza and international security. While, the discourse of 'public health security' is established at the international level, it requires implementation at the domestic and local levels. In the Vietnamese case, pressures from the international sphere coincided with core state interests and domestic sources of political legitimacy, such as protecting economic growth, and maintaining their reputation as competent managers of health emergencies (SARS and H5N1). In the Indonesian case, although the need for *action* established by the WHO discourse of 'health security' was potentially recognised by the Indonesian government, they lacked the ability to fully operationalise this discourse in the domestic environment. In this sense, the path of least resistance for the Indonesian central government was to use its foreign policy freedom (and sovereign legitimacy) at the WHA to cajole the international community into providing domestically appealing forms of aid (such as antivirals and access to pandemic vaccines).

This situation challenges the logic of the original securitisation agenda at the World Health Organisation. Rather than the discourse of health security forcing countries to act because of the inherent danger that their ongoing outbreaks cause to 'international security', the affected countries have followed policy pathways which are politically and materially viable; securitising infectious disease issues when and how they are able to do so.

Implications of competing referents

The second major analytical focal point which arises from the cases is the choice of referents which were appealed to by both governments. Attempts to securitise global health discourses involve the securitisation of multiple and possibly competing referent objects. The referent object of many of the WHO's securitising acts was 'global public health' (see the title of the 2007 World Health Report: *Global Public Health Security*). For the Vietnamese, 'economic growth' was the primary stated referent, but it is likely that such rhetoric stemmed from an underlying need amongst Communist Party elites to protect the 'performance legitimacy' of the Party and the Vietnamese political system more broadly. Finally, the referent of the securitising speech acts emanating from the Indonesian Government in the international arena cannot be clearly identified, and could broadly include claims regarding the threat to Indonesian sovereignty, the health and welfare of its citizens, and the economic productivity of the poultry sector. Such a milieu underscores the difficulty, perhaps incoherency, in seeking to catalogue clearly definable referents which are valued by neatly delineated audiences.

The influence of competing referents also challenges the efficacy of the international securitisation of public health. Once security responses are legitimated in the context of infectious disease issues, then the operationalisation of that logic is taken out of the hands of the original securitising actors. When local securitising processes occur, reproducing international discourses, they will use referents and language that are unique to the social and political context of the audience they are trying to convince. These referents may be incompatible with the intent of those which established the original securitisation and may be tied to the mechanisms of state control and legitimation explored previously. The use of referents which appeal to specific domestic audiences is not merely an exercise in gaining acceptance of externally conceived policies. Rather, it has a profound effect on the qualities of subsequent policy and action. Motives for state control and the mechanisms of that control are thus central in understanding implementation of global health discourses at the domestic level.

The role of audience acceptance

This highlights the issue of audience acceptance and how that may proceed under different political structures. As noted above, securitising H5N1 globally requires not only convincing state level elites that emergency action needs to be taken, but that states such as Indonesia and Vietnam allocate the resources and organisational capacity to respond, and that responses are sufficient to meet the threat. Domestic securitisation in the Indonesian case involved engaging with the politics of elite relationships between the centre and periphery, long known to be a challenge for central Indonesian elites. In this sense, the Indonesia case illustrates how centre-periphery relations and domestic political factors present in client patron societies impact on the process of securitisation by influencing audience dialogue and securitising rhetoric.

For example, provincial and village elites in Indonesia (and in other Southeast Asian polities like Cambodia) are viewed as key sources of knowledge by local people, and therefore they can hold a powerful place as 'communicators' to traditional rural or agriculturally based constituencies.[107] Provincial elites can be seen therefore as 'gatekeepers' of interaction between central elites and provincial constituencies potentially holding significant securitising power in choosing to accept or resist securitising rhetoric. While similar relationships exist at the commune and provincial level in Vietnam, these are mitigated by strong party control of both the administrative apparatus and social movements such as the Vietnam Youth Union. This acts as a disciplining force, by rewarding dissemination of central messages and reducing the incentive to prioritise local concerns. In this sense 'audience' acceptance should take into account the influential and powerful role of provincial elites, and their relationship to the State, in what could be described as a local politics of audience dialogue. Such dynamics do not fit well into the 'Westphalian straitjacket' constricting securitisation theory. Situations where people do not have the degree of access to other forms of information (such as national or international media) as do audiences in democratic and industrialised contexts, and where mobilising and expressing forms of dissent is difficult, may not fit into the paradigmatic understanding of securitisation theory.

Such social structures have implications not only for when and how audiences 'accept' a securitising act, but also for the act itself. The coherency of a securitising act is reliant on a shared context between speaker and audience; where that context is established by both historical experience and shared understanding of linguistic meaning.[108] In Indonesia, the peculiar social and political circumstances of the audience altered the central government's approach to the security implications of the avian influenza epidemic. Furthermore, the post-colonial rhetoric contained in both the speech and symbolic action of the government was a semantic repertoire which could be readily and easily understood by the Indonesian polity. The process in Indonesia thus highlights the truly inter-subjective and contingent nature of securitising processes.

In Vietnam, our analysis concurs with aspects of Vuori's analysis of the role of 'audience acceptance' in authoritarian polities. Securitising speech and action is useful, not only to reproduce political order and to renew discipline where challenges are evident (such as local resistance to poultry culling) but also to serve as a form of communication between the VCP and the people.[109] While securitising H5N1 served a number of international and domestic political goals for the VCP, the global public health message delivered to the masses by central and provincial officials is arguably also a way for the VCP to build and maintain bonds with the 'masses' audience. Securitising H5N1 therefore serves a dual role: at the international level, to protect Vietnam's reputation as competent regional citizen, and at the domestic level, to legitimate the VCP as it 'secures' and 'stabilises' the economy and populace from the ravages of avian influenza.

Implications for the health securitisation agenda

Given the importance of domestic factors in shaping policy responses, we believe there are some stark implications for advocates of the health securitisation agenda. The promise of framing avian influenza as a threat to international security was that it would bypass the normal processes of contestation and compromise which characterise the diffusion of global governance mechanisms into domestic policy. In reality, the performative force of the global public health security discourse seems to be heavily dependent on its alignment with domestic circumstances. In Vietnam, the demands of 'international security' coincided with pre-existing motivations for 'regime security'; where securitising avian influenza served a number of domestic and international political goals. Alternatively, as has seemed to be the case in Indonesia, the logic of security can be distorted into a case for ignoring or subverting the 'global health security' discourse itself. In effect, Indonesia broke free of the new 'rules' established by the initial securitisation of infectious disease at the global level, which were themselves established by breaking free of longstanding norms of humanitarianism.

Such an example underscores concerns regarding the basic precepts of securitisation, which define security practice as a condition of exceptionality from 'normality'.[110] As Vuori suggests, and as we have found, actions which most liberal-democratic states would regard as security practice can be highly normalised in certain political and social contexts. In the international sphere, however, security language is frequently invoked to emphasise the state's right to pursue its interests, ignore international practice and expect non-interference in its internal affairs. The resultant effect of speaking security in an international context may have been a rhetorical structure which promotes the use of drastic action contrary to established international practice, in order to secure the position of the actor (in this case the government of Indonesia). Rather than promoting a period of global cooperation on health issues, our analysis suggests that securitising moves in the cases above have encouraged the prioritisation of domestic political concerns and reinforced *realpolitik* in international engagements on global health issues.

Further empirical work into the operationalisation of the global securitisation of health is thus required in order to fully explore the methods and meanings behind such securitisation. If, empirically, it is deemed that the global discourse of health securitisation is being reproduced at the domestic level in ways counterproductive to the good health of the world's citizens, then caution should be exercised in its extension.

Conclusion

Securitising global public health in general, and infectious disease in particular, functions on the assumption that domestic states have the motivation and capacity to enact policy change. Our case analysis has illustrated that a state's desire and capacity to securitise infectious disease is complex and can not be assumed. It is beyond the scope of the article to analyse the complex causal relationships around whether and how states like Indonesia and Vietnam 'successfully' securitised H5N1 or not. What our analysis has shown, however, is that local securitisation processes that operationalise international public health discourses use referents and language that are unique to the social and political context of the 'audience' they are appealing to, and that these factors have important implications for subsequent policy. Importantly, domestic referents of infectious disease may be incompatible with the policy goals which underpin health securitisation at the international level. We have illustrated that mechanisms of state control and legitimation are important factors that influence and coopt moves to securitise at the domestic level. We also identified important variances in the construction and identification of audiences via our comparative analysis of transitional (Indonesia) and non-democratic (Vietnam) cases. In doing so, we advocate a heightened awareness and understanding of audience situatedness particularly in non-Western, non-democratic and transitional states, to better grasp the policy challenges of implementing global health discourses at the domestic level.

Theoretical critiques of securitisation have focused on deficiencies and tensions in the basic articulations of the theory of securitisation, and how these operate when applied to empirical cases.[111] We believe, that while furthering the discussion surrounding how securitisation can be operationalised, we are also calling into question some of the assumptions underlying the fluidity of securitisation processes between the international and domestic levels. As Hoogensen has argued, 'new security research is demonstrating that important articulations of security emanate from sources other than the state and the international system.'[112] The WHO's role in securitising infectious disease is a significant and important example. Our article suggests that domestic political structures may have a more complex facilitating role to play in the securitisation process than currently detailed in the Copenhagen School's securitisation framework. Further differentiation of the impact of domestic political structures on securitisation processes is therefore an important avenue for the ongoing development of securitisation studies.

Notes

* The authors would like to acknowledge Sara E. Davies and Martin Weber for their comments on a previous version, as well as the contributions of three anonymous reviewers.

1 Robin A Weiss and Anthony J. McMichael, 'Social and environmental risk factors in the emergence of infectious diseases', *Nature Medicine*, 10 (2004).

2 Laurie Garrett, *HIV and National Security: Where are the Links?* (New York: Council on Foreign Relations, 2005); and Peter Piot, 'Global AIDS Pandemic: Time to Turn the Tide', *Science*, 288 (2000).

3 Commission on Human Security, *Human Security Now* (New York: Commission on Human Security, 2003), p. 96.

4 Barry Buzan, Ole Wæver and Jaap de Wilde, *Security: A New Framework For Analysis* (London: Lynne Rienner Publishers, 1998), p. 25.

5 Other facilitating conditions posited by McInnes suggest that in order for a disease to be recognised as a security issue: 'it must have *substantial political effect*; it cannot be dealt with nationally or has *implications beyond national borders*; and it has *legitimacy* as a security issue – a claim is made that the issue can be presented as a threat in security terms.' (emphasis in original); Kelley Lee and Colin McInnes, 'A conceptual framework for research and policy', in Ingram (ed.), *Health, Foreign Policy and Security: Towards a Conceptual Framework for Research and Policy* (London: Nuffield Trust, 2004), p. 15.

6 Colin McInnes, *Health, Security and the Risk Society* (London: The Nuffield Trust, 2005), p. 13; Bill Durodié, 'The Concept of Risk' (London: The Nuffield Trust, 2005).

7 Christian Enemark, *Disease and Security: Natural Plagues and Biological Weapons in East Asia* (London: Routledge, 2007), p. 8.

8 Excluding HIV/AIDS, these diseases account for a very small number of deaths when compared to malaria, cholera or tuberculosis, see Roger I Glass, 'Perceived Threats and Real Killers', *Science*, 304 (2004).

9 For the limits of the risk society, see Ulrich Beck, *Living in the World Risk Society*, Speech delivered 15 February 2006, London School of Economics and Political Science, London. Transcript available at: {http://www.lse.ac.uk/collections/LSEPublicLecturesAndEvents/events/2006/20051215t1424z001.htm} accessed on 17 September 2008, p. 18.

10 Buzan, Wæver and de Wilde, *Security*, p. 31.

11 Thierry Balzacq, 'The Three Faces of Securitization: Political Agency, Audience and Context', *European Journal of International Relations*, 11 (2005), p. 182.

12 Holger Stritzel, 'Towards a Theory of Securitization: Copenhagen and Beyond', *European Journal of International Relations*, 13 (2007), p. 369.

13 Lene Hansen, 'The Little Mermaid's Silent Security Dilemma and the Absence of Gender in the Copenhagen School', *Millenium: Journal of International Studies*,

29 (2000); and Bill McSweeney, 'Durkheim and the Copenhagen school: A response to Buzan and Wæver', *Review of International Studies*, 24 (1998); Michael C. Williams, 'Words, Images, enemies: Securitization and International Politics', *International Studies Quarterly*, 47 (2003).

14 Claire Wilkinson, 'The Copenhagen School on Tour in Kyrgyzstan: Is Securitization Theory Useable Outside Europe?', *Security Dialogue*, 38 (2007), p. 8.

15 Ibid., p. 7.

16 Ibid.

17 Anna Grzymala-Busse and Pauline Jones Luong, 'Reconceptualizing the State: Lessons from Post-Communism', *Politics and Society*, 30 (2002).

18 Kathleen Collins, 'Clans, Pacts and Politics in Central Asia', *Journal of Democracy*, 13 (2002); and Nicole Jackson, 'Human Trafficking in Post-Soviet Central Asia: A Critique of the Securitisation Framework', in Curley and Siu-lun (eds), *Security and Migration in Asia: The Dynamics of Securitisation* (London: Routledge, 2008).

19 Priyankar Upadhyaya, 'Securitisation Matrix in South Asia; Bangladeshi Migrants as Enemy Aliens', in Caballero-Anthony, Emmers and Acharya (eds), *Non-Traditional Security in Asia. Dilemmas in Securitization* (Aldershot: Ashgate, 2006).

20 Ibid.

21 Barry Buzan and Ole Wæver, *Regions and Powers: The Structure of International Society* (Cambridge: Cambridge University Press, 2003).

22 Gunhild Hoogensen, 'Bottoms Up! A Toast to Regional Security', *International Studies Review*, 7 (2005), pp. 271–2.

23 Balzacq, 'The Three Faces of Securitization: Political Agency, Audience and Context', p. 172.

24 Ibid., p. 180.

25 Ibid., p. 184.

26 Juha A. Vuori, 'Illocutionary Logic and Strands of Securitization: Applying the Theory of Securitisation to the Study of Non-Democratic Political Orders', *European Journal of International Relations*, 14 (2008).

27 Ibid., p. 69.

28 Ibid., p. 68.

29 Ibid.

30 See Ibid; Mely Caballero-Anthony, Ralf Emmers and Amitav Acharya (eds), *Non-traditional security in Asia: dilemmas in securitization* (Aldershot: Ashgate, 2006); and Melissa Curley and Siu-lun Wong (eds), *Security and Migration in Asia: The Dynamics of Securitisation* (London: Routledge, 2008).

31 Joseph Liow, 'Malaysia's Approach to Indonesian Migrant Labour: Securitization, Politics, or Catharsis?', in Caballero-Anthony, Emmers and Acharya (eds), *Non-Traditional Security in Asia: Dilemmas in Securitization* (Aldershot: Ashgate, 2006); see also Introduction, Conclusion and chapter by Elizabeth Wishnick, 'The Securitisation of Chinese Migration to the Russian Far East', in Curley and Siu-lun (eds), *Security and Migration in Asia: The Dynamics of Securitisation* (London: Routledge, 2008).

32 Vuori, 'Illocutionary Logic and Strands of Securitization', p. 69.

33 Ibid. This is precisely the contradiction identified in Joseph Liow's critique of the securitisation framework in his examination of Malaysia's approach to Indonesian migrant labour Liow, 'Malaysia's Approach to Indonesian Migrant Labour', pp. 61–2.

34 Vuori, 'Illocutionary Logic and Strands of Securitization', p. 70.

35 Kelley Lee and David P Fidler, 'Avian and pandemic influenza: Progress and problems with health governance', *Global Public Health*, 2 (2007), p. 218.

36 Recent advances within the International Health Regulations, although extending the WHO's powers, do not fundamentally change the reliance on states to accurately report see Ibid., p. 221.

37 Kelley Lee, 'Understandings of global health governance: the contested landscape' in Kay and Williams (eds), *Global Health Governance: Crisis, Institutions and Political Economy* (London: Palgrave Macmillan, 2009).

38 Sara E Davies, 'Securitizing Infectious Disease', *International Affairs*, 84 (2008); and Stefan Elbe, 'Should HIV/AIDS be securitized? The ethical dilemmas of linking HIV/AIDS and security', *International Studies Quarterly*, 50 (2006).

39 World Health Organisation, *World Health Report 2007: A Safer Future – Global Public Health Security in the 21st Century* (Geneva: World Health Organisation, 2007).

40 Davies, 'Securitising infectious disease', p. 301.

41 Lee and Fidler, 'Avian and pandemic influenza', p. 221.

42 The majority of studies have focused on the discourse in developed countries or at the international level. See Alexander Kelle. *Discourses on the Securitisation of Public Health – a Survey of Four Countries* (2006), available at: {http://www.brad.ac.uk/acad/sbtwc/regrev/kelle_securitisationPH.pdf} accessed on 11 March 2009).

43 J Rushton, R Viscarra, E Guerne Bleich and A McLeod, 'Impact of avian influenza outbreaks in the poultry sectors of five South East Asian countries (Cambodia, Indonesia, Lao PDR, Thailand, Viet Nam) outbreak costs, responses and potential long term control', *World's Poultry Science Journal*, 61 (2005), pp. 492–93.

44 Ibid., pp. 496, 499.

45 World Health Organisation, *WHO/WPRO – Officially Confimed Human Influenza A/H5N1 Cases (23 August 2007)*, available at: {http://www.wpro.who.int/sites/csr/data/data_Tables.htm} accessed on 31 August 2007.

46 Data extracted from World Health Organisation, *WHO/WPRO – Human Avian Influenza A/H5N1 Cases by Onset Date*, available at: {http://www.wpro.who.int/sites/csr/data/data_Graphs.htm} accessed 10 September 2007.

47 Alessandro Cristalli and Ilaria Capua, 'Practical Problems in Controlling H5N1 High Pathogenicity Avian Influenza at Village Level in Vietnam and Introduction of Biosecurity Measures', *Avian Diseases*, 51 (2007), p. 462.

48 See Ministry of Health (MOH) and Ministry of Agriculture and Rural Development (MARD), *Vietnam: Integrated National Plan for Avian Influenza Control and Human Pandemic Influenza Preparedness and Response* (Vietnam: Socialist Republic of Vietnam, 2006), p. 1.

49 Tuong Vu, *The Political Economy of Avian Influenza Response and Control in Vietnam*, STEPS Working Paper 19 (Brighton: STEPS Centre, 2009), p. 15.

50 Dennis Normile, 'Vietnam Battles Bird Flu . . . and Critics', *Science*, 309 (2005) p. 368.

51 'Prompt action ordered to contain bird flu', *Saigon Times Daily* (9 February 2004); 'Gov't acts strongly against bird flu – Int'l organizations help Vietnam fight epidemic', *Saigon Times Daily* (5 February 2004).

52 Normile, 'Vietnam Battles Bird Flu', pp. 368–70.

53 Hong Van, 'Ministry requests VND100 billion to vaccinate fowls', *Saigon Times Daily* (26 May 2005).

54 Son Nguyen, 'Awareness the key deadlock', *Saigon Times Daily* (4 November 2005); Hong Van and Bac Cuong, 'Ten Provinces Report Bird Flu, Pandemic Feared Nearing', *Saigon Times Daily* (14 November 2005); and Hong Van and Minh Ngoc, 'Retailers in city plan to take poultry meat off shelves', *Saigon Times Daily* (9 November 2005).

55 Bac Cuong and Hong Van, 'Gov't meets to lay out emergency plan to fight bird flu', *Saigon Times Daily* (18 October 2005); and Hong Van, 'City, neighbouring provinces join forces to bird flu', *Saigon Times Daily* (25 November 2005).

56 Cuong and Van, 'Gov't meets to lay out emergency plan to fight bird flu'; Son Nguyen, 'More resources needed to contain bird flu', *The Saigon Times Daily* (21 January 2005); Hong Van, 'Vietnam culls 90,000 fowls in one day', *Saigon Times Daily* (30 November 2005); 'Fight against bird flu continues', *Vietnam News Agency Bulletin* (27 April 2005); and 'Deputy PM calls on people to fight bird flu', *Vietnam News Agency Bulletin* (13 March 2007).

57 Bracketed comments are from original Resolution 15/2005/NQ-CP, 'Resolution on Urgent Measures to Prevent the Avian Influenza Epidemic (H5N1) and Type-A (H5N1) Human Influenza Pandemic', (Government of the Socialist Republic of Vietnam, 2005).

58 'Deputy PM calls on people to fight bird flu', *Vietnam News Agency Bulletin* (13 March 2007).

59 Fiona Fleck, 'How SARS changed the world in less than six months', *Bulletin of the World Health Organisation*, 81 (2003), p. 626.

60 Zachary Abuza, *Renovating politics in contemporary Vietnam* (Boulder: Lynne Rienner Publishers, 2001), p. 21.

61 Regina M Abrami, 'Vietnam in 2002: On the Road to Recovery', *Asian Survey*, 43 (2003), p. 91.

62 Abuza, *Renovating politics in contemporary Vietnam*, p. 22.

63 See Ministry of Health (MOH) and Ministry of Agriculture and Rural Development (MARD), *Integrated National Operational Program for Avian and Human Influenza* (Vietnam: Socialist Republic of Vietnam, 2006), p. i.

64 'Flu pandemic could kill more people than expected: Deputy PM', *Thanh Nien Daily* (9 November 2005).

65 See MOH and MARD, *Integrated National Operational Program*, p. 7.

66 Nguyen, 'More resources needed to contain bird flu'.

67 MOH and MARD, *Vietnam: Integrated National Plan for Avian Influenza Control*, p. 11.

68 World Health Organisation, *Global Tuberculosis Control: Surveillance, Planning, Financing – WHO Report 2007* (Geneva: World Health Organisation, 2007), pp. 153, 156; and Joint UN Programme on HIV/AIDS (UNAIDS) and World Health Organisation, *AIDS Epidemic Update – December 2006* (Geneva: World Health Organisation, 2006), p. 30. The authors are aware that PEPFAR funding of up to US $36 million was provided to Vietnam during the same period, but this was targeted aid rather than an investment from existing government revenue.

69 Area-culling involves the practice of identifying cases of avian influenza in poultry and then destroying all poultry within a certain radius of the infected flock (usually 3–5km), regardless of whether they exhibit signs of infection.

70 It is difficult to reconcile the notion of economic prosperity being 'existentially threatened', indeed Buzan, Wæver and de Wilde acknowledge the controversy in their chapter on economic referents in *Security*. Although 'economic loss . . . (is) . . . part of the ordinary business of life, it is a matter not of degree but of a possible collapse of welfare' (Buzan et al., *Security*, p. 102); in this sense, the claim made by the Vietnamese government is consistent with the use of the term 'existentially threatened' as described by Buzan et al.

71 Hong Van, 'Neighbors clash over poultry transport precautions', *The Saigon Times Daily* (14 Janaury 2005); Vu, *The Political Economy of Avian Influenza in Vietnam*, p. 46.

72 Vu, The Political Economy of Avian Influenza in Vietnam, p. 46.

73 Vu's recent study highlights this ongoing tension, but re-affirms that 'tough measures' were taken by the central government, in some cases to the detriment of disease control policies (ibid.). Also see Hong Van, 'Health Official Calls for More International Aid', Saigon Times Daily (3 November 2005).

74 Sedyaningsih, Isfandari, Setiawaty, Rifati, Harun, Purba, Imari, Giriputra, Blair, Putnam, Uyeki and Soendoro, 'Epidemiology of Cases of H5N1 Virus Infection in Indonesia, July 2005–June 2006', Journal of Infectious Diseases, 196 (2007), p. 522; and Smith, Naipospos, Nguyen, de Jong, Vijaykrishna, Usman, Hassan, Nguyen, Dao, Bui, Leung, Cheung, Rayner, Zhang, Poon, Li, Nguyen, Hien, Farrar, Webster, Chen, Peris and Guan, 'Evolution and adaptation of H5N1 influenza virus in avian and human hosts in Indonesia and Vietnam', Virology, 350 (2006), p. 264.

75 World Health Organisation, Cumulative Number of Confirmed Human Cases of Avian Influenza A/(H5N1) Reported to WHO, available at: {http://www.who. int/csr/disease/avian_influenza/country/cases_table_2009_03_30/en/index.html accessed 3 April 2008.

76 Yang Yang, M Elizabeth Halloran, Jonathan D Sugimoto and Ira M Longini, 'Detecting Human-to-Human Transmission of Avian Influenza A (H5N1)', Emerging Infectious Diseases, 13 (2007).

77 Rendi A Witular, 'Govt confirms bird flu after long cover-up', Jakarta Post (26 January 2004), p. 1.

78 The bird flu scare', Jakarta Post (27 January 2004), p. 6.

79 Zakki P Hakim, 'Bird flu in RI limited to poultry only, for now', Jakarta Post (6 October 2004), p. 13; LKBN Antara, 'Regional Govts Spearheads of Fight Against Bird Flu, Minister Says', LKBN Antara (15 February 2006); and LKBN Antara, 'Agriculture Minister: Only H5N1 virus infected poultry to be culled', LKBN Antara (21 February 2006).

80 LKBN Antara, 'WB Regrets Cut in Funds for Bird Flu Control in Indonesia', LKBN Antara (24 August 2006); and World Bank, Spending for Development: Making the Most of Indonesia's New Opportunities – Indonesia Public Expenditure Review 2007 (Washington: World Bank, 2007), p. 56.

81 Arie Rukmantara, 'Committee to Prevent Pandemic', Jakarta Post (7 January 2006), p. 2.

82 Indonesian National Committee for Avian Influenza Control and Pandemic Influenza Preparedness, Committee Membership, available at: {http://www.kom-nasfbpi.go.id/aboutuscom_eng.html} accessed 11 September 2007.

83 'Minister: Govt Not to Change Policy to Combat Bird Flu', LKBN Antara (28 March 2006); R. A Witular, 'Mass Cull Unfeasible: Minister', Jakarta Post (12 November 2005), p. 1; E. C Komandjaja, 'WHO Urges Solid Action Plan to Prevent Bird Flu', Jakarta Post (21 February 2004), p. 4.

84 Alan Sipress, 'Indonesia Neglected Bird Flu until Too Late, Experts Say', Washington Post (20 October 2005), p. A01.

85 'Caging bird flu', Jakarta Post (21 September 2005), p. 6; Sari P. Setiogi and Multa Fidrus, 'Bird flu outbreak devastating small poultry farms', The Jakarta Post (13 February 2004), p. 3; 'Certain regions not handling bird flu seriously: President', LKBN Antara (28 November 2005).

86 Paul Forster, The Political Economy of Avian Influenza in Indonesia, STEPS Working Paper 17, (Brighton: STEPS Centre, 2009).

87 Martin Enserink, 'Indonesia Earns Flu Accord At World Health Assembly', Science, 316 (2007), The Lancet, 'Global solidairty needed in preparing for pandemic influenza', The Lancet, 369 (2007).

88 Siti Fadilah Supari, *Statement by the Minister of Health of the Republic of Indonesia H.E Dr Siti Fadilah Supari at the 60th World Health Assembly*, available at: {http://www.mission-indonesia.org/modules/news.php?lang=en&newsid=154 &PHPSESSID=4aflc5827352dcbde4a38f046688c368} accessed 8 October 2007; William New, *WHO Kicks Off Talks On Flu Pandemic, Benefits, Access To Vaccines*, available at: {http://www.ip-watch.Org/weblog/2007/11/21/who-kicks-off-talks-on-flu-pandemic-benefits-access-to-vaccines/} accessed on 12 March 2008.

89 Mark Forbes, 'US dismisses bird flu claims', *Sydney Morning Herald* (21 February 2008), p. 9, Enserink, 'Indonesia Earns Flu Accord At World Health Assembly'. See n. 73 above.

90 Brian Walsh, *Indonesia's Bird Flu Showdown*, available at: {http://www.time. com/time/health/article/0,8599,1619229,00.html) accessed on 12 June 2007.

91 World Health Assembly, 'Pandemic influenza preparedness: sharing of influenza viruses and access to vaccines and other benefits', 2007 (WHA 60.28, 2007).

92 For more on the problems of decentralisation see Vedi R Hadiz, 'Power and Politics in North Sumatra: The Uncompleted Reformasi', in Aspinall and Fealy (eds), *Local Power and Politics in Indonesia: Decentralisation and Democratisation* (Singapore: Institute of Southeast Asian Studies, 2003); and Vedi R Hadiz, 'Decentralization and Democracy in Indonesia: A Critique of Neo-Institutionalist Perspectives', *Development and Change*, 35 (2004).

93 Angel Rabasa and Peter Chalk, *Indonesia's Transformation and the Stability of Southeast Asia* (Santa Monica: RAND Corporation, 2001), pp. 2–3.

94 Ibid., p. 48.

95 Hadiz, 'Decentralization and Democracy in Indonesia', p. 708.

96 'Health Minister Calls for Poultry Ban in Cities', *Jakarta Post* (19 February 2006), p. 1; 'Stamping Out of Poultry Only at Highly Infected Farms', *LKBN Antara* (20 September 2005); and 'Minister: Govt Not to Change Policy to Combat Bird Flu', *LKBN Antara* (28 March 2006).

97 Minako Sakai, 'The Privatisation of Padang Cement: Regional Identity and Economic Hegemony in the New Era of Decentralisation', in Aspinall and Fealy (eds), *Local Power and Politics in Indonesia: Decentralisation and Democratisation* (Singapore: Institute of Southeast Asian Studies, 2003), p. 160.

98 'Agriculture Minister: Only H5N1 virus infected poultry to be culled"; and 'Regional Govts Spearheads of Fight Against Bird Flu, Minister Says', *LKBN Antara*.

99 Declan Butler, 'Q & A: Siti Fadilah Supari', *Nature*, 450 (2007).

100 David Brown, 'Why might constructed nationalist and ethnic ideologies come into confrontation with each other?', *The Pacific Review*, 15 (2002), p. 566.

101 The legal reasoning behind the decision to withhold samples relied on the Convention on Biological Diversity – which asserts the rights of nations not to have their biosphere exploited, and protects them from the practice of pharmaceutical companies manufacturing unaffordable drugs from compounds found in a countries flora or fauna. For a critique of this reasoning, see David P Fidler, 'Influenza Virus Sample Sharing, International Law, and Global Health Diplomacy', *Emerging Infectious Diseases*, 14 (2008).

102 Forster, *Avian Influenza in Indonesia*; and Vu, *Avian Influenza Response and Control in Vietnam*.

103 Stritzel, 'Towards a Theory of Securitization', p. 372.

104 Vuori, 'Illoeutionary Logic and Strands of Securitization', pp. 73, 75.

105 Robert Elson, *The Idea of Indonesia: A History* (Cambridge: Cambridge University Press, 2008), p. 53.

106 This is not to say that all securitising moves by states in international forums are accepted, merely that they possess the legitimacy, formalised by instruments such as the UN charter, to 'make the claim'.

107 See particularly the discussion (pp. 131–5) about relationships between rulers, elites and peasants in Robert E Elson, 'International Commerce, the State and Society: Economic and Social Change', in Tarling (ed.), *The Cambridge History of Southeast Asia* (Cambridge: Cambridge University Press, 1992).

108 Balzacq, 'The Three Faces of Securitization', p. 183.

109 Vuori, 'Illocutionary Logic and Strands of Securitization', p. 71.

110 Stritzel, 'Towards a Theory of Securitization', p. 367.

111 For theoretical perspectives see Balzacq, 'The Three Faces of Securitization'; and Stritzel, 'Towards a Theory of Securitization'; and for empirical analyses of non-democratic, non-Western cases see Vuori, 'Illocutionary Logic and Strands of Securitization'; and Wilkinson, 'The Copenhagen School on Tour in Kyrgyzstan'.

112 Hoogensen, 'Bottoms Up! A Toast to Regional Security?', p. 269.

Part 8

H1N1

41

INFLUENZA PANDEMICS

Past, present and future challenges

Antoine Flahault and Patrick Zylberman

Source: *Public Health Reviews*, 32:1 (2010), 319–40.

Abstract

Influenza epidemics occur regularly and prediction of their conversion to pandemics and their impact is difficult. Coordination of efforts on a global scale to control or reduce the impact is fraught with potential for under and overreaction. In light of the 1956 pandemic and more recently the SARS and H1N1 pandemics, the public health community took steps toward strengthening global surveillance and a coordinated response in keeping with the continuing memory of the tragedy seen in 1918. The scientific, professional, and technical resources of the 21st century are now advanced far beyond those then available. The H1N1 pandemic which commenced in 2009 progressed differently than predicted; its course was difficult to predict with any degree of certainty. Public responses to national immunization programs against the H1N1 virus have been weak. International movement of diseases can lead to creation of new endemic areas and continuous spread such as that which happened with West Nile Fever and Chikungunya. The lessons learned and the public and political responses to each actual or threatened pandemic will serve public health well in dealing with future challenges.

Introduction

The first influenza pandemic of the 21st century which started in May of 2009 and swept through the Northern Hemisphere in two waves, receding after the autumn of 2009, but still circulating widely, made its mark on the history of epidemics.[1] This pandemic threat again raised global concerns stemming from memories of previous pandemics, principally the 1918 "Swine Flu" which killed many tens of millions of people.[2,3]

Influenza A (H1N1) is the first for which a worldwide response was prepared in a coordinated, planned and organised fashion. Some countries reacted to the threat of Swine Flu in 1976, and prepared massive immunization programs in anticipation of a 1918 type pandemic, but the disease did not spread and political and public confidence in the public health agencies was reduced.[4]

For many other emerging large outbreaks (e.g., influenza, AIDS, SARS, dengue fever or Chikungunya) during the 20th century, there was little or no advanced preparation. SARS was an example of a potential pandemic for which the scientific community and international public health efforts were poorly prepared. It was not until the last wave of the epidemic, in May 2003, that the first scientific articles on SARS were published.[5,6] However, for influenza A (H1N1), in May 2009, less than one month after the initial cases presented in the Mexican alert, nearly all the international media as well as medical and scientific reviews were publishing a flood of articles throwing light, sometimes contradictory but always useful, on decision-making at the local, regional and international levels.

Preparations had been made on a global scale for the emergence of a pandemic influenza of the A (H5N1) avian influenza virus that was rampant mainly in Southeast Asia in 2006–2007. This virulent strain was much feared owing to its rare but dreaded transmission from infected birds to man, and high mortality rate (59 percent), with 262 deaths out of 442 reported cases (cumulative cases from 2003 to September 2009).[7]

A new influenza A (H1N1) strain emerged from North America, in late April 2009, identified subsequently as a potential pandemic. More than eight months after it was identified, it was still not known, even very roughly, how many people had been affected throughout the world. As many countries have stopped counting cases, the proportion of mild or asymptomatic cases remained unknown. Most developed countries have taken precautions that seem disproportionate in light of the experience in the Southern Hemisphere during the Austral winter (June–September 2009).[8] Nearly everywhere, vaccination priorities were in turmoil. The politicians' and manufacturers' race against time to produce vaccines seemed to have been won by October of 2009. The first batches were available in the Northern Hemisphere by the start of the autumn-winter wave. This wave came earlier than the regular seasonal influenza. Industrialised countries, in which extensive preparation was undertaken for this pandemic, were, therefore, well-prepared, whereas the needs of the developing countries were not being addressed.

The start of the H1N1 pandemic in April 2009 in the Americas

A new strain of the influenza A (H1N1) virus was first identified in April 2009 and was soon considered to have pandemic potential. Although a significant proportion of people over age 50 showed a residual immunity, nobody knew whether they would really be protected. The age distribution of H1N1 pandemic cases in the United States population was very similar to that for seasonal H1N1 influenza recorded over recent years.[9] Incidence was highest in the 5–24 age group, followed by the 0–4, and then by the 25–49 and lowest among the mature adults and elderly.[10] The wave was fairly moderate in size but with unusually higher mortality among children and young adults than during seasonal influenza outbreaks.[11] Among the very elderly, the mortality was lower than that expected from seasonal influenza.

At the end of the spring and during the summer of 2009, North America experienced an unusually high number of influenza cases for the season. The virus was then projected into all countries by infected air travellers. Fear was raised concerning serious economic consequences for tourism, international trade and the possibility of a blockade on air travel for health reasons. Reassuring reports on the lack of severity in the great majority of cases of infection caused by this virus quickly avoided the suspension of flights. During the austral winter of 2009, the clinical attack rate (percentage of people suffering from influenza symptoms) did not appear to have exceeded 10 to 15 percent in the Southern Hemisphere. However, there are very few data on asymptomatic or mildly symptomatic infections in these areas of the world.[12] In cases where the number of deaths and number of cases are known with reasonable precision (New Caledonia, La Réunion, Mauritius and New York),[13] the mortality directly attributable to the H1N1pdm virus was roughly estimated at about 1 in 10,000 clinical cases. Death was usually caused by viral pneumonia leading to acute respiratory distress syndrome (ARDS) which is a very rare occurrence with seasonal influenza (probably less than one death in a million cases).[13]

According to the Centers for Disease Control and Prevention (CDC), nearly one third of deaths were found to have had an invasive bacterial co-infection mostly caused by pneumococcus.[14] In a series of 722 patients hospitalised in intensive care units in Australia and New Zealand with confirmed H1N1pdm, 20 percent had bacterial superinfections.[15] However, indirect mortality, usually recorded by death statistics, had not yet been estimated in most parts of the world, although a few countries such as the US reported mortality rates above the threshold from October of 2009, through surveillance of pneumonia and influenza mortality.[16] During seasonal influenza, less than 10 percent of this indirect excess mortality which is statistically estimated is usually identified by clinicians and reported in death certificates.

In May of 2009, the WHO announced that there had been 30,000 confirmed cases of H1N1 pandemic influenza, but the same day, the CDC estimated around a million cases.[17,18] In October of 2009, the CDC's estimation of the total number of cases in the US was between 14 and 22 million, with 63–153 thousand hospitalizations and 2,500 to 6,000 deaths, underscoring the very imprecise methods of estimation.[19] These are huge discrepancies which are well known in the world of official statistics. This example is given because the numbers come from what is considered to be the most authoritative epidemiologic surveillance body. Everyone is in a state of confusion. In

France, as in other countries, the "sentinel" doctors do not have the means to confirm the virology of the suspected clinical cases that they report via Internet.[20] As for developing countries, how can those who, for example, do not have official records of births and deaths identify the causes of mortality, let alone estimate morbidity during such an epidemic?

1969–2009: the long GAP between pandemics

There has been a long gap between influenza pandemics during the past forty years. The Sentinelles network set up in November of 1984 by Epidemiology Centre for Causes of Death (INSERM) and Pierre et Marie Curie University, with the support of the Director of Health at the French Ministry of Health and the French Institute for Public Health Surveillance, monitors, detects and forecasts (over a three week period) changes in the course of winter influenza outbreaks. Every year, between November and March, a unimodal influenza epidemic wave sweeps through the whole of France. On average, three million clinical cases are examined by general practitioners, of about six million infections overall.[21,22] These seasonal influenza outbreaks are closely synchronized on both sides of the Atlantic. There is less than a week's delay between the peak mortality attributed to influenza and pneumonia in France and in the US.[23]

Since 1977, seasonal influenza has seen the co-circulation of the A (H3N2) subtype which emerged in 1968 in Hong Kong, the A (H1N1) subtype which re-emerged in 1977 from the former USSR, and Influenza B. Seasonal influenza primarily affects young people (median age around 25 years old) but mainly kills the elderly (90 percent of deaths in those above 75 years old). However, as mentioned above, it is estimated that deaths attributable to influenza (primary or secondary cause) account for less than 10 percent of excess mortality recorded in developed countries. In France, 600 deaths on average are recorded each year by the INSERM, but excess mortality related to influenza is estimated at 6,000, with the young being affected most, both in France and in the US, as compared to the predominance of elderly deaths in the usual seasonal influenza.[24]

A similar order of magnitude is given by US mortality data, from which a total of 36,000 average annual excess deaths is estimated.[25,26] Taking direct and indirect causes together, excess mortality caused by seasonal influenza in rich countries is around one in 1,000 infections.[27]

The fairly rapidly ageing population in these countries probably accounted for a slight increase in these figures during the 2000s. The new antiviral drugs that have been put on the market as preventive or curative measures (oseltamivir and zanamivir) have not yet proved to be a fully satisfactory remedy against seasonal influenza. Very little research is being carried out to try to gain a better understanding of how the virus spreads, in particular by ways other than air-borne infection. In developed countries, preventive measures are focused on

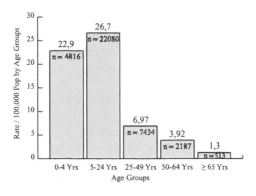

Figure 1 Novel H1N1 Confirmed and Probable Case Rate in the United States, 2009, by Age Group.
Source: CDC[10] 2009 H1N1 Early outbreak and disease characteristics. Available from: http://www.cdc.gov/H1N1FLU/surveillanceqa.htm

vaccinating persons at risk: elderly persons over 65 and people suffering from certain long-term conditions for whom vaccination is recommended.

No country has attempted to prevent the onset of these winter epidemics using a mass immunization strategy. In Japan, vaccination of children was recommended in the 1970s–1980s until it was stopped without rigorous evaluation, despite good arguments that it could be worthwhile.[28] CDC recommends annual immunization of children from 6 months to 19 years of age along with pregnant women and people over age 50, people with chronic illnesses, health care workers, people in chronic care facilities and other risk groups with seasonal flu vaccine.[29] Between 1969 and 2009, during the long period between pandemics, health systems coped, without undue problems, with seasonal outbreaks of influenza (as well as gastroenteritis) that most winters placed strain on the health services, and brought about excess direct medico-economic costs and indirect costs in terms of sick leave and loss of productivity.

1918–1919: the quintessential image of a pandemic

Since the bird flu scare in 2004, there has been considerable speculation about the severity of a future influenza pandemic which, it is said, could be just as deadly as the 1918–1919 influenza pandemic. SARS (severe acute respiratory syndrome) had already struck in 2003 like a "dress rehearsal", with 8,096 cases detected in 26 countries and 774 deaths.[30] Is such a comparison justified? It assumes that certain major questions still pending have been resolved. What micro-organism caused the 1918 pandemic? Sequencing the virus in 2005 provides an answer, but only for the autumn 1918 wave. The samples used by geneticists all came from patients who died in September 1918. The virus responsible for the influenza symptoms arising in spring and summer of 1918 has not yet been identified. Furthermore, sequencing does not reveal anything about the geographic origin of the virus.[31,32] Did it come from China,[33] the US or Europe?[2,34,35] Was it a "new" disease in 1918? Why was it so virulent (Table 1)?[36] Why was mortality so high among young adults?

The A (H1N1) "Spanish" influenza epidemic, the first influenza pandemic of the 20th century, wrought havoc on the world population between May–June of 1918 and April of 1919. It killed at least 50 million people, five times as many as those who died fighting in the First World War. Many deaths were the result of secondary bacterial infections (pneumonia, bronchopneumonia) that were particularly serious in those suffering from pulmonary pathology (tuberculous patients).[37,38] More than 600,000 people died in the US directly or indirectly because of the epidemic. The excess mortality was about 260,000 in France, nearly 220,000 in Great Britain and an equivalent number in Germany during the deadly wave in autumn 1918. Average mortality was nearly 2.5 percent in the US and 4 percent in Europe. Some "naïve" populations such as the Western Samoans (then controlled by New Zealand) suffered terrible mortality (22 percent).[2,39]

The characteristics of the pandemic are well known: mortality rate 5 to 20 times higher than expected, high proportion of complications, unusually high mortality in the 15–39 year old age group, three successive waves within 8 to 9 months, the only influenza outbreak of its kind on record.[31,40] It is sometimes said that these influenza characteristics were unknown at the time.[39] In France, however, in 1919, the Préfecture de la Seine started publishing statistics on the epidemic in Paris and the War Ministry followed suit in 1922.[41-43] Apart from the virology aspects (the virus was not identified in pigs until 1931 and in man until 1933) and despite reservations about the accuracy of the statistics at the time, the descriptive epidemiology of "Spanish" flu was determined almost immediately.

Table 1 Mortality during the three influenza pandemics of the 20th century in the United States.

	Excess mortality during the pandemic season (all causes)	Excess mortality: gross for 100,000 inhabitants (all causes)
1918–1919 A(H1N1)	~ 500,000	530
1957–1958 A(H2N2)	~ 60,000	40
1968–1969 A(H3N2)	~ 40,000	18

Source: Yin S.[36] Avian flu and influenza pandemics. Washington: Population Reference Bureau; 2006. 11 January. 2006.

Most historians now attribute the speed of infection to the significant increase in maritime and rail transport related to the world war. However, the phenomenon was not new. An influenza pandemic had swept Europe from December of 1781 to August of 1782. Although mortality was low (mainly the elderly), the attack rate was very high: three quarters of the population of Europe may have been affected. The virus is thought to have come from Central Asia and it took eight months to travel the 5,000 kilometres that separate the Urals from Portugal.[44] Its journey was greatly assisted by the use of rivers and seas (the Baltic and Mediterranean) for transport and trade, much more so than by the difficult, slower land routes (across the Alps and Pyrenees).

The emergence of a new virus was, therefore, associated with the expansion of transport due to "globalisation" in the 18th century, or rather "Europeanisation". When he founded Saint Petersburg in 1703, Peter the Great wanted the city to open "a window on Europe", which turned out to be only too true in 1781. The connection has only recently been made. The idea of the contagious nature of influenza first had to be accepted. In 1781–1782, the scientists of the Enlightenment, who set great store by meteorological and climatic explanations, were at first disconcerted by the way the epidemic moved east to west, in the opposite direction from the prevailing winds. Suspicions arose that influenza might be contagious and then, in 1889–1890, the propagation of the virus along land and maritime routes convinced contemporaries that influenza was indeed contagious.[44,45]

Today, this is the quintessential image of the epidemic: a health crisis as well as a socioeconomic crisis, causing massive destruction and massive disorganisation. It is a persistent topic in literature: Lucretius, Boccaccio, Defoe, as well as nearer-to-home Artaud, Giono, Camus and many others have drawn on Thucydides and his famous description of the plague of Athens (possibly smallpox, an infectious respiratory disease).[46] An epidemic not only results in suffering caused by the propagation of an infection, but also in the disintegration of power, social structures and customs which ensues: "human society *in extremis*".[47] The Thucydides' paradigm, whether it is real or imaginary, forms the basis for all current anti-pandemic plans.

1957–1958 and 1968–1970: too little too late

The 1957–1958 pandemic has been called the first pandemic of the era of modern virology,[48] and when the A (H3N2) subtype emerged in 1968–1969 causing the third pandemic of the 20th century, virology was a well established discipline. Antiviral drugs were mass produced (amantadine and rimantadine, since abandoned as viruses became resistant and rare, and from which severe undesirable neurological side effects occurred) and there were modern intensive care facilities, at least in developed countries.

The Hong Kong 1968–1970 influenza pandemic passed almost unnoticed, even though it spread worldwide in less than two years given the already significant increase in intercontinental travel.[49,50] Hong Kong was the hub of air travel to the whole of Asia. The attack rate conformed to the models drawn up in the 1980s (40–50 percent with slightly under half being mild or asymptomatic cases) and a mortality rate of 2 to 4 in one thousand. Excess mortality in France stood at 30,000 deaths (five times higher than the rate for seasonal influenza), deaths that then passed unnoticed; they were identified retrospectively in a review of the surge of mortality data for the heat wave in August of 2003, which caused the premature death of 15,000 vulnerable elderly persons.[51] Retrospective analysis reveals infection rates five to six times greater than that for seasonal influenza but with moderate virulence. H3N2 has replaced H2N2 which has not been identified in France since January of 1969, at the start of the pandemic wave.

In 1968, as in 1957, annual vaccination against seasonal influenza was well established. Technical problems (inadequate monitoring, limited production capacity, inadequate clinical test methodology, still unexplored strategies for reducing antigen doses) and legal problems (safety standards) prevented vaccination from being fully available in developed countries. Government action foundered on the logistics and organisation of the campaign. In the US, in 1968 as well as 1957, "too little vaccine was administered too late."[52] In 1957, 49 million doses were available in the US at the peak of the epidemic: only half were used. In 1968–1969, only 15 million doses were delivered at the peak of the epidemic. The health services proved unable to organise themselves in time. Most of these obstacles have now been overcome. The problems are now "political and economic" and involve either reduction of the time necessary for putting products on the market or equity in distributing doses.[53] In December of 2009, social issues surrounding vaccine were also at the height of public attention in France, including popular reluctance to mass immunization, widespread fear of adverse effects of the vaccine, and circulation of rumours on the Internet, including that of a "vast conspiracy" attributed to various sources.[54,55]

1976: the epidemic that never was

The advent of the Asian flu in 1957–1958 recalled the events of the 1918 influenza pandemic to professional and public attention, appearing as the quintessential image of modern pandemics. Subsequent anti-pandemic scenarios were largely based on the "1918-like" scenario. Not knowing what new measures to take when confronted by the originality of unexpected situations, we draw on what Paul Valéry called our "imaginary memories".[56] This reflects the reaction of the US government to the outbreak of "swine flu" at the Fort Dix base of the U.S. Army in New Jersey.

Between January 19th and February 9th, 1976, 230 new recruits between 17 and 21 years old showed signs of respiratory infection. Thirteen were admitted to the hospital. On February 4th, one of the patients died (viral pneumonia). The outbreak fizzled out in February, but the virus was identified as the same A (H1N1) subtype as the Spanish influenza virus which had not been around since 1920.[57] Experts became increasingly concerned about the co-circulation of the two subtypes, A H1N1 and A H3N2. A H3N2 had been dominant since 1968, but would it be able to form a barrier against H1N1? Was there a risk of the two viruses merging?[48] Current sources tend to convey a conflicting picture of the learned opinions at the time. According to Richard Krause, then Director of the National Institute for Allergies and Infectious Diseases (NIAID), in February, experts from the CDC, NIAID and Merck agreed that there was a risk of a pandemic "perhaps similar to the pandemic of 1918".

There was considerable alarm.[58] Yet, in his memorandum addressed to the White House, Dr David Sencer, Director of the CDC, "specifically under-emphasized the specter of the 1918 pandemic",[59] but nonetheless underscored a "strong possibility" for a pandemic "antigenically related" to 1918.[60] On the other hand, Dr Walter Dowdle, chief of the virology section at CDC at the time the A/New Jersey/1976 subtype was isolated, claims that, on the 10th of March, 1976, "the Army provided data to the US Advisory Committee on Immunization Practices that confirmed person-to-person transmission of swine influenza virus. The single death from swine flu loomed large, although most cases were mild. No one at the advisory committee meeting equated the disease potential of this [1976] virus with 1918."[61]

What measures should the country take in the absence of tangible signs of an imminent epidemic? Experts had difficulty in quantifying a vague pos-sibility. The press and Congress toyed with the image of the Spanish flu and its horrors like a poisonous prophecy. Dr Theodore Cooper, Assistant Secretary for Health, made the connection between swine flu and 1918 in a note addressed to the White House. Basing himself on a fashionable theory, he wrote that severe epidemics or influenza epidemics occur approximately every 10 years. In parallel, he sent President Gerald Ford a copy of *Epidemic and Peace, 1918*, by Alfred Crosby – one of the first books, if not the first, to describe Spanish flu from a historical point of view – that was published at the time when the first cases occurred.[62] Cooper's father, himself a doctor, had told him about certain painful reminiscences such as soldiers burying flu victims *en masse* in Pennsylvania where he grew up. Events which might possibly happen suddenly became a real threat based on past events, which he remembered vividly. True-to-life, memories were regarded as a sound basis for predicting the future. Calculating probabilities was never part of the decision to launch a preventive mass vaccination campaign in 1976. "Expertise counts for a lot," wrote the two historians of swine flu, "but only by way of informing subjective judgement." In their view, the subjective probability (the image of 1918) would "in any case" have won the day.[60]

The vaccination programme was launched in October but stopped sud-denly in December after 532 cases of Guillain-Barré syndrome occurred (25 deaths). The programme covered nearly 25 percent (45 million) of the US population. The epidemic petered out, but criticism was virulent. "The CDC lost its innocence", it was said, and with it, its influence.[60] It would experience great difficulty in recovering. Public opinion and the scientific community accused it of having overreacted for sordidly political reasons.[59] In the Presidential elections in November, Gerald Ford was defeated and Jimmy Carter became the new President. Was it a desperate attempt by Ford to re-establish his authority before the elections by a spectacular operation? It was said that only two aspects of this episode had anything to do with science: the identification of the A-subtype swine flu in February and the confirmation that an increased risk of Guillain-Barré syndrome was associated with the vaccination. Apart from this, "everything else was political".[63] The 1976 influenza outbreak is, therefore, the first politicised historical pandemic, "the first time [the government] had been blamed for an epidemic that did not take place".[58] The US strongly encouraged Canada to adopt the immunization for swine flu as well, but Canadian authorities deemed it better to wait and see if the epidemic spread out of Fort Dix, and just then all immunization was called off when the series of complications of the immunization began to appear in the US.[64]

What about the next one?

Can the management of a predicted risk be planned given the scientific uncertainties described above, in particular relating to morbidity and mortality estimates? Much depends on the current pandemic: either the health system infrastructures hold, before, during and after the event, thanks to the efforts made, or they give way in places because the pandemic has medical consequences that are greater than predicted or because its impact on the socioeconomic organisation is more severe, undermining people's confidence. Governments will, in any case, wish to at least conserve a high level of vigilance by setting up measures for preparedness, and if possible, to be even better prepared for the next crisis which could be just as dangerous for the people as for the economy.

Scientists will also have great scope for new discoveries that they will not fail to exploit. The latest pandemic could well transform the "science of influenza". It could give us a better understanding of the mechanisms leading to mutations and recombinations of influenza viruses and it could provide real experience of effective barrier measures – in particular vaccination – against seasonal epidemics, measures that could be implemented if the epidemic recurs and which would allow us to stop a strain with pandemic potential at the source. Rapid diagnostic tests would then be available in the future to identify the viral subtype.

Interdisciplinary observatories using the most up-to-date information could be set up in several places throughout the world, not only in developed countries. These "telescopes observing life", would be able to detect epidemics and epizootics. They would provide precise information almost in real time on seroprevalence rates, on virulence indicators, on the diversity of viruses circulating, and on the distribution of risk factors within the population, including those based on known genetic polymorphisms, not to mention on the state of perception, beliefs, attitudes and behaviour of people exposed to the risk of epidemic.

It is a long haul from 2010 to 2025

There are major gaps in knowledge to be filled in the field of viral respiratory infections and influenza in particular. Little is known about contagion mechanisms or the contribution played by touch contamination (i.e., fomites such as flat surfaces, door handles, etc.). There is a lack of rigorous evaluation of the efficacy of surgical masks worn by contagious persons or of alcohol-based gel hand sanitizer. The appropriateness, timing, duration and social and economic consequences of closing schools have not been evaluated. There is little information on the "altruistic" efficacy of vaccinating health personnel[65,66]; only a few trials have been carried out in retirement homes, not all of which were conclusive.[67]

No trial vaccination has, thus far, been attempted as a barrier against any seasonal influenza epidemic.[68,69] The link between Guillain-Barré syndrome and vaccination is still in dispute, not to mention the quantification of the risk.[70,71] The efficacy of antiviral drugs for serious cases and for reducing mortality has not been satisfactorily evaluated, nor has their mass use outside theoretical computer simulations. We do not know what impact treatment with preventive doses as post-exposure prophylaxis will have on the emergence of resistant strains. The natural history of influenza is still largely unknown. What are the determinants of clinical forms of the influenza syndrome? Little is known about the case mix or the distribution of clinical forms related to the infection. Little is known about the viral variability.[10] Even less is known about the determinants of the severity of the influenza. Why does Acute Respiratory Distress Syndrome (ARDS) occur? Why does secondary invasive bacterial infection occur? Why is 90 percent of mortality due to seasonal influenza not identified by doctors (only 10 percent of influenza-related deaths are recorded as being caused (either primary or secondary) by influenza in death certificates)? We know nothing about the physiopathological mechanisms of this high mortality nor the efficacy of antiviral drugs for preventing or even treating these severe cases nor how and when antibiotics can be used in the treatment of complications, or bacterial vaccines in their prevention. Respiratory complications of influenza are the major causes of death both in seasonal and pandemic situations; medical facilities are confronted with ARDS. Secondary bacterial invasive infections may mask the primary influenza infection, and thus may not be identified medically. It is estimated that influenza is recorded as either the primary or secondary cause of death in only 10 percent of influenza related deaths.[72-74]

However, the route is also technological and political. Between 2010 and 2025, the major international observatories mentioned above may at last be set up to monitor the emergence of epidemics. They will be designed as a grid covering the whole of the world in the same way as meteorological stations and will be linked to a World Health Organisation that is more reactive, better informed and equipped with better resources.

The role of the WHO

Governments set great store through vaccination against pandemic influenza for public health reasons as well as for economic reasons. "Much is riding on the success of vaccination – as well as preventing illness and saving lives, some economists say that curbing the pandemic could prevent hefty financial losses."[75] Beyond this is the competition between the various powers for world leadership in the fight against pandemic risk – whoever successfully manages both the health crisis and the economic crisis will prevail. There is, however, another question, of even greater importance.

On the 17th of September, 2009, the United Nations sent Health Ministries worldwide the conclusions of a report (ordered in July by the Secretary General) in the form of a cry for help. Eighty-five of the poorest countries in the world could not afford vaccines. "The virus could destroy a burgeoning economy or democracy," claimed the WHO, in the purest veins of Thucydides' paradigm.[76] In the context of the concomitant financial crisis and recession, the WHO is well aware that obtaining the support of the rich countries may well prove to be very difficult.

The WHO rather lost its way during the 1980s with respect to influenza policy. Since 1995, it has rebuilt its monitoring and alert systems: the new Division of Communicable Diseases was created (1996), the Global Outbreak Alert and Response Network was set up (2001) and new international health regulations were issued in 2005 (came into effect in 2007) which relieve governments of their veto on epidemiological information. This new era – a "sort of second birth"[77] – was demonstrated by its bold strategy deployed during the SARS epidemic when a global alert,[78] without prior agreement from governments, was issued on the 12th of March, 2003, along with a travel advisory on the 24th of April, advising against travel to Beijing and the Shanxi province in China, as well as Toronto, Canada, while there was open confrontation with the Chinese government regarding the statistics and the progress of the epidemic.

Today, all governments swear to maintain the closest cooperation possible with the WHO. Did Dr Margaret Chang take the trouble to specify in her statement of the 11th of June, 2009 that the WHO does not recommend any uniform scheme and that the order of the day is "adaptation to the local situation"?[17] Even so, the old attitudes reappear. "What really matters is what individual countries are doing on the ground to tackle the disease – and that is not dictated by WHO, but determined by national governments."[79]

The slightest attempt by the WHO to take technical control of operations is immediately censured: down with "world government"!

Controversial allegations that some WHO advisors have conflicts of interest have clouded the public's perception of the H1N1 pandemic of 2009.[80,81] This may partially explain low rates of uptake of the vaccine in many countries. These issues will undoubtedly affect future policy formulation and public attitudes in threatened pandemic situations. Seasonal flu vaccine for risk groups has been accepted as a basic preventive health measure in many health systems, e.g., UK. The H1N1 vaccination rate is estimated by CDC at 75 million or close to 25 percent of the US population, well below figures of 114 million for seasonal flu immunization.[82]

The pharmaceutical industry also has its own strategy which is different from that of the WHO. The WHO asked manufacturers to donate about 10 percent of their vaccine production to low-income countries (400 million doses out of 5 billion). Six manufacturers out of thirty agreed. GlaxoSmithKline and Sanofi-Aventis said that they would donate 150 million doses. Novartis said they would consider discounts if necessary but did not offer to provide the vaccine free of charge, as a rebuff to Ban Ki-Moon, who, on the 19th of May, called on the directors of the pharmaceutical groups for "world solidarity," as well as to Margaret Chan who made the same plea two weeks later.

The day after the United Nations press release, nine countries solemnly promised to release 10 percent of their stock of vaccines to the WHO.[83] Will this be enough? Will this come in due time? The world's vaccine production capacity will be insufficient in any case, as the WHO well knows. The WHO is gambling high on the political question of equity. This will decide the leadership stakes during the current pandemic and in the future.

Summary and conclusions

The 1918 Swine flu pandemic has left an important legacy, much like the Black Plague did four centuries earlier. The folk and political memory of 1918 influenced modern virological and epidemiological thinking when facing potentially robust if not disastrous epidemics during the latter part of the 20th century. The 1976 non-pandemic which caused a national mobilisation in the US with mass immunization resulted in a serious reduction in credibility of the public health community and governmental action in epidemic control.

Subsequent influenza pandemics energised national governments to review their public health structure and laboratory support, and encouraged international agencies to prepare for possible future influenza pandemics, especially in their capacity for rapid production of vaccines, in addition to the seasonal influenza vaccines now accepted as essential to normal public health practice.

When in May of 2009, the H1N1 influenza appeared and was declared to have pandemic potential, WHO and national governments globally prepared to address the worst case scenarios, taking into account millions of possible cases and deaths. In June of 2010, WHO reported that the global H1N1 pandemic included some 18 thousand deaths and the virus is still circulating, though at much reduced levels compared to those in the fall of 2009. Enormous stockpiles of vaccine and Tamiflu went largely unused with poor levels of acceptance in the general public and even among health care providers. These stocks were then donated or sold inexpensively to developing countries.

The role of international cooperation and that of WHO in this pandemic needs to be re-examined. The lack of public response to available immunizations points to an important credibility issue, and the sharing of available vaccine with developing countries requires international attention. It is likely that, after 2010, the experience of H1N1 pandemic influenza will be passed through a fine sieve throughout the world. Although it is difficult to anticipate the conclusions of this analysis at this stage, it is probable that in the future, we will want to be better prepared for the emergence of such epidemics. We will not focus solely on the particularly virulent strains such as H5N1, rather taking measures against a subtype H1N1 pandemic influenza that is predominantly benign (apart from a fairly low proportion of serious cases) but nevertheless significant at the country scale and able to affect health, society and the global economy.

Acknowledgments

The authors wish to thank Beverley Tebby for her help in translation. They are also grateful to Ted Tulchinsky and the referees for their help, advice and patience.

Conflicts of interest

None declared.

References

1. World Health Organization. Pandemic (H1N1) 2009 – update 105. Available from URL: http://www.who.int/csr/don/2010_06_18/en/ (Accessed 19 June, 2010).
2. Barry J. M. The great influenza: the epic story of the deadliest plague in history. New York: Penguin Viking; 2004.
3. Taubenberger J. K., Morens D. M. 1918 influenza: the mother of all epidemics. Emerg Infect Dis. 2006;12:15–22. Available from URL: http://www.cdc.gov/ncidod/EID/vol12no01/05-0979.htm (Accessed 19 June, 2010).
4. Dowdle W. R. Pandemic influenza: confronting a re-emergent threat. The 1976 experience. J Infect Dis 1997;176 Suppl-1:S69–72. Available from URL: http://www.ncbi.nlm.nih.gov/pubmed/9240699 (Accessed 18 June, 2010).

5. Fouchier R. A. M., Kuiken T., Schutten M., van Amerongen G., van Doornum G. J. J., van den Hoogen B. G. et al. Aetiology: Koch's postulates fulfilled for SARS virus. Nature 2003:423:240. Available from URL: http://www.nature.com/nature/journal/v423/n6937/pdf/423240a.pdf (Accessed 18 June, 2010).
6. World Health Organization. Severe Acute Respiratory Syndrome (SARS) – multi-country outbreak. Update 31, 16 April 2003. Available from URL: http://www.who.int/csr/don/2003_04_16/en/ (Accessed 18 June, 2010).
7. World Health Organization. Cumulative number of confirmed human cases of Avian influenza A/(H5N1) reported to WHO. (24 September, 2009). Available from URL: http://www.who.int/csr/disease/avian_influenza/country/cases_table_2009_09_24/en/index.html (Accessed 18 June, 2010).
8. Bishop J. F., Murnane M. P., Owen R. Australia's winter with the 2009 pandemic influenza A (H1N1) virus. N Engl J Med. 2009;361:2591–4. Available from URL: http://content.nejm.org/cgi/reprint/NEJMp0910445.pdf (Accessed 18 June, 2010).
9. de Lamballerie X. Personal communication, June, 2010.
10. Centers for Disease Control and Prevention. 2009 H1N1 early outbreak and disease characteristics. Available from URL: http://www.cdc.gov/h1n1flu/surveillanceqa.htm (Updated 27 October, 2009 and accessed 18 June, 2010).
11. Paris correspondents. First worldwide profile of swine flu victims. Herald Sun (Victoria, Australia). August 26, 2009. Available from URL: http://www.heraldsun.com.au (Accessed 18 June, 2010).
12. Ross T., Zimmer S., Burke D., Crevar C., Carter D., Stark J., et al. Seroprevalence following the second wave of pandemic 2009 H1N1 influenza. PLoS Curr Influenza. 24 Feb, 2010: RRN1148 Available from URL: http://www.ncbi.nlm.nih.gov/pubmed/20191082 (Accessed 18 June, 2010).
13. Flahault A. First estimation of direct H1N1pdm virulence: From reported non consolidated data from Mauritius and New Caledonia. PLoS Curr Influenza. 2009 Aug 23:RRN1010. Available from URL: http://www.ncbi.nlm.nih.gov/pubmed/20020674 (Accessed 18 June, 2010).
14. Centers for Disease Control and Prevention. Bacterial coinfections in lung tissue specimens from fatal cases of 2009 pandemic Influenza A (H1N1) – United States, May–August 2009. MMWR Morb Mort Wkly Rep. 2009; 58:1–4. (early release) Available from URL: http://www.cdc.gov/mmwr/pdf/wk/mm58e0929.pdf (Accessed 18 June, 2010).
15. The ANZIC Influenza Investigators. Critical care services and 2009 H1N1 influenza in Australia and New Zealand. N Engl J Med. 2009;361:1925–34. Available from URL: http://content.nejm.org/cgi/content/full/361/20/1925 (Accessed 18 June, 2010).
16. Reed C., Angulo F. J., Swerdlow D. L., Lipsitch M., Meltzer M. I., Jemigan D., Finelli L. Estimates of the prevalence of pandemic (H1N1) 2009, United States, April–July 2009. Emerg Infect Dis. 2009;15: December. Available from URL: http://www.cdc.gov/eid/content/15/12/pdfs/2004.pdf (Accessed 18 June, 2010).
17. World Health Organization. Transcript of statement by Margaret Chan, Director-General of the World Health Organization. 11 June, 2009. Available from URL: http://www.who.int/mediacentre/influenzaAH1N1_presstranscript_20090611.pdf (Accessed 18 June, 2010).
18. Centers for Disease Control and Prevention. Centers for Disease Control and Prevention. 2009 H1N1 flu: situation update. Available from URL: http://www.cdc.gov/h1n1flu/update.htm (Accessed 20 June, 2010).

19. Centers for Disease Control and Prevention. CDC Estimates of 2009 HlNl influenza cases, hospitalizations, and deaths in the United States, April–December 12, 2009. Available from URL: http://www.cdc.gov/h1n1flu/estimates/April_December_12. htm#Table (Accessed 18 June, 2010).

20. Boussard E., Flahault A., Vibert J. F., Valleron A. J. Sentiweb: French communicable disease surveillance on the world wide web. BMJ. 1996;313:1381–4. Available from URL: http://www.bmj.com/cgi/content/full/313/7069/1381 (Accessed 18 June, 2010).

21. Sentinelles. Réseau Sentinelles France (weekly epidemiologic record for France). Available from URL: http://www.sentiweb.org/ (Accessed 18 June, 2010).

22. Paget J., Marquet R., Meijer A. van der Velden K. Influenza activity in Europe during eight seasons (1999–2007): an evaluation of the indicators used to measure activity and assessment of the timing, length and course of peak activity (spread) across Europe. BMC Infect Dis. 2007;7:141 Available from URL: http://www. ncbi.nlm.nih.gov/pubmed/18047685 (Accessed 18 June, 2010).

23. Viboud C., Boëlle P. Y., Pakdaman K., Carrat F., Valleron A. J., Flahault A. Influenza epidemics in the United States, France, and Australia, 1972–1997. Emerg Infect Dis. 2004;10:32–9. Available from URL: http://www.ncbi.nlm.nih. gov/pubmed/15078594 (Accessed 18 June, 2010).

24. Lemaitre M., Carrat F. Comparative age distribution of influenza morbidity and mortality during seasonal influenza epidemics and the 2009 HlNl pandemic. BMC Infectious Diseases. 2010;10:162 doi: 10.1186/1471-2334-10-162. Available from URL: http://www.biomedcentral.com/content/pdf/1471-2334-10-162.pdf (Accessed 20 June, 2010).

25. Thompson W. W., Shay D. K., Weintraub E., Brammer L., Cox N., Anderson L. J., et al. Mortality associated with influenza and respiratory syncytial virus in the United States. JAMA. 2003;289:179–86. Available from URL: http://jama. ama-assn.org/cgi/content/abstract/289/2/179 (Accessed 19 June, 2010).

26. Centers for Disease Control and Prevention. Seasonal influenza (flu); Estimating deaths from seasonal influenza in the United States. Available from URL: http:// www.cdc.gov/flu/about/disease/us_flu-related_deaths.htm (Accessed 19 June, 2010).

27. Carrat F., Valleron A. J. Influenza mortality among the elderly in France, 1980–90: how many deaths may have been avoided through vaccination? J Epidemiol Community Health. 1995;49:419–25. Available from URL: http://www.ncbi.nlm. nih.gov/pubmed/7650467 (Accessed 18 June, 2010).

28. Reichert T. A., Sugaya N., Fedson D. S., Glezen W. P., Simonsen L., Tashiro M. The Japanese experience with vaccinating schoolchildren against influenza. New Engl J Med. 2001; 344:889–96. Available from URL: http://content.nejm. org/cgi/content/short/344/12/889 (Accessed 18 June, 2010).

29. Centers for Disease Control. Key facts about seasonal flu vaccine. Available from URL: http://www.cdc.gov/Flu/protect/keyfacts.htm (Posted 16 October, 2009 and accessed 18 June, 2010).

30. Skowronski D. M., Astell C., Brunham R. C., Low D. E., Petric M., Roper R. L., et al. Severe acute respiratory syndrome (SARS): A year in review. Annu Rev Med. 2005;56:357–81. Available from URL: http://www.ncbi.nlm.nih.gov/sites/ pubmed (Accessed 18 June. 2010).

31. Morens D. M., Taubenberger J. K. Understanding influenza backward. JAMA. 2009;302:679–80. Available from URL: http://www.ncbi.nlm.nih.gov/sites/pubmed (Accessed 18 June, 2010).

32. Taubenberger J. K. Genetic characterisation of the 1918 'Spanish' influenza virus. In Phillips H., Killingray D., editors. The Spanish influenza pandemic of 1918–19. New perspectives. London: Routledge; 2003:39–46, p. 43. Available from URL: http://www.questia.com/PM.qst?a=o&d=104243843 (Accessed 18 June, 2010).

33. Ohadike D. C. Diffusion and physiological responses to influenza pandemic of 1918–1919 in Nigeria. Social Science and Medicine. 1991;32:1393–9. Available from URL: http://www.sciencedirect.com/ (Accessed 18 June, 2010).

34. Delater Dr. La grippe dans la nation armée de 1918 à 1921. Revue d'hygiene. 1923;45:409–634.

35. Oxford J. S., Sefton A., Jackson R., Innes W., Daniels R. S., Johnson NPAS. World War I may have allowed the emergence of "Spanish" influenza. Lancet Infect Dis. 2002;2:111–4. Available from URL: http://www.ncbi.nlm.nih.gov/pubmed/11901642 (Accessed 18 June, 2010).

36. Yin S. Avian Flu and Influenza pandemics. Washington: Population Reference Bureau; 2006. Available from URL: http://www.prb.org/Articles/2006/AvianFluand-InfluenzaPandemics.aspx (Accessed 18 June, 2010).

37. Defressine and Violle, La prophylaxie et le traitement de la grippe, C. R. hébdo, séances Acad. Sci., 1918; 167: 503; and J. Castaigne, Chronique, J. Méd. franç., 1919; 8: 11–14. In: Phillips H., Killingray D. The Spanish influenza pandemic of 1918–19: new perspectives. London: Routledge; 2003.

38. Johnson NPAS. The overshadowed killer. Influenza in Britain in 1918–19. In: Phillips H., Killingray D., editors. The Spanish influenza pandemic of 1918–19: new perspectives. London: Routledge; 2003:132–55, pp.137–38.

39. Becker J. J. La grippe espagnole, memoire d'une guerre. Liberation. 9 October, 2009. Available from URL: http://www.liberation.fr/societe/0101596047-la-grippe-espagnole-memoire-d-une-guerre (Accessed 18 June, 2010).

40. Taubenberger J. K., Morens D. M. 1918 influenza: the mother of all pandemics, Emerg Infect Dis. 2006;12:15–22. Available from URL: http://www.cdc.gov/ncidod/eid/vol12no01/pdfs/05-0979.pdf (Accessed 18 June, 2010).

41. Préfecture de la Seine. Épidémie de grippe à Paris, 30 juin 1918–26 avril 1919. Paris: Imprimerie des Beaux-Arts; s.d. [1919]. (Service de la statistique municipale; 2e année, no. 2).

42. Ministére de la Guerre. Statistiques médicales. I – Données statistiques relatives à la guerre 1914–1918, Paris, 1922.

43. Phillips H., Killingray D., editors. The Spanish influenza pandemic of 1918–19: new perspectives. London: Routledge; 2003.

44. Patterson K. D. Pandemic influenza, 1700–1900: a study in historical epidemiology. Totowa, NJ: Rowman and Littlefield; 1986.

45. Hays J. N. Epidemics and pandemics: Their impact on human history. Santa Barbara (CA): ABC-CLIO Inc; 2005:88–89.

46. Thucydides, The Peloponesian War (circa 400 BC), translated by Crawley R., edited by Wick T. E., New York: Modern Library. 1982.

47. Burrow J. A history of histories. Epics, chronicles, romances & inquiries from Herodotus & Thucydides to the twentieth century. London: Penguin Books; 2009.

48. Kilbourne E. D. Influenza pandemics of the 20th century. Emerg Infect Dis. 2006;12:9–14. Available from URL: http://www.ncbi.nlm.nih.gov/pubmed/16494710 (Accessed 19 June. 2010).

49. Viboud C., Grais R. F. Lafont B. A., Miller M. A., Simonsen L. Multinational impact of the 1968 Hong Kong influenza pandemic: evidence for a smoldering pandemic, J. Infect. Dis. 2005; 192: 233–48. Available from URL: http://www.ncbi.nlm.nih.gov/pubmed/15962218 (Accessed 10 June, 2010).

50. Gensheimer K. F., Fukuda K., Brammer L., Cox N., Patriarca P., Strikas R. A. Preparing for pandemic influenza: the need for enhanced surveillance. Emerg Infect Dis. 1999;5:297–9. Available from URL: http://www.ncbi.nlm.nih.gov/pubmed/10221887 (Accessed 10 June, 2010).

51. Valleron A. J., Boumendil A. Epidemiology and heat waves: analysis of the 2003 episode in France. C R Biol. 2004;327:1125–41. Available from URL: http://www.ncbi.nlm.nih.gov/sites/pubmed (Accessed 19 June 2010).

52. Boffey P. M. Swine flu vaccination campaign: the scientific controversy mounts. Science. 1976;193:559–63. Available from URL: http://www.ncbi.nlm.nih.gov/pubmed/17759577 (Accessed 19 June, 2010).

53. Stöhr K., Esveld M. Public health: Will vaccines be available for the next influenza pandemic? Science. 2004;306. 24 2195=6. Available from URL: http://www.ncbi.nlm.nih.gov/pubmed/15618505 (Accessed 19 June, 2010).

54. Schwarzinger M., Flicoteaux R., Cortarenoda S., Obadia Y., Moatti J. P. Low acceptability of A/H1N1 pandemic vaccination in French adult population. Did public health policy fuel public dissonance? PLoS One. April 2010; 5:e1099. Available from URL: http://www.ncbi.nlm.nih.gov/pubmed/20421908 (Accessed 19 June, 2010).

55. Setbon M., Raude J. Factors in Vaccination intention against the pandemic influenza A (H1N1). Eur J Publ Health. 5 May, 2010 [e pub ahead of print] Available from URL: http://www.ncbi.nlm.nih.gov/pubmed/20444821?dopt=Abstract (Accessed 19 June, 2010).

56. Valéry P. Regards sur le monde actuel (1931), in Oeuvres, ed. J. Hytier, t. II, Paris: Gallimard (Pléiade), 1960, p. 917.

57. Gaydos J. C., Top F. H., Hodder R. A., Russell P. K. Swine influenza A outbreak, Fort Dix, New Jersey, 1976. Emerg Infect Dis 2006; 12:23–8. Available from URL: http://www.ncbi.nlm.nih.gov/pubmed/16494712 (Accessed 19 June, 2010).

58. Krause R. The swine flu episode and the fog of epidemics. Emerg Infect Dis. 2006;12:40–3. Available from URL: http://www.ncbi.nlm.nih.gov/pubmed/16494715 (Accessed 19 June, 2010).

59. Sencer D. J., Millar J. D. Reflections on the 1976 swine flu vaccination program. Emerg Infect Dis 2006;12:29–33. Available from URL: http://www.ncbi.nlm.nih.gov/pubmed/16494713 (Accessed 19 June, 2010).

60. Neustadt R. E., Fineberg H. V. The epidemic that never was: policy-making in the swine flu scare. New York: Vintage Books; 1983.

61. Dowdle W. R. Influenza pandemic periodicity, virus recycling, and the art of risk assessment. Emerg Infect Dis. 2006;12:34–9. Available from URL: http://www.ncbi.nlm.nih.gov/pubmed/16494714 (Accessed 18 June, 2010).

62. Crosby A. W. Epidemic and peace, 1918. Westport: Greenwood Press; 1976.

63. Dowdle W. R. The 1976 experience. J Infect Dis. 1997;176(suppl 1):S69–72. Available from URL: http://www.journals.uchicago.edu/doi/abs/10.1086/514180 (Accessed 19 June, 2010).

64. Tulchinsky T. H. Personal communication, April, 2010.

65. Thomas R. E., Jefferson T., Lasserson T. J. Influenza vaccination for healthcare workers who work with the elderly. The Cochrane Collaboration, John Wiley & Sons Limited; 2010. Available from URL: http://www.thecochranelibrary.com/ SpringboardWebApp/userfiles/ccoch/file/CD005187.pdf (Accessed 20 June, 2010).

66. Hayward A. C., Harling R., Wetten S., Johnson A. M., Munro S., Smedley J., et al. Effectiveness of an influenza vaccine programme for care home staff to prevent death, morbidity and health service use among residents: cluster randomized controlled trial. BMJ. 2006;333:1241. Available from URL: http://www.bmj.coin/ cgi/content/abstract/333/7581/1241 (Accessed 20 June, 2010).

67. Lemaitre M., Meret T., Rothan-Tondeur M., Belmin J., Lejonc J. L., Luquel L., et al. Effect of influenza vaccination of nursing home staff on mortality of residents: a cluster-randomized trial. J Am Geriatr Soc. 2009;57:1580–6. Available from URL: http://www3.interscience.wiley.coni/journal/122538809/abstract? CRETRY=1- &SRETRY=0 (Accessed 20 June, 2010).

68. Centers for Disease Control and Prevention. Seasonal influenza vaccination health resources for professionals: 2009–10 recommendations of the Advisory Committee on Immunization practices (ACIP). Available from URL: http://198.246.98.21/flu/ professionals/vaccination/index.htm (Accessed 20 June, 2010).

69. La Montagne J. R., Noble G. R., Quinnan G. V., Curlin G. T., Blackwelder W. C., Smith J. I., et al. Summary of clinical trials of inactivated vaccine – 1978. Rev. Infect. Dis. 1983;5:723–36. Available from URL: http://www.ncbi.nlm.nih. gov/pubmed/6353529 (Accessed 20 June, 2010).

70. Stowe J., Andrews N., Wise L. Miller E. Investigation of the temporal association of Guillain-Barré syndrome with influenza vaccine and influenza-like illness using the United Kingdom general practice research database. Am J Epidemiol. 2009;169:382–8. Available from URL: http://aje.oxfordjournals.org/cgi/content/ full/kwn310 (Accessed 20 June, 2010).

71. Hurwitz E. S., Schonberger L. B., Nelson D. B., Hollman R. C. Guillain-Barre syndrome and the 1978–1979 influenza vaccine. N Engl J Med. 1981;304:1557– 61. Available from URL: http://content.nejm.org/cgi/content/abstract/304/26/1557 (Accessed 20 June, 2010).

72. Patel M. Dennis A., Flutter C., Khan Z. Pandemic (H1N1) 2009 influenza. Br J Anaesth. 2010;104:128–42. Available from URL: http://www.ncbi.nlm.nih.gov/ pubmed/20053625 (Accessed 20 June 2010).

73. Kumar A., Zarychanski R., Pinto R., Cook D. J., Marshall J., Lacraoix, et al. Critically ill patients with 2009 influenza A(H1N1) infection in Canada. JAMA. 2009;302:1872–9. Available from URL: http://www.ncbi.nlm.nih.gov/sites/pubmed (Accessed 20 June, 2009).

74. Centers for Disease Control and Prevention. Seasonal influenza (flu); Estimating deaths from seasonal influenza in the United States. Available from URL: http://www.cdc.gov/flu/about/disease/us_flu-related_deaths.htm (Accessed 19 June, 2010).

75. Shetty P. H1N1 vaccine could staunch further financial loss. Lancet Infect Dis. 2009;9:592. Available from URL: http://www.thelancet.com/journals/laninf/article/ PIIS1473-3099(09)70243-9/fulltext (Accessed 20 June, 2010).

76. Syal R. Swine flu 'could kill millions unless rich nations give £900m'. The Observer. 20 September, 2009. Available from URL: http://www.guardian.co.uk/world/2009/ sep/20/swine-flu-costs-un-report (Accessed 20 June, 2010).

77. Murard L. L'organisation internationale de la lutte contre les épidémies (1851–2005). In: Flahault A., Zylberman P. Editors. Des épidémies et des hommes. Paris; De La Martinière; 2008. (pp. 83–92).

78. World Health Organization. WHO extends its SARS-related travel advice to Beijing and Shanxi province in China and to Toronto, Canada. Available from URL: http://www.who.int/ (Accessed 20 June, 2010).

79. Triggle N. What comes next in the flu fight? BBC News. 11 June, 2009. Available from URL: http://news.bbc.co.uk/2/hi/health/8093482.stm (Accessed 20 June, 2010).

80. Godlee F. Editorial: Conflicts of interest and pandemic flu. BMJ. 2010;340:c2947. Available from URL: http://www.bmj.com/cgi/content/full/340/jun03_4/c2947 (Accessed 20 June, 2010).

81. World Health Organization. WHO Director General's letter to BMJ editors. 8 June, 2010. Available from URL: http://www.who.int/mediacentre/news/statements/2010/letter_bmj_20100608/en/index.html (Accessed 20 June, 2010).

82. Roos R. US H1N1 vaccine uptake estimated at 75 million. CIDRAP. Available from URL: http://www.cidrap.umn.edu/cidrap/content/influenza/swineflu/news/feb0410-vac.html (Accessed 20 June, 2010).

83. Public Health Agency of Canada. Government of Canada announces significant contribution to WHO global pandemic relief efforts. News release. 28 January, 2010. Available from URL: http://www.phac-aspc.gc.ca/media/nr-rp/2010/2010_0128-eng.php (Accessed 20 June, 2010).

42

THE 2009 H1N1 INFLUENZA OUTBREAK IN ITS HISTORICAL CONTEXT

Derek Gatherer

Source: *Journal of Clinical Virology*, 45 (2009), 174–8.

Abstract

Of the 16 known serotypes of influenza A haemagglutinin, 6 have been isolated from humans at the molecular level (H1, H2, H3, H5, H7, H9). 3 of these have been involved in past pandemics (H1, H2, H3). Traditional pandemic surveillance has focussed on monitoring antigenic shift, meaning the re-assortment of novel haemagglutinins into seasonal human influenza A viruses during rare events of double infection with seasonal and zoonotic strains. H5, from avian H5N1 influenza, has been the major cause for concern in recent years. However, the 2009 H1N1 zoonotic event demonstrates that even serotypes already encountered in past human pandemics may constitute new pandemic threats. The protein sequence divergence of the 2009 zoonotic H1 from human seasonal influenza H1 is around 20–24%. A similar level of divergence is found between the 2009 H1 and European swine flu. By contrast, its divergence from North American swine flu strains is around 1–9%. Given that the divergence between H1 and its nearest serotype neighbour H2 is around 40–46%, the 2009 H1 may be broadly considered as halfway towards a new serotype. The current situation is one of antigenic pseudo-shift.

1. Introduction: the basic biology of influenza

Influenza A (Family *Orthomyxoviridae*, Genus *Influenzavirus A*) is currently the greatest pandemic disease threat to humankind. Its rivals for this title (HIV-1, Ebola, SARS, pneumonic plague) have higher mortality if untreated, but either lack influenza's rapid inter-personal transmission (HIV-1) or its widespread seasonal distribution (Ebola, SARS, pneumonic plague). Influenza A is unique among the major pandemic threats in that it could potentially infect 30% of the world's population within a matter of months. Even at a conservative overall mortality rate of 2%, it would result in around 135 million deaths worldwide within the first year of a new pandemic outbreak. This is about 4 times the total mortality attributed to HIV-1 in the last 30 years.

Influenza's endemic reservoir is in aquatic wildfowl, many of which are migratory. Containment of the disease outside of mammals is therefore virtually impossible. Once a novel strain of influenza has crossed the species barrier from birds into a mammalian host, it may persist in that new host species for many decades. Molecular evidence exists for the presence of influenza A in at least 18 mammalian species (Table 1). It is also capable of transmission between mammals, and the current influenza A H1N1 2009 outbreak is now known to have originated in pigs.[2,3]

The orthomyxoviruses are single-stranded RNA viruses of the negative strand variety, and include the *Isavirus* and *Thogotovirus* genera. The first of these causes anaemia in fish, and the latter includes several tick-borne mammalian encephalitis viruses which can be clinically serious. In addition to these there are several unclassified orthomyxoviruses and three genera of influenza viruses: A, B and C. The last two are clinically milder than influenza A, but influenza B is nevertheless severe enough to be included in seasonal vaccination programmes. The absence of life-long immunity is a major contributor to influenza A's pandemic potential, and features of the influenza virus make design of a vaccine that would confer immunity against all strains, highly problematic.[4]

The first difficulty is that the majority of the cellular immune response to an influenza virus infection is directed against two proteins on the virus's surface, haemagglutinin and neuraminidase. Influenza strains are therefore usually broadly categorised according to their serotype for these two proteins; for instance the current outbreak is H1N1, and previous pandemics have involved H3N2 and H2N2. There are in total 16 serotypes of haemagglutinin, and 9 serotypes of neuraminidase. Haemagglutinin functions in the binding of the virus to its putative target cell, whereas neuraminidase plays a role in exit of the virus from the cell in preparation for another round of infection. Haemagglutinin in particular has a high amino acid substitution rate in its epitope regions. The ratio of non-synonymous substitutions to synonymous substitutions (*omega*) significantly exceeds 1 at several amino acid positions, indicating a selective advantage for novel amino acid sequences in this region.[6,8] This appears to be directly related to evasion of the host immune system. This process of evolution of a single haemagglutinin serotype is often referred to in the influenza literature as *antigenic drift*,[4] although this is something of a misnomer given that *drift* is used by evolutionary biologists to refer to *neutral evolution*, meaning evolution in the absence of selective pressures. On the contrary, influenza A haemagglutinin evolution is a mixture of functional constraint and positive selection for variability in epitope regions. Antigenic "drift" can render immunity acquired in one influenza season, either by

Table 1 Species distribution of haemagglutinin serotypes from the NCBI Influenza Resource (http://www.ncbi.nlm.nih.gov/genomes/FLU/Database, accessed 3rd June 2009). Note that serotypes 1–5, 7, 9, 10 and 13 have all been found at least once in mammals.

Species	H1	H2	H3	H4	H5	H6	H7	H8	H9	H10	H11	H12	H13	H14	H15	H16	Total
Avian	93	105	265	212	1918	370	509	26	904	86	88	44	39	3	6	14	4,682
Blow fly					1												1
Camel	1																1
Canine	8																8
Cat							7										7
Civet					1												1
Equine			164				17										181
Ferret	1																1
Giant anteater	1																1
Human	1802	106	4610		224		8		8								6,758
Leopard					6												6
Mink			1		1					1							3
Muskrat				1													1
Plateau pika					1												1
Racoon dog					1												1
Seal			2	1			2										5
Stone marten		1															1
Swine	419	2	238	2	12				28								701
Tiger					7												7
Whale					7								1				8
Total	2325	214	5280	216	2179	370	543	26	940	87	88	44	40	3	6	14	12,375

infection with the virus or by vaccination, useless in a short period of time. Repeated seasonal vaccination for vulnerable groups has therefore become a necessary public heath policy.

A second and more serious problem is a result of the fact that the influenza genome, although small – encoding just 11 proteins – is divided into 8 segments. In the rare event of a double infection with two different strains of influenza into a single host, re-assortment of the genome segments can occur, producing a series of completely novel combinations of genome segments in the progeny viruses. When the double infection is with viruses originating in different species, for instance if a patient has a human seasonal influenza simultaneous with a zoonotic influenza such as porcine or avian influenza, such re-assorted strains may be the source of new pandemic influenza variants incorporating haemagglutinin and/or neuraminidase proteins against which hosts may have virtually no immunity. This sudden introduction of completely new serotypes of haemagglutinin into circulating human viruses is referred to as *antigenic shift*. Although serotypes H1, H2 and H3 are the only ones known to have been involved in influenza pandemics, molecular evidence exists for the occasional infection of humans with avian viruses containing H5, H7 and H9. The prospect of an antigenic shift involving any of these is of major concern in pandemic surveillance. The current H1N1 outbreak is now known to involve a re-assorted virus produced from two kinds of porcine influenza, one of which is itself already a "triple re-assortant" strain containing segments originating ultimately in human seasonal H3N2 influenza and in avian influenza as well as porcine influenza.[2]

2. The lessons of past pandemics

The "Spanish Flu" of 1918–1920 is the earliest known pandemic for which hard molecular evidence exists for the involvement of influenza A. Work is currently underway to isolate influenza haemagglutinin sequences from clinical material dating from the previous pandemic event of 1889–1890.[1] This is widely regarded as an influenza pandemic on clinical, epidemiological and some limited serological grounds. Prior to this date, identification of influenza relies on diagnostic detective work in medical records. The similarity of the symptoms of influenza to other feverish respiratory viruses inevitably renders some of this a little speculative, but nevertheless candidate previous widespread influenza outbreaks have been identified in 1173, 1510, 1580, 1729, 1781 and 1830. The term influenza was only used to describe these pandemics from the 18th century onwards (although it had previous medical use dating back to the 14th century to describe epidemics in general), and the earliest case description that satisfies modern clinicians is that of the French physician Molineux in 1694.[5]

The 1918–1920 H1N1 Spanish Flu, which killed 40 million people worldwide is informative as a "worst case scenario" for a flu pandemic. The H1 haemagglutinin in this pandemic may have been of avian origin, and the disease was first detected in the USA in prisons and military bases. Troop movements during the First World War appear to have been a major cause of its global distribution. Antigenic drift subsequent to the initial antigenic shift is the likely cause of the several waves of renewed virulence shown by the virus. Spanish Flu illustrates both the potential of influenza for morbidity and mortality and also the tendency of severe pandemics to occur in several waves as the virus adapts to its new human hosts. After 1920, some gaps exist in the molecular sequence record, but H1N1 was certainly a regular seasonal influenza from 1934 until the mid-1950s. It then reappeared in 1977–1978 and current human seasonal H1 proteins belong to the same lineage that has been circulating at least since the 1930s. Figure 1 shows a phylogenetic tree of the haemagglutinin proteins of all H1N1 strains circulating in humans since the Spanish Flu. The 1918 protein is an outgroup, and the remainder of the sequences are either seasonal H1N1 from the 1934/1977 lineage or zoonotic strains.

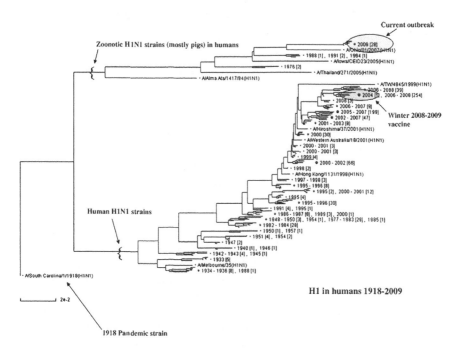

Figure 1 Phylogenetic tree of H1 haemagglutinin sequences in influenza A H1N1 strains infecting humans from 1918 to the present day. 3 clades can be seen: (1) the 1918 pandemic strain which is an outlier; (2) strains circulating seasonally since at least the 1930s (lower of 2 major clades); (3) zoonotic strains (upper clade). The positions of the current outbreak and the most recent vaccine strains are indicated. Tree drawn using the NCBI Influenza Virus Resource tools: (http://www.ncbi.nlm.nih.gov/genomes/FLU/Database).

Between the temporary disappearance of H1 in the 1950s and its reappearance in the 1970s, there were two further pandemics: the 1957–1958 H2N2 "Asian Flu" with 1.5 million fatalities worldwide and the 1968–1969 H3N2 "Hong Kong Flu" with 1 million fatalities worldwide. H2 has been absent from human populations since the late 1960s, but H3, like H1, persists in a seasonal human influenza evolving by antigenic drift. The fact that both H1 and H2 have in the past disappeared – in the former case only temporarily – from human populations demonstrates that previous candidate pandemics of influenza may have involved haemagglutinin serotypes not currently found in humans. Although only H1, H2, H3, H5, H7 and H9 are known to have infected humans, there is no particular reason to exclude the possibility that humans have in the past been, or may in the future be, infected with the remaining 10 serotypes. Any pandemic involving a haemagglutinin serotype not seen in the last century, will almost certainly be very severe.

3. Porcine influenza in pigs and humans: (pseudo)-serotypes and (pseudo)-pandemics

The association of the origins of the current outbreak with the Mexican pig farming region raised immediate suspicions that porcine influenza was involved, and it was soon demonstrated that the nearest relative of the strains isolated in the latest outbreak was the triple re-assortant porcine influenza that had caused considerable problems for pig farmers for several years.[2,3] The new strain incorporated the results of a further re-assortment event, thus generating a quadruple re-assortant virus with genome segments traceable to two major lineages of porcine influenza as well as avian and human influenzas.

Porcine influenza demonstrates two major clades in its haemagglutinin protein evolution, associated with what are termed "Classic North American Swine Flu" and "Eurasian Swine Flu" (Figure 2). In addition there are other porcine influenza haemagglutinins of more uncertain affinities, possibly resulting from independent re-assortment events with avian H1 haemagglutinins. Of all the proven 18 mammalian hosts for influenza, pigs will most readily transmit to humans. Molecular evidence exists for several porcine influenza strains in humans since the 1980s, and all of these have haemagglutinin proteins belonging to the Classic North American Swine Flu lineage. Until the present outbreak however, no cases of porcine influenza were capable of sustained human-to-human transmission. Table 2 shows that the amino acid divergence between haemagglutinin proteins from classic and Eurasian swine flu strains is 20–25%, approximately the same as either class differ from seasonal human H1, but considerably less than the average 40–46% divergence between H1 and H2 haemagglutinin proteins.

At the time of writing (3rd June 2009), it remains unclear if the current outbreak will achieve pandemic status. Although the World Health Organization has reached alert level 5, indicating "pandemic imminent", and this

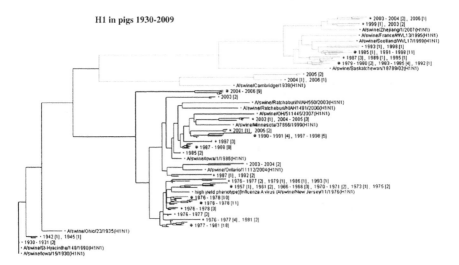

Figure 2 Phylogenetic tree of H1 haemagglutinin sequences in influenza A H1N1 strains infecting pigs from 1930 to the present day. 3 clades can be seen: (1) some early swine flu strains from 1930 to 1945, which are outliers; (2) "Classic" North American swine flu (lower of 2 major clades); (3) atypical swine flu (upper clade, in yellow), including "Eurasian" swine flu and some further atypical strains, including one from 1930 and a group from 2004 to 2006. Tree drawn using the NCBI Influenza Virus Resource tools: (http://www.ncbi.nlm.nih.gov/genomes/FLU/Database).

may rise to level 6, "pandemic underway", if the rate of infection climbs, several criteria may not yet have met the definition of a pandemic used in much of the influenza literature. For instance, mortality is so far low (113 deaths from 17,436 cases as of 2nd June 2009), and the 1977–1978 Russian Flu is sometimes not recognised as a pandemic on account of its low mortality and restricted preferred host range (predominantly children and young adults). Furthermore, previous pandemics have involved antigenic shift: H1 for Spanish Flu, H2 for Asian Flu and H3 for Hong Kong Flu. The current outbreak is serotype H1 and thus by this criterion not an antigenic shift. However, as a Classic North American Swine Flu H1, it is rather different to the H1 haemagglutinins that have seasonally circulated in human since the 1930s. Table 2 shows the percentage identity between the sequences in the tree. The divergence between the various H1 proteins and H2 is 40–46% while the divergence between human and porcine H1 is less than 25%. Nevertheless, this is clearly rather more than the 9–15% between seasonal human H1s. A useful comparison may be made with the relationships between haemagglutinin proteins within each of the two lineages, Victoria and Yamagata, of influenza B (data not shown). The influenza B haemagglutinin have intra-lineage similarities at less than 4% divergence, with sequence divergence in

341

Table 2 Number of amino acid substitutions per site over a 561 residue alignment between representative influenza A haemagglutinin proteins. Analyses were conducted using the Poisson correction method in MEGA4.[7,9] Divergences of 20–40% are unshaded and those of >40% are shaded. Representative sequences are (1) 2009 H1N1: ACR09372 A/Mexico/3955/2009, (2) 1976 swine in humans: ACQ99821 A/New Jersey/8/1976, (3) 1977 human pandemic: ABD60933 A/USSR/92/77, (4) 2008 seasonal H1: ACJ73758 A/California/07/2008, (5) 1935 human H1: ABD62781 A/Melbourne/35, (6) 1957 H2 pandemic: BAC43764 A/Kayano/57, (7) 2006 avian H2: CAQ77186 A/wigeon/Norway/10_1783/2006, (8) 2009 classic swine: ACR01025 A/swine/Alberta/OTH-33-8/2009, (9) 1986 classic swine: ABY81426 A/swine/Iowa/1/1986, (10) 1939 Euroswine: BAA0718 A/swine/Cambridge/1939, (11) 1994 Euroswine: AAD05215 A/swine/Scotland/410440/94, and (12) 2006 Euroswine: ACN72617 A/swine/Hungary/19774/2006. Note that the inter-serotype distance (H1 vs. H2) is always greater than 40%, whereas intra-H1 serotype distances range from just 1% between the latest outbreak and recent strains of swine flu, to 25% between classic swine flu and European swine flu and the same between classic swine flu and seasonal human influenza.

		1	2	3	4	5	6	7	8	9	10	11
1	2009 H1N1											
2	1976 swine in humans	0.09										
3	1977 human pandemic	0.23	0.18									
4	2008 seasonal H1	0.24	0.21	0.10								
5	1935 human H1	0.20	0.16	0.09	0.15							
6	1957 H2 pandemic	0.45	0.41	0.44	0.43	0.41						
7	2006 avian H2	0.44	0.41	0.44	0.44	0.40	0.05					
8	2009 classic swine	0.01	0.10	0.24	0.25	0.20	0.46	0.45				
9	1986 classic swine	0.09	0.04	0.20	0.22	0.18	0.41	0.41	0.10			
10	1939 Euroswine	0.21	0.17	0.11	0.16	0.07	0.42	0.42	0.21	0.19		
11	1994 Euroswine	0.25	0.20	0.05	0.11	0.11	0.45	0.45	0.25	0.22	0.13	
12	2006 Euroswine	0.24	0.20	0.22	0.24	0.21	0.41	0.41	0.25	0.19	0.22	0.24

inter-lineage comparisons at 6–7% on average. The original Lee strain of influenza B from 1940 is approximately 7% divergent to modern samples of either influenza B lineage. By comparison, influenza A HA sequences are 75–76% divergent from influenza B HA. The arrival of porcine H1 in human influenza viruses may be most accurately described as an antigenic pseudo-shift or para-shift.

Therefore the current H1N1 outbreak, although a zoonotic influenza originating in a re-assortment event and exhibiting sustained human-to-human transmission for the first time, may have insufficiently divergent haemagglutinin to be regarded as an antigenic shift, and may be insufficiently virulent ultimately to enter the annals of major pandemics. However, its importance should not be discounted. For the first time, the full repertoire of molecular biology has been applied to a novel form of influenza spreading on a global scale. At the time of writing (3rd June 2009), it appears that rapid molecular analysis and diagnosis coupled to effective clinical and public health methods have at the very least substantially slowed the progress of the outbreak. None of this was possible in 1957 or even in 1977. This provides an important dress rehearsal for potential H5N1 outbreaks. We still cannot stop the arrival of antigenically shifted pandemic influenzas, but in the past we were unaware of their existence until they were already upon us. In future, we are at least likely to see the dust of an approaching pandemic rising in the distance, giving us crucial time to react preventatively.

Finally, the next few months should reveal the answers to several questions: (1) Will antigenic drift sharpen the virulence of the outbreak, as it did in 1918–1920? (2) Will there be double infections with seasonal influenzas increasing the possibility of further re-assortant strains incorporating elements of swine flu with seasonal H1 and H3, again potentially increasing virulence? (3) Will swine flu settle into a seasonal pattern in humans, alongside the more established seasonal strains? If so, it may substantially increase the costs of vaccine development. The major legacy of 2009 porcine H1N1 may be economic as much as medical.

Conflict of interest statement

The author has no conflict of interest.

References

1. Altschuler E. L., Kariuki Y. M., Jobanputra A. Extant blood samples to deduce the strains of the 1890 and possibly earlier pandemic influenzas. *Med Hypotheses* 2009.
2. Dawood F. S., and Team. Emergence of a novel Swine-Origin influenza A (H1N1) virus in humans. *N Engl J Med* 2009.
3. Fraser C., Donnelly C. A., Cauchemez S., Hanage W. P., Van Kerkhove M. D., Hollingsworth T. D., et al. Pandemic potential of a strain of influenza A (H1N1): early findings. *Science* 2009.

4. Hay A. J., Gregory V., Douglas A. R., Lin Y. P. The evolution of human influenza viruses. *Phil Trans R Soc Land B: Biol Sci* 2001;**356**:1861–70.
5. Potter C. W. A history of influenza. *J Appl Microbiol* 2001;**91**:572–9.
6. Suzuki Y. Positive selection operates continuously on hemagglutinin during evolution of H3N2 human influenza A virus. *Gene* 2008;**427**:111–6.
7. Tamura K., Dudley J., Nei M., Kumar S. MEGA4: molecular evolutionary genetics analysis (MEGA) software version 4.0. *Mol Biol Evol* 2007;**24**:1596–9.
8. Wolf Y. I., Viboud C., Holmes E. C., Koonin E. V., Lipman D. J. Long intervals of stasis punctuated by bursts of positive selection in the seasonal evolution of influenza A virus. *Biol Direct* 2006;**1**:34.
9. Zuckerkandl E., Pauling L. Evolutionary divergence and convergence in proteins. In: Bryson V., Vogel H., editors. Evolving genes and proteins. New York: Academic Press; 1965. p. 97–166.

43

THE STATE'S ROLE AND HEALTH
– SWINE FLU AS A CASE STUDY

F. Sim and P. Mackie

Source: *Public Health*, 123:8 (2009), 521–2.

In England, the Secretary of State for Health recently announced a review of public health policy.[1] The review has three main components: consideration of the state's role in relation to people's health, especially in relation to prevention of ill-health; lessons to be learned about influencing healthier lifestyle choices; and the role of the government and NHS in enhancing service delivery to improve people's health and wellbeing. The review is due to report this autumn. At present, independent of the vagaries of the Political system, almost any work scheduled to be completed later this year has some doubt hanging over it cast by the influenza pandemic. Depending upon which projections you decide to heed, the progress of many scheduled programmes in the near future may be impeded. So perhaps it could be fruitful to take a look at the pandemic from the perspective of the Review: we hope we shall be forgiven for writing on the subject again.

Firstly then, what is the role of the state? From what we have seen to date, the role is rather substantial so far, insofar as the UK and many other countries are concerned. Nationwide protocols have been developed, which are reliant upon health professionals adhering to them and patients in turn listening to government and health professionals. Take, for example, the supply of antiviral agents, which have (correctly in our view) been centrally controlled so as to ensure supplies are available when and by whom they are needed whilst seeking to protect against the development of antiviral resistance. However, centrally set policy occasionally runs into difficulty, as for example, when a health minister contradicted her government's advice with regard to the advisability of lifestyle changes for pregnant women.[2] It also lacks the flexibility that autonomous health professionals usually view as important, removing the degree of professional discretion in clinical decision making that is normally available. Universal policy can also increase health inequalities, unless special provision is made to promote access to those least able to use services. The simple answer is that the state's role is one of ethical governance; it must act to support the health and wellbeing of its people.[3] Because the short term imperative of a pandemic accords well with the timeframe of government policies, the state's role is potentially readily reconcilable with the ethical position. Contrast this with the challenge of tackling obesity or other 'lifestyle epidemics', and the state's ethical role in governance becomes more problematic to implement, since government is resistant to tackling longer term challenges.

As we write the number of cases reported worldwide is several thousand and in the UK we have seen a substantial increase in cases, with the accompanying incidence of mortality. Deaths have shocked the public, because the disease has mostly been very mild. The media response has been generally responsible, attributing deaths to serious underlying medical conditions, until the realisation emerged that the disease could strike down otherwise healthy people. A few years ago we published a series of papers about the SARS[4] outbreak of 2003, during which mainly previously fit young adults were affected. Whilst overall, H1N1 is much milder than SARS, the propensity to infect and afflict young otherwise fit people does not sit well with our modern expectation of health and ill health. In recent times in the developed world, only HIV/AIDS has struck a comparably young population without underlying health problems. In considering reports of earlier influenza pandemics, the numbers of deaths reported can be viewed with a detachment brought about by the passage of time. In those days, we tell ourselves, it was only to be expected that the 'flu would kill large numbers of people: now we live in a different era when life expectancy is much greater and pharmacological intervention much more advanced. Unlike the present pandemic, victims of earlier epidemics were not portrayed on TV and details of their lives shared by the mass media as they are today. So, rather than a detached awareness of the possibility of death unless it affected one's own family or close circle, we are now seeing much closer to home the impact of 'flu on other ordinary people.

Deaths from 'flu in previously well people come as a nasty surprise to lay and professional people alike. For the ordinary man or woman in the street, when the level of media interest is so high, it is difficult to gauge the risk to themselves and their family. So, too, for clinical health professionals, who work with the threat of contracting H1N1 and the very small risk of serious disease or death. Until a vaccine becomes widely available, we would all benefit from access to reliable modelling of risk, so that both professionals and public can understand the probability of severe morbidity or mortality during the present H1N1 pandemic. Expecting people to make sensible and informed decisions and choices without such information is problematic. This impacts on the second element of the government's Review: if government really aspires to enable people to make healthier choices, it must provide the information with which such choices can be made consistently, and in ways

346

that are readily accessible and comprehensible to as many of us as possible. The current 'buzz words' for achieving this are social marketing, though it is too soon to judge its impact.[5]

As for front line services, provision exists in the community and in hospitals. A well-informed public will use services appropriately, making use of local services rather than hospitals much of the time. Local services need to be sensitive to the diverse needs of local people, so that only if local services cannot cope with demand or a patient's clinical condition demands it, should people be using hospital provision. Experience since 1948 in the UK National Health Service has shown that this is one of the most difficult things to achieve: during a pandemic, the system will be tested again and we shall not attempt to predict the performance of the NHS. There is, however, evidence of the preparedness of primary care, which suggests grounds for optimism.

References

1. Speech by the Rt Hon Alan Johnson M. P., Secretary of State for Health, 19 March 2009 at the Royal Society of Arts: Nanny state, Nudge state or No state?.
2. Swine flu pregnancy tips reissued. Available from: <http://news.bbc.co.uk/1/hi/health/8157755.stm>; 19 July 2009 [accessed 31.07.09].
3. Public Health. Ethical issues. Nuffield Council on bioethics. Available from: <www.nuffieldbioethics.org/go/ourwork/publichealth/publication_451.html>; 2007 [accessed 31.07.09].
4. Olowokure B., Roth C. Severe acute respiratory syndrome (SARS): reshaping global public health. *Public Health* 2006:**120**(1):3–5.
5. Lowry R. J. In: Douglas Evans W., Hastings Gerard, editors. *Book review: public health branding – applying marketing for social change*. Oxford: Oxford University Press, ISBN 978 0 19 923713 5: 2008. *Public Health* 2009:**123**(8):576.

44

ANTIVIRALS FOR PANDEMIC INFLUENZA

A triumph of policy over evidence?

Matthew Thompson and Carl Heneghan

Source: *Trends in Pharmacological Sciences*, 31:9 (2010), 391–3.

Introduction

In 1918 the influenza A (H1N1) virus, as it came to be known, caused a massive and historic outbreak involving mammals (mainly pigs), and killed millions of people [1]. Although humans subsequently developed immunity to that particular strain, the virus has continued to cause infections because of its remarkable ability to rearrange its genes sufficiently to cause changes in virus structure, allowing it to evade existing immune responses. Minor rearrangements of virus genes through antigenic drift are relatively frequent and result in small changes in the surface molecules, just enough to cause influenza outbreaks in some people – known as 'seasonal influenza'. However, every few decades the virus undergoes a major genetic rearrangement through antigenic shift, creating a new virus to which very few people have any immunity. This results in 'influenza pandemics', the last of which occurred in 1968–1969. The recent pandemic is caused by a novel descendant of the 1918 virus, called H1N1 2009 (Pandemic H1N1) which spread rapidly because most people have little pre-existing immunity.

Efficacy of neuraminidase inhibitors against seasonal and pandemic flu

Antiviral medications, particularly the neuraminidase inhibitors (NIs) (Box 1), are the chief tool that clinicians use for fighting flu. But how effective are the NIs at preventing flu in healthy people and treating people affected with flu? In terms of preventing influenza in people who are exposed to the virus, the only completed trials to date have involved seasonal flu. A recent systematic review

---

Box 1. How do NIs work?

Influenza viruses are transmitted by droplets (from coughing or sneezing) and bind to sialic (neuraminic) acid molecules on the surface of respiratory epithelium cells. After being absorbed into the cell, virus particles enter the nucleus to make viral RNA, which directs the replication of new virus components. The newly formed virus particles assemble near the surface of the infected cells, where they bud through the cell membrane and are the released, free to infect other cells. The release of new viruses from infected cells relies on a crucial virus enzyme called neuraminidase, which allows the virus to free itself from the sialic (neuraminic) acid coating on the surface of the cells. NIs block the action of the viral neuraminidase, thus preventing the release and spread of new viruses.

---

in adults found that NIs provide effective postexposure prophylaxis against laboratory confirmed cases of seasonal influenza, but no effect on reducing the numbers of flu-like illnesses or asymptomatic influenza [2,3]. Another systematic review focusing on children showed that a 10-day course of NIs reduced the risk of developing influenza by 8% after introduction of symptomatic influenza into households [4]. This equates to a 'number needed to treat' of 13 to prevent one additional household child with symptomatic influenza. Given that antivirals have a significant, albeit small, effect on reducing spread of seasonal influenza, why then did they seem to have a limited effect on containing pandemic influenza? Firstly, trials demonstrate they are less effective at preventing flu-like illness rather than proven influenza [3–5]. During an influenza pandemic, the proportion of patients presenting with flu-like illness who have proven influenza (rather than another virus) should be high. However, during the H1N1 2009 pandemic, only 5–6% of patients in the community with flu-like illness and 10% of those admitted tested positive for influenza [6,7]. In other words, most people had another respiratory pathogen, against which NIs would have no effect. Secondly, because shedding of influenza virus occurs before symptoms develop, transmission could be taking place before prophylaxis can be given.

In terms of treating patients with influenza, the only trial data available examined the efficacy of NIs in seasonal influenza rather than pandemic influenza. Overall, the effects of NIs on resolution of flu symptoms prove somewhat disappointing. In adults, oseltamivir and zanamivir show a significant reduction in duration of influenza-like illness by about 1 day compared with placebo [3]. In children, four trials found a reduction in median time to resolution of symptoms or return to normal activity, which ranged from 0.5 to 1.5 days [4].

Other trials have looked at how effectively NIs reduce complications of influenza, such as pneumonia. A systematic review of trials carried out on seasonal influenza found that oseltamivir does not significantly reduce the rate of complications or rates of hospitalisation in adults with confirmed seasonal influenza [3]. Trials in children (again with seasonal influenza) show no beneficial effects on reducing pneumonia or hospitalisation, partly because trials were underpowered to assess these outcomes [4]. In children, NIs provide limited effect on reduction of antibiotic use; one randomized trial found a 10% reduction in overall antibiotic use in children with confirmed influenza given osteltamivir [risk difference (RD) = 0.10, 95% CI 0.19–0.01, $P = 0.03$], but not in those given zanamivir [4]. In one trial, oseltamivir did reduce the incidence of otitis media from 31% to 15% in children aged < 5 years (RD = 0.16, 95% CI 0.29 to 0.04, $P = 0.009$) [4].

The data on side effects of NIs are surprisingly incomplete, given their extensive use. Although both osteltamivir and zanamivir are generally well tolerated, nausea occurs in an additional one in 20 children given oseltamivir [4].

Although most strains of H1N1 2009 appear to be sensitive to NIs, evidence from good-quality trials on their effects on clinically important outcomes have been sparse. There is some evidence from observational studies on patients hospitalised with H1N1 2009 (including those with critical illness) that antiviral treatment might be beneficial [8]. Guidelines for the management of the more serious H5N1 avian flu recommend treatment with oseltamivir, as this infection carries a high (60%) mortality rate from respiratory complications. Given the high mortality rate, it has only been possible to rely on observational data for this infection [9].

Why treat everyone with swine flu?

Early on in the current pandemic, the UK adopted a policy of offering treatment to everyone with suspected H1N1 2009 [10]. The rationale behind this policy was threefold. Firstly, there was evidence early on that pandemic influenza was sensitive to NIs. Secondly, in the early stages of the pandemic there was likely to be insufficient clinical information to determine whether large numbers of otherwise healthy adults and children would have serious outcomes. Thirdly, because NIs are ideally administered within 48 hours of the onset of symptoms, waiting to see which patients develop severe illness could risk delaying treatment. As a result, the number of patients with influenza-like illness requesting NIs grew considerably in the summer of 2009, threatening to overwhelm primary care services in the UK. In response, the National Pandemic Flu Service was set up, using telephone or internet based algorithms to identify patients with influenza-like illness and facilitate access to NIs from pharmacies or distribution centres. As one measure of its success, the UK health secretary noted on 23 July 23 2009 that more than 5,500 people received antiviral drugs on the first day of the service.

A 'treat everyone' approach might not have been justified. By mid-2009, the WHO guidance was modified to recommend using NIs only for patients in high-risk groups or with severe symptoms [11]. Furthermore, it had become increasingly clear that H1N1 2009 was generally a mild illness [12]. Indeed, the policy in the UK contrasted with that of the US, Canada, Ireland and Australia, where NIs were recommended only to patients in high-risk groups, or those with severe symptoms. Why then did the UK adhere to a health policy approach that seemed so out of step with similar western countries? As early as June 2009, an independent expert medical advisory panel set up by the UK Department of Health had warned that the widespread use of NIs could do more harm than good, advice that was seemingly ignored [13]. It is also possible that health officials did not take into account the most up to date information on efficacy of the antivirals as they became available (e.g. updated systematic reviews). More controversial explanations are that policy makers lacked acceptable alternative strategies and were eager to be seen to be 'doing something', or that there was pressure to use the stockpiles of tens of millions of doses of NIs before they expired [14].

Lessons for the future

Further epidemics and pandemics of influenza and other infections are inevitable, so what can we learn from the 2009 influenza pandemic? First, generating clear and comprehensive evidence on the effectiveness and safety of drugs that might be recommended as key treatments is essential. This should include expediting systematic reviews and Cochrane reviews, and in some cases pressing for full data from any poorly reported trials and individual patient data [15]. The decisions to use valuable (both financially and therapeutically) pharmacological resources should be based on the best available (independent) evidence. Secondly, the research community and funders need to be poised to be able to react rapidly, identifying key research gaps and generating new evidence where needed. For example, the large numbers of patients receiving NIs could have provided early evidence for their effects on important outcomes in the pandemic (e.g. hospitalisation) and side effects within a short time. Thirdly, clinicians were hamstrung by the lack of robust diagnostic capacity to differentiate pandemic influenza from other respiratory illnesses, thus the majority of NIs were used by patients who did not have influenza [7]. Once again, systematically identifying evidence for the optimum clinical diagnostic criteria, as well as the most appropriate point of care tests (or the key research needed to generate these) is essential. Finally, adopting the ideal health policy for such events will always be a fine balancing act between acting too strongly versus too cautiously. However, policy should be informed by evidence and continually updated based on emerging new evidence.

Conflicts of interest

The authors have no conflicts of interest to declare.

References

1 Zimmer, S. M. and Burke, D. (2009) Historical perspective – emergence of Influenza A (H1N1) viruses. *N. Engl. J. Med.* 361, 279–285

2 Tappenden P., *et al.* Oseltamivir, amantadine, and zanamivir for the prophylaxis of influenza. http://www.nice.org.uk/nicemedia/pdf/InfiuenzaProphylaxisAssessm entReport.pdf. Accessed Nov 11, 2009

3 Jefferson, T. *et al.* (2009) Neuraminidase inhibitors for preventing and treating influenza in health adults: systematic review and metaanalysis. *BMJ* 339, b5106

4 Shun-Shin, M. *et al.* (2009) Neuraminidase inhibitors for treatment and prophylaxis of influenza in children: systematic review and metaanalysis of randomised controlled trials. *BMJ* 339, b3172

5 Burch, J. *et al.* (2009) Prescription of anti-influenza drugs for healthy adults: a systematic review and meta-analysis. *Lancet* 9, 537–545

6 Health Protection Agency weekly reports, week ending 10 September 2009

7 Elliot, A. J., Powers, C. and Thornton, A. *et al.* (2009) Monitoring the emergence of community transmission of influenza A/H1N1 2009 in England: a cross-sectional opportunities survey of self sampled telephone callers to NHS Direct. *BMJ* 339, b3403

8 Uyeki, T. (2009) Antiviral treatment for patients hospitalised with 2009 pandemic influenza A (H1N1). *N. Engl. J. Med.* 23, e110

9 World Health Organisation: Clinical management of human infection with avian influenza A (H5N1) virus. Accessed 12 May 2010 http://www.who.int/csr/disease/ avian_influenza/guidelines/ClinicalManagement07.pdf

10 Pandemic flu: a national framework for responding to an influenza pandemic. http:// www.dh.gov.uk/en/Publicationsandstatistics/Publications/Publicationspolicyand- guidance/DH_080734. Accessed 12 November 2009

11 WHO guidelines for pharmacological management of pandemic (H1N1) 2009 influenza and other influenza virus. 20 August 2009. www.who.int/csr/resources/ publications/swineflue/h1n1_use_antivirals-20090820/index.html

12 Garske, T. *et al.* (2009) Assessing the severity of the novel influenza A/H1N1 pandemic. *BMJ* 339, b2840

13 Experts warned dispersal of Tamiflu would do more harm than good. Guardian. co.uk Sunday 16th August 2009, www.guardian.co.uk/world/2009/aug/16/swine- flu-tamifu-helpline-paracetamol

14 Jack, A. (2009) Pandemic Flu. Flu's unexpected bonus. *BMJ* 339, b3811

15 Doshi, P. (2009) Neuraminidase inhibitors: the story behind the Cochrane review. *BMJ* 339, b5164

45

THE VAGARIES OF PUBLIC
SUPPORT FOR GOVERNMENT
ACTIONS IN CASE OF A
PANDEMIC

*Karen M. Hilyard, Vicki S. Freimuth, Donald Musa,
Supriya Kumar and Sandra Crouse Quinn*

Source: *Health Affairs*, 29:12 (2010), 2294–301.

Abstract

Government health measures in a pandemic are effective only
with strong support and compliance from the public. A survey
of 1,583 US adults early in the 2009 H1N1 (swine influenza)
pandemic shows surprisingly mixed support for possible government efforts to control the spread of the disease, with strong
support for more extreme measures such as closing borders and
weak support for more basic, and potentially more effective,
policies such as encouraging sick people to stay home from
work. The results highlight challenges that public health officials
and policy makers must address in formulating strategies to
respond to a pandemic before a more severe outbreak occurs.

Although far smaller and less severe than other influenza pandemics of the
past century,[1] the 2009 H1N1 (swine flu) pandemic and the virus that caused
it remain a concern for public health officials for three reasons. First, unlike
typical influenza outbreaks, H1N1 caused proportionally more hospitalizations and deaths among those under age sixty-five,[1] and certain groups, such
as people with obesity, appeared to be at risk for severe complications not
previously seen in influenza.[2] Second, the World Health Organization (WHO)
believes that H1N1 could mutate into a more dangerous form,[3] such as the
1918 avian flu that killed fifty million people, many of whom were ages 20–40

and were previously healthy.[4] And third, although the H1N1 pandemic turned out not to be severe, public health officials discovered problems with their initial efforts to mitigate the spread of the disease and increase public support for those efforts.

Greater public awareness of flu pandemics as a result of the H1N1 outbreak provided a unique opportunity to evaluate strategies that officials might use in a more severe pandemic. We began a longitudinal assessment of public support for government action just after the virus emerged in Mexico and in several areas in the United States. That was early in the outbreak, before the development of a vaccine, the identification of groups that should receive the vaccine first in cases of scarcity, and the beginning of the fall flu season in the northern hemisphere.

Using a representative, nationwide survey, we sought to determine levels of US public support for proposed government actions to fight a pandemic. We also looked for important predictors of public support. This paper reports the results of the first wave of our study—a window into the early stages of pandemic response.

Government policies

Governments around the world were initially uncertain about the virulence of H1N1, so protection measures varied widely, from the routine to the draconian. In Mexico City, where the virus first emerged, officials canceled both private and public events, earning praise from international health experts despite failing to slow the transmission of the disease.[5]

China quarantined all Canadian and Mexican nationals. Hong Kong quarantined all guests at any hotel where even a single guest was diagnosed with H1N1. Singapore quarantined everyone arriving from Mexico. Many Asian nations subjected everyone arriving from abroad, and all schoolchildren, to routine temperature monitoring. They also required hospital staff and visitors to use protective clothing.[6]

To remove any possible threat of the virus's spreading from pigs to humans, Egypt slaughtered all of its more than 300,000 pigs.[7] The European Union's health commissioner warned people not to travel to the United States or Mexico.[8]

In the United States, initial reactions included closing schools with one or more cases of flu and encouraging people to practice good hygiene habits and to engage in "social distancing," or limiting their contact with other people. As the pandemic progressed and school closures appeared ineffective, sick people were encouraged to stay home from work or school until twenty-four hours after their symptoms had subsided.[9] They were also advised to avoid going to health care facilities unless their symptoms became severe.[10]

Vaccine was rushed into production and distribution, undergoing the standard Food and Drug Administration (FDA) approval process but at an accelerated pace.[11] Health care workers, children, and pregnant women were given priority for the first available vaccines. Later, numerous state and local health departments offered vaccines free to the general public.[12]

More-extreme policies in the federal plan for responding to the flu pandemic included widespread closings of schools, stores, churches, and public facilities; quarantines of suspected cases; and closing borders, which would include a ban on immigration. The government never took these steps, but they remain options for future pandemics.

Experience and research

Understanding predictors of public support for government action is critical in a pandemic because empirical evidence shows that public health measures can greatly mitigate the spread of disease. In the 1918 influenza pandemic, US cities where public health interventions were introduced quickly and continued for longer periods had transmission rates that were 30–50 percent lower than those in cities that responded more slowly and less forcefully.[13]

Experience with SARS

Computer simulations and real-world experience with severe acute respiratory syndrome (SARS) show that social distancing can prevent or slow disease transmission[14,15] as long as at least 60 percent of the population complies with the policy.[16] Implementing social distancing seems like common sense, and the policy was used successfully in Asia during the SARS epidemic. However, such policies may work in group-oriented Asian cultures but not in more individualistic countries such as the United States, Australia, and Western Europe.[17]

Canada used quarantine successfully in the Toronto area during the SARS outbreak, but SARS never threatened the general population there. About one-third of the approximately 23,000 people quarantined—some of them at their own request—were health care workers. Guarantees of paid sick leave while in quarantine were critical factors in Canadians' compliance with the policy.[18]

Responses to H1N1 pandemic

Abundant data are available about the public's perceptions of risk, individual preventive behavior, and use of vaccine in the 2009–10 H1N1 pandemic.[19,20] However, relatively little research has been conducted on public support for government action in a pandemic, and most of that work predates the H1N1 outbreak. Some respondents did not know what the word *pandemic* meant, and none had experienced H1N1.

The limited pre-H1N1 data show that 70–80 percent of US respondents favored compulsory quarantine for flu patients in a pandemic.[21,22] Robert Blendon and coauthors[23] also reported that a large majority of working adults could stay home from work for up to ten days, and more than half could stay home for a month, without serious financial problems.

It is important to note that the questions that elicited those responses asked what people could do rather than what they would do. The questions thus did not address important intangible barriers to social distancing, including respondents' perceptions of contagion risk and policy effectiveness, fear of job loss, and objections to policies based on civil liberty or mental health grounds.

Attitudes toward setting vaccination priorities

Attitudes toward rationing or prioritizing of vaccines are another area in which little research has been conducted. Both Hye-Jin Paek and her coauthors[22] and Catherine DesRoches and her colleagues[24] found that just over half the public would support government policies limiting the vaccine to high-risk groups.

An emerging virus would require the rapid development of a new vaccine, perhaps bypassing standard testing protocols. Both Sandra Crouse Quinn and her coauthors[25] and Paek and her coauthors[22] found fewer than 40 percent would support vaccines that had not yet been fully approved. Other surveys conducted before[21,23,24] and during[19,20] the H1N1 outbreak did not address this question.

Role of current study

Our study examined levels of support for all of these actual and hypothetical policies in the early weeks of the outbreak, when concerns about the virus's potential severity were high. Controlling for demographic and attitudinal factors to see the effect of each variable separately, we examined how risk perception, concern about H1N1, trust in the government's handling of the crisis, and perceived fairness predicted support for government action.

Additionally, we examined attitudes about new or not-fully-approved vaccines and medicines—as noted, a topic that few previous surveys had covered. We also examined support for more-moderate measures such as encouraging sick people to stay home from work, and more-extreme measures such as quarantines and border closings.

Our study took place during the initial stages of the H1N1 epidemic, which is typically a pivotal time. In an epidemic's initial stages, no one knows what trajectory the disease will take;[26] the public may be complacent even as public health officials are increasingly alarmed. Thus, our study took a snapshot of the time when uncertainty was highest, instead of gauging public response to a severe but hypothetical pandemic or documenting behavior and attitudes once people began to realize that the 2009 pandemic would be mild.

With a more virulent strain of influenza, the outcome could have been much different, and public compliance might have been a deciding factor in the outbreak's severity. Therefore, our data are especially instructive in anticipating initial public responses to government action in future pandemics.

356

Study data and methods

From June 3 to July 6, 2009, we surveyed a nationally representative, random sample of 1,543 adults, including oversamples of African Americans and Hispanics. We weighted all analyses to make them demographically representative of the US population as reported by the May 2009 Current Population Survey (CPS).

Survey instrument and measures

Our survey instrument described H1N1 as "the current influenza outbreak" and used the term *swine flu* rather than H1N1. We developed measures of support for eight actual or potential government actions using a four-point scale ranging from "strongly oppose" to "strongly favor" (Exhibit 1). Based on the clustering of the distributions, we dichotomized responses to oppose (strongly oppose or oppose) or favor (strongly favor or favor).

Predictors of support for pandemic policies were standard demographic characteristics and self-reported attitudes regarding H1N1, including respondents' perceptions of their susceptibility and the pandemic's severity, and

Exhibit 1 Americans' support for government actions regarding swine flu, 2009.

Do you favor or oppose the following type of action that the government has done or might do?	Weighted (%)		
	Unweighted (number)	Strongly oppose/oppose	Strongly favor/favor
Quarantining those who might have been exposed to the flu to limit their contact with others	1,524	22.1	77.9
Helping people give health care to sick family members at home rather than having them be in the hospital	1,519	24.7	75.3
Giving out medicines or vaccines to people at a designated public location	1,515	25.3	74.7
Closing the borders to visitors from countries with outbreaks of flu	1,521	28.5	71.5
Encouraging people to stay home from work	1,527	50.2	49.8
Setting priorities to determine who gets limited supplies of vaccines or drugs	1,520	51.8	48.2
Closing schools, stores, places of worship, and other places where people gather	1,519	55.8	44.2
Offer people vaccines or drugs that are new and not yet approved	1,520	78.3	21.7

Source: Authors' analysis.

respondents' concern about getting the disease. Additional independent variables included respondents' confidence in the government's handling of the pandemic, measured by indexing perceived levels of government openness, honesty, commitment, caring and concern, and competence in addressing H1N1; the extent to which respondents believed that the government's response was in their personal best interest; and the degree to which respondents believed that the government would protect them from swine flu.[27,28] We calculated a mean score for the trust scale and categorized responses above that score as indicating high trust, and those below that score as indicating low trust.

We also measured respondents' perception of how fairly all groups of Americans were treated with regard to H1N1, constructing a scale from four questions that asked about fairness, equal access to antiviral drugs and vaccines, and respondents' degree of confidence that they would receive equal treatment in a quarantine. For the analysis, we divided the responses at the median value into categories of less and more perceived fairness. In addition, we asked respondents whether they "personally had ever experienced discrimination or been hassled when seeking health care because of your race, ethnicity or color," and we categorized the responses as "yes" or "no."

Data analysis

We used the statistical software Stata, version 10.1, for complex survey analysis procedures incorporating weighting and stratification variables. For categorical measures in the bivariate analysis, we used adjusted Pearson chi-square tests. We examined the relationships between support for government actions and both demographic and attitudinal measures through binary logistic regression for dichotomous outcomes. In all analyses, a p value of < 0.05 indicated a significant finding.

Results

Overall support for government action

Respondents' views of some policies were nearly evenly divided (Exhibit 1). Slightly fewer than half supported encouraging people to stay home from work when sick; closing schools, stores, places of worship, and other gathering places; and setting priorities to determine who would get limited supplies of vaccines or drugs.

On the other hand, strong majorities supported quarantining people exposed to the flu to limit their contact with others; closing borders to visitors from countries with flu outbreaks; helping people care for sick family members at home so they wouldn't have to go to the hospital; and distributing medicines or vaccines at designated public locations. Only about one in five respondents supported offering people new vaccines or drugs that had not yet been approved.

Our next step was to determine which demographic characteristics, such as age or race, and which attitudes, such as risk perception or trust, were most closely associated with support for these policies. Although public health messages often target specific demographic groups where particular risks or attitudes are more prevalent, ultimately, the goal is to change the attitudes and behaviors of individuals. Messages that focus on attitudes can reach individuals in multiple population groups simultaneously. We report attitudinal data for the entire sample in Exhibit 2, demographic predictors of support in Appendix Supplement 1, and attitudinal predictors of support in Appendix Supplement 2.[29]

Generally, we found that although few people saw themselves as highly susceptible to H1N1, almost half felt that the pandemic could be severe and had concerns about getting the disease. A majority trusted the government's ability to handle the pandemic and treat people fairly.

Predictors of support for various strategies

In an initial bivariate analysis (see Appendix Supplements 1 and 2),[29] we found that some demographic and attitudinal variables were associated with support levels for particular policies. For example, higher trust in the government's handling of the pandemic appeared to be related to support for closing borders.

Exhibit 2 Americans' attitudinal characteristics regarding H1N1, 2009.

Characteristic	Unweighted (number)	Weighted (%)
Perceived susceptibility to H1N1		
Less susceptibility	1,273	85.8
More susceptibility	244	14.2
Perceived severity of H1N1		
Less severe	874	58.0
More severe	650	42.0
Concern about getting H1N1		
Less concern	804	53.8
More concern	723	46.2
Trust in government's handling		
Less trust	579	40.9
More trust	353	59.1
Fairness of treatment of all groups		
Less fairness	587	38.4
More fairness	909	61.6
Ever experienced discrimination		
No	1,329	87.6
Yes	202	12.4

Source: Authors' analysis.
Notes: Totals vary because of missing data. See the Study Data and Methods section for definitions.

However, to make meaningful use of the data, it is important to go beyond bivariate analysis and evaluate each predictor individually, with all other variables being equal. We therefore used logistic regression to control for all other demographic and attitudinal variables,[30] singling out critical predictors of support that policy makers and public health officials should focus on (see Appendix Supplement 3).[29] We detail the results of this more precise analysis below.

- STAYING HOME: Significant predictors of support for the government's encouraging people to stay home from work when sick were age, amount of education, and level of trust in the government. Adults age 65 and older were only half as likely as those ages 18–34 to favor a policy of staying home from work. Those having a bachelor's degree were about twice as likely to favor the policy as those with less than a high school education. Finally, those with greater trust (versus less trust) that the government would handle the H1N1 pandemic well were more likely to support staying home from work.

- QUARANTINE: Significant predictors for support of a quarantine included sex, with women about one and a half times more likely than men to favor quarantining. Support was also associated with the attitudinal characteristics of greater perceived susceptibility, greater perceived severity, and more concern about H1N1, as well as greater trust in the government's handling of the pandemic.

- BORDER CLOSINGS: Women were significantly more likely than men to support closing the borders, as were those ages 35–64 versus those ages 18–34, and those reporting greater—versus less—perceived severity of H1N1. However, Hispanics were significantly less likely to support border closings than white non-Hispanics. Those with a bachelor's degree were less likely to support border closings than those with a high school education or less.

- CLOSING GATHERING PLACES: We found support for closing schools and other gathering places from those with greater perceived susceptibility, greater perceived severity, and greater perceived government fairness. People age 65 and older were less likely than those ages 18–34 to favor these closings.

- CARING FOR PEOPLE AT HOME: Both people ages 35–64 and those over age 65 were more likely to support helping people care for sick family members at home, compared to people ages 18–34. People who reported that they had been discriminated against in receiving health care were more likely to support this policy than were those who reported experiencing no discrimination.

- USE OF NEW VACCINES: Support for offering new and not-yet-approved vaccines or drugs was not associated with any independent variable in the bivariate analysis. However, we found one significant predictor in the regression analysis: Women were significantly less likely than men to favor offering unapproved medicines.

- RATIONING VACCINE: Significant predictors of support for setting priorities in case of limited supplies of vaccines and drugs included income, with both those earning $50,000–$74,999 a year and those earning at least $75,000 a year more likely to favor setting priorities than people earning under $25,000. Education was also a significant predictor: Those who had a bachelor's degree were twice as likely to favor setting vaccine priorities as those with less than a high school education. Attitudinal predictors of setting vaccine priorities included greater trust in the government's handling of H1N1 and greater perceived government fairness.
- PUBLIC DISTRIBUTION OF VACCINE: Finally, significant predictors of support for distributing medicines and vaccines at designated public locations were having attended some college (as opposed to having less than a high school education) and having greater trust in the government's handling of the pandemic.

Policy implications

Compared to other studies before and after the pandemic, our data captured a pivotal time in the H1N1 outbreak: It was real, not hypothetical—the World Health Organization had just declared a pandemic—yet no one at that time could predict with any accuracy how severe the outbreak would be.

Overall levels of support for government policies were somewhat counter-intuitive, both in terms of which policies were supported and in the splintered patterns of support among demographic and attitudinal groups. Once other variables were controlled for, the people who opposed particular policies were often a patchwork of different demographic groups and attitudes. That creates a major challenge in directing communication and education efforts to the right people.

Opposition levels

One finding that is particularly important for public health officials is that even the policies with the highest levels of support in our study were still opposed by roughly one-quarter of the respondents. Several basic, common-sense efforts to mitigate the spread of the disease—such as staying home from work while sick, or closing schools and other public gathering places—had surprisingly weak support, with fewer than half of the respondents in favor. It is even more surprising that although only 49.8 percent supported encouraging people to stay home from work, 71.5 percent supported closing borders. Social distancing is considered to be far more effective in a pandemic than closing borders, so this relatively low level of support for staying home from work presents a critical communication challenge for public health officials.

- OPTIMISTIC BIAS: Several factors may play a role here. First is optimistic bias, the well-documented tendency for individuals to believe that they are less vulnerable to common risks than other people are, despite statistical evidence to the contrary. Especially early in the pandemic, people whose communities had not experienced the disease might have been less willing to accept the inconvenience or intrusion of policies that they felt were unnecessary for them.

- ECONOMIC CONSIDERATIONS: Second, the response to the policy of staying home may be purely economic, because large numbers of people cannot work from home, will not be paid if they do not report to work, and don't have paid sick days or are discouraged from using them. Similarly, school and day care closings could force parents to stay home from work, leading them to disapprove of those closings.

- MIXED MOTIVATIONS: Third, it is possible that strong support for closing borders has little to do with trying to mitigate the pandemic. Instead, it could indicate anti-immigrant sentiment, especially since we conducted our survey on the heels of the outbreak's beginnings in Mexico.

Lack of support for closing public places

Only 44.2 percent of our respondents supported closing schools, day care facilities, places of worship, and stores in a pandemic. Given that many studies show schools as vectors of infection transmission, weak support for this policy is cause for concern. Policy makers should support solid research on the efficacy and timing of school closures in a pandemic, to acquire evidence that will support the policy of keeping children home.

However, it is also possible that answers to the survey question were affected by its mingling of religion, commerce, and education. This potential flaw should be corrected in future studies.

Typically, the components of risk perception—in this case, perceived susceptibility to disease and perceived severity of the disease—affect whether someone win take steps to mitigate risk. Indeed, support for a quarantine and for closing schools, stores, and places of worship was associated with higher perceived risk. However, increased perceived risk had no apparent impact on support for staying home from work; only about half of the people in any group supported this measure.

Workers' economic motivations

Officials responsible for giving the public information about risk should realize that even messages that raise levels of perceived risk may not translate into support for the policy of staying home. This is not to say that risk perception does not play a role, but that the most salient risk for many individuals is to livelihood, rather than health.

Lower socioeconomic groups are usually assumed to be less able to work from home or take sick leave, but a wide variety of jobs cannot easily be performed away from the job site. Even corporate executives are subject to cultural norms encouraging people to report to work even when they are sick, or discouraging or limiting the use of leave time when children are sick or child care is unavailable.

A February 2010 study by the Institute for Women's Policy Research, based on statistics from the Centers for Disease Control and Prevention (CDC), found that an estimated eight million of the twenty-six million US adults thought to have contracted H1N1 worked while sick with the virus. Although the reasons for this cannot be determined, the institute blamed a lack of paid sick leave—which may disproportionately affect women, members of minority groups, and younger workers in low-wage jobs.[31]

Canadian public health officials found that addressing these issues was essential to the success of the SARS quarantine. Without laws and support mechanisms in place to make it financially feasible for workers to stay home when they are sick, efforts to increase public support for such policies may be futile.

Communication strategies

In designing messages to promote compliance with policies in a pandemic, public health officials typically look at predictors of support and tailor messages to several audiences. However, it is worth noting that our survey found wide variability in levels of support and little consistency in the variables that predicted support. Factor analysis failed to reveal relationships between what might appear to be similar policies, so policy makers should not simply assume that there are logical continuums of support from less restrictive to more restrictive, or least effective to most effective, policies. Our results argue instead for a granular examination of each policy and each group.

For example, although women were far more likely than men to support quarantines and border closings, two methods of potentially separating the sick from the well, they were not significantly more likely to support other such policies, such as staying home from work when sick, closing schools and gathering places, or caring for the sick at home. It is possible that respondents perceived quarantines and border closings as things that other people might be subject to, whereas the three remaining policies seemed more likely to be applied to the respondents themselves.

Whatever the explanation, it is clear that no inferences should be made about support for one policy based on support for what public health officials may believe to be a similar policy.

Age differences

Compared to the referent group of those ages 18–34, those over age 65 were far less likely to support social distancing and yet far more likely to support caring for the sick at home. There are various possible explanations for these differences, and it is not clear which of them is more likely. Perhaps older people have a more traditional work ethic when it comes to job absences, or perhaps they are more isolated and therefore place more importance on maintaining social connections at church and other gathering places. They may also have more experience or confidence in caring for the sick, and be more wary of hospitals as vectors for germs, compared to younger people.

People ages 35–64 also tended to support caring for the sick at home, but they did not agree with the older respondents on other questions. However, they were more likely than younger adults to support border closings. Again, no simple pattern emerges.

Trust in government

Of the attitudinal characteristics, perceived severity and perceived trust in the government's handling of H1N1 were the two most influential predictors of support for government action. Yet although those who perceived the severity of the crisis to be high were significantly more likely than others were to support quarantines, closing borders, and closing schools and public gathering places, perceived severity appeared to have no impact on other mitigation policies. Trust in the government was linked to support for staying home from work, quarantines, prioritizing limited supplies of medicine, and distributing medicines publicly, but not to support of not-fully-approved medicines or closing borders.

Based on these data, public health officials can make no assumptions about how a given group will respond to a policy. Instead, officials should set strategies on a group-by-group and policy-by-policy basis.

Changing attitudes in the face of a real threat

Our results contrast with the more consistent levels of support across demographic and attitudinal groups seen in surveys conducted prior to H1N1,[22,23] when the idea of a pandemic was hypothetical. That change suggests that the reality of H1N1 prompted quite different responses to potential policies and more varied responses across demographic groups. It may also represent confusion, as people grappled with unfamiliar policies and issues.

Conclusion

Three important considerations for public health officials emerge from this study. First, greater consistency in support for government action is seen in hypothetical situations than in an actual pandemic. Second, during the actual H1N1 pandemic, no clear patterns of support emerged by demographic groups or attitudinal groups, nor could policies be easily grouped or counted on to evoke similar responses. Third, the economic risks of compliance with government action in a pandemic may trump the health risks of noncompliance.

For public health officials, these findings mean that data collected prior to a pandemic might not be applicable when a real pandemic hits. Campaigns to increase support for government action need to be conducted at a detailed level, paying close attention to differences among attitudinal and demographic groups on a policy-by-policy basis. Finally, people's fears about losing their income or job must be addressed if a high degree of compliance with government policies is to be achieved.

However, in the early stages of a pandemic, communication alone is unlikely to persuade people to risk their jobs or their ability to get food or medical attention. The economic, logistical, and political consequences of keeping people home from work and school, closing businesses, closing borders, and dramatically changing the way health care is delivered in a pandemic cannot simply be an afterthought.

Before a severe pandemic strikes, policy makers must revisit their plans for dealing with pandemics and devise strategies that most people can realistically follow, as well as sufficient financial and legal supports to facilitate compliance.

Acknowledgements

This paper was funded through the Center for Public Health Practice by the Centers for Disease Control and Prevention (CDC), Cooperative Agreement No. 1P01TP000304-01. Its contents are solely the responsibility of the authors and do not necessarily represent the official views of the CDC. Donald Musa, Supriya Kumar, and Sandra Crouse Quinn were also supported by the Research Center of Excellence in Minority Health and Health Disparities. National Institutes of Health (NIH-NCMHD: 2P60MD000207-08).

Notes

1 World Health Organization. Pandemic (H1N1) 2009—update 94 [Internet]. Geneva: WHO; 2010 Apr 1 [cited 2010 Apr 7]. Available from: http://www.who.int/csr/don/2010_04_01/en/index.html

2 Centers for Disease Control and Prevention. Intensive-care patients with severe novel influenza A (H1N1) virus infection—Michigan, June 2009. MMWR Morb Mortal Wkly Rep. 2009;58(27):749–52.

3 Schlein L. WHO: H1N1 influenza pandemic to last another year. Voice of America [Internet]. 2009 Dec 29 [cited 2010 Feb 3]. Available from: http://www1.voanews.com/english/news/H1N1-Influenza-Pandemic-Year-29Dec09-80282967.html

4 Morse S. S., Garwin R. L., Olsiewski P. J. Next flu pandemic: what to do until the vaccine arrives? Science. 2006; 314(5801):929.

5 Stern A. M., Markel H. What Mexico taught the world about pandemic influenza preparedness and community mitigation strategies. JAMA. 2009;302(11):1221–2.

6 Ong C. W. M., Ho K. Y., Hsu L. Y., Lim A. Y. T., Fisher D. A., Tambyah P. A. Reacting to the emergence of swine-origin influenza A H1N1. Lancet Infect Dis. 2009;9(7):397–8.

7 Ballantyne C. Will Egypt's plans to kill pigs protect it from swine—sorry, H1N1 flu? Sci Am News Blog [blog on the Internet]. 2009 May 1 [cited 2010 Oct 25]. Available from: http://www.scientificamerican.com/blog/post.cfm?id=will-egypts-plans-to-kill-pigs-prot-2009-05-01

8 Associated Press. Swine flu prompts EU warning on travel to US. MSNBC.com [Internet]. 2009 Apr 27 [cited 2010 Feb 18]. Available from: http://www.msnbc.msn.com/id/30431245/

9 Neale T. CDC eases swine flu school closure guidance. MedPage Today [serial on the Internet]. 2009 Aug 7 [cited 2010 Feb 18]. Available from: http://www.medpagetoday.com/InfectiousDisease/URItheFlu/15435

10 Centers for Disease Control and Prevention. CDC guidance for responses to influenza for institutions of higher education during the 2009–2010 academic year [Internet]. Atlanta (GA): CDC; 2010 Feb 22 [cited 2010 Oct 25]. Available from: http://www.cdc.gov/h1n1flu/institutions/guidance/

11 Masterson K. Swine flu vaccine trials begin testing volunteers. National Public Radio [Internet]. 2009 Aug 10 [cited 2010 Mar 25]. Available from: http://www.npr.org/templates/story/story.php?storyId=111743491

12 Ruiz R. Behind the H1N1 vaccine shortage. Forbes [Internet]. 2009 Oct 30 [cited 2010 Mar 25]. Available from: http://www.forbes.com/2009/10/27/swine-flu-vaccine-lifestyle-health-h1n1-shortage.html

13 Bootsma M. C. J., Ferguson N. M. The effect of public health measures on the 1918 influenza pandemic in U.S. cities. Proc Natl Acad Sci U S A. 2007;104(18):7588–93.

14 Glass R. J., Glass L. M., Beyeler W. E., Min H. J. Targeted social distancing design for pandemic influenza. Emerg Infect Dis. 2006;12(11):1671–81.

15 Ferguson N. M., Cummings D. A. T., Fraser C., Cajka J. C., Cooley P. C., Burke D. S. Strategies for mitigating an influenza pandemic. Nature. 2006;442(7101):448–52.

16 Rothstein M. A., Talbott M. K. Encouraging compliance with quarantine: a proposal to provide job security and income replacement. Am J Public Health. 2007; 97(Suppl 1):S49–56.

17 Wang T. H., Wei K. C., Hsiung C. A., Maloney S. A., Eidex R. B., Posey D. L., et al. Optimizing severe acute respiratory syndrome response strategies: lessons learned from quarantine. Am J Pub Health. 2007;97:S98–100.

18 DiGiovanni C., Conley J., Chiu D., Zaborski J. Factors influencing compliance with quarantine in Toronto during the 2003 SARS outbreak. Biosecur Bioterror. 2004;2(4):265–72.

19 SteelFisher G. K., Blendon R. J., Bekheit M. M., Lubell K. The public's response to the 2009 H1N1 influenza pandemic. New Engl J Med. 2010; 362(22):e65.

20 Maurer J., Harris K. M., Parker A., Lurie N. Does receipt of seasonal influenza vaccine predict intention to receive novel H1N1 vaccine: evidence from a nationally representative survey of U.S. adults. Vaccine. 2009;27(42):5732–4.

21 Blendon R. J., DesRoches C. M., Cetron M. S., Benson J. M., Meinhardt T., Pollard W. Attitudes toward the use of quarantine in a public health emergency in four countries. Health Aff (Millwood). 2006;25(2):w15–25.

22 Paek H. J., Hilyard K., Freimuth V. S., Barge J. K., Mindlin M. Public support for government actions during a flu pandemic: lessons learned from a statewide survey. Health Promot Pract. 2008;9(4 Suppl):60S–72S.

23 Blendon R. J., Koonin L. M., Benson J. M., Cetron M. S., Pollard W. E., Mitchell E. W., et al. Public response to community mitigation measures for pandemic influenza. Emerg Infect Dis. 2008;14(5):778–86.

24 DesRoches C. M., Blendon R. J., Benson J. M. Americans' responses to the 2004 influenza vaccine shortage. Health Aff (Millwood). 2005;24(3):822–31.

25 Quinn S. C., Kumar S., Freimuth V. S., Kidwell K., Musa D. Public willingness to take a vaccine or drug under emergency use authorization during the 2009 H1N1 pandemic. Biosecur Bioterror. 2009;7(3):275–90.

26 Cohen J. Past pandemics provide mixed clues to H1N1's next moves. Science. 2009;324(5930):996–7.

27 Meredith L. S., Eisenman D. P., Rhodes H., Ryan G., Long A. Trust influences response to public health messages during a bioterrorist event. J Health Commun. 2007;12(3):217–32.

28 Peters R. G., Covello V. T., McCallum D. B. The determinants of trust and credibility in environmental risk communication: an empirical study. Risk Anal. 1997;17(1):43–54.

29 To access the Appendix, click on the Appendix link in the box to the right of the article online.

30 Hosmer D. W., Lemeshow S. Applied logistic regression. 2nd ed. New York (NY): Wiley; 2000.

31 Schnirring L. Study links pandemic spread to gaps in paid sick leave. CIDRAP News [serial on the Internet]. 2010 Feb 16 [cited 2010 Feb 25]. Available from: http://www.cidrap.umn.edu/cidrap/content/influenza/biz-plan/news/feb1610sickleave-jw.html

46

POTENTIAL FOR A GLOBAL DYNAMIC OF INFLUENZA A (H1N1)

Antoine Flahault, Elisabeta Vergu and Pierre-Yves Boëlle

Source: *BMC Infectious Diseases*, 9:129 (2009), 11 pp.

Abstract

Background: Geographical and temporal diffusion patterns of a human pandemic due to Swine Origin Influenza Virus (S-OIV) remain uncertain. The extent to which national and international pandemic preparedness plans and control strategies can slow or stop the process is not known. However, despite preparedness efforts, it appears that, particularly in the USA, Mexico, Canada and the UK, local chains of virus transmission can sustain autonomous dynamics which may lead to the next pandemic. Forecasts of influenza experts usually rely on information related to new circulating strains.

Methods: We attempted to quantify the possible spread of the pandemic across a network of 52 major cities and to predict the effect of vaccination against the pandemic strain, if available. Predictions are based on simulations from a stochastic SEIR model. Parameters used in the simulations are set to values consistent with recent estimations from the outbreak in Mexico.

Results: We show that a two-wave pandemic dynamic may be observed in Southern hemisphere because of seasonal constraints for a maximum value of the basic reproductive number ($R_{0, max}$) within a city equal to 1.5 and a mean generation interval (G1) of 2 days. In this case and in the absence of vaccination, attack rates may reach 46% when considering a completely susceptible population. More severe scenarios characterized by higher values of $R_{0, max}$ (2.2) and G1 (3.1) yield an attack rate of 77%. By extrapolation, we find that mass vaccination in all countries (i.e. up to 50% of the population) implemented 6 months after the start of the pandemic may reduce the cumulative number of cases by 91% in the case of the low transmissible strain ($R_{0, max} = 1.5$). This relative reduction is only 44% for $R_{0, max} = 2.2$ since most of the cases occur in the first 6 months and so before the vaccination campaign.

Conclusion: Although uncertainties remain about the epidemiological and clinical characteristics of the new influenza strain, this study provides the first analysis of the potential spread of the pandemic and first assessment of the impact of different immunization strategies.

Background

Within 15 days of the WHO's raising the pandemic threat level to 6, more countries are affected by the new Swine Origin Influenza Virus (S-OIV) further raising concerns that S-OIV may be the next pandemic influenza strain. Active autonomous chains of transmission have been reported in several countries, such as Mexico, the USA, Canada, Spain and the UK. Most information about the virus and disease so far suggests a regular influenza process with many characteristics similar to those documented in past influenza pandemics [1]. Estimates of reproductive rates, higher than for seasonal influenza, are consistent with past pandemics [2,3]. Even if the possibility of a 1918-like scenario seems unlikely with the current circulating virus, the severity of the disease remains uncertain. Importantly, the underlying pathologies and causes of death in patients with S-OIV remain poorly documented, making the future burden of any pandemic uncertain. A major public health question as the disease continues to spread is identifying the likely course of the pandemic as well as possible control measures and their likely impact. Mathematical modelling has proven effective in retrospectively predicting the global circulation of the 1968–69 influenza pandemic, starting from Hong Kong and using coupled local epidemic processes [4,5]. Here, we aim at predicting the pattern of global spread of the potential S-OIV pandemic flu and at estimating the effect of vaccination campaigns under different scenarios.

Methods

The model implements a metapopulation approach [4–6] where coupling between cities is through transportation (data on daily passengers flows from [7]). It simulates the spread of a pandemic through a worldwide network of 52 major cities. In each city, the progression of the disease is tracked by defining four disease states (Susceptible, Exposed, Infectious, Removed; S, E, I, R) and the transition rates between them. The exposed individuals (E) are not infectious and are assumed to travel whereas infectious individuals (I) do not travel. We adopt a stochastic framework in discrete time (with half-day time step), similar to [5], to capture effects of chance, especially at the source where the number of cases is still small. For each city i in the

369

absence of any intervention, epidemic dynamics are described by the equations below (t tracks the time of the epidemic's spread at the population level whereas τ indicates the time since individual contamination):

$$S_i(t + 1) = S_i(t) - \text{Bin}(\beta_i(t), S_i(t))$$

$$E_i(0, t + 1) = \text{Bin}(\beta_i(t), S_i(t))$$

$$E_i(\tau + 1, t + 1) = E_i(\tau, t) - \sum_j \text{Bin}(\sigma_{ij}/n_i, E_i(\tau, t)) + \sum_j \text{Bin}(\sigma_{ij}/n_j, E_j(\tau, t))$$

$$- \sum_j \text{Bin}(\gamma(\tau), \text{Bin}(\sigma_{ij}/n_j, E_j(\tau, t))) - \text{Bin}\left(\gamma(\tau), E_i(\tau, t) - \sum_j \text{Bin}(\sigma_{ij}/n_i, E_i(\tau, t))\right)$$

$$I_i(\tau + 1, t + 1) = I_i(\tau, t) - \text{Bin}(\delta(\tau), I_i(\tau, t)) + \text{Bin}\left(\gamma(\tau), E_i(\tau, t)\right)$$

$$- \sum_j \text{Bin}(\sigma_{ij}/n_i, E_i(\tau, t))\bigg) + \sum_j \text{Bin}(\gamma(\tau), \text{Bin}(\sigma_{ij}/n_j, E_j(\tau, t)))$$

$$\tag{1}$$

Coupling of local epidemic dynamics is described by population flows from city i to city j (σ_{ij}). Transition probabilities between states are captured by distributions $\gamma(\tau)$ (from E to I) and $\delta(\tau)$ (from I to R). $\beta_i(t) = \sum_\tau \beta s_i(t) I_i(\tau, t)/n_i$ is the probability that a susceptible individual becomes infected at $t + 1$ and is proportional to the basic transmission rate ($\beta = R_{0,\,max}/mean\ infectious\ duration$) modulated by the seasonality (s) and the proportion of infectious (I/n). State variables in equation (1) are updated through random variables following Binomial distributions (Bin) which represent, in the order in which they appear in the equations: the number of new infections, the number of travelling latent subjects (in- and out-flows), the number of new infectious individuals coming from other cities, the number of new infectious individuals remaining in the city of origin, and the number of newly recovered individuals.

Parameter values were chosen according to qualitative knowledge or quantitative estimates. Consistent with early estimates of the basic reproductive number from data from the outbreak in Mexico [2,3], two plausible pandemic profiles were tested: in the first, a maximum (i.e. the value at the peak of transmissibility) basic reproductive number ($R_{0,\,max}$) value of 1.5 was assumed [3] whereas in the second a higher $R_{0,\,max}$, equal to 2.2, was chosen [2]. For the first case, the mean generation interval (GI) was assumed to equal 2 days (based on [3]) corresponding to mean exposed and infectious durations equal to 0.7 and 1.9 days respectively whereas in the second case, the GI was set to 3.1 (a value suggested in [2]) and the mean exposed and infectious durations were set equal to 1.45 and 2.9 days respectively. In both cases appropriate distributions of progression probabilities $\gamma(\tau)$ (with τ_{max} equal to 1 and 2 for the first and second pandemic profiles respectively) and $\delta(\tau)$ (with τ_{max} equal to 4 and 7 respectively) were defined. As the average sojourn time in the exposed state for the first pandemic profile is less than a day, a time step of 0.5 days was adopted in order to correctly reproduce fast dynamic processes. The remaining parameters were identical for both pandemic profiles as detailed below. The observed seasonality in influenza transmission was incorporated using a step function: from October to March in the Northern hemisphere and the rest of the year in the Southern hemisphere the transmissibility (s) is maximum and equal to 1. The minimum value was set at 0.4. In the tropics, transmissibility was assumed constant over the year and equal to 0.7. Since no information is available on the existence of cross-immunity from past flu infections, the initial proportion of susceptible individuals was set to 100%. In agreement with current knowledge and data [3], the case fatality rate was assumed equal to 0.003. Deaths were counted but not subtracted from the number of infectious individuals since this does not appreciably impact on the dynamics of infectious individuals. Under-reporting was not addressed and no asymptomatic cases were considered. The pandemic originated in Mexico City where 20 cases were assumed to be present on 1 April.

Several scenarios for vaccination, introduced 6 months after the start of the pandemic, were tested for each of the two pandemic profiles. As little is known about the efficacy of a future vaccine, coverage and efficacy were combined into a unique intervention parameter through their product. Each vaccination scenario was defined by the duration of vaccination campaign and the number of cities where vaccination is implemented (all the cities or cities in developed countries only). Given that the objective is to immunize a predetermined proportion (pv) of susceptibles (with respect to the number of vaccine doses available at a given date) and that it seems reasonable to assume that only a maximum proportion (α, put equal to 0.01) of current susceptibles can be vaccinated daily, we fixed the duration (d) of the vaccination campaign at the value satisfying the equation $pv = 1 - (1 - \alpha)^d$.

First, we assumed that the vaccine was available in developed countries only and that the vaccination campaign lasted 15 days (corresponding to a proportion completely immunized in developed countries of 14%). In the second and the third scenarios, vaccination was implemented in all cities of the network over 35 and 70 days respectively (corresponding to global immunization rates of 30% and 50% respectively). Results are expressed as means calculated over 500 runs for each scenario.

Results and discussion

According to simulations from our model including a seasonal forcing in flu transmission, for $R_{0, max} = 1.5$ without any preventive or control measures, the pandemic would exhibit two waves (one in 2009 with a first Southern sub-wave and a second Northern sub-wave and the other in 2010), mainly owing to two successive epidemic events in Southern cities. In addition, the pattern would be different with respect to the zone considered (Figure 1). In contrast to the South, one massive epidemic would occur in the Northern hemisphere during the winter following the first Southern peak. In tropical cities activity would be moderate, spanning a much longer time period. The two-waves spread has indeed been described among the "signature features of influenza pandemics" [1]. In the case of a more transmissible viral strain ($R_{0,\,max}$ = 2.2), both the first Southern wave and the following Northern wave would be tremendous in size, affecting the vast majority of susceptible individuals of these zones (86%, Table 1 and Figure 2). In this case, the same virus would not spread the following year as a result of depletion of susceptibles.

Owing to the scale used in Figure 1, influenza transmission during the first three months after pandemic onset is not visible on these graphs. However, simulated dynamics show early influenza activity with a daily worldwide incidence lower than 1/100000, which is consistent with the present situation (52160 cases of influenza A(H1N1) in 99 countries on 22 June 2009).

In the case of a moderately transmissible virus with $R_{0,\,max}$ = 1.5, 46% of the population would be infected worldwide by the end of 2010, mostly in Northern and Southern zones (Table 1), if no preventive or control measure were implemented. This proportion would increase to 77% in the case of a higher $R_{0,\,max}$ = 2.2. Although these attack rates may be over-estimated because of the assumption of an entirely susceptible and completely mixing population, the predicted values are not unrealistic compared with past pandemics. However, it is difficult to provide a more accurate prediction since no information is available on the existence of cross-immunity from past flu infections.

The impact of vaccination differs according to the pandemic profiles and intervention scenarios. For the first pandemic profile ($R_{0,\,max}$ = 1.5 and GI = 2), making vaccine available in developed countries only and vaccinating 14% of the population does not change the global pattern of pandemic spread but reduces the global attack rate by 20% (Figure 3 and Table 1). The benefit, in terms of number of cases, is noteworthy in the Northern zone (where most developed countries are located) but is quite low in the Southern and Tropical regions (Table 1). In the third and fourth vaccination scenarios, where vaccination is implemented in all countries (30% and 50% of susceptibles are vaccinated respectively), the pandemic exhibits only a first wave and mainly in Southern cities (Figures 4 and 5). Mean global attack rates are significantly lower (9% and 4% respectively) and benefits are more homogeneously distributed among zones. However, the pandemic burden in the South is still important since the arrival of an effective vaccine 6 months after the start of the pandemic is unable to prevent the first wave in this region. Significant decreases in the global pandemic burden could be recorded for even smaller immunization propor-tions: if 20% (or 25%) of susceptibles are vaccinated, the mean global attack rate decreases to 21% (or 16%) (results not shown in Table 1).

A GLOBAL DYNAMIC OF INFLUENZA A (H1N1)

No. new cases / 100 000

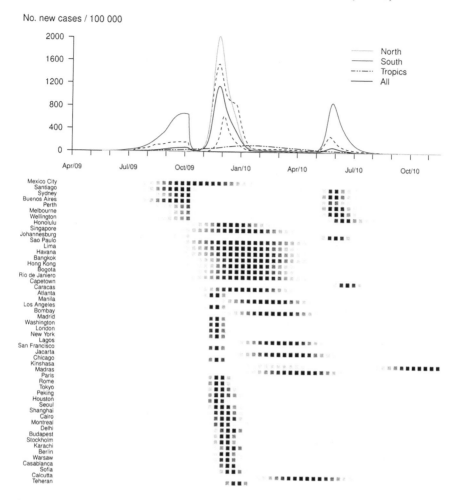

Figure 1 Baseline scenario, no vaccination ($R_{0, max}$ = 1.5 and GI = 2).
Dynamics of the pandemic starting from Mexico City, in late March 2009, in the absence of preventive and control measures. The upper panel represents average daily incidences for Northern (green), Southern (blue), tropical (black) and all (red) cities. Plain lines correspond to means and dashed lines (for the global curve only) to .05 and .95 pointwise quantiles calculated on 500 simulation runs. The lower panel illustrates the spread of the virus through the 52 cities of the network; the predicted probability of influenza activity is represented for each city (from 0 (white) to 1 (black)).

373

Table 1 Forecasted total attack and mortality rates for two pandemic profiles ($R_{0, max}$ = 1.5 and GI = 2 versus $R_{0, max}$ = 2.2 and GI = 3.1).

Scenario	Total attack rate (%)		Total attack rate North (%)		Total attack rate South (%)		Total attack rate Tropics (%)		Mortality rate (%)	
	$R_{0, max}$ = 1.5 GI = 2	$R_{0, max}$ = 2.2 GI = 3.1	$R_{0, max}$ = 1.5 GI = 2	$R_{0, max}$ = 2.2 GI = 3.1	$R_{0, max}$ =1.5 GI = 2	$R_{0, max}$ = 2.2 GI = 3.1	$R_{0, max}$ = 1.5 GI = 2	$R_{0, max}$ = 2.2 GI = 3.1	$R_{0, max}$ = 1.5 GI = 2	$R_{0, max}$ = 2.2 GI = 3.1
No vaccination	46	77	62	86	58	86	19	62	0.14	0.23
Vaccination in developed countries (14%)	37	71	47	74	55	86	17	62	0.11	0.21
Vaccination in all countries (30%)	9	51	11	45	32	86	2	52	0.03	0.15
Vaccination in all countries (50%)	4	43	1	31	32	86	2	52	0.01	0.13

Means of attack and mortality rates in the absence of any intervention and under different vaccination scenarios are calculated on 500 simulation runs for each scenario.

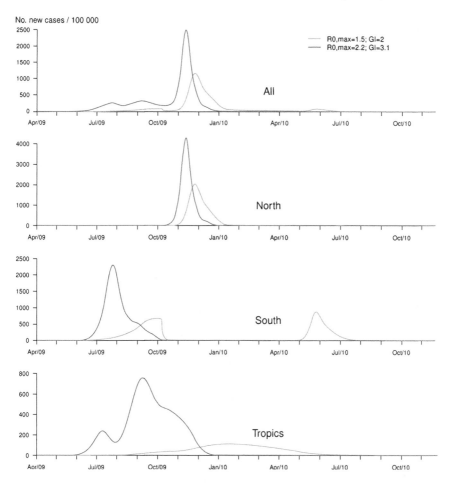

Figure 2 Comparison between baseline scenarios ($R_{0,\,max}$ = 1.5 and GI = 2 versus $R_{0,\,max}$ = 2.2 and GI = 3.1), no vaccination.
Dynamics of the pandemic starting from Mexico City, in late March 2009, in the absence of preventive and control measures for two pandemic profiles ($R_{0,\,max}$ = 1.5 and GI = 2 (lighter); versus $R_{0,\,max}$ = 2.2 and GI = 3.1 (darker)). Graphs represent average daily incidences calculated on 500 simulation runs: for all cities of the network (upper panel) and specifically for cities in each zone (North, South and Tropics; lower panels).

No. new cases / 100 000

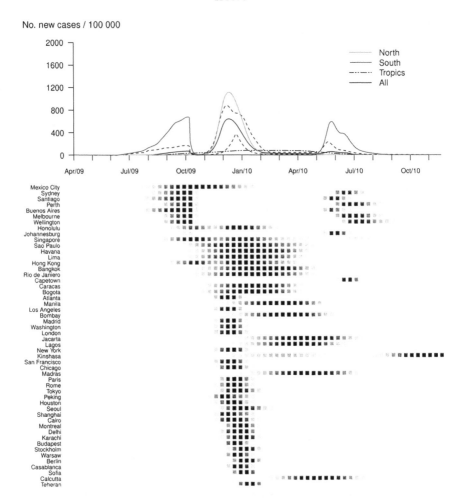

Figure 3 Vaccination in developed countries only, 14% of population are immunized
    ($R_{0, max}$ = 1.5 and GI = 2).

Dynamics of the pandemic starting from Mexico City, in late March 2009, with vaccine available
only in developed countries 6 months after pandemic onset. Fourteen percent of the population
in developed countries are vaccinated at a daily rate of 1%. The upper panel represents average
daily incidences for Northern (green), Southern (blue), tropical (black) and all (red) cities. Plain
lines correspond to means and dashed lines (for the global curve only) to .05 and .95 pointwise
quantiles calculated on 500 simulation runs. The lower panel illustrates the spread of the virus
through the 52 cities of the network; the predicted probability of influenza activity is represented
for each city (from 0 (white) to 1 (black)).

No. new cases / 100 000

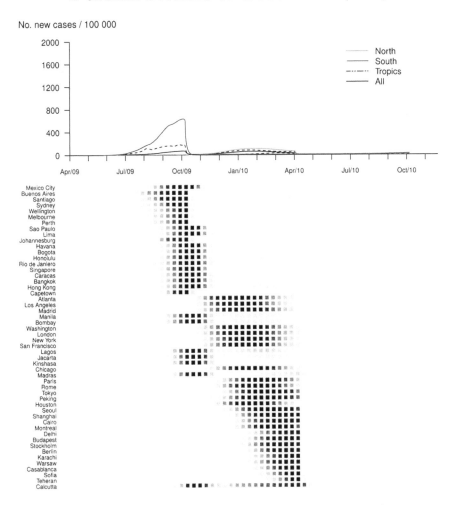

Figure 4 Vaccination in all countries, 30% of population are immunized ($R_{0, max}$ = 1.5 and GI = 2).

Dynamics of the pandemic starting from Mexico City, in late March 2009, with vaccine available in all countries 6 months after the pandemic onset. Thirty percent of worldwide population are vaccinated at a daily rate of 1%. The upper panel represents average daily incidences for Northern (green), Southern (blue), tropical (black) and all (red) cities. Plain lines correspond to means and dashed lines (for the global curve only) to .05 and .95 pointwise quantiles calculated on 500 simulation runs. The lower panel illustrates the spread of the virus through the 52 cities of the network; the predicted probability of influenza activity is represented for each city (from 0 (white) to 1 (black)).

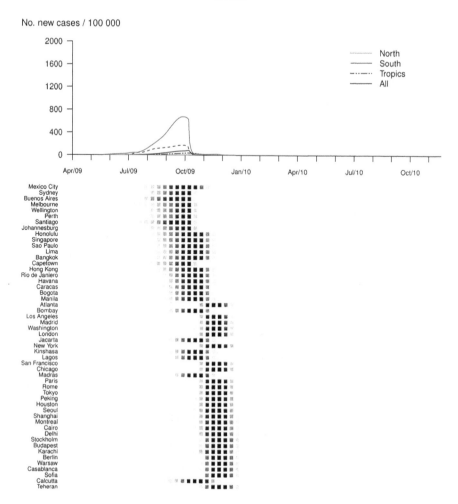

Figure 5 Vaccination in all countries, 50% of population are immunized ($R_{0, max}$ = 1.5 and GI = 2).

Dynamics of the pandemic starting from Mexico City, in late March 2009, with vaccine available in all countries 6 months after the pandemic onset. Fifty percent of worldwide population are vaccinated at a daily rate of 1%. The upper panel represents average daily incidences for Northern (green), Southern (blue), tropical (black) and all (red) cities. Plain lines correspond to means and dashed lines (for the global curve only) to .05 and .95 pointwise quantiles calculated on 500 simulation runs. The lower panel illustrates the spread of the virus through the 52 cities of the network; the predicted probability of influenza activity is represented for each city (from 0 (white) to 1 (black)).

The impact of vaccination is globally diminished in the case of a more transmissible influenza virus and a longer mean infectious duration ($R_{0, max} = 2.2$ and GI = 3.1) (Table 1 and Figure 6). Even in the presence of a mass vaccination campaign (50% of population immunized), 43% of the population would still contract the infection. This is again explained by the fact that the large majority of cases (all the cases in the Southern cities) occur in the first 6 months, before the onset of vaccination.

In addition to intrinsic differences in the dynamics of the two pandemic scenarios (induced by different values of $R_{0, max}$ and of GI duration), the

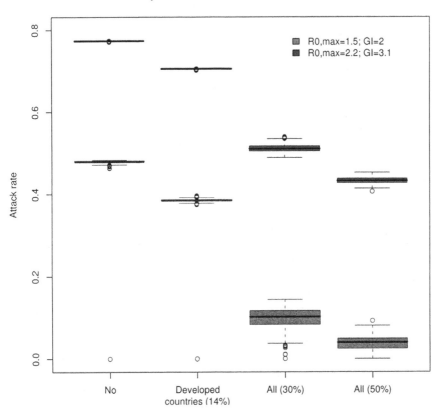

Figure 6 Comparison of vaccination impact ($R_{0, max}$ = 1.5 and GI = 2 versus $R_{0, max}$ = 2.2 and GI = 3.1).

Box-plots represent simulated distributions of attack rates over 500 simulation runs for two pandemic profiles and four vaccination scenarios (no vaccination; vaccination of 14% of population in developed countries only, vaccination of 30% of population worldwide and vaccination of 50% of population worldwide). The vaccine was considered available 6 months after pandemic onset.

two-waves or one-wave patterns are partly due to seasonal forcing. As specified in the Methods, we considered that the transmissibility was 2.5 times greater during the influenza season in Northern and Southern zones (6 months in each hemisphere) than the rest of the year. In tropical regions the transmissibility was set to a constant throughout the year equal to 70% of the transmissibility during the influenza season in the North and South. The choice of a step function to represent variation in transmissibility and of the ratios between epidemic and non-epidemic seasons has a non-negligible impact on the simulated dynamic pattern. Further investigations are needed to evaluate their importance on the dynamics of the new circulating H1N1 strain.

All simulations are performed in the stochastic framework which allows capturing various effects of chance, especially at the source where the number of cases is still small. Results on final pandemic burdens, although based on stochastic runs, are quite stable and concentrated around the mean as illustrated in Figure 6.

As little information exists on the efficacy of any future vaccine, coverage and efficacy were summarized by a single parameter representing the proportion of the population effectively immunized. This approach is a rough approximation to reality and can be interpreted in several ways. For example, a 14% vaccine-induced immunity in the population may be the result of vaccinating 20% of population with a 70% effective vaccine or of vaccinating 70% of over 60 year-olds, assuming that the latter make up 20% of the population of developed countries. It will be possible to refine this approach as age-dependent initial natural immunity and transmissibility are further characterized. Beyond the specific case of vaccination, this kind of scenario could represent any preventive and control measure designed to protect susceptible individuals.

Finally, it is interesting to note that a scenario starting in Mexico City was already identified in previous work [8] exploring possible pandemic profiles. Here we refine our model used in [8] by adopting a stochastic framework and adapting this scenario to parameter estimates closer to those currently reported. Although the prediction concerning the Mexico City pandemic outlined in our previous study could have been altered by using a different classification method, it nevertheless remains that this scenario seemed to be a typical one. Our first prediction in [8] did not indicate a rule for identifying a pandemic-source location but it did provide some insight on how a pandemic would spread if starting in such a place. Ultimately, this finding was not surprising since Mexico City is well connected to the rest of the world and belongs to the tropical zone where viral strains circulate all year. These are two important characteristics for "successful" influenza spread.

Conclusion

Although much remains to be done to characterize the new strain further, this study, based on models including estimates close to recently published data, shows that a multi-wave pandemic with a large attack rate is possible and may be curtailed using different immunization strategies.

Competing interests

The authors declare that they have no competing interests.

Authors' contributions

AF conceived the study. AF, EV and PYB developed the mathematical model. EV performed simulations. AF, EV and PYB analyzed the results. AF and EV drafted the manuscript. All authors read and approved the final manuscript.

References

1. Miller M. A., Viboud C., Balinska M. Simonsen L.: **The Signature Features of Influenza Pandemics – Implications for Policy.** *N Engl J Med* 2009, **360(25)**:2595–2598.
2. Boëlle P. Y., Bernillon P., Desenclos J. C.: **A preliminary estimation of the reproduction ratio for new influenza A(H1N1) from the outbreak in Mexico, March–April 2009.** *Euro Surveill* 2009, **14(19)**:pii: 19205.
3. Fraser C., Donnelly C. A., Cauchemez S., hanage W. P., Van Kerkhove M. D., *et al.*: **Pandemic Potential of a Strain of Influenza A (H1N1): Early Findings.** Science 2009, **324(5938)**:1557–1561.
4. Rvachev L., Longini I. M.: **A mathematical model for the global spread of influenza.** *Math Biosci* 1985, **75(1)**:3–22.
5. Cooper B. S., Pitman R. J., Edmunds W. J., Gay N. J.: **Delaying the international spread of pandemic influenza.** *PLoS Med* 2006, **3(6)**:e212.
6. Flahault A., Vergu E., Coudeville L., Grais R. F.: **Strategies for containing a global influenza pandemic.** *Vaccine* 2006, **24(44–46)**:6751–6755.
7. Grais R. F., Ellis J. H., Glass G. E.: **Assessing the impact of airline travel on the geographic spread of pandemic influenza.** *Eur J Epidemiol* 2003, **18(11)**:1065–1072.
8. Kernéis S., Grais R. F., Boëlle P. Y., Flahault A., Vergu E: **Does the effectiveness of control measures depend on the influenza pandemic profile?** *PLoS ONE* 2008, **3(1)**:e1478.

Pre-publication history

The pre-publication history for this paper can be accessed here:

http://www.biomedcentral.cpm/1471-2334/9/129/prepub

47

STRENGTHENING THE INTERNATIONAL HEALTH REGULATIONS

Lessons from the H1N1 pandemic

Kumanan Wilson, John S. Brownstein and David P. Fidler

Source: *Health Policy and Planning*, 25:6 (2010), 505–10.

The International Health Regulations (2005) [IHR(2005)] repre-sent a potentially revolutionary change in global health governance. The use of the regulations by the World Health Organization (WHO) to respond to the outbreak of pandemic influenza A 2009-H1N1 highlights the importance of the regulations to protecting global health security. As the 2009-H1N1 pandemic illustrated, the IHR(2005) have provided a more robust framework for responding to public health emergencies of international concern (PHEICs), through requiring reporting of serious disease events, strength-ening how countries and WHO communicate concerning health threats, empowering the WHO Director-General to declare the existence of PHEICs and to issue temporary recommendations for responding to them, and requiring countries not to implement measures that unnecessarily restrict trade and travel or infringe on human rights. However, limitations to the effectiveness of the IHR(2005) revealed in the 2009-H1N1 pandemic include con-tinuing inadequacies in surveillance and response capacities within some countries, violations of IHR(2005) rules and a potentially narrowing scope of application only to influenza-like pandemic events. These limitations could undermine the IHR(2005)'s potential to contribute to national and global efforts to detect and mitigate future public health emergencies. Support for the IHR(2005) should be broadened and deepened to improve their utility as a tool to strengthen global health security.

Introduction

Following the SARS outbreak in 2003 and concerns about an influenza pandemic in 2004–05 after avian influenza A (H5N1) emerged, the World

Health Organization (WHO) adopted in May 2005 the revised International Health Regulations [IHR(2005)] (WHO 2005). The revised regulations were the product of a decade-long revision process within WHO that substantially changed this international legal regime by expanding its scope of application, the obligations of States Parties and WHO's powers to respond to public health emergencies. The IHR(2005) figured prominently in the WHO's response to the influenza A (H1N1) outbreak (Fidler 2009; Katz 2009). For the first time since the IHR(2005) entered into force in June 2007, WHO utilized the regulations to create an Emergency Committee to advise the WHO Director-General, declare a public health emergency of international concern and issue temporary recommendations on increasing surveillance and on the need to avoid unnecessary trade, travel and human rights restrictions.

The use of the IHR(2005) during the 2009-H1N1 influenza outbreak has raised questions about whether the regulations functioned as intended. Initial analysis suggests that the IHR(2005) worked well in the 2009-H1N1 outbreak (Fidler 2009; Katz 2009). This event, however, also revealed concerns about the realization of the regulations' full potential. These concerns include narrow interpretations of the WHO Director-General's power to declare a public health emergency of international concern, the lack of coordinated and adequately-funded global support for IHR(2005) implementation by developing countries, the relationship between the IHR(2005) and WHO's pandemic influenza alert system and the ability of countries to violate the IHR(2005)'s rules on measures affecting trade, travel and human rights with relative impunity.

The power to declare a public health emergency of international concern

One of the IHR(2005)'s innovations is the concept of a 'public health emergency of international concern' (PHEIC). Rather than requiring States Parties only to report cases of specific diseases, the regulations mandate reporting of any natural or manmade disease event—biological, chemical or radiological—that may constitute a PHEIC. The IHR(2005) contain a decision instrument that guides States Parties through the process of determining whether they must report a disease event to WHO (Fidler 2003; Baker and Fidler 2006). The regulations deem any case of human influenza caused by a new virus subtype as a potential PHEIC that must be reported to WHO, which therefore requires that States Parties report cases of novel influenza viruses, such as 2009-H1N1, to WHO. Under the IHR(2005), the WHO Director-General is empowered to analyse information received from States Parties and non-governmental sources in order to determine, with the advice of an Emergency Committee, whether a disease event actually constitutes a PHEIC, as Director-General Margaret Chan did in the case of the 2009-H1N1 threat.

The PHEIC declaration in the 2009-H1N1 outbreak revealed the significance of this aspect of the IHR(2005). Such a declaration requires the WHO Director-General to issue temporary recommendations on how countries should respond to the PHEIC. The PHEIC declaration for the 2009-H1N1 outbreak did not prove controversial; in fact, the controversy generated by WHO's pandemic influenza alert system largely overshadowed the PHEIC declaration (Fidler 2009). Nevertheless, the first PHEIC declaration raises some questions about this power.

The first-ever PHEIC declaration draws attention to other significant disease events that the WHO Director-General has not considered PHEICs under the approach adopted in the IHR(2005), perhaps providing insight into the scope of the PHEIC-declaration power. Serious public health events, including the emergence and spread of XDR-TB (Calain and Fidler 2007; Wilson *et al.* 2007), significant cholera outbreaks and the export of melamine-contaminated food (Bell 2008), did not lead to the convening of the Emergency Committee or a PHEIC declaration by the WHO Director-General. In considering whether the XDR-TB problem warranted PHEIC treatment, the Global Task Force on TB stated that 'the IHR Emergency Committee and temporary recommendations are really intended for outbreaks of acute disease, rather than the "acute-on-chronic" situation of MDR-TB and XDR-TB' (Global Task Force on XDR-TB 2006). Similar reasoning might explain the lack of PHEIC attention given to the melamine problem, but nothing in the IHR(2005) textually supports this reasoning. Further, it does not explain the non-use of a PHEIC declaration with respect to the rapid spread of acute outbreaks of cholera, especially given the IHR(2005)'s identification of cholera as a pathogen of international concern [Annex 2 of the IHR(2005)].

This admittedly brief experience with the IHR(2005) suggests that WHO practice might limit PHEIC declarations to a very small number of infectious diseases with characteristics resembling novel human influenza viruses or SARS. This narrow scope reflects a conservative approach to the political and epidemiological discretion the IHR(2005) provide the Director-General in determining the existence of a PHEIC. Too much caution might, however, prevent the IHR(2005) from being used more strategically to draw attention to serious public health harms that require international action and assistance.

Preparing for a public health emergency: surveillance and response capacities

The IHR(2005) require States Parties to develop and maintain minimum core capacities, to conduct surveillance and to respond to public health threats from the local to the national levels [Annex 1 of the IHR(2005)]. States Parties had to assess their capabilities in these realms by 2009 and must be compliant with these obligations by 2012 (with the option for time extensions). The 2009-H1N1 outbreak revealed continuing problems with surveillance and response capacities in many countries, and these problems connect to growing concern that many States Parties will not be able to comply with their minimum core capacity requirements by the deadline, even with allowed extensions (Calain 2007a,b).

For example, the response to the 2009-H1N1 influenza outbreak underscores the importance of countries developing real-time, comprehensive clinical surveillance in order to rapidly identify outbreaks that might occur. The lack of readily available, high-quality surveillance in Mexico may have contributed to delays in identifying the outbreak and mischaracterization of the virus's severity. The inability to estimate accurately a proper denominator for the number of affected individuals in Mexico resulted in a grossly inflated mortality rate associated with 2009-H1N1 (Garske et al. 2009). As a result, recognition of the strain's novelty, its sustained human-to-human transmission and its virulence was delayed, which made interventions recommended in WHO's influenza pandemic preparedness plan (e.g. ground-level containment, social distancing and distribution of anti-virals) more difficult. The WHO pandemic influenza strategy hinges on the ability of countries to detect, at the earliest stages, the emergence of a novel pathogen with efficient human-to-human transmission (Ferguson et al. 2005; Longini et al. 2005).

However, complying with the IHR(2005)'s surveillance and response capacity obligations generates challenges and tensions, especially for developing and least-developed countries. First, as the 2009-H1N1 outbreak illustrated, many developing and least-developed countries are far from being able to comply with the IHR(2005)'s minimum core capacity mandates, and no coordinated, adequately funded global health initiative is underway to deliver assistance to such countries to implement the IHR(2005). Support for implementation of the IHR(2005) is often voiced, as illustrated by the creation of a WHO collaborating centre on IHR(2005) implementation at the US Centers for Disease Control and Prevention[1] and by the inclusion of IHR(2005) implementation support in the new US National Health Security Strategy (US Department of Health and Human Services 2009). However, to date, these and other expressions of support for IHR(2005) implementation have not coalesced into coordinated, funded global action.

Second, some view the minimum core capacity mandates as potentially distorting national public health priorities by requiring developing countries to expend resources for potential PHEICs, which are of great concern to wealthier nations, at a time when resources for public health emergencies of local concern are scarce and diminishing (Lancet 2004; Calain 2007a). The controversy over the sharing of avian influenza H5N1 samples and benefits derived from research on such samples (e.g. vaccines), including the rejection of the applicability of the IHR(2005), reflects a developing-country sense of the inequity in the way the current system operates (Garrett and Fidler 2007; Fidler 2008). Similarly, problems experienced with creating more developing-country access to vaccine for 2009-H1N1 revealed the IHR(2005)'s lack of relevance to addressing questions of equity and fairness in access to disease-response technologies (Fidler 2010).

Relationship between the IHR(2005) and the
WHO pandemic alert system

The IHR(2005)'s role in the global handling of the 2009-H1N1 outbreak was obscured by the controversies that erupted over the application of WHO's influenza pandemic alert system, through which the WHO Director-General can determine various alert phases in order to stimulate governments to prepare for or respond to a pandemic. The management of the 2009-H1N1 outbreak by WHO created confusion about the relationship between the IHR(2005) and the influenza pandemic alert system. Legally speaking, the IHR(2005) contain no provisions that mention, let alone authorize, anything connected with the influenza pandemic alert system. The argument that the decision to raise the alert levels constitutes a temporary recommendation under the IHR(2005) is not persuasive for two reasons. First, the WHO Director-General only sought the Emergency Committee's advice two out of the three times she raised the pandemic alert levels. The IHR(2005) require Emergency Committee input before the Director-General issues any temporary recommendations. Second, WHO never included the country-level actions contained within the alert system's levels in listing the temporary recommendations made under the IHR(2005). Thus, what happened in the 2009-H1N1 context raises questions about the explicit legal propriety of using the IHR(2005)'s Emergency Committee to advise on raising pandemic influenza alert levels.

Potential violations of the IHR(2005)

The 2009-H1N1 outbreak also produced behaviour by some countries that raised questions about their compliance with the IHR(2005). The IHR(2005)'s purpose is 'to prevent, protect against, control and provide a public health response to the international spread of disease in ways that are commensurate with and restricted to public health risks, and which avoid unnecessary interference with international traffic and trade' (article 2). In addition, 'States Parties shall treat travelers with respect for their dignity, human rights and fundamental freedoms and minimize any discomfort or distress associated with such measures' (article 32). States Parties applying measures that are more restrictive of trade and intrusive for travellers than recommendations issued by WHO must provide WHO with the public health rationale and scientific evidence justifying such measures (article 43) (von Tigerstrom 2005).

Examples of potential violations of these obligations arose during the 2009-H1N1 outbreak. Despite WHO's determination that travel advisories and restrictions were not necessary, many countries used such measures in responding to the outbreak. Other countries implemented restrictions on pork products exported by countries affected by 2009-H1N1 cases even though WHO and the World Animal Health Organization (OIE) repeatedly stated that such restrictions were not justified. Controversies also arose from the isolation or quarantine of individuals and groups arriving from, or associated with, 2009-H1N1-affected countries—policies that were also inconsistent with WHO recommendations (Gostin 2009). In one case, WHO requested a country's public health rationale and scientific justification for its actions, in accordance with the IHR(2005).

For the most part, the countries engaging in actions that potentially violated the IHR(2005) did so without suffering serious consequences. Like most international agreements, the IHR(2005) do not contain a mandatory dispute settlement process or enforcement mechanism. The larger concern with these potential violations is that they occurred during an outbreak of a comparatively mild virus, creating the possibility of more widespread violations if a more dangerous virus emerges and spreads. More unnecessary trade, travel and human rights restrictions could undermine incentives States Parties have to comply with their obligations to report public health events that may constitute PHEICs. Under this scenario, the IHR(2005) are at risk of unravelling through systematic violations, in much the same way as earlier versions of the regulations did. However, it is important to recognize that in the absence of the IHR(2005), it is possible that these restrictions would have been more widespread.

Strategies for supporting the IHR(2005)

The problems identified above should not detract from the importance of the IHR(2005). The use of the IHR(2005) during the 2009-H1N1 outbreak revealed the revised regulations as a considerable improvement over the previous governance approaches, particularly in the flow of information between countries and WHO. The issues identified in this article indicate, however, that WHO and the States Parties face challenges in strengthening implementation of and compliance with the IHR(2005) (Box 1).

In terms of the WHO Director-General's power to declare a PHEIC, consideration should be given to making more robust use of the IHR(2005) for public health threats. PHEIC declarations could prove useful in other contexts by drawing attention and assistance to efforts to prevent the spread of serious transboundary public health harms. The WHO Director-General could also make use of the power to issue standing recommendations under the IHR(2005) as part of strategics to improve how countries deal with different types of serious international public health danger.

The relationship between the IHR(2005) and the WHO pandemic alert system should be clarified so that questions about, or challenges to, the use of the Emergency Committee established under the regulations do not create

---

Box 1. Key points

Improvements in the response to 2009-H1N1 resulting from the coming into force of the IHR(2005)

- Clear reporting requirements for countries.
- Identification of national focal points for communication with WHO.
- Integration of information received from States Parties and non-governmental sources.
- Use of the Director-General's power to declare a PHEIC.
- Issuance of temporary recommendations concerning the management of the pandemic.
- Monitoring responses for unnecessary trade, travel and human rights restrictions.

Areas where the IHR(2005) should be supported

- Technical and financial support to developing and least-developed countries to assist them in meeting surveillance and response capacity requirements of IHR(2005).
- Consideration of using the power to declare PHEICs for a broader range of global health threats.
- Development of mechanisms to improve compliance with the IHR(2005) and WHO recommendations issued thereunder.

---

political and legal complications in the midst of a potential emergency. The efficiency of using the Emergency Committee for advising the Director-General on declaring a PHEIC, issuing temporary recommendations and raising pandemic phase levels is obvious, but the lack of legal authority for the Emergency Committee to provide advice on pandemic phase levels should be addressed, perhaps through a resolution of the World Health Assembly or a formal amendment to the regulations.

In terms of reducing potential violations of the IHR(2005)'s rules on trade and travel measures, amending the IHR(2005) to include an enforcement mechanism or penalties for violations would not be possible politically. The Director-General could, however, implement more strongly the requirement in the IHR(2005) mandating that States Parties provide the public health rationale and scientific evidence justifying trade and travel restrictions not conforming to WHO recommendations. Such action could include asking the Review Committee established under the IHR(2005) to provide its views on the justifications for trade and travel restrictions that do not conform to WHO recommendations. In addition, States Parties could make expedited use of the good offices of the Director-General for resolving disputes raised by restrictive trade and travel measures. Finally, WHO, OIE and the World Trade Organization could explore strategies to reduce trade reactions to PHEICs and other public health threats that are not supported by public health principles or scientific evidence, perhaps through formation of a co-operative mechanism to respond in real time to alleged violations of trade and health rules during international public health events.

Perhaps the most pressing need for new strategic action concerns the danger that many States Parties, especially developing and least-developed countries, will not be in compliance with their minimum core obligations on surveillance and response capacities by the deadlines established in the IHR(2005). Key to progress on these obligations is technical assistance and financial resources from developed countries, the availability of which would be linked to measurable improvements in the minimum core surveillance and response capacities mandated by the regulations. Creation and operation of assistance mechanisms could be supported and coordinated by WHO and powerful global health partners, such as the World Bank, the Group of 20 and philanthropic organizations (e.g. Gates and Rockefeller Foundations).

The 2009-H1N1 outbreak highlighted the potential the revolutionary change in international law the IHR(2005) represent, but it also revealed problems that require immediate attention. Stronger global health security will require strategic advances in the implementation of, and compliance with, the IHR(2005). Without such advances, the problems seen during the 2009-H1N1 outbreak may multiply exponentially if the world community faces a more dangerous influenza virus or some other virulent microbial surprise.

Acknowledgements

Dr Wilson is supported by a Canada Research Chair in public health policy. Dr Brownstein is supported by the National Library of Medicine, National Institutes of Health and by research funding from Google.org. Dr Brownstein is the co-creator of The HealthMap Project. Professor Fidler is the James Louis Calamaras Professor of Law and Director of the Center on American and Global Security at Indiana University.

Endnote

1 Statement by Under Secretary Tauscher on Biological Weapons, 9 December, 2009, at http://www.america.gov/st/texttrans-english/2009/December/20091210142708xjs nommis0.2277948.html.

References

Baker M. G., Fidler D. P. 2006. Global public health surveillance under new international health regulations. *Emerging Infectious Diseases* **12**: 1058–55.

Bell D. M. 2008. Of milk, health and trade security. *Far Eastern Economic Review* **171**: 34–7.

Calain P. 2007a. From the field side of the binoculars: a different view on global public health surveillance. *Health Policy and Planning* **22**: 13–20.

Calain P. 2007b. Exploring the international arena of global public health surveillance. *Health Policy and Planning* **22**: 2–12.

Calain P., Fidler D. P. 2007. XDR tuberculosis, the new International Health Regulations, and human rights. *Global Health Governance* **1** (1). Online at: http://ghgj.org/Calain%20and%20Fidler%20article.pdf, accessed 23 June 2010.

Ferguson N. M., Cummings D. A., Cauchemez S. *et al.* 2005. Strategies for containing an emerging influenza pandemic in Southeast Asia. *Nature* **437**: 209–14.

Fidler D. P. 2003. Emerging trends in international law concerning global infectious disease control. *Emerging Infectious Diseases* **9**: 285–90.

Fidler D. P. 2008. Influenza virus samples, international law, and global health diplomacy. *Emerging Infectious Diseases* **14**: 88–94.

Fidler D. 2009. H1N1 after action review: learning from the unexpected, the success and the fear. *Future Microbiology* **4**: 767–9.

Fidler D. P. 2010. International law and equitable access to vaccines and antivirals in the context of 2009-H1N1 influenza. In: Institute of Medicine. *The Domestic and International Impacts of the 2009-H1N1 Influenza A Pandemic: Global Challenges. Global Solutions.* Washington. DC: National Academies Press.

Garrett L., Fidler D. P. 2007. Sharing H5N1 viruses to stop a global influenza pandemic. *PLoS Medicine* **4**: e330.

Garske T., Legrand J., Donnelly C. A. *et al.* 2009. Assessing the severity of the novel influenza A/H1N1 pandemic. *British Medical Journal* **339**: b2840.

Gostin L. O. 2009. Influenza A(H1N1) and pandemic preparedness under the rule of international law. *Journal of the American Medical Association* **301**: 2376–8.

Katz R. 2009. Use of revised international health regulations during influenza A (H1N1) epidemic. *Emerging Infectious Diseases* **15**: 1165–70.

Lancet. 2004. Public-health preparedness requires more than surveillance. *Lancet* **364**: 1639–40.

Longini I. M., Jr., Nizam A., Xu S. *et al.* 2005. Containing pandemic influenza at the source. *Science* **309**: 1083–7.

US Department of Health and Human Services. 2009. *National Health Security Strategy of the United States of America.* December 2009.

von Tigerstrom B. 2005. The revised International Health Regulations and restraint of national health measures. *Health Law Journal* **13**: 35–76.

WHO. 2005. *Fifty-eighth World Health Assembly Resolution WHA58.3: Revision of the International Health Regulations.* Geneva: World Health Organization.

WHO Global Task Force on XDR-TB. 2006. Control of XDR-TB. Update on progress since the Global XDR-TB Task Force Meeting: 9–10 October 2006. Geneva.

Wilson K., Gardam M., McDougall C., Attaran A., Upshur R. 2007. WHO's response to global public health threats: XDR-TB. *PLoS Medicine* **4**: e246.

Part 9

BIOTERRORISM

48

PUBLIC HEALTH AND NATIONAL SECURITY IN THE GLOBAL AGE

Infectious diseases, bioterrorism, and *realpolitik*

*David P. Fidler**

Source: *George Washington International Law Review*, 35:4 (2003), 787–856.

Introduction: linking public health and national security

In the not too distant past, attempts to connect public health and national security would have raised eyebrows and perhaps condescending sympathy from experts in both areas. The discipline of public health focuses on "what we, as a society, do collectively to assure the conditions in which people can be healthy."[1] Although public health has long been an issue in international relations,[2] public health studies have had a strong domestic focus. For example, public health law texts "in the United States from the twentieth century . . . contain little or no discussion of international considerations."[3] Even when public health analysis ventures beyond the domestic to consider international aspects of population health, the issues examined, such as the cross-border transmission of infectious diseases,[4] do not typically involve the problems at the heart of national security studies, such as the military balance of power. By contrast, the study of national security traditionally has concentrated analysis on external threats, mainly of a military nature, to a country's interests, security, and survival.[5] Historically, analysts in this field have not studied public health problems as national security threats.

Arguments linking public health and national security have, however, become frequent in the past seven to eight years.[6] Increased concerns about the proliferation of biological weapons and the potential for bioterrorism have brought national security and public health closer together than has traditionally been the case. The perpetration of bioterrorism in the United States in October 2001 brought the public health-national security connection more prominence

393

and policy attention. This Article examines the linkage of public health and national security in order to understand the origins, nature, and future implications of this new development in the foreign policy arena.

Analyzing the public health-national security linkage is important for many reasons. This linkage connects, for example, public health with developments in the area of security studies[7] and debates about the nature and meaning of national security.[8] Different perspectives on what "security" means compete for attention, and the literature that brings public health and national security together forces those in public health to contemplate these different perspectives and how they relate to the public health mission of protecting population health. The linkage also challenges those studying national security to consider issues, such as the relationship of public health to a state's material capabilities, previously alien to national security debates. The different perspectives on the meaning of security further relate to larger theoretical concepts concerning the structure and dynamics of international relations. The linking of public health and national security thus raises deeper theoretical issues and controversies about world politics in the global era.

First, using the literature that posits and analyzes the public health-national security linkage, this Article examines the emergence of the concept of "public health security," which refers to the policy areas in which national security and public health concerns overlap (Part I). Delineating the overlap requires defining both "public health" and "national security," which proves difficult with both terms. Second, in connection with defining security, this Article examines four different conceptions of security—the *realpolitik*, common, human, and ecological security perspectives—and how these conceptions produce different visions of public health security (Part II). This analysis focuses on the two dominant themes in the literature on the public health-national security linkage: the threats posed by emerging and reemerging infectious diseases and biological weapons. Contrary to most of the literature on the public health-national security linkage, I argue that the *realpolitik* security perspective is relevant to thinking about how to conceptualize public health security.

Finally, this Article assesses how recent events involving the United States inform the scope and substantive concept of public health security, and what these developments tell us about the relationship between public health and theories of international relations (Part III). This Article argues that the evidence to date indicates that the *realpolitik* perspective on national security is driving the development of the concept of public health security in the United States. This part of the Article concludes by examining whether the conceptual and practical analyses of *realpolitik*-driven notions of public health security hold deeper implications for understanding public health in the age of the globalization of infectious diseases and point to the economic, military, and geopolitical interests of the great powers determining the direction of infectious disease diplomacy.

I. The public health-national security linkage develops

A. Public health as a national security concern?

Public health problems, especially infectious diseases, have been the focus of diplomatic activity among states since at least the mid-nineteenth century.[9] The prevention and control of infectious diseases has, therefore, been a *foreign policy* concern of states for a long time. Public health as a foreign policy concern is not the same thing, however, as public health constituting an issue of *national security*. Traditionally, for most states, national security is one of the most important, if not the most important, foreign policy concern.[10] Although public health has been the subject of diplomatic activity for over 150 years, other foreign policy concerns, such as the balance of military power and international trade, have been more important to statecraft than public health.[11] The novelty of the recent literature on infectious diseases as a national security issue rests in elevating public health from an obscure, neglected foreign policy area to the heights of the "high politics" of national security.

Analysis of national security historically paid no attention to public health.[12] Similarly, the public health discipline has been uninterested in whether its domain connects to discourse on national security. This mutual neglect holds true even for the most obvious threat linking national security and public health—biological weapons. Although biological weapons have been on the national security agenda of states since at least the prohibition of the use of biological weapons in 1925,[13] national security analysts and international relations specialists did not devote much attention to these weapons until the 1990s. National security analysis during the Cold War focused most of its energy on the relative strengths and weaknesses of American and Soviet nuclear[14] and conventional[15] weapons. The United States' unilateral renunciation of offensive biological weapons in the late 1960s[16] further pushed biological weapons into the shadows of national security analysis. From the public health perspective, concerns about Soviet biological weapons stimulated some public health preparedness efforts in the first decade after World War II,[17] but this activity faded from the public health agenda until the latter half of the 1990s when the role of public health in bioweapons policy emerged from obscurity.

B. The emergence of public health-national security linkage arguments

The first development that began to bring health and security together was the general broadening of security studies in the 1980s and first half of the 1990s through which analysts began to consider "nonmilitary security threats, such as environmental scarcity and degradation, the spread of disease, over population, mass refugee movements, nationalism, terrorism, and nuclear catastrophe."[18] Dennis Altman also noted this shift in observing that attempts to redefine security often added "issues of health generally, and epidemics of infectious diseases more specifically" to the list of new security threats.[19] In the latter half of the 1990s, governmental, intergovernmental, non-governmental, and academic statements, policies, and analyses began to flesh out the linkage between health and security. Much of this analysis appeared before the events on September 11th and anthrax attacks in the United States in 2001, so those historic events do not inform a great deal of the linkage literature. The development of the public health-national security linkage in the 1990s flows from four important causes: (1) the devastating scale of the HIV/AIDS pandemic in the developing world;[20] (2) the recognition of the global problem of emerging and reemerging infectious diseases;[21] (3) renewed concerns about the proliferation of biological weapons by states;[22] and (4) increased fears about the use of biological weapons by terrorists.[23]

From a governmental perspective, the best-known linkage arguments came from the Clinton administration, which claimed that emerging and re-emerging infectious diseases, especially HIV/AIDS, constituted a national security threat and foreign policy challenge for the United States.[24] The previous Democratic administration under Jimmy Carter sought to elevate the foreign policy importance of health in the late 1970s.[25] The Reagan administration ordered "federal agencies to develop a model that could predict the global spread of AIDS and its demographic effects,"[26] and Congress held hearings in the late 1980s on the threat HIV/AIDS posed to international development efforts in the developing world.[27]

The Clinton administration's arguments that infectious diseases should be a U.S. foreign policy concern were not novel. The linkage between infectious diseases and national security, however, sets the Clinton administration's policy initiative apart. The infectious disease-national security connection crystallized when the Central Intelligence Agency's National Intelligence Council issued a report in January 2000 entitled *The Global Infectious Disease Threat and Its Implications for the United States*, which presented infectious diseases as a national security threat to the United States.[28] The argument from the world's remaining superpower that pathogenic microbes represented a *national security threat* raised the profile of infectious diseases within the United States government and beyond. This development was without precedent in U.S. national security discourse.

Another event without precedent occurred in January 2000 when the United Nations (U.N.) Security Council focused on the HIV/AIDS crisis in sub-Saharan Africa.[29] Never before had the U.N. Security Council debated the security problems created by a microbial foe. The U.N. had been fighting HIV/AIDS from the original efforts of the World Health Organization's Global AIDS Programme, established in 1986 through the creation in 1996 of the multi-organizational UNAIDS.[30] The elevation of the HIV/AIDS catastrophe in sub-Saharan Africa to an issue of international peace and security at the

U.N. Security Council level, however, was a profoundly different kind of intergovernmental treatment of an infectious disease problem. The World Health Organization also began to frame its reinvigorated efforts on infectious diseases in terms of "global health security," consciously appropriating the concept of security to promote global infectious disease control.[31]

Calls for the United States and other leading states to see infectious diseases as a national security issue came from journalists and non-governmental organizations (NGOs). Journalist Laurie Garrett argued that the United States had to pay more attention to emerging infectious diseases as a matter of foreign policy and national security.[32] Think tanks engaged in the issue as well. The Chemical and Biological Arms Control Institute (CBACI) and the Center for Strategic and International Studies (CSIS) International Security Program issued a report in January 2000 that focused on health as a global security challenge.[33] CBACI followed up this initial report with a second publication in December 2001 entitled *Health, Security, and U.S. Global Leadership*.[34] The International Crisis Group—a NGO devoted to strengthening the capacity of the international community to prevent and contain conflict— issued a report in June 2001 called *HIV/AIDS as a Security Issue*.[35] The Council on Foreign Relations and the Milbank Memorial Fund produced a document in May 2001 calling for the United States to place more foreign policy attention on infectious diseases and international health cooperation, arguing that "[s]upporting public health worldwide will enhance U.S. national security."[36] In 2003, RAND supported and published as report entitled *The Global Threat of New and Reemerging Infectious Diseases: Reconciling U.S. National Security and Public Health Policy*.[37]

Academics also contributed to thinking about the linkage between public health and national security. Dennis Pirages argued, for example, that pathogenic microbes might constitute the greatest threat to security and stability in the post-Cold War world.[38] He observed that "[t]he greatest challenges to human well-being in the next century are more likely to come directly from nature than from the malignant designs of malevolent dictators."[39] Andrew Price-Smith developed empirical analysis indicating that infectious disease prevalence in a country negatively affects state capacity, suggesting that infectious diseases in many developing countries may contribute to poverty, state failure, and national and regional destabilization.[40] Price-Smith used his empirical evidence to argue that infectious diseases constitute both a direct and indirect threat to the security of nation-states in the global age.[41]

This overview of leading examples of the public health-national security linkage literature does not suggest that everyone participating in the discourse accepted that infectious diseases constituted a national security threat, or even that establishing the linkage was easy or persuasive. Despite the Clinton administration's claim that infectious diseases, especially HIV/AIDS in sub-Saharan Africa, represented a national security threat to the United States, the administration behaved in ways that indicated it did not practice what it preached. The most glaring discrepancy on this issue came in the hard line the Clinton administration took against developing countries, such as South Africa, that sought to increase access to antiretroviral therapies for HIV/ AIDS-ravaged populations.[42]

Reviewing the National Intelligence Council's report on *The Global Infectious Disease Threat and Its Implications for the United States* in *Foreign Affairs*, Philip Zelikow argued: "The analysis is fascinating, and the case for international humanitarian action is compelling. But why invoke the "national security" justification for intervention? The case for direct effects on U.S. security is thin."[43] Frustration also accompanied efforts to delineate the linkage. CBACI and the CSIS International Security Program engaged in an eighteen-month research project on the question of whether the "growing number of intersections between health and security issues create a national security challenge for the United States" only to conclude that "we still cannot provide a definitive answer."[44] The report on the proceedings of a June 2001 CBACI workshop on health and security also highlighted continuing uncertainty about linking national security and public health.[45]

The anthrax attacks in the United States in 2001 changed the landscape of the linkage discourse in ways still being felt. The threat of biological weapons proliferation and bioterrorism constituted part of the arguments that infectious diseases represented a national security threat to the United States and other countries in the pre-anthrax attack literature; but many in the national security and public health communities did not believe that states or terrorists[46] would use biological weapons against the United States or any other country. When bioterrorism visited the United States less than a month after the September 11th terrorist attacks, the national security threat of bioterrorism specifically and biological weapons generally became terrifyingly clear to every American as well as people in other countries.

C. The concept of "public health security"

The emergence of policy and academic literature analyzing the nexus between public health and national security suggests that a new concept of "public health security" has entered both the public health and national security communities—communities that have traditionally had little to do with each other. Public health security consists of the policy areas in which national security and public health concerns overlap (see Figure 1). The literature on the public health-national security linkage does not argue that the public health and national security worlds are synonymous but rather attempts to demonstrate that they intersect. The analytical challenge comes in defining the extent to which public health and national security overlap as policy endeavors and the importance of the overlap for policy purposes.

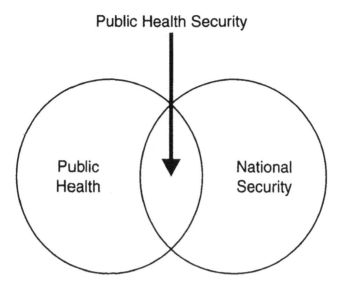

Figure 1 Public Health Security.

Is "public health security" a narrow concept, dealing only with the threat of biological weapons, or does it include challenges posed by emerging and reemerging infectious diseases generally? The public health-national security linkage literature attempts, for the most part, to construct a generous overlap that includes both biological weapons and infectious disease threats, which produces a broad conception of public health security. This broad conception contains a more diverse set of substantive issues (e.g., biological weapons *and* naturally occurring infectious diseases) than a narrow notion (e.g., biological weapons only).

Identifying the scope and substance of public health security depends, however, on how one defines "national security" and "public health." Although most people have a rough idea what national security means, the concept of public health causes confusion.[47] Public health is often mistaken for health care[48] or, more specifically, health care for the poor.[49] According to Lawrence Gostin, experts distinguish public health from health care in several respects:

> Public health focuses on: (1) the health and safety of populations rather than the health of individual patients; (2) prevention of injury and disease rather than treatment and care; (3) relationships between the government and the community rather than the physician and patient; and (4) population-based services grounded on the scientific methodologies of public health (e.g., biostatistics and epidemiology) rather than personal medical services.[50]

Thus, public health differs fundamentally from health care because of its focus on population health and the responsibility of the government in protecting populations from health threats.

Distinguishing public health from health care proves helpful in understanding what public health involves, but the concept remains difficult because most contemporary definitions of "public health" and "health" are broad. The definition of health in the Constitution of the World Health Organization (WHO) captures this expansive conception of public health: the WHO defines health to include not only the absence of disease but also the physical, mental, and social well-being of human beings.[51] Other experts have also stressed the expansive nature of public health, illustrated by the argument that "[s]ocial justice is the main pillar of public health."[52] Although many have criticized the expansive view of public health,[53] most public health literature acknowledges that public health today is a broad field encompassing infectious and non-communicable diseases, physical and mental health, prevention and treatment of diseases, and policy activities at the local, national, international, and global levels.[54]

The public health-national security linkage literature does not involve the entirety of contemporary public health concepts, so concerns about the expansive definition of public health do not prove debilitating in this context. The linkage literature focuses exclusively on infectious disease threats and does not mention the significant global health problems caused by non-communicable diseases, such as those connected with tobacco consumption.[55] Many areas of contemporary public health practice that involve significant and growing national and global morbidity and mortality are not within the emerging public health security concept.

The scope and substance of the concept of "national security" also raises controversies. National security and international relations experts have engaged in a debate for two decades (if not longer) on how they should define "national security" and "security."[56] Part II below explores this debate because the various concepts of security create different visions of public health security. The broad conception of public health security found in the public health-national security linkage literature incorporates, therefore, expanded notions of what should constitute security in the global age. To understand public health security as a concept, we need to delve into the different perspectives on the meaning of security in the context of international relations.

II. Concepts of security

One reason why some experts resist the public health-national security linkage is that it forces us to think hard about the meaning of "national security" in the context of the globalization of infectious disease. Like any prominent terms in policy and academic discourse, "national security" and "security" have been sources of definitional controversy. Understanding the debate

Table 1 Four concepts of security.

Security concept	Basic focus	Theoretical source	Security objective
Realpolitik	Power politics among states	Realism	Security for the state (national security)
Common security	The individual, democracy, and interdependence	Liberalism	Security among states for the benefit of individuals (international security)
Human security	Structural injustice and transnationalism	Critical theory/social constructivism	Security for individuals and communities through transnational civil society action (global security)
Ecological security	Biological/ environmental threats	Ecology/ Evolutionary theory	Sustainable equilibrium between the natural environment, pathogens, and human populations (epidemiological security)

about the security concept is important in evaluating public health security as an evolving area of foreign policy concern. In this Part, I present four different concepts of security and connect them with the discourse on the public health-national security linkage.[57] Table 1 summarizes the main elements of the four security concepts.

A. Four concepts of security

1. The realpolitik perspective—protecting national security

The traditional framework for analyzing security comes from the international relations theory called *realism*.[58] Realism holds that the anarchical nature of the international system means that states are the primary actors[59] and the states seek power in order to survive and be secure.[60] As a result, realism defines security as "national security"—the security of the state. Threats to national security are exogenous and come from rival states that likewise are seeking power and security in anarchy. Realists believe that international cooperation is little more than an exercise in expedience and that cooperative arrangements break down once the national interests of states change.[61] Self-help in the face of the dangerous world of international politics is the only reliable strategy for a state.[62] Under realism, the pursuit of national security involves power politics among states, creating the "security dilemma" that other states will perceive one state's effort to achieve national security as constituting a threat, necessitating their response, which the first state will view as a threat, and so on.[63] In this world view, states achieve national security by maintaining military power and other forms of material power (e.g., economic and technological prowess)[64] and preserving a balance of power among competing states.[65] The great powers maintain international or systemic security and order through maintenance of a balance of power.[66]

For realism, power manifests itself through material capabilities in many contexts—political, economic, and military. As Jeffrey Legro and Andrew Moravcsik argued, "[r]ealists have long insisted that control over material resources in world politics lies at the core of realism. . . . material resources constitute a fundamental 'reality' that exercises an exogenous influence on state behavior no matter what states seek, believe, or construct."[67] Under realism, the most important measure of power in the anarchy of international relations historically has been military power.[68] Under realist thinking, achieving national security requires the creation and maintenance of national power in the form of various kinds of material capabilities. Realism traditionally focused little or no attention on politics, economics, or culture within states[69]—except to the extent such internal matters connect to material capabilities the state needs to survive and be secure in the dangerous game of power politics.

2. The common security perspective—achieving international security

Although the *realpolitik* perspective on security has dominated security studies in the post-World War II period, critics have attacked it as being inadequate to explain security in an interdependent and globalized world.[70] Theorists can trace theoretical dissatisfaction with the *realpolitik* concept of national security to the origins of international relations theory. Immanuel Kant opposed, for example, balance of power politics and the focus on the state's security because these produced war and human misery rather than order and security.[71] After World War II, Edward Carr argued that the state had become an anachronism for providing security because the state could no longer, by itself, provide its citizenry with any kind of security, be it military, economic, or political.[72] Carr urged people to think of security without relying on the traditional *realpolitik* notions of power, sovereignty, and borders.[73] A different challenge to prevailing notions of national security appeared in the human rights movement after World War II. Drawing on the experience of Nazi Germany, post-war human rights advocates believed that how a government treated its citizens was an indicator of the likelihood that the government would become a menace not only to its own people but also international peace.[74] Human rights were, in other words, important for national security thinking.

Challenges to realism's conception of national security developed more systematically in the 1970s and the 1980s, when international relations specialists began to question the realist paradigm of security. Jessica Mathews argued that "[i]n the 1970s the concept [of national security] was expanded to include international economics as it became clear that the U.S. economy was no longer the independent force it had once been, but was powerfully affected by the economic policies in dozens of other countries."[75] In 1983 Richard Ullman noted that "[o]ver the past decade or so a vast array of public interest organizations have begun to put forward alternate conceptions of national security . . . devoted to particular issues—limiting population growth, enhancing environmental quality, eradicating world hunger, protecting human rights, and the like."[76] Ullman's analysis challenged the realist approach because he expanded security threats to include events that degraded the quality of life of a state's inhabitants or narrowed the policy choices of a government and non-state actors within a state.[77] Ullman included "decimating epidemics"[78] in the list of events that threaten the quality of life of a state's citizens, directly opening the security debate to public health concerns. In 1987 Caroline Thomas argued that security studies should consider internal security in terms of secure systems of food, health, money, and trade.[79] Thomas' argument also implicates public health by suggesting that health—typically an issue internal to a state of no interest to realists—should be a security concern under an expanded definition of that concept. In 1989 Mathews asserted that "[t]he 1990s will demand a redefinition of what constitutes national security" and advocated expanding the "definition of national security to include resource, environmental and demographic issues."[80]

The security debate expanded again after the Cold War. The full context of this debate in the late 1980s and 1990s is beyond the scope of this Article, but I focus on one perspective that gained stature during this period—the "common security" perspective. This perspective rejected the *realpolitik* emphasis on state power (especially military power) and argued that states face threats the realist framework does not address. Experts pushing the common security agenda frequently mentioned economic and environmental problems as threats to security[81]—threats that interdependence and globalization exacerbate. J. Ann Tickner argued, for example, that "[t]he multidimensionality of security defined in military, economic, and ecological terms, and the interdependence between them is at the heart of common security thinking."[82] As noted above, the efforts to broaden security studies to new challenges created space for public health in the discourse, even if experts did not occupy this space until the latter half of the 1990s. As Altman observed, "[i]n contemporary attempts to redefine security, it is now common to list a number of issues (for example, international terrorism, drug trafficking) to which issues of health generally, and epidemics of infectious diseases more specifically, are often added."[83]

The common security agenda recognized that states remain important actors but emphasized two issues that separated it from realism's perspective on security. First, as Ullman's emphasis on threats to the quality of life indicates,[84] the *security of the individual within the state* interested common security analysts. Tickner noted that most common security proponents stressed the security of the individual,[85] and this emphasis recalls the Kantian effort to refocus attention from the state to the individual as the central concern of foreign policy. Second, common security analysts rejected the "self-help" modus operandi of realism and underscored the importance of international cooperation among states.[86] Emphasis on cooperation was not idealistic but grounded in a realistic understanding of the nature of the threats faced.[87]

These observations suggest that liberalism[88] provides the theoretical foundation for the common security perspective. Liberalism argues that individuals and private groups, not states, are the primary actors in international relations.[89] Although liberalism accepts the importance of states and the reality of states interacting in a condition of anarchy, it does not agree with realism that structural anarchy determines state behavior. In contrast to realism, liberalism looks inside the state to explain behavior in international politics. Moravcsik argues that a core assumption of liberal theory is that states "represent some subset of domestic society, on the basis of whose interests state officials define state preferences and act purposively in world politics."[90] Unlike realism, liberalism "explains policy as a function of social context, and focuses on how domestic conflict, not international anarchy, imposes suboptimal outcomes."[91]

The policy and social preferences of individuals and private groups not only determine state preferences but, through transnational commerce, create a "pattern of interdependent state preferences [that] impose[ ] a binding constraint on state behavior."[92] For liberalism, the key variables in understanding how security, order, and peace can be achieved in anarchy are the form of governments through which individuals and private groups create preferences and how states create patterns of interdependent preferences in the economic realm. Liberalism posits that democratic governments[93] and liberalized trade and economic intercourse[94] provide the best foundations for security and order.

Like liberalism, the common security agenda redirects the focus of security studies from the state to the individual level while accepting the framework of the state and the inter-state system. The common security approach broadens the security agenda to include transnational phenomena that threaten the security of individuals and communities, including drug trafficking, environmental degradation, or disease epidemics. To achieve common security, the state must redefine its security to include the wider range of threats creating insecurity for individuals and cooperate with other states to mitigate such security problems. The common security idea stresses the interdependence of individual, national, and international security in the same fashion as liberalism.

From a public health viewpoint, the common security perspective opens space for discussing health as a security problem. As public health histories record, infectious diseases have had a devastating impact on the quality of life of individuals in most nations.[95] In fact, infectious disease morbidity and mortality far exceed war-related death and disability in human history.[96]

Given the nature of pathogenic microbes, states have to cooperate to mitigate the threat to individuals in their territories from infectious diseases. *National* security in infectious disease terms can only be achieved by states cooperating to create *international* security against microbial threats. The long history of international cooperation on infectious disease control then becomes relevant not only as a foreign policy but also a security issue. The common security perspective creates, thus, something akin to a collective public health security framework in which each state in the international system acknowledges that the public health security of one state is the concern of all and agrees to cooperate in a collective response to pathogenic threats.[97]

3. The human security perspective—constructing global security

The third competing concept is the "human security" perspective.[98] The United Nations Development Programme (UNDP) popularized the concept of "human security" in the first half of the 1990s.[99] According to the UNDP:

> The concept of security has for too long been interpreted narrowly: as security of territory from external aggression, or as protection of national interests in foreign policy or as global security from the threat of nuclear holocaust. . . . Forgotten were the legitimate concerns of ordinary people who sought security in their daily lives.[100]

The UNDP asserted that human security has two main elements: protection from (1) chronic threats, such as hunger, disease, and repression; and (2) sudden and harmful disruptions in the patterns of daily life.[101] Globalization adds to the need to think about security in human rather than state-centric terms: "In the globalizing world of shrinking time, shrinking space and disappearing borders, people are confronting new threats to human security— sudden and hurtful disruptions in the pattern of daily life."[102]

The human security perspective is more critical of the existing structure and dynamics of international relations than the common security perspective. Like common security, human security moves the focus away from the state toward the individual.[103] The common security agenda accepts the reality of the state and the inter-state system and seeks to use them constructively through international cooperation. The human security perspective expresses skepticism about the capacities of the state and the interstate system to provide people-centered security[104] and stresses the need for non-state actors and transnational social movements to engage in the quest for human security.[105] As Tickner observed in discussing critical perspectives on security, "many critics of realism claim that, if security is to start with the individual, its ties to state sovereignty must be severed."[106]

Further, she noted that such critics "claim that the creative energy for reformulating security in less exclusionary terms is coming from social movements which operate across national boundaries and which grow out of a concern for human security defined in economic and ecological as well as political/military terms."[107] With human security, we have traveled far from realism because the state is neither the focus nor the critical actor in the provision of security. The human security perspective contains a vision of security more critical and radical than the common security concept because human security relies on notions of transnational human solidarity that transcend the statist instruments (e.g., the state, international law, and international organizations) the common security outlook utilizes.

Theoretically, the human security perspective connects with post-Marxist critical international theory[108] and social constructivism.[109] Marx and Engels rejected the state and the instruments of inter-state relations (e.g., war, diplomacy, and international law) and condemned them as part of the superstructure of the capitalist exploitation of the working class.[110] The Marxist outlook on security was, thus, radically different from traditional state-centric approaches because it thought *transnationally* along socio-economic lines rather than *internationally* between states. Today, critical international theory shows a similar interest in exposing the injustice inherent in existing political structures, such as the interstate system, and identifying possible emancipatory levers to pull in order to reform radically human affairs.[111]

Social constructivism likewise posits that ideas rather than power shape anarchy. As Alexander Wendt argued, "constructivists argue that material resources [so critical to realism] only acquire meaning for human action through the structure of shared knowledge in which they are embedded."[112] Social constructivists would focus, thus, on the ideational move away from the narrow, realist concept of national security toward more expansive notions of security, such as human security, a shift that illustrates the power of ideas to shape how humans socially construct their relations globally. To borrow from Wendt's version of social constructivism, the move toward human security might represent a shift from a Hobbesian (i.e., foreigner as enemy) to a Kantian (i.e., foreigner as friend) culture of anarchy.[113] Jennifer Brower and Peter Chalk labeled the theoretical approach informing human security the "'globalist' school of thought . . . that asserts that an 'international society' has emerged that integrates communications, cultures, and economics in new ways and in a manner that transcends statecentric relations."[114]

The human security concept opens more space for public health than the common security perspective. The rejection of statist approaches and solutions to human security allows public health problems to be framed as transnational threats to communities and individuals that require transnational responses. Public health, thus, escapes its traditional association with the nation-state[115] and becomes a comprehensive idea that more accurately reflects the nature of health threats in the global era, especially infectious diseases. Not only is the concept of "public health" reconstructed, but this ideational revision allows the new public health perspective to re-evaluate traditional attitudes toward international relations. Foremost in this reevaluation is the empowerment of non-governmental actors in global politics as a strategy to avoid relying on statist models that reproduce structural injustice and violence. The growing interest in the involvement of non-state actors, such as multinational corporations and NGOs, in public health through "global health governance"[116] and "global public-private partnerships for health"[117] resonates with the human security perspective. In addition, Ilona Kickbusch's argument that social constructivism (rather than realism or liberalism) offers the best theoretical framework for global health analysis[118] suggests that the ideas alive in the human security concept relate to emerging themes in global health studies. Thus, the human security perspective aims not for the statist forms *national* or *international* security sought by realism and liberalism respectively but for *global* security focused on people-centered, people-led transnational human relations.

4. The ecological security perspective—maintaining epidemiological security

In his analysis of the globalization of infectious diseases at the end of the twentieth century, Pirages argued that the traditional perspectives on international relations—the realist, liberal, and critical schools of thought—"offer little policy guidance in dealing with issues of twenty-first century globalism."[119] Central to Pirages' disparagement of these theories was the biological threat to the human species posed by emerging and reemerging infectious diseases.[120] In place of traditional approaches to explaining international relations, Pirages offered what he called an "ecological approach":

> A predictive theory of international relations that can account for these biological threats to human security and deal with the causes and myriad human consequences of globalization, including emerging and resurgent infectious diseases, is best grounded in an ecological perspective. This approach stresses the evolutionary interactions among human populations, between them and the physical environment, and between them and pathogenic microorganisms.[121]

According to Sarah Glasgow and Pirages, "ecological security" for any human population depends on maintaining evolutionary equilibrium in four relationships that produce four security modes: (1) between human populations and the sustaining physical environment—environmental security; (2) between human populations and those of other species—species security; (3) among human populations sharing the same ecosystems—military security; and (4) between human populations and pathogenic microorganisms—microsecurity.[122] As a perspective on security, ecological security is broader than even human security because it looks not only at human populations on a global scale, but also the macro and micro natural environments in which human populations live. The security at issue in this perspective is the security of neither states nor individuals but the natural environment that sustains human life. Thus, this approach to security differs from the argument that environmental changes threaten national security by replacing a state-centric, anthropocentric focus with one that concentrates on the ecological/environmental context in which human life transpires.

Ecological security is also broader than human security because its scope incorporates the insecurity of non-human living species and non-living natural resources on a global scale. The theoretical sources for ecological security come from the study of ecology and evolution, producing what Pirages called "an eco-evolutionary point of view that can yield rich insights into the sociopolitical consequences of human interactions with nature and pathogenic microorganisms."[123] In terms of infectious disease threats, ecological security promotes more effective "international management of the epidemiological consequences of globalization,"[124] in essence the pursuit of *epidemiological security*.

Pirages' ecological approach echoes writers who focus not on the security dilemma among states but on "a more wide-ranging 'planetary security dilemma'" that constitutes a crisis originating not in "a *competitive game between states* but rather one that has its source in a *cooperative game against nature.*"[125] It also resonates with those who have argued that traditional concepts of security need to include environmental issues. In a sense, the ecological approach removes the concept of "security" from the structure and dynamics of the anarchical international system and forces people to confront the common nemesis of nature's looming revenge on anthropomorphic abuse of the planet's environment.

B. The four perspectives and the concept of public health security

As noted previously, two themes in the literature on the public health-national security linkage are (1) the threat posed by emerging and re-emerging infectious diseases, and (2) the threat posed by biological weapons through state proliferation and bioterrorism. In this Section, I slot these two threats into the four perspectives on security described in Part II.A. The literature on the security threat posed by infectious diseases does not, for the most part, engage in this type of theoretical analysis. Most of the literature attempts to reach policy-making audiences in the United States, who tend to be more pragmatic and less theoretical, as illustrated by the titles and sub-titles of some of the reports (e.g., *America's Vital Interest in Global Health; The Global Infectious Disease Threat and Its Implications for the United States; Why Health is Important to U.S. Foreign Policy, Health, Security, and U.S. Global Leadership; Reconciling U.S. National Security and Public Health Policy*). One of the reports, *HIV/AIDS as a Security Issue*, almost defies theoretical categorization as it argues that HIV/AIDS represents a personal, economic, communal, national security, and international security threat.[126]

When theoretical matters arise, as they do in some analysis, the arguments note the inadequacy of realism to assist formulating responses to globalized pathogenic threats. As illustrated by Ullman's redefinition of security,[127] academic work often replaces realism's national security perspective with something broader. Pirages dismissed realism as "possibly useful in explaining the machinations of nineteenth-century European autocrats or the behavior patterns of contemporary despots in less industrialized countries" but "of little use in predicting and explaining changes in the contemporary world."[128] Price-Smith argued that "Realist policy prescriptions (which emphasize self-help strategies) will not protect states from the negative consequences of disease resurgence" and that "Liberal theory . . . is likely to provide a better theoretical foundation than Realism for tackling problems posed by the resurgence of infectious disease and other global issues."[129] Brower and Chalk explicitly rejected traditional concepts of security to apply the human security idea to infectious disease threats.[130]

In keeping with the more policy-oriented public health-national security linkage literature, Price-Smith's work points analysis in the direction of the common security perspective with its emphasis on the interdependence of individual, national, and international security.[131] The same emphasis appears in CBACI's observation that the objective is "to enhance the security of individuals, communities, nations, and the international community."[132] Pirages, on the other hand, dismisses liberalism as "not particularly useful in building relevant theory or offering policy guidance for dealing with the mounting biological and ecological challenges to the existing global order."[133]

1. Realpolitik, biological weapons, and infectious diseases

A. BIOLOGICAL WEAPONS

The threat posed by biological weapons fits within the *realpolitik* perspective on national security because such weapons correlate with its emphasis on exogenous military threats to a state's physical and material security. Realism has little trouble accommodating the scenario in which one state uses or threatens to use a biological weapon against another state. Nor does realism have much difficulty accounting for the proliferation of biological weapons in the international system; such proliferation represents the convergence of the security dilemma with advancing biotechnological capabilities on the part of states.

The development of international law regarding biological weapons reflects the realist perspective. States banned the use of biological weapons in the Geneva Protocol of 1925; but the states limited the Protocol's prohibition in two respects: (1) it only applied between states parties to the Protocol,[134] and (2) many states reserved the right to retaliate in kind in response to a first-use of biological weapons by another state party.[135] The Geneva Protocol, in essence, only prohibited the first-use of biological weapons and enforced this prohibition by the threat of retaliation in kind, or biological deterrence. Further, the United States' unilateral renunciation of biological weapons made the prohibition on the development of biological weapons negotiated in the Biological and Toxin Weapons Convention of 1972 possible.[136] This renunciation followed a review by the United States that concluded that biological weapons had little utility as military weapons,[137] and thus—in the realist framework—were expendable because they added little if anything to U.S. material power in international politics. Realism even accounts for the biological weapons proliferation by states that has occurred since states adopted the Biological and Toxin Weapons Convention, as a result of realism's view of the weakness of international law in the face of the competing interests of states.

In addition, realist analysis accommodates arguments that biological weapons may be more attractive to weaker states that confront the overwhelming conventional military superiority of the United States.[138] Experts argued that "it is entirely conceivable that a state threatened militarily by a superior conventional power such as the United States will attempt to deter war, or deter specific military actions, through the threat or use of NBC [nuclear, biological, and chemical] weapons against U.S. or allied civilian or military targets."[139] This "asymmetrical" security dilemma increases the importance of biological weapons and their proliferation in realist thinking.

More difficult from the *realpolitik* perspective is the specter of bioterrorism. Realism's traditional focus has been on states and their interactions in a condition of anarchy, and realism typically downplays the importance of non-state actors, such as multinational corporations and NGOs. Terrorists are non-state actors. The growth of terrorism as a phenomenon in international relations has presented realism with a dilemma because terrorism's increased prominence suggests that (1) states do not have a monopoly on violence in international politics, and (2) the anarchical structure of the international system is not the only source of conflict and violence.

In connection with state-sponsored terrorism, realism's dilemma is attenuated because state sponsorship of unconventional violence fits within the general framework of realist analysis—terrorists are merely instruments of power and violence among competing states. The policy response has been to confront, sometimes with military force, the state sponsors of terrorism.[140] The so-called "new terrorists" who are not necessarily state-sponsored pose a more difficult problem for realism. As Richard Falkenath, Robert Newman, and Bradley Thayer argued:

> [T]here is a growing body of evidence that non-state actors are becoming more interested in causing human casualties on a massive scale. This is a relatively new development, and is poorly understood.

The classic conceptual model of a terrorist organization—that of an established group with limited political aims, a strategy of controlled violence for achieving them, and an interest in self-preservation—appears to be breaking down. New groups are emerging with hazier objectives, shorter life spans, and a more direct interest in violence for its own sake, often for reasons rooted in religious fundamentalism or political radicalism. . . . In short, the nature of terrorism is changing in a way that suggests there will be an expanding range of groups that are both capable of using weapons of mass destruction and interested in inflicting casualties at levels well beyond the terrorist norms of the previous decades.[141]

Until September 11th, "new terrorism" remained manageable for realism because its violence remained isolated and on a small scale (for example, the chemical terrorism of Aum Shinriyko in Japan),[142] not disturbing the machinations of states in the anarchical international system.

One potential feature of the "new terrorism"—bioterrorism—contains, however, the potential to disrupt a state's power and material capabilities *vis-à-vis* other states. Bioweapons pose threats to military assets at home and abroad and thus the ability of a country to use such assets to protect its overseas interests and territorial security. Likewise, the dangers bioweapons pose for disrupting the domestic governance and economic infrastructure that supports military power surpass the dangers created by conventional terrorist weapons. Bioweapons are both weapons of mass disruption as well as weapons of mass destruction. Therefore, domestic military and civilian prevention of and preparedness for bioterrorism becomes important to *realpolitik* thinking about national security.[143]

B. INFECTIOUS DISEASES

The more general threat from infectious diseases proves harder to connect with the *realpolitik* perspective on national security. The literature on the public health-national security linkage posits two kinds of threats from naturally occurring infectious diseases: direct and indirect. The direct threat comes from pathogenic microbes "invading" a state through global travel and trade, undermining military, economic, and political capabilities and thus the state's foundations of power. The indirect threat manifests itself when infectious diseases contribute to "state failure" in other regions of the world, causing military, political, and economic instability that adversely affects the strategic interests of other states. HIV/AIDS in sub-Saharan Africa is an example experts frequently employ in the public health-national security linkage literature to argue that infectious disease problems in other countries represent an indirect national security threat to the United States.[144]

From the *realpolitik* perspective, the "direct threat" argument is hard to maintain in connection with the national security of the great powers, which are the primary focus of realism. HIV/AIDS "invaded" the United States and European nations during the 1980s and caused epidemics. Infectious disease morbidity and mortality, and the economic costs associated with dealing with the consequences, have climbed in the United States[145] and other nations[146] over the past twenty years. The increasing problems associated with microbial invaders specifically and infectious diseases generally did not, however, undermine or challenge the great power status of the United States and countries in Western Europe. Analysts of international politics generally recognized that the United States and Europe grew in absolute and relative power *during* the first two decades of the HIV/AIDS pandemic and the time period associated with emerging and re-emerging infectious diseases.[147] For the United States as a great power, the microbial incursion of HIV/AIDS and other pathogens has not affected its ability to defend the nation against external attack or project its power in other regions of the world. As Price-Smith concluded, "the globalization of disease is not a direct threat to the security of industrialized nations at the present time."[148]

The "direct threat" thesis holds true, however, for realist analysis applied to many developing countries. The military, economic, and governance devastation being wrought by HIV/AIDS in sub-Saharan Africa demonstrates that infectious diseases can directly undermine material sources of a state's power, particularly its economic capabilities. Robert Ostergard argued, for example, that "African countries differ from most of the rest of the world in that the HIV/AIDS pandemic has reached a level of concern to them that would warrant perceiving the virus as a *direct* security threat."[149] Similarly, Price-Smith has analyzed how HIV/AIDS constitutes a direct and indirect national security threat to South Africa.[150]

The *realpolitik* perspective is not, thus, theoretically resistant to incorporating infectious disease threats, whether endogenously or exogenously driven, to a state's material capabilities and power. The infectious disease/state power dynamic has not received much realist attention because it has not, and does not presently, adversely affect the great powers, upon which most realist analysis focuses. Analysts are, however, beginning to employ traditional realist approaches to HIV/AIDS, as illustrated by Nicholas Eberstadt's argument that "[d]riven by the spread of the disease in the region's three largest countries—China, India, and Russia—the coming Eurasian pandemic threatens to derail the economic prospects of billions and alter the global military balance of power."[151]

The *realpolitik* perspective can incorporate public health as an element of material state power, much in the same way it does military, economic, demographic, and technological contributions to a state's national security. Realism has no theoretical trouble accepting Price-Smith's argument that "it must be understood that any agent that directly threatens to destroy a significant proportion of a state's population constitutes a direct threat to that state's national security."[152] Thus, realist analysis of the South African government's failure to confront South Africa's HIV/AIDS crisis[153] would condemn President

Mbeki and his advisors for undermining South Africa's military, economic, demographic, and political power in international politics.

The South African example indicates that direct threats from infectious diseases are not beyond the *realpolitik* perspective on national security as is generally claimed in the public health-national security linkage literature. This position holds true even for great powers such as the United States because it is not inconceivable that pathogenic microbes could cause extensive damage to American power in a manner similar to what South Africa currently suffers. Capabilities to handle infectious diseases—public health capacity— represent a material capability of a state and fall within the narrow national security perspective of *realpolitik*.

Perhaps only highly transmissible and virulent infectious diseases could cause significant damage to U.S. material capabilities and power, which limits realism's interest in public health capabilities to "strategic diseases"— those which have the potential to inflict serious harm on U.S. military, economic, demographic, and political capabilities.[154] At present, the list of strategic diseases under a realist national security perspective is short, perhaps containing only two infectious diseases—smallpox used as a biological weapon[155] and pandemic influenza as a naturally occurring threat.[156] Pathogens genetically engineered to be more transmissible, virulent, or resistant to existing vaccines and drugs[157] would also come within realism's concept of public health security.

As Kenneth Waltz argued, "[a] key proposition derived from realist theory is that international politics reflects the distribution of national capabilities, a proposition daily borne out."[158] HIV/AIDS invaded both the United States and South Africa with divergent effects on the material sources of national power because of, among other things, differences in national public health capacity. The presence of public health capacity mitigates the impact of infectious diseases on sources of U.S. power, while the absence of such capacity in South Africa contributes to the devastation HIV/AIDS inflicts on the South African military, economy, population, and governing elite.

Further, the United States and European countries applied their national economic and technological capabilities to develop antiretroviral drugs and, through their use, transform an incurable, fatal disease into a medical condition that can, in many circumstances, be handled as a chronic condition.[159] The great powers engaged in self-help to produce this transition in HIV/AIDS, and the progress they have made against HIV/AIDS has not been dependent on international cooperation or international institutions, such as WHO or UNAIDS. By contrast, South Africa lacks the material capabilities to handle its HIV/AIDS epidemic through self-help. The U.S. and South African experiences with HIV/AIDS reflect the distribution of national public health and other material capabilities, which realists can analyze.

My argument differs from Price-Smith's observation that "infectious disease constitutes a real threat to the national security of all states, but particularly those that are most vulnerable to the ravages of disease—that is, states with low endogenous capacity"[160] because Price-Smith rejects realism and uses a national security concept broader than *realpolitik*.[161] Similarly, my analysis challenges other writers, such as Brower and Chalk, who reject traditional concepts of security in order to adopt more expansive notions of security.[162] My thesis contends that realism is relevant for thinking about the direct threats infectious diseases pose to states in the global era.

Much of the literature on the public health-national security linkage works hard to make the case that infectious disease-related damage in developing countries threatens the national security of the United States and other developed countries. The persuasiveness of this "indirect threat" thesis is, however, questionable from the *realpolitik* perspective on national security. Whether HIV/AIDS cripples Botswana or contributes to instability in southern Africa does not address the main concern of the realist—does the weakening of individual African countries or regional instability in sub-Saharan Africa threaten U.S. military or strategic interests (for example, access to critical resources or essential markets)? The answer to these questions would be in the negative because sub-Saharan Africa is not currently either strategically or economically vital to the great powers. In this regard, Eberstadt provides a classic *realpolitik* analysis of HIV/AIDS in sub-Saharan Africa:

> Africa's AIDS catastrophe is a humanitarian disaster of world historic proportions, yet the economic and political reverberations from this crisis have been remarkably muted outside the continent itself. The explanation for this awful dissonance lies in the region's marginal status in global economics and politics. By many measures, for example, sub-Saharan Africa's contribution to the world economy is less than Switzerland's. In military affairs, no regional state, save perhaps South Africa, has the capacity to conduct overseas combat operations, and indeed sub-Saharan African governments are primarily preoccupied with local troubles. The states of the region are thus not well positioned to influence events much beyond their own borders under any circumstances, good or ill—and the cruel consequence is that the world pays them little attention.[163]

Ostergard similarly argued:

> The end of the global ideological tug-of-war between the USA and former Soviet Union marginalised Africa in US foreign policy and in the international community and consequently marginalized Africa's social problems, not least of which was the growing HIV/AIDS epidemic. The spread of HIV/AIDS in Africa was not a *direct* security threat to the West in any sense of the word.[164]

414

The Group of Eight (G-8) countries' response at their 2002 summit in Canada to pleas for help and partnership from African leaders illustrates the ambivalence of the hegemons toward Africa's plight with HIV/AIDS. While the G-8 countries pledged $20 billion for reducing the threat to their security of weapons and materials of mass destruction,[165] they offered no new money for the fight against HIV/AIDS in sub-Saharan Africa.[166] This result is consistent with a realist perspective on national security: the threat from weapons of mass destruction, including biological weapons, constitutes a graver concern for the great powers than HIV/AIDS in Africa.[167] Even though September 11th may have taught the lesson that "failed states are a national security problem,"[168] realists would see a myriad of "internal" factors that contribute to "state failure" in sub-Saharan Africa, which limits the credibility of elevating infectious disease over other causal factors, such as poverty, civil war, or ethnic hatred.

Perhaps sensing the difficulty of the "hard case" of the indirect threat thesis, the public health-national security linkage literature often turns its attention to the indirect threat to U.S. military and strategic interests posed by infectious disease problems in countries experts perceive are strategically important to U.S. national security interests—Russia, India, and China. Citing Russia, India, and China, CBACI argued, for example, that "[d]eclining health trends *in countries of strategic importance* where conflict and instability could have profound consequences for regional and global security are particularly disturbing."[169] Again, this emphasis on infectious disease problems in strategically important countries illustrates that realism is not theoretically resistant to incorporating public health considerations into power-political calculations at the heart of the *realpolitik* perspective on national security, even in the context of indirect infectious disease threats.

These observations converge to produce a *realpolitik* policy stance on the threat of infectious diseases generally. Public health is important to preserving material sources of military and economic power at home and to projecting both kinds of power abroad, and public health cooperation with strategically important countries may be necessary to prevent instability that may threaten a country's national security and foreign policy objectives. Problems and instability caused by infectious diseases in countries or regions marginal to great power interests do not register significantly in *realpolitik*'s linkage of public health and national security.

2. Common security, biological weapons, and infectious diseases

A. BIOLOGICAL WEAPONS

Because the common security perspective does not deny that traditional military attacks on the physical integrity of a state can occur, it can accommodate the threat of state use of biological weapons. The common security perspective differs from *realpolitik*'s power-oriented approach by stressing the importance of creating and strengthening international cooperative norms and regimes to deter the development and proliferation of bioweapons by states, such as the Biological and Toxin Weapons Convention. Such international cooperation becomes critical when factoring in biotechnology's inherent "dual use" nature, growing global diffusion and rapid development of genetic engineering technologies. Such advances in biotechnology increase the threat of bioweapon proliferation and heighten the need for sustainable international cooperation on biological weapons.

The non-state actor wrinkle posed by bioterrorism that causes realism some difficulty is more easily incorporated into the common security perspective because it recognizes non-traditional threats to national security, whether those threats come from terrorism or environmental degradation. The common security perspective would focus on both domestic public health preparedness (because protecting the quality of life of the citizenry from threats is an objective of common security) and international cooperation on preventing and preparing for bioterrorism (because self-help against bioterrorism would prove futile in a globalized world).

B. INFECTIOUS DISEASES

The common security perspective also distinguishes itself from *realpolitik* in how it relates to the direct and indirect threats posed by infectious diseases generally. The common security perspective—with its shift of focus from state power to individual quality of life—is more sensitive to the threats pathogenic invaders pose to the populations of nation-states, both developed and developing. In connection with HIV/AIDS, Soloman Benetar sounded this theme in arguing that South Africa had to engage in a "shift in expenditure from security against war towards expenditure that could reduce threats from social disintegration, if we are to move towards safer and more secure societies."[170] Nor can the common security perspective cabin its concern for countries devastated by infectious diseases to those that are "strategic" because such a perspective relates to rejected balance-of-power thinking.

Because liberal theory informs the common security perspective, economic development internally and economic interdependence between peoples (not between governments) are important strategic objectives. As public health studies show, rising infectious disease morbidity and mortality create increasing economic costs to domestic economies,[171] and these costs represent not only lost economic opportunities but also indicators of a declining quality of life. The belief in economic interdependence among peoples is not based on charity but on the mutual economic need societies have for each other. In other words, economic interdependence contains, purposefully, selfish as well as altruistic motivations. The emphasis on economic interdependence means that liberalism as a theory of international relations encourages global trade and travel, which constitute important vectors in spreading microbial pathogens around the planet.[172] Therefore, the common security perspective contains a tension between promoting economic interdependence among nations and shielding populations from infectious disease threats.

The trade-public health nexus becomes, thus, central to the common security perspective.[173] The public health-national security literature stresses one aspect of this nexus—the economic opportunities the United States loses because of the economic impact of infectious diseases in the developing world. Jordon Kassalow argued, for example, that the "[l]ack of attention to the burden of disease in these [developing] countries, which receive 42 percent of U.S. exports, may depress demand for those goods and services and thus threaten the jobs of Americans."[174] Another aspect of the trade-public health linkage—the importation of infectious diseases through trade and travel—also appears frequently in the public health-national security linkage literature.[175] A final aspect involves the extent to which international regimes liberalizing trade recognize the need for countries to restrict trade for public health purposes.[176]

Infectious diseases also provide the common security perspective with an "amplifier" for its broader approach to security. As literature on emerging and reemerging infectious diseases notes, many factors contribute to disease emergence, reemergence, and spread—from poverty to environmental degradation.[177] Infectious diseases provide an excellent focus for the common security perspective because it brings other non-traditional threats into view, which connect to the broad concept of "public health." Notions of "environmental security" can, thus, easily overlap with the concept of public health security because of the close relationship between environmental conditions and the protection of population health.[178]

In addition, infectious diseases fit the common security framework well because, as public health experts often opine, the global challenge of infectious diseases can only be addressed through expanded and deepened international cooperation.[179] The common security perspective's emphasis on international cooperation among states and non-state actors helps distinguish it from the skepticism of such cooperation found in realism.

3. *Human security, biological weapons, and infectious diseases*

A. BIOLOGICAL WEAPONS

Locating the threats from biological weapons within the human security perspective proves more difficult than one at first might believe.[180] The human security perspective seeks to move security analysis away from the kind of narrow, statist thinking realism adopts, but this move creates difficulties for dealing with the development and deployment of biological weapons by states. State-based threats do not disappear even if the human security perspective wishes to move beyond state-centric analysis of security. The proper policy response for human security thinking presumably would be to see non-state actors, especially transnational civil society movements, as critical to curtailing the development and deployment of biological weapons by states.[181]

417

The human security perspective's attachment to the normative role of non-state actors does not include bioterrorists, whose malevolent use of microbes not only strikes at state institutions and power but also threatens the health and well-being of communities and individuals. The human security perspective would perhaps be more sensitive than *realpolitik* and common security approaches to the "root causes" of terrorism and terrorist interest in biological weapons. In other words, states cannot secure human security until the states mitigate the underlying social injustices that feed terrorism. Again, the main actors in such mitigation efforts are not states and international organizations but civil society groups operating transnationally.

B. INFECTIOUS DISEASES

In terms of direct and indirect threats from infectious diseases generally, the human security perspective's focus on the transnational unity of peoples make it receptive to arguments that greater global solidarity is needed to confront the problems pathogenic microbes pose. This perspective would sharpen analytical focus on transnational problems that exacerbate infectious disease spread, such as poverty, racism, gender oppression, inequitable access to health technologies and services, and ecosystem destruction.[182]

While the human security perspective would find rich veins of transnational injustice to mine, its normative public health edge is more difficult to pin down. Classically, experts view public health as a "public good," which private actors have neither adequate incentives nor resources to produce. The responsibility for public health falls, then, to the state.[183] The human security perspective is, however, determined not to be state-centric analytically or normatively. Globally, the human security perspective posits that non-state actors and transnational movements will play a leading role in improving human welfare rather than state institutions. The increasing attention being paid to the role of non-state actors in "public-private partnerships"[184] producing "global public goods for health"[185] and "global health governance"[186] may provide evidence of the human security perspective's insights on the public health-security linkage that cannot be dismissed out of hand.

More generally, experts have expressed concern that the expansive scope of human security itself threatens to scuttle its relevance for discussing security threats. Ostergard argued that raising issues such as disease, crime, drugs, and pollution "to the level of a security problem is almost meaningless" because "[c]hanging their status from problems of good governance to a security threat diminishes their distinct importance."[187] Ostergard asserts that "[i]f all human maladies are a security threat (as the UNDP seems to propose), then the potential for complacency or apathy becomes the real threat."[188] The expansive scope of human security creates a problem of prioritization—in the vast universe of "new security threats," what should be addressed first? Price-Smith argued that "the threats to the health of populations from infectious diseases (such as HIV/AIDS) are far more immediately destructive than are migration and resource scarcities, and thus states should accord a position of prominence among the new security threats of the twenty-first century."[189] Placing infectious diseases higher on the list of new security threats runs, however, headlong into the daunting list of political, economic, social, and epidemiological causes behind the emergence and re-emergence of pathogenic threats. What causes on this foreboding list are to be given priority?

As noted earlier, realism can incorporate the destructiveness of infectious diseases in its theoretical perspective on security, but it is less clear whether the underlying theories informing the human security perspective—critical international theory and social constructivism—provide reasons why public health deserves greater attention than other problems affecting human security. As I have argued elsewhere, neither of these theories proves very helpful in developing normative blueprints that would assist infectious disease control specifically or global health advocacy generally.[190]

4. *Ecological security, biological weapons, and infectious diseases*

The ecological security perspective would see biological weapons, whether in the form of state or terrorist deployment or use, as part of the biological and ecological perils that face the human race and the global ecosystem that supports it. Ecological security's concern with biological weapons would be greatest in connection with highly contagious pathogens, such as smallpox, or genetically-engineered pathogens that might, upon release, not only kill humans in large numbers but throw ecological and evolutionary processes into disequilibrium, triggering other eco-evolutionary threats to humankind and the natural world. The introduction of smallpox into a world with increasingly large and vulnerable human immune-compromised populations (e.g., those living with HIV/AIDS) would be an eco-evolutionary nightmare of the first order.

Although ecological security views biological weapons as a potential threat, its approach to security would focus more attention on the problems caused by pathogenic microbes generally. Compared to the morbidity and mortality created by infectious diseases (e.g., HIV/AIDS, tuberculosis, and malaria), actual or foreseeable deaths and illness from biological weapons remain small.[191] Further, the eco-evolutionary complexity of emerging and re-emerging infectious diseases make this pathogenic challenge much more a source of global epidemiological insecurity than biological weapons. Part of this eco-evolutionary complexity involves the interaction of human technology (e.g., antimicrobial drugs) with the evolutionary capabilities of the microbial world. Drug resistance in the pathogens that cause AIDS, tuberculosis, malaria, and other infectious diseases represents global epidemiological insecurity that needs urgent attention.[192] These observations make clear that ecological security reverses the public health security priorities of realism by making the general infectious disease threat primary and the biological weapons threat secondary.

5. Differing concepts of public health security

As the previous paragraphs demonstrate, the four visions of security—*realpolitik*, common security, human security, and ecological security—translate into different concepts of public health security. The *realpolitik* perspective on public health security is narrowest, followed in breadth by the common and human security perspectives, with ecological security being the broadest vision. One lesson learned from slotting the public health-national security linkage literature into the four concepts of security is that theorists cannot dismiss realism from discourse concerning public health security as such literature has generally done.

As noted above, much of the public health-national security linkage literature attempts to move U.S. national security thinking away from *realpolitik* to something closer to the common security perspective. As Pirage's and Price-Smith's dismissals of realism illustrate, most experts leave realism behind in discussing how to deal with threats from infectious diseases and biological weapons.[193] Realism's ability to incorporate public health concerns as part of its power-oriented outlook is, however, more robust than its dismissal suggests. In Part III below, when attention turns from theory to practice, the relevance of realism comes more into focus because *realpolitik* is determining the scope and substance of the concept of public health security in the most important country in this debate, the United States.

III. The emerging scope and substance of public health security in the United States

Having laid out four concepts of security and translated these into different visions of "public health security," this Article endeavors to discern from recent events the emerging scope and substance of public health security as this concept relates to the United States. Admittedly, this enquiry is American-centric, but the public health-national security linkage literature concentrates, for the most part, on the United States;[194] thus, my focus parallels the literature informing this Article. In addition, the United States has taken a lead role in shaping the concept of public health security because it has been the victim of bioterrorism. Finally, as the world's leading economic and military power, trends and developments in the United States have global importance, and this fact holds true in connection with the development of the public health security concept as well.

A. The threat from biological weapons

The threat from biological weapons dominates the emerging concept of public health security in the United States. As indicated before, pre-September

420

11th and pre-anthrax literature on the public health-national security linkage included the biological weapons threat; but the terrorist attacks against New York and Washington, D.C. and the subsequent bioterrorism profoundly changed the political landscape of the public health-national security debate. Terrorists directly attacked the United States with unconventional weapons—hijacked passengers planes and anthrax-laced letters. Not since World War II had a group attacked the territory of the United States with such death and destruction as occurred on September 11th. Never before had the United States experienced biological terror within its borders of the sophisticated, widespread kind fomented by the anthrax attacks.[195] These ominous events shattered American complacency about national security in the post-Cold War era.

The resulting domestic and foreign policy responses in connection with biological weapons connect to the *realpolitik* perspective on national security in a number of ways. In terms of foreign policy, the threat from biological weapons to the national security of the United States has become central to U.S. post-September 11th strategic thinking. The strategic importance of the biological weapons threat became clear in President Bush's January 2002 State of the Union Address, when he named the "axis of evil" as the main threat to U.S. national security in the forthcoming years.[196] This "Bush Doctrine" also featured in the national security strategy released by the Bush administration in September 2002, which stated "[w]e must be prepared to stop rogue states and their terrorist clients before they are able to threaten or use weapons of mass destruction against the United States and our allies and friends."[197] The Bush administration's *National Strategy to Combat Weapons of Mass Destruction*, released in December 2002, also argued that weapons of mass destruction "in the possession of hostile states and terrorists represent one of the greatest security challenges facing the United States."[198] Substantively, the Bush Doctrine holds that oppressive states that seek to develop weapons of mass destruction, including biological weapons, and that support terrorism constitute threats to U.S. national security.[199] The Bush Doctrine draws together national security concerns about "rogue states," state-sponsored terrorism, and the growing state and terrorist interest in weapons of mass destruction. Echoing the *realpolitik* perspective on national security, the Bush Doctrine views national security threats as exogenous, connected to state behavior, and aimed at the physical territory and foreign strategic assets of the United States and its allies.[200]

The manner in which the United States has implemented the Bush Doctrine also reflects realism. As the world's military hegemon, the United States dominates the "war on terrorism" in Afghanistan and elsewhere. One of the earliest casualties of this war was the Taliban government of Afghanistan. The United States and its allies destroyed an existing government that harbored terrorists responsible for attacking the United States. In March and April 2003, the United States waged war against Iraq to destroy its capabilities to develop weapons of mass destruction. Even when military action is not likely against members of the "axis of evil," as appears to be the case with North Korea, the United States is not shying away from confrontation with states that fit the characteristics laid out in the Bush Doctrine.

A key development in this regard is the Bush administration's arguments that the United States can use force preemptively against threats posed by an enemy's possession of weapons of mass destruction:

> The United States has long maintained the option of preemptive actions to counter a sufficient threat to our national security. The greater the threat, the greater the risk of inaction—and the more compelling the case for taking anticipatory action to defend ourselves. . . . [I]n an age where enemies of civilization openly and actively seek the world's most destructive technologies, the United States cannot remain idle while dangers gather.[201]

The military victory in Iraq, in all likelihood, has strengthened the Bush administration's commitment to the doctrine of preemptive self-defense in connection with threats posed by states seeking or possessing weapons of mass destruction.

In terms of other concerns about weapons of mass destruction, the United States—much to the consternation of its allies—has exhibited strong unilateralism, or self-help. Contrary to common security preferences for international cooperation, the United States effectively killed ongoing diplomatic negotiations to strengthen the Biological and Toxin Weapons Convention through a verification protocol.[202] The United States also flexed its muscle by successfully leading the ouster of the director-general of the Organization for the Prohibition of Chemical Weapons under the Chemical Weapons Convention of 1993.[203] On nuclear weapons, the United States unilaterally withdrew from the Anti-Ballistic Missile Treaty of 1972 and continued plans to develop a "national missile defense" system.[204] All these moves represent strong and controversial examples of self-help in the face of threats from weapons of mass destruction.

On the domestic front, the *realpolitik* perspective is evident in the massive federal government effort to strengthen "homeland security" against threats from other states, terrorists, and weapons of mass destruction.[205] The concept of homeland security involves protecting the territory and people of the United States from attack and preparing them in case of attack.[206] While the Bush Doctrine constitutes part of public health security because of its efforts to prevent and deter attacks involving weapons of mass destruction, homeland security efforts in the United States provide the emerging concept of public health security with significant content. From the Defense Against Weapons of Mass Destruction Act of 1996[207] through the Public Health Security and Bioterrorism Preparedness and Response Act of 2002,[208] the United States has tried to improve its domestic preparedness against potential state or terrorist uses of biological and other weapons of mass destruction.[209] The domestic preparedness effort went into overdrive after the anthrax attacks, and homeland security policy in the United States today places strategic attention on improving the nation's public health capabilities.[210] Congress has appropriated significant funding for improving U.S. public health systems against biological weapon attacks (e.g., $2.9 billion for fiscal 2002[211]) and passed important new legislation on bioterrorism.[212] Further, President Bush requested $5.9 billion for fiscal 2003 to strengthen national defenses against biological terrorism.[213] The federal government rapidly developed contingency plans for dealing with a possible smallpox attack,[214] including acquisition of millions of doses of smallpox vaccine[215] and the crafting of a smallpox vaccination strategy.[216]

Most of the biological weapons' component of homeland security policy deals only with the United States. The billions Congress has appropriated for public health improvements will be spent entirely at home to protect the American homeland. The United States recognizes a foreign component of biodefense in the need to coordinate with other countries, as the Ottawa Plan,[217] the G-8 Global Partnership Against the Spread of Weapons and Materials of Mass Destruction,[218] and the international cooperation elements of National Strategy for Homeland Security[219] indicate; but this international coordination is classically realist in its expediency—the United States now has significant national security interests in international coordination on biodefense. Further, as the United States' rejection of the proposed protocol to the Biological and Toxin Weapons Convention and the voluntary nature of the Ottawa Plan and G-8 commitments suggest, the United States does not seek to bind its hands through international legal commitments in the pursuit of public health security against biological weapons.

Although one can connect the movement to strengthen homeland security against biological weapons in the United States to the *realpolitik* perspective on national security, this movement also raises some questions for realism. As indicated in the earlier discussion of different concepts of security, critics have argued that realism has become antiquated as a theory of national security because of its emphasis on the utility of military power and the projection of military power abroad. Homeland security policies on biodefense that involve strengthening the nation's public health system seem to underscore the futility of relying primarily on military power to defend a nation's security. The U.S. public health system now joins the military forces as national security assets, which is something new in national security thinking in the United States. Further, the military might of the United States cannot physically shield the U.S. population from biological attack because borders have become too porous. The sharp distinction between the domestic and the international in realist thinking does not, in the scenario of biological weapons, seem sustainable.

These caveats are important, but the problem of biological weapons does not stump realist thought. The U.S. military and diplomatic responses to the September 11th attacks indicate that the United States flexed its military power to deter any state from sponsoring or harboring terrorists hostile to the United States. Military prowess remains critical to defending the United States from future terrorist attacks, whether or not they involve biological weapons.[220] Realism teaches exactly this lesson.

Realism can also accommodate the movement toward "homeland security" with its internal as opposed to external focus. Realism's focus on the material capabilities of a state includes not only military power and its projection overseas but also other material sources of power—economic, technological, political, and demographic.[221] During the Cold War, the United States engaged in many internal efforts to maintain and increase U.S. power *vis-à-vis* its adversaries, especially the Soviet Union. The civil defense program to protect U.S. citizens and other assets in case of nuclear attack is one example. The building of the U.S. interstate highway system also exemplified concerns about military defense in case of attack against the United States. Another example comes from the U.S. space program, into which Congress poured billions of dollars because of its importance in the ongoing power struggle on Earth and in space with the Soviet Union. The United States undertook to vet mergers and acquisitions of U.S. companies by foreign enterprises for national security reasons.[222] Maintaining a national market open to international trade also had strategic rationale—to provide weaker allies in close geographical proximity to Soviet power (e.g., recovering West European countries and Japan) with a source of economic development and growth through access to the U.S. domestic market. In short, realism's focus on exogenous threats does not mean that it has no theoretical sensitivity to guarding and nurturing internal economic, technological, governance, and population assets that provide the foundation for U.S. power and its projection abroad. Homeland security efforts to strengthen national public health capabilities represent the latest effort to improve and protect internal material capabilities in order to protect U.S. power internationally.

B. The threat from infectious diseases generally

As the public health-national security linkage literature illustrates, experts have been trying to convince the United States government that the direct and indirect threats posed by infectious diseases generally constitute national security concerns. Prior to September 11th and the anthrax attacks, these arguments were more prominent in the linkage discourse. These attacks so altered the national security landscape in the United States, however, that the bio-weapon threat overshadows perceived threats from infectious diseases generally. As mentioned earlier, the attention given and resources pledged at the G-8 summit in June 2002 to fighting weapons of mass destruction dwarfed the issue of helping Africa deal with its HIV/AIDS crisis.[223] Infectious disease problems in the developing world did not rate high on the U.S. national security agenda before the anthrax attacks, despite Clinton administration rhetoric to the contrary. After the attacks, however, such problems may be even less important to U.S. national security and foreign policy.[224] As Richard Parker noted, these attacks threaten the "ability to maintain interest in the seemingly more long-term and distant security concerns of issues such as HIV/AIDS."[225]

As analyzed above, arguments that infectious diseases coming from other countries through international trade and travel constitute a direct national security threat to the United States were not persuasive. "Germs don't recognize borders" did not impress the national security community in the United States, and the seismic shift precipitated by the anthrax attacks reinforces this skepticism. At the time of this writing, for example, the global spread of Severe Acute Respiratory Syndrome (SARS)—a new, contagious disease causing severe public health and economic problems in Asia and Canada[226]— was not being discussed in the United States as a national security issue, except in connection with how SARS may affect U.S. military efforts in Iraq.[227] The emerging concept of public health security in the United States only weakly recognizes the national security importance of the globalization of infectious diseases.

This argument does not mean that the globalization of infectious diseases is entirely absent from the post-anthrax U.S. *foreign policy* agenda. The Bush administration's national security strategy includes frequent references to the foreign policy importance of HIV/AIDS,[228] and President Bush's announcement in January 2003 of an Emergency Plan for AIDS Relief represented a dramatic proposal for increased U.S. humanitarian assistance to nations in Africa and the Caribbean significantly affected by HIV/AIDS.[229] As indicated earlier in this Article, not all foreign policy issues rise, however, to the level of being national security concerns. As a consequence, global infectious disease problems do not feature strongly in the emerging scope and substance of public health security in the United States.

The problems caused by the globalization of disease for the United States feature in public health security discourse in a different, more indirect way. A theme in the public health literature on biological weapons is the benefits that biodefense efforts would produce for public health generally. For example, money spent to improve infectious disease surveillance to detect acts of bioterrorism also improves public health capabilities to conduct infectious disease surveillance generally, and *vice versa*.[230] This biodefense/public health synergy plays out both domestically and internationally, but the bulk of the political attention and public money in the United States is going into *domestic* public health programs that create biodefense and public health synergies *domestically*. The importance of international and global surveillance (and the cooperation these activities entail) receives recognition most strongly in connection with efforts to bolster domestic biodefense (e.g., the Ottawa Plan and proposed Global Pathogen Surveillance Act[231]), with general infectious disease problems as a secondary concern. The benefits for international public health generally produced by national biodefense efforts represent a positive externality produced by biodefense policy. This situation accords with the *realpolitik* perspective on national security—international cooperation is expedient when it contributes to the preservation of a state's national security.

Similarly, the indirect threat to U.S. national security from the effects of infectious diseases in other countries argued in the public health-national security linkage literature features only weakly in the emerging concept of public health security in the United States. Even with weak recognition, realism's distinctive imprint can be discerned. Increasing U.S. concern about emerging and reemerging infectious diseases in the 1990s coincided with important developments in global public health generally. Most prominent has been a shift toward economic and utilitarian frameworks for thinking about global public health problems. The World Bank's *World Development Report 1993: Investing in Health*[232] marks perhaps the beginning of this trend away from the traditional "health for all" ideology of the WHO based in the belief that health is a fundamental human right.[233] The Institute of Medicine's 1997 publication *America's Vital Interest in Global Health* followed the economic line when it stressed "enhancing our economy" as a strategic rationale for U.S. involvement in global health.[234]

The more recent *Report of the Commission on Macroeconomics and Health*[235] perhaps represents a new high-water mark in shifting analytical and ideological approaches to global public health problems toward economics and away from rights-based perspectives. The Commission on Macroeconomics and Health (CMH) frames health as both an input and output of economic development.[236] The CMH *Report* details the drag that infectious diseases create for developing-country economies and urges developed nations to promote economic development by investing in the public health of developing countries.[237] The CMH *Report* does not directly form part of the public health-national security linkage literature because it does not discuss public health threats in the context of security. Viewed through the competing perspectives on national security presented earlier, the CMH *Report* would fall into the common security perspective because the *Report*'s economic approach, recommendations for international cooperation, and support for the participation of non-state actors echo liberalism.

The emphasis on the economic damage infectious diseases can inflict on countries, especially developing states, resonates with realism's interest in the material capabilities of the state. As indicated above, the devastating impact of HIV/AIDS on the military forces, economies, and governance systems of countries in sub-Saharan Africa represents a direct national security threat to those countries under the tenets of *realpolitik* because HIV/AIDS is destroying the material sources of state power. The scale of the devastation wrought by HIV/AIDS has reached the level where even the world's hegemon, the United States, has become more engaged, as suggested by the Emergency

Plan for AIDS Relief. This engagement does not, however, mean that the United States government believes that HIV/AIDS in sub-Saharan Africa directly threatens U.S. national security.[238]

A simple comparison of funds allocated and proposed by the federal government provides a window on where HIV/AIDS problems overseas sit as a national security priority in the United States. Prior to the announcement of the Emergency Plan for AIDS Relief, the United States pledged $500 million to the Global Fund to Fight AIDS, Tuberculosis, and Malaria (Global Fund), compared to $19.5 billion in fiscal year 2002 and a proposed $37.7 billion for fiscal year 2003 for homeland security and $1.4 billion in fiscal year 2002 and a proposed $5.9 billion for domestic biodefense for fiscal year 2003.[239] Further, the United States pledged $10 billion toward the $20 billion G-8 Global Partnership Against the Spread of Weapons and Materials of Mass Destruction in June 2002.[240] The Emergency Plan for AIDS Relief would, if enacted by Congress, increase the U.S. financial contribution to international HIV/AIDS efforts to $3 billion annually starting in fiscal 2004 through fiscal 2008. Although a significant increase over prior funding levels, the Emergency Plan for AIDS Relief is still small compared to U.S. spending on perceived direct threats to U.S. national security.

Lurking within the economic analysis and public health policy recommendations of the CMH, the World Bank, and donors such as the United States is another feature that contains hints of *realpolitik*. The CMH *Report* recommends conditioning financial aid to developing countries wracked by infectious diseases on those countries using the money appropriately.[241] The money should come, in other words, with strings attached. The policy framework that emerges from the CMH, World Bank, and great-power donors constitutes what can be called "structural adjustment for public health." As literature on World Bank and International Monetary Fund structural adjustment policies argues, conditionality for loans and grants represents the exercise of power by the strong against the weak.[242] The Emergency Plan for AIDS Relief will also utilize conditions in distributing funds. President Bush proposed that only $1 billion of the $15 billion initiative be earmarked for the Global Fund,[243] and distribution of that $1 billion is to be "conditioned on the Fund showing results."[244] Under the President's Plan, the United States would distribute the remaining $14 billion through bilateral aid efforts not through international institutions. Consistent with *realpolitik*, the Emergency Plan for AIDS Relief represents a shift away from the multilateralism of the Global Fund toward the unilateral exercise of U.S. financial power. Advocates for the Global Fund have criticized the unilateralism animating the Emergency Plan for AIDS Relief.[245]

Even those not inclined to see realism as helpful in understanding U.S. attitudes toward the indirect threat of infectious diseases sense that the great powers need to throw their weight around in helping developing countries in terms of public health. Price-Smith observes, for example, that the international norm against intervention in the domestic affairs of sovereign states hampers the ability of developed countries to assist some developing nations. He writes: "In the case of states such as South Africa and Zimbabwe, where there remains an enduring culture of denial regarding HIV/AIDS, this means that the international community has little choice but to stand by and watch the ruling elites of these countries preside over the destruction of their populaces."[246] He further noted that "the governments of Russia and China have opposed the inclusion of public health matters within the global security agenda on the ground that such an inclusion would result in increased intervention within their internal affairs."[247] The only alternatives available to the developed world are to use "a carrot-and-stick approach, with financial and technological incentives use to obtain compliance from recalcitrant regimes"[248] or to make additional financial assistance "to non-compliant regimes conditional on effective action to slow the spread of contagion within national borders."[249]

Realists do not, however, have much tolerance for the principle of non-intervention when they perceive that other countries threaten a state's national interests. The emerging concept of public health security suggests that the United States might seek to intervene more dramatically if infectious diseases in other countries threaten, directly or indirectly, its military, technological, and economic power. The Emergency Plan for AIDS Relief provides evidence of the United States' willingness to exercise its power unilaterally in contexts where infectious diseases and foreign policy overlap.

The growing involvement of non-states actors in global public health policy, as recognized by analysis of "public-private partnerships" and "global health governance," might appear to cause some difficulties for the thesis that the *realpolitik* perspective informs the emerging concept of public health security in the United States. The involvement of non-state actors—multinational pharmaceutical corporations, NGOs, and philanthropic foundations—is, without question, a feature of global public health today. The legislation proposed to implement the Emergency Plan for AIDS Relief expressly supports, for example, the use of non-state actors in the fight against HIV/AIDS.[250]

The involvement of non-state actors does not, however, stump the realist. For example, Bill Gates' prominence in global public health today[251] represents, in some degree, how uninterested the great powers have been and perhaps remain in the health matters the Gates Foundation funds. More substantively, the realist emphasis on states as the main actors does not mean states cannot utilize non-state actors to pursue *realpolitik* policies. The realist focus on military power, for example, does not mean that the instruments of military power have to be entirely developed or owned by governments. For-profit manufacturers of military technology have been critical to the development of U.S. military power. The U.S. government used such non-state actors to achieve its overriding goal of military power and security. Similarly, the great powers can utilize non-state actors, both for-profit and non-profit, in their attempts to deal with foreign policy challenges posed by infectious diseases. Non-state actors are, thus, simply material assets that states expediently use to address perceived threats to their security and national interests.

C. The emerging concept of public health security: the relationship between public health and realpolitik

Section III.B argued that the concept of public health security in the United States reflects the *realpolitik* perspective on national security much more than other conceptions of security. Again, this argument questions the dismissal of realism seen in much of the pre-September 11th and pre-anthrax literature on the public health-national security linkage. Perhaps the *realpolitik* tenor of the emerging U.S. concept of "public health security" flows from the short-term policy responses to the historic terrorist attacks on the United States in September and October 2001 and will eventually mellow into a broader concept, informed by other more expansive conceptions of security in the global age. In this section, I explore whether *realpolitik*-driven public health security notions have deeper implications for understanding public health in the age of the globalization of infectious disease.

Realism as a theory of explaining international relations generally has not informed, and still does not inform, analysis of global public health.[252] Ulysses Panissett's review of theories of international health identified conceptual categories that do not connect at all with the basic tenets of realism.[253] One of the most prominent of these theories—that international health is public health activities for the poor[254]—diverges dramatically from the state-centered, power-driven, and skepticism-laden realist outlook on international politics. In fact, one of the reasons why the discipline of international relations has ignored public health as a field of study may stem from the public health's attachment to (1) issues and methodological approaches not related to great-power politics, international order, and national security, and (2) improving health conditions in poor, weak countries at the periphery of realism's central concern with the great powers.

The selfish interests and schemes of the great powers mark, however, the field of international health. Specifically, international health's roots are in the *economic, military, and geopolitical concerns of the great powers*. International health diplomacy arose in the mid-nineteenth century because the European great powers were increasingly concerned about the direct threat "Asiatic diseases," such as cholera, posed to their foreign trade and domestic economic interests. Trade and economics drove international health cooperation among the European powers not altruistic concern with the health of non-European peoples.[255] The international health cooperation attempted in the nineteenth century was not expressly connected to notions of national security, but the European great powers made infectious disease control a foreign policy issue, especially as connected with trade and commercial matters.

The selfish interests of the great powers characterize other aspects of public health's development in the nineteenth century and early twentieth century. European militaries adopted sanitary reforms to mitigate the adverse effects of infectious diseases on military preparedness and effectiveness before governments began to do the same for civilian populations,[256] illustrating how realism can incorporate public health concerns.

The great powers also perceived public health as related to their efforts to project power in other parts of the world, whether through imperialism or spheres of influence. European interest in tropical medicine resulted from the threat infectious diseases posed to imperial ventures (e.g., the establishment of the London School of Hygiene & Tropical Medicine).[257] U.S. concerns with yellow fever in the Americas stemmed from its effort to maintain military and economic hegemony in the Western hemisphere.[258]

These historical examples show how public health played a role in important nineteenth and early twentieth century contexts relevant to realist thinking: preservation of military power, protection and expansion of economic and commercial power, and projection of national power and influence overseas. The great powers did not sustain these public health activities during most of the twentieth century because they reduced the threat and burden of infectious diseases to their militaries, economies, and societies through *domestic* public health reform and the development of powerful health technologies, such as antibiotics and vaccines.[259] Whether public health improvements on infectious diseases in the United States and European countries in the first half of the twentieth century owed anything to international health cooperation and international health regimes is doubtful.[260] As the engagement of the great powers waned, international health policy morphed into more humanitarian modes of activity, such as providing technical assistance to improve public health in poor countries.[261] The proclamation of health as a fundamental human right in the constitution of the World Health Organization in 1946[262] symbolizes the shift from the *realpolitik* origins of international health statecraft toward a humanitarian, rights-based ethos.

The public health-national security linkage literature suggests that the universalist, right-to-health ideology that guided international public health in the WHO's first five decades is, controversially, giving way to arguments centered again on the self-interests of the great powers. In their different ways, the public health-national security linkage literature and the World Bank 1993 *World Development Report*'s and the CMH *Report*'s economic approaches to global public health problems attempt to provide the great powers of the international system with direct, selfish motivations to engage more intensively in international health activities. *America's Vital Interest in Global Health* lists three strategic rationales for United States' engagement: "protecting our people," "enhancing our economy," and "advancing our international interests."[263] The document *Why Health is Important to U.S. Foreign Policy* also provides a classic example of this phenomenon because it argues that the United States needs to make health a foreign policy concern out of "narrow self-interest" and "enlightened self-interest."[264]

The pattern that emerges from these contemporary efforts to reengage the great powers in international health could be taken directly from the pages of nineteenth century international health diplomacy because we see again the emphasis on *economic, military, and geopolitical aspects* of infectious disease threats from the perspective of the great powers. The public health-national security linkage literature emphasizes that the United States should see infectious diseases as a national security threat because it is once again vulnerable to the importation of infectious diseases from countries, especially developing countries. The literature also stresses the increasing economic costs of emerging and reemerging infectious diseases on international trade and commerce. The public health-national security arguments frequently include concerns about infectious disease threats to military preparedness and effectiveness for the United States, developing countries, and U.N. peace-keeping missions. Finally, this literature stresses the infectious disease threat to strategic areas of the world in which the United States needs to protect its interests and project influence, such as Russia and China.

The parallels between nineteenth century international health diplomacy and the contemporary public health-national security literature are telling in their appeal to the economic, military, and geopolitical interests of the great powers. The parallels between history and contemporary events raise a number of questions for those interested in global public health. Despite over 150 years of international health activity, is the twenty-first century public health advocacy really affected by nineteenth century *realpolitik* arguments? The realist would answer this question in the affirmative because realism stresses that the anarchical structure of the international system creates repetition in state behavior over time. In other words, the feeling of *déjà vu* comes naturally to the realist.

The parallels reviewed above more fundamentally challenge those seeking to broaden the concept of public health security through the common, human, and ecological security approaches. In terms of the common security approach, this framework does not abandon the concept of the national interest because states remain central to the normative liberal project informing this perspective. The common security objective is to broaden the parameters of the "national interest" to accommodate new kinds of challenges to the nation that go beyond traditional state-based threats. The parallels between nineteenth century motivations and the public health-national security literature suggest, however, that the core questions remain narrow and selfish—how are diseases predominantly originating in other countries adversely affecting a great power's military, economic, and geopolitical interests?

Those in favor of the human security agenda may experience either delight or dismay at the parallels outlined above. Critical international theorists would see such parallels as further evidence that the statist status quo is fundamentally unjust and incapable of significant self-reform. Social constructivists might despair that the concept of "public health security" is being socially constructed (again) in the image of *realpolitik* rather than an image more conducive to human solidarity or emancipation through health protection and promotion.

Neither critical international theory nor social constructivism seems, at present, capable of producing an alternative blueprint that would have credibility and traction in the current public health security context. The human security approach fostered by these two theories has not, to date, come to grips with the dual nature of public health in the global age—all disease is local and global. Public-private partnerships involving global NGOs can contribute to public health improvements, but the heavy lifting of public health at the national and local level remains a "public good" that governments must shoulder.

Does public health have a built-in need for statist architecture that critical international theory and social constructivism seek either to circumvent or overcome? Does public health in some fashion confront what Philip Allott called the "tyranny of the actual"?[265] Does public health have to follow the path taken by liberalism in accepting the anarchical and statist nature of international relations but trying to ameliorate the dangerous and violent tendencies of such a structure for human relations? The public health-national security linkage literature's resonance with common security concepts suggests that public health's best hope rests in liberalism and not more radical theories of human emancipation. This conclusion is basically the one Price-Smith reached in his analysis.[266]

The *realpolitik* imprint on the emerging concept of public health security in the United States also confronts notions of ecological security with difficulties. Ecological security would stress general infectious disease threats more than those from biological weapons, but the opposite is in fact happening in the United States. Ecological security thinking could dismiss these developments as further examples of the inability of statespersons to see the eco-evolutionary threats to the human race, but ecological security does not necessarily help us understand why *realpolitik* has and continues to influence global public health activities.

As with critical international theory and social constructivism, the ecological approach to security does not provide a clear blueprint for policy action. Pirages stressed that "the international management of the epidemiological consequences of globalization" must be a top priority "for the emerging council of the global village."[267] Pirages does not describe the governance structure and dynamics of this "council," but presumably he does not mean either states interacting in a condition of anarchy or international organizations. Perhaps this "council" notion ties into developments in global public health, such as public-private partnerships and global health governance; but whether these new features of global public health activism reflect the eco-evolutionary approach of ecological security thinking is doubtful.

As argued in this Article, realism rather than the other theories of international relations currently shapes the scope and content of public health security in the United States. The historic terrorist attacks in the United States have much to do with this stark imprint of *realpolitik* on the public health-national security nexus, but the reasons for the deep nature of the imprint may not all be connected with those awful events. The sobering parallels between nineteenth century international health statecraft and arguments in the public health-national security linkage literature perhaps provide a window on understanding how adversely the anarchical structure of international relations— the central focus of realism—affects global public health efforts.[268]

The typical mantra, seen in the common security perspective and in literature on the globalization of infectious diseases, is that only international cooperation can produce adequate responses to threats posed by biological weapons and the globalization of infectious diseases. The *realpolitik* imprint on public health security in the United States calls this mantra into question. The reductions in infectious disease morbidity and mortality achieved in the era of the globalization of infectious diseases in the latter half of the nineteenth and first half of the twentieth centuries suggests that the strategic driver was not international cooperation but domestic public health reforms—in other words, self-help.[269]

Other problems exist with the common security approach's call for more international cooperation on public health. The exact nature of the international cooperation needed is rarely specified. The emerging concept of public health security in the United States does not reject international cooperation but views it as an expedient means to prevent and control public health threats to U.S. territory and economic, military, and geopolitical power and interests. In other words, international cooperation involves the exercise of national power to achieve selfish ends.

In his classic work *The Twenty Years' Crisis*, E. H. Carr noted that liberal states have had a tendency to use the "harmony of interests" doctrine to justify their exercises of power in pursuit of selfish ends.[270] The "harmony of interests" doctrine generally holds that whatever is in the national interest of one state is also in the interest of the rest of the world.[271] The divergent interests of states usually reveal the "harmony of interests" to be the argument of strong, status quo states.[272] The appearance of the "harmony of interests" doctrine in the public health-national security linkage literature should come, then, as no surprise. *Why Health is Important to U.S. Foreign Policy* argues that "U.S. leadership in international health affairs can provide an unequivocally positive framework for pursuing what is in our interest as well as that of the world."[273] The U.S. Office of Global Health Affairs likewise marries U.S. national interests with universal purpose in arguing that "[a]ctive U.S. engagement in global health is *in the interest of U.S. diplomacy and national security; it also is simply the right thing to do.*"[274] The many controversies surrounding U.S. foreign policy on global health issues, from criticism of strong U.S. support for patent rights over greater access to infectious disease drugs to complaints about the funding the United States provides the Global Fund, demonstrate that the "harmony of interests" language in the public health-national security literature suffers the fate of this doctrine identified by Carr—states have divergent rather than harmonious interests.

One of the problems confronting reliance on the liberal preference for international law and international organizations in the public health context is the recognized weaknesses of such institutions during the post-World War II period. Realist analysis suggests that regime formation and maintenance depends on hegemonic leadership—hegemons exercise their power to make regimes work.[275] The hegemons bear greater costs and produce benefits for others, but the key element in successful international regimes is hegemonic commitment. Experts widely recognize that the WHO suffered in the post-World War II period from a sometimes ambivalent, sometimes hostile relationship with the great powers, especially the United States.[276] The public health-national security linkage literature recognizes the importance of the power dynamic in regime sustainability by arguing that the leadership of the United States in global health is critical.

Similarly, advocates for global health have often argued that public health needs to be higher on the political and diplomatic agenda of important, powerful countries, especially the United States.[277] In short, public health needs to move from "low politics" (e.g., humanitarianism) to "high politics" (e.g., national security).[278] A higher political profile for public health will, however, bring it into direct contact with the volatile and power-laden politics generated by states interacting in a condition of anarchy. As the emerging concept of public health security shows, the United States has put public health on the national security agenda but not in the way the public health-national security linkage literature necessarily advocated. Realist analysis holds that the *realpolitik* imprint on the public health security concept in the United States was predictable, and those advocates of putting public health into "high politics" who would recoil from the dominance of realism did not understand the game they wanted to join. The anarchical structure and dynamics of international politics constitute a virus to which public health is not immune when health and security converge.

Conclusion

This Article's argument that the *realpolitik* perspective on national security is relevant to understanding global infectious disease problems and now dominates the public health security concept in the United States does not mean that other perspectives on the public health-national security nexus disappear and become irrelevant. Realism has lost much of its theoretical credibility in the eyes of critics.[279] *Realpolitik* had its day in the sun during the Cold War, the argument goes; and today the states need new, more sophisticated and persuasive explanations of globalization. In this sense, the *realpolitik* imprint on public health security in the United States bucks not only the normative thrust of the public health-national security linkage literature but also the dressing-down of realism in international relations theory. Perhaps public health security in the image of *realpolitik* will have its brief day in the sun and fade as the attacks of September and October 2001 loosen their grip on U.S. domestic politics and foreign policy.

The development of a public health security concept in the United States that bears the imprint of realism might, however, be an indication that public health as a discipline in the global age will feature what Stanley Hoffmann called the "permanent dialogue" between the liberal Kant and the realist Rousseau in international relations theory.[280] This dialogue is not a conversation with which many in the public health world have experience, and the challenge becomes to ensure that those already participating in the dialogue hear what public health advocates have to say about the threats from infectious diseases. Whether hearing constitutes listening remains for history to determine.

Notes

* An earlier version of this Article was delivered at a seminar at the London School of Hygiene and Tropical Medicine on May 30, 2002. Support for the research and writing of this article was provided by a Fulbright New Century Scholarship.

1 INSTITUTE OF MEDICINE, THE FUTURE OF PUBLIC HEALTH 1 (1988); *see also* Mark A. Rothstein, *Rethinking the Meaning of Public Health*, 30 J.L. MED., & ETHICS 144 (2002) (discussing the meaning of "public health").

2 David P. Fidler, *The Globalization of Public Health: The First 100 Years of International Health Diplomacy*, 79 BULL. WORLD HEALTH ORG. 842 (2001).

3 David P. Fidler, Tony D. Perez, & Martin S. Cetron, *International Considerations, in* LAW IN PUBLIC HEALTH PRACTICE 93, 93 (R. A. Goodman et al. eds., 2002).

4 *See, e.g.*, Arthur L. Reingold & Christina R. Phares, *Infectious Diseases, in* INTERNATIONAL PUBLIC HEALTH 139 (Michael H. Merson et al. eds., 2001).

5 CHEM. & BIOLOGICAL ARMS CONTROL INST. & CTR. FOR STRATEGIC & INT'L STUDIES INT'L SEC. PROGRAM, CONTAGION AND CONFLICT: HEALTH AS A GLOBAL SECURITY CHALLENGE 2 (2000) [hereinafter CONTAGION AND CONFLICT] ("Historically, the concept of national security has focused on the use of military power to protect national borders and interests abroad."); Dennis Altman, *Understanding HIV/AIDS as a Security Issue, in* HEALTH IMPACTS OF GLOBALIZATION: TOWARDS GLOBAL GOVERNANCE 33–34 (Kelley Lee ed., 2003) ("For most of the twentieth century, the impact of two world wars and the succeeding 50 years of the Cold War meant that security remained defined almost entirely in military terms."); Press Release, Council on Foreign Relations, Council Establishes Senior Fellowship in Global Health and Foreign Policy with a Grant from the Bill & Melinda Gates Foundation (Apr. 25, 2003), *at* http://www.cfr.org ("Widespread disease such as HIV/AIDS and SARS relate directly to U.S. national security in ways that were unimaginable just a few years ago.").

6 CONTAGION AND CONFLICT, *supra* note 5, at vii (arguing that "today's world, in which globalization and the information revolution bring people and problems together in surprising ways, finds health and security intersecting with greater frequency"). The leading developments in this linkage are analyzed in Section I.B *infra*.

7 Joseph S. Nye, Jr. & Sean M. Lynn-Jones, *International Security Studies: A Report on the State of the Field*, INT'L SECURITY, Spring 1988, at 5; Stephen M. Walt, *The Renaissance of Security Studies*, 35 INT'L STUD. Q. 211 (1991); David A. Baldwin, *Security Studies and the End of the Cold War*, 48 WORLD POL. 117 (1995).

8 John Baylis, *International and Global Security in the Post-Cold War Era, in* THE GLOBALIZATION OF WORLD POLITICS: AN INTRODUCTION TO INTERNATIONAL RELATIONS 253 (John Baylis & Steve Smith eds., 2d ed. 2001); Roland Paris, *Human Security: Paradigm Shift or Hot Air?*, INT'L SECURITY, Fall 2001, at 87.

9 NEVILLE M. GOODMAN, INTERNATIONAL HEALTH ORGANIZATIONS AND THEIR WORK (2d ed. 1971); NORMAN HOWARD-JONES, THE SCIENTIFIC BACKGROUND OF THE INTERNATIONAL SANITARY CONFERENCES, 1851–1938 (1975); Fidler, *supra* note 2, at 842.

10 The editors of a casebook on national security law emphasize the importance of national security when they argue that "[i]n a world that bristles with animosity and danger, an inadequate national defense would jeopardize our lives and ideals." NATIONAL SECURITY LAW 1 (Steven Dycus et al. eds., 2d ed. 1997).

11 Kelley Lee & Anthony Zwi, *A Global Political Economy Approach to AIDS: Ideology, Interests and Implications, in* HEALTH IMPACTS OF GLOBALIZATION: TOWARDS GLOBAL GOVERNANCE 13, 13 (K. Lee ed., 2003) (noting that "little attention has been devoted to health in the I[nternational] R[elations] field"); Ilona Kickbusch, *Global Health Governance: Some Theoretical Considerations on the New Political Space, in* HEALTH IMPACTS OF GLOBALIZATION: TOWARDS GLOBAL GOVERNANCE 192, 192 (Kelley Lee ed., 2003) (noting "the gulf that divides scholars of policy/International Relations and public health.").

12 CONTAGION AND CONFLICT, *supra* note 5, at vii ("Health has rarely, if ever, been defined as a national security issue.").

13 Geneva Protocol for the Prohibition of the Use in War of Asphyxiating, Poisonous or Other Gases, and of Bacteriological Methods of Warfare, June 17, 1925, 94 L.N.T.S. 65 [hereinafter Geneva Protocol].

14 Lawrence Freedman, *The First Two Generations of Nuclear Strategists, in* MAKERS OF MODERN STRATEGY FROM MACHIAVELLI TO THE NUCLEAR AGE 735 (Peter Paret ed., 1986).

15 Michael Carver, *Conventional Warfare in the Nuclear Age, in* MAKERS OF MODERN STRATEGY FROM MACHIAVELLI TO THE NUCLEAR AGE 779 (Peter Paret ed., 1986).

16 Jonathan B. Tucker, *A Farewell to Germs: The U.S. Renunciation of Biological and Toxin Warfare*, INT'L SECURITY, Summer 2002, at 107.

17 Elizabeth Fee & Theodore M. Brown, *Preemptive Biopreparedness: Can We Learn Anything from History?*, 91 AM. J. PUB. HEALTH 721 (2001).

18 Paris, *supra* note 8, at 97.

19 Altman, *supra* note 5, at 34.

20 UNAIDS, REPORT ON THE GLOBAL HIV/AIDS EPIDEMIC 2002, at 44 (2002) ("Twenty years after the world first became aware of AIDS, it is clear that humanity is facing one of the most devastating epidemics in human history."); *see also* UNAIDS, AIDS EPIDEMIC UPDATE: DECEMBER 2002, at 3 (2002) (discussing the grim statistics on the scale of the HIV/AIDS pandemic, and in particular, listing

numbers of people infected with and living with HIV/AIDS and the number of deaths from AIDS).

21 WORLD HEALTH ORGANIZATION, WORLD HEALTH REPORT 1996: FIGHTING DISEASE, FOSTERING DEVELOPMENT, at v (1996) [hereinafter WORLD HEALTH REPORT 1996] (arguing that the world stands "on the brink of a global crisis in infectious disease" because "[i]nfectious diseases are attacking us on multiple fronts"); *see also* WORLD HEALTH ORGANIZATION, REMOVING OBSTACLES TO HEALTHY DEVELOPMENT: REPORT ON INFECTIOUS DISEASES (1999) (containing more information on the global crisis in emerging and re-emerging infectious diseases).

22 John Bolton, Remarks to the 5th Biological Weapons Convention RevCon Meeting (Nov. 19, 2001), *at* http://www.state.gov/t/us/rm/janjuly/6231.htm (last visited Jan. 3, 2003) (raising U.S. concerns about biological weapons proliferation by states).

23 MICHAEL T. OSTERHOLM & JOHN SCHWARTZ, LIVING TERRORS: WHAT AMERICA NEEDS TO KNOW TO SURVIVE THE COMING BIOTERRORIST CATASTROPHE (2000).

24 U.S. NATIONAL SCIENCE AND TECHNOLOGY COUNCIL COMMITTEE ON INTERNATIONAL SCIENCE, ENGINEERING, AND TECHNOLOGY (CISET) WORKING GROUP ON EMERGING AND RE-EMERGING INFECTIOUS DISEASES, INFECTIOUS DISEASES—A GLOBAL THREAT (1995); *see also* INSTITUTE OF MEDICINE, AMERICA'S VITAL INTEREST IN GLOBAL HEALTH (1997) [hereinafter AMERICA'S VITAL INTEREST IN GLOBAL HEALTH] (arguing that the interests of the United States are best served through decisive action to promote health around the world).

25 NEW DIRECTIONS IN INTERNATIONAL HEALTH COOPERATION: A REPORT TO THE PRESIDENT (1979).

26 Loch K. Johnson & Diane C. Snyder, *Beyond the Traditional Intelligence Agenda: Examining the Merits of a Global Public Health Portfolio, in* PLAGUES AND POLITICS: INFECTIOUS DISEASE AND INTERNATIONAL POLICY 214, 217 (Andrew Price-Smith ed., 2001); *see also* Altman, *supra* note 5, at 35 (noting evidence "that officers in the Central Intelligence Agency (CIA) have been pushing their superiors to consider the impact of HIV/AIDS on national and global stability since 1990").

27 *AIDS and the Third World: The Impact on Development, Hearing Before the Select House Comm. on Hunger*, 100th Cong. (1988).

28 NATIONAL INTELLIGENCE COUNCIL, THE GLOBAL INFECTIOUS DISEASE THREAT AND ITS IMPLICATIONS FOR THE UNITED STATES (National Intelligence Estimate 99-17D, January 2000), *at* http://www.cia.gov/cia/publications/nic/report/nie99-17d. html (last visited Jan. 2, 2003).

29 The U.N. Security Council met on January 10, 2000 to discuss "The Situation in Africa: the Impact of AIDS on Peace and Security in Africa." *Round-Up: Developments throughout Africa, Renewed Violence in Middle East Among Key Issues for Security Council in 2000*, U.N. SCOR, U.N. Doc. SC/6987 (2000), *at* http://www.un.org/documents/roundup.htm (last visited Jan. 2, 2003). In a follow-up action to this meeting, the U.N. Security Council passed Resolution 1308 in July 2000 on the impact of HIV/AIDS on international peacekeeping efforts. S.C. Res. 1308, U.N. SCOR, U.N. Doc. S/Res/1308 (2000).

30 UNAIDS, *What UNAIDS Does, at* http://www.unaids.org/about/what.asp (last visited Jan. 2, 2003).

31 World Health Organization, *Global Health Security: Epidemic Alert and Response*, World Health Assembly Resolution WHA54.14 (2001); *Global Health Security*, 76 WKLY. EPIDEMIOLOGICAL REC. 166 (2001); *see also* Emma Rothschild, *What is Security?*, 124 DAEDALUS 58 (1995) (commenting on the appropriation of "security" as a policy strategy).

32 LAURIE GARRETT, THE COMING PLAGUE: NEWLY EMERGING DISEASES IN A WORLD OUT OF BALANCE (1994); Laurie Garrett, *The Return of Infectious Disease*, 75

FOREIGN AFF. 66 (1996); LAURIE GARRETT, BETRAYAL OF TRUST: THE COLLAPSE OF GLOBAL PUBLIC HEALTH (2000) [hereinafter BETRAYAL OF TRUST].

33 CONTAGION AND CONFLICT, *supra* note 5.

34 JONATHAN BAN, HEALTH, SECURITY, AND U.S. GLOBAL LEADERSHIP (2001).

35 INTERNATIONAL CRISIS GROUP, HIV/AIDS AS A SECURITY ISSUE, *at* http://www.crisisweb.org/projects/showreport.cfm?reportid=321 (last visited Jan. 2, 2003).

36 JORDON S. KASSALOW, WHY HEALTH IS IMPORTANT TO U.S. FOREIGN POLICY (2001), *at* http://www.milbank.org/reports/Foreignpolicy.html (last visited Jan. 2, 2003).

37 JENNIFER BROWER & PETER CHALK, THE GLOBAL THREAT OF NEW AND REEMERGING INFECTIOUS DISEASES: RECONCILING U.S. NATIONAL SECURITY AND PUBLIC HEALTH POLICY (2003).

38 Dennis Pirages, *Microsecurity: Disease Organisms and Human Well-Being*, 18 WASH. Q. 5 (1995); Dennis Pirages, *Ecological Theory and International Relations*, 5 IND. J. GLOBAL LEGAL STUD. 53 (1997) [hereinafter Pirages, *Ecological Theory*].

39 Pirages, *Ecological Theory, supra* note 38, at 55.

40 ANDREW T. PRICE-SMITH, THE HEALTH OF NATIONS: INFECTIOUS DISEASE, ENVIRONMENTAL CHANGE, AND THEIR EFFECTS ON NATIONAL SECURITY AND DEVELOPMENT 49–77 (2002).

41 *Id.*

42 Caroline Thomas, *The Politics of Access to Drugs, in* HEALTH IMPACTS OF GLOBALIZATION: TOWARDS GLOBAL GOVERNANCE 182–185 (Kelley Lee ed., 2003) (analyzing the exercise of U.S. power against developing country efforts to increase access to medicines, including antiretrovirals for treatment of HIV/AIDS).

43 Philip Zelikow, *Book Review*, 79 FOREIGN AFF. 154, 154 (2000).

44 CONTAGION AND CONFLICT, *supra* note 5, at vii.

45 BAN, *supra* note 34, at 9 ("[T]he traditional national security establishment is not wholly convinced that framing . . . health issues in security terms is useful. Many feel that drawing this relationship dilutes or stretches the parameters of what should fall under the rubric of national security to a point that may be counterproductive. This view maintains that national security should be largely confined to military affairs–protecting borders, fighting wars, and devising military strategy.").

46 Jonathan B. Tucker, *Lessons from the Case Studies, in* TOXIC TERROR: ASSESSING TERRORIST USE OF CHEMICAL AND BIOLOGICAL WEAPONS 249, 267 (Jonathan B. Tucker ed., 2000) [hereinafter *Lessons*] (arguing that "[b]ased on historical trends identified in this study, however, only a tiny minority of terrorists will seek to inflict indiscriminate fatalities [with chemical or biological weapons], and few if any of them will succeed[ ]").

47 Michael H. Merson, Robert E. Black, & Anne J. Mills, *Introduction* to INTERNATIONAL PUBLIC HEALTH, at xvii (Michael H. Merson et al. eds., 2001) ("The term *public health* evokes different ideas and images. One is often asked: Is it a profession, a discipline, or a system? Is it concerned primarily with health care of the poor? Does it mean working in an urban clinic, or providing clean water and sanitation?"); BETRAYAL OF TRUST, *supra* note 32, at 6 ("[T]he new century finds experts at odds over the mission of public health. No two deans of the West's major schools of public health agree on a definition of its goals and missions.").

48 JAMES A. TOBEY, PUBLIC HEALTH LAW 10 (2d ed. 1939) (differentiating public health law from law relating to medicine); LAWRENCE O. GOSTIN, PUBLIC HEALTH LAW: POWER, DUTY, RESTRAINT 3–4 (2000) (attempting to distinguish public health law from health care law).

49 BETRAYAL OF TRUST, *supra* note 32, at 8 ("In the United States 'public health' had become—incorrectly—synonymous with medicine for poor people. Few Americans at the millennium thought of 'public health' as a system that functioned in their interests. Rather, it was viewed as a government handout for impoverished people.").

50 Lawrence O. Gostin, *Public Health Law: A Renaissance*, 30 J.L. MED., & ETHICS 136, 136 (2002).

51 *Constitution of the World Health Organization, July 22, 1946, in* WORLD HEALTH ORGANIZATION, BASIC DOCUMENTS 1, 1 (40th ed. 1994). WHO has discussed making this expansive definition of health even broader by including spiritual health in the definition. *See also Review of the Constitution and Regional Arrangements of the World Health Organization: Report of the Special Group*, WHO Doc. EB101/7 (Nov. 14, 1997).

52 Merson, Black, & Mills, *supra* note 47, at xviii.

53 BETRAYAL OF TRUST, *supra* note 32, at 8 (criticizing the Institute of Medicine's broad definition of public health, *see supra* note 1 and accompanying text, as revealing "no agreement about what constituted 'public health' other than assuring that people were healthy"); Rothstein, *supra* note 1, at 145, 147 (criticizing the Institute of Medicine's definition of public health as "a vague definition that fails to indicate the primary objective or scope of public health" and opposing "the use of the term 'public health' as an open-ended descriptor of widely divergent efforts to improve the human condition").

54 *Public Health: An Introduction, reprinted in* DAVID P. FIDLER, INTERNATIONAL LAW AND PUBLIC HEALTH: MATERIALS ON AND ANALYSIS OF GLOBAL HEALTH JURISPRUDENCE 3, 4 (2000) ("The modern view of health is broad. It goes beyond individual diseases or viruses and includes all of the aspects of life that can affect our physical, mental, or social well-being.").

55 Press Release, World Health Organization, WHO Atlas Maps Global Tobacco Epidemic 82 (Oct. 15, 2002), *at* http://www.who.int/inf-fs/en/fact221.html (last visited Jan. 2, 2003) (describing a "galloping worldwide epidemic" in tobacco-related diseases, which currently kill 4.9 million people per annum globally and which are projected to kill 8.4 million people a year by 2020, with the developing countries bearing 70% of the projected mortality); *see also* WORLD HEALTH ORGANIZATION, WORLD HEALTH REPORT 1997: CONQUERING SUFFERING, ENRICHING HUMANITY (1997) (discussing the global scale of non-communicable disease problems).

56 Richard Ullman, *Redefining Security*, INT'L SECURITY, Summer 1983, at 129; Jef Huysmans, *Security? What Do You Mean? From Concept to Thick Signifier*, 4 EUR. J. INT'L RELATIONS 226 (1998).

57 These four concepts of security do not necessarily exhaust the possible perspectives that exist about what "security" means or should mean. Roland Paris noted, for example, that the terms human security, common security, global security, cooperative security, and comprehensive security have all been developed to "encourage policymakers and scholars to think about international security as something more than the military defense of state interests and territory." Paris, *supra* note 8, at 87. In addition, other theories of international relations, such as feminism, offer perspectives on security not utilized in this Article. J. ANN TICKNER, GENDER IN INTERNATIONAL RELATIONS: FEMINIST PERSPECTIVES ON ACHIEVING GLOBAL SECURITY (1992). I select the concepts and theories used in this Article because they appear, to me, to be the most relevant for illuminating the public health-national security linkage.

58 For overviews of the realist theory of international relations, see Scott Burchill, *Realism and Neo-Realism, in* THEORIES OF INTERNATIONAL RELATIONS 67 (Scott

Burchill & Andrew Linklater eds., 1996); REALISM: RESTATEMENTS AND RENEWAL (Benjamin Frankel ed., 1996); Timothy Dunne & Brian C. Schmidt, *Realism, in* THE GLOBALIZATION OF WORLD POLITICS: AN INTRODUCTION TO INTERNATIONAL RELATIONS 141 (John Baylis & Steve Smith eds., 2d ed. 2001).

59 KENNETH N. WALTZ, THEORY OF INTERNATIONAL POLITICS 93–97 (1979) (discussing why states are the primary actors in the anarchic structure of international relations); Benjamin Frankel, *Restating the Realist Case: An Introduction, in* REALISM: RESTATEMENTS AND RENEWAL, at xiv–xv (Benjamin Frankel ed., 1996) (noting realism's premise that states are the central actors in an anarchic world); John J. Mearsheimer, *The False Promise of International Institutions*, INT'L SECURITY, Winter 1994/1995, at 5, 10 (noting as one of realism's assumptions that the international system is anarchic and that states are the main political units of that system).

60 HANS J. MORGENTHAU, POLITICS AMONG NATIONS 5 (5th ed. rev. 1978) (arguing that, under realism, "statesmen think and act in terms of interest defined as power"); WALTZ, *supra* note 59, at 113 (arguing that "[i]nternational politics is the realm of power"); Frankel, *supra* note 58, at xv (noting the realist assumption that states seek to maximize their security or power).

61 Mearsheimer, *supra* note 59, at 12 (noting that, under realism, the self-interested behavior of states limits their ability to cooperate).

62 WALTZ, *supra* note 59, at 111 (arguing that states in anarchy "must rely on the means they can generate and the arrangements they can make for themselves. Self-help is necessarily the principle of action in anarchy").

63 Dunne & Schmidt, *supra* note 58, at 153 (discussing the security dilemma in the context of realist theory).

64 Jeffrey W. Legro & Andrew Moravcsik, *Is Anybody Still a Realist?*, INT'L SECURITY, Fall 1999, at 5, 17 (arguing that, under realism, a state's influence is proportional to its underlying power, defined as access to various material resources and capabilities, which includes, but is not limited to, military power).

65 WALTZ, *supra* note 59, at 116–28 (discussing the importance of the balance of power to a structural theory of international politics); Steven L. Lamy, *Contemporary Mainstream Approaches: Neo-Realism and Neo-Liberalism, in* THE GLOBALIZATION OF WORLD POLITICS: AN INTRODUCTION TO INTERNATIONAL RELATIONS 185 (John Baylis & Steve Smith eds., 2d ed. 2001) (noting realism's emphasis on the balance of power as the central mechanism for international order).

66 HEDLEY BULL, THE ANARCHICAL SOCIETY: A STUDY OF ORDER IN WORLD POLITICS 206–07 (1977) (arguing that the great powers manage international order through, among other things, preserving the general balance of power).

67 Legro & Moravcsik, *supra* note 64, at 18; *see also* WALTZ, *supra* note 59, at 131 (discussing the relevant material capabilities of states as including "size of population and territory, resource endowment, economic capability, military strength, political stability and competence").

68 Lamy, *supra* note 65, at 185 (noting that traditional realists and neo-realists agree on the importance of military power to a state's security and survival).

69 Anne-Marie Slaughter, *International Law and International Relations*, 285 RECUEIL DES COURS 9, 33–34 (2000) (noting the realist premise that states are "rational unitary actors who are functionally identical," like billiard balls colliding with one another in the international system).

70 J. Ann Tickner, *Re-visioning Security, in* INTERNATIONAL RELATIONS TODAY 175, 179 (Ken Booth & Steve Smith eds., 1995) ("The realist preoccupation with cross-border conflict and military power defined in terms of the interests and security of the great powers has come under a great deal of criticism from those who

argue that its worldview is a poor fit with contemporary reality."); JAN A. SCHOLTE, GLOBALIZATION: A CRITICAL INTRODUCTION 207–08 (2000) (noting how globalization has broadened "the security agenda beyond military matters alone").

71 Howard Williams & Ken Booth, *Kant: Theorist Beyond Limits, in* CLASSICAL THEORIES OF INTERNATIONAL RELATIONS 71 (Ian Clark & Iver B. Neumann eds., 1996).

72 EDWARD H. CARR, NATIONALISM AND AFTER 38 (1945) [hereinafter NATIONALISM AND AFTER].

73 *Id.* at 39–72.

74 Anne-Marie Slaughter, *A Chance to Reshape the UN*, WASH. POST, April 13, 2003, at B7 (arguing that "the very origins of the Universal Declaration of Human Rights reflect at least in part the recognition that Hitler's horrific abuses of his own people foreshadowed the threat he posed to the rest of the world[ ]"). The preamble of the European Convention for the Protection of Human Rights and Fundamental Freedoms also expressed this perspective as the signatory governments reaffirmed "their profound belief in those Fundamental Freedoms which are the foundation of justice and peace in the world and are best maintained on the one hand by an effective political democracy and on the other by a common understanding and observance of the Human Rights upon which they depend". European Convention for the Protection of Human Rights and Fundamental Freedoms, Nov. 4, 1950, 213 U.N.T.S. 222.

75 Jessica R. Mathews, *Redefining Security*, 68 FOREIGN AFF. 162, 162 (1989).

76 Ullman, *supra* note 56, at 152

77 *Id.* at 133.

78 *Id.*

79 CAROLINE THOMAS, IN SEARCH OF SECURITY: THE THIRD WORLD IN INTERNATIONAL RELATIONS (1987).

80 Mathews, *supra* note 75, at 162.

81 BARRY BUZAN, PEOPLE, STATES, AND FEAR: AN AGENDA FOR INTERNATIONAL SECURITY STUDIES (1991) (arguing for including economic and environmental issues in security studies); Thomas Homer-Dixon, *On the Threshold: Environmental Changes as Causes of Acute Conflict*, INT'L SECURITY, Fall 1991, at 76 (arguing the linkage between environmental conditions and violence); Jessica Mathews, *The Environment and International Security, in* WORLD SECURITY: TRENDS AND CHALLENGES AT CENTURY'S END (Michael Klare & David Thomas eds., 1991) (arguing for including environmental and demographic concerns in discourse on security); THOMAS HOMER-DIXON, ENVIRONMENT, SCARCITY, AND VIOLENCE 166 (1999) (linking environmental conditions with conflicts over scarce resources).

82 Tickner, *supra* note 70, at 182.

83 Altman, *supra* note 5, at 34.

84 Ullman, *supra* note 56, at 133–35.

85 Tickner, *supra* note 70, at 182 (arguing that all proponents of the common security approach emphasize the security of the individual and call into question the state as the provider of security).

86 As Mathews argued in connection with environmental challenges, "the need for new diplomacy and for new institutions and regulatory regimes to cope with the world's growing environmental interdependence is even more compelling." Mathews, *supra* note 75, at 174.

87 Tickner, *supra* note 70, at 181–82 ("Common security assumes that there are global dangers which threaten the entire system and which cannot be solved by boundary protection; by emphasizing common dangers, it bases its appeal for co-operative behaviour, not on altruism, but on a larger sense of collective self-interest.").

88 Scott Burchill, *Liberal Internationalism, in* THEORIES OF INTERNATIONAL RELATIONS 28 (Scott Burchill & Andrew Linklater eds., 1996) (providing an overview of liberalism as a theory of international relations); *see also* Timothy Dunne, *Liberalism, in* THE GLOBALIZATION OF WORLD POLITICS: AN INTRODUCTION TO INTERNATIONAL RELATIONS 163 (John Baylis & Steve Smith eds., 2d ed. 2001).

89 Andrew Moravcsik, *Taking Preferences Seriously: A Liberal Theory of International Politics*, 51 INT'L ORG. 513, 516 (1997).

90 *Id.* at 518.

91 *Id.* at 537.

92 *Id.* at 520.

93 *Id.* at 531 (arguing that liberal theory holds that "aggressive behavior . . . is most likely in undemocratic or inegailitarian polities where privileged individuals can easily pass costs on to others").

94 *Id.* at 530 (arguing that liberal theory posits that "the more diversified and complex the existing transnational commercial ties and production structures, the less cost-effective coercion is likely to be").

95 GEORGE ROSEN, A HISTORY OF PUBLIC HEALTH (1958); DOROTHY PORTER, HEALTH, CIVILIZATION, AND THE STATE (1999).

96 PRICE-SMITH, *supra* note 40, at 2 ("Throughout recorded history, infectious disease has consistently accounted for the greatest proportion of human morbidity and mortality, surpassing war as the foremost threat to human life and health."). Two examples from the twentieth century illustrate this fact. Experts estimate that smallpox alone killed 500 million people during the twentieth century. DAVID KOPLOW, SMALLPOX: THE FIGHT TO ERADICATE A GLOBAL SCOURGE 1 (2002). The 1918–1919 influenza pandemic killed between an estimated 20 and 100 million people in a short period of time. GINA KOLATA, FLU: THE STORY OF THE GREAT INFLUENZA PANDEMIC OF 1918 AND THE SEARCH FOR THE VIRUS THAT CAUSED IT 4–7 (1999).

97 Here I borrow from the definition of "collective security" in Adam Roberts & Benedict Kingsbury, *Introduction: The UN's Roles in International Society since 1945, in* UNITED NATIONS, DIVIDED WORLD 30 (Adam Roberts & Benedict Kingsbury eds., 1993).

98 Paris, *supra* note 8, at 87 (providing a detailed analysis of the "human security" concept). My presentation of human security differs from Paris' analysis because I connect the concept to underlying theories of international relations, critical international theory and social constructivism. I take this approach to avoid the problems created by the expansive way in which human security is often presented. As Paris critically observed, "if human security means almost anything, then it effectively means nothing at all." *Id.* at 93. My approach captures the central focus of human security literature on the security of individuals and communities but adds a prescriptive focus that such security is to be achieved transnationally by non-state actors rather than internationally by states and international organizations. This prescriptive focus is what separates human security from common security conceptually.

99 UNITED NATIONS DEVELOPMENT PROGRAMME, HUMAN DEVELOPMENT REPORT, 1994 (1994).

100 *Id.* at 22.

101 *Id.* at 23. Under this approach, UNDP identified seven core elements of human security: (1) freedom from poverty (economic security); (2) access to food (food security); (3) access to health services and protection from disease (health security); (4) protection from environmental degradation (environmental security); (5) protection against violent threats to personal safety (personal security); (6) protection for

indigenous cultures and ethnic communities (community security); and (7) protection of civil and political rights and freedom from political oppression (political security). *Id.* at 24–25.

102 UNITED NATIONS DEVELOPMENT PROGRAMME, HUMAN DEVELOPMENT REPORT: GLOBALISATION WITH A HUMAN FACE 3 (1999).

103 BROWER & CHALK, *supra* note 37, at 4–5 ("The key idea behind human security . . . is the focus on the *individual* as the primary object of security.").

104 *Id.* at 4 ("Such statecentric paradigms are clearly unable to deal with issues that originate within national borders but whose effects transcend international boundaries and affect the security of people worldwide.").

105 *Id.* at 6 (arguing that "human security stresses the potential for individual/ communitarian cooperation that is undertaken to achieve (absolute) gains that will be to the benefit of all.").

106 Tickner, *supra* note 70, at 189.

107 *Id.* at 190.

108 Richard Devetak, *Critical Theory, in* THEORIES OF INTERNATIONAL RELATIONS 145 (Scott Burchill & Andrew Linklater eds., 1996) (discussing critical international theory generally); *see also* Stephen Hobson & Richard Wyn Jones, *Marxist Theories of International Relations, in* THE GLOBALIZATION OF WORLD POLITICS: AN INTRODUCTION TO INTERNATIONAL RELATIONS 200, 214–16 (John Baylis & Steve Smith eds., 2d ed. 2001).

109 Alexander Wendt, *Anarchy is What States Make of It: The Social Construction of Power Politics*, 46 INT'L ORG. 391 (1992) (discussing social constructivism as a theory of international relations) [hereinafter *Anarchy*]; Jeffrey T. Checkel, *The Constructivist Turn in International Relations Theory*, 50 WORLD POL. 324 (1998); ALEXANDER WENDT, SOCIAL THEORY OF INTERNATIONAL POLITICS (1999); Steve Smith, *Reflectivist and Constructivist Approaches to International Relations, in* THE GLOBALIZATION OF WORLD POLITICS: AN INTRODUCTION TO INTERNATIONAL RELATIONS 224, 242–46 (John Baylis & Steve Smith eds., 2d ed. 2001).

110 VENDULKA KUBÁLKOVÁ & A. A. CRUICKSHANK, MARXISM AND INTERNATIONAL RELATIONS (1985) (discussing Marxist international relations theory); Hobson & Jones, *supra* note 108, at 203–05.

111 Devetak, *supra* note 108, at 165 (arguing that critical international theory differs radically from other theories because it "seeks to bring about radical change; it seeks to remove those unnecessary constraints on universal freedom"); Hobsen & Jones, *supra* note 108, at 215 (noting that "[c]ritical theorists have made some of their most important contributions through their explorations of the meaning of emancipation").

112 Alexander Wendt, *Constructing International Politics*, INT'L SECURITY, Summer 1995, at 71, 73.

113 WENDT, *supra* note 109, at 246–308 (analyzing the Hobbesian, Lockean, and Kantian cultures of anarchy).

114 BROWER & CHALK, *supra* note 37, at 4.

115 Theoretically and practically, public health is closely associated with the state. Theoretically, public health is considered a "public good," a service or resource that only the government can supply adequately and consistently. Arguments that the government has the primary responsibility for public health illustrate this theoretical position. INSTITUTE OF MEDICINE, *supra* note 1, at 7–10 (discussing the role of government in the public health mission); GOSTIN, *supra* note 48, at 4 (arguing that "[p]ublic health activities are a special responsibility of the government"). The focus in public health histories on the development of government policy and activities further underscores the special role that the state plays in traditional

conceptions of public health. *See generally* ROSEN, *supra* note 95; PORTER, *supra* note 95; PETER BALDWIN, CONTAGION AND THE STATE IN EUROPE, 1830–1930 (1999).

116 RICHARD DODGSON ET AL., GLOBAL HEALTH GOVERNANCE: A CONCEPTUAL REVIEW (World Health Org., Key Issues in Global Health Governance Discussion Paper No. 1, 2002) (discussing global health governance); KELLY LOUGHLIN & VIRGINIA BERRIDGE, GLOBAL HEALTH GOVERNANCE: HISTORICAL DIMENSIONS OF GLOBAL GOVERNANCE (World Health Org., Key Issues in Global Health Governance Discussion Paper No. 2, 2002); DAVID P. FIDLER, GLOBAL HEALTH GOVERNANCE: OVERVIEW OF THE ROLE OF INTERNATIONAL LAW IN PROTECTING AND PROMOTING GLOBAL PUBLIC HEALTH (World Health Org., Key Issues in Global Health Governance Discussion Paper No. 3, 2002); Kickbusch, *supra* note 11, at 192.

117 Kent Buse & Gill Walt, *Globalisation and Multilateral Public-Private Partnerships: Issues for Health Policy, in* HEALTH POLICY IN A GLOBALISING WORLD 41 (Kelley Lee et al. eds., 2002) (discussing global public-private partnerships for health); PUBLIC-PRIVATE PARTNERSHIPS FOR PUBLIC HEALTH (Michael Reich ed., 2002); Roy Widdus, *Public-Private Partnerships for Health: Their Main Targets, Their Diversity, and Their Future Directions*, 79 BULL. WORLD HEALTH ORG. 713 (2001).

118 Kickbusch, *supra* note 11, at 195 (arguing that the social constructivist framework "offers the best theoretical starting point to help understand the dynamics of global health governance"). *But see* David P. Fidler, *Disease and Globalized Anarchy: Theoretical Considerations on the Pursuit of Global Health*, 1 SOC. THEORY & HEALTH 21, 32–33, 37 (forthcoming 2003) (arguing that using social constructivism as the theoretical vehicle for global health advocacy faces serious problems).

119 Pirages, *Ecological Theory, supra* note 38, at 54.

120 *Id.* at 53.

121 *Id.* at 56.

122 Sarah Glasgow & Dennis Pirages, *Microsecurity, in* PLAGUES AND POLITICS: INFECTIOUS DISEASE AND INTERNATIONAL POLICY 195, 198 (Andrew T. Price-Smith ed., 2001).

123 Pirages, *Ecological Theory, supra* note 38, at 59.

124 *Id.* at 63.

125 IAN CLARK, THE HIERARCHY OF STATES: REFORM AND RESISTANCE IN THE INTERNATIONAL ORDER 62 (1989); *see also* Matthew Paterson, *Green Politics, in* THEORIES OF INTERNATIONAL RELATIONS 252 (Scott Burchill & Andrew Linklater eds., 1996) (discussing "green political theory" and international relations).

126 INTERNATIONAL CRISIS GROUP, *supra* note 35, at i–ii.

127 Ullman, *supra* note 56.

128 Pirages, *Ecological Theory, supra* note 38, at 54.

129 PRICE-SMITH, *supra* note 40, at 183.

130 BROWER & CHALK, *supra* note 37, at 1–12.

131 Price-Smith adopts Ullman's definition of security in his analysis, demonstrating that Price-Smith rejects the traditional realist framework for thinking about security in connection with infectious diseases. *Id.* at 119.

132 BAN, *supra* note 34, at 71.

133 Pirages, *Ecological Theory, supra* note 38, at 55.

134 Geneva Protocol, *supra* note 13 (stating that the states parties "agree to be bound as between themselves").

135 A number of states parties to the Geneva Protocol entered reservations that declared that the Protocol would cease to be binding if another state party violated its terms. DOCUMENTS ON THE LAWS OF WAR 144–146 (Adam Roberts & Richard Guelff eds., 2d ed. 1989) (listing reservations to the Geneva Protocol).

136 Convention for the Prohibition of the Development, Production, and Stockpiling of Bacteriological (Biological) and Toxin Weapons and on Their Destruction, Apr. 10, 1972, 11 I.L.M. 309.

137 *Lessons, supra* note 46, at 249–67.

138 RICHARD A. FALKENRATH, ROBERT D. NEWMAN & BRADLEY A. THAYER, AMERICA'S ACHILLES HEEL: NUCLEAR, BIOLOGICAL, AND CHEMICAL TERRORISM AND COVERT ATTACK 221–25, 228–29 (1998) (discussing the attractiveness of nuclear, biological, and chemical weapons in asymmetrical conflict with the United States).

139 *Id.* at 222.

140 One of the best known examples of the use of military force against a state sponsor of terrorism is the U.S. military strikes against Libya in 1986 following a Libyan-sponsored terrorist attack against U.S. military personnel in Berlin.

141 FALKENRATH, NEWMAN & THAYER, *supra* note 138, at 169–70.

142 David E. Kaplan, *Aum Shinriyko, in* TOXIC TERROR: ASSESSING TERRORIST USE OF CHEMICAL AND BIOLOGICAL WEAPONS 207 (Jonathan B. Tucker ed., 2000); William Rosenau, *Aum Shinriyko's Biological Weapons Program: Why Did It Fail?*, 24 STUD. CONFLICT & TERRORISM 289 (2001).

143 Richard A. Falkenrath, *Problems of Preparedness: U.S. Readiness for a Domestic Terrorist Attack*, INT'L SECURITY, Spring 2001, at 147.

144 Robert L. Ostergard, *Politics in the Hot Zone: AIDS and National Security in Africa*, 23 THIRD WORLD Q. 333, 346 (2002) ("The HIV/AIDS epidemic is perhaps the greatest security threat from disease since the bubonic plague ravaged Europe between 1346 and 1351."); Altman, *supra* note 5, at 36–40 (analyzing HIV/AIDS as an exemplar of a new kind of security threat); PRICE-SMITH, *supra* note 40, at 123–24 (citing various arguments about the threat HIV/AIDS poses to U.S. foreign policy and national security); BROWER & CHALK, *supra* note 37, at 31–60 (analyzing HIV/AIDS in South Africa).

145 DEPARTMENT OF HEALTH AND HUMAN SERVICES & CENTERS FOR DISEASE CONTROL AND PREVENTION, ADDRESSING EMERGING INFECTIOUS DISEASE THREATS: A PREVENTION STRATEGY FOR THE UNITED STATES (1994); DEPARTMENT OF HEALTH AND HUMAN SERVICES & CENTERS FOR DISEASE CONTROL AND PREVENTION, PREVENTING EMERGING INFECTIOUS DISEASES: A STRATEGY FOR THE 21ST CENTURY (1998).

146 WORLD HEALTH REPORT 1996, *supra* note 21, at 15 ("During the past 20 years, at least 30 new diseases have emerged to threaten the health of hundreds of millions of people.").

147 Francis Fukuyama, *The End of History?*, NAT'L INT., Summer 1989, at 3, 3 ("The triumph of the West, of the Western *idea*, is evident first of all in the total exhaustion of viable systematic alternatives to Western liberalism."); Samuel P. Huntington, *The Clash of Civilizations?*, 72 FOREIGN AFF. 22, 39 (1993) ("The West is now at an extraordinary peak of power in relation to other civilizations.").

148 PRICE-SMITH, *supra* note 40, at 179.

149 Ostergard, *supra* note 144, at 347.

150 ANDREW T. PRICE-SMITH, PRETORIA'S SHADOW: THE HIV/AIDS PANDEMIC AND NATIONAL SECURITY IN SOUTH AFRICA (Chem. and Biological Arms Control Inst., Health and Security Series Special Report No. 4, 2002) [hereinafter PRETORIA'S SHADOW].

151 Nicholas Eberstadt, *The future of AIDS*, 81 FOREIGN AFF. 22, 22 (2002).

152 PRETORIA'S SHADOW, *supra* note 150, at 3–4.

153 *Id.* at 34 ("Historically, South Africa's ruling ANC party has shown itself to be less than apt when it comes to formulating a coherent and effective national policy to address the HIV/AIDS epidemic").

154 Although not using realism as a framework, Price-Smith's analysis is again relevant because he identifies, as a task for future research, the need "to distinguish pathogens that generate great mortality and/or morbidity in a population and significantly affect state capacity (e.g., HIV/AIDS and the malaria and tuberculosis pathogens) from relatively innocuous or rare pathogens (e.g., rhinovirus and legionella)." PRICE-SMITH, *supra* note 40, at 180–81.

155 The rapid development of a smallpox vaccination policy by the Bush administration after the events of September 11th and the anthrax attacks illustrates the threat the U.S. government perceives smallpox used as a weapon to be. U.S. CENTERS FOR DISEASE CONTROL AND PREVENTION, PROTECTING AMERICANS: SMALLPOX VACCINATION POLICY (Dec. 13, 2002), *available at* http://www.bt.cdc.gov/agent/smallpox/vaccination/pdf/vaccination-program-statement.pdf [hereinafter PROTECTING AMERICANS: SMALLPOX VACCINATION POLICY].

156 The Ottawa Group, made up of the Group of Seven ministers of health and the Mexican minister of health and established to explore ways to improve collaboration on preparing for bioterrorism after September 11th and the anthrax attacks, has added international cooperation on preparedness for pandemic influenza to its agenda. U.S. DEPARTMENT OF STATE, FACT SHEET RELEASED BY THE U.S. DELEGATION TO THE 5TH REVIEW CONFERENCE OF THE BWC (Nov. 14, 2002).

157 JUDITH MILLER, STEPHEN ENGELBERG & WILLIAM BROAD, GERMS: BIOLOGICAL WEAPONS AND AMERICA'S SECRET WAR 81 (2001) ("With the right equipment, military scientists could make a pathogen much hardier or even more lethal. Researchers might use the new techniques to turn harmless germs into killers. Overall, the advances [in genetic engineering] threatened to tip the balance between offense and defense decisively in favor of the attacker. Genetic manipulation made it possible to redesign bugs like anthrax so that they could evade vaccines, one of the best protections against a biological weapon.").

158 Kenneth Waltz, *Structural Realism after the Cold War*, INT'L SECURITY, Summer 2000, at 5, 5.

159 U.S. CENTERS FOR DISEASE CONTROL AND PREVENTION, HIV/AIDS UPDATE—A GLANCE AT THE EPIDEMIC, *available at* http:www.cdc.gov/nchstp/od/news/At-a-Glance.pdf (last visited Jan. 3, 2003) ("During the mid-to-late 1990's, advances in HIV treatments led to dramatic declines in AIDS deaths and slowed progression from HIV to AIDS [in the United States].").

160 PRICE-SMITH, *supra* note 40, at 119.

161 *Id.* at 119, 183 (adopting Ullman's rejection of realism's conception of security and his broader definition of security and expressly rejecting realism as a theoretical approach to disease threats); PRETORIA'S SHADOW, *supra* note 150, at 3 (accepting the broadening of the definition of national security "to include such phenomena as terrorism, resource scarcity, migration, and now threats to population health").

162 *See* BROWER & CHALK, *supra* note 37, at 1–12.

163 Eberstadt, *supra* note 151, at 23.

164 Ostergard, *supra* note 144, at 339.

165 GROUP OF EIGHT, THE G8 GLOBAL PARTNERSHIP AGAINST THE SPREAD OF WEAPONS AND MATERIALS OF MASS DESTRUCTION (June 27, 2002), *at* http//www.g8.gc.ca/kan_docs/globpart-e.asp (last visited Jan. 3, 2003) [hereinafter G8 GLOBAL PARTNERSHIP].

166 GROUP OF EIGHT, G8 AFRICA PLAN (June 27, 2002), *at* http://www.g8.gc.ca/kan_docs/afraction-e.asp (last visited Jan. 3, 2002).

167 A similar realist analysis can be undertaken concerning the financial difficulties facing the Global Fund to Fight AIDS, Malaria, and Tuberculosis and the substance of President Bush's Emergency Plan for AIDS Relief. David P. Fidler,

Racism or Realpolitik? The HIV/AIDS Catastrophe in Sub-Saharan Africa and U.S. Foreign Policy, J. GENDER, RACE & JUST. 97 (2003).

168 Stephen M. Walt, *Beyond Bin Laden: Reshaping U.S. Foreign Policy*, INT'L SECURITY, Winter 2001/2002, at 56, 62.

169 BAN, *supra* note 34, at 14 (emphasis added). The same emphasis, especially on China, India, and Russia, can be found in other writings on the public health-national security linkage. CONTAGION AND CONFLICT, *supra* note 5; NATIONAL INTELLIGENCE COUNCIL, *supra* note 28; KASSALOW, *supra* note 36; Eberstadt, *supra* note 151 at 22–23 (emphasizing Russia, China, and India's problems with HIV/AIDS over sub-Saharan Africa's); NATIONAL INTELLIGENCE COUNCIL, THE NEXT WAVE OF HIV/AIDS: NIGERIA, ETHIOPIA, RUSSIA, INDIA, AND CHINA (Intelligence Community Assessment 2002-04D, Sept. 2002) [hereinafter THE NEXT WAVE].

170 Soloman R. Benetar, *South Africa's Transition in a Globalizing World: HIV/ AIDS as a Window and Mirror*, 77 INT'L AFF. 347, 347–75 (2001).

171 COMMISSION ON MACROECONOMICS AND HEALTH, MACROECONOMICS AND HEALTH: INVESTING IN HEALTH FOR ECONOMIC DEVELOPMENT 22 (2001) ("The economic costs of avoidable disease, when taken together, are staggeringly high.").

172 INSTITUTE OF MEDICINE, EMERGING INFECTIONS: MICROBIAL THREATS TO HEALTH IN THE UNITED STATES 77–84 (1992) [hereinafter EMERGING INFECTIONS] (discussing international travel and commerce as factors in global spread of infectious diseases).

173 M. Kent Ranson et al., *The Public Health Implications of Multilateral Trade Agreements*, in HEALTH POLICY IN A GLOBALISING WORLD 18 (Kelley Lee et al. eds., 2002); Meri Koivusalo, *Assessing the Health Policy Implications of the WTO Trade and Investment Agreements*, in HEALTH IMPACTS OF GLOBALIZATION: TOWARDS GLOBAL GOVERNANCE 161 (Kelley Lee ed., 2003); WORLD HEALTH ORGANIZATION & WORLD TRADE ORGANIZATION, WTO AGREEMENTS AND PUBLIC HEALTH—A JOINT STUDY BY THE WHO AND WTO SECRETARIATS (2002).

174 KASSALOW, *supra* note 36.

175 CONTAGION AND CONFLICT, *supra* note 5, at 4–5 (discussing impact of economic globalization on spread of infectious diseases).

176 Ranson et al., *supra* note 173, at 18; Koivusalo, *supra* note 173, at 161; WORLD HEALTH ORGANIZATION & WORLD TRADE ORGANIZATION, *supra* note 173; DAVID P. FIDLER, INTERNATIONAL LAW AND INFECTIOUS DISEASES 114–168 (1999) (analyzing international trade law and infectious disease control).

177 EMERGING INFECTIONS, *supra* note 172, at 34–112 (analyzing the many factors of infectious disease emergence).

178 *See, e.g.*, Y. Von Schirnding, W. Onzivu, A. O. Adede, *International Environmental Law and Global Public Health*, 80 BULL. WORLD HEALTH ORG. 970 (2002); David P. Fidler, *Challenges to Humanity's Health: The Contributions of International Environmental Law to National and Global Public Health*, 31 ENV. L. REV. 10,048 (2001).

179 U.S. DEPARTMENT OF HEALTH AND HUMAN SERVICES & CENTERS FOR DISEASE CONTROL AND PREVENTION, PROTECTING THE NATION'S HEALTH IN AN ERA OF GLOBALIZATION: CDC's GLOBAL INFECTIOUS DISEASE STRATEGY 5 (2002) ("Although safeguarding U.S. health is a domestic goal, its achievement requires international action and cooperation. This is because U.S. health and global health are inextricably linked.").

180 Brower and Chalk list biowarfare and bioterrorism as one element of the threats infectious diseases pose to human security, but their discussion of these threats is cursory compared to the attention they pay to infectious diseases generally, especially HIV/AIDS. *See* BROWER & CHALK, *supra* note 37, at 10–11 (on biowarfare and bioterrorism), 72–73 (on bioterrorism).

181 The human security perspective is thus likely to see promise in efforts such as the Bioweapons Prevention Project, which "is dedicated to reinforcing the norm against the weaponization of disease. It is a global civil society activity that tracks governmental and other behaviour under the treaties that codify the norm. It nurtures and is empowered by an international network, and acts both through that network and its publications." Bioweapons Prevention Project, *at* http://www.bwpp.org/ (last visited Jan. 3, 2003).

182 *See, e.g.*, BROWER & CHALK, *supra* note 37, at 13–30 (analyzing factors associated with the increased incidence and spread of infectious diseases).

183 See *supra* note 115.

184 *See supra* note 117.

185 Ilona Kickbusch & Kent Buse, *Global Influences and Global Responses: International Health at the Turn of the Twenty-First Century, in* INTERNATIONAL PUBLIC HEALTH: HEALTH ECONOMIC AND PUBLIC HEALTH PERSPECTIVES 727–28 (Michael H. Merson et al. eds., 2001) (discussing health as a "global public good"); GLOBAL PUBLIC GOODS FOR HEALTH (Richard Smith et al. eds., 2003).

186 *See supra* note 116.

187 Ostergard, *supra* note 144, at 336; *see also* Paris, *supra* note 8, at 93 (arguing that "if human security means almost anything, then it effectively means nothing").

188 Ostergard, *supra* note 144, at 337.

189 PRICE-SMITH, *supra* note 40, at 3.

190 *See* David P. Fidler, *The Globalization of Public Health: Emerging Infectious Diseases and International Relations*, 5 IND. J. GLOBAL LEGAL STUD. 11, 46–50 (1997) (analyzing the potential contribution of critical international theory to understanding the globalization of public health and the problem of emerging infectious diseases); Fidler, *supra* note 118, at 33 (arguing that social constructivism "provides no blueprint for selecting what ideas to construct and how such ideas should be constructed").

191 The anthrax attacks in the United States in October and November 2001 resulted in twenty-two cases and five deaths. Daniel B. Jernigan et al., *Investigation of Bioterrorism-Related Anthrax, United States, 2001: Epidemiologic Findings*, 8 EMERGING INFECTIOUS DISEASE 1019 (2002), *at* http://www.cdc.gov/ncidod/EID/vol8no10/02-0353.htm (last visited Jan. 3, 2003). According to UNAIDS, 3.1 million people died from HIV/AIDS in 2002. UNAIDS, AIDS EPIDEMIC UPDATE: DECEMBER 2002, at 3 (2002).

192 WORLD HEALTH ORGANIZATION, GLOBAL STRATEGY FOR CONTAINMENT OF ANTIMICROBIAL RESISTANCE (2002); David P. Fidler, *Antimicrobial Resistance: A Challenge for Global Health Governance, in* HEALTH IMPACTS OF GLOBALIZATION: TOWARDS GLOBAL GOVERNANCE 144 (Kelley Lee ed., 2003).

193 Altman briefly notes the relevance of the realist framework when he argues that, in the HIV/AIDS-security debate, "the primary concern is for the 'security' of the rich world, not for those already infected and those most at risk of infection. Yet if self-interest leads to a greater realism about HIV, it could not only improve prevention efforts, it may help break down stigma that remains a major part of the problem for those already infected." Altman, *supra* note 5, at 43.

194 *But see* PRICE-SMITH, *supra* note 40 (focusing on South Africa). Price-Smith's analysis of South Africa is "the first in a series that looks at the health and security interactions in a number of countries" that CBACI will publish in the future. *Id.* at iv.

195 The United States experienced bioterrorism previously when the Rajneeshee cult in Oregon contaminated salad bars in an attempt to influence a local election in the early 1980s. W. Seth Carus, *The Rajneeshees, in* TOXIC TERROR: ASSESSING

TERRORIST USE OF CHEMICAL AND BIOLOGICAL WEAPONS 115 (Jonathan B. Tucker ed., 2000). This bioterrorism incident was, however, not understood as such until years later, remained local in nature, and did not terrorize the nation as a whole.

196 President George W. Bush, State of the Union Address (Jan. 29, 2002), *available at* http://www.whitehouse.gov/news/releases/2002/01/20020129-11.html (last visited Jan. 3, 2003).

197 NATIONAL SECURITY STRATEGY OF THE UNITED STATES OF AMERICA 14 (2002).

198 NATIONAL STRATEGY TO COMBAT WEAPONS OF MASS DESTRUCTION 1 (2002).

199 NATIONAL SECURITY STRATEGY OF THE UNITED STATES OF AMERICA, *supra* note 197, at 13–14.

200 NATIONAL STRATEGY TO COMBAT WEAPONS OF MASS DESTRUCTION, *supra* note 198, at 1 ("We must accord the highest priority to the protection of the United States, our forces, and our friends and allies from the existing and growing WMD threat.").

201 NATIONAL SECURITY STRATEGY OF THE UNITED STATES OF AMERICA, *supra* note 197, at 15; *see also* NATIONAL STRATEGY TO COMBAT WEAPONS OF MASS DESTRUCTION, *supra* note 198, at 1 ("We will not permit the world's most dangerous regimes and terrorists to threaten us with the world's most destructive weapons.").

202 Graham Pearson, *Report from Geneva: The Biological and Toxin Weapons Convention*, 54 CBW CONVENTIONS BULL. 13 (2001); Barbara Hatch Rosenberg, *Allergic Reaction: Washington's Response to the BWC Protocol*, ARMS CONTROL TODAY, July–Aug. 2001, *at* http://www.armscontrol.org/act/2001_07-08/rosenbergjul_aug01.asp (last visited Jan. 3, 2003) (discussing the U.S. rejection of the protocol to the Biological and Toxin Weapons Convention); KATHLEEN C. BAILEY, NAT'L INST. FOR PUB. POLICY, WHY THE UNITED STATES REJECTED THE PROTOCOL TO THE BIOLOGICAL AND TOXIN WEAPONS CONVENTION (Oct. 2002), *available at* http://nipp.org/Adobe/Toxin%20Weapons2.pdf (last visited Nov. 8, 2003).

203 Seth Brugger, *Chemical Weapons Convention Chief Removed at U.S. Initiative*, ARMS CONTROL TODAY, May 2002, *available at* http://www.armscontrol.org/act/2002_05/opcmay02.asp (last visited Jan. 3, 2003).

204 *Special Section: The U.S. Decision to Withdraw from the ABM Treaty*, ARMS CONTROL TODAY, Jan.–Feb. 2002, *available at* http://www.armscontrol.org/act/2002_01-02/specjanfeb02.asp (last visited Jan. 3, 2003).

205 OFFICE OF HOMELAND SECURITY, NATIONAL STRATEGY FOR HOMELAND SECURITY (2002).

206 *Id.* at 5 ("Our great power leaves these enemies with few conventional options for doing us harm. One such option is to take advantage of our freedom and openness by secretly inserting terrorists into our country to attack our homeland. Homeland security seeks to deny this avenue of attack to our enemies and thus to provide a secure foundation for America's ongoing global engagement.").

207 Defense Against Weapons of Mass Destruction Act of 1996, Pub. L. 104–201, 110 Stat. 2715.

208 Public Health Security and Bioterrorism Preparedness and Response Act of 2002, Pub. L. 107–188, 116 Stat. 594.

209 *See also* Falkenrath, *supra* note 143.

210 OFFICE OF HOMELAND SECURITY, *supra* note 205, at 41–45 (describing efforts to be made to prepare the United States for responding to emergencies caused by terrorist attacks, including preparing public health and health care providers for catastrophic terrorism).

211 Press Release, U.S. Department of Health and Human Services, Bioterror Funding Provides Blueprint to Build a Strong New Public Health Infrastructure (Jan. 25,

2002), *available at* http://www.hhs.gov/news/press/2002pres/20020125.html (last visited Jan. 3, 2003).

212 Public Health Security and Bioterrorism Preparedness and Response Act of 2002, *supra* note 208.

213 OFFICE OF HOMELAND SECURITY, *supra* note 205, at 68.

213 U.S. CENTERS FOR DISEASE CONTROL AND PREVENTION, SMALLPOX RESPONSE PLAN AND GUIDELINES, *at* http://www.bt.cdc.gov/agent/smallpox/response-plan/index. asp (last visited Jan. 3, 2003).

215 Press Release, U.S. Department of Health and Human Services, HHS Awards $428 Million Contract to Produce Smallpox Vaccine (Nov. 28, 2001), *at* http:// www.hhs.gov/news/press/2001pres/20011128.html (last visited Jan. 3, 2003).

216 President George W. Bush, Remarks by the President on Smallpox Vaccination (Dec. 13, 2002), *available at* http://www.whitehouse.gov/news/releases/2002/12/20021213-7. html (last visited Jan. 3, 2003); PROTECTING AMERICANS: SMALLPOX VACCINATION POLICY, *supra* note 155.

217 Press Release, U.S. Department of Health and Human Services, Secretary Thompson Joins Health Ministers in "Ottawa Plan": Countries Forge New Partnerships to Strengthen Public Health and National Security (Nov. 7, 2001), *available at* http://www.hhs.gov/news/press/2001press/20011107a.html (last visited Jan. 3, 2003).

218 G8 GLOBAL PARTNERSHIP, *supra* note 165.

219 OFFICE OF HOMELAND SECURITY, *supra* note 205, at 61 (noting that "the United States will seek to establish cooperative endeavors with Canada and Mexico for cross-border efforts to detect biological weapons attacks; eventually, these programs may be expanded to include other friendly nations").

220 Barry R. Posen, *The Struggle Against Terrorism: Grand Strategy, Strategy, and Tactics*, INT'L SECURITY, Winter 2001/2002, at 39.

221 WALTZ, *supra* note 59, at 131.

222 Exon-Florio Amendment, 50 U.S.C. § 2170 (1996).

223 *See supra* notes 158–59 and accompanying text.

224 David P. Fidler, *Bioterrorism, Public Health, and International Law*, 3 CHI. J. INT'L L. 7, 25 (2002) (arguing that "[i]nfectious disease problems in the developing world will be even less important to the United States in the post-anthrax world than they were previously").

225 Richard Parker, *The Global HIV/AIDS Pandemic, Structural Inequalities, and the Politics of International Heath*, 92 AM. J. PUB. HEALTH 343, 346 (2002).

226 For statistics on the SARS epidemic as of April 23, 2003, see World Health Organization, Cumulative Number of Reported Probable Cases of Severe Acute Respiratory Syndrome (SARS), *at* http://www.who.int/csr/sarscountry/2003_04_23/ en/ (last visited Apr. 24, 2003). As of April 23, 2003, the United States had reported only thirty-nine probable SARS cases and no deaths. *Id.*

227 *U.S. Issues a Middle East Laundry List*, CINCINNATI POST, Apr. 19, 2003, at A9 [2003 WL 2915696] ("The Pentagon also is wary of SARS, clipping all but essential travel to Asia and keeping movement of troops in the region to a minimum. A particular fear is that the virus will somehow be transmitted to U.S. troops in or bound for Iraq."). At least two developing countries, Malaysia and the Philippines, considered SARS to be a national security issue. *See* Raissa Robles, *Returning Filipinos Greeted by Masked Medics, not Smiles; Airport Authorities Go on Full Alert in Manila to Bar SARS Carriers from Slipping into the Country for the Easter Holidays*, SOUTH CHINA MORNING POST, Apr. 14, 2003, at 3 [2003 WL 17705027] (noting that, in the Philippines, "SARS is now regarded as a national security threat after the World Health Organisation listed

the Philippines as one of 30 countries 'with suspected or probable SARS cases' . . ."); Monique Chu, *Malaysia Freezes Visas for Taiwnese, Citizens of HK, China, Vietnam, Canada*, TAIPEI TIMES, Apr. 12, 2003 [2003 WL 4152230] (reporting on Malaysia's handling of SARS as a national security issue); Annie Freeda Cruez, *SARS: Four More Families Placed Under Home Quarantine*, THE NEW STRAIT TIMES, Apr. 8, 2003, at 1 [2003 WL 3361418] (reporting that the Malaysian government "viewed the spread of SARS as serious and as threat to national security").

228 NATIONAL SECURITY STRATEGY OF THE UNITED STATES OF AMERICA, *supra* note 197, at vi ("We will also continue to lead the world in efforts to reduce the terrible toll of HIV/AIDS and other infectious diseases."), 19 ("We will ensure that the WTO intellectual property rules are flexible enough to allow developing nations to gain access to critical medicines for extraordinary dangers like HIV/AIDS, tuberculosis, and malaria."), 22 (noting funding increases to poor countries for HIV/AIDS), 23 (stating that growth and development in countries afflicted by HIV/AIDS and other epidemics is threatened and that the United States strongly backed the new global fund for HIV/AIDS), 27 (noting that the spread of HIV/AIDS is on the U.S.-China foreign policy agenda).

229 George W. Bush, State of the Union Address (Jan. 28, 2003), *at* http://www. whitehouse.gov/news/releases/2003/01/20030128-19.html (last visited Feb. 3, 2003). President Bush proposed spending $15 billion over five years to assist African and Caribbean nations badly affected by HIV/AIDS. *Id.* The Emergency Plan would approximately triple U.S. financial support for international HIV/AIDS assistance. THE WHITE HOUSE, FACT SHEET: THE PRESIDENT'S EMERGENCY PLAN FOR AIDS RELIEF (Jan. 29, 2003), *at* http://www.state.gov/p/af/rls/fs/17033pf. htm (last visited Jan. 30, 2003). For the legislation introduced in Congress to implement the Emergency Plan for AIDS Relief, see the United States Leadership Against HIV/AIDS, Tuberculosis, and Malaria Act of 2003, H.R. 1298, 108th Cong. (2003). The House of Representatives passed this bill on May 1, 2003. Juliet Eilperin & Amy Goldstein, *House Passes $15 Billion AIDS Bill*, WASH. POST, May 2, 2003, at A01.

230 World Health Organization, *Report by the Secretariat: Deliberate Use of Biological and Chemical Agents to Cause Harm: Public Health Response*, WHO Doc. A55/20, Apr. 16, 2002, *at* http://www.who.int/gb/EB_WHA/PDF/WHA55/ea5520.pdf (last visited Jan. 3, 2003) (stressing importance of strengthening general public health capabilities to deal with threats from deliberate use of biological or chemical agents).

231 Global Pathogen Surveillance Act of 2002, S. 2487, 107th Cong. (2002); *see also* Global Pathogen Surveillance Act of 2003, S. 871, 108th Cong. (2003).

232 WORLD BANK, WORLD DEVELOPMENT REPORT 1993: INVESTING IN HEALTH (1993).

233 *Constitution of the World Health Organization*, *supra* note 51, at 1 (proclaiming that "[t]he enjoyment of the highest attainable standard of health is one of the fundamental rights of every human being without distinction of race, religion, political belief, economic or social condition").

234 AMERICA'S VITAL INTEREST IN GLOBAL HEALTH, *supra* note 24, at Chapter 5; *see also* U.S. DEPARTMENT OF HEALTH AND HUMAN SERVICES OFFICE OF GLOBAL HEALTH AFFAIRS, GLOBAL HEALTH CORE MESSAGES, *at* http://www.globalhealth. gov/quotes.shtml#nationalsecurity (last visited Jan. 3, 2003) [hereinafter OFFICE OF GLOBAL HEALTH AFFAIRS] ("The United States cannot afford an isolationist approach to health, as America's economic well-being depends on the well-being of our partner nations. *Healthy populations and healthy economies are vital for a healthy world economy and strong markets*.") (emphasis in original).

235 Commission on Macroeconomics and Health, *supra* note 171.

236 *Id.*

237 *Id.*

238 The proposed legislation to implement the Emergency Plan for AIDS Relief has Congress making findings that HIV/AIDS constitutes threat to "personal security" (sec. 2(6)) and "economic security" (sec. 2(7)); "poses a serious security issue for the international community" (sec. 2(10)); and is a major "national security" crisis (sec. 301(a)). The United States Leadership Against HIV/AIDS, Tuberculosis, and Malaria Act of 2003, *supra* note 229. From the *realpolitik* perspective, the finding that HIV/AIDS in the developing world is a national security crisis for the United States is not credible. The notion of a national security crisis would, however, be accurate under *realpoltiik* for those countries whose economic, military, and governance capabilities are being devastated by HIV/AIDS. *See supra* note 149 and accompanying text.

239 Michael E. O'Hanlon et al., Protecting the American Homeland: A Preliminary Analysis 138 (2002).

240 *G-8 Global Partnership Against the Spread of Weapons and Materials of Mass Destruction Before the House Comm. on Int'l Relations*, 107th Cong. (July 25, 2002) (testimony of Alan P. Larson, Under Secretary for Economic, Business, and Agricultural Affairs, U.S. Dep't of State), *at* http://www.state.gov/e/rls/rm/2002/12190pf.htm (last visited Sept. 11, 2002).

241 Commission on Macroeconomics and Health, *supra* note 171, at 5 ("Where countries are not willing to make a serious effort, though, or where funding is misused, prudence and credibility require that large-scale funding should not be provided.").

242 Caroline Thomas, *Poverty, Development, and Hunger, in* The Globalization of World Politics: An Introduction to International Relations 559, 566–569 (John Baylis & Steve Smith eds., 2d ed. 2001) (analyzing structural adjustment lending in the developing world); Bob Deacon, *Social Policy in a Global Context, in* Inequality, Globalization, and World Politics 211, 220 (Andrew Hurrell & Ngaire Woods eds., 1999) (noting that "[t]he impact of the IMF and World Bank structural adjustment programmes in developing countries has . . . generated a vast and critical development studies literature"); David P. Fidler, *A Kinder, Gentler System of Capitulations? International Law, Structural Adjustment Policies, and the Standard of Liberal, Globalized Civilization*, 35 Tex. Int'l L.J. 387, 404 (2000) (arguing that "[t]he system of SAPs [structural adjustment policies] reflects the exercise of hegemonic power in the international system by globalized states.").

243 *See also* The United States Leadership Against HIV/AIDS, Tuberculosis, and Malaria Act of 2003, *supra* note 229, at sec. 202(d) (1) (appropriating $1 billion for the Global Fund).

244 The White House, *supra* note 229. The proposed implementing legislation for the Emergency Plan for AIDS Relief also contains conditions on U.S. contributions to the Global Fund. *See* The United States Leadership Against HIV/AIDS, Tuberculosis, and Malaria Act of 2003, *supra* note 229, at sec. 202(c)(4)(A)(i)–(iii), (v) (limiting U.S. contributions to the Global Fund to no more than 33% of the total funds contributed to the Fund from all other sources; withholding contributions if the Global Fund provides assistance to a country determined by the United States to have provided support for international terrorism; and withholding contributions if the expenses of the Global Fund exceed 10% of the total expenditures for the Global Fund for any 2-year period; withholding contributions if the salary of any individual employed by the Global Fund exceeds the salary of the Vice President of the United States). The proposed implementing legislation also provides that

not less than 33% of the amounts appropriated for HIV/AIDS prevention shall be expended for abstinence-until-marriage programs. *Id.* at sec. 403(a). On the controversy surrounding the abstinence-until-marriage provision, see Eilperin & Goldstein, *supra* note 229, at A1.

245 Mark Heywood of the South African Treatment Action Coalition stated his concerns that the funds made available for the Emergency Plan for AIDS Relief would be spent bilaterally rather than through the Global Fund. Laurie Garrett & Samson Mulugeta, *AIDS Plan Offers Hope—But Some Activists Worry Global Funds May Not Reach Victims*, NEWSDAY, Jan. 30, 2003, *available at* http://www. newsday.com/news/health/ny-woaids303109187jan30.01.1801554.story?coll=ny% 2Dhealth%2Dheadlines (last visited Feb. 3, 2003). Rachel Cohen of Médecins Sans Frontierès' Campaign for Access to Essential Medicines warned that U.S. unilateralism on HIV/AIDS will squander money and lose lives and argued that the United States should "redirect more of the promised funds to existing multilateral funding bodies, rather than waste time and money on creating new ones." Press Release, Médecins Sans Frontierès, MSF Welcomes President Bush's Commitment to Scale-Up Access to Affordable AIDS Treatment, But Warns US Against Breaking Promises, Taking a Unilateral Approach (Jan. 30, 2003), *at* http:// www.msf.org (last visited Feb. 3, 2003).

246 PRICE-SMITH, *supra* note 40, at 136.

247 *Id.* China's initial secretive and uncooperative approach to the SARS outbreak reflected this perspective because "[t]he Chinese government often treats disease epidemics as state secrets and a national security concern and have been extremely cautious about reporting the SARS epidemic to the public." Robert J. Saiget, *China SARS Cases Expected to Rise as Epidemic Not Controlled, WHO Says*, AGENCE FRANCE-PRESSE, Mar. 28, 2003 [2003 WL 2765562].

248 PRICE-SMITH, *supra* note 40, at 136.

249 *Id.* at 137.

250 *See* The United States Leadership Against HIV/AIDS, Tuberculosis, and Malaria Act of 2003, *supra* note 229, at sec. 2, para. 21(F) (finding that a comprehensive, long-term, and international response to HIV/AIDS includes "encouraging active involvement of the private sector, including businesses, pharmaceutical and biotechnology companies, the medical and scientific communities, charitable foundations, private and voluntary organizations and nongovernmental organizations, faith-based organizations, community-based organizations, and other nonprofit entities").

251. BILL & MELINDA GATES FOUNDATION, STRIVING FOR GLOBAL HEALTH EQUITY, *at* http://www.gatesfoundation.org/globalhealth/infectiousdiseases/default.htm (last visited Jan. 3, 2003) ("The Bill & Melinda Gates Foundation has committed more than $1 billion to projects focused on the prevention and control of infectious disease.").

252 Fidler, *supra* note 190, at 38 n.115 (noting that "public health has rarely, if ever, been discussed in any realist analysis of international relations").

253 ULYSSES B. PANISSET, INTERNATIONAL HEALTH STATECRAFT: FOREIGN POLICY AND PUBLIC HEALTH IN PERU'S CHOLERA EPIDEMIC 23–88 (2000) (critiquing theories of international health).

254 *Id.* at 33–56 (analyzing perspective that international health is public health activities for the poor).

255 GOODMAN, *supra* note 9, at 329; Norman Howard-Jones, *Origins of International Health Work*, BRIT. MED. J. 1032, 1035 (1950).

256 JOHN HUTCHINSON, CHAMPIONS OF CHARITY: WAR AND THE RISE OF THE RED CROSS 126, 348–49 (1996).

257 Philip H. Manson-Bahr, History of the School of Tropical Medicine in London 31 (1956) (arguing that, in the late 1890s, British political officials and physicians realized that "[i]nstruction in tropical medicine was urgently necessary in this country as it was the centre of a great and growing tropical Empire").

258 Medical Museum of the Armed Forces Institute of Pathology, Yellow Fever 1 (1964) (observing that "the history of its [yellow fever's] control and cure is written in the annals of the United States Army"); Medical Museum of the Armed Forces Institute of Pathology, Conquerors of Yellow Fever 1 (1964) ("Among the triumphs of military medicine, few can equal the conquest of yellow fever by medical officers of the United States Army.").

259 Fidler, *supra* note 190, at 26–30.

260 Fidler, *supra* note 116, at 45.

261 Howard-Jones, *supra* note 255, at 1036 (noting this shift in the work of the Health Organization of the League of Nations, which promoted programs under "which the more advanced countries could, through an international agency, confer benefits upon countries whose technical resources were more limited").

262 *Constitution of the World Health Organization, supra* note 51, at 1.

263 Institute of Medicine, *supra* note 24, at Chapters 4–6.

264 Kassalow, *supra* note 36. Such arguments from self-interest for the United States to increase its involvement in international health matters are not new. In 1971, Representative Hugh L. Carey, arguing in favor of the proposed International Health Agency Act of 1971, said the following:

> Again as a practical matter it is in our self-interest to find and fight disease in foreign lands as a safeguard for our own population. Pandemic diseases respect no borders. . . . A second practical consideration is that improved health among the developing peoples abroad means more viable young nations and betters hopes for a peaceful environment throughout the world. I submit that health care is our lowest cost form of international security and protection against war and violence. . . . Third, improved health overseas in all age brackets means expanding consumer markets and increased trade for U.S. products.

See Hearing on H.R. 10042 Before the House Subcomm. on Int'l Orgs. & Movements of the Comm. on Foreign Affairs, 92nd Cong. 5 (1971) [hereinafter *1971 Hearings*].

265 Philip Allott, *The Concept of International Law,* 10 Eur. J. Int'l L. 31, 49 (1999).

266 Price-Smith, *supra* note 40, at 183.

267 Pirages, *Ecological Theory, supra* note 38, at 63.

268 For more on the problems anarchy poses for global public health, see Fidler, *supra* note 118.

269 Interestingly, Robert Koch, one of the leading scientists behind the triumph of germ theory in the late nineteenth century, argued that, concerning cholera, all "these international efforts are quite superfluous" and that the best approach would be for each country to engage in self-help: "seize cholera by the throat and stamp it out." Howard-Jones, *supra* note 9, at 76.

270 E. H. Carr, The Twenty Years' Crisis, 1919–1939: An Introduction to the Study of International Relations 41–62 (1939).

271 *Id.* at 55 ("The politician pursues the concrete interest of his country, and assumes (if he makes the assumption at all) that the interest of the world as a whole is identical with it.").

272 *Id.* at 51–53.

273 Kassalow, *supra* note 36.

274 OFFICE OF GLOBAL HEALTH AFFAIRS, *supra* note 234. Representative Donald M. Fraser made essentially the same "harmony of interests" argument in 1971 when he claimed that "sound health of the human body" represents "[a] positive goal consistent with American ideals and shared by most of the people of the world." *See 1971 Hearings, supra* note 264, at 2.

275 Mearsheimer, *supra* note 59, at 9–14.

276 Leon Gordenker, *The World Health Organization: Sectoral Leader or Occasional Benefactor?, in* U.S. POLICY AND THE FUTURE OF THE UNITED NATIONS 167 (Roger A. Coate ed., 1994); FREEMAN H. QUIMBY, THE POLITICS OF GLOBAL HEALTH, SUBCOMM. ON NAT'L SECURITY & SCIENTIFIC DEVS. OF THE HOUSE COMM. ON FOREIGN AFFAIRS 75 (1971) ("The United States is the chief contributor to WHO and is also one of the chief sources of complaint—principally with its heavy share of the financial burden as matched against its lack of direct control over the WHO programs.").

277 Ilona Kickbusch, *Influence and Opportunity: Reflections on the U.S. Role in Global Public Health*, 21 HEALTH AFF. 131 (2002). Again, arguments for the elevation of health on the agenda of U.S. foreign policy are not new. *See, e.g., 1971 Hearings, supra* note 264, at 1 (congressional hearings on proposed legislation to create "an international health agency in the Federal Government in order to permit greater American involvment in furnishing health assistance to the developing world"); NEW DIRECTIONS IN INTERNATIONAL HEALTH COOPERATION, *supra* note 25, at 2 (recommending in 1978 "that international health be elevated to an active and positive concern of all U.S. Government agencies, and particularly, that in the State Department, international health should play a strong role in the basic human needs strategy of U.S. foreign policy").

278 Altman, *supra* note 5, at 46 (arguing for "the need to put global health onto the table of 'high polities'").

279 Legro & Moravcsik, *supra* note 64, at 6–9.

280 Stanley Hoffmann, *Rousseau on War and Peace, in* STANLEY HOFFMANN, JANUS AND MINERVA: ESSAYS IN THE THEORY AND PRACTICE OF INTERNATIONAL POLITICS 25, 47 (1987).

49

BIOTERRORISM AS A FOREIGN POLICY ISSUE

Marc L. Ostfield

Source: *SAIS Review*, 24:1 (2004), 131–46.

Bioterrorism, the intentional release of biological pathogens, is distinct from other forms of terrorism in several important ways. Bioterrorist attacks are silent, low in cost and easy to replicate in multiple sites, and respect no geographical boundaries. With no central point of impact, explosion, or assault, the bioterrorist attack exists wherever and whenever one person transmits the infectious agent to another. But rather than recognizing the critical differences between nuclear, chemical, and biological attacks, analysts frequently group them into categories like "CBRN" (Chemical, Biological, Radiological, and Nuclear)—making it seem as if terrorist use of biological agents is merely another variant on a basic theme. This article details the differences that set bioterrorism apart, and discusses a number of implications for foreign policy decision makers, who ideally should be involved in planning for both the prevention and response to bioterrorism. Bioterrorism's distinctive foreign policy ramifications mean that those in the foreign policy establishment must work closely with public health leaders and others addressing national security to ensure effective strategies to address bioterrorism exist.

Few would disagree with the assertion that bioterrorism is a major foreign policy concern. Numerous articles and books have been written about terrorism, its impact, and its challenges for foreign policy. Yet when one explores the specific foreign policy aspects of *biological* terrorism, it becomes clear that addressing bioterrorism will require an enhanced perspective and unique approach on the part of the foreign policy establishment.

Discussions about combating bioterrorism have primarily taken place in two separate realms: public health and law enforcement/national defense.

While each realm has important components to contribute to an overall strategy, the unique features of bioterrorism and its almost immediate international impact require a coherent, thoughtful foreign policy component to any comprehensive response. The international reaction to Severe Acute Respiratory Syndrome (SARS) highlighted the critical linkages between public health and foreign policy. Strategies to combat bioterrorism further clarify those links, and reveal the unique ways in which foreign policy decision makers can form bridges not only between nations, but also across disciplines. By developing methods to facilitate effective international responses to bioterrorism, policymakers seeking to make the world safer in the face of the intentional release of a biological agent simultaneously provide ancillary benefits to global health systems that protect against infections diseases.

What is "bioterrorism"?

Bioterrorism is the threat or actual use of biological agents, designed—as with most types of terrorism—to advocate political, religious, or social statements to governments or populations by attacking primarily civilian targets.[1] Biological agents of specific concern for human health—viruses, bacteria, and toxins—include those causing smallpox, anthrax, plague, tularemia, botulinum toxin, and viral hemorrhagic fevers (for example, Ebola virus). These diseases can cause widespread panic and extensive loss of life, and have the clear potential to overwhelm health care systems. As such, they require specific and comprehensive preparations to manage the consequences in the event of an attack. In addition to threats to human health, bioterrorism can also include the use of biological agents to attack animals and plants, including livestock and food crops.

Some have argued that biological agents are not very useful for military strategy because they may be too unpredictable, or too dependent on other uncontrollable factors.[2] These very features, however, are exactly what make biological agents appealing as a method of terrorism. While naturally-occurring infectious diseases spread relatively slowly, the intentional release of pathogens can lead to massive disease outbreak among large numbers of people simultaneously.[3] Even an inept attempt at using biological agents is capable of causing great panic and even greater publicity, all of which may serve the terrorists' goals. Biological terrorism, by its very nature, is a form of terrorism particularly well-suited to inspire fear and chaos.

Despite a few key events (see sidebar)—including the 1984 Rajneeshee use of salmonella[4] and the well-publicized anthrax attacks of 2001[5]—documented instances of bioterrorism have been remarkably few. However, analysts expect such attacks to increase in frequency. "A bioterrorism attack against the civilian population in the United States is inevitable in the 21st century," Dr. Anthony Fauci of the U.S. National Institute of Allergies and Infectious

Diseases asserted in 2001. "The only question is which agent(s) will be used and under what circumstances will the attack(s) occur."[6]

The unique characteristics of bioterrorism

Bioterrorism differs from nuclear or chemical terrorism in a number of significant ways.

Lack of geographical boundaries   With a contagious agent such as smallpox or pneumonic plague, it is impossible to define the geographical boundary of an attack. In other words, rather than a central point of impact, explosion, or assault, the bioterrorist attack exists wherever and whenever one person transmits the infectious agent to another. Following a bombing or even a chemical release, it is usually possible to define the perimeter of the affected area and identify a central target point. The unique nature of bioterrorist attacks, though, makes such delineation and identification nearly impossible.

Silent attack—Because the initial "assault" is silent, the onset of a bioterrorist attack may not be known until the infection is widespread. Unlike most nuclear or chemical auacks, there is typically no dramatic signal to mark the onset of a biological attack. Only when emergency rooms or clinics begin to report suspicious cases, or unusually large numbers of patients, will authorities become aware of the possibility of a bioterrorist attack and begin to investigate.

Difficulty in identifying perpetrators   The lag between an initial attack and the emergence of symptoms gives the attackers a type of head start, greatly complicating efforts to identify and apprehend the perpetrators. The task is made even more complex if the terrorists design the outbreak to appear not the result of a premeditated plan but rather as a naturally occurring phenomenon.

Unclear intent   It may be difficult, or even impossible to determine whether a bioterrorist attack is intentional or not. Depending on the biological agent used, it could easily look like a naturally occurring, albeit unusual, outbreak. The 1984 Rajneeshee salmonella attack in Oregon, for example, was not seen as intentional for more than a year.[7]

Non-specificity of symptoms   Some of the key biological agents likely to be used in a bioterrorist attack—such as smallpox, anthrax, tularemia, plague, and brucellosis—initially produce fairly nonspecific symptoms. It is unlikely, then, that even well-prepared clinicians would identify one of these illnesses without some additional evidence of an attack.

Toxicity   Biological agents are substantially more toxic per agent weight, and are often seen as more lethal than chemical agents.[8]

Low cost of production   Biological agents are also less expensive to acquire or manufacture than nuclear or chemical materials. According to Scott Layne and colleagues, "It costs about $1 million to kill one person with a nuclear weapon, about $1,000 to kill one person with a chemical weapon, and about $1 to kill one person with a biological weapon."[9] The low cost of producing and distributing dangerous biological agents broadens the spectrum of terrorist groups that are able to obtain and use them, making prevention far more difficult.

Health workers as first responders   The "first responders" to a bioterrorist attack are the primary care physicians and nurses staffing hospital emergency rooms and clinics—not the police, firefighters, and military personnel who would likely be the first to the scene of an explosion or chemical attack.

Easy replication   Even given government knowledge that a biological attack has taken place, it is still relatively easy for the same or other groups to replicate the attack, either simultaneously in multiple sites or repeatedly in one site. Thus, there is great potential to overwhelm medical systems in many places at once.

Inhibition of prosocial response   During disasters, both natural and deliberate, there is a tendency for people to engage in prosocial (altruistic and empathic) behavior. This tendency, however, would serve to further spread the contagious, lethal organisms (for example, smallpox) released by a bioterrorist attack. Because such an attack is not necessarily as obvious or visibly dangerous as a nuclear or chemical attack, the public would be less likely to stay away, thus increasing the efficacy of the attack.[10]

These various characteristics of bioterrorism attacks not only differentiate them from nuclear and chemical concerns, but also raise a number of questions with distinct foreign policy implications.

CBRN, CBW, and WMD: Terminology as destiny in combating bioterrorism?

One of the problems in discussing the foreign policy implications of bioterrorism is that numerous thinkers and writers have conflated the various forms of terrorism, creating a sort of "alphabet soup" that muddles the issues. Rather than recognizing the critical differences between nuclear, chemical, and biological attacks, analysts frequently lump them together into categories like "CBRN" (Chemical, Biological, Radiological, and Nuclear) weapons, or "CBW" (Chemical and Biological Weapons), or "WMD" (Weapons of Mass Destruction). The lexical merger of these very distinct forms of attack makes it seem as if the use of biological agents is merely another variant on a basic theme.

In far too many instances, discussions about biological terrorism simply mimic the thinking about responses to nuclear or chemical terrorism as if these several forms only involve different formulations of the same fundamental

Historical uses of biological agents as weapons

Using biological agents to infect an enemy or other target is not a new concept. It is thought that Assyrians in the sixth century BC poisoned enemy wells with rye ergot—causing hallucinations, severe gastrointestinal problems, a burning sensation in limbs and extremities (Saint Anthony's Fire), and a variant of gangrene.[1] Reports indicate that, in the Middle Ages, Tartar armies in what is now Ukraine hurled plague-infected corpses into a city under siege (Kaffa, now Feodosia) to create pervasive and devastating illness and death.[2] The victims of this attack ended up carrying the plague back to Italy from where it spread throughout Europe as the "Black Death" and killed almost one-third of the medieval European population.[3] The plague in Europe also provided a convenient mechanism for blaming a country's enemies for increasing health problems. In fourteenth century Europe, for example, some Christian religious leaders alleged that Jews were causing plague by poisoning wells. These allegations sparked violent pogroms against Jewish communities.[4]

There are several instances in history of smallpox being used as a biological weapon. It is believed that in the fifteenth century, the Spanish explorer Pizarro gave smallpox-contaminated articles of clothing to natives in South America.[5] Two centuries later, in North America, the British armies during the French and Indian War gave smallpox-infested blankets to Native Americans, decimating the tribes; some have argued that this aided the successful British attack on Fort Carillon.[6]

The 20th century's first use of bioweapons occurred during World War I when German undercover agents are reported to have used glanders[7] to infect livestock being transported to France.[8] Beginning in the 1930's, Japan experimented with biological agents on more than 10,000 prisoners of war and others in China—and used anthrax, cholera, and plague in attacks on a dozen Chinese cities. Some reports have suggested that the Soviet Union attempted to use tularemia against the German forces during the battle of Stalingrad.[9]

Work in the United States on a biological weapons program began in 1943, investigating the use of anthrax, plague, tularemia, Q fever, botulinum toxin, brucellosis, Venezuelan equine encephalitis, and other pathogens. All research on the use of biological agents for offensive purposes, however, was discontinued in 1969. In 1972, the U.S.—along with more than 100 other nations—signed the Biological and Toxin Weapons Convention (BWC), a treaty banning an entire class of weapons. The treaty prohibits stockpiling or possession of biological agents except for those used in defensive research.

Although the former Soviet Union had signed the BWC, their research and development of biological weapons continued into the 1990's. In

1979, a biological weapons plant in Sverdlovsk (now Yekaterinburg) in the former Soviet Union accidentally released airborne anthrax spores; in 1992, Russia acknowledged that the release and human and animal deaths were indeed related to military microbiology research.[10]

In a famous incident in London in 1978, Bulgarian dissident Georgi Markov was stabbed with a weapon disguised as an umbrella which injected ricin toxin into his leg as he waited for a bus. He died after several days. The assassination, it was later revealed, had been carried out by the Bulgarian secret service.[11] In Japan, Aum Shinrikyo, the apocalyptic religious sect responsible for the sarin gas attack in the Tokyo subway system in 1995, was also pursuing biological weapons. They had previously attempted to disperse botulinum toxin and anthrax in Tokyo's city center.

The U.S. in the 20th century has not been immune to deadly attacks using biological agents. In 1984, followers of the Bhagwan Shree Rajneesh used salmonella to contaminate salad bars in Oregon in an attempt to influence the outcome of a local election. No one died, although 750 people became ill.[12] The attack was not seen as intentional for more than a year.[13] Most recently, the anthrax attacks in 2001 killed five, sickened 22, shut down government and other buildings for months, involved, thousands of health care, environmental, and law enforcement personnel in the response and aftermath, and resulted in tens of thousands of people taking antibiotics.[14,15]

Notes

1 U.S. Army Medical Research Institute of Infectious Diseases. Mark Kortepeter, George Christopher, Ted Cieslak, Randall Culpepper, Robert Darling, Julie Pavlin, John Rowe, Kelly McKee, Jr., and Edward Eitzen, Jr., eds., *USAMRIID's Medical Management of Biological Casualties Handbook, Fourth Edition* (International Medical Publishing, 2001).

2 Transmission patterns of *Y. Pestis* (the organism which causes plague) would indicate that it is likely that the plague-infected corpses were not the only cause of the plague epidemic among the besieged Genoese. It is possible that deteriorating sanitation and hygiene in the city under siege actually contributed to a more naturally occurring flea-rodent transmission vector. A. G. Robertson, "From Asps to Allegations: Biological Warfare in History," *Military Medicine* 160, no. 8 (1995): 369–373. Nevertheless, the use of plague-infected corpses did become a war strategy for a time—and is depicted on some tapestries from the Middle Ages. James Poupard and Linda Miller, "History of Biological Warfare: Catapults to Capsomeres" in Raymond Zilinskas, ed., *The Microbiologist and Biological Defense Research: Ethics, Politics and International Security* (New York: New York Academy of Sciences, 1992), 10–11. Christopher, George, Theodore Cieslak, Julie Pavlin and Edward Eitzen "Biological Warfare: A Historical Perspective," *JAMA* 278, no 5 (1997): 412.

3 Mark G. Kortepeter, Theodore J. Cieslak, and Edward M. Eitzen, "Bioterrorism," *Environmental Health* 63, no. 6 (2001): 21.

4 John Ellis van Courtland Moon, "Biological Warfare Allegations: the Korean War Case" in Raymond Zilinskas, ed., *The Microbiologist and Biological Defense Research: Ethics, Politics and International Security* (New York: New York Academy of Sciences, 1992), 54.

5 Don L. Noah, K. D. Huebner, R. G. Darling, and J. F. Waeckerle, "The History and Threat of Biological Warfare and Terrorism," *Emergency Medicine Clinics of North America* 20, no. 2 (2002).

6 George W. Christopher, Theodore Cieslak, Julie Pavlin, and Edward M. Eitzen, Jr., "Biological Warfare—A Historical Perspective," *JAMA* 278, no. 5 (1997): 412–417.

7 Glanders is a contagious, frequently fatal bacterial disease of horses and other equine species—and can also be naturally contracted by goats, dogs, and cats. The disease is communicable to humans through direct and prolonged contact (via the skin and mucous membranes), and can be fatal.

8 *USAMRIID's Medical Management of Biological Casualties Handbook, Fourth Edition.*

9 Britt Durham, "The Background and History of Manmade Disasters," *Topics in Emergency Medicine* 24, no. 2 (2002): 2.

10 Matthew Meselson, Jeanne Guillemin, Martin Hugh-Jones, Alexander Langmuir, Ilona Popova, Alexia Shelokov, and Olga Yampolskaya, "The Sverdlovsk Anthrax Outbreak of 1979." *Science* 266, no. 5188 (Nov 18, 1994): 1202–8.

11 *USAMRIID's Medical Management of Biological Casualties Handbook, Fourth Edition.*

12 Richard Preston, *The Demon in the Freezer* (New York: Random House, 2002).

13 Christopher F. Chyba, "Toward Biological Security," *Foreign Affairs* 81, no. 3 (May/June 2002): 129.

14 Elin Gursky, Thomas Inglesby, and Tara O'Toole, "Anthrax 2001: Observations on the Medical and Public Health Response," *Biosecurity and Bioterrorism* 1 no. 2 (2003).

15 David Heyman, Jerusha Achterberg, and Joelle Laszlo, "Lessons from the Anthrax Attacks: Implications for U.S. Bioterrorism Preparedness," *CSIS Report* (April 2002).

weapon.[11] Yet biological agents as weapons differ markedly—in production, prevention, and protection—from the nuclear and chemical weapons with which they are often paired.

The use of shorthand reference terms like WMD, CBW, and CBRN promotes confusion and can shape perceptions and realities of how governments prepare for and respond to bioterrorism. In his new book, *Living Terrors*, Osterholm argues that "the overuse of the term 'weapons of mass destruction' (WMD) has done a great deal to stunt the necessary attention to the looming threat of biological terrorism."[12] The term "WMD" makes the military and the police responsible for defense against bioterrorism, Osterholm insists. And that means, he says, "our priorities are really screwed up."

The challenge of bioterrorism is not about "arms control" as we traditionally envision it, nor about weapons as we typically conceive of them.[13] Yet writers and policymakers tend to apply terms such as "arms control" and "nonproliferation" equally when discussing either nuclear weapons or biological pathogens. While it is true that there is a connection between controlling bioweapons overall and combating bioterrorism,[14] preventing bioterrorism is much more than simply maintaining control over biological pathogens. To consign foreign policy's actions on bioterrorism prevention to the realms of arms control and nonproliferation means that foreign policy is limited to a handful of strategic options among its full range of policy capabilities, and dangerously oversimplifies the problems posed by bioterrorism.

Law enforcement, national security, and (oh, yes) public health

Even though law enforcement and the military have been the primary government agencies charged with dealing with terrorism, the public health system must be primarily responsible for developing systems to prevent, identify, respond, and recover from a bioterrorism attack. However, because policymakers and writers still merge strategies to combat bioterrorism with those designed to handle nuclear and chemical weapons, we confront a response mechanism designed and managed primarily within a military deterrence and law enforcement framework. Deterrence and law enforcement are indeed critical components in responding to terrorism, including bioterrorism. Their primary focus is on keeping dangerous materials out of the hands of those who would use them to cause harm, and on identifying and apprehending the perpetrators. These are valuable—indeed critical—functions in preventing and responding to terrorism. In the case of a bioterrorist attack, though, the public health system will be present on the front lines, and will be the one that ultimately helps a community or a nation get through a bioterrorist attack. Some already call for greater recognition of the importance of both aspects:

> If the true dimensions of the challenge posed by infectious and pathogenic organisms are to be understood and factored into viable policy responses, it is vital that more comprehensive and inclusive analyses of *both* disease *and* security be adopted.[15]
>
> [Emphasis in original]

The importance of public health and infectious disease response systems, though, is not usually reflected in discussions about foreign policy work or strategy. A review of the literature on bioterrorism reveals that the vast majority has been published within the medical and public health realms. From 2001 to 2003 alone, there have been hundreds of articles about bioterrorism in numerous publications, including *Emerging Infectious Diseases,*

Public Health Reports, the *Journal of the American Medical Association (JAMA)*, and others.[16]

Within the foreign policy literature in the same time period, there have been numerous articles about terrorism and counterterrorism in publications such as *Foreign Affairs, Foreign Policy*, and *International Security*. If we refine our search to bioterrorism in the foreign policy realm, however, discussion usually takes place in a context of a broader discussion about CBRN, CBW, or WMD, and typically uses the analogies of chemical and nuclear weapons as surrogates for articulating what is needed to combat biological terrorism. In other words, the foreign policy literature seems to perpetuate the conflation of distinct forms of terrorism.[17]

Over the past several years, *Foreign Affairs*, for example, has published several prominent articles about terrorism. Since the late 1990's, just two of these articles have focused specifically on bioterrorism, and only one of these was written by a scholar working within the foreign policy/national security realm.[18] Similar reviews of other journals over the same period reveal a number of articles about terrorism in general or about counterterrorism strategies, policies, or politics, but little substantive discussion or recognition of either the distinct nature of bioterrorism or of its specific foreign policy implications. If nations are to combat bioterrorism effectively, however, it is necessary to recognize and articulate the particular ways in which bioterrorism is indeed a foreign policy issue.

The foreign policy implications of combating bioterrorism

It is in the interest of all states to reduce the chances of terrorists using biological agents, and a key way to reduce the risk is to build the systems now to prevent and respond to a bioterrorist attack. In the case of bioterrorism, effective strategy hinges on a robust capacity to control access to dangerous pathogens, identify an outbreak quickly, and work efficiently to mitigate its impact.

Preparing for and identifying a bioterrorist attack

There are a number of foreign policy implications involved in preparing for and identifying a bioterrorism attack. Successful prevention necessitates a close working relationship on an international level to build and sustain the capacity for effective disease surveillance, so as to better ensure timely and effective detection of suspicious outbreaks. Because of the cross-border implications of a bioterrorist attack, countries must have systems in place *before an attack occurs*. Given that it can take less than thirty-six hours to cross the globe, and that some infectious diseases have lengthier incubation periods, the problems of bioterrorism do not simply concern those nations that share common borders.

The key to international cooperation is the *sensitivity* of public health systems (that is, their ability to quickly and accurately identify an unusual or suspicious illness), and the *connectivity* of national and international public health systems (that is, the speed and efficiency of conveying this information both domestically and internationally).[19] The ability to communicate the information internationally is particularly crucial. This means that Ministries of Foreign Affairs (MFAs) must partner *now* with Ministries of Health (MOHs) and with international health organizations to develop the necessary cross-border systems for the sharing of information and intelligence about disease patterns or related information.[20] In addition, MFAs can help facilitate the sharing of appropriate scientific and laboratory information to help strengthen disease research and monitoring systems within the broader context of relationships between countries. But, the interagency collaborative process is often difficult, and can require learning new systems, a new vernacular, and even new assumptions.

International movement along these lines has already begun. The November 2001 formation of the Global Health Security Action Group (GHSAG)—composed of Health Ministers from Canada, France, Germany, Italy, Japan, Mexico, the United Kingdom, and the United States who have come together to combat bioterrorism and promote greater health security—is an important step toward creating the vital bridge between public health and foreign policy. In the United States, a particularly encouraging element has been the close collaboration between the U.S. Department of Health and Human Services (HHS) and the U.S. Department of State on U.S. involvement in GHSAG. During a September 2003 international bioterrorism exercise involving the Ministries of Health of all eight GHSAG nations, for example, HHS encouraged the State Department's participation, thus demonstrating its growing recognition of the critical collaboration necessary in implementing a rapid foreign policy response to an international health emergency. An important next step will be for the other GHSAG member nations to involve more directly and explicitly their MFAs in GHSAG issues and events.

It is equally important to use mechanisms like GHSAG to develop and promote new strategies in public health, law enforcement, emergency response, or international collaboration. In this way, entities like GHSAG can become models for effective international or regional cooperation. In most instances, bilateral health cooperation can be part of a larger pattern of building trust and confidence between nations. Such efforts—perhaps between China and Taiwan, the United States and Russia, or India and Pakistan—can help bridge gaps and possibly lead to even greater subsequent collaboration and interaction on other issues.

Another key aspect to preventing bioterrorism is maintaining control over those dangerous pathogens that can have the greatest impact as terrorist weapons. This is an area that has already received substantial attention in the foreign policy arena, and builds on the foundation of other non-proliferation efforts. The United States and other nations should continue to work multilaterally, sharing lessons learned from around the world in identifying effective statutory approaches to maintaining better control over biological pathogens. The 150 States Parties to the Biological Weapons Convention (BWC), for example, are working to improve national implementation measures, including penal legislation, and also to enhance biosecurity. The BWC discussions are also focusing attention on disease surveillance, unusual and suspicious outbreaks, and the establishment of codes of conduct for scientists. In 2002, the United States passed the Public Health Security and Bioterrorism Preparedness and Response Act (the Bioterrorism Act), which strengthened mechanisms of protection in response to the anthrax attacks of fall 2001. As the Bioterrorism Act is implemented in the United States, and as government, academia, and private industry assess its impact and effectiveness, it may prove a useful springboard for international discussion of policy responses.

The need for better and more timely information about disease patterns and suspicious outbreaks is not only the responsibility of the public health system, but also of national intelligence agencies. Some of these agencies will thus need to enhance their data collection and analysis methodologies, and will need to develop new analytical strategies, talents, and mandates. Making greater use of a range of epidemiological reports, learning about the public health screening systems in other countries, and researching the range of conditions that can have an impact on disease patterns (in order to identify aberrations) must all be integrated into relevant intelligence operations.

There also exists the need to develop internationally recognized systems for microbial forensics—systems by which evidence from a bioterrorist attack can be linked to its source and possibly its perpetrators in an attempt to make the attack attributable.[21] This will entail building a "comprehensive molecular fingerprint database of the most threatening bioagents and [using] such information to track samples and attribute sources."[22] Developing such a system, however, will require sharing data *now* from specimen inventories worldwide—and, in particular, cooperation with states of the former Soviet Union.

Domestic decisions, international implications

Some nations, including the United States, build stockpiles of vaccines and medical treatments, or develop large-scale vaccination programs against diseases such as smallpox in preparation for possible bioterrorist attacks. At first glance, this may seem like a purely domestic decision. The choices nations make about stockpiles and vaccination, however, can have an impact on the decisions of other nations, or on relationships between countries.

Some argue for a more rapid implementation of the current U.S. efforts to provide voluntary smallpox vaccination for health care workers, asserting that the nation is extraordinarily vulnerable to a bioterrorist smallpox attack until the completion of the program's next phase, in which ten million health care workers in the United States will be vaccinated.[23] If such a vaccination program is implemented fully within the United States, however, a number of significant foreign policy implications arise.

Following through on the program, particularly with a rapid and aggressive expansion, will send powerful messages about U.S. preparedness and deterrence—and will also prompt a number of questions, some with bearing on U.S. foreign policy. Will increased U.S. vaccination, for example, lead to increased demand worldwide for vaccine as other countries expand their vaccination programs? What immediate impact will this have on the worldwide options, currently relatively limited, for commercial access to smallpox vaccine? Will this also lead nations to request smallpox vaccine directly from the U.S. stockpile or from the stockpiles of other countries? Will it increase pressure on nations to augment the very limited supplies in the World Health Organization (WHO) smallpox vaccine reserve?

Calls for expanded vaccination efforts can also raise questions, for example, about international travel for the recently inoculated. After inoculation, an individual still harbors vaccinia, the virus used in the smallpox vaccine, for twenty-one days, and could transmit it to an individual in another country. What are the foreign policy implications of this danger, particularly in a country without its own supplies of Vaccinia Immune Globulin (VIG) used to treat certain serious adverse reactions to smallpox vaccination?[24] As is evident, domestic decisions to move toward mass vaccination can touch very directly on foreign policy concerns and decisions; thus, the debates about these issues must also involve foreign policy thinkers and policymakers.

An important aspect of the foreign policy implications of preventing and protecting against bioterrorism is that policymakers are presented with a situation in which the solution benefits all sides—a so-called "win-win" situation. In the nonproliferation realm, the phrase "dual use" means that material or technologies can serve both civilian and military purposes. In the context of combating bioterrorism, however, "dual use" refers to methods of fighting bioterrorism that will be equally invaluable in confronting the challenges of infectious diseases worldwide. The dual application of strategies for combating bioterrorism means that the programs, though costly, can make substantial and highly welcome contributions to global health.

Some have argued that policymakers must rectify the "imbalance" between devoting resources to combating bioterrorism and to controlling naturally occurring infectious disease outbreaks.[25] This, though, is a false and misleading distinction, presuming that resources for measures to prevent and respond to bioterrorism are somehow not simultaneously supporting the development of robust public health systems. This dichotomous viewpoint seems to derive from the same conflation of "CBRN" counterterrorism strategy, from the false presumption that a country should combat bioterrorism in the same manner it would combat nuclear and chemical attacks, primarily with law enforcement and defense approaches. Instead, the recognition of bioterrorism—and, more broadly, health—as foreign policy concerns helps to reframe the notion of "dual use" in effective approaches to combating bioterrorism.

Often, discussions about national security focus on those countries with the industrial power to intimidate, and the military might to threaten their neighbors. A bioterrorist attack, though, need not involve nations with advanced military power; on the contrary, one nightmare bioterrorism scenario involves the release of a contagious biological agent in a crowded urban area of a densely populated developing nation—without the public health and scientific infrastructure necessary to identify and quickly respond to the attack.

> Indeed, countries that do not pose an obvious military security danger may be the ones most likely to pose a disease risk, owing to poorly developed and underfunded public health systems. Such possibilities will need to be recognized and factored into strategic threat analyses.[26]

Immediate response to a bioterrorist attack

There are also foreign policy implications for the strategies that nations contemplate or implement as an *immediate response* to a bioterrorist attack. It is clear that rapid response to a bioterrorist attack is vital. Studies by the U.S. Centers for Disease Control and Prevention (CDC) indicate deaths from a bioterrorist attack can be reduced if intervention begins quickly.[27] Thus, the critical component of successful prevention is rapid detection and reporting from the front lines of the healthcare system.[28]

To be maximally effective, international cooperation and communication is necessary to identify suspicious outbreaks as quickly as possible. A single case in one country may not be particularly notable, but a handful of cases scattered over several countries represents a meaningful and significant pattern. The sooner nations can coordinate the sharing of health-related information, the faster countries can respond and mitigate the impact of a bioterrorist attack. Nations must be willing to share sensitive data about disease patterns within their borders. Regional cooperation—and regional intelligence and data sharing—can help identify suspicious patterns faster and more effectively. Countries are now beginning to discuss or develop networks for health-related data sharing in Southeast Asia, in Central America, and in Central Asia. These are important first steps, and should be supported and emulated by other countries.

In addition to the timely sharing of data, countries need to consider sharing technical and material resources to respond to a bioterrorist attack. Will one country share vaccine or medicines from its stockpiles if another country is attacked? Can some countries safely assume that they will receive such help—and as such not build their own stockpiles? Can Canada, for example, rely on the fact that it is in the U.S. interest to move quickly to stop any spread of smallpox in Canada before it can spread to the United

States? If Canada, in this hypothetical example, is planning to rely on U.S. supplies of vaccine, what are the implications then for the amounts needed in the U.S. stockpile? What will be the role of the vaccine in the WHO reserve? Most importantly, what can and should countries do now to identify possible ways to share resources and to develop the necessary logistics and implementation strategies in case of an attack?

In the event of a bioterrorist attack—particularly one involving a contagious disease such as smallpox—it is likely that some countries would recommend possible movement restrictions (perhaps voluntary) within their borders or internationally. By reducing the numbers of people on the move, public health systems would have a better chance of slowing the spread of the disease, and of more effectively implementing an emergency vaccination or treatment strategy. Limits on movement, however, can have substantial international implications. Will some countries contemplate closing their borders in the event of an attack? Would international air travel and trade be suspended? How will these decisions be made, and who will make them? During the SARS outbreak in 2003, Canada protested strongly when WHO issued a travel advisory counseling against travel to particular locations in Canada. Will WHO issue travel advisories in the case of a smallpox attack on one or more countries? Will WHO's actions receive international support? Does a WHO travel advisory constitute what some have referred to as the "quarantine of an entire country"? What about the fact that many nations may look to WHO for guidance and information in order to help them set their own policies?

Immediate response strategies address other areas of international concern, particularly international access to resources and facilities. The U.S. Department of Defense has laboratory facilities overseas, but these are limited and may not be available to the United States in an attack. Agreements between nations for cooperation and sharing of lab resources are vital. In the event of a bioterrorist attack anywhere in the world, there must be reference labs available and accessible in a number of countries, so that no single country's resources are overwhelmed with international samples and requests.

Conclusion

In the final analysis, one particularly pressing issue surfaces: the need to better integrate public health more fully into foreign policy discussions and decisions. It is inadequate to leave the foreign policy aspects of bioterrorism solely to the arms control, nonproliferation, defense, or law enforcement realms of foreign policy.[29,30] Instead, there must be greater emphasis on health as a foreign policy concern. In the unclassified report in 2000, *The Global Infectious Disease Threat and Its Implications for the United States*, the U.S. National Intelligence Council emphasized that infectious diseases endanger U.S. citizens domestically and in other countries, threaten U.S. military forces overseas, and have the potential to exacerbate societal and political tensions in the hardest hit countries in the developing and former communist worlds, while also increasing political tensions in and among some developed countries. To reduce the dangers, governments must work to create and then strengthen bridges *between* the realms of foreign policy and public health. This remains true for the United States as well as for other nations.

Surprisingly, particularly for those involved in government and policymaking, the problem of integrating bioterrorism into foreign policy work does not seem to be an issue of turf battles. Instead, successful integration requires overcoming preconceived notions about responses to terrorism in general, and challenging assumptions that combating biological terrorism follows the same model as combating nuclear or chemical terrorism. Collaboration between the foreign policy, public health, and defense establishments is not only possible and productive, it is absolutely vital.

A robust, concerted effort to combat bioterrorism will have substantial and meaningful ancillary benefits, particularly the overall strengthening of public health diagnosis and response systems worldwide. In addition to helping protect nations from bioterrorism, these systems will work more broadly to combat the global threat of infectious diseases.

The consequences of a bioterrorist attack could be both devastating and widespread, and not limited to a particular nation or even a clearly defined geographical area. Because of the particular characteristics of bioterrorism, the challenge is a uniquely international one. As such, it must involve the recognition of bioterrorism and health security as vital foreign policy concerns coupled with enhanced cooperation and sharing of information and resources between nations. Without such a collaborative, international approach, no nation can consider itself safe from the threat of bioterrorism.

Notes

The views expressed in this article are those of the author and do not reflect the official policy or positions of the U.S. Department of State or the U.S. Government.

1 There are three other (and sometimes overlapping) classifications of ways that biological agents can be used to inflict harm: (1) *Biological Warfare* is the use of biological agents targeting soldiers, armed forces, or government resources that can impede a country's capacity to defend itself or respond to an attack; (2) *Biological Crime* is when biological agents are threatened or used to achieve individual aims such as revenge or financial advantage; and (3) *Biological Accident*, the unintentional release of agent from laboratory or other specialized facility.
2 Richard Danzig and Pamela Berkowsky, "Why Should We Be Concerned About Biological Warfare?" *JAMA* 278, no 5 (1997): 431–432.
3 Richard A. Falkenrath, "Confronting Nuclear, Biological and Chemical terrorism," *Survival* 40, no. 3 (Autumn 1998): 45.
4 In 1984, followers of the Bhagwan Shree Rajneesh used salmonella to contaminate salad bars in various Oregon restaurants in an attempt to influence the outcome of a local election. For more, see Richard Preston, *The Demon in the Freezer* (New Yolk: Random House, 2002).

5 Elin Gursky, Thomas Inglesby, and Tara O'Toole, "Anthrax 2001: Observations on the Medical and Public Health Response," *Biosecurity and Bioterrorism* 1 no. 2 (2003).

6 Anthony Fauci, "Infectious Diseases: Considerations for the 21st Century," *Clinical Infectious Diseases* 32 (2001): 678.

7 Richard Preston, *The Demon in the Freezer.*

8 Britt Durham, "The Background and History of Manmade Disasters," *Topics in Emergency Medicine* 24, no. 2 (2002): 2.

9 Scott P. Layne and Tony J. Beugelsdijk, "High-Throughput Laboratories for Homeland and National Security," *Biosecurity and Bioterrorism* 1, no. 2, (2003): 1.

10 Molly J. Hall, Anne E. Norwood, Robert J. Ursano, and Carol S. Fullerton, "The Psychological Impacts of Bioterrorism," *Biosecurity and Bioterrorism* 1, no. 2, (2003): 142.

11 Christopher F. Chyba, "Toward Biological Security," *Foreign Affairs* 81, no. 3 (May/June 2002): 129.

12 Laurie Garrett, "The Nightmare of Bioterrorism," *Foreign Affairs* 80, no. 1 (January/February 2001): 88–89.

13 Michael Moodie, "Reducing the Biological Threat: New Thinking, New Approaches," *CBACI, Special Report 5* (Spring 2003).

14 Barry Kellman, "An International Criminal Law Approach to Bioterrorism," *Harvard Journal of Law & Public Policy* 25, no. 2 (Spring 2002): 721–742.

15 Jennifer Brower and Peter Chalk, *The Global Threat Of New And Reemerging Infectious Diseases: Reconciling U.S. National Security And Public Health Policy* (Santa Monica, CA: RAND, 2003), 12.

16 *Science, American Journal of Infection Control, Health Care Management, Lancet, Nursing, Journal of the American Pharmaceutical Association, Emergency Medicine Services, and Clinical Infections Diseases,* among others.

17 This issue of conflating chemical, biological, and nuclear issues is not unique to foreign policy publications, though. A recent article in *Biosecurity and Bioterrorism*, a relatively new journal looking specifically at bio issues, talked extensively about responding to events involving CBRNE (Chemical, Biological, Radiological, Nuclear, or high-yield Explosive) weapons—with limited separation of the unique aspects of bioterrorism. Hall, et al. "The Psychological Impacts of Bioterrorism."

18 Christopher Chyba, Co-Director of the Center for International Security and Cooperation at Stanford. The other article was written by Laurie Garrett, a science and medical writer for the New York City area newspaper, *Newsday*—and adapted from her 2000 book on global public health. See Christopher F. Chyba, "Toward Biological Security," *Foreign Affairs* 81, no. 3 (May/June 2002): 122–136; LaurieGarrett, "The Nightmare of Bioterrorism."

19 Christopher F. Chyba, "Biological Terrorism and Public Health," 96.

20 MFAs themselves could also typically benefit from greater internal interdisciplinary interaction. In other words, it is important for the people working on counter-terrorism, arms control, nonproliferation, political-military affairs, and international health, for example, to ensure productive, ongoing, collaborative efforts to combat bioterrorism.

21 Randall S. Murch, "Microbial Forensics: Building a National Capacity to Investigate Bioterrorism," *Biosecurity and Bioterrorism* 1, no. 2 (2003).

22 Scott P. Layne, and Tony J. Beugelsdijk, "High-Throughput Laboratories for Homeland and National Security."

23 As of September, 2003, about 38,000 health care workers in the United States had been vaccinated against smallpox, while the first phase of the program to be

471

completed by early 2003 called for 500,000 to be vaccinated, with an additional 10 million health workers to be vaccinated by the end of 2003. The final phase would make the vaccine available for the general population. See William J. Bicknell, and Kenneth D. Bloem, "Smallpox and Bioterrorism: Why the Plan to Protect the Nation is Stalled and What to Do," *Cato Institute, Briefing Paper 85* (September 2003).

24 VIG is produced from plasma from the blood of those who have received the smallpox vaccine more than once (usually many times). Because few people around the world have developed immunity against smallpox so far, there are very limited supplies of VIG worldwide.

25 Brower and Chalk, *The Global Threat Of New And Reemerging Infectious Diseases.* (2003): 106.

26 Ibid: 106.

27 Christopher F. Chyba, "Biological Terrorism and Public Health," 100–101.

28 David A. Ashford, Robyn M. Kaiser, Michael E. Bales, Kathleen Shutt, Amee Patrawalla, Andre McShan, Jordan W. Tappero, Bradley A. Perkins, and Andrew L. Dannenberg, "Planning Against Biological Terrorism: Lessons from Outbreak Investigations," *Emerging Infectious Diseases* 9, no. 5 (May 2003): 515.

29 John J. Hamre, "National Leadership in Confronting Bioterrorism," *Public Health Reports* 116, Supplement 2, (2001): 114.

30 Amy E. Smithson, "International Cooperation to Prevent Biological Weapons Research and Development," *Public Health Reports* 116, Supplement 2, (2001): 23–26.

50

BIOLOGICAL TERRORISM

Gregory J. Moran, David A. Talan and
Fredrick M. Abrahamian

Source: *Infectious Disease Clinics of North America*, 22:1 (2008), 145–87.

The realities of the current world situation dictate that people prepare for bioterrorism. If an attack were to occur, many people could become ill in a very short time, putting an enormous, if not overwhelming, strain on local health care facilities [1]. The emergency department will be among the first areas affected by a large influx of patients, including the truly sick and the worried well [2]. The expertise of emergency physicians and infectious disease specialists will be critical to effective planning and execution of an effective response to a bioterrorism event. Many principles used to prepare for an outbreak caused by terrorists would also be applicable to developing a response to a natural outbreak, such as an influenza pandemic (eg, Avian influenza) or severe acute respiratory syndrome epidemic [3].

Critical actions in the early stages of an event include identifying the causative agent and, if necessary, initiating infection control measures to decontaminate victims and prevent further spread of the disease [4]. Priority must be given to protecting health care workers so they can continue to care for those affected by the attack. Resources must be mobilized to increase surge capacity of emergency departments, hospitals, and clinics [5]. Large-scale vaccination programs may need to be initiated or prophylactic antibiotics distributed to a large number of individuals within a very short period.

Although many potential problems associated with a bioterrorist attack seem intimidating, certain preparations could improve the ability to deal with this event. Physicians should be familiar with their contacts in the local public health department so that any suspicious illness can be reported promptly. Specific plans for bioterrorism should be incorporated in disaster planning [6]. Important topics would include infection control measures, communication with key agencies such as public health and law enforcement, mobilization of laboratory and pharmacy resources, plans for processing large numbers of patients, and increased security.

A wide range of microorganisms could potentially be used as weapons of mass destruction. The ideal agent for bioterrorism would be capable of producing illness in a large percentage of those exposed, be disseminated easily to expose large numbers of people (eg, through aerosol), remain stable and infectious despite environmental exposure, and be available to terrorists for production in adequate amounts. Fortunately, very few agents have these characteristics.

As part of their preparations for a possible bioterrorism event, the Centers for Disease Control and Prevention (CDC) have identified several organisms that are believed to have the greatest potential for use in this capacity [7]. Those believed to be top priority for preparations because of their suitability for weaponization and lethality are classified as category A agents. Several other organisms (categories B and C) are believed to be lower priority for specific preparations, but are recognized as possible bioterrorism agents. Box 1 lists the agents classified by the CDC as having potential for use in bioterrorism.

The potential for these agents to be turned into weapons varies considerably. Some are highly lethal but designated as lower-priority agents because they are unstable in the environment or would be difficult to disseminate effectively. Many of these agents cause nonlethal illness. Although highly lethal infections would create the most terror in the population, agents causing nonlethal illness could certainly provide significant social disruption, which would satisfy terrorist goals.

This article addresses some general issues related to preparing an effective response to bioterrorism. It also reviews the characteristics of organisms and toxins that could be used for bioterrorism, including clinical features, management, diagnostic testing, and infection control (Table 1).

Why biological terrorism?

Biological agents have several features that might make them more attractive to terrorists compared with conventional explosives, chemical weapons, or nuclear weapons. One advantage of biological agents is that they can inflict devastating damage even when used in minuscule amounts. They are odorless and easily concealed and are therefore difficult to detect. Enough botulinum toxin could be carried in one's pocket to kill millions of people if properly dispersed. Because biological agents do not trigger metal detectors, a terrorist could board a commercial airplane and transport the agent to any city in the world, where civilian populations are largely unprotected from this kind of attack.

Although access to hazardous biological agents is now more restricted than in the past, many agents are easy to obtain, certainly much more so than materials such as plutonium that could be used for other weapons of mass destruction. A biological weapon may be more difficult to prepare than a

---

Box 1. Agents with potential for use in biological terrorism

Category A

Easy to disseminate; cause high morbidity and mortality; and require specific enhancements of CDC's diagnostic capacity and enhanced disease surveillance

    Anthrax
    Plague
    Smallpox
    Hemorrhagic Fevers
    Botulism
    Tularemia

Category B

Somewhat easy to disseminate; cause moderate morbidity and low mortality; and require specific enhancements of CDC's diagnostic capacity and enhanced disease surveillance

    Coxiella burnetii (Q fever)
    Brucella species (brucellosis)
    Burkholderia mallei (glanders)
    Alphaviruses
    Venezuelan encephalomyelitis
    Eastern and Western equine encephalomyelitis
    Ricin toxin from *Ricinus communis* (castor beans)
    Epsilon toxin of *Clostridium perfringens*
    Staphylococcus enterotoxin B
    Food or waterborne agents
    Salmonella species
    Shigella dysenteriae
    Escherichia coli O157:H7
    Vibrio cholerae
    Cryptosporidium parvum

Category C

Emerging pathogens that could be engineered for mass dissemination in the future because of availability; ease of production and dissemination; and potential for high morbidity and mortality and major health impact

    Nipah virus
    Hantaviruses
    Tickborne hemorrhagic fever viruses
    Tickborne encephalitis viruses
    Yellow fever
    Multidrug-resistant tuberculosis

Table 1 Agents of bioterrorism.

Disease	Clinical presentation	Diagnostic tests	Person-to-person transmission	Treatment	Vaccine/prophylaxis
Anthrax	Inhalation: fever, malaise for 1–2 days followed by respiratory distress, shock May have meningitis. Highly fatal if untreated Cutaneous: red papule progressing to shallow ulcer or blister, then black eschar	CXR may show wide mediastinum Gram-positive bacilli in blood, CSF, or skin lesion CSF may be bloody Blood culture is highest yield for inhalation anthrax	No	Ciprofloxacin or doxycycline plus one to two other drugs Other active drugs include penicillin, clindamycin, rifampin, vancomycin, imipenem Levofloxacin or moxifloxacin probably also effective	Prophylaxis: ciprofloxacin or doxycycline for 60 days (30 days if given with vaccine) Bioport vaccine 0.5 mL SC at 0, 2, 4 weeks, 6, 12, 18 months, then annual boosters
Botulism	Cranial nerve palsies (particularly involving eyes) progressing to descending paralysis Paralysis lasts for weeks to months.	Diagnosis mostly clinical Mouse bioassay using patient serum takes several days, not widely available	No	Primarily ventilator support Antitoxin can prevent further progression, but will not reverse paralysis	None
Brucellosis	Fever, chills, anorexia, malaise May last weeks to months	Blood culture (slow-growing; notify laboratory if suspected) or serology Leukocyte counts variable CXR nonspecific	No Culture specimens may pose risk to laboratory workers	Doxycycline or fluoroquinolone plus rifampin	Doxycycline or fluoroquinolone plus rifampin for 6 weeks No vaccine available

Disease	Symptoms	Diagnosis	Risk / Isolation	Treatment	Prophylaxis / Vaccine
Cholera	Severe watery diarrhea	Stool culture with special media	Rare. Use body fluid precautions	Fluids, ciprofloxacin or doxycycline	Prophylaxis: ciprofloxacin or doxycycline. Two-dose vaccine, not highly effective
Glanders (Burkholderia mallei)	Tender skin nodules, septicemia, pneumonia	Serology (not widely available). Blood culture often negative	Low risk, but respiratory isolation recommended. Culture specimens may pose risk to laboratory workers	Doxycycline, TMP/SMX, chloramphenicol, fluoroquinolones, or aminoglycosides	Doxycycline, TMP/SMX, macrolides, or fluoroquinolones can be used for prophylaxis. No vaccine
Pneumonic plague	Fever, chills, malaise, cough, respiratory distress, hemoptysis, meningitis, sepsis. Highly fatal if untreated	Gram-negative coccobacilli in blood, sputum, lymph node aspirate. Safety-pin appearance with Wright or Giemsa stain. ELISA antigen test and serology using ELISA or IFA also available	High risk. Use respiratory droplet isolation	Streptomycin, gentamicin, doxycycline, or chloramphenicol	Doxycycline or quinolone for 6 days. Killed vaccine for bubonic plague, not effective against aerosol exposure (no longer manufactured)
Q fever (Coxiella burnetii)	Fever, chills, headache, sometimes pneumonia. Mortality is low	Serology. Titers may not be elevated until 2–3 weeks into illness	No. Culture or tissue specimens may pose risk to lab workers.	Tetracycline or doxycycline	Tetracycline or doxycycline for 5 days for prophylaxis. Single dose inactivated whole cell vaccine, not licensed in United States

Table 1 (cont'd)

Disease	Clinical presentation	Diagnostic tests	Person-to-person transmission	Treatment	Vaccine/prophylaxis
Ricin	Fever, dyspnea, vomiting, diarrhea, shock	CXR may show pulmonary edema Serology (not widely available)	No	Supportive	No vaccine or prophylaxis available
Smallpox	Fever, malaise, headache for 1–2 days, followed by papular rash progressing to vesicles and pustules.	Scabs or pustular fluid can be forwarded to CDC through local public health dept Can test vesicular fluid locally to exclude varicella	High risk Use strict respiratory isolation Identify any possible contacts Specimens can pose risk to laboratory workers	Supportive Cidofovir may be useful, but not tested	Vaccinia vaccine can prevent illness in contacts up to several days after exposure
Staphylococcal enterotoxin B	Sudden onset of fever, headache, myalgias, vomiting, diarrhea, dry cough Usually resolves within a day	Urine antigen, ELISA of nasal swab (not widely available)	No	Supportive	No vaccine

Disease	Clinical Features	Diagnosis	Person-to-Person Transmission	Treatment	Prophylaxis/Vaccine
Tularemia	Fever, malaise, prostration, headache, weight loss and non-productive cough	CXR may show infiltrate, hilar adenopathy, or effusion Culture and gram stain of blood or sputum may show small, faintly staining, slow growing gram-negative coccobacilli. Serology usually positive after 1–2 weeks	No Culture specimens may pose risk to laboratory workers	Streptomycin, gentamicin, doxycycline, chloramphenicol, or fluoroquinolones	Doxycycline or ciprofloxacin for 14 days Investigational live attenuated vaccine
Venezuelan, Eastern, or Western equine encephalitis	Most have mild syndrome of fever, headache, and myalgia Rarely progresses to encephalitis	Serology of CSF or serum	Only via vector. Isolation not necessary	Supportive	Inactive vaccines for VEE, EEE, WEE are poorly effective Live vaccine for VEE has high incidence of side effects
Viral hemorrhagic fevers (eg, Ebola)	Fever, prostration, myalgia, conjunctival injection, petechial rash, bleeding Most are highly fatal	Thrombocytopenia Identification of virus requires special testing at CDC	Moderate risk Primarily transmitted through body fluids, but strict respiratory isolation is recommended	Primarily supportive Ribavirin may be effective for some, including Congo-Crimean HF, Lassa fever	No prophylaxis or vaccine available

Abbreviations: CDC, Centers for Disease Control and Prevention; CSF, cerebrospinal fluid; CXR, chest x-ray; EEE, Eastern equine encephalitis; ELISA, enzyme-linked immunosorbent assay; HF, hemorrhagic fever; IFA, indirect fluorescent antibody; SC, subcutaneous; TMP/SMX, trimethoprim-sulfamethoxazole; VEE, Venezuelan equine encephalomyelitis; WEE, Western equine encephalomyelitis.

simple pipe bomb, but could often be prepared with only basic microbiology skills. Biological agents are also more difficult to trace because there is a delay between release of the agent and the first development of symptoms. A terrorist could release a biological agent in a major metropolitan area and be on another continent before anyone knows an attack occurred.

Biological agents certainly have the capacity to produce terror. Even if only a few people actually become ill, an entire city (or even country) could be disrupted if people believe they have been exposed to a deadly organism, such as Ebola virus or plague. In addition to preparing for the medical emergency, preparing for the panic and chaos that a bioterrorism attack would cause is also important. Thousands of people, ill or healthy, could descend on emergency departments and clinics, convinced they are about to die.

Probable scenarios and likely problems

One possible scenario for a large-scale biological attack would be aerosolized dispersal of a biological agent, such as from an airplane flying over a populated area or a small device planted in a ventilation system or crowded location. Fortunately, very few biological agents remain infectious after prolonged exposure to air and sunlight, making a large-scale attack difficult.

Because most illnesses caused by biological agents involve incubation periods, several days are likely to elapse before people become sick. In addition, because the victims will probably seek medical care at different facilities, some time may pass before the medical community is even aware that anything unusual has occurred. The epidemiologic pattern could be an early sign that an attack has occurred, but with patients presenting at different locations, often with relatively nonspecific signs and symptoms, suspecting that an act of terrorism has occurred will be difficult until the number of victims becomes significant.

In addition to the challenge of treating illnesses, clinicians will be faced with serious logistical problems if they receive a multitude of victims. Personnel, medications, and other resources are likely to be insufficient [8]. Prophylactic therapies are effective against some biological agents. However, knowing that doxycycline or ciprofloxacin can prevent illness in people exposed to anthrax will not help when immediate demand exceeds available supply. The federal government has stockpiles of antibiotics, as do many large cities, but rapid distribution to large numbers of people will be difficult. Shortages of medicine could exacerbate the panic and chaos caused by the attack, not only among the victims streaming into emergency departments and hospitals but also among health care personnel.

Because some of the diseases caused by biological agents can be spread person-to-person, isolation of victims may be necessary, which will be another formidable challenge, especially with thousands of victims [9]. Many facilities do not have enough isolation beds even for their current needs [10], so patients will probably have to be cohorted in designated wards. Use of portable high-efficiency particulate air (HEPA) filters may also be useful in an outbreak situation [11].

Emergency department surveillance for bioterrorism events

As the front line of clinical medicine, emergency departments are key to an effective surveillance program [12]. Emergency physicians (and infectious disease specialists) must continue to be on the lookout for unusual syndromes or clusters of illness that could represent a natural or intentional outbreak.

Surveillance systems have been greatly expanded in recent years in response to concerns about bioterrorism. Many emergency departments are now part of regional syndromic surveillance systems [13]. Computerized emergency department information systems that continuously collect information have facilitated inclusion of many facilities in these types of systems and facilitate surveillance with minimal resource commitment. Systems that require human involvement to actively collect data or enter it into a dedicated system are likely to be abandoned or become less effective after many years of data collection with no real events [14]. Systems that run continuously in the background are more efficient and allow generation of data on the background incidence and variability of different clinical syndromes. Additional benefits of these systems include improved recognition of naturally occurring outbreaks and facilitation of research with large emergency department databases. These systems are generally designed so that individual patient identifiers are not sent to the central database, but public health reporting is exempted from Health Insurance Portability and Accountability Act (HIPAA) requirements for patient consent to share information [15].

Although syndromic surveillance systems could be useful in detecting disease outbreaks, the usefulness of these systems is unproven. Syndromic surveillance has been found to correlate with activity of some common viruses, such as influenza and respiratory syncytial virus (RSV) [16], but the more difficult task of detecting the first cases of a new outbreak has not been seen. Even with these surveillance systems in place, the initial detection of a bioterrorism event may still result from laboratory identification of anthrax, smallpox, plague, or Ebola virus. It is unlikely that any syndromic surveillance system would have detected the United States mail-related anthrax cases of 2001 before the first case was identified through laboratory testing of cerebrospinal fluid (CSF). Unfortunately, microbiologic identification in the laboratory usually takes a couple of days, during which the outbreak may spread beyond easy containment. Investing in rapid laboratory testing methods that could be performed during emergency department evaluation might improve early detection. The real test will be when the next outbreak or bioterrorism event occurs.

The presence of syndromic surveillance systems does not remove the obligation of individual physicians to be vigilant for unusual clinical presentations and notify the local public health department if an infectious disease is suspected that could pose a threat to public health.

Agents with potential use as biological weapons

Some biological agents can be fatal, such as anthrax, botulinum toxin, and the viruses that cause hemorrhagic fevers, but terrorists could also meet their goals simply through making many people ill. Diseases such as brucellosis and tularemia are rarely lethal but can wreak havoc in a community if enough people are afflicted.

Fortunately, most biological agents cannot be dispersed effectively through aerosol. Many are not stable enough to withstand temperature changes, exposure to sunlight, and drying. Anthrax is often cited as an agent likely to be used for bioterrorism because spores are stable for many years, even in extreme environments. The spores are also of an optimal size $(1-2 \ \mu m)$, which allows them to be inhaled into the lungs and deposited in the alveolar spaces. Most viral agents, such as those that cause hemorrhagic fevers and encephalitis, are unstable and therefore would be difficult to disperse through aerosolized large-scale attacks, but smallpox virus can remain viable after many years of storage. Bacterial agents vary in their stability during storage and dispersal. Although toxins such as botulinum toxin and staphylococcal enterotoxin B can remain stable for many years in storage, they can be difficult to disperse effectively to cause illness in a large population.

The agents designated by the CDC as category A are believed to be the greatest threat because of ease of dissemination or transmission, high mortality rate, potential major impact on public health, ability to incite panic and social disruption, and the requirement for additional major public health preparedness measures (see Box 1).

Category B agents would be moderately easy to disseminate, would cause moderate morbidity and low mortality, and would require specific enhancements of the CDC's diagnostic capacity and disease surveillance capabilities. The agents classified by the CDC as category C are emerging pathogens that could someday be engineered for mass exposure because of availability, ease of production and dissemination, and potential for high morbidity and mortality. Preparedness for category C agents requires ongoing research to improve disease detection, diagnosis, treatment, and prevention. Which newly emergent pathogens terrorists might use is impossible to know in advance. For detection and response to these agents, a strong public health infrastructure is essential. It is also important for physicians to notify the local health department if unusual patterns of illness are observed.

Category A agents

Anthrax

History and significance

Bacillus anthracis could be considered to be the perfect agent for bioterrorism. It occurs naturally as a zoonotic disease of persons who handle contaminated animal products, such as hair or hides. It forms spores that are stable over long periods and can withstand exposure to air, sunlight, and even some disinfectants. Anthrax was studied as a possible weapon by the United States when it had an active biological weapons program, and has been weaponized by other countries [17]. Anthrax bacteria are easy to cultivate in the microbiology laboratory and can be readily induced to produce spores. The Soviet Union produced weaponized anthrax in ton quantities during the cold war era. An outbreak of inhalational anthrax occurred near a Soviet bioweapons facility at Sverdlovsk in 1979, resulting in 77 infections and 66 deaths, with some victims becoming ill up to 6 weeks after exposure [18]. The Japanese cult group Aum Shinrikyo attempted several attacks with anthrax in the 1990s but were unsuccessful [19].

Anthrax became the most notorious bioterrorism agent after October 4, 2001, when a 63-year-old man died of inhalational anthrax that was traced to intentional exposure through the United States mail [20,21]. This instance represented the first inhalation anthrax case in the United States since 1976 [22]. Ultimately, 18 cases of anthrax (11 inhalational and 7 cutaneous) were confirmed. More than 30,000 people who were potentially exposed received postexposure prophylaxis, and none developed inhalational anthrax.

Clinical presentation

Anthrax can present as three distinct clinical syndromes in humans: cutaneous, inhalation, and gastrointestinal. Cutaneous anthrax, the most common naturally occurring form, is usually spread through contact with infected animals, particularly cows, sheep, and horses, or their products. Cutaneous anthrax (Figure 1) typically produces large black eschars on the skin, but in early stages may appear as papules that progress to vesicles. Patients may also experience lymphadenopathy, fever, malaise, and nausea. Local cutaneous anthrax has a mortality rate of less than 1% if treated but can occasionally become systemic, with mortality rates approaching 20% [23].

Gastrointestinal anthrax is rare in humans. It is acquired by ingesting inadequately cooked meat from infected animals. As the ingested spores germinate, the infected person may develop ulcers in the mouth or esophagus, or may develop lesions lower in the intestinal tract that caused them to

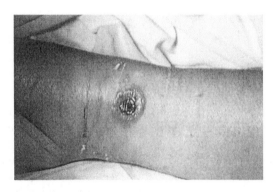

Figure 1 Anthrax skin lesion. (*Courtesy of* Centers for Disease Control and Prevention/ Dr. Philip S. Brachman.)

present with abdominal pain, fever, and diarrhea that progresses to a sepsis syndrome with high mortality.

A far greater threat is posed by the inhalational form of anthrax. This type of anthrax, also known as woolsorter's disease when it occurs naturally, is only rarely seen among wool or tannery workers, but is the form of anthrax most likely to be spread through a terrorist attack. Inhalational anthrax can be rapidly fatal once symptoms begin.

The victims of the 2001 anthrax attack presented with a fairly consistent clinical syndrome [24–26]. Symptoms began as a nonspecific prodrome resembling influenza, with malaise, dry cough, and mild fever. This progressed to chills, sweats, nausea, and vomiting, with development of chest pain and respiratory distress. Almost all patients had some abnormality on chest radiograph or CT scans, including infiltrates, pleural effusion, or mediastinal widening. Some patients developed meningitis. Inhalation anthrax can sometimes present without the usual symptoms of chest pain and shortness of breath [27]. The illness often progressed to septic shock and death approximately 24 to 36 hours after the appearance of respiratory distress.

Before the events of 2001 in the United States, almost all cases of inhalational anthrax were fatal when treatment was initiated after development of significant symptoms. The case fatality rate was 45% among the 11 confirmed inhalational cases resulting from bioterrorism in the fall of 2001, largely attributed to earlier and more aggressive supportive care and antibiotic therapy [22,28].

Diagnosis

Generally, diagnosis must be suspected on clinical grounds for treatment to be initiated in time to be beneficial. By the time the disease is confirmed through laboratory tests, many patients will be beyond help [29]. *B anthracis* is detectable through Gram stain of the blood and blood culture on routine media, but often not until the patient is seriously ill. An enzyme-linked immunosorbent assay (ELISA) for the anthrax toxin exists, but most hospital laboratories do not have it readily available. The organism may also be identified in CSF, because approximately 50% of cases have hemorrhagic meningitis [30]. Chest films may show a widened mediastinum and pleural effusions [31], but those findings are not universal and are usually seen late in the disease.

Infection control precautions

Anthrax does not spread person-to-person, and standard precautions are recommended. However, persons who present shortly after exposure may still be contaminated with spores. Any persons coming into direct contact with a substance alleged to be anthrax spores should simply bathe with soap and water and store contaminated clothing in a plastic bag, but decontamination procedures for other persons in the area should not be necessary. Disinfectants such as bleach solutions can be used to decontaminate inanimate objects, but are not recommended for skin.

Treatment and prophylaxis

The mainstay of treatment is antibiotic therapy, but the regimen should be started as early as possible to be effective. Although penicillin is usually regarded as the preferred treatment for naturally occurring anthrax [32], penicillin-resistant strains are known to occur, and the belief is that terrorists would be likely to use a more resistant strain (although this was not the case in the 2001 attack). Penicillin is not recommended as empiric treatment until susceptibility of the organism is known. *B anthracis* is also susceptible to tetracyclines, erythromycin, chloramphenicol, gentamicin, and fluoroquinolones. Initial empiric treatment with ciprofloxacin or another fluoroquinolone is recommended until susceptibility is known [33]. Supportive therapy to maintain the airway, replenish fluids, and alleviate shock is also crucial. Because spores can be dormant for a long time, a 60-day course of antibiotics is recommended for treating anthrax.

In patients who were exposed to anthrax but are not yet sick, illness and death can be prevented with prophylactic antibiotics. The CDC recommends ciprofloxacin (500 mg orally twice daily) or doxycycline (100 mg orally twice daily) as first-line prophylaxis after inhalational exposure to anthrax, and for presumptive treatment of mild symptoms after anthrax exposure. If anthrax exposure is confirmed, antibiotics should be continued for at least 60 days in all exposed individuals, and patients should be followed up closely after antibiotics are discontinued.

A vaccine for anthrax, derived from an attenuated anthrax strain, has been licensed by the U.S. Food and Drug Administration since 1970 [34].

This vaccine has been used mostly for military personnel, and might not be generally available to the public in adequate amounts in the event of a large biological attack. The vaccine is given repeatedly in a series of six subcutaneous injections over 18 months and can cause several adverse effects [35]. It is not licensed for use against inhalational anthrax exposure, but some limited animal data suggest protection [36]. Attempts to develop a better vaccine have met with technical problems and political interference [37].

Several anthrax hoaxes have been perpetrated in many United States cities, both before and after the 2001 attacks. Public health officials, working with law enforcement and first-response personnel, should determine the necessity for decontamination and prophylactic therapy after these alleged exposures. Until the substance can be identified, chemoprophylaxis is a reasonable precaution if the threat is credible. Good communication among public health, law enforcement, and clinicians caring for persons who may have been exposed is critical for appropriate management.

Plague

History and significance

Few illnesses carry as many terrifying connotations for the general public as plague, caused by the gram-negative bacillus *Yersinia pestis*. The "Black Death" killed millions of people throughout Europe in the fourteenth century. A more recent pandemic originated in China and spread worldwide at the turn of the twentieth century. Bubonic plague is the most common naturally occurring form. It is a zoonotic infection spread from the rodent reservoir to man through the bites of infected fleas. Plague, like anthrax, also has a pneumonic form, which can be transmitted through inhalation of droplets spread by cough or, in the event of a terrorist attack, through inhalation of an aerosol containing *Y pestis*. As with anthrax, the pneumonic form of the disease is far more dangerous. Left untreated, pneumonic plague is nearly always fatal within 2 days of onset of symptoms.

Plague is more difficult to use as a biological weapon than anthrax because *Y pestis* is susceptible to drying, heat, and ultraviolet light. However, unlike anthrax, secondary cases may result from person-to-person transmission. Attempts to use plague as a biological weapon date back to the ancient practice of flinging plague-infected corpses over the walls of cities under siege. The Japanese attempted to use plague as a biological weapon by releasing infected fleas over cities in Manchuria during World War II, but dissemination attempts met with limited success. The United States did not develop plague as a potential weapon because of its persistence in the environment and the possibility of noncombatant and friendly casualties after an attack. The Soviet Union reportedly developed dry, antibiotic-resistant, environmentally stable forms of *Y pestis* that could be disseminated as an aerosol [38].

Clinical presentation

Bubonic plague begins as painful adenopathy several days after the infecting flea bite. Without treatment, the illness progresses within several days to septicemia. Approximately 5% to 15% of patients will develop a secondary pneumonia that can spread plague through droplets from coughing.

Aerosol dispersal with resulting pneumonic plague would be more likely in a bioterrorism attack. After an incubation period of 2 to 3 days, patients who have pneumonic plague typically develop fulminant pneumonia, with malaise, high fever, cough, hemoptysis, and septicemia with ecchymoses and extremity necrosis. Findings on chest radiographs are generally typical of patients who have pneumonia. The disease progresses rapidly, leading to dyspnea, stridor, cyanosis, and septic shock. Death is normally the result of respiratory failure and circulatory collapse [39].

Diagnosis

A presumptive diagnosis can often be made by identifying *Y pestis* in Gram's, Wayson's, or Wright-Giemsa stain of blood, sputum, or lymph node aspirate samples. A definitive diagnosis is generally made with culture studies. An ELISA test for plague exists, but it is not widely available. Direct fluorescent antibody staining of the capsular antigen is also available. Buboes may be aspirated with a small-gauge needle, but incision and drainage should not be performed because of the risk for aerosolization of the organism. The organism has a characteristic bipolar "safety pin" appearance.

Hematologic studies will show leukocytosis with left shift. Bilirubin levels and serum aminotransferases are often elevated. Antibody studies are not useful for diagnosing disease during the acute phase. Blood, sputum, bubo aspirate, and CSF cultures on normal blood agar media are often negative at 24 hours but positive by 48 hours. The colonies of *Y pestis* are usually 1 to 3 mm in diameter and have been described as having a "beaten copper" or "hammered metal" appearance [36].

Infection control precautions

Unlike pulmonary anthrax, pneumonic plague is very contagious. Strict respiratory isolation is necessary until infected patients have undergone treatment for at least 3 days. Unfortunately, because the initial presentation resembles that of severe pneumonia caused by other agents, the actual diagnosis may not be known for several days. Therefore, patients who present with fulminant pneumonia after a suspected biological attack should be held in respiratory isolation until the cause has been determined.

Treatment and prophylaxis

Early treatment with antibiotics, within 24 hours of the appearance of symptoms, is crucial to the survival of patients who have pneumonic plague. Streptomycin is the traditional preferred agent but may not be readily available in some facilities. Doxycycline, gentamicin, ceftriaxone, chloramphenicol, and fluoroquinolones should also be effective. Treatment should be continued for a minimum of 10 days, or for 4 days after clinical recovery. Patients who have mild illness can be treated with oral doxycycline or fluoroquinolones.

Persons exposed to plague should receive postexposure prophylaxis with doxycycline (100 mg twice daily) or a fluoroquinolone for 6 days. Medical personnel who practice good infection control precautions should not require prophylaxis. A recombinant vaccine is under development and seems to protect against pneumonic plague.

Smallpox

History and significance

Smallpox (variola) is a DNA orthopoxvirus that has been a scourge to humans throughout recorded history. No nonhuman reservoirs or human carriers exist for smallpox; the disease survives through continual person-to-person transmission. The first documented epidemic of smallpox was during the Egyptian-Hittite war in 1350 BC. The mummy of Ramses V has lesions that suggest he died of smallpox at the age of 35 years in 1143 BC. Smallpox was used inadvertently as a biological weapon when Cortez introduced it to the new world in 1520, devastating much of the native population. The English used smallpox intentionally during the French and Indian war in 1754 when tainted blankets were distributed to Native Americans, with up to 50% mortality in many tribes. The last case of wild smallpox occurred in Somalia in 1977, although a few small outbreaks have occurred related to laboratory exposure. The disease was declared eradicated by the World Health Organization (WHO) in 1980 and routine vaccination was stopped soon after.

Because of its propensity for secondary human-to-human transmission, smallpox is one of the most feared agents that could be unleashed in a biological attack [40]. Because vaccination is no longer given, most persons today are susceptible to infection. Even those who were vaccinated as children are likely to be susceptible, because immunity wanes over time.

Stocks of variola virus are supposedly stored at only two WHO-approved storage facilities: the CDC in Atlanta and the NPO (Scientific and Production Association) in the Novosibirsk region of Russia. The Soviet Union may have developed stockpiles of weaponized smallpox and experimented with genetic manipulation of the virus [38]. Many believe that some virus samples may be in the hands of potential terrorists. Because the virus is difficult to obtain, an intentional smallpox exposure would require extensive resources that might be out of reach for small groups.

Clinical presentation

The incubation period associated with smallpox is approximately 12 days. Smallpox begins with a febrile prodrome a few days before the rash that may also be accompanied by chills, head and body aches, nausea, vomiting, and abdominal pain [41]. The characteristic rash develops on the extremities and spreads centrally. Skin lesions evolve slowly from macules to papules to vesicles to pustules, with each stage lasting 1 to 2 days. Unlike chickenpox, all smallpox lesions are at the same stage of development. The first lesions are often on the oral mucosa or palate, face, or forearms. The vesicles or pustules tend to be distributed centrifugally, with the greatest concentration on the face and distal extremities, including the palms and soles. Vesicles and pustules are deep-seated, firm, or hard, round, well-circumscribed lesions; they are sharply raised and feel like small round objects embedded under the skin (Figure 2). As they evolve, the lesions may become umbilicated or confluent and will scab over in 1 to 2 weeks, leaving hypopigmented scars.

If a biological attack is not known to have occurred, some early smallpox cases are likely to be mistaken for chickenpox or other diseases. Chickenpox differs from smallpox in that the prodrome is milder, the vesicles are superficial (ie, easily collapse on puncture) and predominate on the trunk as opposed to the distal extremities, and active and healing lesions occur simultaneously.

Mortality is reported as approximately 30% overall among unvaccinated persons, but this reflects historical data in populations without modern medical care. Mortality is higher in infants and elderly individuals, and would

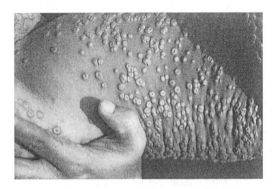

Figure 2 Smallpox skin lesions on the trunk. (*Courtesy of* Centers for Disease Control and Prevention/James Hicks.)

likely be much lower among healthy adults and older children. Death occurs late in the first week or during the second week of the illness and is caused by the toxemia induced by the overwhelming viremia. A rare hemorrhagic form occurs with extensive bleeding into the skin and gastrointestinal tract followed almost universally by death within a few days.

Diagnosis

The diagnosis of smallpox can be confirmed with electron microscopy or gel diffusion on vesicular scrapings, but these modalities are not available in most hospital laboratories. If smallpox is suspected, the laboratory must be notified to take proper precautions. Smallpox specimens should be handled under biosafety level 4 conditions. Because testing for varicella virus is usually available, a vesicular eruption in which varicella cannot be identified should alert clinicians to possible smallpox. Specimens could then be forwarded for testing at a specialized laboratory, such as at the CDC or U.S. Army Medical Research Institute of Infectious Diseases (USAMRIID). Electron microscopy cannot reliably differentiate between variola, vaccinia (cowpox), and monkeypox. New polymerase chain reaction (PCR) techniques that can rapidly diagnose smallpox may soon be available.

Infection control precautions

Identification of even a single case of smallpox would signal an infectious disease emergency of worldwide significance. Clinicians who suspect smallpox should immediately contact their local health department and their hospital infection control officer. The local health department will immediately contact the state public health department and the CDC. The most important issue concerning smallpox would be containment of any subsequent outbreak. If an initial outbreak cannot be contained within a single community, an arduous worldwide eradication effort may need to be begun anew.

Smallpox is readily transmitted person-to-person through respiratory droplets. Because delays in the initial diagnosis are likely, some secondary exposures may already have occurred by the time smallpox virus is identified as the cause of illness. Although people are generally not considered infectious until the rash begins, they can shed virus in early stages of the rash before it can be readily identified as smallpox.

Aggressive quarantine measures will be necessary to prevent further spread. Anyone who has had direct contact with an infected person should undergo strict quarantine with respiratory isolation for 17 days. In large-scale outbreaks, infected individuals may need to be kept at home.

Virions can also remain viable on fomites for up to 1 week. All laundry, including bedding of infected individuals, should be autoclaved or washed in hot water with bleach. Standard hospital antiviral surface cleaners are adequate for disinfecting surfaces (eg, counters, floors). Viable virus has been found in scabs that have been stored for up to 13 years, so meticulous decontamination is crucial. If possible, all bodies should be cremated to prevent subsequent exposure of individuals who have had contact with the deceased, such as funeral home workers.

Treatment and prophylaxis

No known effective treatment exists against smallpox. The drug cidofovir, used to treat cytomegalovirus infections, may be active against variola virus, but no data currently show the drug's efficacy in humans. Management of cases will be largely supportive care.

A vaccine based on the vaccinia virus is effective for immunizing against smallpox, and has been the mainstay of smallpox control. Unlike many other vaccines, smallpox vaccine can be effective in preventing disease even up to several days after exposure. Although stockpiles of the vaccine were low after routine vaccination ceased in the 1980s, concern about bioterrorism has prompted recent development of more modern vaccine manufacturing methods and creation of new stockpiles.

Smallpox vaccination is not without risk [42]. Risks are higher for those who have never been previously vaccinated. Complications from the use of the current smallpox (vaccinia) vaccine range from the relatively benign autoinoculation and generalized vaccinia through the more severe progressive vaccinia. The most serious complications include postvaccinial encephalopathy and encephalitis, but fortunately these are rare [43]. Because vaccinia is a live virus, potential exists for secondary transmission after vaccination [44]. In the era of routine smallpox eradication, the only contraindications to vaccination were pregnancy, certain immunocompromised conditions, and eczema. In the setting of a bioterrorism-related smallpox outbreak, those believed to have been exposed to the virus would have no absolute contraindications to vaccination.

In 2002, president Bush announced a program for the vaccination of health care workers against smallpox. The goal was to vaccinate 500,000 health care workers, but only a very small number actually received the vaccine. Many health care workers declined vaccination because of concerns about adverse reactions [45]. An advisory panel recommended against routine vaccination of emergency physicians because of concern that even a small risk for adverse reactions outweighed the minimal benefit that could be expected from smallpox vaccination in the absence of smallpox transmission anywhere in the world [46]. In the event of even a single smallpox case or a credible imminent threat, the benefits of smallpox vaccination would become clearer. Performing a rigorous scientific analysis of the risks and benefits for smallpox vaccination is impossible, because the true risk of a smallpox attack is unknown. The probability that any individual physician would be among those to see the first few cases of a smallpox outbreak is extremely low. Because smallpox vaccine can provide protection up to several days after exposure, a strategy to ensure timely vaccination of exposed health care workers and the general public if a smallpox case is identified would avoid the risk for unnecessary adverse reactions to smallpox vaccine while smallpox does not exist. Emergency and infectious disease physicians should work with public health authorities to ensure that these mechanisms are in place.

The Advisory Committee on Immunization Practices (ACIP) and the Health care Infection Control Practices Advisory Committee (HICPAC) recommend that each acute-care hospital identify health care workers who can be vaccinated and trained to provide direct medical care for the first smallpox patients requiring hospital admission and to evaluate and manage patients who are suspected as having smallpox [47]. When feasible, the first-stage vaccination program should include previously vaccinated health care personnel to decrease the potential for adverse events. Additionally, persons administering smallpox vaccine in this pre-event vaccination program should be vaccinated.

Smallpox vaccine is administered by using the multiple-puncture technique with a bifurcated needle packaged with the vaccine and diluent. According to the product labeling, 2 to 3 punctures are recommended for primary vaccination and 15 for revaccination. A trace of blood should appear at the vaccination site after 15 to 20 seconds; if no trace of blood is visible, an additional 3 insertions should be made by using the same bifurcated needle without reinserting the needle into the vaccine vial. If no evidence of vaccine take is apparent after 7 days, the person can be vaccinated again. Optimal infection-control practices and appropriate site care should prevent transmission of vaccinia virus from vaccinated health care workers to patients. Health care personnel providing direct patient care should keep their vaccination sites covered with gauze in combination with a semipermeable membrane dressing to absorb exudates and provide a barrier for containment of vaccinia virus to minimize the risk of transmission. The dressing should also be covered by a layer of clothing [48].

Viral hemorrhagic fevers

History and significance

Like plague, the viral hemorrhagic fevers, which include Ebola and Marburg disease, Lassa fever, and Bolivian hemorrhagic fever, incite fear in the general public. Many of these viruses cause rapidly progressive illnesses that carry extremely high mortality rates. Viral hemorrhagic fevers can be spread in various ways. Lassa fever, for instance, is usually spread through the ingestion of food contaminated with rodent urine, although person-to-person transmission through contact with urine, feces, or saliva can also occur.

Yellow fever and dengue (Flaviviridae) are probably the archetypical diseases of this group but are not considered significant bioterrorism threat agents.

Hantavirus (Bunyaviridae) is enzootic in rodents. West Africa's Lassa fever, and Argentine, Bolivian, Brazilian, and Venezuelan hemorrhagic fevers (Arenaviridae) are also enzootic in rodents within their respective areas. The most publicized viral hemorrhagic fevers are the Ebola and Marburg (Filoviridae) viruses. These viruses produce grotesquely lethal diseases, making them favorites with the popular media. The reservoir and natural transmission of Ebola and Marburg are unknown, but they are readily transmittable through infected blood and tissue. Aerosols may be formed naturally when infectious body fluids are expelled or, in the case of hantavirus, when rodent feces and urine are resuspended from movement in the area. Laboratory cultures can yield sufficient concentrations of organisms to provide a credible terrorist weapon if disseminated as an aerosol [36].

Clinical presentation

The clinical presentations of different viral hemorrhagic fevers vary, but all can involve diffuse hemorrhage and bleeding diatheses. The incubation periods of the hemorrhagic fevers range from 4 to 21 days. The more severe fevers, such as Ebola, generally have shorter incubation periods. Patients typically present with a nonspecific prodrome that includes fever, myalgia, and prostration. On physical examination, the only findings may be conjunctival injection, mild hypotension, flushing, and scattered petechiae. Laboratory testing may show thrombocytopenia or other signs of disseminated intravascular coagulation or elevated levels of liver enzymes or creatinine. Within hours or days after the initial presentation, patients will experience a quick deterioration of their status, followed by mucous membrane hemorrhage and shock, often with signs of neurologic, pulmonary, and hepatic involvement [49].

Diagnosis

Specific tests for some hemorrhagic fevers exist but are not available at most hospital laboratories. Specific identification requires ELISA detection of antiviral IgM antibodies or direct culture of the viral agent from blood or tissue samples. These tests can only be performed at specialized laboratories, such as those available at CDC or USAMRIID. If the agent remains unknown, it may be visualized through electron microscopy (Figure 3) followed by immunohistochemical techniques. The laboratory should be notified if Ebola or Marburg viruses are suspected because specimens should be handled under biosafety level 4 precautions.

Infection control precautions

Contact precautions are necessary for all health care personnel managing persons who have hemorrhagic fever [50]. All body fluids should be considered

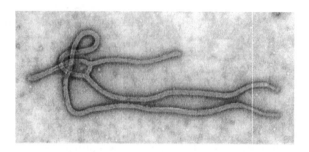

Figure 3 Electron micrograph of Ebola virus. (*Courtesy of* Centers for Disease Control and Prevention/Cynthia Goldsmith.)

infectious. In several outbreaks in Africa, hospital personnel were able to prevent transmission to themselves and other patients simply through wearing gowns, gloves, and masks. Respiratory isolation, however, may be necessary for patients who experience massive hemorrhage into the lungs. Aerosol transmission of hemorrhagic fever has been shown in animal studies but does not appear to be a significant mode among humans. Under ideal conditions, each patient should be cared for in a private room. The room should be entered through an adjoining anteroom that is used for decontamination and hand washing.

Treatment and prophylaxis

Good supportive care is the mainstay of therapy for patients who have any viral hemorrhagic fever. Special care must be taken during fluid resuscitation, because fluid transudation into the lungs will occur in some patients. In addition, because the risk for hemorrhage is high among these patients, caution is also necessary when placing intravenous and other lines. For patients who have Lassa fever, Bolivian hemorrhagic fever, Congo-Crimean hemorrhagic fever, or Rift Valley fever, the antiviral agent ribavirin may offer some benefit [49].

Botulism

History and significance

Botulism is a syndrome caused by exposure to one or more of the seven neurotoxins produced by the bacillus *Clostridium botulinum*. The botulinum toxins are among the most potent toxins in existence. They are 100,000 times more toxic per microgram than the nerve agent sarin, which was used by the cult Aum Shinri Kyo in their terrorist attack in the Tokyo subway system in 1995. Theoretically, enough toxin is present in a single gram of crystallized botulinum toxin to kill more than 1 million people.

Most cases of naturally occurring botulism result from the ingestion of improperly prepared or canned foods; the disease is also associated, although rarely, with infected wounds or abscesses related to injection drug use. Terrorists could conceivably contaminate food supplies with the botulinum toxins or initiate a large-scale attack by dispersing the toxins through aerosol over a vast area [51]. Despite efforts to produce an effective botulinum toxin weapon, botulism is unlikely to ever be effectively deployed as a weapon of mass destruction. Aerosol delivery would require large quantities of toxin at the optimal time, because botulinum toxin quickly degrades in the environment and is rendered nonlethal within minutes after release. Municipal water reservoirs are most likely safe from contamination by terrorists, because ton quantities of toxin would be necessary due to the effects of dilution. Botulinum toxin is not stable for extended periods in water, and chlorination provides an effective means of destruction.

Clinical presentation

Unlike most other bioterrorism-related illness, botulism has a fairly characteristic presentation and therefore can usually be diagnosed from the clinical signs and symptoms alone. The clinical syndrome is similar regardless of whether the botulinum toxins are ingested or inhaled. Once absorbed, the toxins block the cholinergic synapses and thereby interfere with neurotransmission. After an incubation period of 1 to 5 days, patients generally present with neurologic manifestations. Bulbar palsies are extremely common, with ocular signs such as diplopia and mydriasis. Other bulbar effects may include dysarthria and dysphagia. Eventually, patients will experience progressive weakness, followed by skeletal muscle paralysis. The cause of death is usually respiratory failure. On physical examination, infected patients are generally afebrile, alert, and oriented. They may have postural hypotension, and some complain of dry mouth.

Diagnosis

Laboratory testing is generally not helpful. The diagnosis usually must be made on clinical and epidemiologic grounds. Botulinum toxins are generally difficult to detect, and most patients do not have antibody responses because the amount of toxin required to produce clinical symptoms is so small. Some bioassay tests are available, such as a mouse bioassay, in which the specimen is injected into mice that are then observed for changes. These assays are labor-intensive and take several days, and are only available in a few laboratories.

Infection control precautions

Standard universal procedures should be taken whenever a patient presents with botulism. Patients who may have the toxin on their skin as a result of aerosol exposure should bathe thoroughly with soap and water and discard their clothes.

Treatment and prophylaxis

The mainstay of treatment is hemodynamic and ventilatory support. Most patients who have botulism will survive if they are given proper ventilatory assistance. Full recovery, however, generally takes several weeks or months, during which the patient is required to remain on a ventilator, because new synapses must grow to replace the ones damaged by the botulinum toxin. Unfortunately, this strategy would present insurmountable logistical problems in the event of a terrorist attack, when hundreds or thousands of people may be afflicted with respiratory failure. Mechanical ventilators will be in short supply, and bag-ventilation would be impractical for weeks to months. The sudden demand for limited resources could make proper care for the many victims nearly impossible.

A trivalent equine botulinum antitoxin is available from the CDC and some state health departments [52]. Unfortunately, it is effective only in preventing further deterioration; it will not reverse muscle weakness that has already developed. It would not be available in adequate amounts to treat the number of people resulting from a large-scale exposure. Because the antitoxin is a horse serum product, skin testing for horse serum sensitivity is recommended before the drug is administered. A newer human botulism immunoglobulin has been shown to be effective for infant botulism [53], and would probably also be effective for preventing progression of botulism related to bioterrorism events.

Tularemia

History and significance

Otherwise known as *rabbit* or *deer fly fever*, tularemia is usually contracted after contact with infected animals or from the bites of infected deer-flies, mosquitoes, or ticks. It can also be caused by the ingestion of contaminated food and water and the inhalation of contaminated air. The causative organism, *Francisella tularensis*, is a small, intracellular gram-negative coccobacillus. *F tularensis* remains viable for weeks in water, soil, carcasses, and hides, and for years in frozen meat. It is easily killed by heat and disinfectants but can survive for months in temperatures of freezing and below.

F tularensis was weaponized by the United States in the 1950s and 1960s during the offensive biowarfare program, and other countries are also suspected to have weaponized the organism. *F tularensis* could potentially be stabilized for weaponization and produced in either a wet or dried form for delivery in a terrorist attack [54]. As few as 10 to 50 organisms may cause disease if inhaled or injected intradermally; however, approximately 10^8 organisms are required to cause infection after oral ingestion.

Clinical presentation

Tularemia can manifest in several ways, depending on the route of infection. Ulceroglandular tularemia resulting from contact with infected animals is the most common form, accounting for up to 85% of cases. This form manifests as fever, chills, headache, malaise, an ulcerated skin lesion, and painful regional lymphadenopathy. Skin ulcers typically begin in the area of exposure to the organism, most commonly on the hands.

Typhoidal tularemia, which is caused by infectious aerosols, is the form most likely to appear after a terrorist attack. After an incubation period of 2 to 10 days, most victims present with fever, headache, chills, myalgia, nausea, vomiting, and diarrhea. They may also have cough and other respiratory symptoms. Initial laboratory evaluations are generally nonspecific. Approximately 80% of patients will have pneumonia. These nonspecific signs and symptoms would make a specific diagnosis of tularemia difficult in the event of a terrorist attack, leading to increased mortality. Case fatality rates of untreated naturally acquired typhoidal cases is approximately 35%, compared with 1% to 3% for appropriately treated cases.

Diagnosis

Tularemia can be diagnosed through culturing the organism from blood, ulcers, conjunctival exudates, sputum, gastric washings, and pharyngeal exudates, although culture is difficult and the yield is low. The organism grows poorly on standard media but can be grown on media containing cysteine or other sulfhydryl compounds (eg, glucose cysteine blood agar, thioglycollate broth). The laboratory should be notified if tularemia is suspected, because the organism represents a hazard to laboratory personnel. Culture should only be attempted using biosafety level 3 precautions.

Tularemia is usually diagnosed serologically using bacterial agglutination or ELISA. Antibodies to *F tularensis* appear within the first week of infection, but levels adequate to allow confidence in the specificity of the serologic diagnosis (titer > 1:160) do not appear until more than 2 weeks after infection [55]. Cross-reactions can occur with other organisms, such as *Brucella, Proteus,* and *Yersinia*. Because antibodies may persist for years after infection, serologic diagnosis depends on a fourfold or greater increase in the tularemia tube agglutination or microagglutination titer during the course of the illness. Titers are usually negative during the first week of infection, become positive during the second week in 50% to 70% of cases, and achieve a maximum level in 4 to 8 weeks [56].

Infection control precautions

Although person-to-person transmission of tularemia is rare, health care personnel should follow standard universal precautions whenever managing patients who have the disease.

Treatment and prophylaxis

The traditional treatment for patients who have tularemia is a 10- to 14-day course of streptomycin, but this agent may not be readily available in the event of an attack. Other agents that have proven effective against the disease include gentamicin, tetracycline, chloramphenicol, and fluoroquinolones [57]. Ciprofloxacin or doxycycline could be used for postexposure protection against tularemia, based on in vitro susceptibilities. A 2-week course should be effective as postexposure prophylaxis when given within 24 hours of aerosol exposure.

Category B agents

Coxiella burnetii *(Q fever)*

History and significance

Not all potential agents of bioterrorism cause fulminant, life-threatening illnesses; some produce milder, longer-lasting illnesses. Q fever is a good example of the latter. The disease has a long incubation period, after which it tends to produce nonspecific, fairly mild symptoms. Only very rarely is it fatal. However, a terrorist group could still disrupt and terrify a community by causing nonfatal illness.

Q fever is an acute or chronic zoonotic illness caused by the rickettsial organism *Coxiella burnetii*. The illness was described during a 1935 outbreak in Queensland, Australia, and was called Q (query) fever because the origin was not currently identified.

Q fever occurs worldwide and usually results from exposure to infected livestock such as sheep, cattle, or goats. Infected animals are usually asymptomatic; parturient animals may have large numbers of organisms present in the placenta, resulting in environmental contamination. Humans typically become infected through inhaling aerosols containing *C burnetii*. The organism proliferates in the lung and then spreads through the bloodstream.

C burnetii has a spore-like form that can survive for weeks or months in the environment. The organism can survive heat and drying and can be disseminated through airborne spread. *C burnetii* is highly infectious to humans; a single viable organism is adequate to cause infection. Because of these characteristics, it is considered suitable for use as a bioweapon.

Clinical presentation

The presenting symptoms of Q fever are nonspecific. In fact, many infections appear to be asymptomatic. In those who become ill, the most common findings are fever, chills, and headache. Onset may be sudden or gradual, and the incubation period can vary considerably from approximately 10 days up to several weeks. Most patients have a self-limited febrile illness that resolves within 1 or 2 weeks. Overall mortality is low: 2.4% in one large series of hospitalized patients [58]. However, many patients report malaise and fatigue that persist for months.

Q fever may manifest as pneumonia. Many patients who have Q fever have radiographic evidence of pneumonia but no cough. If cough is present, it is usually nonproductive. Severe headache is frequently associated with Q fever pneumonia. Hepatic transaminase levels are frequently elevated, but the peripheral white blood cell count is usually normal. Some patients have a rapidly progressing pneumonia syndrome similar to Legionnaire's disease. Although Q fever pneumonia may have various radiographic appearances, multiple rounded opacities (often pleural-based) are a suggestive pattern. Pleural effusion (usually small) is found in approximately one third of cases [59].

Q fever can also have various chronic manifestations, including endocarditis, intravascular infection, hepatitis, and osteomyelitis. Endocarditis typically involves abnormal or prosthetic valves but can sometimes develop in normal valves. *C burnetii* will not grow in routine blood cultures, so culture-negative endocarditis is a typical clinical picture. Liver involvement may manifest as acute hepatitis or as a fever of unknown origin, with granulomas found on liver biopsy.

Diagnosis

Most laboratories do not have the facilities to isolate *C burnetii*. Serologic testing through complement fixation, indirect fluorescent antibody (IFA) or ELISA is the mainstay of diagnosis for Q fever. However, titers may not be elevated until 2 to 3 weeks into the illness. Convalescent titers characteristically show a fourfold increase 2 or 3 months after onset of illness.

Infection control precautions

Human-to-human spread of Q fever does not seem to occur, and therefore isolation is not required. However, tissues from patients who have Q fever may pose a threat to laboratory workers and should be processed under biosafety level 3 conditions.

Treatment and prophylaxis

Several antibiotics have activity against *C burnetii* and seem to shorten the duration of illness. Antibiotics also seem to prevent illness when given during the incubation period [60]. Tetracyclines are most commonly used for treatment. Other drugs that have been used include macrolides, quinolones, chloramphenicol, rifampin, and trimethoprim-sulfamethoxazole. The optimal duration of therapy is unclear. Treatment for uncomplicated infections or prophylaxis is generally given for 5 to 7 days. Prolonged combination treatment (eg, doxycycline plus a quinolone or rifampin) is usually given for chronic infection such as endocarditis. A vaccine against Q fever is being used in Australia but is not licensed in the United States [61].

Brucella *species (brucellosis)*

History and significance

Brucellosis is a zoonotic infection that can have various manifestations in humans. *Brucella* species are small, aerobic, slow-growing gram-negative coccobacilli. The genus *Brucella* is divided into several species on the basis of preferred animal hosts and other features. The main manifestations in animals are abortion and sterility. Humans can become infected from (1) direct contact with animal secretions through breaks in the skin, (2) infected aerosols, or (3) ingestion of unpasteurized dairy products. Brucellae are facultative intracellular pathogens, and replication and spread seem to occur through lymphatics and hematogenous dissemination. *Brucella* species can survive for many weeks in soil or water. *B suis* was weaponized by the United States in the 1940s and 1950s; other countries are also suspected to have weaponized brucellae. Brucella organisms are highly infectious when aerosolized; consequently, inhalation will be the most likely route of infection during a terrorist attack. The organism could be spread as a slurry in bomblets or as a dry aerosol [61].

Clinical presentation

Clinical symptoms of brucellosis are varied and nonspecific. Like Q fever, brucellosis can begin insidiously, with an influenza-like illness. Symptoms generally begin 2 to 4 weeks after exposure, but the incubation period can be 8 weeks or more. The infection tends to localize in tissues with large numbers of macrophages, such as lung, spleen, liver, central nervous system (CNS), bone marrow, and synovium. Symptoms vary because of the widespread nature of infection. In most instances, the intermittent fever phase lasts for several weeks, followed by a period of remission, during which symptoms may wane or disappear altogether. The fever and other symptoms then recur. This pattern of periodic febrile waves and remission can last for months or even years. Although chronic cases of brucellosis can be very debilitating, the disease is rarely fatal. Fever, chills, sweats, anorexia, headache, and malaise are common manifestations. Although patients may complain of many symptoms, physical findings are often lacking.

Liver involvement is common, although transaminase levels are usually only mildly elevated. Hepatic granulomas are characteristic of some species, such as *B abortus*. Several skeletal complications are also found, including arthritis, osteomyelitis, and tenosynovitis. Large weight-bearing joints (eg, sacroiliac, hips, knees, ankles) are most commonly involved. Hematologic findings include anemia, leukopenia, and thrombocytopenia. The rare serious complications of brucellosis include endocarditis and CNS infection. Although depression and difficulty concentrating are common complaints in patients who have brucellosis, direct invasion of the CNS (eg, meningitis, encephalitis) occurs in fewer than 5% of infected individuals [62]. Endocarditis occurs in fewer than 2% of cases but is responsible for most deaths.

Diagnosis

Brucellosis can be diagnosed through isolation of the organism in cultures or by serology. Because brucellae are slow-growing, the laboratory should be alerted to hold culture specimens for at least 4 weeks if brucellosis is suspected. Cultures of bone marrow have a higher yield than blood. Rapid bacterial identification systems used by many laboratories may reduce the time to isolation, but misidentification of brucellae with these systems has been reported [63]. A presumptive diagnosis can be made on the basis of high or rising antibody titers. Most patients who have infection have titers higher than 1:160. Febrile agglutinin tests are not adequately sensitive. PCR techniques may soon yield a rapid method of diagnosing brucellosis.

Infection control precautions

Because human-to-human transmission seems to be rare, isolation is not necessary. However, the organisms are highly infectious through aerosol, and culture specimens may pose a threat to laboratory workers. The laboratory should be notified if brucellosis is suspected; laboratory biosafety level 2 or 3 precautions are recommended. Contact isolation should be used for patients who have open draining lesions.

Treatment and prophylaxis

Although most patients will recover without treatment, antibiotics reduce the severity and duration of illness. Many antibiotics have in vitro activity, but those with good intracellular penetration are most effective clinically.

Combination treatment is most effective. Doxycycline plus rifampin for 6 weeks is the most commonly used regimen. Gentamicin or streptomycin is sometimes included in the regimen for more severe infections such as endocarditis. No effective human vaccine is available for brucellosis.

Antibiotics will unlikely prevent disease if given before the onset of symptoms, although the optimal regimen is unknown. Because of the long incubation period, the opportunity for prophylaxis is greater with brucellosis than for some other agents with shorter incubation periods, such as anthrax or tularemia. An economic model estimated that the economic impact of a bioter-rorist attack with brucellosis on a population of 100,000 people would be approximately $478 million. Timely intervention with antibiotic prophylaxis could reduce the economic impact through preventing illness [64].

Burkholderia mallei *(glanders)*

History and significance

Glanders is a disease of horses, mules, and donkeys caused by the bacterium *Burkholderia mallei* (previously known as *Pseudomonas mallei*). The infection can also occur in humans and other animals. Human infection is rare but can be severe. *B mallei* is a nonmotile, gram-negative bacillus. The route of naturally occurring infection is unclear, but infection is believed to occur through broken skin or nasal mucosa contaminated with infected material. Infection also seems to occur through an aerosol route, as evidenced by infections in laboratory workers from routine handling of cultures [65,66]. Its ability to cause serious illness and infect through aerosol indicate that *B mallei* may have potential use in bioterrorism. In fact, this organism has been used as a bioweapon; animals were deliberately infected with glanders during World War I [67].

Melioidosis is a human illness caused by *B pseudomallei*, which is clinically similar to glanders but does not seem to be particularly infectious through aerosol.

Clinical presentation

Infection from inoculation through a break in the skin typically results in a tender nodule with local lymphangitis. Inoculation of the eyes, nose, and mouth can result in mucopurulent discharge with ulcerating granulomas. With systemic invasion, a generalized papular or pustular eruption is frequent. This septicemic form is often fatal within 7 to 10 days. The incubation period after infection through inhalation (most likely in a bioterrorism event) is approximately 10 to 14 days. The most common manifestations include fever, myalgias, headache, and pleuritic chest pain. Lymphadenopathy or splenomegaly may be present. The disease often manifests as pneumonia [65].

Diagnosis

The organism can be difficult to identify. Blood cultures are usually negative, except in the terminal stages of septicemia. Automated bacterial identification systems used in many laboratories may not correctly identify *B mallei*. Serologic tests will usually show a rise in titers by the second week, but agglutination titers are not very specific. Complement fixation titers are more specific but less sensitive. Serologic tests are not standardized or widely available. *B mallei* and *B pseudomallei* cannot be distinguished morphologically, but a PCR procedure has been developed that can differentiate the two [68].

Infection control precautions

Because person-to-person transmission can occur, isolation is indicated. Culture specimens pose a threat to laboratory personnel, and therefore the laboratory should be notified if *B mallei* is suspected. Biosafety level 3 precautions are indicated.

Treatment and prophylaxis

The paucity of human cases has prevented any systematic study of treatment. Sulfadiazine has been effective in experimental animal infections and humans. Agents known to be effective for human melioidosis include tetracyclines, trimethoprim-sulfamethoxazole, amoxicillin-clavulanate, and chloramphenicol. In vitro, *B mallei* is susceptible to aminoglycosides, macrolides, quinolones, doxycycline, piperacillin, ceftazidime, and imipenem [69]. No vaccine is available.

Alphaviruses

History and significance

Venezuelan Equine Encephalomyelitis and Eastern and Western Equine Encephalomyelitis (VEE, EEE, and WEE, respectively) are mosquito-borne viral infections found in North and South America. EEE occurs primarily along the eastern and gulf coasts of the United States. Although human illness is rare, the case-fatality rate can be as high as 50% to 70%. WEE viruses are found primarily west of the Mississippi. During an epidemic, WEE infection rates are much higher than for EEE, but the case fatality rate is much lower (approximately 3%–4%). Outbreaks occur primarily in the summer, and equine cases greatly outnumber human cases. VEE occurs in many areas of South and Central America, and outbreaks have occurred in North America.

These alphaviruses are limited in their geographic distribution by the mosquito vector, and therefore finding these viruses outside the endemic areas should arouse suspicion of an intentional release. All of these viruses are highly infectious through aerosol. Because they are stable during storage and can be produced in large amounts with unsophisticated equipment, they are regarded as having potential for weaponization [61].

Clinical presentation

Most infections with these viruses result in nonspecific symptoms of fever, headache, and myalgia. Only a fraction of individuals infected will experience progression to frank encephalitis. Viral encephalitides should be included in the differential diagnosis of nonspecific viral syndromes after a possible bioterrorism event. Reports of ill horses in the vicinity would obviously suggest an equine encephalitis virus. Whether aerosol exposure, as in a bioterrorism event, would lead to a pattern of symptoms different from that of the mosquito-borne illness is unknown.

EEE is the most severe of these infections, with high mortality rates and high rates of neurologic sequelae [70]. WEE and VEE have lower rates of progression to neurologic symptoms. Infants and elderly individuals are more prone to developing encephalitis. In people who develop encephalitis, the initial viral prodrome is followed by confusion and somnolence, which may progress to coma. Peripheral blood counts often show leukopenia in the early stages of illness, which can progress to leukocytosis. CSF protein is elevated, and lymphocytic pleocytosis is usually present.

Diagnosis

Virus can sometimes be isolated from blood during the early stages of illness, but viremia has usually resolved by the time symptoms of encephalitis develop. Virus can sometimes be isolated from CSF or postmortem brain tissue. The specific viral pathogen is generally identified through serologic testing of the CSF or serum (or both), but these results will not be available until later. Virus-specific IgM antibodies can be detected with ELISA [71]. Subsequent testing of convalescent serum may confirm the diagnosis but will not be helpful in initial management. Physicians should attempt to obtain enough CSF for specialized testing if encephalitis is a diagnostic possibility. Experimental PCR assays have been developed for several viral pathogens and will likely become more standardized and readily available in the future.

Infection control precautions

Isolation is not necessary since person-to-person transmission does not occur.

Treatment and prophylaxis

No specific treatment for these viral encephalitides. Treatment is supportive. Inactivated vaccines are available for EEE, WEE, and VEE, but none is widely used because of problems with poor immunogenicity and need for multiple doses. A live attenuated vaccine is available for VEE but has a high incidence of side effects, such as fever, headache, and malaise. Newer vaccines using recombinant technology are in development.

Ricin toxin from ricinus communis (castor beans)

History and significance

Ricin is a protein toxin derived from the castor bean plant. Castor beans are easily obtained worldwide, and it is relatively easy to extract the toxin. One million tons of castor beans are processed annually in the production of castor oil worldwide; the waste mash from this process is approximately 5% ricin by weight. Ricin was used in the assassination of Bulgarian exile Georgi Markov in London in 1978. Markov was attacked with a specially engineered weapon disguised as an umbrella, which implanted a ricin-containing pellet into his leg [72].

Ricin toxin is somewhat less toxic by weight compared with botulinum toxin or staphylococcal enterotoxin B, but can be produced in large quantities easily. Ricin toxin is stable and can be disseminated as an aerosol. It is toxic through several routes of exposure, including respiratory and gastrointestinal.

Clinical presentation

Ricin toxin inhibits protein synthesis. When inhaled as an aerosol, the toxin can produce symptoms within 4 to 8 hours. Typical symptoms include fever, chest tightness, cough, dyspnea, nausea, arthralgias, and profuse sweating. With a sublethal dose of toxin, the symptoms should improve within several hours. In animal studies, lethal doses produced necrosis of the respiratory tract and alveolar filling in 36 to 72 hours after exposure.

When ingested, ricin causes severe gastrointestinal symptoms, such as nausea, vomiting, and diarrhea. With large toxin exposures, this may be associated with gastrointestinal hemorrhage and hepatic, splenic, and renal necrosis. Death can occur from hypovolemic shock [73]. Ricin toxin may also cause disseminated intravascular coagulation, microcirculatory failure, and multiple organ failure if given intravenously in laboratory animals.

Diagnosis

Diagnosis of ricin poisoning would be primarily clinical and epidemiologic. ELISA testing can be performed on serum, but this modality would not be widely available in most laboratories [74]. Acute and convalescent sera could be obtained from survivors to measure antibody response for diagnostic confirmation.

Infection control precautions

This toxin-mediated syndrome has no potential for person-to-person spread. Patients who are grossly contaminated may need to change their clothes and wash with soap and water.

Treatment and prophylaxis

Treatment of ricin poisoning is supportive. Respiratory support may be needed for pulmonary edema. Gastric decontamination with charcoal may have some benefit for ingestions. Fluids may be required to replace gastro-intestinal losses. Vaccines against ricin toxin are currently under development [75].

Epsilon toxin of Clostridium perfringens

History and significance

Clostridium perfringens is an anaerobic, gram-positive, spore-forming bacillus. This ubiquitous organism is present in soil throughout the world and has been found in the stool of virtually every vertebrate organism ever tested [76]. *Clostridium* species can produce various toxins, and these are responsible for illness. Enterotoxin-producing strains of *C perfringens* type A cause a mild form of food poisoning that is common worldwide. Large amounts of this toxin could be produced for intentional exposure.

Clinical presentation

Within hours of exposure, gastrointestinal symptoms such as watery diarrhea, nausea, and abdominal cramps will develop. Fever is rare. Spontaneous resolution typically occurs within a day, and fatalities are rare. The *C perfringens* enterotoxin can act as a superantigen and is a potent stimulator of human lymphocytes. Large exposure through aerosol or ingestion could lead to more severe systemic symptoms.

Diagnosis

Enterotoxin can be detected in stool with latex agglutination or ELISA, but these tests are not widely available. Cultures are not of value because *C perfringens* is normally found in stool.

Infection control precautions

Because this is a toxin-mediated syndrome, no potential exists for person-to-person spread.

Treatment and prophylaxis

Treatment is supportive.

Staphylococcus enterotoxin B

History and significance

Staphylococcal enterotoxin B (SEB) is a common cause of food poisoning caused by a heat-stable toxin produced by the ubiquitous organism *Staphylococcus aureus*. The toxin is relatively stable in aerosols (more stable than botulinum toxin); even low doses can cause symptoms when inhaled. Although rarely fatal, a high percentage of those exposed could become seriously ill within a few hours. It could also be used to contaminate food or water supplies.

Clinical presentation

SEB is a potent activator of T cells, and most of the clinical manifestations are mediated by the patient's own immune system. Symptoms begin 3 to 12 hours after exposure. Typical symptoms are high fever, headache, myalgia, prostration, and dry cough. Vomiting and diarrhea may result from swallowed toxin. Patients may be incapacitated for up to 2 weeks. In severe cases, pulmonary edema or adult respiratory distress syndrome may develop. In rare cases, death occurs from dehydration.

Diagnosis

The diagnosis of SEB intoxication is primarily clinical and epidemiologic. Practically speaking, a specific diagnosis of SEB would be very difficult. The symptoms are nonspecific and overlap with many other clinical syndromes, including those of other bioterrorism agents. Because of the short incubation period, this agent is more likely to cause a sudden cluster of cases in a localized area compared with many other bioterrorism agents. The toxin may be identified with ELISA of nasal swabs after aerosol exposure, or the antigen can be detected in urine [61]. Neither of these tests is readily available.

Infection control precautions

Because this is a toxin-mediated syndrome, no potential exists for person-to-person spread. However, if patients are grossly contaminated after a recent exposure, health care workers could be exposed to the toxin on skin or clothing. A simple change of clothes and shower with soap and water would provide adequate decontamination.

Treatment and prophylaxis

Treatment is supportive. Some patients may require rehydration for fluid losses, although care must be taken to avoid pulmonary edema in more severe intoxications. Ventilatory support may be required in severe cases. Vaccines are under development.

Food-borne and waterborne pathogens

History and significance

Although most agents considered more likely to be used for bioterrorism would be disseminated through aerosol, food- or waterborne agents could be used. In fact, Shigella and Salmonella have already been used in intentional exposures in the United States. Shigella was used to contaminate donuts given to fellow workers by a disgruntled employee and caused 12 cases of diarrhea [77]. Salmonella was used by a religious commune in Oregon to contaminate local salad bars, leading to more than 750 cases of gastroenteritis [78].

Food- and waterborne agents would be less likely than airborne agents to be involved in a large-scale attack, because it is more difficult to expose large numbers of people. Standard treatment of municipal water supplies would preclude survival of most biologic agents and inactivates most biological toxins. Food-borne outbreaks are generally limited to small groups of people. However, more centralized processing of foods for mass marketing may increase the potential for widespread food-borne outbreaks, as has been shown by multistate outbreaks of Listeria and Salmonella resulting from contamination in food-processing facilities [79,80].

Salmonella species, *Shigella dysenteriae, Escherichia coli* O157:H7, and *Vibrio cholerae* are all bacterial causes of food-borne gastroenteritis. *Salmonella, Shigella,* and *E coli* all cause illness sporadically in the United States [81]. Cholera is a cause of severe gastroenteritis in developing countries but is only occasionally imported into the United States.

Cryptosporidium parvum is a protozoal organism that is also associated with diarrhea. *C parvum* can be spread by contamination of food or water and has been involved in outbreaks related to swimming pools. Because it is resistant to chlorine, *C parvum* can survive in swimming pools and municipal water supplies. *C parvum* was associated with a massive outbreak caused by contamination of the municipal water supply in Milwaukee, Wisconsin, in 1993 [82]. More than 400,000 people became ill, resulting in more than 40,000 health care visits and 4000 hospitalizations.

Clinical presentation

These infections generally present with diarrhea, sometimes associated with nausea, vomiting, fever, and abdominal cramps. The incubation period is approximately 1 to 3 days. Gastroenteritis caused by *Shigella* is often associated with blood or mucus in the stool. *Salmonella typhi* and *S paratyphi* can produce a typhoidal syndrome, with gradual onset of fever, headache, malaise, myalgias, and constipation. Diarrhea is uncommon. Cholera is associated with severe watery diarrhea, which can cause death from dehydration within hours.

E coli O157:H7 is notable for being associated with bloody diarrhea, but Salmonella or Shigella can also be associated with this condition [83]. *E coli* O157:H7 produces a Shiga toxin associated with development of hemolytic uremic syndrome (HUS) [84]. HUS is characterized by hemolytic anemia, thrombocytopenia, and renal insufficiency. Approximately 6% of people with bloody diarrhea caused by *E coli* O157:H7 will develop HUS, but the rate is higher (about 10%) in children younger than 10 years. The mortality rate associated with HUS is 3% to 5%.

C parvum typically causes watery diarrhea associated with crampy abdominal pain. The incubation period is usually approximately a week but can sometimes extend up to several weeks. Illness can sometimes last for many weeks.

Diagnosis

Routine stool cultures for enteropathogens will identify agents such as *Salmonella* and *Shigella*. Many laboratories do not routinely test for *E coli* O157:H7 and other Shiga toxin–producing strains of *E coli*, so the laboratory should be notified if this agent is suspected (eg, afebrile patient with bloody diarrhea). *E coli* O157:H7 appears as a colorless colony on sorbitol MacConkey agar. These colonies can be tested for O157 antigen using a commercial kit. Stool cultures can also be tested directly for Shiga toxin using a commercial kit. *V cholerae* requires special media to grow, so the laboratory should be notified if cholera is suspected. *C parvum* can be identified with a modified acid-fast stain of stool or with fluorescent stain.

Infection control precautions

Standard body fluid precautions should prevent spread of these organisms. Patients should be instructed to be extra vigilant about handwashing after using the bathroom.

Treatment and prophylaxis

Treatment of these infections is generally supportive. Most infections with *Salmonella* and *Shigella* are self-limited and will resolve without specific treatment within a few days. Antimicrobial treatment may reduce the duration and severity of symptoms. *Salmonella* is susceptible to quinolones, azithromycin, and third-generation cephalosporins. Resistance to trimethoprim-sulfamethoxazole seems to be increasing, and antimicrobial-resistant organisms seem likely to be used in a bioterrorism event. *Shigella* is susceptible to fluoroquinolones, trimethoprim-sulfamethoxazole, and azithromycin. *E coli* O157:H7 infection should not be treated with antimicrobials or antimotility agents, because treatment may increase toxin production and thereby increase the risk for hemolytic uremic syndrome. Treatment of cholera typically requires large amounts of intravenous fluids and replacement of electrolytes. Oral administration of ciprofloxacin or doxycycline is effective for cholera. No antimicrobial agent has proven efficacy for *C parvum* infection, although paromomycin and azithromycin have been used in patients who have AIDS experiencing chronic diarrhea caused by this organism.

Category C agents

Nipah virus

History and significance

In April 1999, an outbreak of 257 cases of encephalitis (100 fatal) was reported in Malaysia [85]. A previously unrecognized paramyxovirus called *Nipah* was identified as the cause. Pigs appeared to be the primary source of human infection in this outbreak.

Clinical presentation

Patients in the reported outbreak presented with fever, headache, and myalgias and eventually developed signs of meningitis or encephalitis. A few patients had respiratory symptoms.

Diagnosis

Identification of Nipah virus requires specialized testing in a reference laboratory, such as the CDC or USAMRIID. IgM antibodies can be detected in blood and CSF. Better diagnostic tests for this recently discovered agent are under development [86].

Infection control precautions

Person-to-person spread of Nipah virus has not been identified. However, virus has been isolated from respiratory secretions and urine of patients infected with Nipah virus [87]. Pending further study of the potential for person-to-person spread, strict isolation would be prudent for patients suspected of being infected with this virus.

Treatment and prophylaxis

Treatment is primarily supportive. A small, open-label trial conducted during the outbreak in Malaysia showed a 36% reduction of mortality among patients who had acute Nipah virus encephalitis with ribavirin [88].

Hantaviruses

History and significance

Hantaviruses are in the family Bunyaviridae, which also comprises California encephalitis virus and several hemorrhagic fever viruses. Hantaviruses are found in many rodent species worldwide. Hantavirus and several related viruses cause a syndrome of fever, thrombocytopenia, and renal insufficiency; the disease occurs primarily in Eastern Asia. Sin nombre virus (SNV), a similar virus, was identified as the cause of several cases of severe pulmonary edema and shock (hantavirus pulmonary syndrome) in the southwestern United States in 1993 [89]. Aerosols of virus-contaminated rodent urine or feces seemed to be the mechanism of transmission in these cases. Because aerosol transmission is possible, the virus is believed to have potential for weaponization.

Clinical presentation

Hantavirus pulmonary syndrome (HPS) begins with a viral prodrome of fever and myalgias. Respiratory symptoms, including cough and dyspnea, begin after several days. Laboratory investigations may reveal an elevated hematocrit, leukocytosis, mild thrombocytopenia, and elevated liver transaminases. In severe cases, the illness progresses to pulmonary edema, with respiratory failure and shock [90].

Diagnosis

Hantaviruses are difficult to isolate in viral culture. In the acute phase of the disease, the clinical diagnosis may be confirmed through serology or PCR. ELISA and IFA are available to identify antibody to hantaviruses [91]. An immunoblot assay is also available.

Infection control precautions

Person-to-person transmission of naturally occurring SNV in the United States has not been identified. However, it has been identified in Argentina, including a fatal infection in a physician who also transmitted the virus to his family [92,93]. Because of the potential for person-to-person spread of a virus used in an intentional attack, using respiratory isolation would be prudent for persons who have suspected HPS related to a bioterrorism event.

Treatment and prophylaxis

Treatment of HPS is primarily supportive. Extracorporeal membrane oxygenation has been used in severe cases [94]. An open-label trial of ribavirin for HPS failed to show any benefit. Controlled trials of ribavirin are ongoing. Vaccines are under development.

Other agents

Several arthropod-borne viruses might have potential for use as bioweapons, including the flaviviruses that cause yellow fever and tick-borne encephalitis. Person-to-person transmission of flaviviruses does not appear to occur, except through the arthropod vectors.

Yellow fever is a mosquito-borne virus of historical interest because of large outbreaks that played a role in development of the Americas. The disease has been greatly diminished through mosquito control and vaccination, although sporadic outbreaks still occur. The severity of illness can range from a mild self-limited viral syndrome to a fatal hemorrhagic fever [95]. After an incubation period of several days, symptoms begin as fever, headache, and myalgias. Conjunctivitis, relative bradycardia, and leukopenia may be present. Jaundice occurs secondary to hepatitis, and gastrointestinal bleeding may also occur. Death can occur 7 to 10 days after onset. Treatment of yellow fever is supportive. The illness is preventable with the attenuated 17D vaccine, which produces immunity in approximately 95% of those vaccinated.

Tick-borne encephalitis occurs in many areas of Europe and Asia. Infection can also occur from consumption of unpasteurized milk products. Most infections are asymptomatic or only mildly symptomatic, but a small fraction of infected individuals can develop encephalitis. Only approximately 1% of encephalitis cases are fatal, mostly in elderly individuals [96]. No specific therapy exists for flavivirus encephalitis.

Multidrug-resistant tuberculosis has become a significant problem in many areas of the world over the past several decades. Although illness progression and person-to-person transmission occur slowly, the ability to disseminate through aerosol and difficulty treating multidrug-resistant strains could make the organism attractive as a bioweapon. Treatment options for highly resistant strains are severely limited [97].

Summary

Various agents have potential for use as weapons of bioterrorism. Knowledge of the likely organisms may be useful in preparations to mitigate the effects of a bioterrorism event. Recognizing the clinical presentation of these organisms could help physicians identify infection quickly, allowing more appropriate management and possible prophylaxis of other individuals who may have been exposed. Although many of these agents do not have specific treatments, those that do are important to recognize. Which infections require isolation is also important to know because of potential for person-to-person spread.

If a bioterrorism event occurs, the expertise of emergency physicians and infectious disease specialists will be critical to mitigate the effects of the disaster. Emergency physicians will be on the front line when large numbers of ill and potentially contagious patients present for care. Infectious disease specialists will be essential in providing expertise for specialized diagnostic testing, identifying treatment options when resources may be limited, and advising on infection control and prophylaxis. Disaster planning for bioterrorism should incorporate consideration of surge capacity, infection control, and mobilization of resources for vaccination, antimicrobial treatment, and prophylaxis for large numbers of people.

References

[1] Keim M., Kaufmann A. F. Principles for emergency response to bioterrorism. Ann Emerg Med 1999;34(2):177–82.

[2] Richards C. F., Burstein J. L., Waeckerle J. F., et al. Emergency physicians and biological terrorism. Ann Emerg Med 1999;34(2):183–90.

[3] Tham K. Y. An emergency department response to severe acute respiratory syndrome: a prototype response to bioterrorism. Ann Emerg Med 2004;43(1):6–14.

[4] Macintyre A. G., Christopher G. W., Eitzen E., et al. Weapons of mass destruction events with contaminated casualties: effective planning for health care facilities. JAMA 2000;283(2):242–9.

[5] Rubinson L., Nuzzo J. B., Talmor D. S., et al. Augmentation of hospital critical care capacity after bioterrorist attacks or epidemics. Crit Care Med 2005;33(10): 2393–403.

[6] Wetter D. C., Daniell W. E., Treser C. D. Hospital preparedness for victims of chemical or biological terrorism. Am J Public Health 2001;91(5):710–6.

[7] Centers for Disease Control and Prevention. Biological and chemical terrorism: strategic plan for preparedness and response. MMWR Recomm Rep 2000; 49(RR04):1–14.

[8] Hupert N., Wattson D., Cuomo J., et al. Anticipating demand for emergency health services due to medication-related adverse events after rapid mass prophylaxis campaigns. Acad Emerg Med 2007;14(3):268–74.

[9] Rothman R. E., Irvin C. B., Moran G. J., et al. Respiratory hygiene in the emergency department. Ann Emerg Med 2006;48(5):570–82.

[10] Moran G. J., Fuchs M. A., Jarvis W. R., et al. Tuberculosis infection control practices in United States emergency departments. Ann Emerg Med 1995;26(3): 283–9.

[11] Mead K., Johnson D. An evaluation of portable high-efficiency particulate air filtration for expedient patient isolation in epidemic and emergency response. Ann Emerg Med 2004;44(6):635–45.

[12] Moran G. J., Kyriacou D. N., Newdow M. A., et al. Emergency department sentinel surveillance for emerging infectious diseases. Ann Emerg Med 1995; 26(3):351–4.

[13] Moran G. J., Talan D. A. CDC update commentary: public health surveillance for smallpox—United States, 2003–2005. Ann Emerg Med 2007;50(1):52–4.

[14] Moran G. J., Talan D. A. CDC update commentary—syndromic surveillance for bioterrorism following the attacks on the world trade center—New York City, 2001. Ann Emerg Med 2003;41(3):417–8.

[15] U.S. Dept. of Health and Human Services. HIPAA. Available at: http://www.hhs.gov/ocr/hipaa/. Accessed December 7, 2007.

[16] Bourgeois F. T., Olson K. L., Brownstein J. S., et al. Validation of syndromic surveillance for respiratory infections. Ann Emerg Med 2006;47(3):265–71.

[17] Christopher G. W., Cieslak T. J., Pavlin J. A., et al. Biological warfare, a historical perspective. JAMA 1997;278(5):412–7.

[18] Meselson M., Guillemin J., Hugh-Jones M., et al. The Sverdlovsk anthrax outbreak of 1979. Science 1994;266(5188):1202–8.

[19] Keim P., Smith K. L., Keys C., et al. Molecular investigation of the Aum Shinrikyo anthrax release in Kameido, Japan. J Clin Microbiol 2001;39(12):4566–7.

[20] Bush L., Abrams B., Beall A., et al. Index case of fatal inhalational anthrax due to bioterrorism in the United States. N Engl J Med 2001;345(22):1607–10.

[21] Centers for Disease Control and Prevention. Investigation of bioterrorism-related anthrax, 2001. MMWR Morb Mortal Wkly Rep 2001;50(48):1008–10.

[22] Jernigan J., Stephens D., Ashford D., et al. Bioterrorism-related inhalational anthrax: the first 10 cases reported in the United States. Emerg Infect Dis 2001;7(6):933–44.

[23] Friedlander A. Anthrax. In: Sidell F. R., Takafuji E. T., Franz D. R., editors. Textbook of military medicine: medical aspects of chemical and biological warfare. Washington, DC: TMM Publications; 1997. p. 467–78.

[24] Borio L., Frank D., Mani V., et al. Death due to bioterrorism-related inhalational anthrax: report or 2 patients. JAMA 2001;286(20):2554–9.

[25] Mayer T., Bersoff-Matcha S., Murphy C., et al. Clinical presentation of inhalational anthrax following bioterrorism exposure: report of 2 surviving patients. JAMA 2001;286(20):2549–53.

[26] Centers for Disease Control and Prevention. Considerations for distinguishing influenza-like illness from inhalational anthrax. MMWR Morb Mortal Wkly Rep 2001;50(44):984–6.

[27] Holty J. E., Kim R. Y., Bravata D. M. Anthrax: a systematic review of atypical presentations. Ann Emerg Med 2006;48(2):200–11.

[28] Holty J. E., Bravata D. M., Liu H., et al. Systematic review: a century of inhalational anthrax cases from 1900 to 2005. Ann Intern Med 2006;144(4):270–80.

[29] Moran G. J. Commentary: bioterrorism alleging use of anthrax and interim guidelines for management. Ann Emerg Med 1999;34(2):229–32.

[30] Inglesby T. V., Henderson D. A., Bartlett J. G., et al. Anthrax as a biological weapon: medical and public health management. JAMA 1999;281(18):1735–45.

[31] Kyriacou D. N., Yarnold P. R., Stein A. C., et al. Discriminating inhalational anthrax from community-acquired pneumonia using chest radiograph findings and a clinical algorithm. Chest 2007;131(2):489–96.

[32] Dixon T. C., Meselson M., Guillemin J., et al. Anthrax. N Engl J Med 1999; 341(11):815–26.

[33] Inglesby T. V., O'Toole T., Henderson D. A., et al. Anthrax as a biological weapon, 2002: updated recommendations for management. JAMA 2002;287(17): 2236–52.

[34] Friedlander A. M., Pittman P. R., Parker G. W. Anthrax vaccine. JAMA 1999; 282(22):2104–6.

[35] CDC. Surveillance for adverse events associated with anthrax vaccination—U.S. Dept. of Defense, 1998–2000. MMWR Morb Mortal Wkly Rep 2000;49(16): 341–5.

[36] Darling R. G., Catlett C. L., Huebner K. D., et al. Threats in bioterrorism. I: CDC category A agents. Emerg Med Clin North Am 2002;20(2):273–309.

[37] Willman D. New anthrax vaccine doomed by lobbying; America's sole supplier faced oblivion if its rival's product was adopted. It was time to call on its connections. Los Angeles Times. December 2, 2007;Part A:A1.

[38] Alibek K. Biohazard. New York: Random House; 1999.

[39] Inglesby T. V., Dennis D. T., Henderson D. A., et al. Plague as a biological weapon. JAMA 2000;283(17):2281–90.

[40] Henderson D. A., Inglesby T. V., Bartlett J. G., et al. Smallpox as a biological weapon: medical and public health management. JAMA 1999;281(22):2127–37.

[41] Henderson D. A. Smallpox: clinical and epidemiologic features. Emerg Infect Dis 1999;5(4):537–9.

[42] Bartlett J., Borio L., Radonovich L., et al. Smallpox vaccination in 2003: key information for clinicians. Clin Infect Dis 2003;36(7):883–902.

[43] Centers for Disease Control and Prevention. Update: adverse events following civilian smallpox vaccination—United States, 2003. MMWR Morb Mortal Wkly Rep 2004;53(05):106–7.

[44] Centers for Disease Control and Prevention. Vulvar vaccinia infection after sexual contact with a military smallpox vaccinee—Alaska, 2006. MMWR Morb Mortal Wkly Rep 2007;56(17):417–9.

[45] Kwon N., Raven M. C., Chiang W. K., et al. Emergency physicians' perspectives on smallpox vaccination. Acad Emerg Med 2003;10(6):599–605.

[46] Moran G. J., Everett W. W., Karras D. J., et al. Smallpox vaccination for emergency physicians: joint statement of the AAEM and SAEM. J Emerg Med 2003;24(3):351–2.

[47] Centers for Disease Control and Prevention. Recommendations for using smallpox vaccine in a pre-event vaccination program. Supplemental recommendations of the Advisory Committee on Immunization Practices (ACIP) and the Healthcare Infection Control Practices Advisory Committee (HICPAC). MMWR Recomm Rep 2003;52(RR-7):1–16.

[48] Centers for Disease Control and Prevention. Vaccinia (smallpox) vaccine: recommendations of the Advisory Committee on Immunization Practices (ACIP), 2001. MMWR Recomm Rep 2001;50(RR-10):1–25.

[49] Borio L., Inglesby T., Peters C. J., et al. Hemorrhagic fever viruses as biological weapons. JAMA 2002;287(18):2391–405.

[50] Centers for Disease Control and Prevention. Management of patients with suspected viral hemorrhagic fever. MMWR Morb Mortal Wkly Rep 1995;44(25): 475–9.

[51] Arnon S. S., Schechter R., Inglesby T. V., et al. Botulinum toxin as a biological weapon. JAMA 2001;285(8):1059–70.

[52] Shapiro R. L., Hatheway C., Becher J., et al. Botulism surveillance and emergency response. JAMA 1997;278(5):433–5.

[53] Arnon S. S., Schechter R., Maslanka S. E., et al. Human botulism immune globulin for the treatment of infant botulism. N Engl J Med 2006;354(5):462–71.

[54] Dennis D. T., Inglesby T. V., Henderson D. A., et al. Tularemia as a biological weapon: medical and public health management. JAMA 2001;285(21):2763–73.

[55] Sato T., Fujita H., Ohara Y., et al. Microagglutination test for early and specific serodiagnosis of tularemia. J Clin Microbiol 1990;28(10):2372–4.

[56] Bevanger L., Macland J. A., Naess A. I. Agglutinins and antibodies to *Francisella tularensis* outer membrane antigens in the early diagnosis of disease during an outbreak of tularemia. J Clin Microbiol 1988;26(3):433–7.

[57] Russell P., Eley S. M., Fulop M. J., et al. The efficacy of ciprofloxacin and doxycycline against tularemia. J Antimicrob Chemother 1998;41(1):461–5.

[58] Dupont H. T., Raoult D., Brouqui P., et al. Epidemiologic features and clinical presentation of acute Q fever in hospitalized patients: 323 French cases. Am J Med 1992;93(4):427–34.

[59] Millar J. K. The chest film findings in Q fever—a series of 35 cases. Clin Radiol 1978;329(4):371–5.

[60] Raoult D. Treatment of Q fever. Antimicrob Agents Chemother 1993;37(9):1733–6.

[61] Franz D. R., Jahrling P. B., Friedlander A. M., et al. Clinical recognition and management of patients exposed to biological warfare agents. JAMA 1997;278(5):399–411.

[62] Young E. J. Overview or brucellosis. Clin Infect Dis 1995;21(2):283–9.

[63] Barham W. B., Church P., Brown J. E., et al. Misidentification of *Brucella* species with use of rapid bacterial identification systems. Clin Infect Dis 1993;17(6):1068–9.

[64] Kaufmann A. F., Meltzer M. I., Schmid G. P. The economic impact of a bioterrorist attack: are prevention and postattack intervention programs justifiable? Emerg Infect Dis 1997;3(2):83–94.

[65] Centers for Disease Control and Prevention. Laboratory-acquired human glanders —Maryland, May 2000. MMWR Morb Mortal Wkly Rep 2000;49(24):532–5.

[66] Srinivasan A., Kraus C. N., DeShazer D., et al. Glanders in a military research microbiologist. N Engl J Med 2001;345(4):256–8.

[67] Mobley J. A. Biological warfare in the twentieth century: lessons from the past, challenges for the future. Mil Med 1995;160(11):547–53.

[68] Bauernfeind A., Roller C., Meyer D., et al. Molecular procedure for rapid detection of Burkholderia mallei and Burkholderia pseudomallei. J Clin Microbiol 1998;36(9):2737–41.

[69] Heine H. S., England M. J., Waag D. M., et al. In vitro antibiotic susceptibilities of Burkholderia mallei (causative agent of glanders) determined by broth microdilution and E-test. Antimicrob Agents Chemother 2001;45(7):2119–21.

[70] Deresiewicz R. L., Thaler S. J., Hsu L., et al. Clinical and neurologic manifestations of eastern equine encephalitis. N Engl J Med 1997;336(26):1867–74.

[71] Calisher C. H., El-Kafrawi A. O., Al-Deen Mahmud M. I., et al. Complex-specific immunoglobulin M antibody patterns in humans infected with alphaviruses. J Clin Microbiol 1986;23(1):155–9.

[72] Ricin. In: Woods J. B., editor. Medical management of biological casualties handbook. 6th edition. Fort Detrick (MD): USAMRIID; 2005. p. 93–6.

[73] Challoner K. R., McCarron M. M. Castor bean intoxication. Ann Emerg Med 1990;19(10):1177–83.

[74] Leith A. G., Griffiths G. D., Green M. A. Quantification of ricin toxin using a highly sensitive avidin/biotin enzyme-linked immunosorbent assay. J Forensic Sci Soc 1988;28(4):227–36.

[75] Smallshaw J. E., Richardson J. A., Vitetta E. S. RiVax, a recombinant ricin subunit vaccine, protects mice against ricin delivered by gavage or aerosol. Vaccine 2007;25(42):7459–69.

[76] Lorber B. Gas gangrene and other clostridium-associated diseases. In: Mandell G. L., Bennett J. E., Dolin R., editors. Principles and practice of infectious diseases. 5th edition. Philadelphia: Churchill Livingstone; 2000. p. 2549–61.

[77] Kolavic S. A., Kimura A., Simons S. L., et al. An outbreak of Shigella dysenteriae type 2 among laboratory workers due to intentional food contamination. JAMA 1997;278(5):396–8.

[78] Torok T. J., Tauxe R. V., Wise R. P., et al. A large community outbreak of salmonellosis caused by intentional contamination of restaurant salad bars. JAMA 1997;278(5):389–95.

[79] Centers for Disease Control and Prevention. Emerging infectious diseases: outbreak of Salmonella enteritidis associated with nationally distributed ice cream products—Minnesota, South Dakota, and Wisconsin, 1994. MMWR Morb Mortal Wkly Rep 1994;43(40):740–1.

[80] Centers for Disease Control and Prevention. Multistate outbreak of listeriosis—United States, 2000. MMWR Morb Mortal Wkly Rep 2000;49(50):1129–30.

[81] Centers for Disease Control and Prevention. Diagnosis and management of foodborne illnesses: a primer for physicians. MMWR Recomm Rep 2001;50(RR02):1–69.

[82] Mac Kenzie W. R., Hoxie N. J., Proctor M. E., et al. A massive outbreak in Milwaukee of cryptosporidium infection transmitted through the public water supply. N Engl J Med 1994;331(3):161–7.

[83] Talan D. A., Moran G. J., Newdow M., et al, for the EMERGEncy ID Net Study Group. Etiology of bloody diarrhea among patients presenting to U.S. emergency departments: prevalence of E. coli O157:H7 and other enteropathogens. Clin Infect Dis 2001;32(4):573–80.

[84] Mead P. S., Griffin P. M. Escherichia coli O157:H7. Lancet 1998;352(9135):1207–12.

[85] Centers for Disease Control and Prevention. Update: outbreak of Nipah virus, Malyasia and Singapore, 1999. MMWR Morb Mortal Wkly Rep 1999; 48(16):335–7.

[86] Daniels P., Ksiazek T., Eaton B. T. Laboratory diagnosis of Nipah and Hendra virus infections. Microbes Infect 2001;3(4):289–95.

[87] Chua K. B., Lam S. K., Goh K. J., et al. The presence of Nipah virus in respiratory secretions and urine of patients during an outbreak of Nipah virus encephalitis in Malaysia. J Infect 2001;42(1):40–3.

[88] Chong H. T., Kamarulzaman A., Tan C. T., et al. Treatment of acute Nipah encephalitis with ribavirin. Ann Neurol 2001;49(6):810–3.

[89] Nichol S. T., Spiropoulou C. F., Morzunov S., et al. Genetic identification of a hantavirus associated with an outbreak of acute respiratory illness. Science 1993;262(5135):914–7.

[90] Duchin J. S., Koster F., Peters C. J., et al. Hantavirus pulmonary syndrome: a clinical description of 17 patients with a newly recognized disease. N Engl J Med 1994;330(14):949–55.

[91] Koraka P., Avsic-Zupanc T., Osterhaus A. D., et al. Evaluation of two commercially available immunoassays for the detection of hantavirus antibodies in serum samples. J Clin Virol 2000;17(3):189–96.

[92] Padula P. J., Edelstein A., Miguel S. D., et al. Hantavirus pulmonary syndrome outbreak in Argentina: molecular evidence for person-to-person transmission of Andes virus. Virology 1998;241(2):323–30.

[93] Wells R. M., Sosa Estani S., Yadon Z. E., et al. An unusual hantavirus outbreak in southern Argentina: person-to-person transmission? Emerg Infect Dis 1997; 3(2):171–4.

[94] Fabbri M., Maslow M. J. Hantavirus pulmonary syndrome in the United States. Curr Infect Dis Rep 2001;3(3):258–65.

[95] Monath T. P. Yellow fever: a medically neglected disease. Rev Infect Dis 1987; 9(1):165–75.

[96] Tsai T. F. Flaviviruses. In: Mandell G. L., Bennett J. E., Dolin R., editors. Principles and practice of infectious diseases. 5th edition. Philadelphia: Churchill Livingstone; 2000. p. 1714–36.

[97] Small P. M., Fujiwara P. I. Management of tuberculosis in the United States. N Engl J Med 2001;345(3):189–210.

51

SECURITIZATION OF INTERNATIONAL PUBLIC HEALTH

Implications for global health governance and the biological weapons prohibition regime

Alexander Kelle

Source: *Global Governance*, 13:2 (2007), 217–35.

This article analyzes the extent to which international public health has become securitized and what effects this has on global health governance and the biological weapons control regime. Attempts to securitize public health are traced in the two multilateral discursive spaces of greatest relevance to biological weapons arms control and international public health; the community of state parties to the Biological Weapons Convention, and the World Health Organization. The conclusion is that with respect to public health, the identified securitization moves have led to a strengthening of the state as actor in the provision of international public health. For biological weapons arms control, the impact of the identified securitization moves depends largely on the overall development of the biological weapons control regime.

Public health and biological weapons arms control would appear to be two distinct policy arenas with little, if any, overlap in terms of actors involved, problems to address, and solutions to be proposed to better the human condition. Traditionally, security from biological weapons and security from disease were pursued by different actors on both the domestic and the international level. For the former, biodefense and biological weapons (BW) arms control policies were formulated by the military and diplomatic communities, while responsibility for disease prevention and mitigation fell to the public health sectors of states, or to international organizations such as the World

Health Organization (WHO). This strict separation has become increasingly blurred.

Starting in the mid-1990s, the possibility of terrorism with biological and chemical weapons has evolved into the number one security threat for military planners and decisionmakers in many countries, most notably the United States. This dramatic shift in threat perception, which was fueled first and foremost by the Aum Shinrikyo 1995 sarin gas attack in the Tokyo subway system and the 2001 anthrax letters sent through the US postal service, had two effects that so far have not been thoroughly analyzed. First, it shifted the balance between biodefense and BW arms control in the fight against biological warfare toward biodefense. The process of readjusting this equilibrium in favor of biodefense has brought with it the second effect: the drafting of public health to fight bioterrorism.[1] While biodefense activities had in the past been geared toward hostile states employing BW, and thus had focused on troop protection in the field by the military forces themselves, this approach was no longer deemed valid in the age of global bioterrorist threats. Those who are "at risk from biological warfare" are no longer a subsection of the population—the armed forces—but are now the population as a whole. Consequently, protective measures had to extend to whole populations as well: enter the public health infrastructure. To better capture and analyze the processes related to this "drafting" of the public health sector, or parts thereof, the concept of "securitization" will be applied. As I have argued elsewhere, such securitization moves have been successfully employed in the United States over the past decade.[2]

The term *securitization* was introduced into the security studies discourse during the 1990s by a group of scholars, including Ole Wæver and Barry Buzan.[3] The development of the concept has to be seen in the context of a more general trend to move beyond a focus on the nation-state and on the provision or analysis of military security issues only.[4] To overcome the shortcomings of some competing approaches to broadening the concept of security, Waever and his colleagues proposed to concentrate on the specificity of security studies and reformulate the concept of security on that basis. Two operations are crucial in this context: speech acts (uttering security) and modalities (threat-defense sequences).[5] The process of securitization is initiated through a

> speech act where a securitizing actor designates a threat to a specified referent object and declares an existential threat implying a right to use extraordinary means to fence it off. The issue is securitized— becomes a security issue, a part of what is security—if the relevant audience accepts this claim and thus grants the actor a right to violate rules that otherwise would bind.[6]

If a securitizing speech act is performed successfully—and, as I show in this article, this is by no means always the case—the threat-defense sequence, which has characterized traditional thinking about security, has been success-fully put into action for a new issue, one that was previously separate from the security discourse.

There are thus three elements to the securitization process: a securitizing actor, a referent object to be securitized, and an audience that accepts (or rejects) the securitizing move. Thus, by looking at speech acts, the securitiza-tion concept allows an observer to analyze and link discursive interventions and policy measures beyond those that would normally be considered appro-priate. Usually, such new policy measures would manifest themselves in shifting budgetary priorities.

In applying this framework, I analyze the extent to which threats to public health through the deliberate spread of disease have become securitized. As mentioned above, the emergence of the bioterrorist threat in the mid- to late 1990s has in the United States coincided with a reduced reliance on BW arms control in addressing the specter of biological warfare. Instead, biode-fense measures, with the concomitant securitization of public health, have been placed center stage in the effort to counter the newly identified existen-tial threat of bioterrorism.

In order to trace securitization moves and map the resulting changes in international public health discourse and the implications this has for both the globalization of public health and the international regime to prohibit BW, I provide in the next section an overview of the deliberate spread of disease in the form of biological warfare. In the following two sections I briefly describe the tools to fight both deliberate and natural disease; BW arms control; and international public health prior to the emergence of bio-terrorism as a new existential security threat. My focus in the subsequent section is on the emergence of bioterrorism as security threat and the secur-itization moves in relation to public health on the international level, with emphasis on the two discursive spaces of the WHO and the community of Biological and Toxin Weapons Convention (BWC) member states. I conclude with a discussion of the implications for the global governance of public health and BW arms control that result from the identified public health securitization moves.

Biological warfare as "deliberate disease"

The use of disease-causing biological agents, or pathogens, in warfare goes back at least several hundred years.[7] Biological warfare agents are usually grouped into five categories: (1) bacteria, such as *Bacillus anthracis*, the causative agent of anthrax; (2) viruses, such as the ones that cause smallpox, or Ebola; (3) rickettsiae, such as the organism that causes Q-fever; (4) fungi, such as the *Aspergillus* fungi; and (5) toxins—nonliving products from microorganisms, plants, or animals—such as botulinum toxin, or ricin. Some of these BW agents are mostly incapacitating, while others have a high lethality. Also, some BW agents will be localized in their effects, while others—due to their contagiousness—may cause widespread epidemics. Following from this diversity, biological warfare agents can be employed in a number of attack scenarios.[8]

To make efforts to implement the prohibitory norm against biological warfare even more challenging, the material, technologies, and know-how needed for offensive military BW programs or the pursuit of terrorist BW attacks are of a so-called dual-use character. Not only can they be used for offensive military purposes, but many of the "ingredients" of a BW program have perfectly legitimate civilian applications. Thus, it cannot be deduced from the mere presence of a seed culture of a particular pathogen or a specific type of equipment that a state pursues an offensive BW program.

Furthermore, the nature and scope of biological warfare has changed dramatically as a result of the revolution in the life sciences. As Malcolm Dando has shown for the "three generations of offensive biological warfare programs" of the twentieth century, all the military programs were "developing on the back of growth in scientific knowledge."[9] This pattern seems to continue. As a panel of life sciences experts concluded in a recent assessment of the threat of advanced BW based on biotechnological methods and processes that was conducted for the CIA,

> Classes of unconventional pathogens that may arise in the next decade and beyond include binary BW agents that only become effective when two components are combined ... ; "designer" BW agents created to be antibiotic resistant or to evade an immune response; weaponized gene therapy vectors that effect permanent change in the victim's genetic make up; or a "stealth" virus, which could lie dormant inside the victim for an extended period before being triggered.[10]

Thus, problems in fighting the naturally occurring disease agents of today might be dwarfed by the genetically modified agents of the future, putting an ever increasing burden on biodefense and public health systems.

Fighting deliberate disease through biological weapons arms control

The structure of the BW prohibition regime

The BW prohibition regime rests largely on the 1972 Biological and Toxin Weapons Convention. It is based on the recognition that the use of BW agents constitutes an abhorrent act of warfare and is therefore prohibited. At the same time, peaceful uses of the biosciences are regarded as a legitimate undertaking. According to BWC Article I,

> Each State Party to this Convention undertakes never in any circum-
> stances to develop, produce, stockpile or otherwise acquire or retain:
> (1) Microbial or other biological agents, or toxins whatever their
> origin or method of production, *of types and in quantities that have
> no justification for prophylactic, protective or other peaceful purposes.*
> (Emphasis added)[11]

This so-called general purpose criterion makes it clear that not only are peaceful uses of the biosciences legitimate undertakings for states parties to the BWC, but so are defenses against the threat or use of BW. This principle is rooted in the belief that the peaceful uses of biosciences cannot be taken for granted—be it for the lack of universality in membership or for a state party not living up to the obligations it has assumed.

Central to the normative guidelines for state action contained in the BW control regime is the non-use norm. It is explicitly spelled out in the 1925 Geneva Protocol and implicitly contained in Article I of the BWC.[12] Of particular relevance to the interrelation between biodefense and public health, and the securitization of the latter, are three further regime norms: the co-operation norm contained in Article X of the BWC; the assistance norm as spelled out in BWC Article VII, according to which state parties will come to each other's assistance in case of the use or threat of BW against one of them; and the internalization norm, as stipulated in Article IV of the BWC. According to the latter norm, state parties have to internalize the prohibitions of the BWC and prevent the activities banned under the BWC from taking place on their territory. Yet, how this is to be accomplished is left to the interpretation of state parties.

Efforts to strengthen the BW prohibition regime

The two central weaknesses of the BW control regime—the absence of a verification principle and the lack of precise rules and procedures that would specify how to implement the norms of the regime in everyday state prac-tice—came to the fore soon after entry into force of the BWC in 1975. The confidence-building measures (CBMs) agreed upon during the Second and Third BWC Review Conferences in 1986 and 1991 represent one attempt to remedy these shortcomings. However, as one review of the data submissions up to 2003 has revealed, implementation of the CBMs was poor.[13]

In parallel to these CBMs, a process was initiated that initially looked into the technical feasibility of potential verification measures for the BWC (during 1992–1993) and led to negotiations on a verification protocol, which lasted from 1995 to 2001. Yet, already the formulation of the negotiating mandate proved contentious and allowed for various diverging goals to be pursued in the negotiations.[14] To speed up negotiations, Ambassador Tibor Tóth, chair of the Ad Hoc Group (AHG), developed a compromise text, which he presented to delegations in spring 2001.[15] The July 2001 session of the AHG was scheduled to discuss this compromise text. While there was considerable support for the approach taken by Ambassador Tóth, the United States concluded that the overall approach taken in the negotiations up to that point was flawed and the draft protocol text would reduce and not increase security against BW.

The ensuing sense of failure was compounded during the last day of the Fifth BWC Review Conference when the United States came forward with a proposal to terminate the AHG for good. The content of this proposal ran counter to the tacit understanding not to touch the topic of the AHG in order to avoid a breakdown of the review process as well. Moreover, the United States did not inform any of its allies in advance about the content or timing of the proposal. Not surprisingly, this created the impression that the US delegation was deliberately attempting to wreck the conference. The only way to prevent a diplomatic disaster was to adjourn the conference and reconvene one year later, in November 2002.[16] During this second part of the conference, a set of five measures was agreed on to guide discussions among state parties for the years 2003–2005. One of the measures was international cooperation in the fight against infectious disease.

Public health in the fight against natural diseases

The international public health regime

Although international cooperation to improve public health started in the middle of the nineteenth century, it was the establishment of the WHO in 1948 that marked the birth of today's international public health regime.[17] When the WHO was set up, its members agreed on the principles that "the enjoyment of the highest attainable standard of health is one of the fundamental rights of every human being" and that the "health of all peoples is fundamental to the attainment of peace and security and is dependent upon the fullest cooperation of individuals and States."[18] Despite this lofty rhetoric, including peace and security, Anne-Marie Slaughter reminds us that the WHO falls in the category of more specialized international organizations that "address less overtly 'political' subject areas than international and regional security."[19]

During the first three decades of its existence, the WHO attempted to implement its mandate largely through a disease-oriented policy. This rather technical approach found its expression in the adoption of the International Health Regulations (IHR). In it, WHO member states agreed to two normative guideposts for their public health policy. First, they agreed to notify the WHO of outbreaks of diseases covered by the IHR. Initially six diseases were subject to this notification norm: smallpox, typhus, relapsing fever, cholera, malaria, and yellow fever. After a 1981 modification of the IHR, only the latter three had to be reported to the WHO. The primary goal of the IHR "is to ensure the maximum security against the international spread of diseases with minimum interference with world traffic,"[20] In addition, the IHR was designed to interfere only marginally with how WHO member states organized their domestic health policies. Rather, its primary target has been to prevent the transborder movement of disease-causing organisms. Only a limited set of requirements—this represented the second, much weaker, normative guidepost of the IHR—has been imposed by the IHR on states to undertake certain public health measures at ports and airports. However, as David Fidler summarizes, the "IHR failed massively to achieve their objective."[21] This failure was first and foremost due to the widespread non-compliance of member states with the reporting requirements under the IHR. Second, the large number of newly emerging or reemerging infectious diseases, especially HIV/AIDS, demonstrated the growing irrelevance of the reduced list of diseases that were to be reported. The World Health Assembly (WHA), the WHO's highest governing body, acknowledged this failure in 1995 and tasked the WHO with revising the IHR.[22] In 2001, WHA Resolution 54.14 "supported the ongoing revision, including criteria to define what constitutes a public health emergency of international concern."[23] Based on the work of an intergovernmental working group, the new regulations were adopted by the WHA in May 2005.[24]

From international to global public health?

Programs to eradicate specific diseases have been departing from this inter-state focus of WHO activities and have attempted to interfere much more deeply with capacity-building efforts in member states and the organization of their public health systems. The programs to eradicate smallpox and malaria are two examples of success and failure, respectively, of such pro-grams.[25] A more general shift away from the horizontal strategies based on intergovernmental relations, as embodied in the IHR, was signaled by the "Health for All" declaration agreed on in 1978 in Alma Ata. As Fidler points out with respect to this shift in priorities, "The need of the great powers for the kind of international cooperation embodied in the IHR had all but vanished, leaving the regime without its traditional political engine."[26] This opened the discursive space for addressing and reaffirming health as a funda-mental human right, whose realization cannot be limited to the monitoring and reporting of three communicable diseases. The linkage between health and human rights was further strengthened when the WHO integrated efforts to stop the discrimination of those affected by HIV/AIDS into its policies to address the disease. This clearly represented a further step in eroding the sovereignty of states to deal with a crucial public health issue on their own terms.[27] Calls to that end also came from the international development arena, where in the early to mid-1990s the annual reports of the United

Nations Development Programme (UNDP) started to focus on human security, with health security being one of its core dimensions.[28]

Intergovernmental public health policies came under additional pressure from a number of globalization-related processes. As Richard Dodgson and Kelley Lee point out, "Globalisation has introduced or intensified trans-border health risks," which include "emerging and re-emerging infectious diseases, various non-communicable diseases . . . and environmental change,"[29] In particular, the issue of emerging and reemerging diseases has occupied a large part of public health discourse since the early 1990s, both nationally and internationally.[30] This discourse increasingly involves a multitude of nonstate actors in the form of both health-oriented NGOs and multinational corporations.[31] In general terms, globalization has reduced state capacity to adequately address problems in a variety of issue areas—public health among them.

Acknowledging this decreased state capacity, nonstate actors have been brought into the international public health arena as information providers. This has begun to redirect the discourses and processes of international public health away from a purely state-centric approach. Fidler aptly illustrates this trend with the example of NGO-generated disease surveillance data that are now being utilized by the WHO and fed into its Global Outbreak Alert and Response Network (GOARN). The need to harness this additional source of information was identified early in the process of revising the IHR, but the process for formalizing the use of data from nonstate actors then took on a life of its own. The use of nongovernmental disease surveillance data, started in 1997, was approved by the WHA in 2001 and thus preceded the conclusion of the IHR revision in 2005 by several years.[32]

The emergence of bioterrorism and the securitization of public health

Following the actual emergence of the use of biological agents by criminals or terrorists, an academic discourse on bioterrorism began to form during the 1970s.[33] For the 1970s, Seth Carus reports eight cases of bioagent use, nine for the 1980s. Figures for bioagent incidents skyrocketed during the 1990s, with much of the increase occurring during the second half of the decade. He identifies 153 cases for the 1990s, which brings the total to 180. However, many of these "cases" took place only in the mind of perpetrators or were hoaxes: Carus puts 137 out of the 180 reported cases in the latter category.[34] A group of US scholars investigated twelve of the most plausible cases, but even of these, three turned out to be apocryphal.[35]

The shift in academic and political discourse that sought to establish whether the new fear of bioterrorism was supported by facts or was "hyped"[36] was triggered by the Aum Shinrikyo attack in March 1995. This attack, in which the nerve agent sarin was released in commuter trains of the Tokyo subway system, killed twelve people and injured several hundred more.[37] Beginning in the mid-1990s, that attack—in conjunction with the Oklahoma City bombing—led to calls in the United States for expanded measures to counter potential bioterrorist attacks, including the utilization of the public health system. However, hardly any corresponding efforts to securitize public health were visible at the international level before the fall of 2001.

After the World Trade Center and Pentagon attacks in the United States on September 11, 2001, and the subsequent anthrax letters sent through the US mail, attempts to securitize public health manifested themselves on a number of levels and led to a variety of institutional responses, such as the G8 global health security initiative, and different policy measures at the European Union level. However, the focus here is on the two discursive spaces with the clearest mandate on the international level to address public health and the biological weapons threat—that is, the World Health Organization and the meetings of state parties to the BWC.

The WHO and the securitization of international public health

In spring 2002, in the aftermath of the anthrax attacks in the United States, the WHO secretariat, in preparation for the Fifty-fifth World Health Assembly (WHA), produced a report entitled "Deliberate Use of Biological and Chemical Agents to Cause Harm."[38] The report points out that in response to such an incident, the organization is to "strengthen public health disease alert systems at all levels, as such a system will detect and respond to diseases that may be deliberately caused."[39] In case the United Nations were tasked to investigate a disease outbreak, the report suggested that the

> WHO could be asked to provide technical expertise or to make available its existing resources and mechanisms. Non–public health issues related to investigations of reports on possible use of chemical and bacteriological (biological) or toxin weapons, however, remain the responsibility of the United Nations. If such a request were made, information about the public health response, including the results of epidemiological and laboratory investigations, would be reported by WHO to the government of the country or countries where the event was occurring.[40]

With this statement, the WHO clearly rejects any attempts at international public health being securitized and positions itself outside the BW arms control context. An expansion of the WHO mandate to function as a substitute verification organization for the BWC is rejected.

In the WHA resolution based on this report, member states are urged to adopt national measures regarding disease surveillance, to collaborate in capacity building, and to assist one another in case of a deliberately caused epidemic. These national measures are to be supported by the WHO secretariat through the strengthening of global surveillance mechanisms for infectious disease, the provision of tools and support for member states, and international guidance and technical information that would support public health systems in countering deliberate epidemics.[41]

The Department of Communicable Disease Surveillance and Response in the WHO secretariat had already set up its Programme for the Preparedness for Deliberate Epidemics (PDE) in response to the anthrax attacks in the United States. Following the WHA resolution, PDE was developed into three main areas:[42]

- *International coordination and collaboration.* This involves the contribution of WHO staff to a variety of meetings organized in the context of the BWC, the North Atlantic Treaty Organization, or the Red Cross.
- *National capacity strengthening on preparedness for and response to the deliberate use of bioagents.* In this area, the WHO issued recommendations on the development of guidelines, expert networks, and training. One concrete example is *Guidelines for Assessing National Health Preparedness Programmes for the Deliberate Use of Biological and Chemical Agents.*
- *Public health preparedness for diseases associated with the deliberate use of biological agents.* In this context, "WHO is strengthening selected disease-specific networks, starting with anthrax. Other priority diseases— identified by a WHO risk assessment—include plague, tularemia, brucellosis, glanders, melioidosis, Q fever, typhus fever . . . and smallpox."[43]

All the activities conducted under PDE are being funded by extrabudgetary resources, which are donated by member states with an interest in these issues. The original program budget for the biennium 2002–2003 was below US$1 million,[44] and although this has increased for the period 2004–2005, it still funds only a small team dedicated to preparedness for deliberate diseases.

In parallel to these limited PDE activities, the discourse on the revision of the IHR gained momentum.[45] Following consultations with state parties, the WHO secretariat circulated a first draft of the revised IHR in early 2004.[46] Extensive regional consultations were followed by three rounds of negotiations, which took place in Geneva between November 2004 and May 2005. Already the first draft IHR contained four major new elements that expanded the scope of the IHR considerably. State parties would now be required to "notify all events potentially constituting a public health emergency of international concern"; set up a national IHR focal point; and implement "the minimum core surveillance and response capacities required at the national level in order to successfully implement the global health security, epidemic alert and response strategy." In addition, the revised IHR were conceptualized as the legal framework for that strategy.[47] Although a large part of the discourse on IHR revision was characterised by a consensus on the need to expand the scope of the regulations, just how far such an expansion should go was contested among WHO states parties. Diverging views came to the fore in particular with respect to the question of IHR coverage of chemical, biological, radiological, and nuclear (CBRN) weapons incidents. While some state parties—among them the United States—believed that the IHR could also be utilized to gather information not otherwise obtainable on such incidents, state parties from the developing world, most notably from the Southeast Asian and eastern Mediterranean regional groups, were led in their rejection by Pakistani and Iranian delegates.[48] The evolution of the discourse on notification criteria contained in Annex 2 to the revised IHR is particularly instructive in this regard: the language provided by an Ad Hoc Expert Group report in February 2005 cited the "release into the environment of a chemical or radionuclear agent that has contaminated or has the potential to contaminate a population and/or a large geographical area"[49] as one of the criteria prompting notification to the WHO. In the final version of the IHR, all references to chemical or radionuclear agents have been eliminated, because some delegations argued that their explicit mention would place too much emphasis on CBW scenarios and thus risk going beyond WHO's mandate.[50] Instead, Annex 2 now lists the "spread of toxic, infectious or otherwise hazardous material that may be occurring naturally or otherwise" as one of the criteria for notification.[51] In combination with references to "unexpected and unusual outbreaks of disease" in Annex 2 and in the main body of the text, this wording was able to bridge the divide between those advocating a further-reaching securitization of the revised IHR, including the United States, and those mostly concerned with limiting the degree of transparency that has to be provided under the IHR to information that is "commensurate with and restricted to public health risks,"[52] such as Pakistan. Concerning the role played by the WHO bureaucracy in developing this discourse, all interviewed delegates in Geneva agreed that there were few if any signs that the WHO secretariat was acting in a politically motivated way. However, one delegate cautioned that in addition to a genuine motive in wanting to strengthen the IHR, the WHO might also have been "sniffing the political wind" and may have engaged in "strategic positioning, based on past experience of being left behind."[53] In other words, there have been indicators that the WHO bureaucracy might have been receptive to notions of health security in order to jump on the human security train, in an attempt not to be disconnected from a shifting discourse in the UNDP and the UN system at large. However, attempts of the WHO bureaucracy to side with proponents of stronger securitization moves during the IHR revision could not be ascertained.

The WHO's potential role in the fight against the deliberate spread of disease also featured in the report of the UN Secretary-General's High-Level Panel on Threats, Challenges and Change, which the panel delivered in

December 2004.[54] In Part 2 of the report, "Collective Security and the Challenges of Prevention," several paragraphs address the challenges of poverty reduction, sustainable development, and the prevention of the spread of infectious disease. Under the heading "New Initiatives," the panel argues that "a new global initiative" is required to "rebuild local and national public health systems throughout the developing world."[55] In addition, WHA members are urged to increase GOARN's "capacity to cope with potential disease outbreaks."[56] Last, and more problematic, the panel recommends that "in extreme cases of threat posed by a new emerging infectious disease or intentional release of an infectious agent, there may be a need for cooperation between WHO and the Security Council in establishing effective quarantine measures."[57]

This notion of WHO–Security Council collaboration is reinforced elsewhere in the report, where under the heading "Better Public Health Defenses," the panel suggests that the "Security Council should consult with the WHO Director General to establish the necessary procedures for working together in the event of a suspicious or overwhelming outbreak of infectious disease."[58] As Graham Pearson has pointed out, with this last statement the panel is "treading on dangerous ground," as it threatens to undermine the WHO's "political neutrality and the widespread recognition that its purpose is to provide assistance to its member states when they are faced with outbreaks of disease."[59] However, this far-reaching securitization move of the High-Level Panel was not followed by the UN secretary-general, whose report mentioned the burden of diseases like malaria, HIV/AIDS, and SARS only in a human security context, not in relation to arms control verification activities. Consequently, his recommendation is limited to a call on WHO member states to agree on the revised IHR during the next WHA session.[60]

The discourse on disease surveillance in the BWC intersessional process

When the second part of the BWC Review Conference took place in late 2002, BWC member states decided by consensus to hold annual meetings from 2003 to 2005 that would address, among other things,[61]

> enhancing international capabilities for responding to, investigating and mitigating the effects of cases of alleged use of biological or toxin weapons or suspicious outbreaks of disease [and] . . . strengthening and broadening national and international institutional efforts and existing mechanisms for the surveillance, detection, diagnosis and combating of infectious diseases affecting humans, animals, and plants.[62]

This reduced program of work is a far cry from the comprehensive approach of the Ad Hoc Group to reach agreement on a legally binding protocol.[63]

The discussion on the above-mentioned two agenda items in 2004 led to the inclusion of several substantive paragraphs in the report of the meeting of states parties.[64] In it, BWC member states recognize that

> strengthening and broadening national and international surveillance, detection, diagnosis and combating of infectious disease may support the object and purpose of the Convention; ... the primary responsibility for surveillance, detection, diagnosis and combating of infectious diseases rests with States Parties, while the WHO, FAO [Food and Agriculture Organization] and OIE [World Organisation for Animal Health] have global responsibilities, *within their mandates*, in this regard. The respective structures, planning and activities of States Parties and the WHO, FAO and OIE should be co-ordinated with and complement one another.[65]
>
> (Emphasis added)

The acknowledgment of the existing mandates of WHO, FAO, and OIE stands in marked contrast to the High-Level Panel report, which, if acted upon, would have led to a part of WHO's activities being securitized. The wording in the report of BWC states parties likewise displays greater consciousness in describing the scenarios in which WHO assistance might be required: it refers to all cases of infectious disease outbreak, not—like the panel report repeatedly—to "suspicious" outbreaks. The latter approach implies already a political judgment, which is anathema to the WHO's perception of its role and mandate.

Implications for the global governance of public health and the BW prohibition regime

This article set out to trace the securitization moves that have been made in relation to international public health (IPH) in the two discursive spaces most relevant to the provision of IPH and security from the threat of biological weapons: the WHO and the meetings of BWC states parties.

The securitizing speech acts that have been discussed in relation to the WHO show that the organization has appeared in three different roles or functions in attempts to securitize IPH: in the context of the UN Secretary-General's High-Level Panel, the WHO appeared as the object of securitization; during the IHR revision process, the WHO served both as discursive space in which the securitization of IPH was debated and as a securitizing actor in its own right. With respect to the latter role, it is worth distinguishing between the promotion of the notion of health security in human security terms and securitizing moves that aim at a more traditional understanding of the concept. As the previous discussion showed, what was supported by the WHO secretariat was the former notion, not the latter. This position was motivated by the preservation of its neutrality, in order to be able to continue the broader roles foreseen in its mandate. Being implicated in verifying the use of biological weapons or other aspects of BWC compliance would compromise this neutrality.[66]

Noteworthy in this context is that all references to health security have IPH as referent object—that is, as that which is to be secured, not global public health. The role of states as central actors in IPH has clearly been reaffirmed by the revised IHR: it is *states*, not nonstate actors, that have to provide national focal points for the implementation of IHR and also fulfill minimum standards in disease surveillance and reporting. The WHO and NGOs, like the networks contributing to the WHO's GOARN, have only a supporting role.

From this it follows that IPH has so far been only partially securitized. This assessment is supported by a look at the resource allocation for deliberate epidemics. This area of WHO's activities is closest in substantive terms to BW control mechanisms. However, its resources do not form part of the regular WHO budget, but are funded by interested member states. This leads to an institutionalization on a lower level that is more easily reversible in case the specific interests of the states supporting the program on preventing deliberate epidemics should shift. However, PDE represents yet another area in WHO's portfolio in which intergovernmental mechanisms prevail. As Fidler and others have pointed out, such an intergovernmental approach to global public health problems is leading to suboptimal policy outcomes when compared to an approach that strengthens global governance mechanisms. In light of this, the continued preoccupation of parts of WHO's secretariat with BW-related issues poses an obstacle to the transition from international to global public health.

In sum, the attempts to securitize IPH in the context of the WHO have led to a new mix of horizontal (i.e., intergovernmental) and vertical strategies to provide public health. The state as actor in IPH has been strengthened, while at the same time, the new health regulations reach much deeper into states and affect their preparations for public health emergencies of international concern. The definition of such emergencies, however, appears to be much more oriented toward the US Center for Disease Control's list of bioterrorism agents than those disease-causing agents that have caused the most fatalities over the last decade.

As for the implications of the attempted securitization of international public health for the future of the BW prohibition regime, a first question to consider is whether and to what extent the emergence of the WHO as a new actor who "speaks security" in this area will have an impact on the regime. On first glance, the setting up of new organizational structures dealing with preparedness for deliberate epidemics within the WHO secretariat might indicate the creation of a competing actor to a potential future BWC secretariat. However, as the analysis of WHO involvement in the BWC Ad Hoc Group deliberations and the 2002 report on its PDE activities show, WHO has no intention of taking on the role of verifying the use of BW or other aspects of states' compliance with their obligations undertaken under the BWC. Furthermore, at current levels of funding and manpower allocation, WHO's PDE team would not have the capacity to perform such a function in the first place. In sum, then, the WHO is not an actor that should be expected to influence regime development in a major way.

As discussed in the section on the BWC intersessional process, "enhancing international capabilities for responding to . . . suspicious outbreaks of disease" and "strengthening and broadening . . . the surveillance, detection, diagnosis and combating of infectious diseases" had been selected as issue areas for consideration by BWC states parties for the intersessional process leading up to the 2006 BWC Review Conference. This heightened profile of infectious disease surveillance could positively affect the implementation of three core regime norms: the cooperation norm, the assistance norm, and the internalization norm. However, such a positive effect will depend on the overall approach taken by BWC state parties to utilize the outcomes of the intersessional process. Should BWC state parties, for example, decide to set up a small secretariat to assist state parties in implementing more effectively the provisions of the BWC in general and the recommendations that might flow from the 2003–2005 intersessional process more specifically, such a secretariat could conceivably also take on a few functions that overlap with or utilize the technical assistance WHO provides to its members. It might, for example, tap into the information provided by GOARN and act as a clearing house by assisting member states in identifying, from the wealth of information provided by GOARN, suspicious outbreaks of disease. This would also relieve the WHO of suspicions that it might be misused as a Trojan horse to conduct BWC-related activities in public health guise.

Should the community of BWC state parties not be able to reach consensus during the 2006 Review Conference as to how to build on the work of the intersessional process, the partially securitized IPH regime will not be able to compensate for such a lack of political will. Neither is it to be expected that implementation of the international health regulations will detract from the attention BWC state parties devote to their obligations under this convention. Thus, it will not further weaken the already patchy BWC implementation record of a number of state parties. If, however, the BWC state parties should not be able to utilize the potential contribution of international public health—within the boundaries of the mandate and scope of WHO's activities—through the creation of new organizational structures for the BWC, this would amount to nothing less than another lost opportunity for the strengthening of the BW prohibition regime.

Notes

1 The term is taken from Elin A. Gursky, *Drafted to Fight Terror: U.S. Public Health on the Front Lines of Biological Defense* (Washington, DC: ANSER, 2004).

2 See Alexander Kelle, *Securitization of Public Health in the United States of America: Implications for Public Health and Biological Weapons Arms Control*, Bradford Regime Review Paper No. 2, available at www.brad.ac.uk/acad/sbtwc/regrev/Kelle_SecuritizationinUS.pdf.

3 See Ole Wæver, "Securitization and Desecuritization," in Ronnie D. Lippschutz, ed., *On Security* (New York: Columbia University Press, 1995), pp. 46–86.

4 See, for example, Richard Ullman, "Redefining Security," *International Security* 8, no. 1 (1983): 129–153; and Keith Krause and Michael C. Williams, "Broadening the Agenda of Security Studies: Politics and Methods," *Mershon Review of International Studies* 40, no. 2 (1996): 229–254.

5 Wæver, "Securitization and Desecuritization," p. 51.

6 Ole Wæver, "The EU as a Sovereign Actor: Reflections from a Pessimistic Constructivist on Post-sovereign Security Orders," in Morten Kelstrup and Michael Williams, eds., *International Relations Theory and the Politics of European Integration: Power, Security and Community* (London: Routledge, 2000), p. 251.

7 Mark L. Wheelis, "Biological Warfare Before 1914," in Erhard Geissler and John Ellis van Courtland Moon, eds., *Biological and Toxin Weapons: Research, Development and Use from the Middle Ages to 1945*, SIPRI Chemical and Biological Warfare Studies, No. 18 (Oxford: Oxford University Press, 1999), pp. 8–34.

8 See Dean Wilkening, "BCW Attack Scenarios," in Sidney D. Drell, Abraham D. Sofaer, and George D. Wilson, eds., *The New Terror: Facing the Threat of Biological and Chemical Weapons* (Stanford: Hoover Institution Press, 1999), pp. 76–114.

9 Malcolm Dando, "The Impact of the Development of Modern Biology and Medicine on the Evolution of Offensive Biological Warfare Programs in the Twentieth Century," *Defense Analysis* 15, no. 1 (1999): 51.

10 Central Intelligence Agency, Directorate of Intelligence, *The Darker Bioweapons Future*, unclassified, Washington, DC, 3 November 2003, p. 1, available at www.fas.org/irp/cia/product/bw1103.pdf.

11 The text of the BWC is available in numerous places; see, for example, the website of the United Nations Office in Geneva, www.unog.ch/bwc.

12 For a comprehensive discussion of the normative structure of the BW regime, see Alexander Kelle, "Strengthening the Effectiveness of the BTW Control Regime: Feasibility and Options," *Contemporary Security Policy* 24, no.2 (2003): 95–132.

13 Iris Hunger, *Confidence Building Needs Transparency: A Summary of Data Submitted Under the Bioweapon Convention's Confidence Building Measures, 1987–2003*, September 2005, available at www.biological-arms-control.org/download/hunger_CBM.pdf.

14 Kenneth D. Ward, "The BWC Protocol. Mandate for Failure," *Nonproliferation Review* 11, no. 2 (Summer 2004): 183–199.

15 Jenni Rissanen, "Chair Releases His 'Composite Text' for Verification Protocol," *Disarmament Diplomacy*, no. 55 (March 2001), available at www.acronym.org.uk/bwc/archive.htm? (accessed 1 December 2006).

16 See Jenni Rissanen, "Left in Limbo: Review Conference Suspended on Edge of Collapse," *Disarmament Diplomacy*, no. 62 (January–February 2002): 18–32.

17 Javed Siddiqi, *World Health and World Politics: The World Health Organisation and the U.N. System* (London: Hurst, 1995), pp. 14–20.

18 See the preamble of WHO's constitution, available at http://policy.who.int/cgi-bin/om_isapi.dll?infobase=Basicdoc&softpage=Browse_Frame_Pg42.

19 Anne-Marie Slaughter, *A New World Order* (Princeton: Princeton University Press, 2004), p. 22.

20 See World Health Organization, "International Health Regulations," available at www.who.int/csr/ihr/en.

21 David P. Fidler, *SARS, Governance and the Globalization of Disease* (Basingstoke: Palgrave Macmillan, 2004), p. 35.
22 Ibid., p. 61, footnote.
23 South East Asian Regional Committee, *International Health Regulations: Revision Process*, Document SEA/RC56/4, New Dehli, 4 July 2003, available at http://w3.whosea.org/meeting/rc/rc56/pdf/RC56-4.pdf, p. 1.
24 *Revision of the International Health Regulations*, WHO Doc. WHA58.3, 23 May 2005, available at www.who.int/gb/ebwha/pdf_files/WHA58/WHA58_3-en.pdf.
25 On the malaria program, see Siddiqi, *World Health and World Politics*, pp. 123–191; on smallpox, see F. Fenner et al., *Smallpox and Its Eradication* (Geneva: WHO, 1988).
26 Fidler, *SARS, Governance and the Globalization of Disease*, pp. 40–41
27 J. M. Mann, "Human Rights and Aids: The Future of the Pandemic," in J. M. Mann et al. eds., *Health and Human Rights: A Reader* (London: Routledge, 1999), pp. 216–226.
28 See United Nations Development Programme, *Human Development Report 1994: New Dimensions of Human Security* (New York: United Nations, 1994), pp. 27–28.
29 Richard Dodgson and Kelley Lee, "Global Health Governance. A Conceptual Review," in Rorden Wilkinson and Steve Hughes, eds., *Global Governance: Critical Perspectives* (London: Routledge, 2002), p. 98.
30 See, for example, Institute of Medicine (IOM), *Emerging Infections: Microbial Threats to Health in the United States* (Washington, DC: National Academy Press, 1992); World Health Organization, *World Health Report: Fighting Disease, Fostering Development* (Geneva: WHO, 1996); and IOM, *Microbial Threats to Health: Emergence, Detection, and Response* (Washington, DC: National Academy Press, 2003).
31 On the involvement of the latter, see Yves Beigbeder, *International Public Health: Patients' Rights vs. the Protection of Patents* (Aldershot: Ashgate, 2004).
32 Fidler, *SARS, Governance and the Globalization of Disease*, pp. 66–67.
33 W. Seth Carus, *Bioterrorism and Biocrimes: The Illicit Use of Biological Agents Since 1900* (Washington, DC: National Defense University, February 2001), p. 11; Ron Purver, *Chemical and Biological Terrorism: The Threat According to the Open Literature* (Ottawa: Canadian Security Intelligence Service, June 1995).
34 Ibid., p. 8.
35 Jonathan Tucker, ed., *Toxic Terror: Assessing Terrorist Use of Chemical and Biological Weapons* (Cambridge: MIT Press, 2000).
36 Brad Roberts, ed., *Hype or Reality: The "New Terrorism" and Mass Casualty Attacks* (Alexandria, VA: CBACI, 2000).
37 See Milton Leitenberg, "The Experience of the Japanese Aum Shinrikyo Group and Biological Agents," in Roberts, *Hype or Reality*, pp. 159–170.
38 See WHO document at www.who.int/gb/ebwha/pdf_files/WHA55/ea5520.pdf.
39 Ibid., p. 2.
40 Ibid., p. 3.
41 See www.who.int/gb/ebwha/pdf_files/WHA55/ewha5516.pdf, p. 2.
42 WHO, *Preparedness for Deliberate Epidemics: To Support Member States in Enhancing Their Preparedness and Response Programmes for the Possible Deliberate Use of Biological Agents That Affect Health: Report of Activities for the Biennium 2002–2003*, Doc. WHO/CDS/CSR/LYO/2004.7 (Geneva: WHO, 2004), available at www.who.int/csr/delibepidemics/preparedness/WHO_CDS_CSR_LYO_2004_7.pdf.
43 Ibid., p. 5.
44 Ibid., p. 6.

45 Unless otherwise noted, the following account of the discourse on the revised IHR is based on a number of interviews with national delegates involved in this process. Interviews were conducted in Geneva during the week 5–9 December 2005.

46 See WHO Working Group on the Revision of the International Health Regulations, *International Health Regulations: Working Paper for Regional Consultations*, Doc. IGWG/IHR/Working paper/12.2003 (Geneva: WHO, 12 January 2004).

47 Ibid., pp. 2–3.

48 Interviews with delegates in Geneva, 7 and 8 December 2005.

49 WHO, *Decision Instrument for the Assessment and Notification of Events That May Constitute a Public Health Emergency of International Concern: Report of the Ad Hoc Expert Group on Annex 2*, Doc. A/IHR/IGWG/2/INF.DOC./4 (Geneva: WHO, 22 February 2005), p. 7.

50 Interview with delegate in Geneva, 8 December 2005.

51 WHO, Revision *of the International Health Regulations*, Doc. WHA58.3 (Geneva: WHO, 23 May 2005), p. 46.

52 Ibid., p. 9. See also *Statement for the Record by the Government of the United States of America Concerning the World Health Organizations Revised International Health Regulations* (Geneva: US Mission to the United Nations in Geneva, 23 May 2005), available at www.usmission.ch/Press2005/0523IHRs.htm.

53 Interview with delegate participating in the IHR revision process, Geneva, 8 December 2005.

54 *A More Secure World: Our Shared Responsibility: Report of the Secretary-General's High Level Panel on Threats, Challenges and Change* (New York: United Nations, 2004).

55 Ibid., p. 29.

56 Ibid., p. 29, footnote.

57 Ibid., p. 30.

58 Ibid., p. 47.

59 Graham S. Pearson, *The UN Secretary-General's High Level Panel: Biological Weapons Related Issues*, Strengthening the Biological Weapons Convention Review Conference Paper No. 14 (Bradford: Department of Peace Studies, University of Bradford, May 2005), p. 16.

60 See *In Larger Freedom: Towards Development, Security and Human Rights for All*, Report of the Secretary-General (New York: United Nations, 2005), pp. 20–21.

61 On the split 2001–2002 BWC review conference, see Marie I. Chevrier, "Waiting for Godot or Saving the Show? The BWC Review Conference Reaches Modest Agreement," in *Disarmament Diplomacy*, no. 68 (December 2002–January 2003): 11–16.

62 Final document of the Fifth BWC Review Conference, Doc. BWC/CONF. V/17, p. 3, available at http://disarmament2.un.org/wmd/bwc/pdf/bwccnfv17.PDF.

63 See Kelle, "Strengthening the Effectiveness," note 11.

64 United Nations, *Report of the Meeting of States Parties*, Doc. BWC/MSP/2004-3 (Geneva: United Nations, 14 December 2004), available at www.opbw.org/new_process/msp2004/BWC_MSP_2004_3_E.pdf.

65 Ibid., p. 4.

66 Although intended in no way as a comprehensive answer, this finding also speaks to the issue recently raised by McInnes and Lee concerning the "lack of conceptual clarity over what WHO and others term 'global health security.'" Collin McInnes and Kelley Lee, "Health, Security and Foreign Policy," in *Review of International Studies* 32, no. 1 (2006): 23.

52

THE ROLE OF THE BIOLOGICAL WEAPONS CONVENTION IN DISEASE SURVEILLANCE AND RESPONSE

Christian Enemark

Source: *Health Policy and Planning*, 25:6 (2010), 486–94.

This article assesses the role and significance of the Biological Weapons Convention (BWC) with respect to infectious disease surveillance and response to outbreaks. Increasingly, the BWC is being used as a platform for addressing infectious disease threats arising naturally as well as traditional concerns about malicious dissemination of pathogenic microorganisms. The latter have long had a place on the security agenda, but natural disease outbreaks too are now being partially 'securitized' through the use of the BWC as a forum for exchanging information and ideas on disease surveillance and response. The article focuses on two prominent issues discussed at recent meetings of BWC member states: enhancing capacity for disease surveillance and response; and responding to allegations of biological weapons use and investigating outbreaks deemed suspicious. It concludes, firstly, that the BWC supports the efforts of international health organizations to enhance disease surveillance and response capacity worldwide. And secondly, that the BWC, rather than the World Health Organization (WHO), is the appropriate institution to deal with biological weapons allegations and investigations of suspicious outbreaks. The overall message is that securitization in the health sphere cuts both ways. Adding a security dimension (BW) alongside the task of detecting and responding to naturally occurring disease outbreaks is beneficial, but requiring a non-security organization (the WHO) to assume a security role would be counterproductive.

Key messages

- The 1972 Biological Weapons Convention (BWC) is increasingly being used as a platform for addressing infectious disease threats arising naturally as well as from malicious human action.

- The BWC supports the efforts of international health organizations to enhance disease surveillance and response capacity worldwide. Such support constitutes partial securitization of naturally occurring infectious disease threats.

- The BWC, rather than the World Health Organization (WHO), is the appropriate institution to deal with allegations of biological weapons use and investigations of suspicious outbreaks of disease. Requiring the WHO to perform a security role would undermine the Organization's humanitarian mission and thus diminish its ability to perform effectively.

Introduction

This article assesses the role and significance of an international arms control and disarmament treaty, the 1972 Biological Weapons Convention (BWC), with respect to infectious disease surveillance and response to outbreaks. The BWC is the main instrument of international law banning biological weapons (BW). Increasingly, however, the Convention is being used as a platform for addressing infectious disease threats arising naturally as well as traditional concerns about malicious dissemination of pathogenic micro-organisms. The latter have long had a place on the security agenda, but natural disease outbreaks too are now being partially 'securitized' through the use of the BWC as a forum for exchanging information and ideas on disease surveillance and response. The article focuses on two prominent issues discussed at recent meetings of BWC member states, with particular regard to the views expressed by states in East Asia:[1] enhancing capacity for disease surveillance and response; and responding to allegations of BW use and investigating outbreaks deemed suspicious. It concludes that: the BWC supports the efforts of international health organizations to enhance disease surveillance and response capacity worldwide; and the BWC, rather than the World Health Organization (WHO), is the appropriate institution to deal with BW allegations and investigations of suspicious outbreaks. The overall message of the article is that securitization in the health sphere cuts both ways. Adding a security dimension (BW) alongside the task of detecting and responding to naturally occurring disease outbreaks is beneficial, but requiring a non-security organization (the WHO) to assume a security role would be counterproductive.

The Biological Weapons Convention

In the ongoing struggle between humans and pathogenic microorganisms, the BWC was born in an era very different from the present. The opening of the Convention for signature in 1972 was preceded and facilitated by US President Richard Nixon's decision in 1969 to abandon the American offensive BW programme. In the same year, US Surgeon-General William H Steward testified before Congress that he was ready to 'close the book' on infectious disease (Moore 2001: 1). Such optimism derived from widespread confidence (in the developed world at least) that new and improved antibiotics and vaccines would bring about a lasting victory of man over microbe. Today, however, the BWC operates in an era of emerging and re-emerging infectious diseases which impose a heavy health burden and defy many existing forms of medical treatment. To an increasing extent, the worsening threat of naturally occurring disease outbreaks is being considered alongside traditional BW concerns at meetings of BWC member states. In accordance with an agreement reached at the Fifth BWC Review Conference in Geneva in 2002, member states met in 2004 to 'discuss and promote common understanding and effective action' on:

- strengthening and broadening national and international institutional efforts and existing mechanisms for the surveillance, detection, diagnosis and combating of infectious diseases affecting humans, animals and plants; and
- enhancing international capabilities for responding to, investigating and mitigating the effects of cases of alleged use of biological or toxin weapons or suspicious outbreaks of disease (BWC 2002: 3–4).

Security against BW and security against natural disease outbreaks have traditionally been pursued by different sets of actors on both the domestic and international levels. Biodefence and BW arms control are usually the preserve of the military and diplomatic communities, and disease prevention and mitigation are the responsibility of state public health sectors and international institutions like the WHO. As Alexander Kelle has observed, however, '[t]his strict separation has become increasingly blurred' (Kelle 2007: 217). The 2004 BWC meeting engaged a diversity of individuals, government departments and non-government organizations (NGOs) beyond those few arms control officials usually associated with the Convention and its implementation (United States 2004; European Union 2006: 5). The WHO, the Food and Agriculture Organization, the International Committee of the Red Cross and the World Organization for Animal Heath were granted observer status to participate in the meeting. Also in attendance were 14 NGOs and research institutes (BWC 2004: 2).

Subsequently, at the Sixth BWC Review Conference in 2006, member states agreed that the topic discussions of 2004 'functioned as an important forum for exchange of national experiences and in-depth deliberations among States Parties' (BWC 2006: 19). For this reason they agreed, prior to the Seventh Review Conference in 2011, to 'discuss, and promote common understanding and effective action on':

- in 2009: 'promoting capacity building in the fields of disease surveillance, detection, diagnosis, and containment of infectious diseases'; and
- in 2010: 'Provision of assistance and coordination with relevant organizations ... in the case of alleged use of biological or toxin weapons, including improving national capabilities for disease surveillance, detection and diagnosis and public health systems' (BWC 2006: 21).

This article explores international attitudes to these two issues, as expressed in a BWC context, with particular regard to the views of states in East Asia. The picture that emerges is that the Convention plays a supportive role in championing enhanced disease surveillance and response capacity, and that the BWC is preferable to the WHO as a platform for investigating BW allegations and outbreaks deemed suspicious. Explained in the terms of 'securitization' theory, the partial securitization of disease surveillance and response via the BWC is beneficial. But requiring the WHO to perform a security role would undermine the Organization's humanitarian mission and thus diminish its ability to perform effectively. In other words, in the health sphere, appeals to security can cut both ways.

Infectious diseases and securitization theory

The idea of linking health and security concerns, as a matter of academic analysis and public policy, has received support from two directions. On the one side is the public health sector, some members of which see the language of security as a means of rallying political support and financial resources to address neglected health issues. On the other side is the security sector, where some argue that the impact of particular health challenges is sufficiently serious as to warrant the prioritization traditionally accorded to the use of armed force (Enemark 2009: 195). Infectious disease is the health issue which has received most attention in security-oriented policy documents and scholarly debates. And for the purposes of this article, the infectious disease issue of BW is the vehicle for framing disease surveillance and response in security terms.

The theory of securitization derives principally from the work of Barry Buzan, Ole Waever and Jaap de Wilde (Buzan 1991; Waever 1995; Buzan *et al.* 1998). According to these authors, for threats to count as security issues they must be distinguished from issues that are merely political. Specifically, they have to be 'staged as existential threats to a referent object by a securitizing actor who thereby generates endorsement of emergency measures beyond rules that would otherwise bind' (Buzan *et al.* 1998: 5). This theoretical formula appears to assume that the treatment of an issue can only move from 'politicized' to 'securitized' in a single bound. An alternative view is that only rarely does an issue move from being addressed within the realm of 'normal' politics to suddenly requiring emergency measures (Haacke and Williams 2008: 782). For Rita Abrahamsen, the theoretical insistence on defining security as 'existential threat' and distinguishing sharply between normal, everyday politics and 'emergency action' means that 'many of the processes and modalities whereby issues come to be feared and experienced as potentially dangerous cannot be adequately captured within [the] perspective [of Buzan and his co-authors]' (Abrahamsen 2005: 59). She goes on to argue that most security politics is concerned with mundane risk management rather than emergency action, and that 'security issues can be seen to move on a continuum from normalcy to worrisome/troublesome to risk and to existential threat—and conversely, from threat to risk and back to normalcy' (Abrahamsen 2005: 59). In line with such reasoning that the process of securitization is gradual and incremental, it is plausible to conceive of a political gesture towards security or 'partial' securitization.

Regarding the role of the BWC in disease surveillance and response, an arms control and disarmament treaty is an extraordinary mechanism for addressing naturally occurring health threats. Employing such a mechanism does not, however, constitute an 'emergency measure' as contemplated by securitization theory in its pure form. Nevertheless, it imbues the response process with more of a security flavour and such partial securitization probably enhances that process. As the next section will show, the threats of deliberate and natural disease create a dual imperative for governments and non-government entities to improve disease surveillance and response capabilities: expenditure on (traditional) security grounds to resist BW is more justifiable financially because it promises also to improve defences against disease outbreaks of natural origin; and expenditure on health grounds to resist natural diseases is made more acceptable politically because its applicability also to defending against biological attacks adds a security element.

It is important to note, however, that securitization to any extent and/or in any form is potentially counterproductive or otherwise harmful. Buzan and his co-authors take the view that 'Avoiding excessive and irrational securitization is . . . a legitimate social, political and economic objective of considerable importance' (Buzan *et al.* 1998: 208). In the context of HIV/AIDS, Stefan Elbe has warned of the risk that securitization will push responses to that disease towards military and intelligence organizations and away from organizations best suited to dealing with health issues (Elbe 2006: 119). Acknowledging this risk, the final section of this article argues that it would be counterproductive for the WHO—an organization which avoids politics in order to carry out its humanitarian mission—to assume the security role of responding to BW allegations and investigating disease outbreaks deemed suspicious.

Disease surveillance and response capacity

A recent review of 14 international disease surveillance and response programmes identified deficiencies (particularly in the developing world) in the critical areas of health infrastructure, technical resources, and financial and human resources that pose challenges for effectively detecting and responding to disease outbreaks around the globe (Hitchcock *et al.* 2007: 221–2). Insofar as framing a problem in security terms has the potential to generate greater attention to and financial resources for solving that problem, the partial securitization afforded by discussing disease surveillance and response in a BWC context is a welcome development.

Regardless of whether an outbreak occurs naturally or as a result of BW use, there is a detection and response imperative. For this reason, broadly applicable measures aimed at limiting vulnerability to infectious disease threats are a worthwhile area in which to invest financial resources and political attention. Many of the basic measures needed to protect populations against naturally emerging infectious diseases—for example, syndromic surveillance, diagnostics and medical therapies—are the same as would be required to mitigate a biological attack. The Chinese Communist Party leader Mao Zedong recognized this as far back as 1952 when, amidst the controversy over alleged biological attacks by the USA during the Korean War (to be discussed later in this article), he launched China's first Patriotic Hygiene Campaign. The slogan for the campaign was: 'Mobilise to promote hygiene, to reduce disease, to raise the level of the people's health, and to smash the germ warfare of the American imperialists!' (Huang 2003: 2). More recently, China has stated that the 'fundamental purpose of disease surveillance is to prevent and control the spread of disease, but it is also important in the prevention of bioterrorism attacks' (China 2004: 3). This resonates with the view of the WHO (Cosivi 2005: 151):

"Confronted with the potential threat to global health security by the intentional release of biological agents, the World Health Organization . . . advocates 'dual-use' investment in national, regional and global public health operations and infrastructure for early detection and immediate response. One of the most effective methods of preparedness against deliberate epidemics is to strengthen public health surveillance and response activities for naturally and accidentally occurring diseases."

With highly sensitive and well-connected systems for local disease surveillance in place, outbreaks of deadly, contagious diseases could be detected and contained rapidly wherever in the world they occurred. Enhancing disease surveillance sensitivity requires, for example, training clinicians to recognize the signs and symptoms of diseases they would not normally encounter in their medical practices. It also requires expanded local diagnostic capacity worldwide to ensure existing laboratories are not swamped with samples.

In a highly interconnected world, there is an inevitable international dimension to public health responses. An outbreak event inside one country is potentially a problem for others, especially if the disease in question is contagious. In East Asia, the need to prioritize public health responses to infectious disease outbreaks spans the region. Poorer countries such as Cambodia, Laos and Myanmar are particularly vulnerable to disease outbreaks occurring in their territory because of a paucity of health resources. Wealthier countries like Japan, Singapore and South Korea are also vulnerable despite the higher standards of health care enjoyed by their citizens. This is largely because the public health systems of these countries, less accustomed to infectious disease threats, are ill-prepared for dealing with the morbidity, mortality and social anxiety burden of an outbreak. In the case of China, the largest and most populous country in East Asia, its vulnerability to such an event stems largely from the fact that health resources are allocated so unevenly as to open up gaps in outbreak response capacity. The region as a whole would be better able to resist infectious disease threats if wealthier countries worked to enhance the outbreak response capacity of poorer countries' health systems as well as their own. In addition, well-resourced countries closely connected to but outside East Asia, such as the United States and Australia, have an interest in ensuring an outbreak does not spread within and beyond the region.

Arguments along these lines are routinely advanced at meetings of international health organizations like the WHO. However, the BWC is increasingly being used as an additional forum for states and NGOs to exchange information and ideas on detecting and responding to disease outbreaks, be they of natural or deliberate origin. In addition to standard arms control provisions banning BW possession and proliferation, Article X of the BWC requires that member states 'facilitate, and have the right to participate in, the fullest possible exchange of equipment, materials and scientific and technological information for the use of bacteriological (biological) agents and toxins for peaceful purposes' (BWC 1972). At the Fourth BWC Review Conference in 1996, member states acknowledged 'worldwide concern about new, emerging and re-emerging infectious diseases' and regarded international responses to these as offering 'opportunities for increased cooperation in the context of Article X application and of strengthening the Convention' (BWC 1996: 25). The Conference welcomed efforts to establish a system of global monitoring of disease and encouraged member states to support WHO programmes 'to strengthen national and local programmes of surveillance for infectious diseases and improve early notification, surveillance, control and response capabilities' (BWC 1996: 25).

The 2004 meeting of BWC member states was an opportunity to focus on the details of potential public health capabilities that would be useful in the event of a major disease outbreak, however caused. In one sense, states' contributions to this meeting consisted simply of reports on what each was doing or would do for foreign policy, humanitarian or self-interest reasons. With respect to recent outbreaks of SARS and avian influenza in East Asia, for example, Japan reported that it had 'strengthened national response measures, and during these outbreaks, provided medical equipment and medicines, as well as dispatching experts to affected countries' (Japan 2004). Nevertheless, it was genuinely helpful for individual states to learn more about foreign systems, institutions, laws, policies and capabilities for disease surveillance and response. The message of the USA to other delegates was that the 2004 meeting was an opportunity 'to share insights that will greatly improve the ability of the international community to respond to dangerous outbreaks of disease, whether naturally occurring or deliberate' (United States 2004). The South Korean delegate noted (Republic of Korea 2004) that the meeting:

> "brought us a better understanding of the diverse systems and mechanisms for the surveillance, detection, diagnosis and combating of infectious diseases and for responding to, investigating and mitigating the effects of alleged use of biological weapons or suspicious outbreaks of disease. As a consequence, we now know more clearly what has to be done and what remains to be done for the improved effectiveness of those systems and mechanisms."

Some states, however, were interested in receiving more than just information and ideas. Indonesia, for example, called for enhanced laboratory capacity in developing countries (Indonesia 2004), and Malaysia was adamant that 'the outcome of all research regarding the surveillance, detection, diagnosis and combating of infectious diseases affecting humans, animals and plants should also be made available to all [BWC] states parties on a non-discriminatory basis' (Malaysia 2004). China called for wealthier BWC member states to fund improvements in disease surveillance and response in poorer states, and for assistance (in the form of technology, resources and information) to be provided 'on the basis of equality, cooperation and mutual respect' (BWC 2004: 21–2). China also suggested that BWC member states share their experiences in disease prevention and control by promoting technological cooperation and personnel exchanges (BWC 2004: 27). Some developed countries seemed receptive to such ideas, with the US representative remarking: 'We too see utility in the provision of technical assistance . . . particularly in framing and/or expanding . . . national systems of disease surveillance and response' (United States 2004). Australia in turn took the view that the 2004 meeting of BWC member states had 'usefully informed initiatives to improve disease surveillance and diagnostic laboratory capacity in the Asia-Pacific region' (Australia 2004).

Finally, in a consensus statement on the topic of disease surveillance and response, the BWC member states attending the 2004 meeting recognized that 'strengthening and broadening national and international surveillance, detection, diagnosis and combating of infectious disease may support the object and purpose of the Convention' and that 'scientific and technological developments have the potential to significantly improve disease surveillance and response' (BWC 2004: 4). They consequently 'agreed on the value' of supporting the existing networks of international health organizations 'for the surveillance, detection, diagnosis and combating of infectious diseases' and 'improving . . . national and regional disease surveillance capabilities' (BWC 2004: 4). Subsequently, at the Sixth BWC Review Conference in 2006, the Non-Aligned Movement (NAM)[2] (NAM 2006: 3) urged BWC member states:

"to develop a framework to provide technical and financial resources, including through voluntary contributions, for States Parties to support an international system for the global monitoring of emerging and re-emerging diseases in humans, animals and plants and to support other specific programmes to improve the effectiveness of national and international efforts on the surveillance, diagnosis, prevention and treatment of diseases caused by microbial and other biological agents and toxins, in particular infectious diseases, including collaborative vaccine research and development and relevant training programmes."

In a statement on BWC universality, South Korea[3] suggested that '[m]ore specific programs for the implementation of Article X of the Convention on international cooperation need to be developed (e.g. initiatives for capacity building)' and '[e]xchange/training programs for scientists and the sharing of information through various seminars would offer an attractive incentive for non-Parties to join the Convention' (Republic of Korea 2006: 2–3). Such prescriptions generally found favour at the Conference, the Final Declaration of which encouraged BWC member states 'to continue strengthening existing international organizations and networks working on infectious diseases' and 'to improve communication on disease surveillance at all levels', between themselves and with international health organizations. There was also consensus that wealthier member states should continue supporting, directly and through international organizations, capacity-building in poorer states 'in the fields of disease surveillance, detection, diagnosis and combating of infectious diseases and related research' (BWC 2006: 16). Clearly, the BWC was supporting the efforts of international health organizations to enhance disease surveillance and response capacity worldwide. Partial securitization, effected by discussing natural disease threats alongside BW issues via an arms control and disarmament treaty, appeared to be beneficial.

It is not difficult to see that strong surveillance and response capacity is important to protect not only against disease outbreaks of natural origin but also against the use of BW. And heightened surveillance, in particular, can help distinguish between the two. An increase in illness associated with a biological attack would be more difficult to detect if it occurred during a seasonal surge in naturally occurring infectious disease. For this reason, the WHO emphasizes the importance of routine surveillance for emerging diseases and those prone to epidemics. This would enhance the capacity of public health authorities to detect and investigate outbreaks that are caused deliberately; that is, an unusual disease event would be more easily recognized in the light of background data on the natural behaviour of infectious diseases. Such data include the disease's geographical and seasonal occurrence, and the characteristic epidemiological, demographic and clinical features of an outbreak (WHO 2002: 2–4).

Certain epidemiological features of an outbreak suggesting an unnatural origin might lead to its description as suspicious. In 1979, for example, there was an outbreak of anthrax in Sverdlovsk in the former Soviet Union. Human and animal cases were distributed in a narrow corridor downwind from a military microbiology facility. Also, a biological agent used in a BW attack might differ from one occurring naturally if it has been genetically engineered or has remained genetically stable in laboratory culture for a long time. In the Sverdlovsk anthrax outbreak, victims were simultaneously infected with several strains of *Bacillus anthracis* bacteria; something not normally encountered in natural outbreaks (Wheelis 2000: 596). Labelling a disease outbreak as 'suspicious', however, can be a political judgment as well as a scientific one. As the next section shows, the investigation of such an outbreak or an allegation of BW use is likely to involve trade-offs between security and public health imperatives. For this reason, the WHO is not a suitable investigatory institution. Rather, such investigations should be carried out only under the auspices of the BWC. If the WHO were to assume this extraordinary (security) role, this would likely undermine the credibility and effectiveness of its humanitarian mission. In other words, securitization of the Organization's role in disease surveillance and response via the issue of BW would be an unwelcome development.

BW allegations and suspicious outbreaks

East Asia has been the scene of biological attacks, actual and alleged, at various times during the last century and BW suspicions persist in the region to this day. From the early 1930s and into the Second World War, the Imperial Japanese Army deployed a large-scale BW programme against China, and at the most recent BWC Review Conference the US government publicly accused North Korea of possessing BW (United States 2006: 2). However, BW allegations are notorious for having political motivations, and investigations of disease outbreaks deemed suspicious face formidable evidentiary difficulties. This is aptly demonstrated by the BW accusations levelled against the USA in the early 1950s and the Yellow Rain (toxin warfare) controversy of the early 1980s.

After its 1945 victory over Japan in the Second World War, the US government secretly provided immunity from war crimes prosecution to Japanese army scientists in exchange for their data on BW (Powell 1981). The USA itself was soon afterwards accused of perpetrating biological attacks during the Korean War. In February 1952, North Korean foreign minister Bak Hun Yung and Chinese Premier Zhou Enlai attracted worldwide attention when they made the allegation that the USA deployed BW on an experimental basis in China and North Korea. At the time, Western governments dismissed this as hostile propaganda based on forced confessions from captured US Air Force pilots (Leitenberg 1998: 170, 172). According to one account, the US military believed at the time that a great advantage of biological warfare would be the enemy's difficulty in distinguishing it from naturally occurring diseases, especially given the poor sanitary conditions of the enemy's territory (Endicott and Hagerman 1998: 186). This very factor, however, could be used to support an argument that BW attacks never occurred in China and North Korea. Rather, outbreaks of diseases endemic to the area were probably natural occurrences resulting from the disruption of war, crowding, an increase in the mobility of the population, a breakdown of sanitation, and a lack of pest control and adequate medical services (Wilde and Johnson 1999: 1877–8).

The allegation that the USA deployed BW during the Korean War was most probably a fabrication of huge and elaborate proportions. In January 1998 a reporter for the Japanese newspaper *Sankei Shimbun* published the findings of 12 documents from former Soviet archives which provide detailed evidence that the allegations were contrived (Leitenberg 1998: 185). The documents describe remarkable measures taken by the North Koreans and Chinese, with Soviet advice, to create false evidence to corroborate their charges against the USA. Moreover, publicly available documents from the Russian Foreign Ministry Archive indicate that Soviet officials were involved in managing the North Korean propaganda campaign about US use of BW so as to prevent the falsity of the claims from being revealed (Weathersby 1998: 176–7).

The USA in turn raised allegations of toxin warfare in the Yellow Rain controversy of the early 1980s. Toxins—poisonous substances derived from a biological source (a microorganism, plant, insect or animal)—are covered by the BWC. On 13 September 1981, US Secretary of State Alexander Haig accused the Soviet Union of supplying trichothcccne mycotoxins to its communist allies in Vietnam and Laos for military use against resistance forces in Laos and Cambodia. According to the US government, aircraft were spraying a yellow toxic material that fell like rain, allegedly bringing illness and death to thousands of victims (Robinson *et al.* 1990: 220). The substance became known as Yellow Rain because samples typically consisted of small yellow spots on leaves and bark. However, the physical evidence supporting this allegation was soon subjected to intense scientific scrutiny and criticism. Scientists outside the US government who studied the Yellow Rain samples were able to conclude instead that the alleged victims had mistaken toxin attacks for harmless showers of yellow honeybee faeces containing digested pollen (Tucker 2001: 26).

The Yellow Rain affair could have been addressed through the BWC, which had entered into force in 1975, but it was not. Under Article V, member states 'undertake to consult one another and to cooperate in solving any problems which may arise in relation to . . . the Convention' (BWC 1972). One such problem is the alleged use of biological or toxin weapons. Article VI provides for the investigation of BWC compliance concerns by the United Nations (UN) Security Council, and under Article VII member states undertake to assist one another in the event that biological or toxin weapons are used (BWC 1972). The Article V consultative process has been used only once. In August 1997, BWC member states met for 3 days to discuss an allegation by Cuba that a US government aircraft had deliberately released over the island a crop-destroying pest (*Thrips palmi*) in an attempt to inflict agricultural damage. The US rebutted this allegation, and the report on this consultation was inconclusive 'due, *inter alia*, to the technical complexity of the subject and to the passage of time' (Mathews 2005: 172). Neither Article VI nor Article VII of the BWC has ever been invoked.

For Jonathan Tucker, the *Thrips palmi* allegation experience suggests that 'a mechanism for addressing BWC compliance concerns can be effective only if implemented by an international organization that is seen as independent, objective, and competent' (Tucker 2004: 3). In 1997 the UN Secretary-General had standing authorization under General Assembly Resolution 37/98D (December 1982) to investigate, with the assistance of national technical experts, alleged use of BW. However, this authority has never been exercised, not least because of political sensitivities. China, for example, has expressed concern that no Asian or Latin American experts were involved in drafting Resolution 37/98D. As such, it doubts that the Secretary-General's investigatory authority represents the will of all UN member states (BWC 2004: 38). Regarding a hypothetical UN Security Council investigation under Article VI of the BWC, China has insisted that the state requesting it should provide valid evidence and detailed data to prove that an outbreak of disease is not natural (BWC 2004: 39).

In the face of institutional inertia affecting the BWC, and in line with Tucker's observations, it has been suggested that investigations should instead be conducted by the WHO. Certainly, the WHO already involves itself in BW issues by encouraging disease surveillance to detect suspicious outbreaks and providing advice to its member states on BW preparedness and response programmes. At the 55th World Health Assembly (WHA), Resolution WHA55.16 (18 May 2002) acknowledged that 'the local release of biological . . . material designed to cause harm could have serious global public health implications and jeopardize the public health achievements of the past decades' (WHA 2002). Article 6 of the 2005 International Health Regulations (IHR) requires each WHO member state to notify the Organization of a 'public health emergency of international concern'. Annex 2 of the IHR, dealing with the criteria for notification, includes the 'spread of toxic, infectious or otherwise hazardous material that may be occurring naturally or otherwise' (WHO 2008: 44).

At the 2004 BWC meeting the USA was in favour of 'updating and providing national expertise and laboratory capacity . . . to the World Health Organization' in the context of 'responding to, and working to mitigate the effects of cases of alleged biological weapons use or suspicious outbreaks of disease' (United States 2004). Later that year the report of the UN High-Level Panel on Threats, Challenges and Change recommended that 'in extreme cases of threat posed by a new emerging infectious disease or intentional release of an infectious agent, there may be a need for cooperation between WHO and the Security Council in establishing effective quarantine measures' (UN 2004: 30). This recommendation, clearly aimed at garnering greater resources and authority for dealing with disease emergencies, nevertheless failed to recognize the political distinction that may be drawn between a natural outbreak and a biological attack. Health resources and political responses flow differently depending on whether a disease crisis touches the humanitarian nerve or the security nerve of governments. If WHO resources were used to investigate a politically motivated accusation of BW use, for example, this could tarnish the non-partisan image upon which the Organization relies to work effectively. So much of the access and goodwill accorded the WHO is dependent on its reputation as a neutral, scientific body. Too close an association with the Security Council, the least representative organ of the UN, might make some countries reluctant to co-operate with WHO investigations. This is but one illustration of the potential risks of securitization in the health sphere.

It is important to note also that any security-oriented investigation to confirm or rule out BW use would necessarily occur alongside the public health process of establishing the source of the outbreak and containing the spread of disease. The scientific aspects of both would be identical, although the international politics and forensic imperatives accompanying the former would make a big difference. For intelligence officials interacting with public health professionals, the principal challenge would be to overcome cultural, operational and organizational differences. For example, there are potential incompatibilities between the transparency required for public health agencies to operate freely and the confidentiality requirements of intelligence gathering. Related to this, there are also clear differences between law enforcement and public health. A BW attack is a crime as well as a health problem, and evidence in a criminal investigation must be collected within the constraints of legal rules to ensure any prosecution based upon that evidence can withstand scrutiny in a court. By contrast, public health investigators tend not to be as concerned with strict chain of custody requirements. In these circumstances, a worrying possibility is that containment of a disease outbreak and prompt treatment of patients will be compromised by a simultaneous arms control investigation (Wheelis 2000: 598). Moreover, there are a limited number of professionals worldwide with the expertise required to investigate disease outbreaks, so diverting personnel to a BW investigation could amount to wasting investigation resources.

At the 2004 BWC Meeting of Experts, Cuba and Brazil insisted that the WHO and other international health organizations should work only within their mandate and not be given a role in investigating BW allegations (BWC 2004: 40). Likewise, China's position was that these organizations 'have no right' to carry out such investigations but could 'provide technological assistance' on request (BWC 2004: 42). At the Sixth BWC Review Conference in 2006, the consensus reached was that 'achieving the objectives of the Convention will be more effectively realized . . . through collaboration with relevant regional and international organizations, in keeping within their respective mandates' (BWC 2006: 9). The reference to 'mandates' reflected BWC member states' desire that the WHO maintain a purely humanitarian role, unburdened by the politicization that traditionally accompanies BW allegations. Indeed, this policy is the same when BW issues are discussed in a WHO context. That is, the WHO 'focuses on the possible public health consequences of an incident involving biological . . . agents . . . regardless of whether it is characterized as a natural occurrence, accidental release or a deliberate act' (WHA 2002). As Kelle observes, 'the WHO clearly rejects any attempts at international public health being securitized and positions itself outside the BW arms control context' (Kelle 2007: 225–6).

Conclusion

This article illustrates how injecting a security dimension into disease surveillance and response can cut both ways. Addressing a traditional security issue (BW) alongside the task of detecting and responding to naturally occurring disease outbreaks is beneficial, but requiring a non-security organization (the WHO) to assume a security role would be counterproductive. As a platform for addressing infectious disease threats arising naturally as well as from malicious human action, the BWC supports the efforts of international health organizations to enhance disease surveillance and response capacity worldwide. Although discussions of BW are sometimes seen as an undue distraction from the worsening threat of naturally occurring diseases (McInnes and Lee 2006: 15), states are increasingly promoting and benefiting from a 'dual use' response as envisaged in the BWC discussion process. Such partial securitization of naturally occurring infectious disease threats is to be welcomed. As for investigating BW allegations and disease outbreaks deemed suspicious, however, it would be a bad idea to contaminate the humanitarian, non-political mission of the WHO by saddling it with a security role. The BWC, for all its imperfections, is still the appropriate institution to deal with this vexed aspect of disease surveillance and response. History suggests that BW allegations will always be politicized, and security imperatives could jeopardize public health imperatives if pursued simultaneously.

Nevertheless, there seems to be no clear solution to this dilemma; in practice, and as a matter of international law, BWC-relevant allegations are likely to overlap with core WHO concerns in some way. An IHR notification of a 'public health emergency of international concern', specifically the 'spread of toxic, infectious or otherwise hazardous material that may be occurring naturally or otherwise' (WHO 2008: 44), prompts a WHO disease-control response regardless of whether such spread is occurring 'naturally' or 'otherwise'. However, a state making such a notification could, on the same basis, additionally request a UN Security Council or Secretary-General investigation of alleged BW use. In March 2010, the then Chairman for the BWC meetings later in the year on 'alleged use of biological or toxin weapons' sought to compartmentalize the 'health' and 'security' dimensions of this topic in an advance brief to BWC member states (Chile 2010). Ambassador Carlos Portales of Chile distinguished between 'public health' responses to the 'effects' of alleged BW use, including controlling the spread of disease, and finding the 'cause' (a 'criminal investigation'), including identifying the source of the outbreak (Chile 2010). Unfortunately, this distinction is difficult to maintain when, as is likely to be the case, knowing where and how an outbreak started vitally informs efforts to control the spread of disease.

Following the 2010 BWC discussions, the World Health Assembly and the Seventh BWC Review Conference in 2011 would be timely opportunities for WHO and BWC member states, respectively, to discuss further the dilemmas of responding to BW allegations. One way of protecting the WHO from the political ravages of securitization might be to somehow ensure, as China suggested in 2004 (BWC 2004: 42), that the Organization performs only an advisory rather than an investigatory role. For example, the member states of the WHO and/or BWC could agree on a provision whereby the Security Council or the Secretary-General may request a scientific report from the WHO Director-General on the nature, origins and progress of a disease outbreak which is the subject of a BW allegation. Consistent with the neutrality of the WHO, provision of such a report would require the consent of the state(s) in whose territory the outbreak was occurring, the state(s) alleging BW use and the state(s) accused. Alternatively, the report could be provided to the Security Council or Secretary-General at the discretion of the WHO Director-General, again subject to the consent of those states directly concerned. In both scenarios, the WHO would be expressly prohibited from making any determination of wrongdoing: only the Security Council or Secretary-General would be empowered to do so. Further discussions among BWC and WHO member states might yield more or better ideas for the international handling of BW allegations. As regards the health-security nexus, the guiding principle should be that a stronger and more effective WHO is one less burdened by real and perceived politicization.

Endnotes

1 For the purposes of this article, 'East Asia' comprises 15 countries: Brunei, Cambodia, China (and Taiwan), Indonesia, Japan, Laos, Malaysia, Myanmar, North Korea, Philippines, Singapore, South Korea, Thailand, Timor-Leste and Vietnam.
2 The Non-Aligned Movement (NAM), founded in 1961, comprises 118 developing countries and aims to represent the political, economic and cultural interests of the developing world. The NAM includes every state in East Asia except China, Japan and South Korea.
3 In consultation with Japan, Australia, Canada, Switzerland, Norway and New Zealand.

References

Abrahamsen R. 2005. Blair's Africa: the politics of securitization and fear. *Alternatives* **30**: 55–80.

Australia. 2004. Australian Statement. Meeting of the States Parties to the Convention on the Prohibition of the Development, Production and Stockpiling of Bacteriological (Biological) and Toxin Weapons and on Their Destruction, Geneva.

Buzan B. 1991. *People, States and Fear: An Agenda for International Security Studies in the Post-Cold War Era*. London: Harvester Wheatsheaf.

Buzan B., Waever O., de Wilde J. 1998. *Security: A New Framework for Analysis*. London: Lynne Rienner.

BWC. 1972. Convention on the Prohibition of the Development, Production and Stockpiling of Bacteriological (Biological) and Toxin Weapons and on their Destruction. Online at: http://www.opbw.org/convention/conv.html, accessed 10 May 2009.

BWC. 1996. Final Document. Fourth Review Conference of the States Parties to the Convention on the Prohibition of the Development, Production and Stockpiling of Bacteriological (Biological) and Toxin Weapons and on their Destruction, Geneva.

BWC. 2002. Final Document. Fifth Review Conference of the States Parties to the Convention on the Prohibition of the Development, Production and Stockpiling of Bacteriological (Biological) and Toxin Weapons and on their Destruction, Geneva. BWC/CONF.V/17.

BWC. 2004. Report of the Meeting of Experts. Geneva, Meeting of the States Parties to the Convention on the Prohibition of the Development, Production and Stockpiling of Bacteriological (Biological) and Toxin Weapons and on their Destruction.

BWC. 2004. Report of the Meeting of States Parties. Meeting of the States Parties to the Convention on the Prohibition of the Development, Production and Stockpiling of Bacteriological (Biological) and Toxin Weapons and on their Destruction, Geneva.

BWC. 2006. Final Document. Sixth Review Conference of the States Parties to the Convention on the Prohibition of the Development, Production and Stockpiling of Bacteriological (Biological) and Toxin Weapons and on their Destruction, Geneva.

Chile. 2010. Biological Weapons Convention: Regional Group Meetings, March 2010, Chairman's Speaking Notes (Ambassador Carlos Portales). Online at: http://www.unog.ch/80256EDD006B8954/(httpAssets)/EFCF26EC708AB682C12576F600527FF1/$file/Chairman+talking+points+group+meetings+29-30+March.pdf, accessed 16 June 2010.

China. 2004. Surveillance of Infectious Diseases. Meeting of Experts of the States Parties to the Convention on the Prohibition of the Development, Production and Stockpiling of Bacteriological (Biological) and Toxin Weapons and on Their Destruction, Geneva.

Cosivi O. 2005. Preparedness for deliberate epidemics: the World Health Organization approach. In: Mathews R. J. (ed.). *Proceedings of the Biological Weapons Convention Regional Workshop*. Melbourne: Asia-Pacific Centre for Military Law, University of Melbourne.

Elbe S. 2006. Should HIV/AIDS be securitized? The ethical dilemmas of linking HIV/AIDS and security. *International Studies Quarterly* 50: 119–44.

Endicott S., Hagerman E. 1998. *The United States and Biological Warfare: Secrets from the Early Cold War and Korea*. Bloomington, IN: Indiana University Press.

Enemark C. 2009. Is pandemic flu a security threat? *Survival* 51: 191–214.

European Union. 2006. The Intersessional Programme of Work. Sixth Review Conference of the States Parties to the Convention on the Prohibition of the Development, Production and Stockpiling of Bacteriological (Biological) and Toxin Weapons and On Their Destruction, Geneva. BWC/CONF.VI/WP.8.

Haacke J., Williams P. D. 2008. Regional arrangements, securitization, and transnational security challenges: the African Union and the Association of Southeast Asian Nations compared. *Security Studies* 17: 775–809.

Hitchcock P., Chamberlain A., Wagoner M. V., Inglesby T. V., O'Toole T. 2007. Challenges to global surveillance and response to infectious disease outbreaks of international importance. *Biosecurity and Bioterrorism* 5: 206–27.

Huang Y. 2003. *Mortal Peril: Public Health in China and its Security Implications*. Washington, DC: Chemical and Biological Arms Control Institute.

Indonesia. 2004. Statement by Indonesia. Meeting of the States Parties to the Convention on the Prohibition of the Development, Production and Stockpiling of Bacteriological (Biological) and Toxin Weapons and on their Destruction, Geneva.

Japan. 2004. Statement by H. E. Mr Yoshiki Mine. Meeting of Experts of the States Parties to the Convention on the Prohibition of the Development, Production and Stockpiling of Bacteriological (Biological) and Toxin Weapons and on their Destruction, Geneva.

Kelle A. 2007. Securitization of international public health: implications for global health governance and the biological weapons prohibition regime. *Global Governance* **13**: 217–35.

Leitenberg M. 1998. Resolution of the Korean War biological warfare allegations. *Critical Reviews in Microbiology* **24**: 169–94.

Malaysia. 2004. Statement by the Delegation of Malaysia. Meeting of the States Parties to the Convention on the Prohibition of the Development, Production and Stockpiling of Bacteriological (Biological) and Toxin Weapons and on their Destruction, Geneva.

Mathews B. 2005. Allegations of use. In: Mathews R. J. (ed.). *Proceedings of the Biological Weapons Convention Regional Workshop.* Melbourne: Asia-Pacific Centre for Military Law, University of Melbourne.

McInnes C., Lee K. 2006. Health, security and foreign policy. *Review of International Studies* **32**: 5–23.

Moore P. 2001. *Killer Germs: Rogue Diseases of the Twenty-First Century.* London: Carlton.

NAM. 2006. Article X of the Convention. Sixth Review Conference of the States Parties to the Convention on the Prohibition of the Development, Production and Stockpiling of Bacteriological (Biological) and Toxin Weapons and on their Destruction, Geneva.

Powell J. W. 1981. A hidden chapter in history. *Bulletin of the Atomic Scientists* **37**: 44–52.

Republic of Korea. 2004. Statement by Ambassador CHOI Hyuck. Meeting of the States Parties to the Convention on the Prohibition of the Development, Production and Stockpiling of Bacteriological (Biological) and Toxin Weapons and on their Destruction, Geneva.

Republic of Korea. 2006. Universality of the BWC. Sixth Review Conference of the States Parties to the Convention on the Prohibition of the Development, Production and Stockpiling of Bacteriological (Biological) and Toxin Weapons and on their Destruction, Geneva.

Robinson J., Guillemin J., Meselson M. 1990. Yellow rain in Southeast Asia: the story collapses. In: Wright S. (ed). *Preventing a Biological Arms Race.* Cambridge MA: MIT Press.

Tucker J. B. 2001. The "Yellow Rain" controversy: lessons for arms control compliance. *Nonproliferation Review* **8**: 25–42.

Tucker J. B. 2004. The new BWC process: a preliminary assessment. *Nonproliferation Review* **11**: 1–13.

UN. 2004. *A More Secure World: Our Shared Responsibility.* Report of the High-Level Panel on Threats, Challenges and Change. New York: United Nations.

United States. 2004. U.S. Statement. Meeting of the States Parties to the Convention on the Prohibition of the Development, Production and Stockpiling of Bacteriological (Biological) and Toxin Weapons and on their Destruction, Geneva.

United States. 2004. U.S. Views on Disease Surveillance. Meeting of Experts of the States Parties to the Convention on the Prohibition of the Development, Production and Stockpiling of Bacteriological (Biological) and Toxin Weapons and on their Destruction, Geneva.

United States. 2006. Confronting Noncompliance with the Biological Weapons Convention. Sixth Review Conference of the States Parties to the Convention on the

Prohibition of the Development, Production and Stockpiling of Bacteriological (Biological) and Toxin Weapons and on Their Destruction, Geneva.

Waever O. 1995. Securitization and desecuritization. In: Lipschutz R. D. (ed.). *On Security*. New York: Columbia University Press.

Weathersby K. 1998. Deceiving the deceivers: Moscow, Beijing, Pyongyang, and the allegations of bacteriological weapons use in Korea. *Cold War International History Project Bulletin* **11**: 176–85.

WHA. 2002. Global public health response to natural occurrence, accidental release or deliberate use of biological and chemical agents or radionuclear material that affect health. World Health Assembly Resolution WHA55.16. Geneva: Fifty-Fifth World Health Assembly.

Wheelis M. 2000. Investigating disease outbreaks under a protocol to the Biological and Toxin Weapons Convention. *Emerging Infectious Diseases* **6**: 595–600.

WHO. 2002. *Preparedness for the Deliberate Use of Biological Agents: A Rational Approach to the Unthinkable*. Geneva: World Health Organization.

WHO. 2008. *International Health Regulations (2005)*. 2nd Edition. Geneva: World Health Organization.

Wilde H., Johnson R. N. 1999. Book review: 'The United States and Biological Warfare: Secrets From the Early Cold War and Korea'. *Journal of the American Medical Association* **282**: 1877–8.